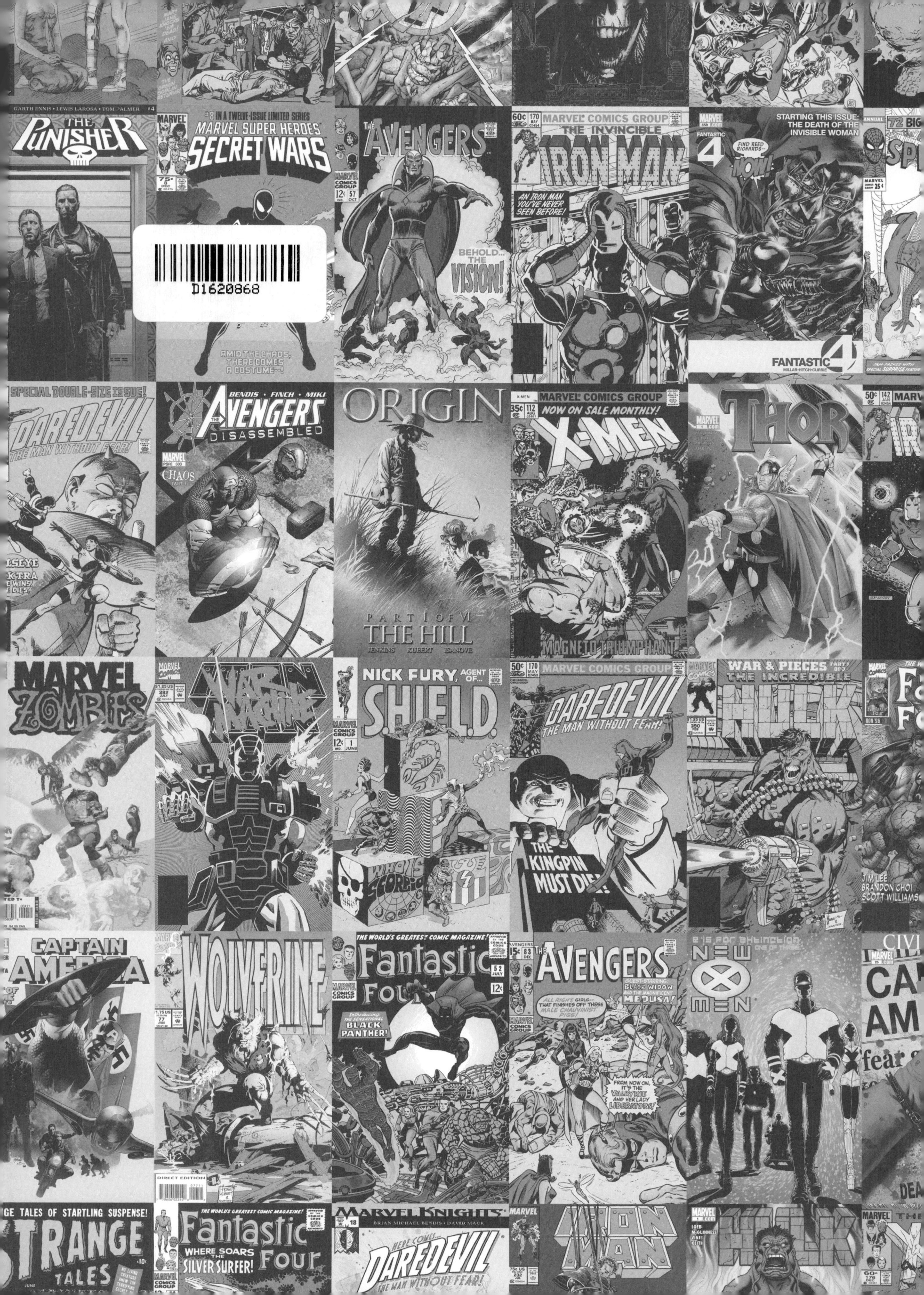
GARTH ENNIS • LEWIS LAROSA • TOM PALMER #4
THE PUNISHER
#8 IN A TWELVE-ISSUE LIMITED SERIES
MARVEL SUPER HEROES SECRET WARS
AMID THE CHAOS, THERE COMES A COSTUME--!
THE AVENGERS
BEHOLD... THE VISION!
MARVEL COMICS GROUP
THE INVINCIBLE IRON MAN
AN IRON MAN YOU'VE NEVER SEEN BEFORE!
STARTING THIS ISSUE: THE DEATH OF THE INVISIBLE WOMAN
FIND REED RICHARDS-- NOW!
FANTASTIC 4
MILLAR-HITCH-CURRIE
SPECIAL DOUBLE-SIZE ISSUE!
DAREDEVIL THE MAN WITHOUT FEAR!
BENDIS • FINCH • MIKI
AVENGERS DISASSEMBLED
CHAOS
ORIGIN
PART I OF VI
THE HILL
JENKINS KUBERT ISANOVE
MARVEL COMICS GROUP
NOW ON SALE MONTHLY!
X-MEN
MAGNETO TRIUMPHANT!
THOR
MARVEL ZOMBIES
WAR MACHINE
NICK FURY, AGENT OF... SHIELD
MARVEL COMICS GROUP
DAREDEVIL THE MAN WITHOUT FEAR!
THE KINGPIN MUST DIE!
WAR & PIECES
THE INCREDIBLE HULK
JIM LEE
BRANDON CHOI
SCOTT WILLIAMS
CAPTAIN AMERICA
WOLVERINE
DIRECT EDITION
THE WORLD'S GREATEST COMIC MAGAZINE!
Fantastic Four
BLACK PANTHER!
THE AVENGERS
ALL RIGHT, GIRLS-- THAT FINISHES OFF THESE MALE CHAUVINIST PIGS!
FROM NOW ON, IT'S THE VALKYRIE AND HER LADY LIBERATORS!
NEW X-MEN
STRANGE TALES
THE WORLD'S GREATEST COMIC MAGAZINE!
Fantastic Four
WHERE SOARS THE SILVER SURFER!
MARVEL KNIGHTS
BRIAN MICHAEL BENDIS • DAVID MACK
HERE COMES... DAREDEVIL THE MAN WITHOUT FEAR!
IRON MAN
HULK

# MARVEL COMICS

# 75 YEARS OF COVER ART

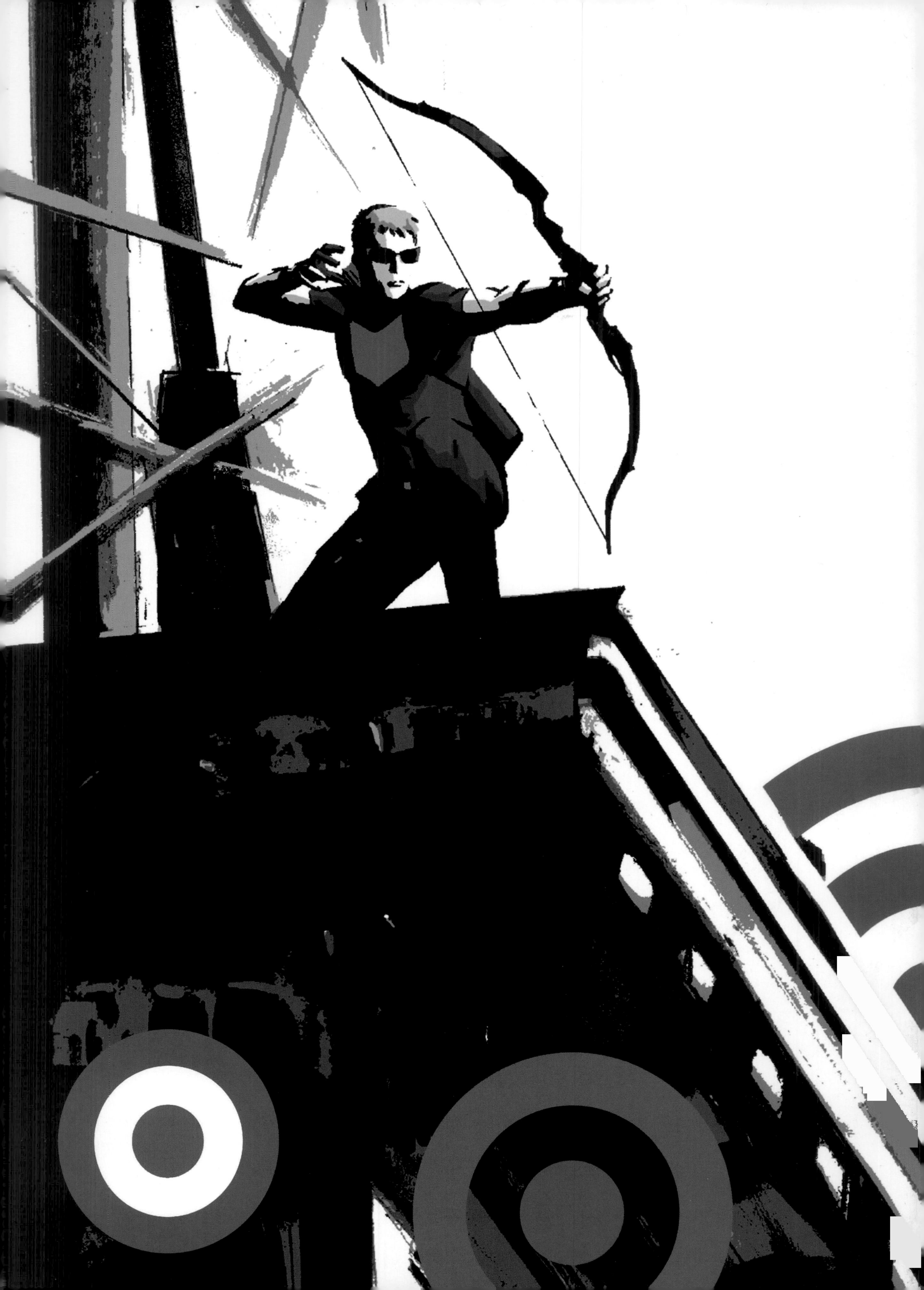

# MARVEL COMICS
## 75 YEARS OF COVER ART

Written by Alan Cowsill
With a Foreword by Adi Granov

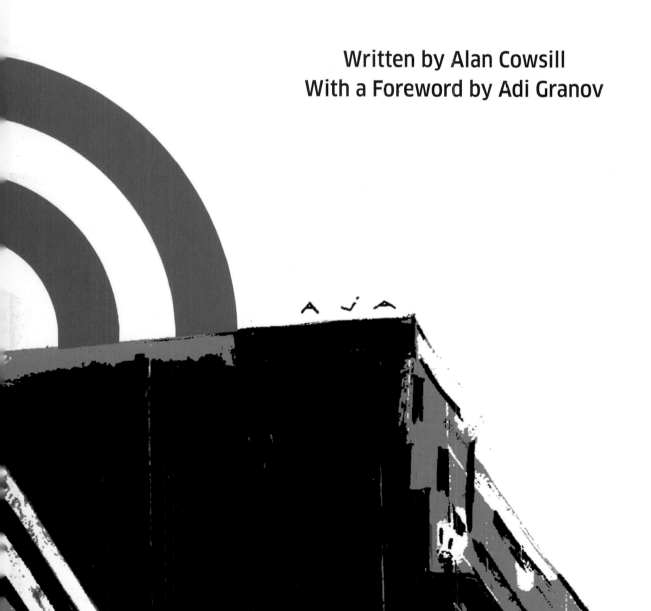

# CONTENTS

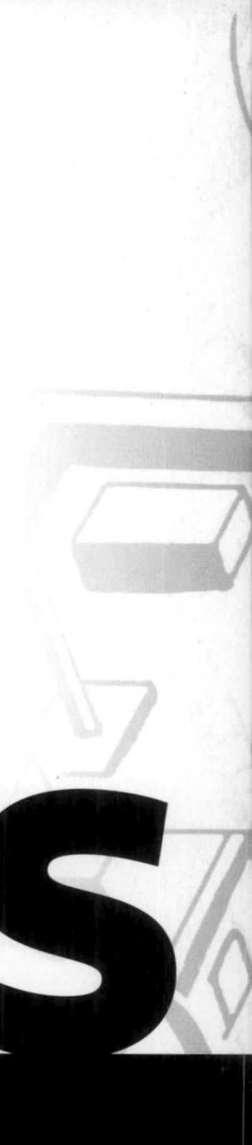

# THE MODERN AGE
## 1986–

# FOREWORD

My career and my life have been intrinsically linked with Marvel Comics covers for a long time now, and they are such a strong presence in my reality that it's difficult to be objective about it. I grew up in former Yugoslavia, and even in those dark days before the internet, we had access to a lot of Marvel comics, and they had a big impact on my young mind. The energy and power of the images, featuring these fantastically iconic characters, was so exciting—a window into a world of action and wonder, of stylized modern mythology. My first job for Marvel, over a decade ago, was creating a cover for Iron Man, and my life was never quite the same again...

The iconography and styles of Marvel covers have been, and are, such strong elements of pop culture throughout the decades—from the legendary *Amazing Fantasy* issue #15 cover by Jack Kirby, through to the trippy *Nick Fury, Agent of S.H.I.E.L.D.* by Jim Steranko and *Elektra* by Bill Sienkiewicz, to *Marvels* by Alex Ross...and with some wonderful deviations such as *Silver Surfer: Parable* by one of my heroes, Moebius. They have reflected and shaped the trends in comic books and entertainment at large—never more so than today, when some of the biggest Hollywood movies are so closely linked with the visual styles of those iconic images.

The covers have traditionally always served as an advertisement for what is inside, but along the way they developed a parallel life of their own. They started to be framed as standalone posters, collected as pieces of fine art, and came to be seen by artists themselves as their opportunity to push a bit farther and show their best work; the covers became just as iconic as the characters they were depicting.

As the printing technology got more sophisticated, so did the covers. No longer restricted by the process, they started to become elaborate, often fully painted artworks that could take as long to create as whole comic issues used to back in the early days.

This was where my story with Marvel began. I was a semi-successful illustrator on the fringes of the industry, but with a fully formed painted style which attempted to fuse the iconography of comics with the style and rendering of poster illustrators from times before. The Marvel guys recognized something in it and asked me to illustrate a few covers. My second ever cover for them was the one of Iron Man punching the ground...I didn't know it at the time but I had stumbled upon a formula which would take the ol' Shell Head and me on a fantastic journey, starting with the "Extremis" book, written by Warren Ellis, through to the *Iron Man* and the *Avengers* movies, countless covers, toys, statues, and pretty much anything you could think of putting an image onto. Over the years I have illustrated covers featuring just about every Marvel character there is. It's the best job in the world!

The book in your hands is a wonderful collection of the most iconic and memorable covers from Marvel's 75 years of making comics, a journey through history featuring our favorite heroes and villains. I am delighted to have contributed to the world of Marvel covers and proud for my work to stand alongside so many amazing illustrations by incredible artists, past and present. To me the most exciting thing is that some of the best covers are yet to be created. I cannot wait!

Adi Granov

MARVEL
PSR 76 421
THE INVINCIBLE
IRON MAN
MILLER
LUCAS
RAPMUND
THE BEST DEFENSE
PART 4

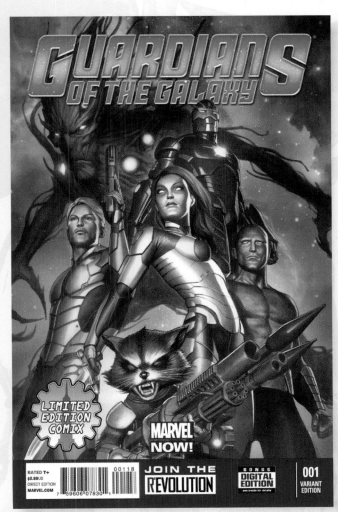

*IRON MAN* **#76**
**March 2004**
**Artist:** Adi Granov

GUARDIANS OF THE GALAXY
LIMITED EDITION COMIX
MARVEL NOW!
RATED T+
$3.99US
DIRECT EDITION
MARVEL.COM
JOIN THE REVOLUTION
BONUS DIGITAL EDITION
001
VARIANT EDITION

*GUARDIANS OF THE GALAXY* **#1**
**May 2013**
**Artist:** Adi Granov

# INTRODUCTION

Whether it was Spidey swinging over New York for the first time on Jack Kirby's cover for *Amazing Fantasy* issue #15 or everyone's favorite Avenger appearing on David Aja's *Hawkeye* issue #1, Marvel has always had a knack for creating covers that not only make readers want to read a comic, but *need* to. Indeed, it was the covers that grabbed me as a kid when the *Mighty World of Marvel* was released in the UK way back in 1972.

Selecting the covers for the book...well, that was a daunting task. Some choices were immediately obvious—debuts such as *Fantastic Four* issue #1 could not be omitted! Others were chosen because they best reflect the era they came from, or because they are perfect examples of an artist's style. Of course, opinion on the "best" will always be divided, but we hope that you enjoy delving into this beautiful book and its wide selection of stunning covers.

The book is divided into four chapters, each one covering a comic book era. Within the chapters, covers have been placed in their Marvel "families." So, the Silver Age *Avengers* titles are placed alongside those featuring Avengers characters. At times, this ordering is broken if a theme, story, or artist unites a selection of covers—as it is the art that comes first. And it is the artists that this book is dedicated to. They are the real stars of the show and the ones who have helped make Marvel a household name, creating some of the greatest works of art from the last 75 years along the way.

Alan Cowsill (author)

# THE GOLDEN AGE

## 1938–1956

**THE 1930s SAW** the new medium of the comic burst into life. Shortly after DC Comics released *Action Comics* issue #1 (June 1938), Marvel Comics—originally known as Timely Comics—unleashed their own Super Heroes into the world in *Marvel Comics* issue #1 (October 1939). The Human Torch and Sub-Mariner were huge hits and soon joined by others such as Captain America and the Destroyer. The stories created during the Golden Age were a clear reflection of the anxiety caused by the Great Depression and the buildup to World War II. Indeed, many of Timely's heroes—such as Captain America—fought the Nazis before America entered the war.

Comic books were a close cousin of pulp magazines such as *Weird Tales* (first published in March 1923). Many artists best known for their work on the pulps, such as Frank R. Paul and Alex Schomburg, brought their eye-catching art styles across to the fledgling comic industry. Young artists such as Jack Kirby and Syd Shores embraced the new art form, creating exciting tales behind colorful, action-packed covers, the likes of which had never been seen before.

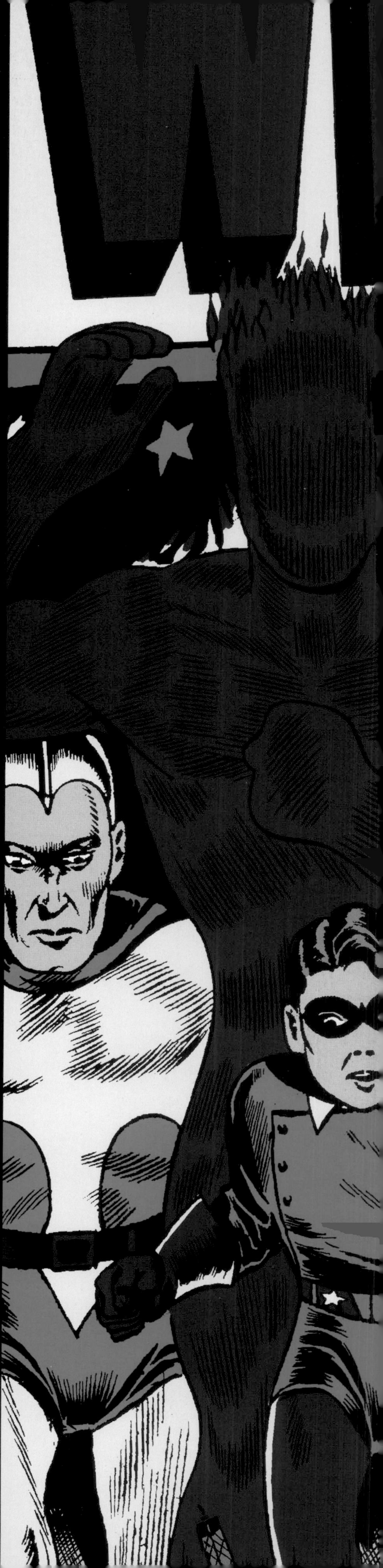

***ALL WINNERS #4*** ▶
**Spring 1942**
**Artist:** Al Avison
*(Cover shown in full on p14)*

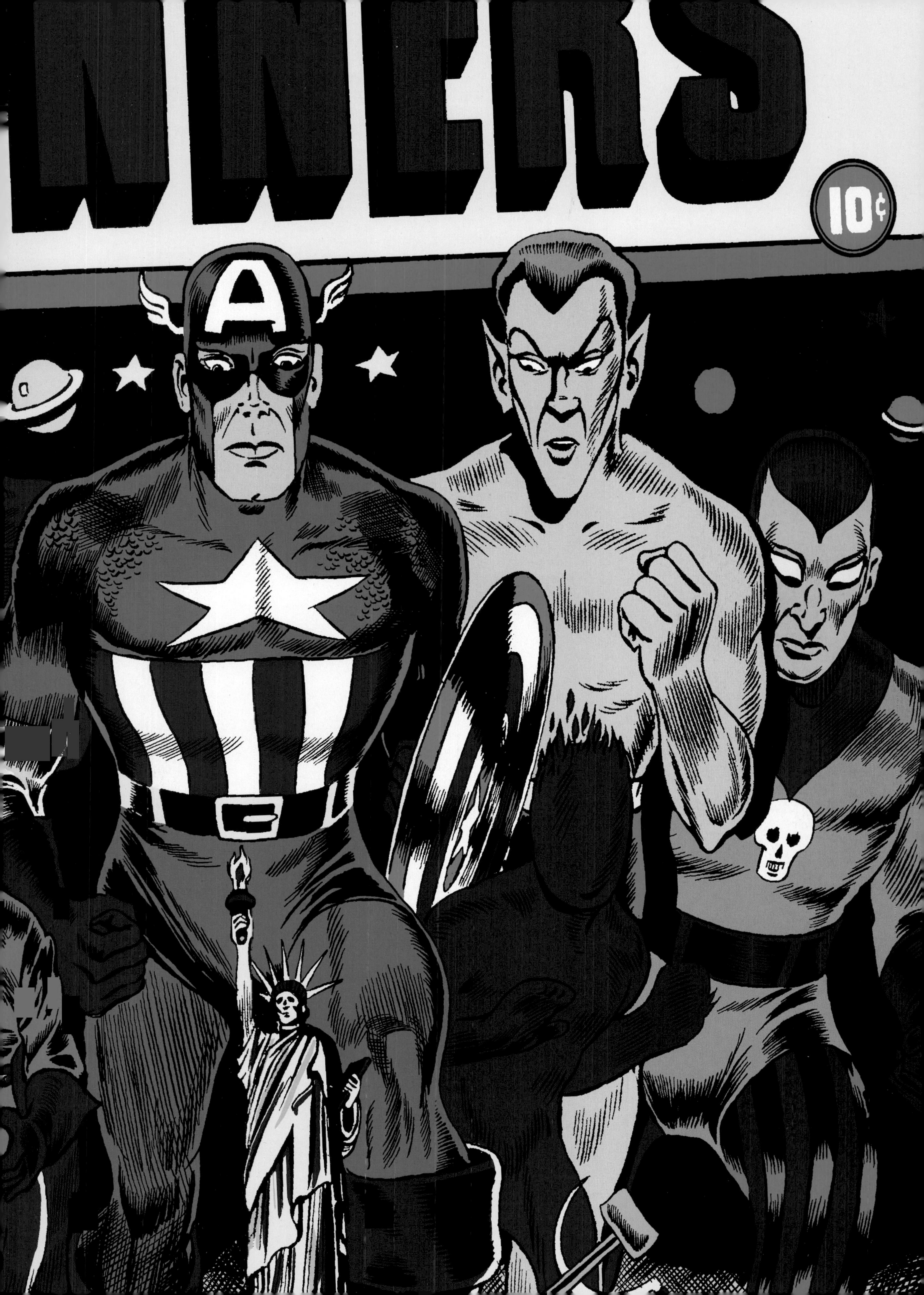
10¢

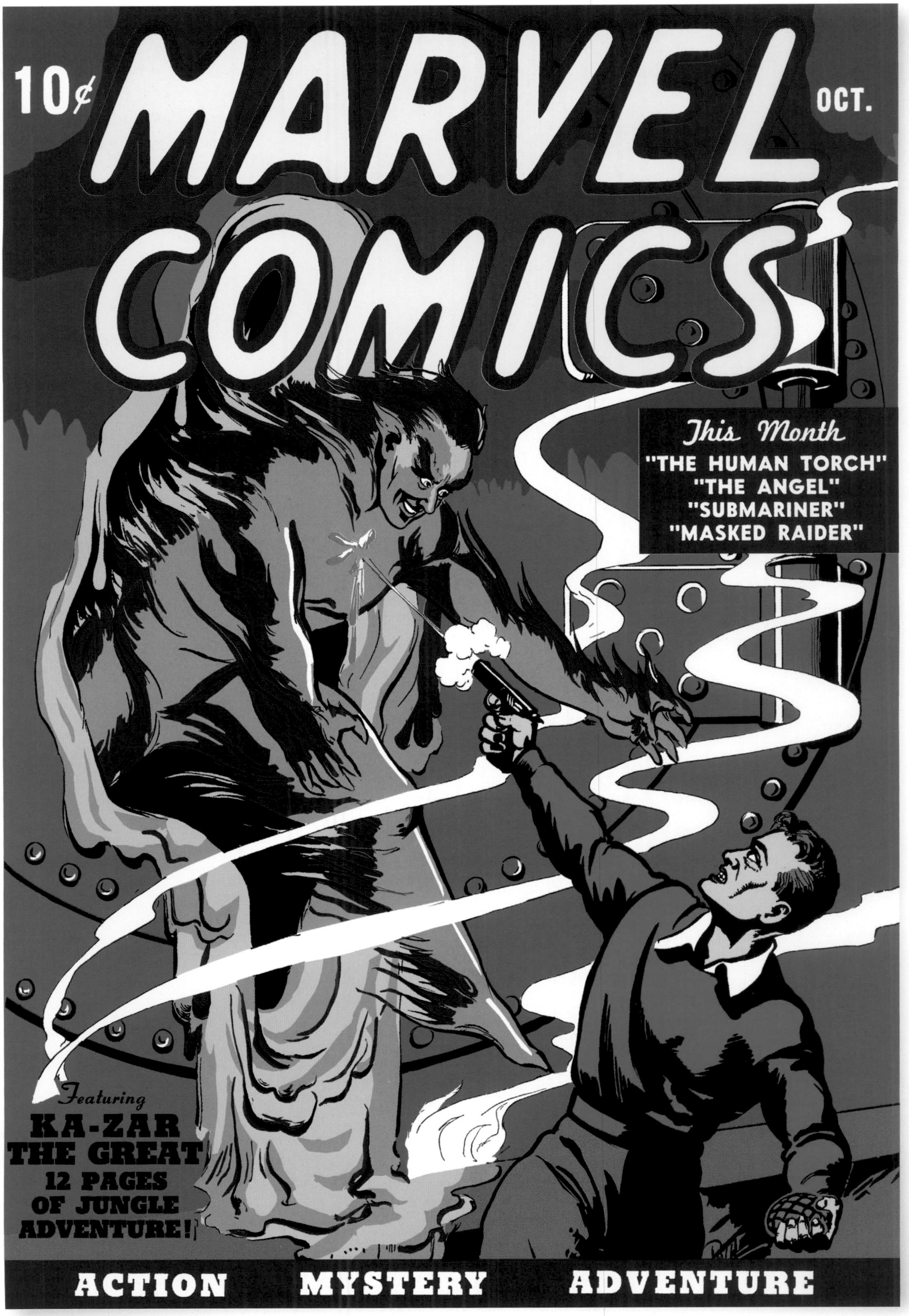
10¢
MARVEL COMICS
OCT.
This Month
"THE HUMAN TORCH"
"THE ANGEL"
"SUBMARINER"
"MASKED RAIDER"
Featuring
KA-ZAR THE GREAT
12 PAGES OF JUNGLE ADVENTURE!
ACTION MYSTERY ADVENTURE

▲ *MARVEL COMICS* #1

**October 1939**
**Artist:** Frank R. Paul

Released by Timely Publishing, *Marvel Comics* issue #1 is the most important cover of all time, as it is the one that launched the company that would become Marvel. Artist Frank R. Paul remains best known for his work on pulp magazines. The monstrous look that Paul gave the Human Torch established the comic as something unique, combining the then-new Super Hero craze with the look of classic pulps.

MARVEL
JANUARY 1941
IN CANADA 15¢
10¢
COMICS
MYSTERY
No. 15
POURING THROUGH the OCEAN TUNNEL CAME the NAZI HORDES!
25,000 FEET
THIS COVER PICTURE IS THE START OF A GREAT NEW ADVENTURE..
TORCH and SUB-MARINER FIGHTING SIDE BY SIDE!!!

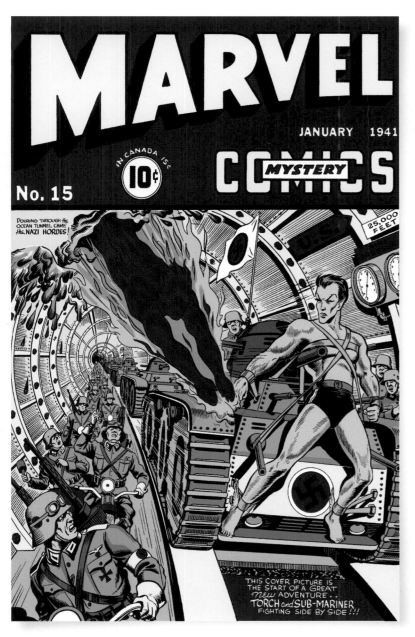

▲ *MARVEL MYSTERY COMICS* #15

**January 1941**
**Artist:** Alex Schomburg

Marvel maestro Stan Lee once said, "Alex Schomburg was to comic books what Norman Rockwell was to the *Saturday Evening Post*." Schomburg excelled at tension, high-tech machinery, and action—and this exciting cover to *Marvel Mystery Comics* shows his style at its best.

MYSTIC
NO. 7
STARRING The DESTROYER
DECEMBER
COMICS
10¢
WAR MINISTER
SECRET PLANS
AS THE DEADLY MONSTERS FROM HITLER'S TRUNK OF TERROR WERE FREED THE DESTROYER PLUNGED DOWN!

▲ *MYSTIC COMICS* #7

**December 1941**
**Artist:** Jack Kirby

While the Destroyer has rarely appeared since the Golden Age, he was one of the most popular characters of the era, and one of the earliest co-created by Stan Lee. This dramatic cover, with its fluid line work and action-packed composition, is a good example of Kirby's early work.

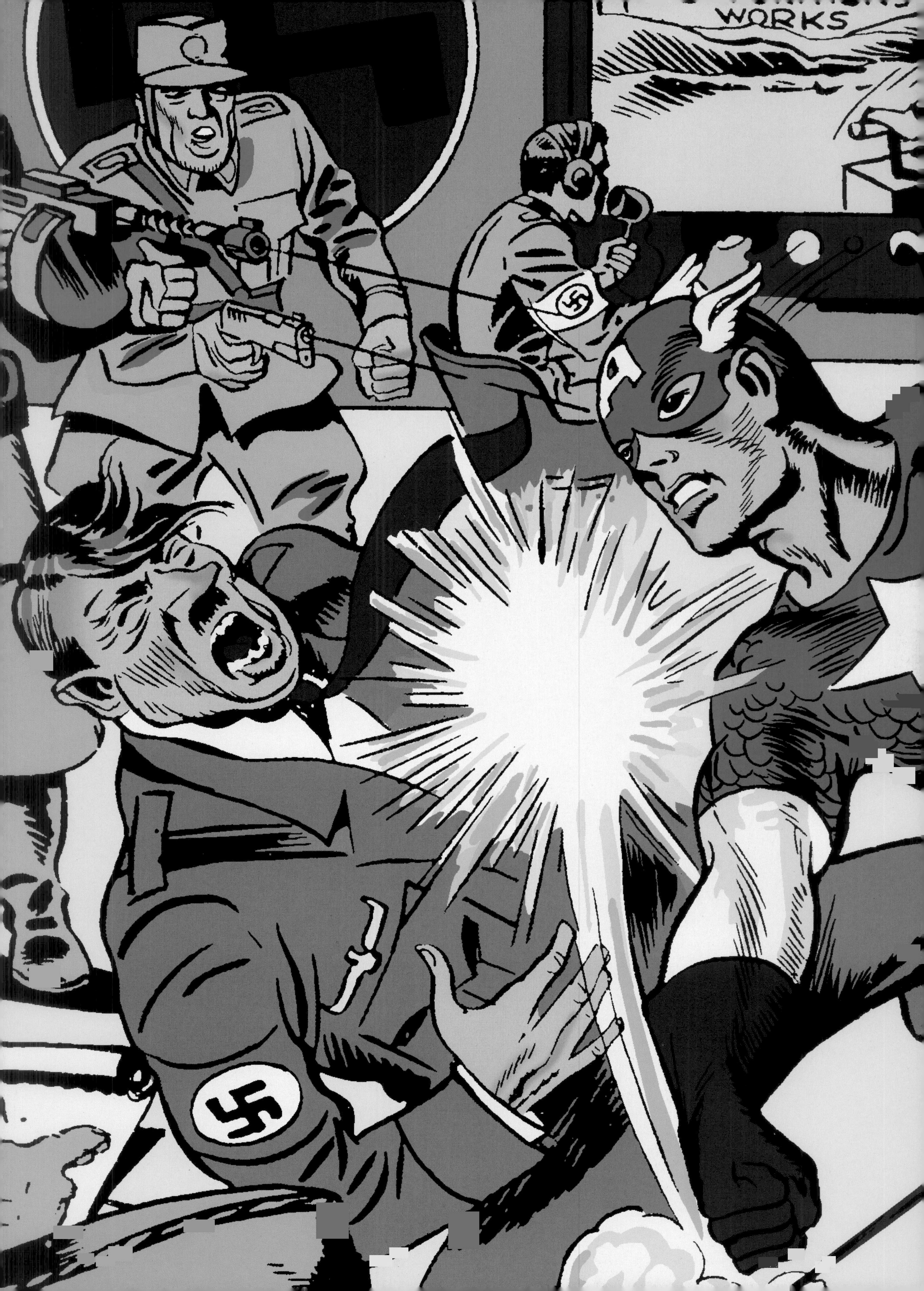
WORKS

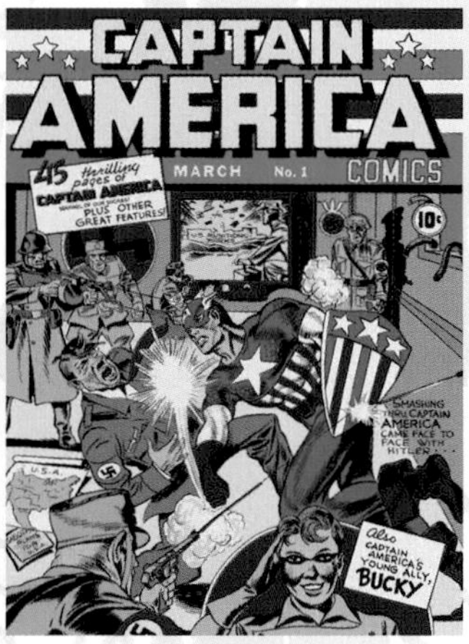
CAPTAIN AMERICA
MARCH
No. 1
COMICS
10¢
SMASHING THRU, CAPTAIN AMERICA CAME FACE TO FACE WITH HITLER
BUCKY

*CAPTAIN AMERICA* **#1**

**March 1941**
**Artist:** Jack Kirby

Writer Joe Simon and artist Jack Kirby were the greatest team to come out of the Golden Age. They created Captain America for Timely in 1941, the patriotic Super Hero reflecting their own hatred of Hitler before the US entered World War II. The cover to the first issue signalled a clear mission statement: This was a book about heroes opposing the rise of fascism.

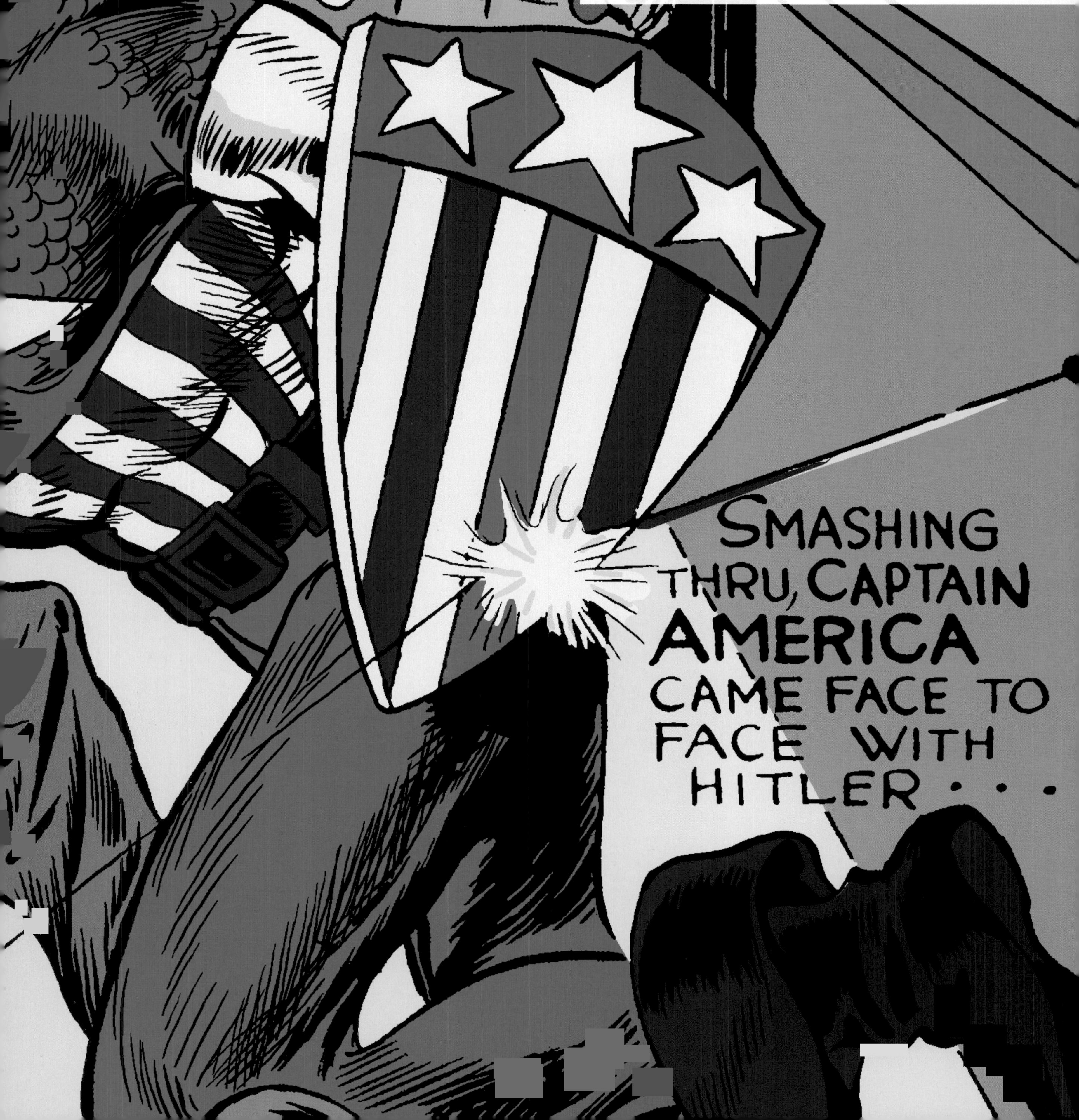
SMASHING THRU, CAPTAIN AMERICA CAME FACE TO FACE WITH HITLER . . .

NO. 32
CAPTAIN
10¢
AMERICA
NOVEMBER
COMICS
THE HUMAN TORCH
IN THIS ISSUE!

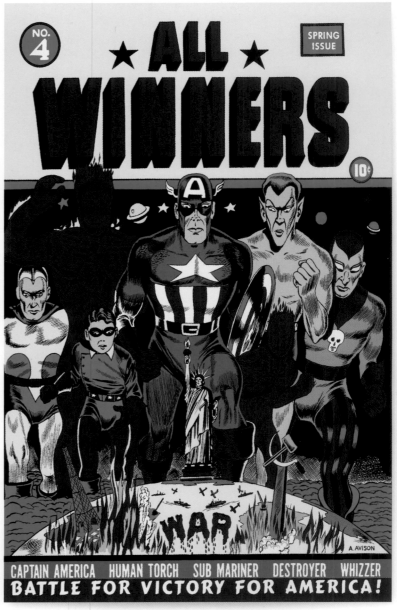

▲ *CAPTAIN AMERICA* #32

**November 1943**
**Artist:** Syd Shores

Syd Shores started his career inking for Jack Kirby, who was a big influence on his own work. He started pencilling when Kirby briefly joined Timely's competition, and Shores was soon creating fantastic covers of his own. This Cap cover is a great example of Shores' work and also foreshadows Bucky's eventual "death" while trying to stop a drone plane, as recounted in *Avengers* issue #4 *(see p23)*.

NO. 4
ALL
SPRING ISSUE
WINNERS
10¢
WAR
A. AVISON
CAPTAIN AMERICA HUMAN TORCH SUB MARINER DESTROYER WHIZZER
BATTLE FOR VICTORY FOR AMERICA!

▲ *ALL WINNERS* #4

**Spring 1942**
**Artist:** Al Avison

This cover reflects the worrying political times more than any other cover of the period, as the heroes march into battle, a burning world below them. Like Syd Shores, Al Avison started as an inker before working as a penciller. The cover also features Whizzer (far left on the cover), the hero Avison helped to create.

HUMAN TORCH
CAPTAIN AMERICA
SUB MARINER
ALL WINNERS
NO. 19
FALL ISSUE
10¢
COMICS
SEE
THE HUMAN TORCH CAPTAIN AMERICA AND SUB-MARINER BATTLE THE WORLD'S MOST FEARFUL VILLAIN IN A COMPLETE, SIZZLING, ACTION THRILLER!

▲ *ALL WINNERS* #19

**Fall 1946**
**Artist:** Al Avison

The post-war years weren't kind to Super Heroes as other genres proved more popular. Timely tried new ways of grabbing the public's attention, though. This classic Al Avison cover showcased the company's most popular heroes as they came together for the very first time to form a supergroup, the All Winners Squad.

ATLAS
BLACK KNIGHT
THE GREATEST KNIGHT OF THEM ALL!
Black Knight
MAY
10¢
APPROVED BY THE COMICS CODE AUTHORITY
THRILLS FROM KING ARTHUR AND HIS KNIGHTS OF THE ROUND TABLE!
STRIKE, BLACK BLADE! THE BLACK KNIGHT CHALLENGES MODRED THE EVIL!
SHARE THE THRILLS WHEN "THE BLACK KNIGHT RIDES!"
SEE THE BLACK KNIGHT COMBAT MODRED THE EVIL IN "THE ABDUCTION OF KING ARTHUR!"
ALSO "THE CRUSADER" IN THIS GREAT ISSUE!

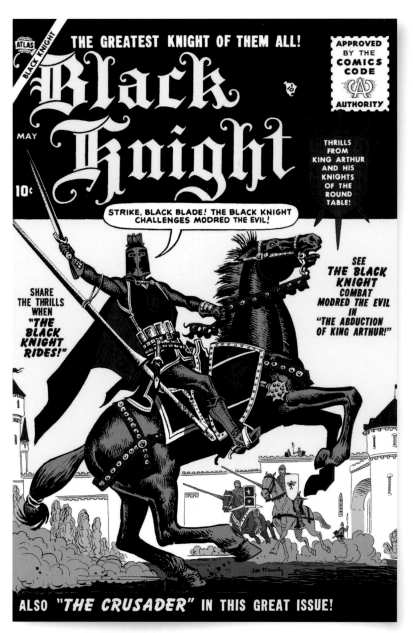

▲ *BLACK KNIGHT* #1

**May 1955**
**Artist:** Joe Maneely

The cover to the first issue of the *Black Knight* remains one of the gems of the decade. It was illustrated by Joe Maneely, a contemporary of Jack Kirby. Stan Lee declared Maneely would have been an all-time great if he hadn't been tragically killed in a train accident in 1958, at the young age of 32. Maneely was a skilled draughtsman and this cover shows his highly detailed style at its best.

STRANGE TALES OF STARTLING SUSPENSE!
STRANGE TALES
10¢
JUNE
NO LIVING CREATURE KNEW THE TERRIFYING SECRET OF "THE ROOM!"
ALSO IN THIS ISSUE
"THE STRANGE MEN!"
"A CALL IN THE NIGHT!"
"THE BEAST!"
KEEP WALKING, RESTON! THAT'S IT... JUST A LITTLE FURTHER! ONE MORE STEP AND ALL YOUR WORRIES WILL BE OVER!
NO...NO! YOU CAN'T MAKE ME GO IN THERE!

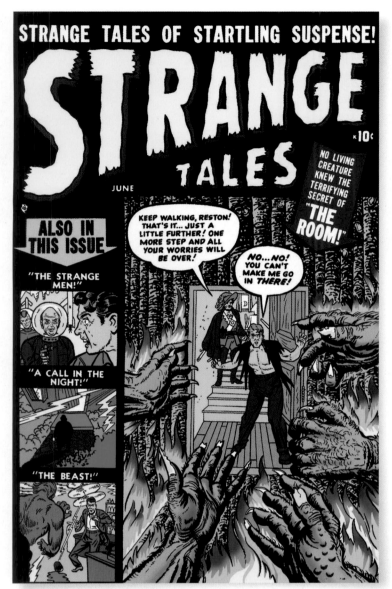

◀ ***STRANGE TALES* #1**

**June 1951**
**Artist:** Carl Burgos

Horror comics were big business in the 1950s, until Fredric Wertham's book *Seduction of the Innocent*, in which he warned about the negative impact of comic books, brought about comic book censorship. Timely produced many horror titles, including the long-running *Strange Tales*. The series' debut issue is a good reflection of their style—weird concepts mixed with bizarre creatures. The cover was illustrated by Carl Burgos, who created the original Human Torch.

10¢
Patsy Walker
NO. 1

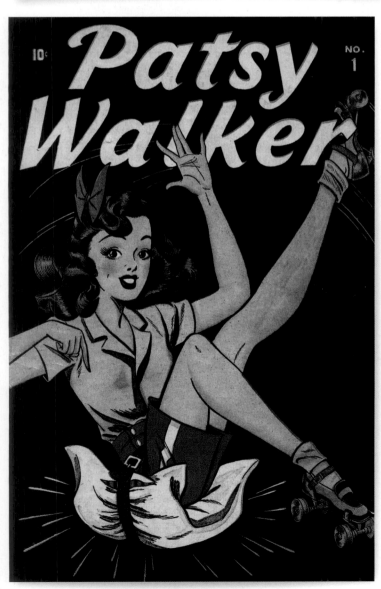

◀ ***PATSY WALKER* #1**

**1945**
**Artist:** Mike Sekowsky

Patsy Walker was created by the pioneering female cartoonist Ruth Atkinson, although Mike Sekowsky illustrated the cover to the first issue. A teen humor comic in the same vein as *Millie the Model*, the cover is a good example of Timely's early female characters as the company experimented with various genres. Patsy Walker later became a fully fledged Super Hero when she took on the role of Hellcat in *Avengers* issue #144 (February 1976).

***MILLIE THE MODEL* #1** ▶

**Winter 1945**
**Artist:** Mike Sekowsky

As the Super Hero craze started to wane, Timely tried to find success in other genres. *Millie the Model* proved to be a hit. The cover of the first issue set the style for Millie's romantic, and sometimes slapstick, adventures. The interior artwork was created by Ruth Atkinson.

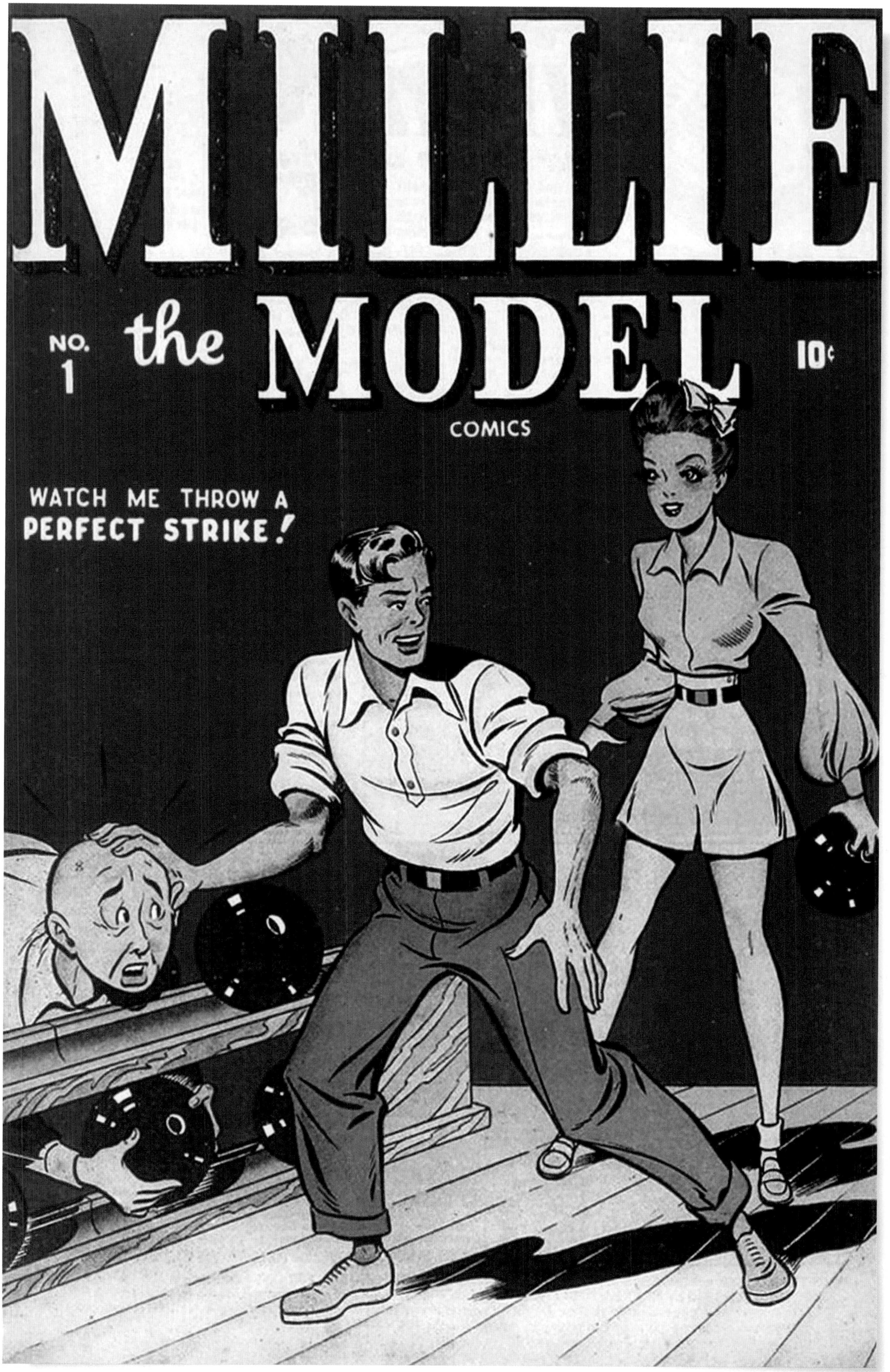
MILLIE the MODEL
NO. 1
10¢
COMICS
WATCH ME THROW A PERFECT STRIKE!

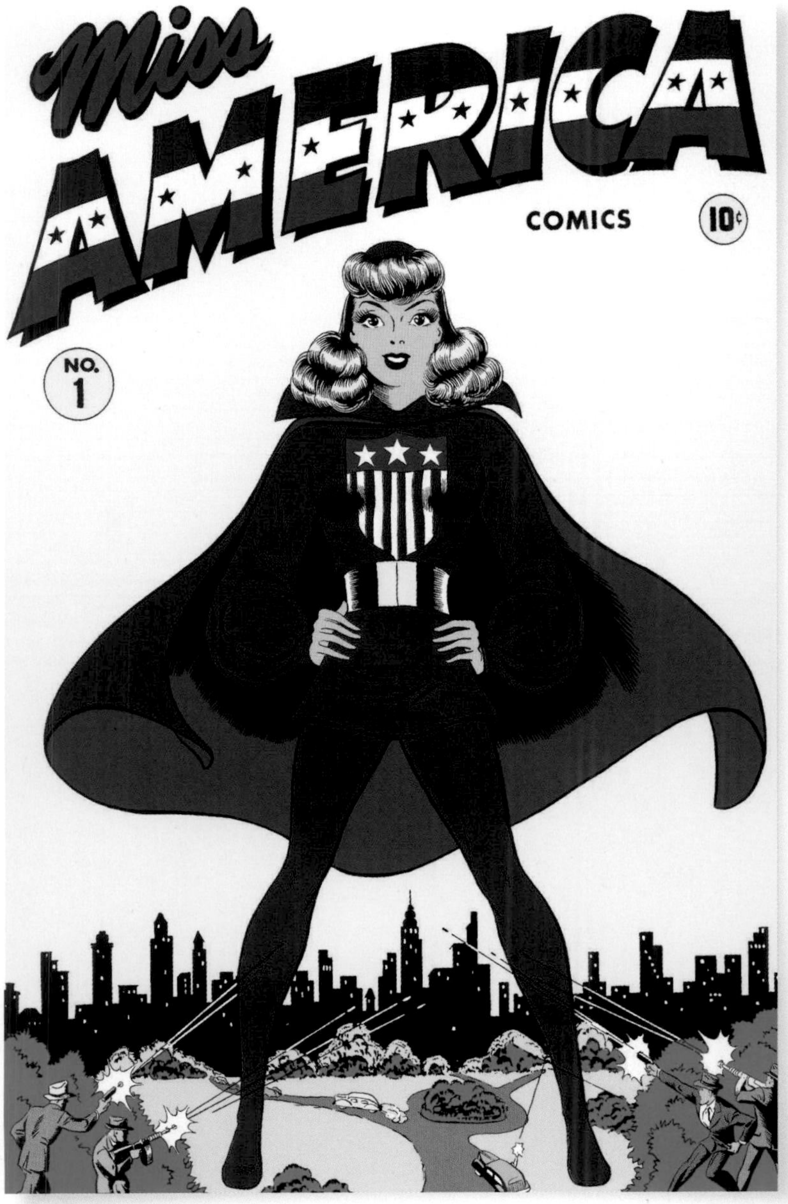
Miss
AMERICA
COMICS
10¢
NO.
1

▲ *MISS AMERICA* #1

**Summer 1944**
**Artist:** Ken Bald or Pauline Loth

Female heroes came into vogue toward the end of the first wave of Super Heroes as the main companies created star-spangled heroines. Timely's take was *Miss America*. The artist of the cover has been disputed in recent times. Some believe it to be Ken Bald, while Vincent Fago (who took on Stan Lee's role while Lee did national service) believed it to be Pauline Loth.

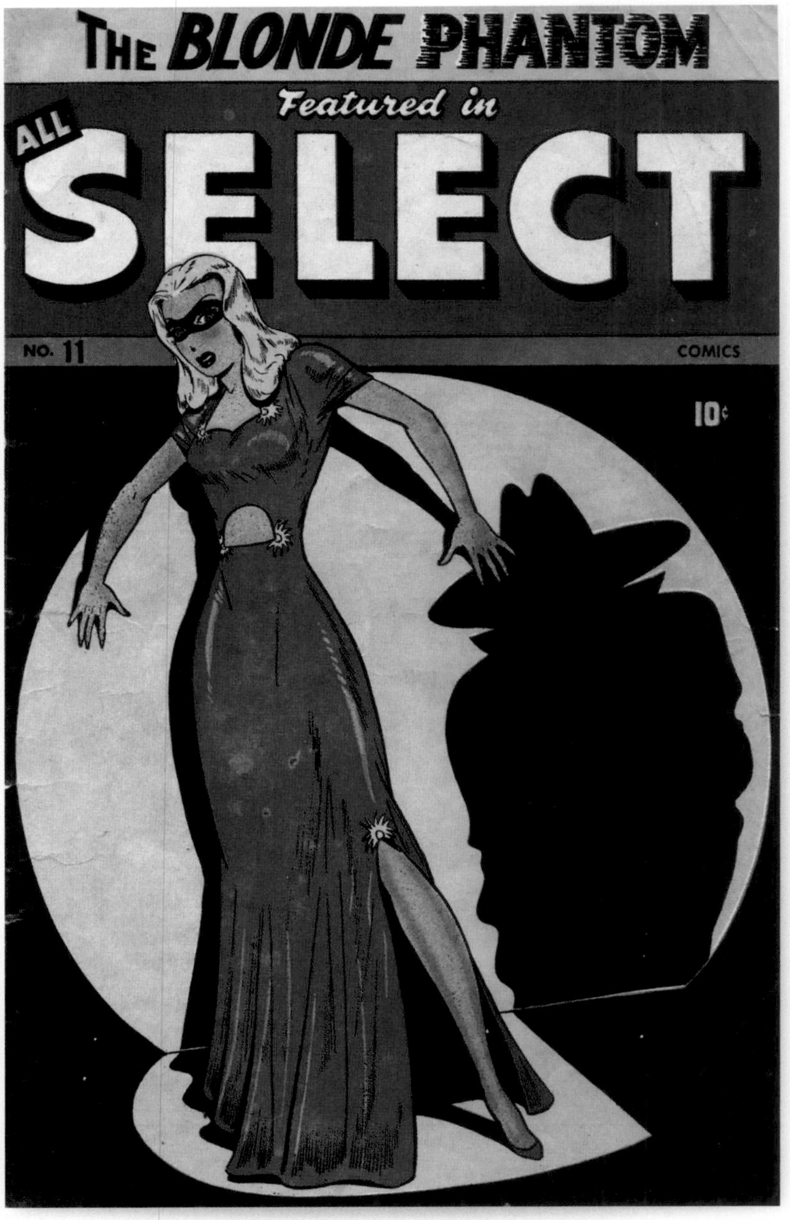
THE BLONDE PHANTOM
Featured in
ALL
SELECT
NO. 11
COMICS
10¢

▲ *ALL SELECT* #11

**Fall 1946**
**Artist:** Syd Shores

Stan Lee and Syd Shores created the Blonde Phantom—and she proved to be a popular femme fatale. Shores produced the stylish cover for her first appearance, bringing a film noir quality to his depiction of the heroine. She was so popular that the magazine was renamed *Blonde Phantom Comics* from the following issue.

MARVEL BOY
DEC.
10¢
HERE HE IS... THE NEWEST, MOST AMAZING CHARACTER IN COMICS!! MARVEL BOY... THE BOY FROM ANOTHER PLANET, AT LAST IN HIS OWN MAGAZINE!
MARVEL BOY TRIES TO SAVE EARTH FROM THE MENACE OF THE "LOST WORLD!"

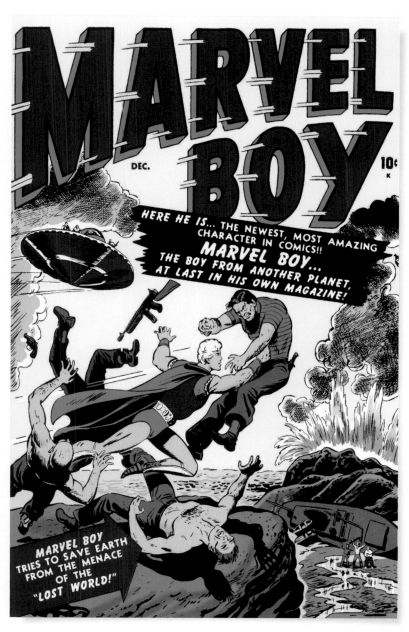

▲ *MARVEL BOY* #1

**December 1950**
**Artist:** Russ Heath

Marvel Boy made his debut in his self-titled comic, with art legend Russ Heath illustrating the cover. While best known for his work on *Sgt. Rock* for DC Comics and *Kid Colt* for Marvel, Heath's cover for *Marvel Boy* is the perfect combination of Super-Hero action and pulp science fiction.

ATLAS
YOUNG MEN
THE HUMAN TORCH RETURNS
DEC.
YOUNG MEN
10¢
ALL NEW STORIES!
LOOK! HE'S BACK FROM THE DEAD! IT'S THE HUMAN TORCH!
SUBMARINER AND CAPTAIN AMERICA ALSO IN THIS ISSUE
SUBMARINER
CAPTAIN AMERICA AND BUCKY

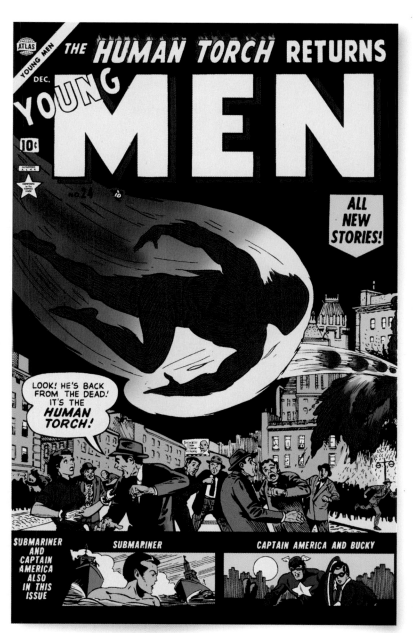

▲ *YOUNG MEN* #24

**December 1953**
**Artist:** Dick Ayers

While Timely's Super-Hero titles faded away in the late 1940s, the heroes made a comeback in *Young Men* #24. Dick Ayers' dynamic cover is more detailed than the earlier Golden Age work and seems a lot closer to the dramatic Super-Hero covers published by the company in the 1960s. In many ways it's a title heralding the start of the Silver Age.

# THE SILVER AGE

**THE SILVER AGE** saw the birth of Marvel Comics, the company that Timely Publishing eventually evolved into. Due to a decline in the general public's love for Super Heroes in the 1950s, Timely published various comic anthologies dealing with genres as varied as funny animal characters, crime, and horror. The Silver Age started with the publication of DC Comics' *Showcase* issue #4 (October 1956), featuring a new incarnation of The Flash and marking the resurgence of the Super Hero. However, for Marvel fans it really began with *Fantastic Four* issue #1 (November 1961; *see p36*). This was the comic that heralded the launch of the Marvel Universe and a bold new style of storytelling.

This new style—combining fantastical, action-packed adventures with down-to-earth drama—was reflected in many of Marvel's covers. Future artistic legends such as Jack Kirby, Steve Ditko, Gil Kane, and John Romita Sr. created work that tapped into the 1960s zeitgeist, helping to make Marvel Comics the coolest kid on the block. By the end of the Silver Age, Spider-Man, the Hulk, Iron Man, and many other Marvel characters were already on their way to becoming cultural icons.

*FANTASTIC FOUR #49* ▶
**April 1966**
**Artist:** Jack Kirby
*(Cover shown in full on p41)*

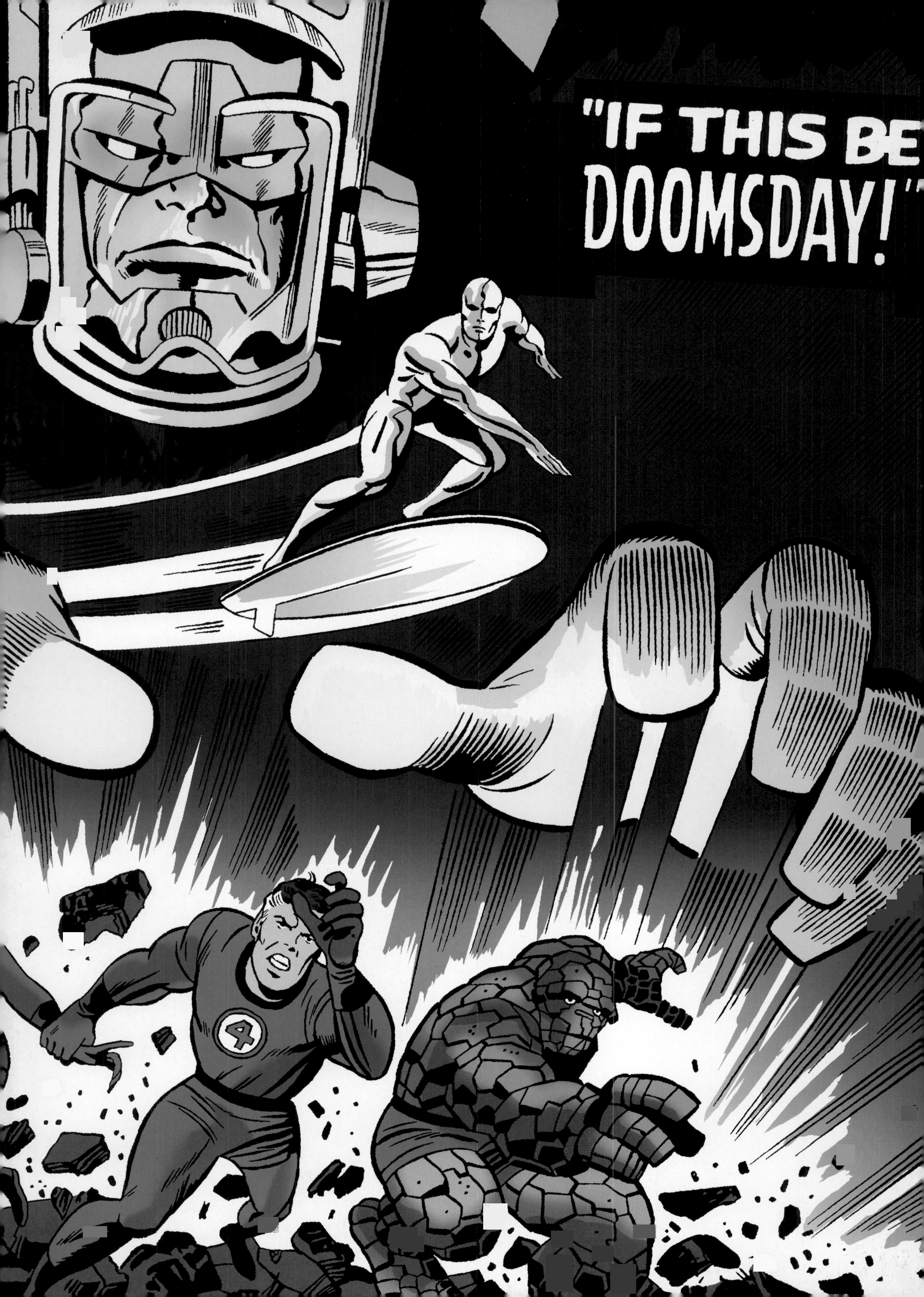
"IF THIS BE DOOMSDAY!"

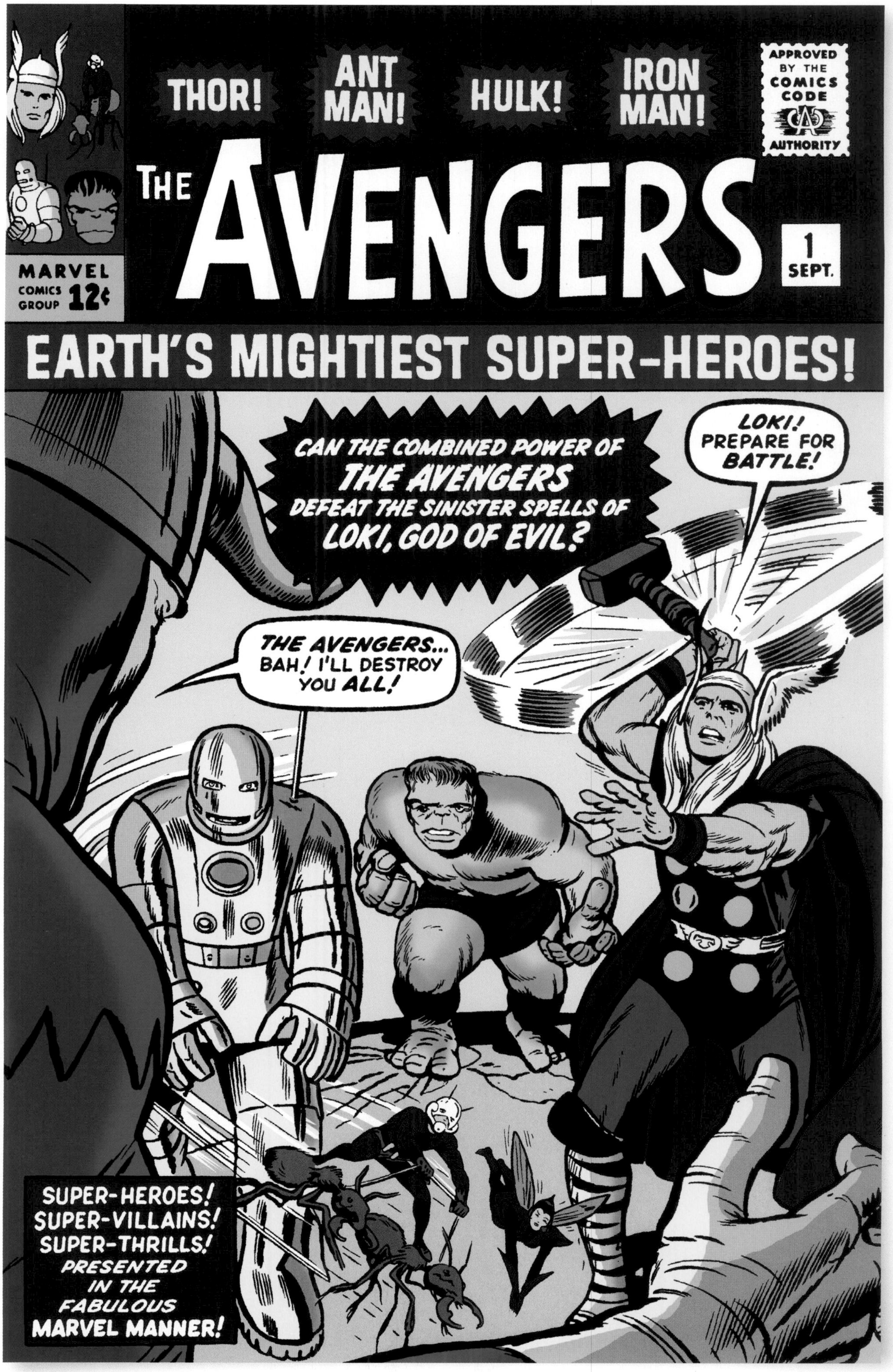
THOR!
ANT MAN!
HULK!
IRON MAN!
APPROVED BY THE COMICS CODE AUTHORITY
THE AVENGERS
MARVEL COMICS GROUP 12¢
1 SEPT.
EARTH'S MIGHTIEST SUPER-HEROES!
CAN THE COMBINED POWER OF THE AVENGERS DEFEAT THE SINISTER SPELLS OF LOKI, GOD OF EVIL?
LOKI! PREPARE FOR BATTLE!
THE AVENGERS... BAH! I'LL DESTROY YOU ALL!
SUPER-HEROES! SUPER-VILLAINS! SUPER-THRILLS! PRESENTED IN THE FABULOUS MARVEL MANNER!

▲ *AVENGERS* #1

**September 1963**
**Artist:** Jack Kirby

By 1963, the Marvel Age of Comics was well underway, with Jack "King" Kirby proving invaluable as he helped build the Marvel Universe. Kirby's cover to the *Avengers*' debut issue brought together Marvel's biggest stars in one, all-powerful super-team. The issue was put together quickly, to replace the late-running *Daredevil* issue #1, but Kirby's artwork made it a smash hit.

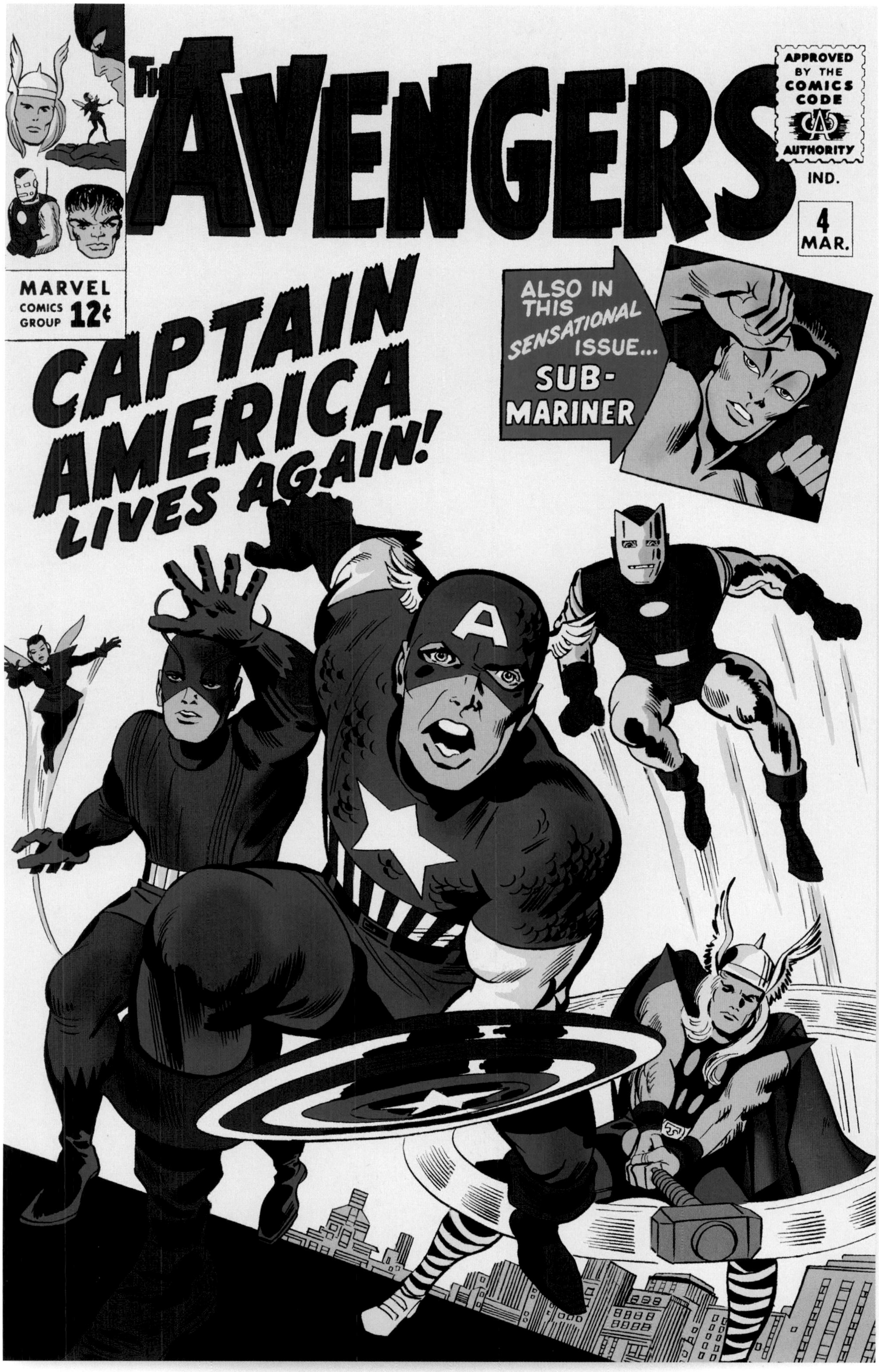

THE AVENGERS
APPROVED BY THE COMICS CODE AUTHORITY
IND.
4 MAR.
MARVEL COMICS GROUP 12¢
CAPTAIN AMERICA LIVES AGAIN!
ALSO IN THIS SENSATIONAL ISSUE... SUB-MARINER


▲ ***AVENGERS* #4**

**March 1964**
**Artist:** Jack Kirby

The Silver Age produced many classic covers. As Marvel found new ways of telling stories, they created dramatic covers to go with them—like this masterpiece featuring the return of Captain America. It wasn't the first time Cap's image had been used on a Marvel comic. *Strange Tales* issue #114 featured Cap fighting the Human Torch, but that Cap had proven to be an imposter. This one was very much the real thing.

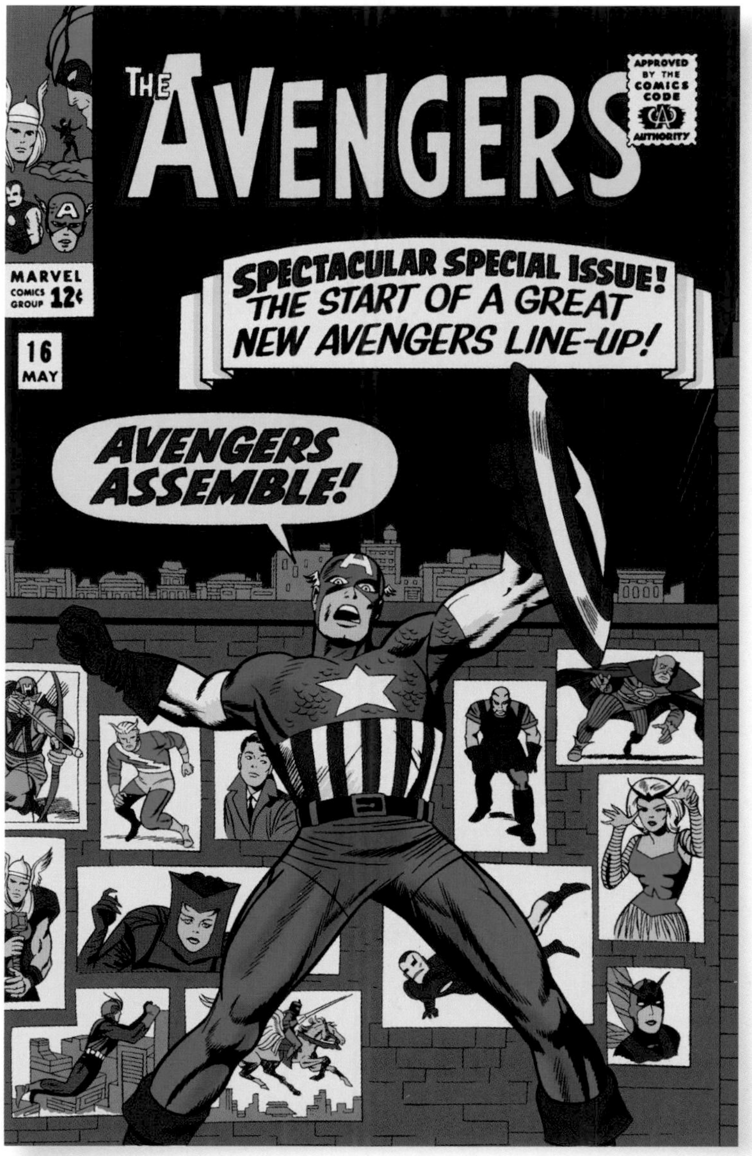

THE AVENGERS
APPROVED BY THE COMICS CODE AUTHORITY
MARVEL COMICS GROUP 12¢
16 MAY
SPECTACULAR SPECIAL ISSUE! THE START OF A GREAT NEW AVENGERS LINE-UP!
AVENGERS ASSEMBLE!


**◀ *AVENGERS* #16**

**May 1965**
**Artist:** Jack Kirby

If a company had a successful team-book, it was unheard of for them to change the formula. Marvel did just that—with only Cap remaining from the original Avengers line-up. The result is an eye-catching cover focusing on Cap as he brought together a new team. Removing established heroes from the cover and title and replacing them with relative unknowns was a groundbreaking move.

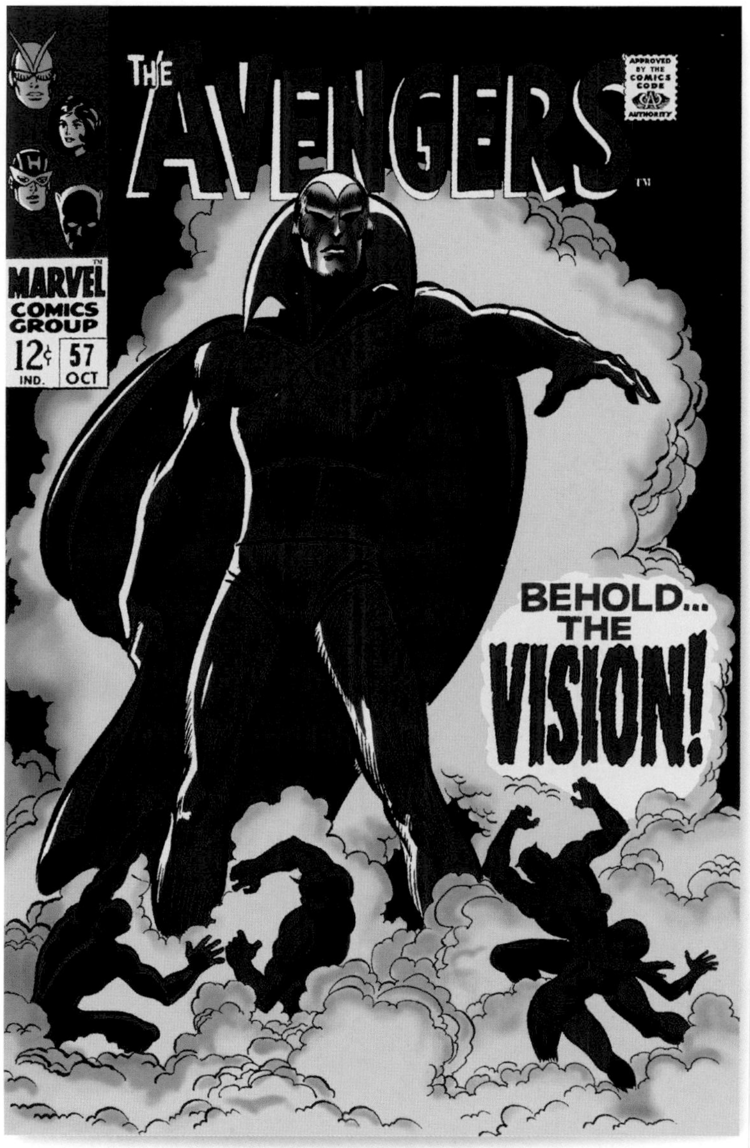

THE AVENGERS
MARVEL COMICS GROUP
12¢ IND. 57 OCT
BEHOLD... THE VISION!


**◀ *AVENGERS* #57**

**October 1968**
**Artist:** John Buscema

John Buscema was a master of form and dynamic poses. The first appearance of the Vision (inked by George Klein) shows just how powerful Buscema could make a simple image. Aided by an eye-catching coloring job, it remains one of the most memorable Avengers' covers and introduced one of the team's greatest heroes.

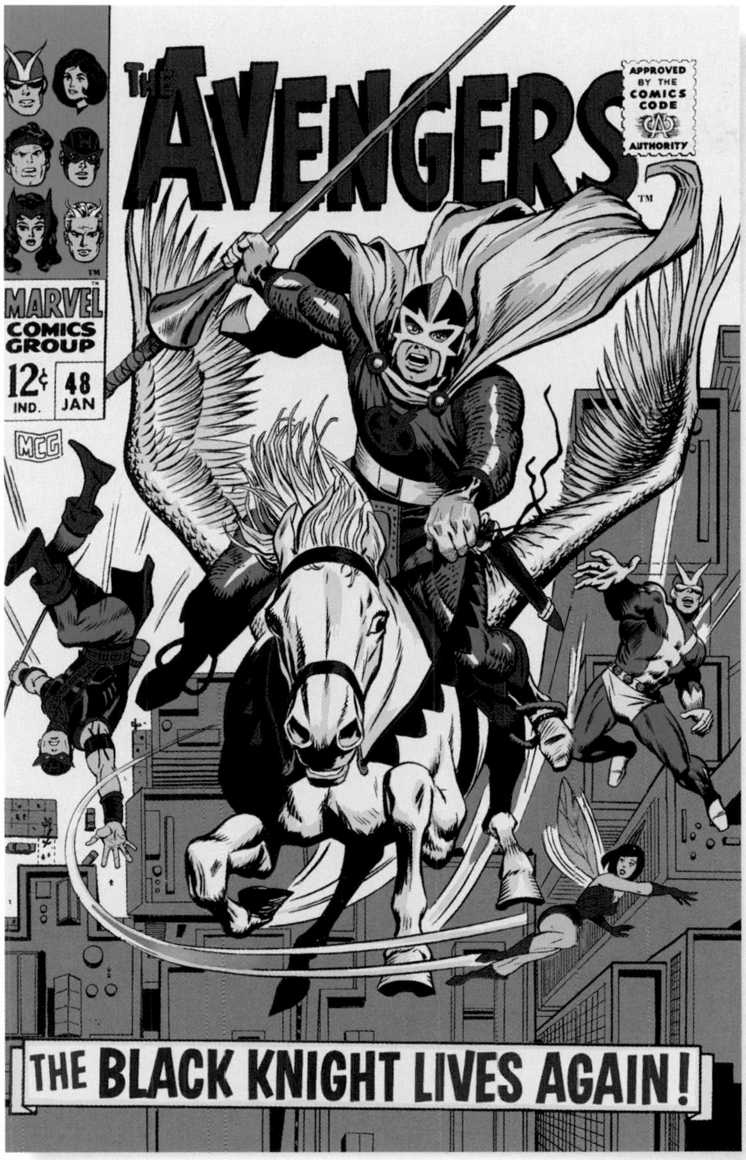
THE AVENGERS
APPROVED BY THE COMICS CODE AUTHORITY
MARVEL COMICS GROUP
12¢ IND.
48 JAN
MCG
THE BLACK KNIGHT LIVES AGAIN!

◀ *AVENGERS* #48

**January 1968**
**Artist:** George Tuska

George Tuska was at the helm for the introduction of a new Black Knight. Best known for his work on Iron Man, Tuska was a Marvel mainstay for much of the Silver Age. This Black Knight was the third incarnation of the character and would become a popular member of the Avengers.

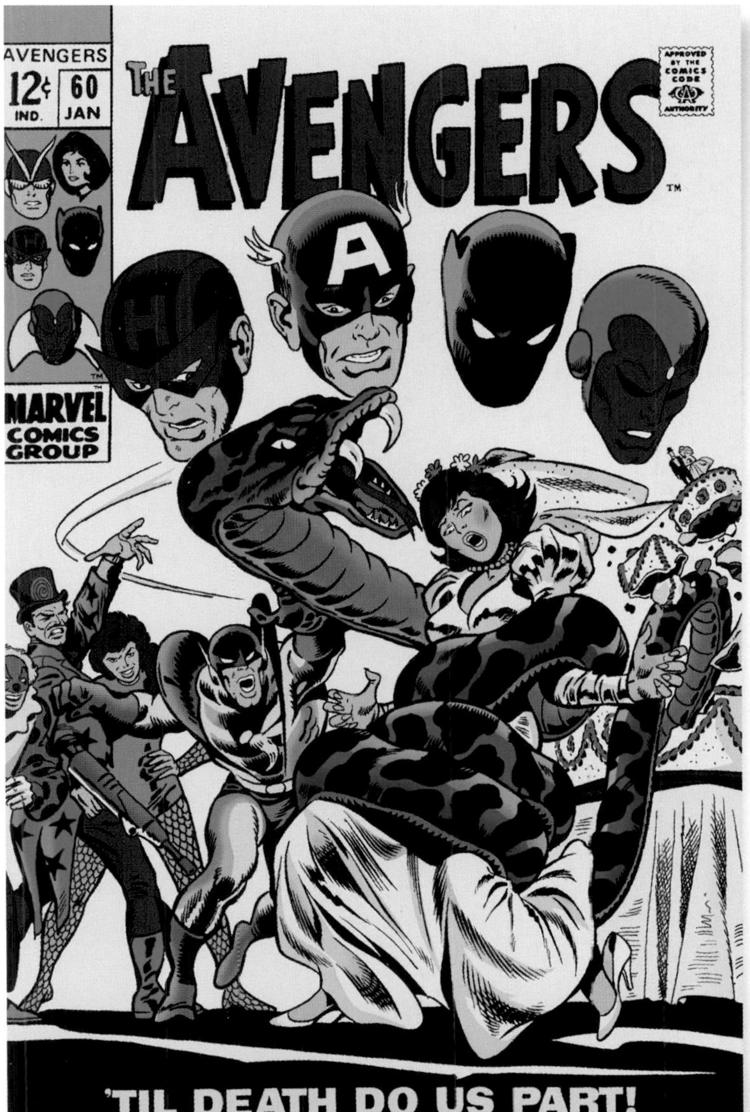
AVENGERS
12¢ IND.
60 JAN
THE AVENGERS
APPROVED BY THE COMICS CODE AUTHORITY
MARVEL COMICS GROUP
'TIL DEATH DO US PART!

◀ *AVENGERS* #60

**January 1969**
**Artist:** John Buscema

Weddings are always stressful—especially for Super Heroes. This John Buscema cover shows the artist at his dynamic best, as the Circus of Crime gatecrashes the Wasp's wedding to Yellowjacket (secretly her long-term beau Henry Pym). It's the sort of mad-but-brilliant concept that made Marvel Comics number one.

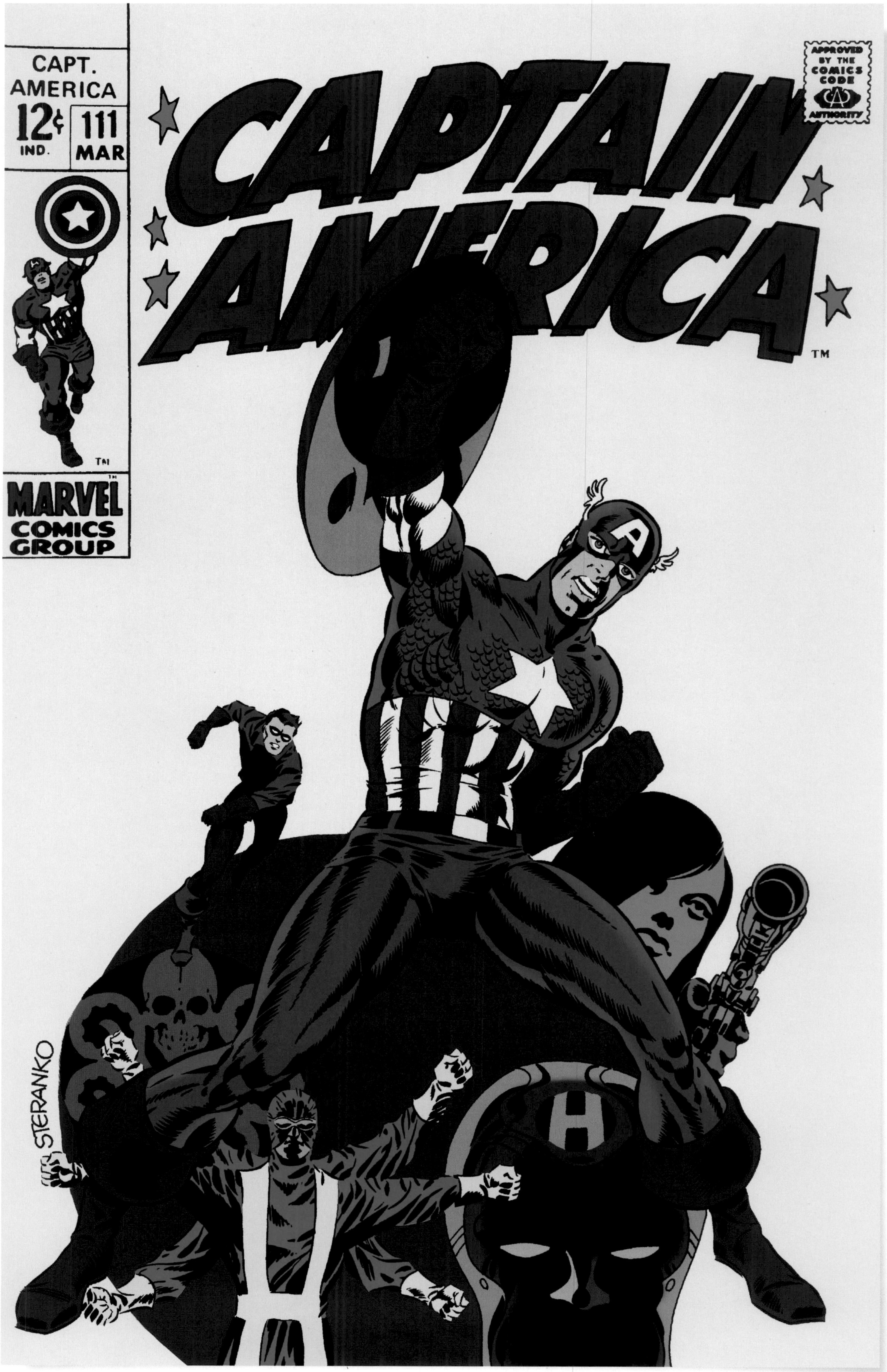
CAPT. AMERICA
12¢ IND.
111 MAR
MARVEL COMICS GROUP
CAPTAIN AMERICA
APPROVED BY THE COMICS CODE AUTHORITY
STERANKO

◀ ***CAPTAIN AMERICA* #111**

**March 1969**
**Artist:** Jim Steranko

Few artists have had such an impact as Jim Steranko. He brought a strong design sense to his work that established Marvel's books as cutting edge. This cover is a perfect example of Steranko's skill as a draftsman, while also including some of the more psychedelic elements often seen in his work.

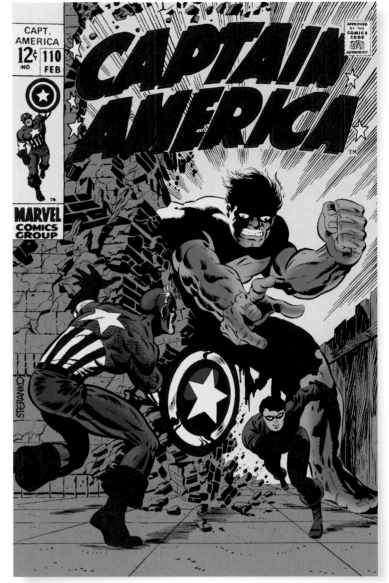

CAPT. AMERICA
12¢ 110 FEB
CAPTAIN AMERICA
MARVEL COMICS GROUP
STERANKO

***CAPTAIN AMERICA* #110** ▶

**February 1969**
**Artist:** Jim Steranko

Steranko drew a mean-looking Hulk—as this atmospheric cover shows. The Hulk is all about anger and raw power—facets that Steranko wonderfully brings out in his portrayal of the green-skinned beast. It's a version that also helps make Captain America look all the more heroic.

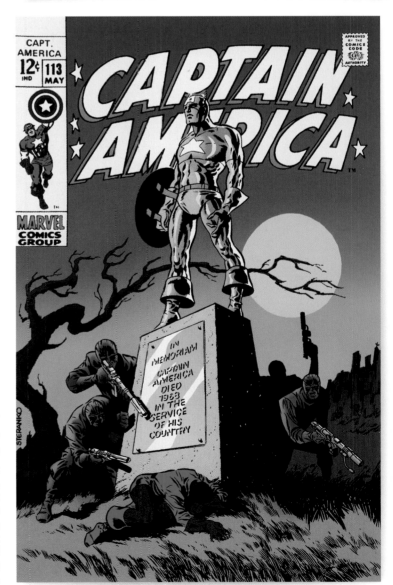

CAPT. AMERICA
12¢ 113 MAY
CAPTAIN AMERICA
MARVEL COMICS GROUP
IN MEMORIAM
CAPTAIN AMERICA
DIED
1968
IN THE
SERVICE
OF HIS
COUNTRY
STERANKO

***CAPTAIN AMERICA* #113** ▶

**May 1969**
**Artist:** Jim Steranko

Another Steranko masterpiece—not that he ever produced anything less. The image of Cap's headstone, with Bucky crying nearby, was sure to grab readers' attention. How can you look at that image and not want to know what was going on inside? That was part of Steranko's brilliance—strong images with even stronger hooks.

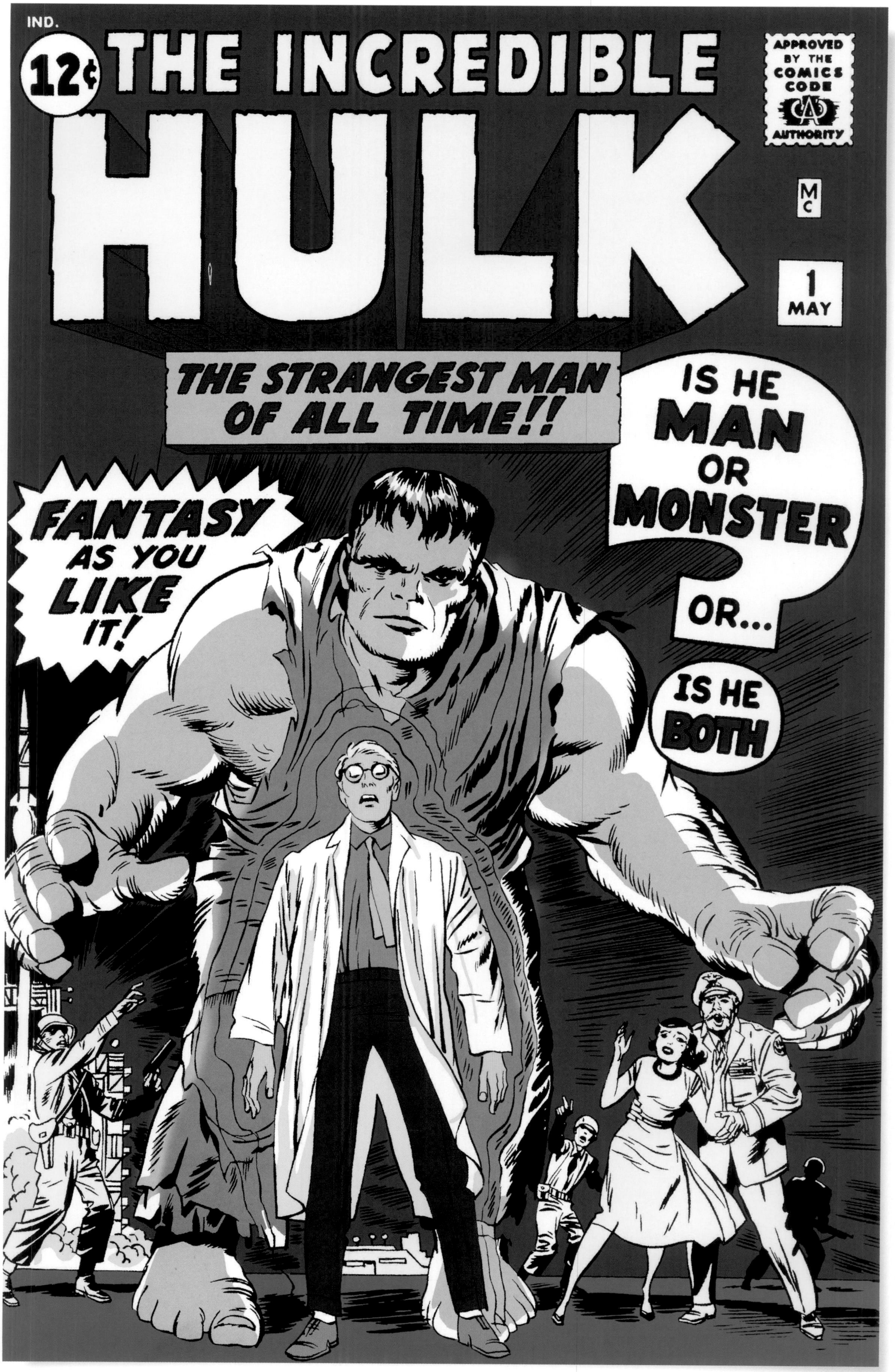
IND.
12¢
THE INCREDIBLE
HULK
APPROVED BY THE COMICS CODE AUTHORITY
MC
1
MAY
THE STRANGEST MAN OF ALL TIME!!
IS HE MAN OR MONSTER OR...
IS HE BOTH
FANTASY AS YOU LIKE IT!

◀ ***INCREDIBLE HULK* #1**

**May 1962**
**Artist:** Jack Kirby

Jack Kirby only illustrated the first five issues of *Incredible Hulk*, but his cover to the debut issue firmly established the concept of the Banner-Hulk transformation and created what was to become an iconic image for Marvel. The taglines help pull the reader in, but it is Kirby's powerful central image of Bruce Banner and the Hulk (gray-skinned in his first appearance) that really makes for a dramatic cover.

HULK
MARVEL COMICS GROUP
12¢ IND.
109 NOV
THE LOST LAND OF KA-ZAR
TRIMPE & SEVERIN

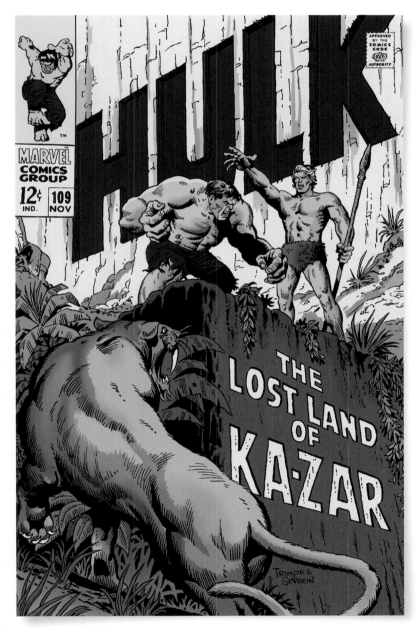

▲ ***INCREDIBLE HULK* #109**

**November 1968**
**Artist:** Herb Trimpe

Herb Trimpe remains best known for his work on the Hulk, a character he illustrated for seven years in the late 1960s/early 1970s. This early cover (inked by John Severin) shows Marvel's keen eye for design in the way they played with the logo and title to add more impact to the finished cover.

INCREDIBLE HULK
15¢ IND.
118 AUG
THE INCREDIBLE HULK
MARVEL COMICS GROUP
TRIMPE
GUEST-STARRING: THE SUB-MARINER!

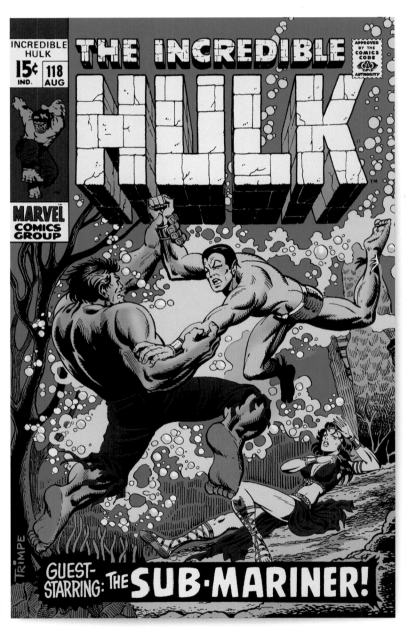

▲ ***INCREDIBLE HULK* #118**

**August 1969**
**Artist:** Herb Trimpe

This early confrontation between the Hulk and Sub-Mariner shows Trimpe at his artistic best. The Sub-Mariner had mostly reformed by this point in Marvel continuity, but a fight between the two heroes was bound to attract the reader—especially as Trimpe manages to convey the power of both characters so well.

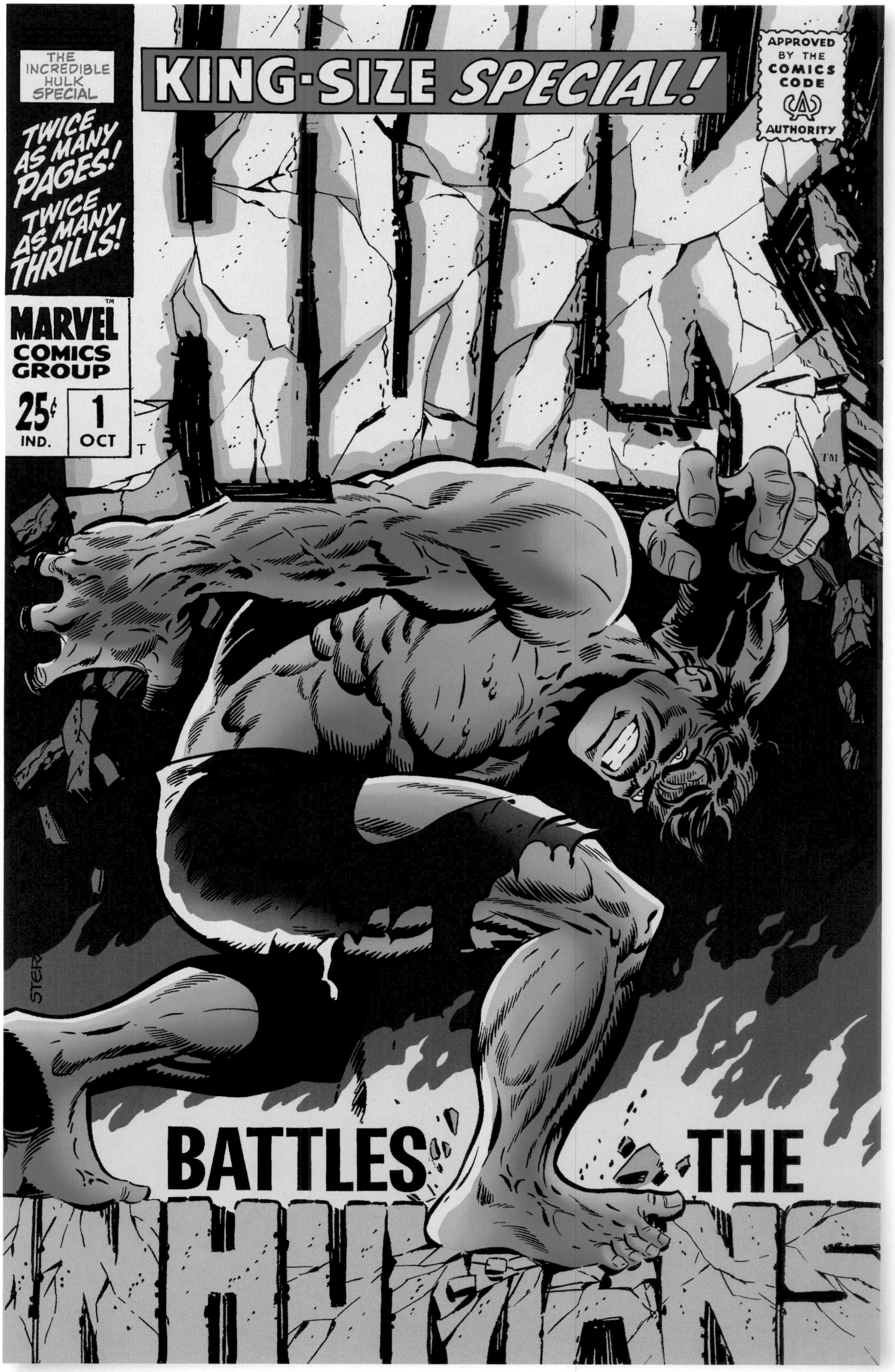
THE INCREDIBLE HULK SPECIAL
KING-SIZE SPECIAL!
APPROVED BY THE COMICS CODE AUTHORITY
TWICE AS MANY PAGES! TWICE AS MANY THRILLS!
MARVEL COMICS GROUP
25¢ IND.
1 OCT
STER
BATTLES THE

▲ *INCREDIBLE HULK KING-SIZE SPECIAL* #1

**October 1968**
**Artist:** Jim Steranko

This cover has proven to be one of the most popular (and copied) covers of all time. It also harbors a secret—the Hulk's head isn't by Steranko. The editor wasn't happy with the original, so he had Marie Severin draw a new head to paste over the original. It's still regarded as an epic work—and the full original was later shown in the UK on *Mighty World of Marvel* issue #129 (March 1979).

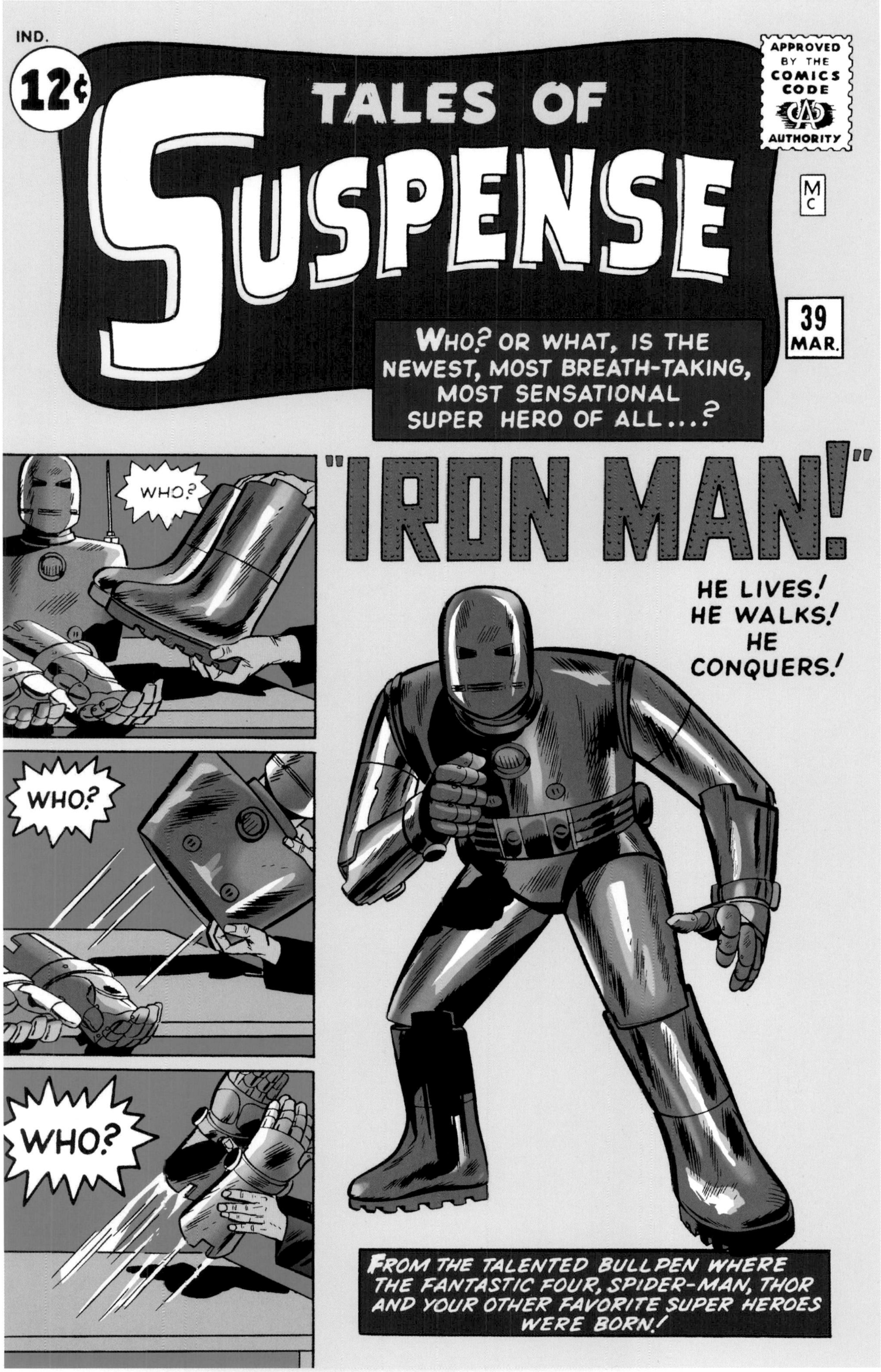
IND.
12¢
TALES OF SUSPENSE
APPROVED BY THE COMICS CODE AUTHORITY
MC
39 MAR.
WHO? OR WHAT, IS THE NEWEST, MOST BREATH-TAKING, MOST SENSATIONAL SUPER HERO OF ALL...?
"IRON MAN!"
WHO?
WHO?
WHO?
HE LIVES! HE WALKS! HE CONQUERS!
FROM THE TALENTED BULLPEN WHERE THE FANTASTIC FOUR, SPIDER-MAN, THOR AND YOUR OTHER FAVORITE SUPER HEROES WERE BORN!

▲ *TALES OF SUSPENSE* **#39**

**March 1963**
**Artist:** Jack Kirby

As Marvel's undisputed artistic "King," Jack Kirby was often tasked with creating the covers of key issues, such as the first appearance of Iron Man. The three-panel breakdown next to the large image of Iron Man provided an eye-catching contrast from the regular full-page cover images, and owed a lot to the magazine's past as a horror anthology.

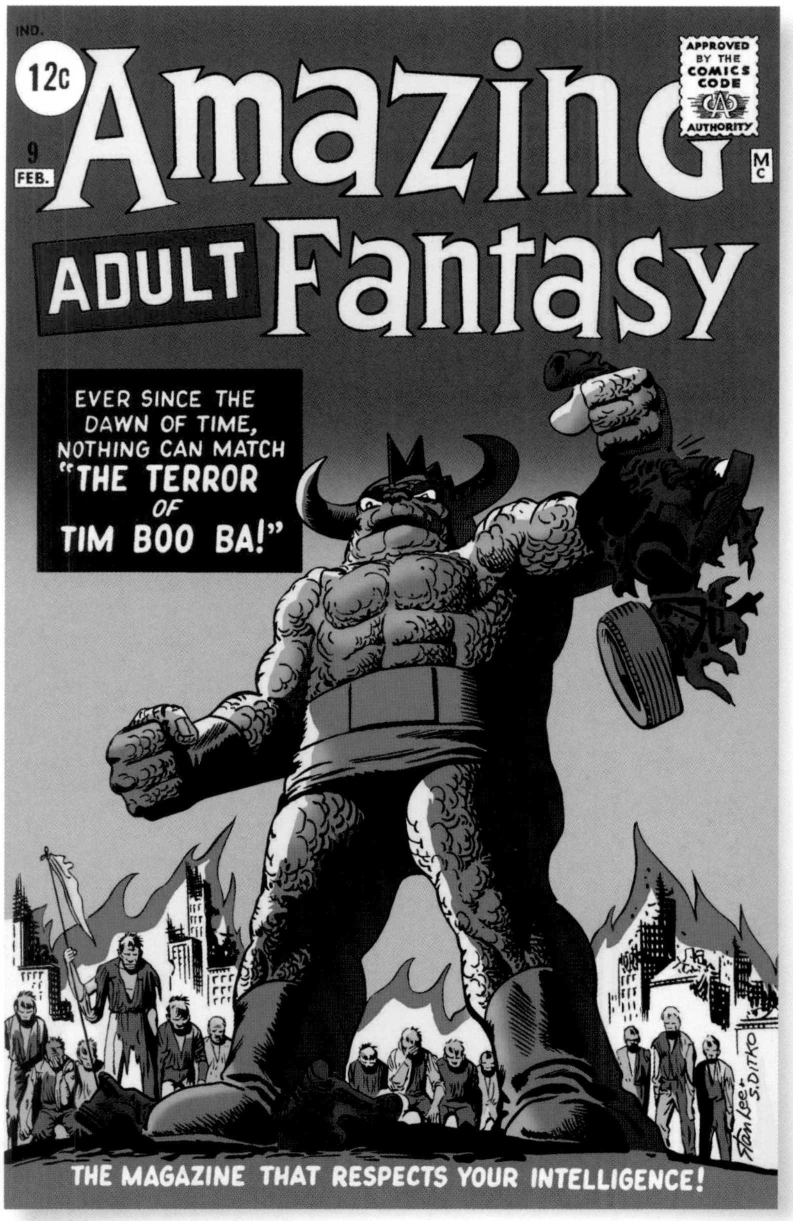
12¢
Amazing
9
FEB.
APPROVED BY THE COMICS CODE AUTHORITY
MC
ADULT Fantasy
EVER SINCE THE DAWN OF TIME, NOTHING CAN MATCH "THE TERROR OF TIM BOO BA!"
THE MAGAZINE THAT RESPECTS YOUR INTELLIGENCE!

▲ *AMAZING ADULT FANTASY* #9

**February 1962**
**Artist:** Steve Ditko

Before Steve Ditko gave Spider-Man his unique look, he brought one of the all-time great monsters to life. Tim Boo Ba was an intergalactic ruler who led a reign of terror across the universe. Ditko was a master of bizarre visuals (as his work on the character Doctor Strange would prove), and Tim Boo Ba is an imposing figure on the cover. The real terror, however, emanates from the slumped forms of his enslaved victims.

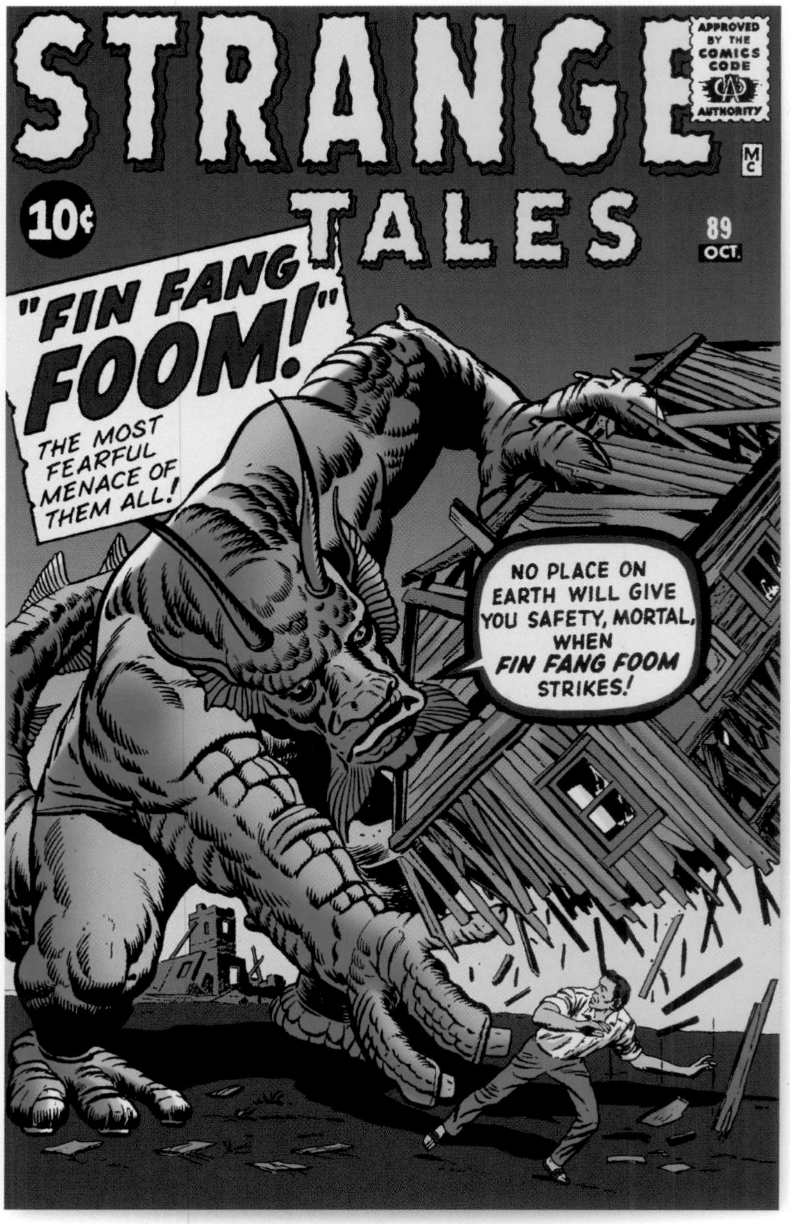
STRANGE TALES
APPROVED BY THE COMICS CODE AUTHORITY
MC
10¢
89
OCT.
"FIN FANG FOOM!"
THE MOST FEARFUL MENACE OF THEM ALL!
NO PLACE ON EARTH WILL GIVE YOU SAFETY, MORTAL, WHEN FIN FANG FOOM STRIKES!

▲ *STRANGE TALES* #89

**October 1961**
**Artist:** Jack Kirby

Rivalling Tim Boo Ba in the great monster stakes is the rather brilliant Fin Fang Foom. This Jack Kirby creation was an ancient dragon (later revealed as an alien) that sought to wreak havoc on the world. The monster's unique look makes for an eye-catching cover. He was one of the few monsters to make the transition to the Marvel Universe, taking on Iron Man and the Hulk years later.

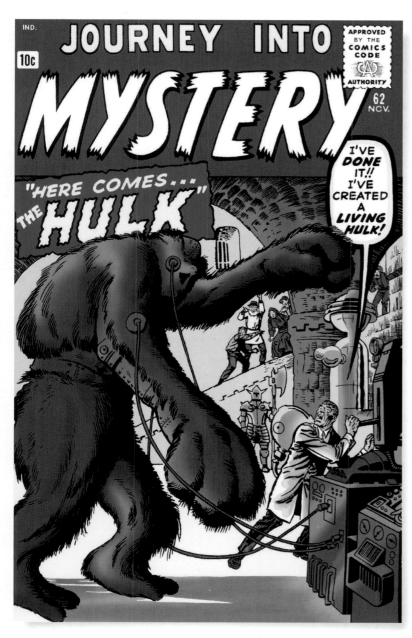

IND.
JOURNEY INTO
10¢
APPROVED BY THE COMICS CODE AUTHORITY
MYSTERY
62 NOV.
"HERE COMES..." THE HULK
I'VE DONE IT!! I'VE CREATED A LIVING HULK!

▲ *JOURNEY INTO MYSTERY* #62

**November 1960**
**Artist:** Jack Kirby

The first Hulk created by Stan Lee and Jack Kirby wasn't the famous green-skinned behemoth, but this alien-would-be conqueror of Earth. It is a sign of Kirby's amazing skill at character design that a number of his early creations, such as Captain America and Fin Fang Foom, later lived on in the Marvel Universe. This Hulk, after a name change to Xemnu, took on the Defenders in *Marvel Feature* issue #3.

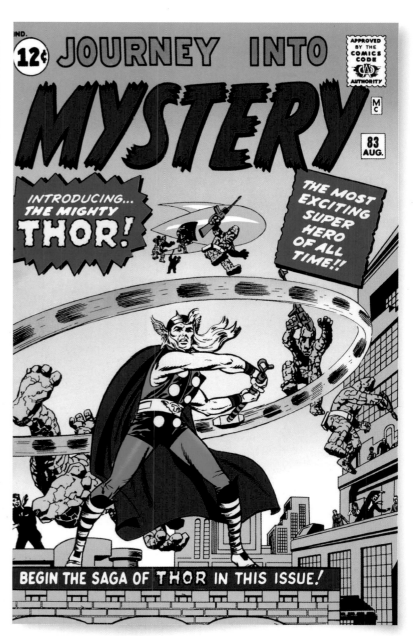

IND.
12¢
JOURNEY INTO
APPROVED BY THE COMICS CODE AUTHORITY
MYSTERY
MC
83 AUG.
INTRODUCING... THE MIGHTY THOR!
THE MOST EXCITING SUPER HERO OF ALL TIME!!
BEGIN THE SAGA OF THOR IN THIS ISSUE!

▲ *JOURNEY INTO MYSTERY* #83

**August 1962**
**Artist:** Jack Kirby

Jack Kirby was perfectly suited to drawing Thor and the gods of Asgard. He had a gift for portraying beings of real power, and heroes don't come much more powerful than the Norse God of Thunder. The cover of Thor's first appearance has rightly become a classic as the Norse god took on the Stone Men of Saturn. It was a nod to the science fiction stories previously seen in the title.

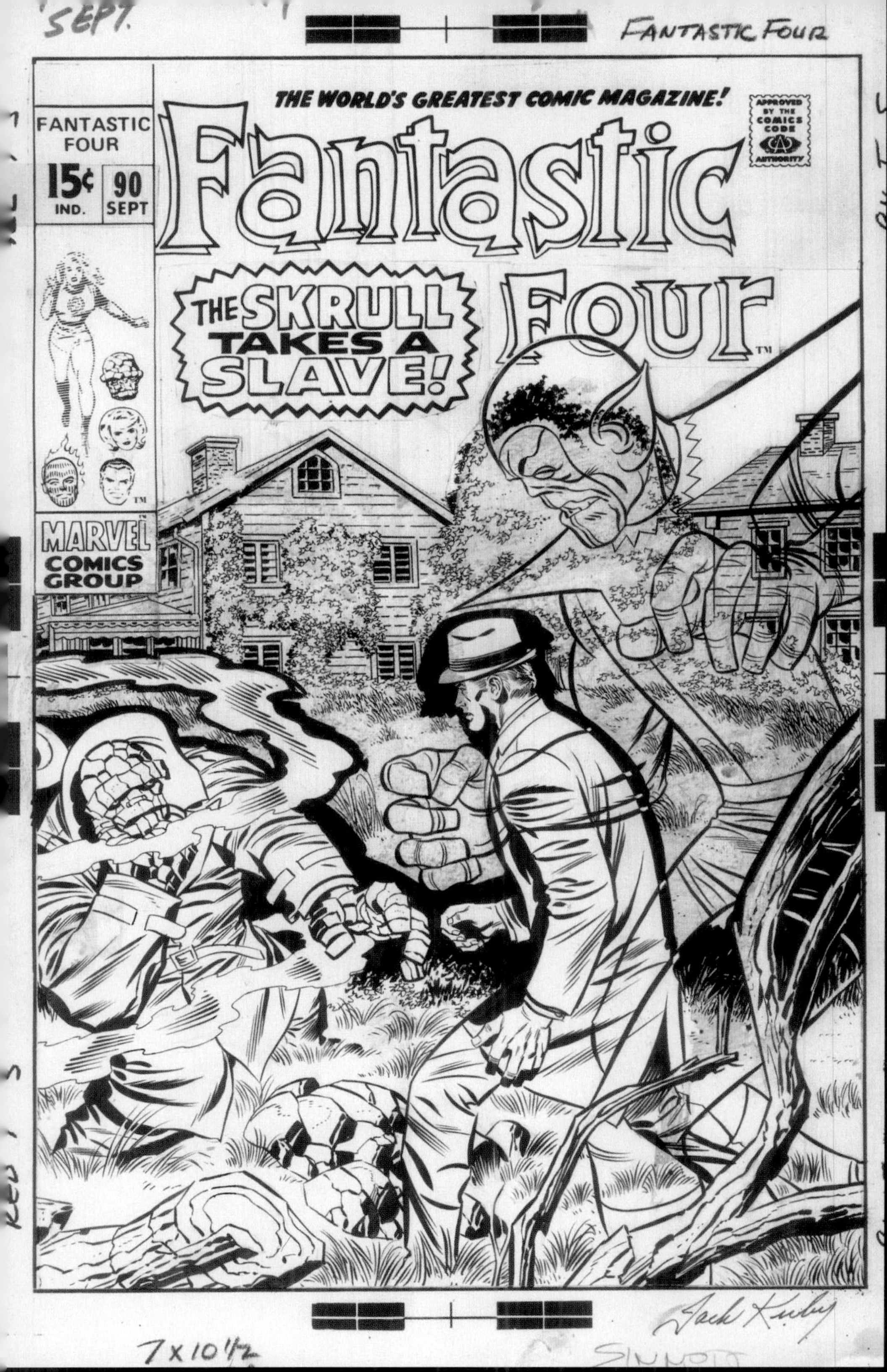
SEPT.
FANTASTIC FOUR
THE WORLD'S GREATEST COMIC MAGAZINE!
FANTASTIC FOUR
15¢ IND.
90 SEPT
APPROVED BY THE COMICS CODE AUTHORITY
Fantastic Four
THE SKRULL TAKES A SLAVE!
MARVEL COMICS GROUP
Jack Kirby
7 x 10½
SINNOTT

1.

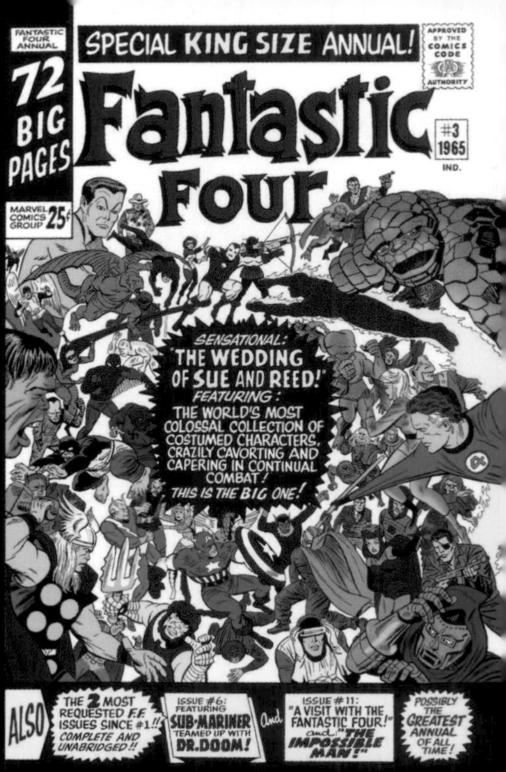
FANTASTIC FOUR ANNUAL
SPECIAL KING SIZE ANNUAL!
APPROVED BY THE COMICS CODE AUTHORITY
72 BIG PAGES
Fantastic Four
#3 1965 IND.
MARVEL COMICS GROUP 25¢
SENSATIONAL: "THE WEDDING OF SUE AND REED!" FEATURING: THE WORLD'S MOST COLOSSAL COLLECTION OF COSTUMED CHARACTERS, CRAZILY CAVORTING AND CAPERING IN CONTINUAL COMBAT! THIS IS THE BIG ONE!
ALSO
THE 2 MOST REQUESTED F.F. ISSUES SINCE #1!! COMPLETE AND UNABRIDGED!!
ISSUE #6: FEATURING SUB-MARINER TEAMED UP WITH DR. DOOM!
and
ISSUE #11: "A VISIT WITH THE FANTASTIC FOUR!" and "THE IMPOSSIBLE MAN!"
POSSIBLY THE GREATEST ANNUAL OF ALL TIME!

2.

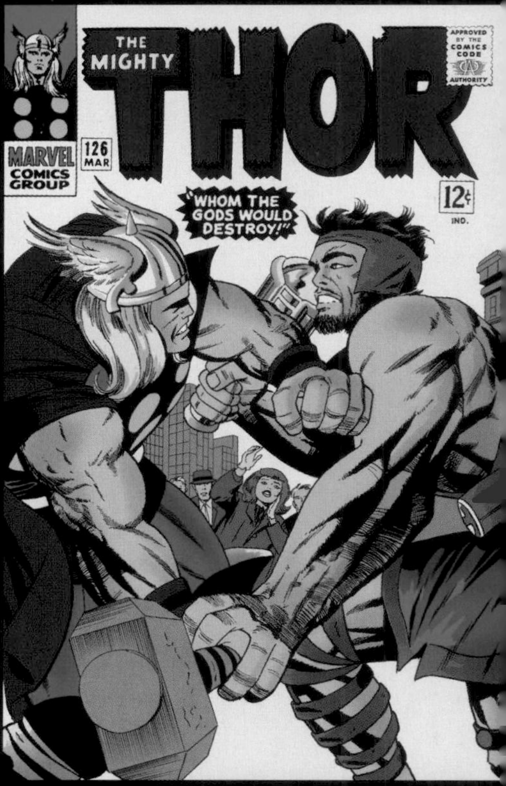
THE MIGHTY THOR
APPROVED BY THE COMICS CODE AUTHORITY
MARVEL COMICS GROUP
126 MAR
12¢ IND.
"WHOM THE GODS WOULD DESTROY!"

3.

# JACK KIRBY

n a career that spanned over seven decades, Kirby is said to nave pretty much created the rules of comic book art. This "King of Comics" helped to create many of Marvel's greatest neroes and produced countless legendary covers. With writer Joe Simon, Kirby helped to create Captain America, bringing a sense of humanity to the Super Hero. He worked on a variety of genres, from romance to monster comics, but it is his work for Marvel for which he is best known. The Fantastic Four, Avengers, Thor, Hulk, and the X-Men are just some of the heroes Kirby created with Stan Lee. Their work laid the foundations of the Marvel Universe and brought a new style of storytelling to the medium—one that mixed bombastic cosmic action with down-to-earth drama

### 1. *FANTASTIC FOUR* #90

**September 1969**

This cover (original artwork shown here) is a good example of the mix of the mundane with the alien that made the title such a smash hit. Kirby loved illustrating The Thing—perhaps because Ben Grimm's background was partially based on the artist's own upbringing in Manhattan's Lower Eastside.

### 2. *FANTASTIC FOUR ANNUAL* #3

**October 1965**

Jack Kirby worked with Stan Lee to create most of Marvel's heroes and villains—and they all came together for the wedding of Mr. Fantastic and the Invisible Woman in this annual

### 3. *THOR* #126

**March 1966**

Kirby's robust style was perfect for portraying characters of real power—and they didn't come more powerful than Thor and his fellow Asgardian gods. This action-filled cover ripples with energy as Thor and Hercules clash.

### 4. *FANTASTIC FOUR* #72

**March 1968**

This cover features two of the elements that Kirby is best known for—the Silver Surfer and the "Kirby Krackle." The latter is an art technique Kirby started to use at this time, using black dots and fractal imagery to denote cosmic energy

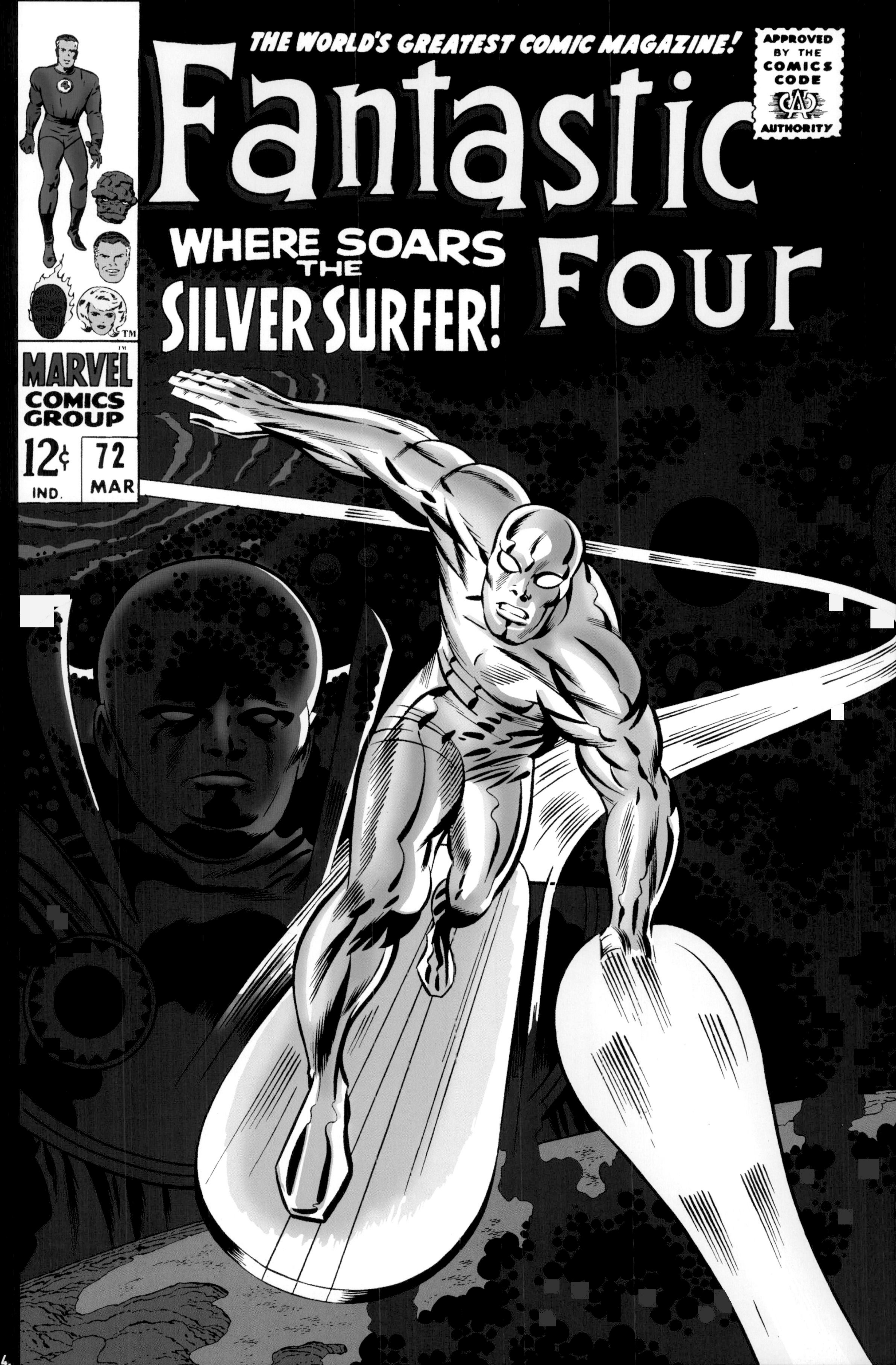
THE WORLD'S GREATEST COMIC MAGAZINE!
APPROVED BY THE COMICS CODE AUTHORITY
Fantastic Four
WHERE SOARS THE SILVER SURFER!
MARVEL COMICS GROUP
12¢ IND.
72 MAR

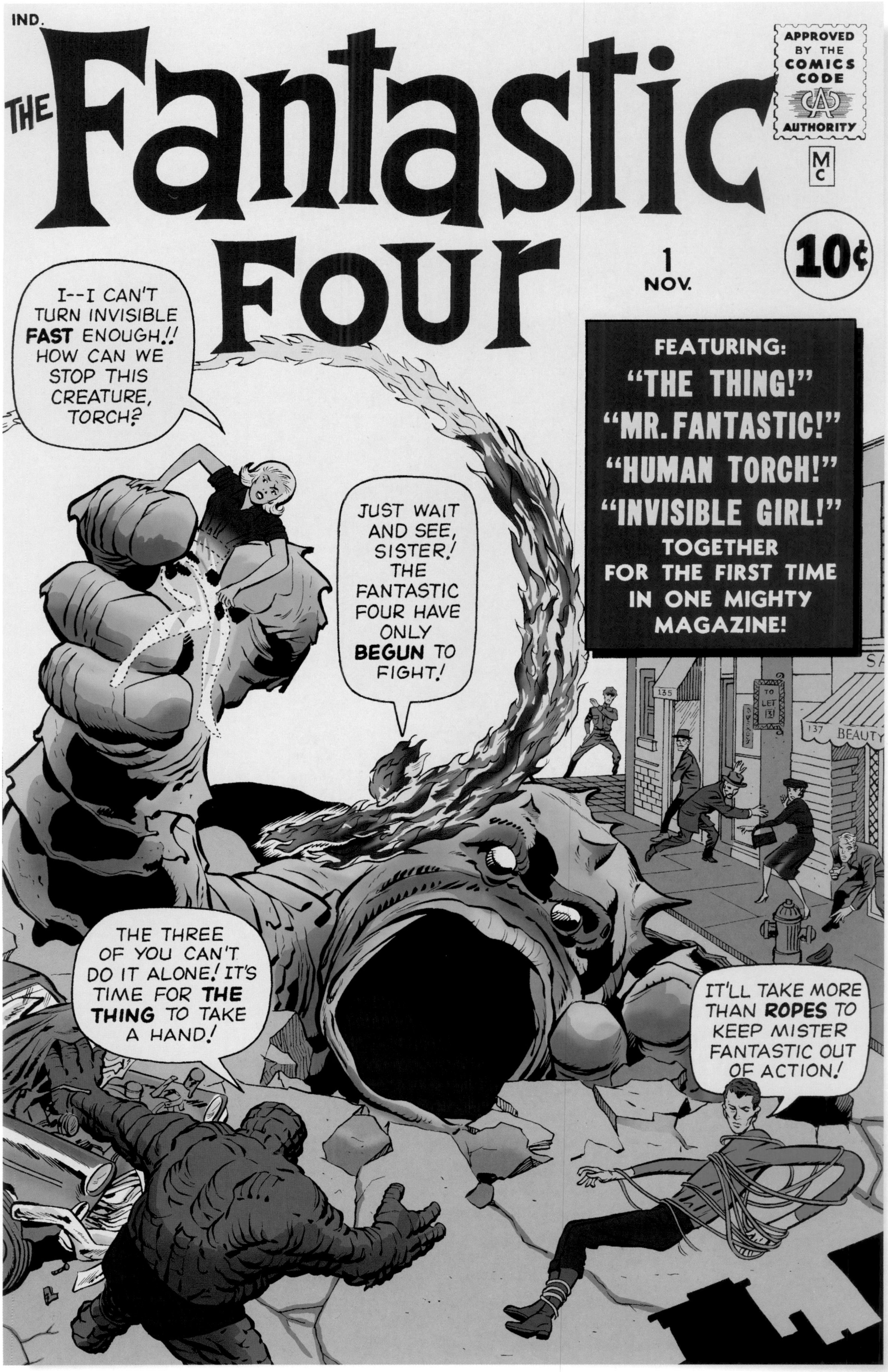
IND.
THE Fantastic FOUR
1
NOV.
10¢
APPROVED BY THE COMICS CODE AUTHORITY
MC
I--I CAN'T TURN INVISIBLE FAST ENOUGH!! HOW CAN WE STOP THIS CREATURE, TORCH?
FEATURING: "THE THING!" "MR. FANTASTIC!" "HUMAN TORCH!" "INVISIBLE GIRL!" TOGETHER FOR THE FIRST TIME IN ONE MIGHTY MAGAZINE!
JUST WAIT AND SEE, SISTER! THE FANTASTIC FOUR HAVE ONLY BEGUN TO FIGHT!
135
TO LET
137
BEAUTY
THE THREE OF YOU CAN'T DO IT ALONE! IT'S TIME FOR THE THING TO TAKE A HAND!
IT'LL TAKE MORE THAN ROPES TO KEEP MISTER FANTASTIC OUT OF ACTION!

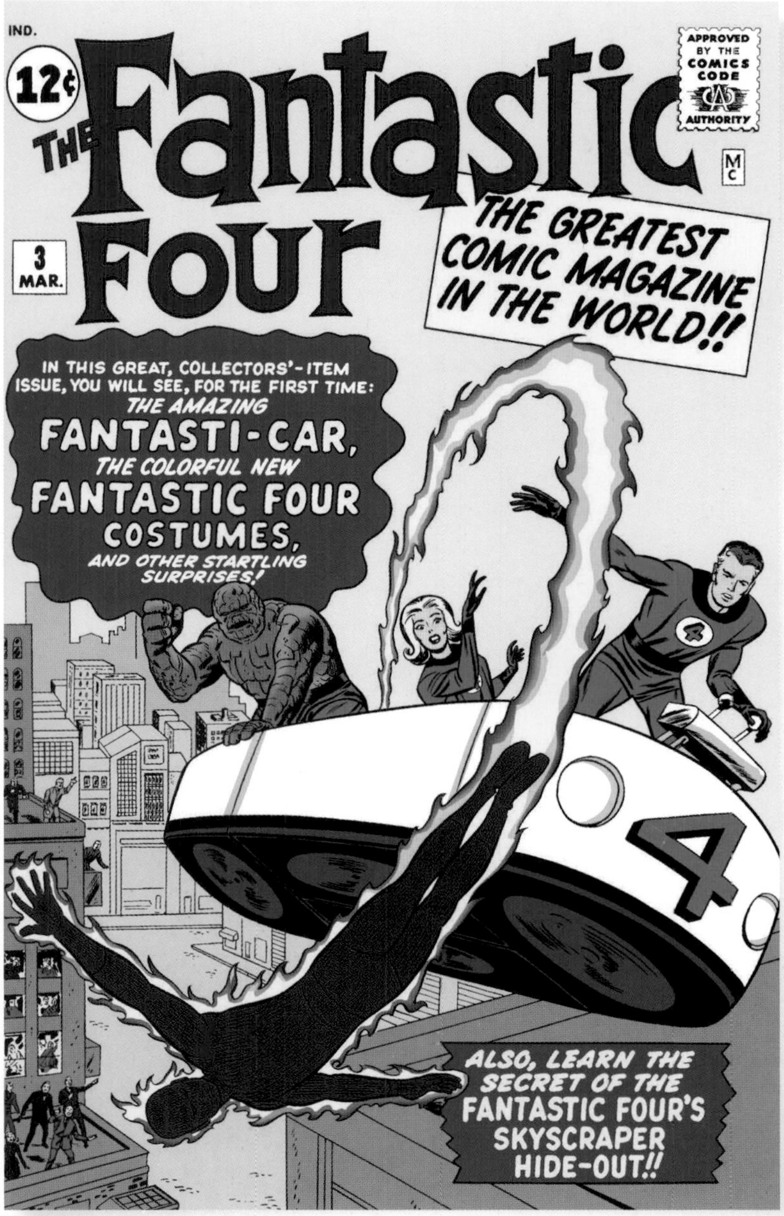
IND.
12¢
APPROVED BY THE COMICS CODE AUTHORITY
THE Fantastic FOUR
3 MAR.
THE GREATEST COMIC MAGAZINE IN THE WORLD!!
IN THIS GREAT, COLLECTORS'-ITEM ISSUE, YOU WILL SEE, FOR THE FIRST TIME: THE AMAZING FANTASTI-CAR, THE COLORFUL NEW FANTASTIC FOUR COSTUMES, AND OTHER STARTLING SURPRISES!
ALSO, LEARN THE SECRET OF THE FANTASTIC FOUR'S SKYSCRAPER HIDE-OUT!!

▲ *FANTASTIC FOUR #3*

**March 1962**
**Artist:** Jack Kirby

Part of *Fantastic Four*'s success was down to the sheer brilliance of Kirby's artwork and his design of the team and their home. The Fantasti-car is revealed on the cover to issue #3, which also has the FF in costume for the first time. It establishes the book as a unique take on Super Heroes.

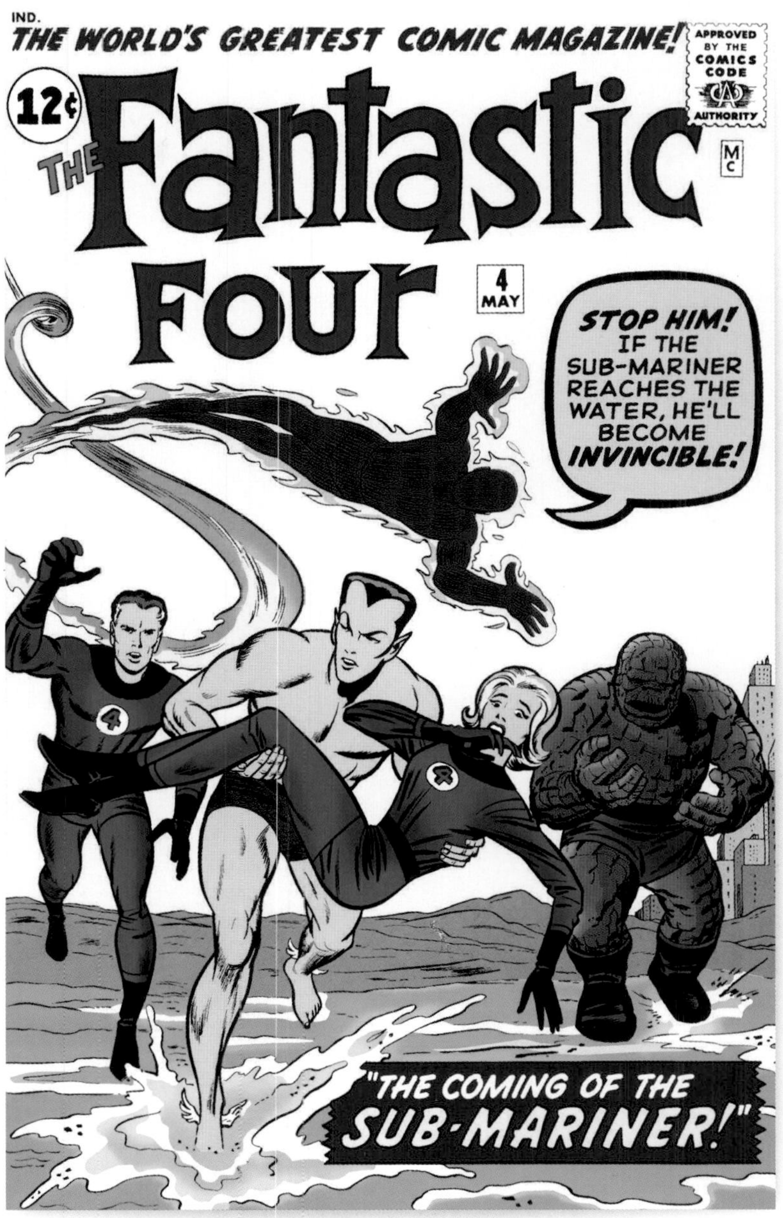
IND.
THE WORLD'S GREATEST COMIC MAGAZINE!
APPROVED BY THE COMICS CODE AUTHORITY
12¢
THE Fantastic FOUR
4 MAY
STOP HIM! IF THE SUB-MARINER REACHES THE WATER, HE'LL BECOME INVINCIBLE!
"THE COMING OF THE SUB-MARINER!"

▲ *FANTASTIC FOUR #4*

**May 1962**
**Artist:** Jack Kirby

The Sub-Mariner made his first Silver Age appearance in this issue. But instead of the hero of old, he was now a villain attempting to destroy the surface world and kidnap Sue Storm. It also proved to be the start of one of Marvel's best love triangles, as Sue Storm found herself torn between the Sub-Mariner and Reed Richards.

◀ *FANTASTIC FOUR #1*

**November 1961**
**Artist:** Jack Kirby

The first issue of *Fantastic Four* heralded the start of the Marvel Universe. It also introduced a new type of storytelling—one that mixed soap opera dramatics with amazing stories and fantastical new heroes. Jack Kirby's cover hints at this new direction, as it portrays regular people with amazing powers, fighting a monstrous foe (later revealed as Giganto, a pawn of the Mole Man).

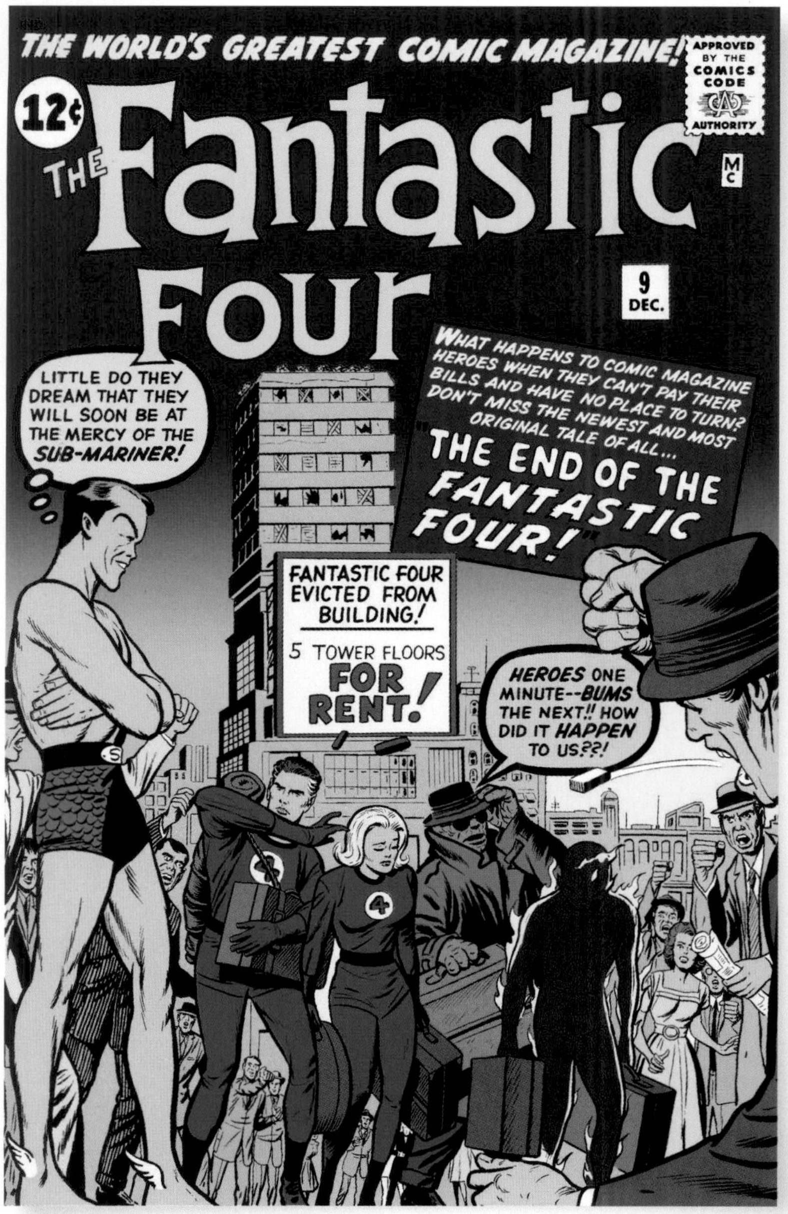
THE WORLD'S GREATEST COMIC MAGAZINE!
APPROVED BY THE COMICS CODE AUTHORITY
12¢
THE Fantastic Four
MC
9 DEC.
LITTLE DO THEY DREAM THAT THEY WILL SOON BE AT THE MERCY OF THE SUB-MARINER!
WHAT HAPPENS TO COMIC MAGAZINE HEROES WHEN THEY CAN'T PAY THEIR BILLS AND HAVE NO PLACE TO TURN? DON'T MISS THE NEWEST AND MOST ORIGINAL TALE OF ALL... "THE END OF THE FANTASTIC FOUR!"
FANTASTIC FOUR EVICTED FROM BUILDING!
5 TOWER FLOORS FOR RENT!
HEROES ONE MINUTE--BUMS THE NEXT!! HOW DID IT HAPPEN TO US??!

▲ *FANTASTIC FOUR* #9

**December 1962**
**Artist:** Jack Kirby

This Kirby creation is pure Hollywood drama as Namor uses his wealth to turn people against the Fantastic Four. The copyline says it all—what happens when the FF can't pay the rent? It was the sort of everyday problem readers could identify with, and it helped make the FF seem more real than many of their contemporaries.

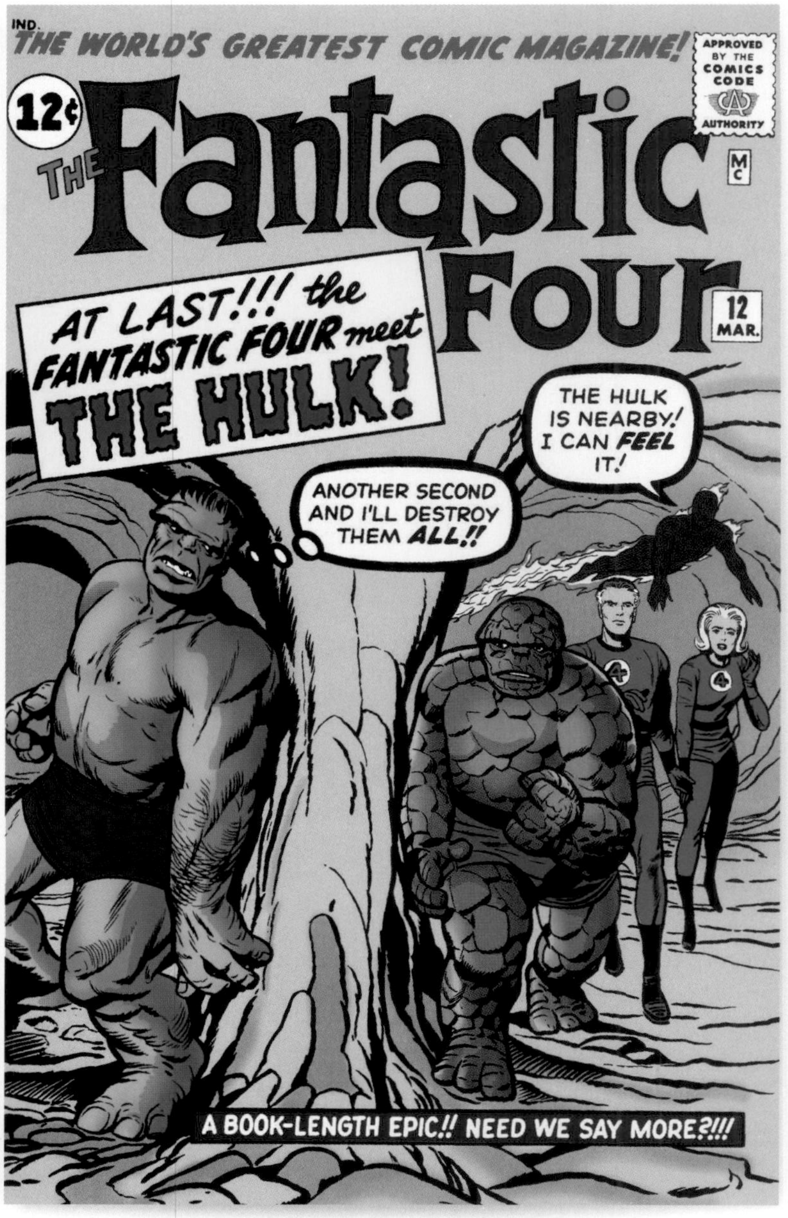
IND.
THE WORLD'S GREATEST COMIC MAGAZINE!
APPROVED BY THE COMICS CODE AUTHORITY
12¢
THE Fantastic Four
MC
12 MAR.
AT LAST!!! the FANTASTIC FOUR meet THE HULK!
THE HULK IS NEARBY! I CAN FEEL IT!
ANOTHER SECOND AND I'LL DESTROY THEM ALL!!
A BOOK-LENGTH EPIC!! NEED WE SAY MORE?!!!

▲ *FANTASTIC FOUR* #12

**March 1963**
**Artist:** Jack Kirby

The Thing fighting the Hulk is a slugfest Marvel fans love. The two met for the first time in this issue—the cover teasing the reader with the prospect of their confrontation. Kirby had already started to mutate the Thing into his well-known rocky form, while his Hulk was all about brute force.

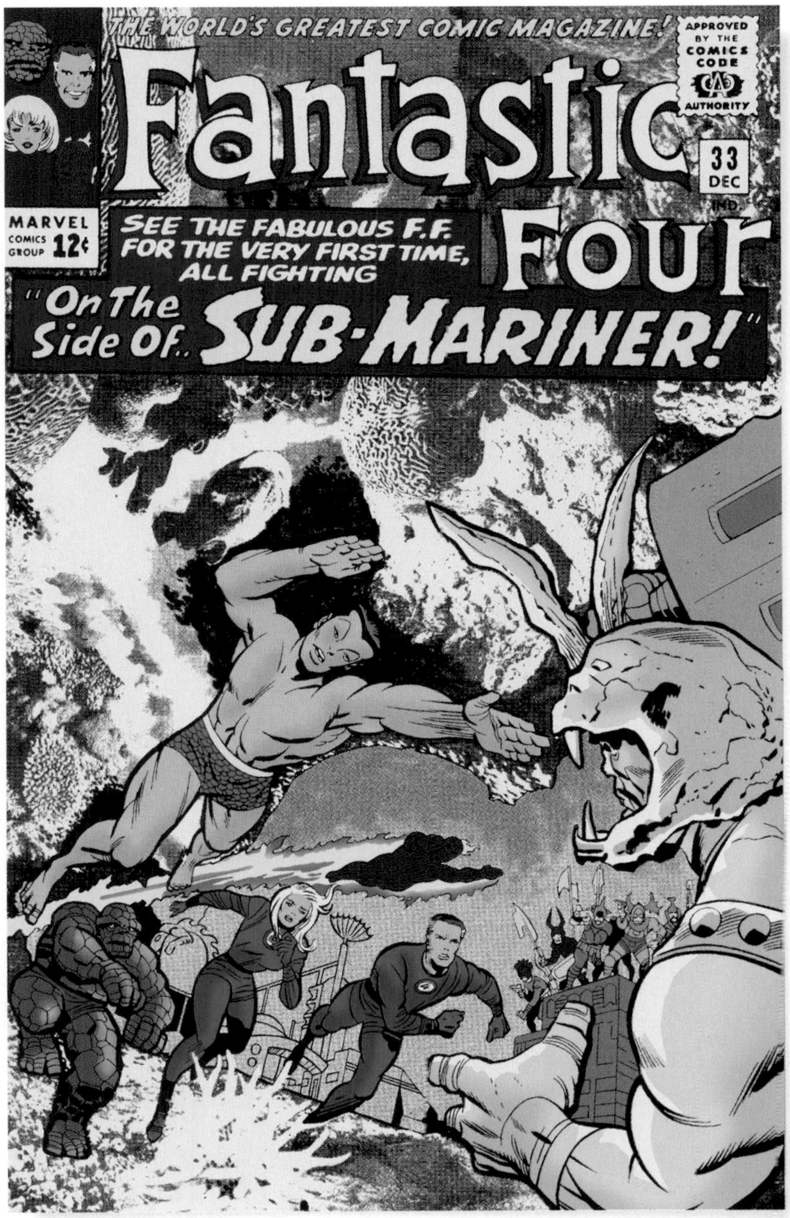
THE WORLD'S GREATEST COMIC MAGAZINE!
APPROVED BY THE COMICS CODE AUTHORITY
Fantastic Four
33 DEC
MARVEL COMICS GROUP 12¢
SEE THE FABULOUS F.F. FOR THE VERY FIRST TIME, ALL FIGHTING
"On The Side Of.. SUB-MARINER!"

▲ *FANTASTIC FOUR* #33

**December 1964**
**Artist:** Jack Kirby

Jack Kirby was constantly experimenting with new ways of creating art, sometimes using collages of photos and artwork to create amazing images. These were rarely used on covers, making the cover for *Fantastic Four* issue #33 all the more special. It is a great example of how Kirby constantly pushed the boundaries of comic cover art.

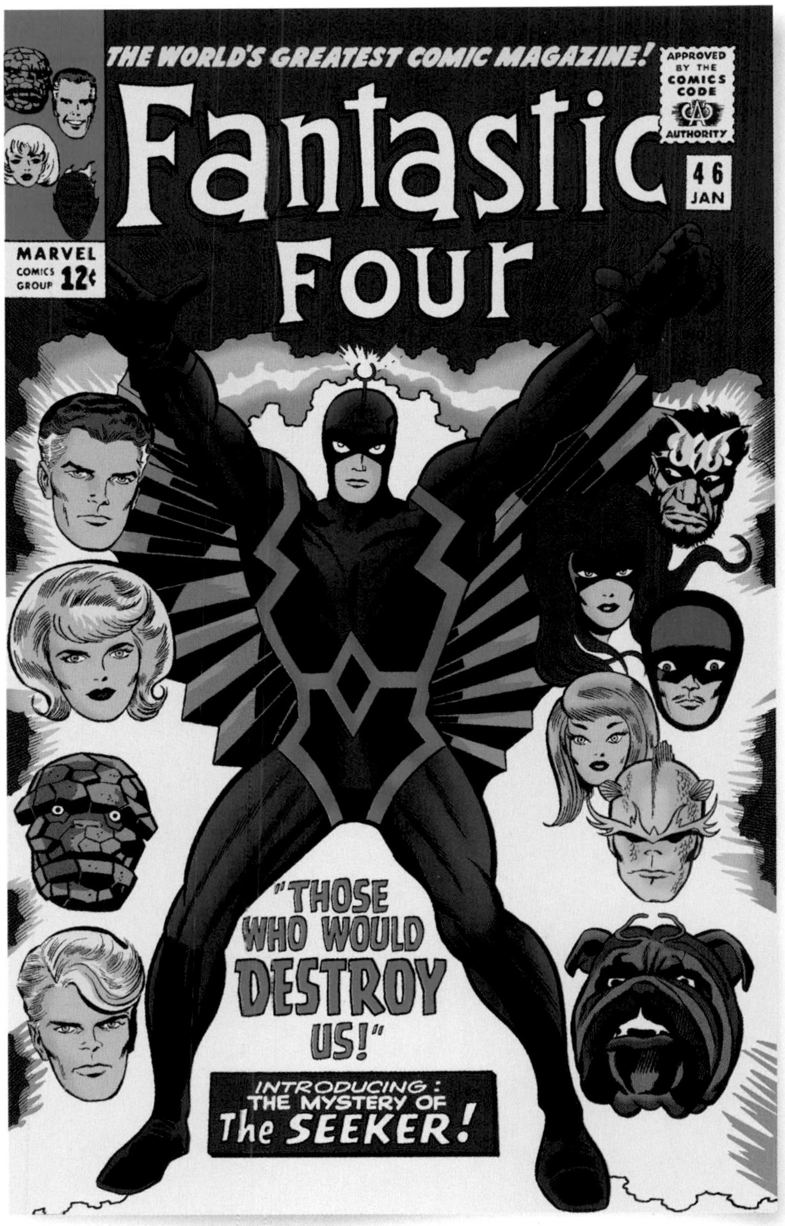
THE WORLD'S GREATEST COMIC MAGAZINE!
APPROVED BY THE COMICS CODE AUTHORITY
Fantastic Four
46 JAN
MARVEL COMICS GROUP 12¢
"THOSE WHO WOULD DESTROY US!"
INTRODUCING: THE MYSTERY OF The SEEKER!

▲ *FANTASTIC FOUR* #46

**January 1966**
**Artist:** Jack Kirby

The first few years of the *Fantastic Four* saw Stan Lee and Jack Kirby at their creative peak. Every issue seemed to introduce stunning concepts and bold new heroes. The Inhumans had made their first appearance in the previous issue, but it is their leader, the stunningly designed Black Bolt, who dominates this cover.

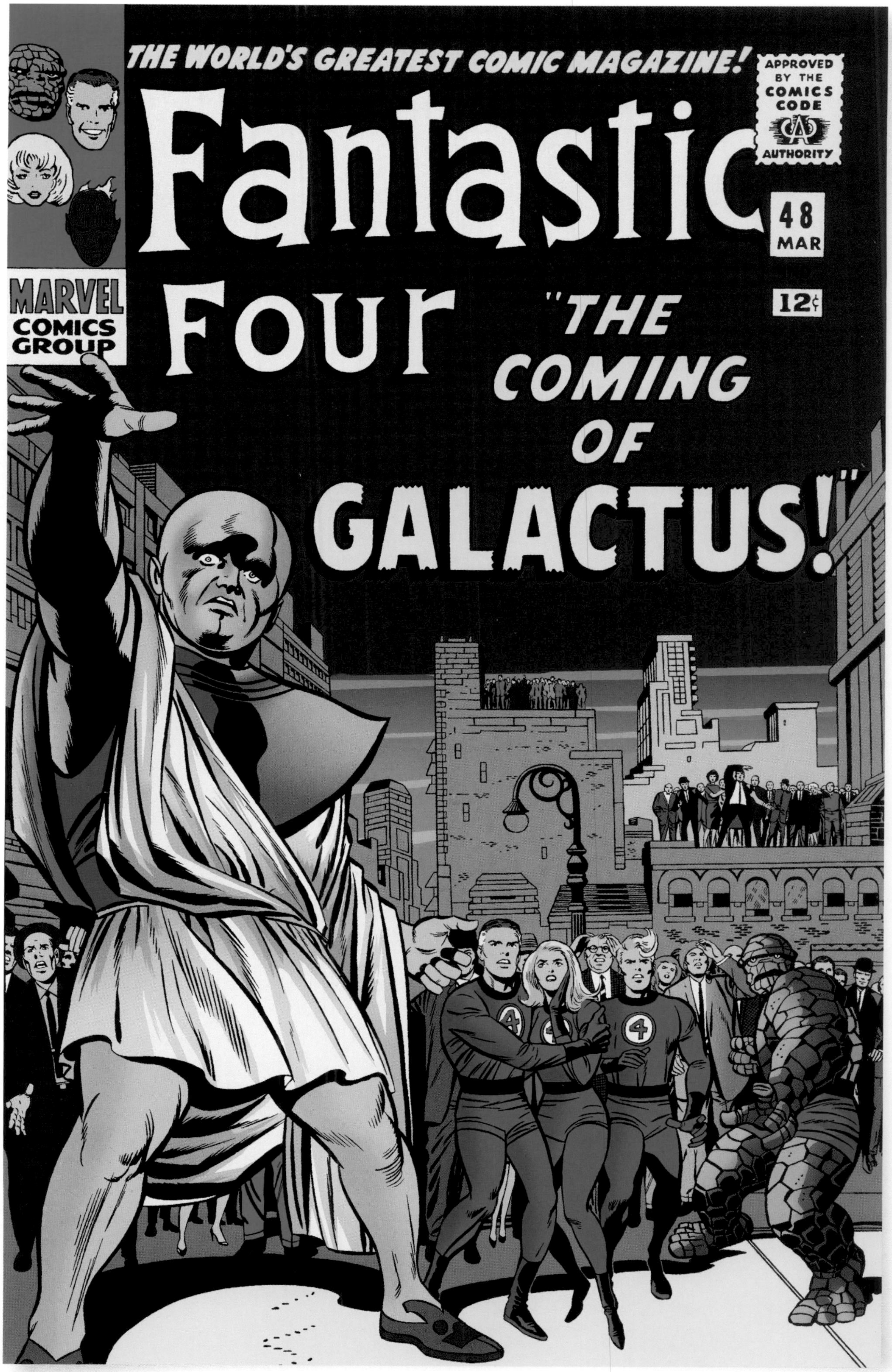
THE WORLD'S GREATEST COMIC MAGAZINE!
APPROVED BY THE COMICS CODE AUTHORITY
Fantastic Four
48 MAR
12¢
MARVEL COMICS GROUP
"THE COMING OF GALACTUS!"

▲ *FANTASTIC FOUR* #48

**March 1966**
**Artist:** Jack Kirby

Stan Lee and Jack Kirby were about to unleash two of their greatest creations onto the world—Galactus and the Silver Surfer—and they needed a multi-part story to do so. This was one of the first times that the Watcher, a cosmic being who appeared at moments of great importance, was used on a cover to increase the tension. His appearance next to a warning of Galactus communicates a real sense of foreboding.

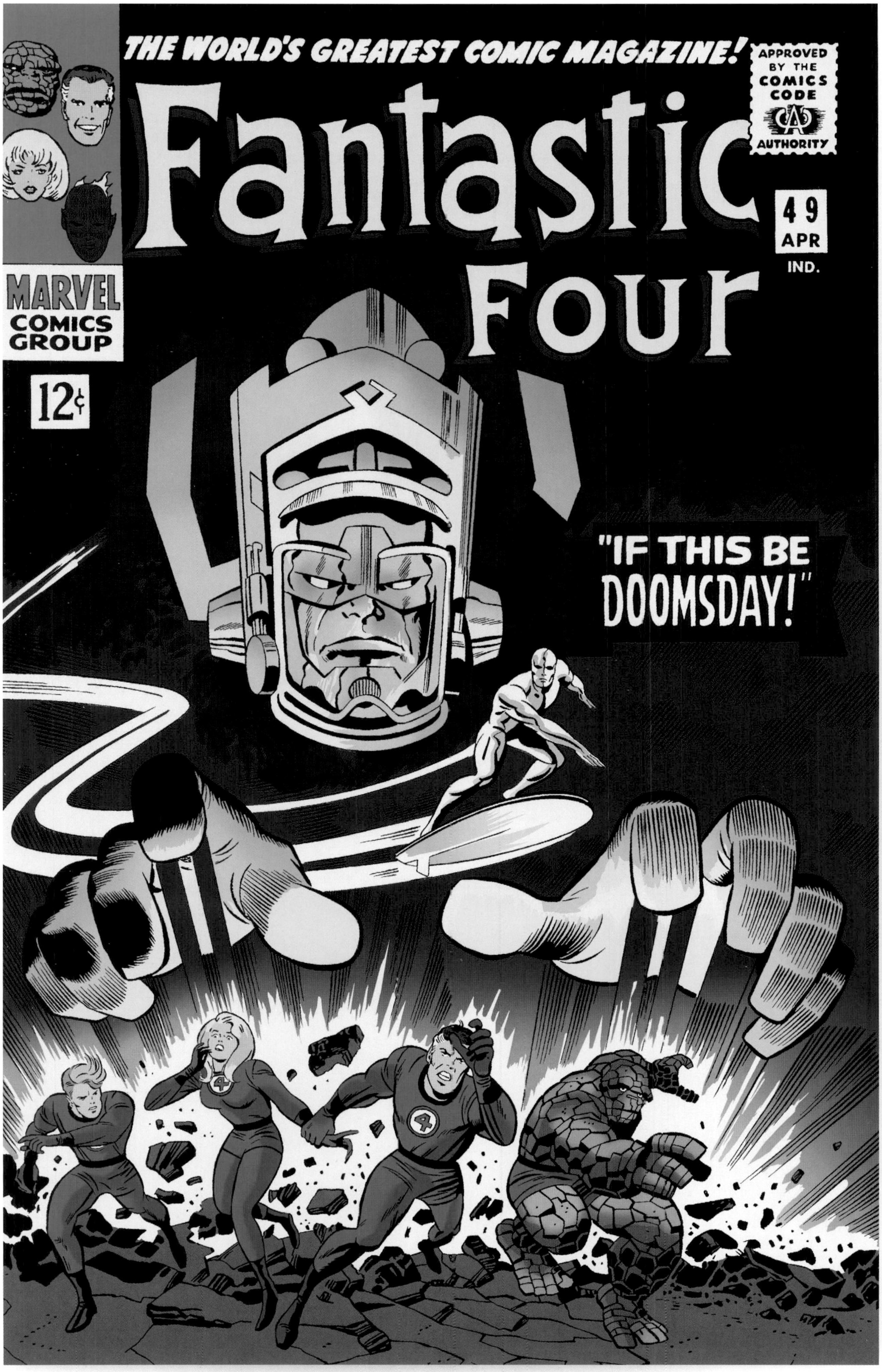
THE WORLD'S GREATEST COMIC MAGAZINE!
APPROVED BY THE COMICS CODE AUTHORITY
Fantastic Four
49 APR IND.
MARVEL COMICS GROUP
12¢
"IF THIS BE DOOMSDAY!"

▲ *FANTASTIC FOUR #49*

**April 1966**
**Artist:** Jack Kirby

Two of Marvel's greatest characters terrorize the Fantastic Four on this cover. The planet-devouring Galactus and his cosmic herald, the Silver Surfer, were the biggest threat the Fantastic Four had ever faced. The apocalyptic tone of the cover brilliantly sets up the saga as the FF try to stop Galactus from destroying Earth. It's an epic that is often regarded as a high point of the Lee/Kirby era.

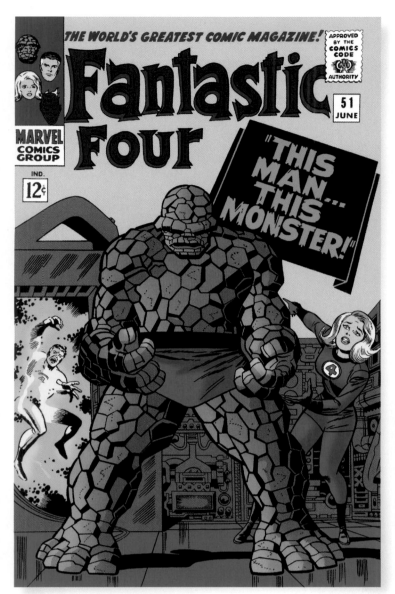

***SUB-MARINER* #1 ▶**

**May 1968**
**Artist:** John Buscema

When Prince Namor, the Sub-Mariner, gained a new series, something special was needed for the first cover. Luckily, John Buscema was on hand to illustrate Namor, producing a simple, yet powerful piece. The prince is shown in all his strength and nobility, while a montage in the background shows his history.

THE WORLD'S GREATEST COMIC MAGAZINE!
APPROVED BY THE COMICS CODE AUTHORITY
Fantastic Four
51 JUNE
MARVEL COMICS GROUP
IND.
12¢
"THIS MAN... THIS MONSTER!"

**◀ *FANTASTIC FOUR* #51**

**June 1966**
**Artist:** Jack Kirby

The Thing was the standout character during Kirby's time on the *Fantastic Four*, and he was often front and center on the covers. Kirby's art perfectly evokes the hero's duality as hero and monster. The issue had a shocking twist though—the Thing that his teammates faced wasn't Ben Grimm, but an imposter.

THE WORLD'S GREATEST COMIC MAGAZINE!
APPROVED BY THE COMICS CODE AUTHORITY
Fantastic
52 JULY
MARVEL COMICS GROUP
12¢
Introducing: THE SENSATIONAL BLACK PANTHER!

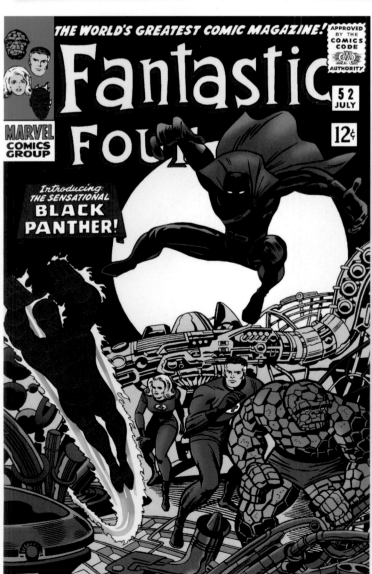

**◀ *FANTASTIC FOUR* #52**

**July 1966**
**Artist:** Jack Kirby

The 1960s was a period of immense social change—something Marvel's stories often reflected. Stan Lee and Jack Kirby provided another example of their understanding of the zeitgeist with The Black Panther, as they introduced the first mainstream African Super Hero. The cover reflects the story inside, with the Black Panther hunting the FF to test his own skills.

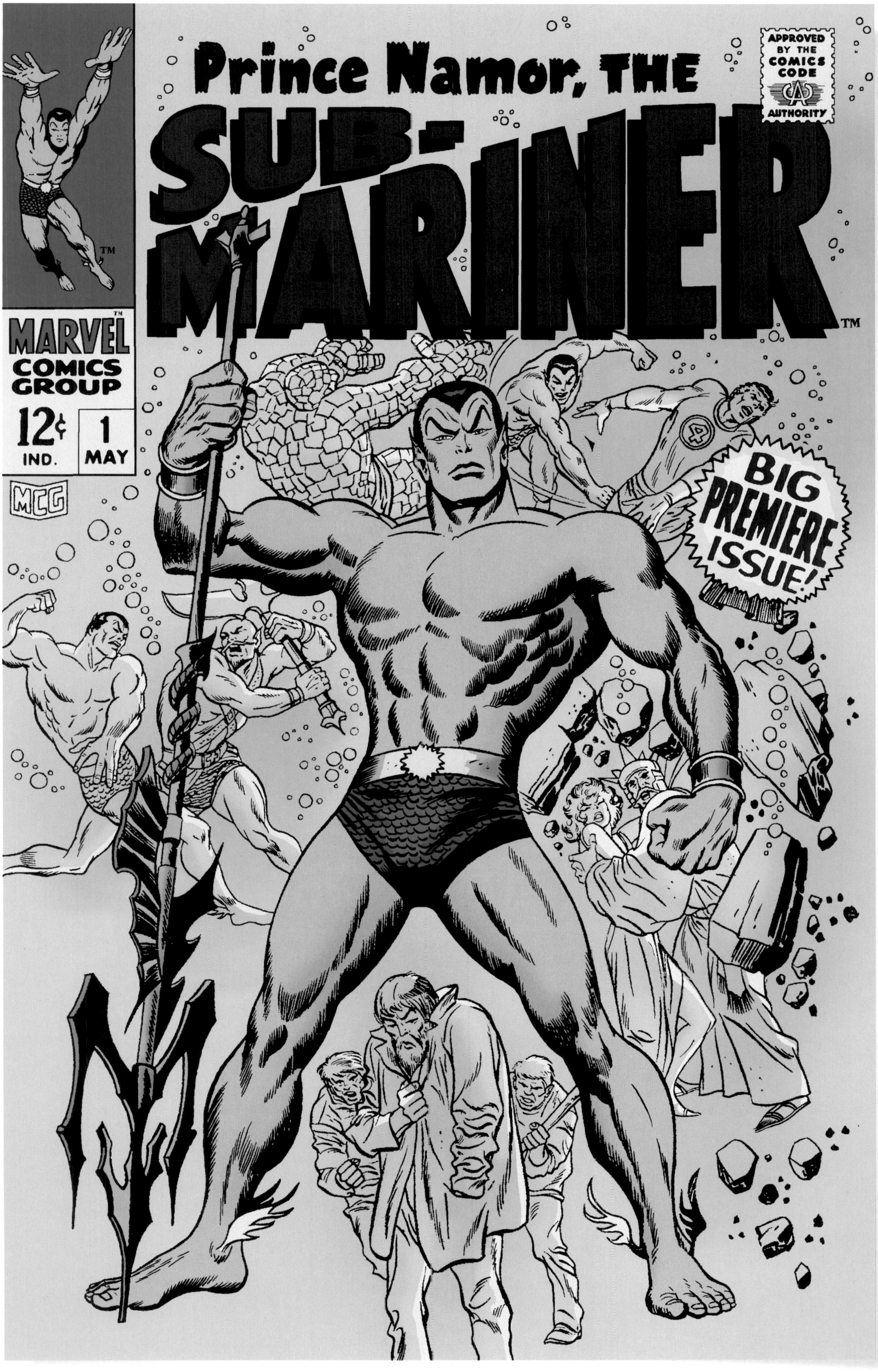
APPROVED BY THE COMICS CODE AUTHORITY
Prince Namor, THE
SUB-MARINER
MARVEL COMICS GROUP
12¢ IND.
1 MAY
MCG
BIG PREMIERE ISSUE!

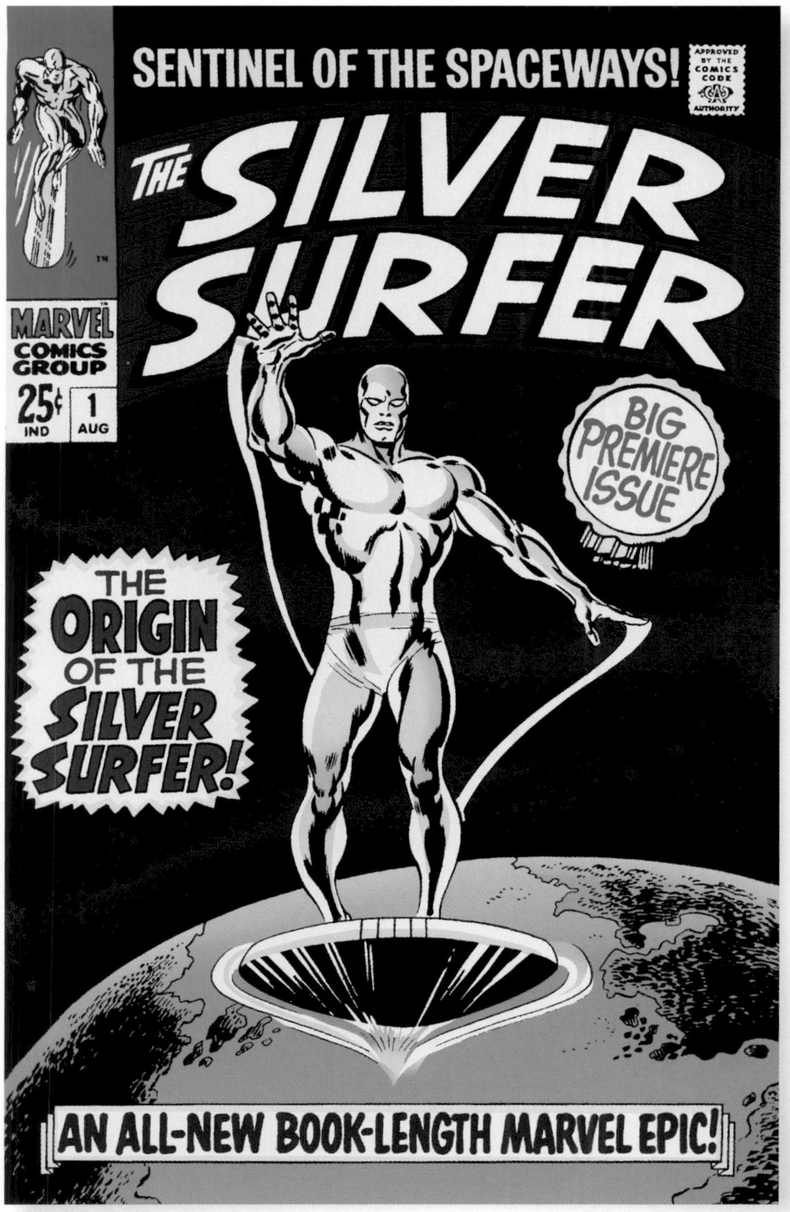
SENTINEL OF THE SPACEWAYS!
APPROVED BY THE COMICS CODE AUTHORITY
THE SILVER SURFER
MARVEL COMICS GROUP
25¢ 1 IND AUG
BIG PREMIERE ISSUE
THE ORIGIN OF THE SILVER SURFER!
AN ALL-NEW BOOK-LENGTH MARVEL EPIC!

▲ *SILVER SURFER* #1

**August 1968**
**Artist:** John Buscema

As soon as the Silver Surfer made his debut in *Fantastic Four* issue #48 (March 1966), he became a fan-favorite. John Buscema brought his art talents to the regular series, creating a heroic, but suitably alien Silver Surfer. The cover-line promises what readers were desperate to learn—the Silver Surfer's backstory.

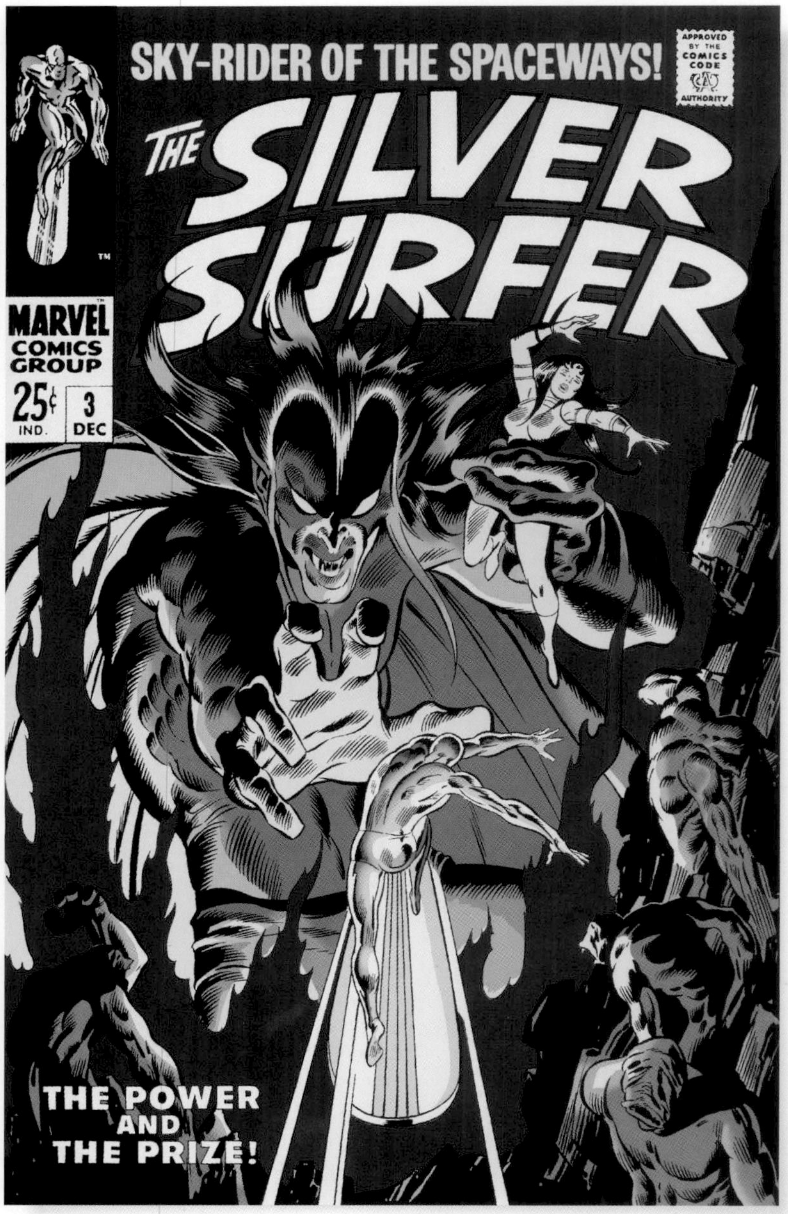
SKY-RIDER OF THE SPACEWAYS!
APPROVED BY THE COMICS CODE AUTHORITY
THE SILVER SURFER
MARVEL COMICS GROUP
25¢ 3 IND. DEC
THE POWER AND THE PRIZE!

▲ *SILVER SURFER* #3

**December 1968**
**Artist:** John Buscema

One of the most memorable *Silver Surfer* covers pits the cosmic hero against Mephisto, Marvel's answer to the Devil. The evil Mephisto made the perfect foil for the pure and noble Silver Surfer. The cover of their first confrontation radiates menace as the Surfer rushes towards Hell to save his true love, Shalla Bal. The twisted souls of the damned framing the scene only add to the sense of danger.

SILVER SURFER
25¢
4
FEB
IND.
SKY-RIDER OF THE SPACEWAYS!
APPROVED BY THE COMICS CODE AUTHORITY
THE SILVER SURFER
MARVEL COMICS GROUP

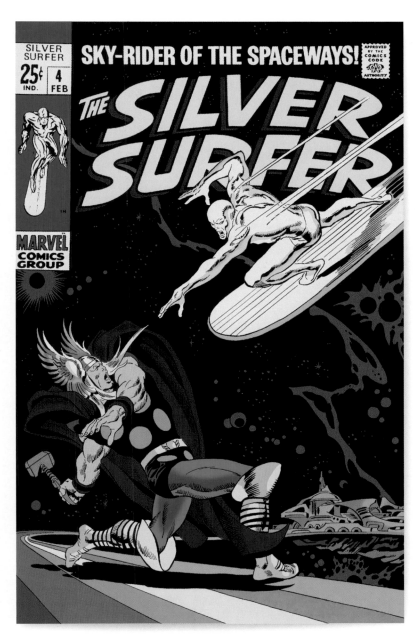

▲ *SILVER SURFER* #4

**February 1969**
**Artist:** John Buscema

Buscema was a master of exciting and dynamic cover composition, and this face-off between Thor and the Surfer perfectly radiates the power of the two heroes. It draws the reader's eye into the heart of the action, and leaves them really needing to know what would happen when the two titans clashed.

HERE COMES...
DAREDEVIL
APPROVED BY THE COMICS CODE AUTHORITY
1 APR.
IND.
MARVEL COMICS GROUP 12¢
THE MAN WITHOUT FEAR!
REMEMBER WHEN WE INTRODUCED... SPIDER-MAN
NOW WE CONTINUE THE MIGHTY MARVEL TRADITION WITH... DAREDEVIL!!
...A WORTHY COMPANION MAGAZINE TO SUCH ALL-TIME GREATS AS THE FABULOUS FANTASTIC FOUR!
IN THIS ISSUE YOU WILL MEET...
The Most UNUSUAL HERO of all
MATT MURDOCK
"FUN-LOVING" FOGGY NELSON
GORGEOUS KAREN PAGE
CAN YOU GUESS WHY DAREDEVIL IS DIFFERENT FROM ALL OTHER CRIME-FIGHTERS...?

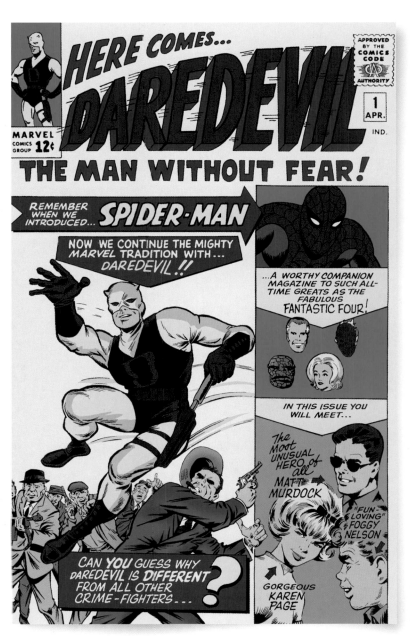

▲ *DAREDEVIL* #1

**April 1964**
**Artists:** Jack Kirby and Bill Everett

Bill Everett was the main artist on *Daredevil's* debut issue, but when he fell behind schedule, Jack Kirby was called in to help out. The cover and issue included work by both of them, and Steve Ditko and inker Sol Bodsky also contributed. The cover uses elements of Marvel's old romance comics and makes the most of Spider-Man and the Fantastic Four's success to help sell the new hero.

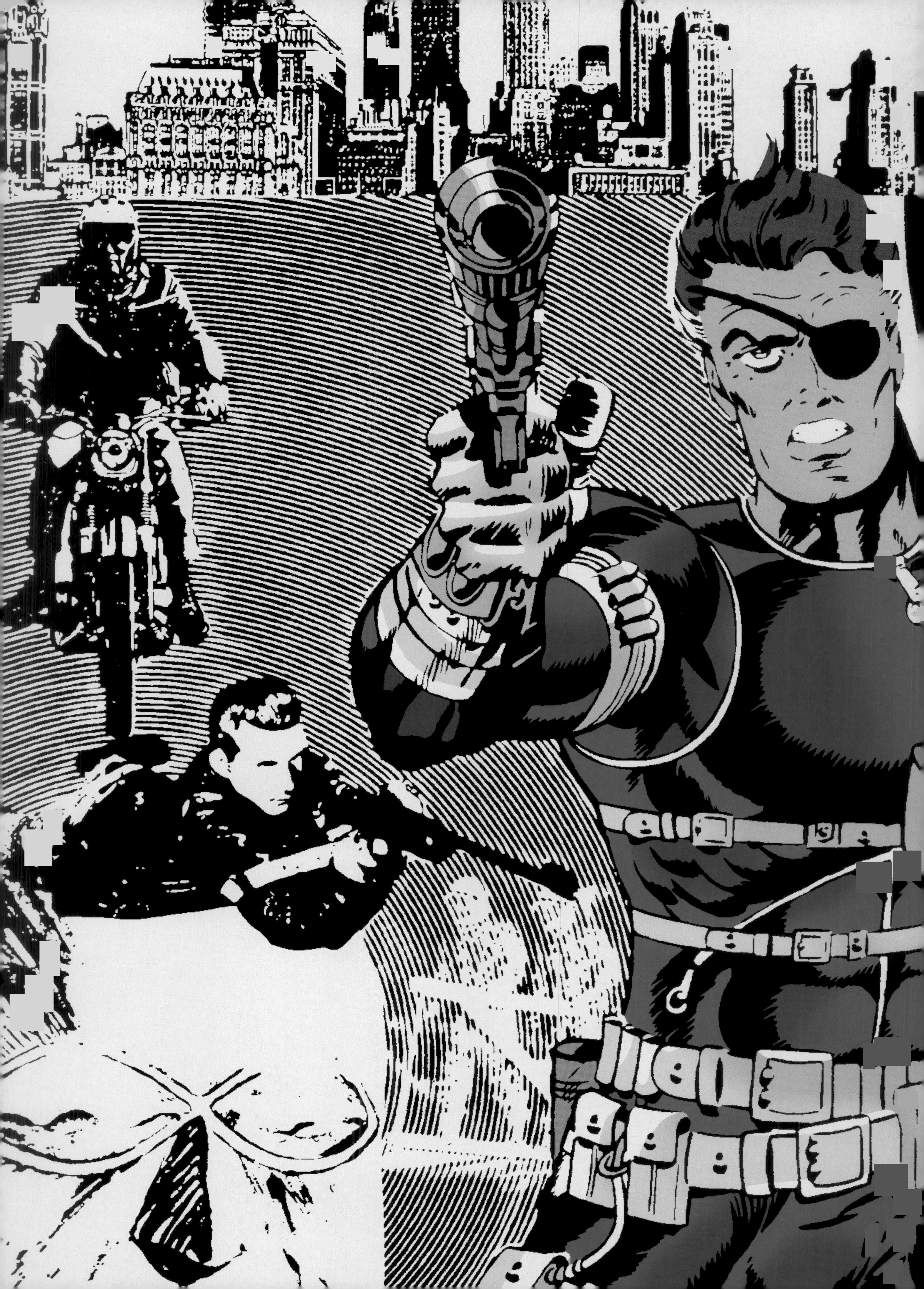

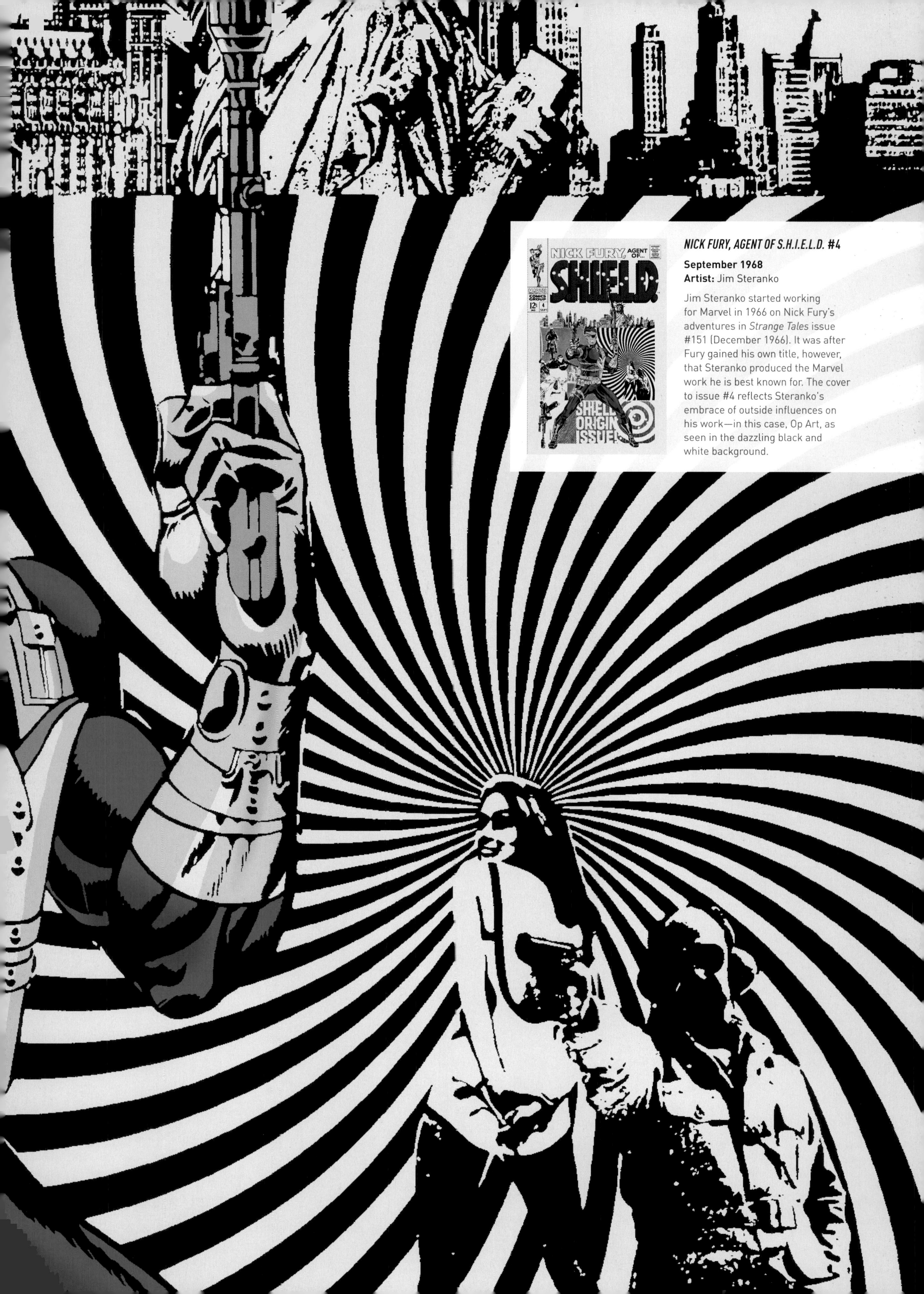
NICK FURY, AGENT OF...
S.H.I.E.L.D.
MARVEL COMICS GROUP
12¢
4
SEPT
SHIELD ORIGIN ISSUE!

***NICK FURY, AGENT OF S.H.I.E.L.D. #4***

**September 1968**
**Artist:** Jim Steranko

Jim Steranko started working for Marvel in 1966 on Nick Fury's adventures in *Strange Tales* issue #151 (December 1966). It was after Fury gained his own title, however, that Steranko produced the Marvel work he is best known for. The cover to issue #4 reflects Steranko's embrace of outside influences on his work—in this case, Op Art, as seen in the dazzling black and white background.

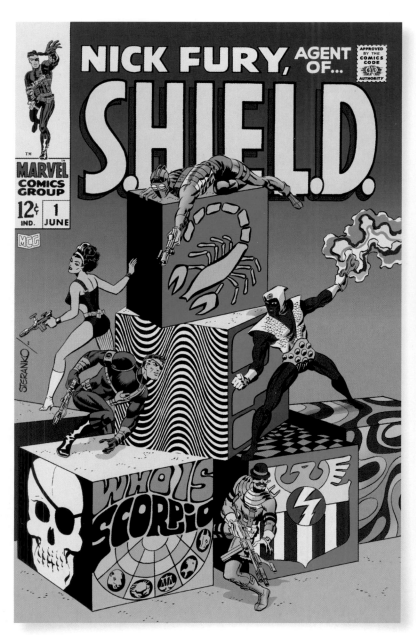

NICK FURY, AGENT OF...
S.H.I.E.L.D.
APPROVED BY THE COMICS CODE AUTHORITY
MARVEL COMICS GROUP
12¢ IND.
1 JUNE
WHO IS SCORPIO
STERANKO

▲ ***NICK FURY, AGENT OF S.H.I.E.L.D.* #1**

**June 1968**
**Artist:** Jim Steranko

When Jim Steranko was given a full comic to illustrate, he created one of the most-revered series in the medium. The cover to the first issue saw Steranko use text as part the main image—creating a new element of cover design in the process and producing a cover the like of which had never been seen before at Marvel.

NICK FURY, AGENT OF...
S.H.I.E.L.D.
APPROVED BY THE COMICS CODE AUTHORITY
MARVEL COMICS GROUP
12¢ IND.
3 AUG
RIP
BLACK HUGH RAVENLUCK
1758-1905
STERANKO

▲ ***NICK FURY, AGENT OF S.H.I.E.L.D.* #3**

**August 1968**
**Artist:** Jim Steranko

This Steranko cover highlights his skill as a colorist as well as an artist. With echoes of the classic novel *Hound of the Baskervilles*, the story had Nick Fury traveling to Scotland to help an old war colleague. Steranko's use of moody colors complements his pencils to give the cover a dark and sinister atmosphere.

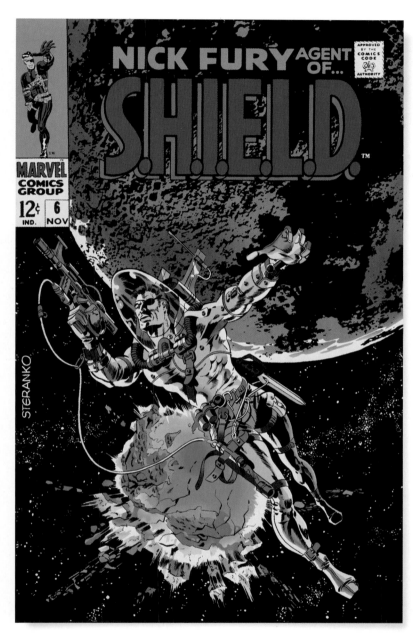

NICK FURY AGENT OF...
S.H.I.E.L.D.
MARVEL COMICS GROUP
12¢ 6
IND. NOV
STERANKO

▲ *NICK FURY, AGENT OF S.H.I.E.L.D.* **#6**

**November 1968**
**Artist:** Jim Steranko

Although Steranko stopped handling the interior artwork with this issue, he did create one of his best covers. This striking image of Nick Fury in space, with the moon looming behind him, was produced at the height of the Space Race. With the Earth exploding in the distance, it's the kind of high-impact, beautifully drawn cover that Steranko excelled at.

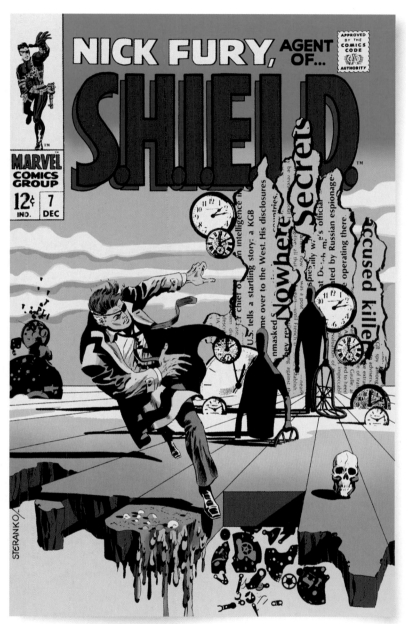

NICK FURY, AGENT OF...
S.H.I.E.L.D.
MARVEL COMICS GROUP
12¢ 7
IND. DEC
Nowhere
Secrets
STERANKO

▲ *NICK FURY, AGENT OF S.H.I.E.L.D.* **#7**

**December 1968**
**Artist:** Jim Steranko

Jim Steranko's last cover for the title (except for the collections) owes something to the work of Salvador Dali, with its melting landscape and nightmarish figures. Steranko eventually returned to the more lucrative world of advertising, but his comic art remains some of the best to have ever graced the medium.

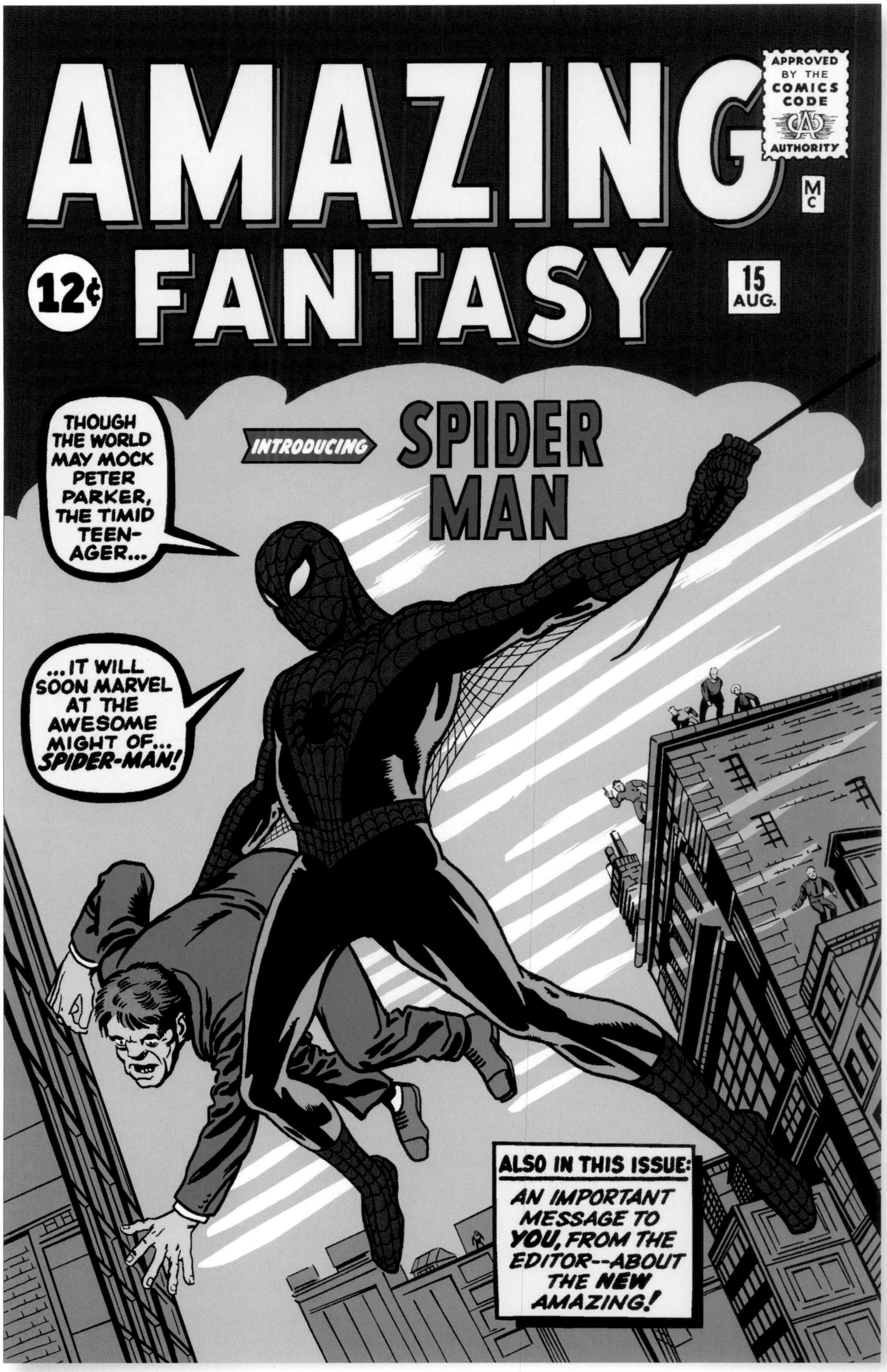

AMAZING FANTASY
APPROVED BY THE COMICS CODE AUTHORITY
MC
12¢
15 AUG.
INTRODUCING SPIDER MAN
THOUGH THE WORLD MAY MOCK PETER PARKER, THE TIMID TEEN-AGER...
...IT WILL SOON MARVEL AT THE AWESOME MIGHT OF... SPIDER-MAN!
ALSO IN THIS ISSUE: AN IMPORTANT MESSAGE TO YOU, FROM THE EDITOR--ABOUT THE NEW AMAZING!


▲ *AMAZING FANTASY* #15

**August 1962**
**Artist:** Jack Kirby

While Steve Ditko illustrated Spider-Man's first appearance, Marvel boss Stan Lee didn't think his original cover was heroic enough and got Jack Kirby to provide a fresh take. Kirby's image is arguably the most famous in Marvel's history and shows the creators at their game-changing best. At the time, the consensus was that teenage heroes couldn't be the main character. Spidey's success changed that idea forever.

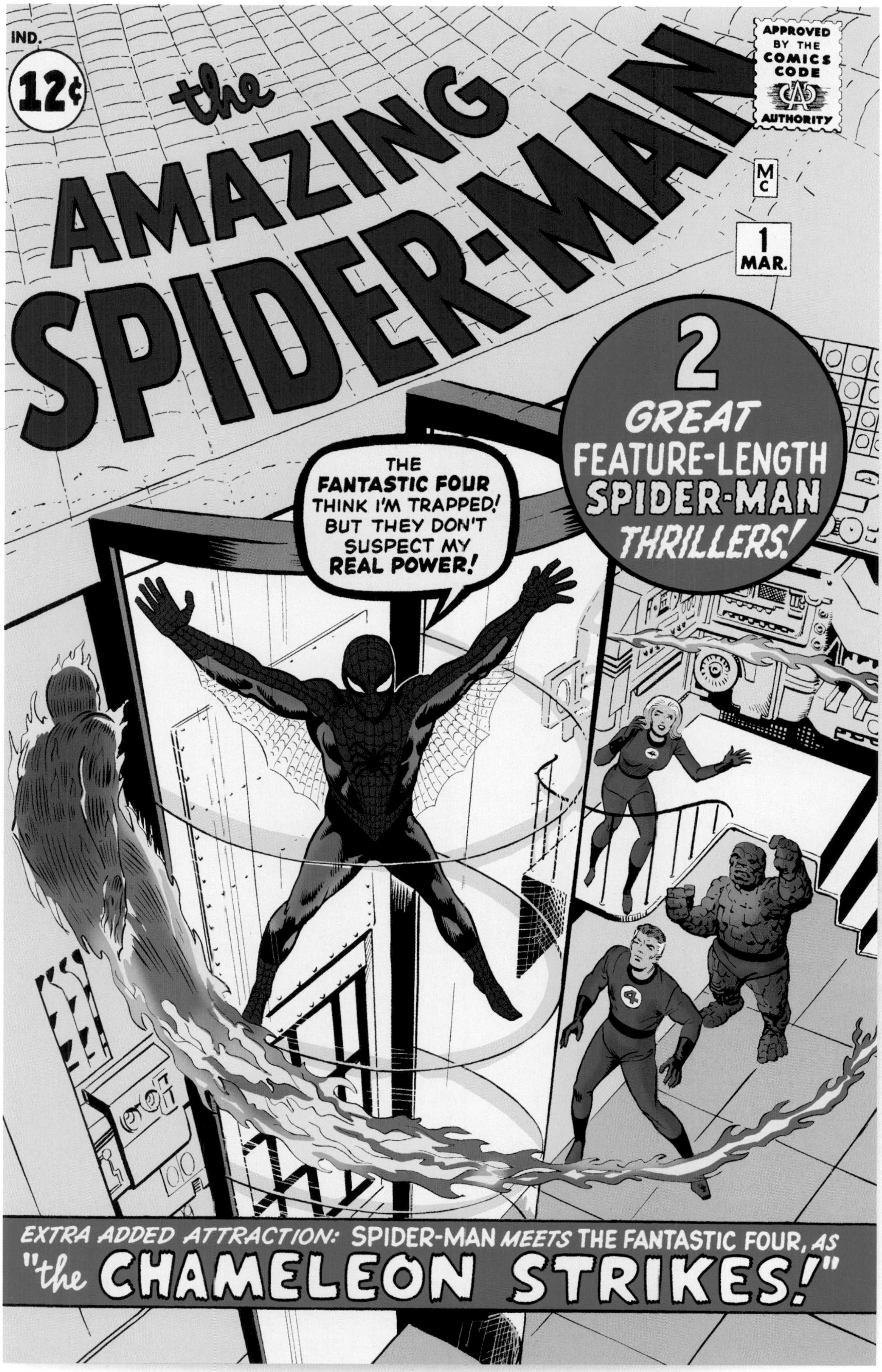
IND.
12¢
the
AMAZING
SPIDER-MAN
APPROVED BY THE COMICS CODE AUTHORITY
MC
1 MAR.
2 GREAT FEATURE-LENGTH SPIDER-MAN THRILLERS!
THE FANTASTIC FOUR THINK I'M TRAPPED! BUT THEY DON'T SUSPECT MY REAL POWER!
EXTRA ADDED ATTRACTION: SPIDER-MAN MEETS THE FANTASTIC FOUR, AS
"the CHAMELEON STRIKES!"

▲ ***AMAZING SPIDER-MAN* #1**

**March 1963**
**Artists:** Jack Kirby and Steve Ditko

Jack Kirby and Steve Ditko joined forces for the cover of *Amazing Spider-Man* issue #1, with Ditko inking Kirby's heroic-looking pencils. The image of Spidey meeting the Fantastic Four was commercially a strong one. The FF had proven to be a big hit and having them on the cover would help attract readers to the new book. It was also a sign of the interconnected universe that would help make Marvel so popular.

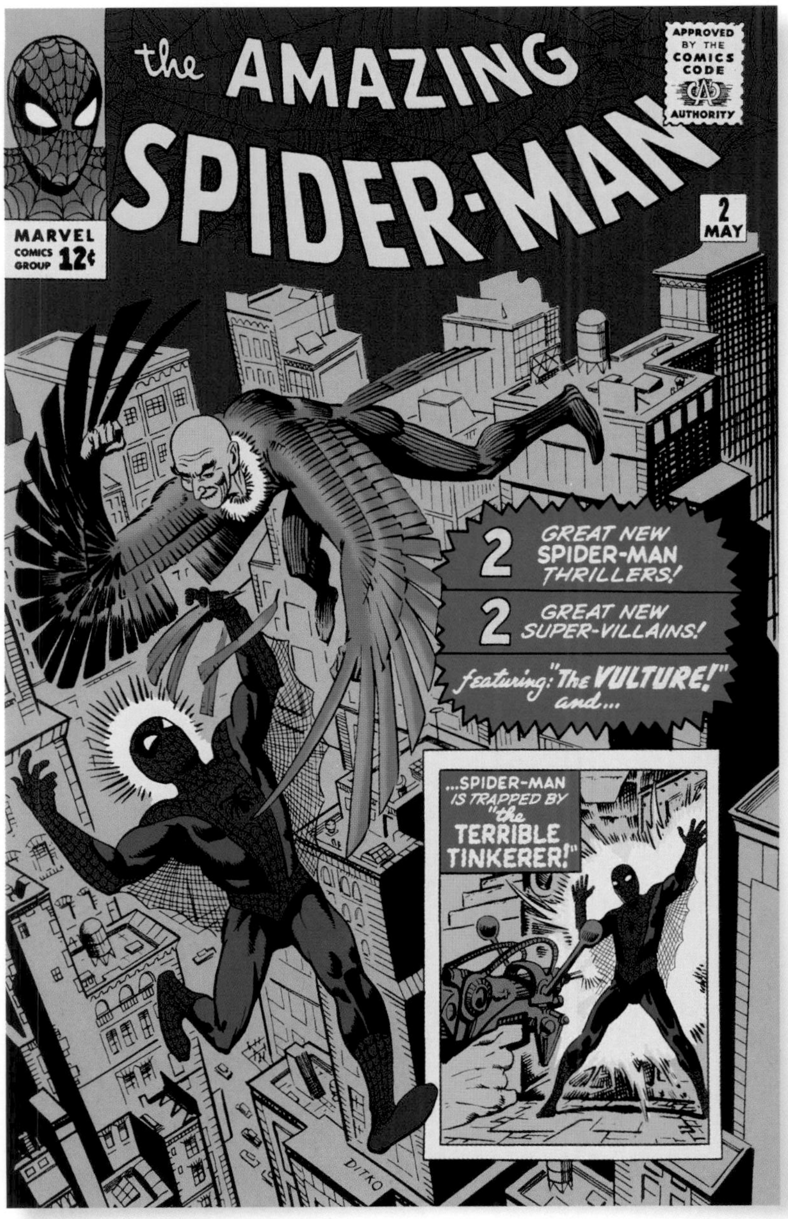
the AMAZING
SPIDER-MAN
APPROVED BY THE COMICS CODE AUTHORITY
MARVEL COMICS GROUP 12¢
2 MAY
2 GREAT NEW SPIDER-MAN THRILLERS!
2 GREAT NEW SUPER-VILLAINS!
featuring: "The VULTURE!" and...
...SPIDER-MAN IS TRAPPED BY "the TERRIBLE TINKERER!"
DITKO

▲ *AMAZING SPIDER-MAN #2*

**May 1963**
**Artist:** Steve Ditko

Steve Ditko's first published Spider-Man cover pits the hero against Vulture. Ditko played a big part in Spidey's early success and his visuals for the webslinger's foes gave each villain a unique look. The Vulture looks exceptionally menacing here, with Spidey apparently on the verge of plummeting to his death.

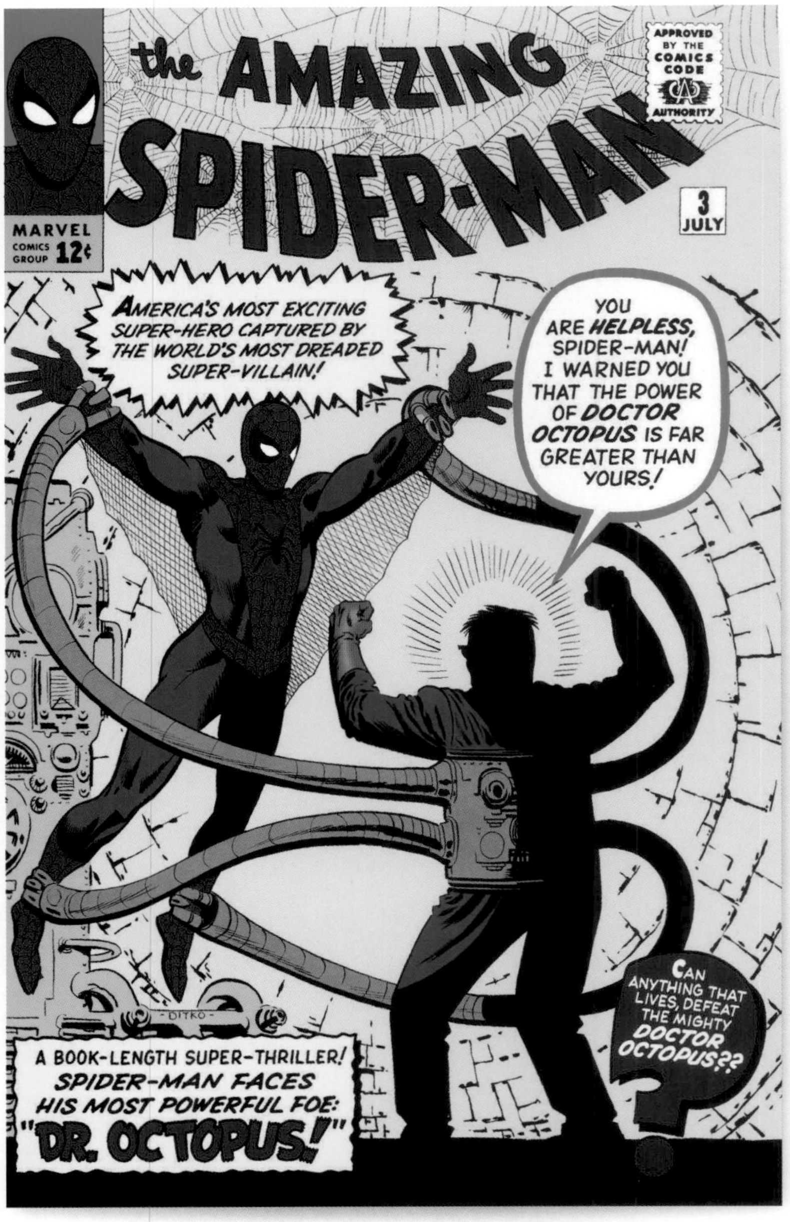
the AMAZING
SPIDER-MAN
APPROVED BY THE COMICS CODE AUTHORITY
MARVEL COMICS GROUP 12¢
3 JULY
AMERICA'S MOST EXCITING SUPER-HERO CAPTURED BY THE WORLD'S MOST DREADED SUPER-VILLAIN!
YOU ARE HELPLESS, SPIDER-MAN! I WARNED YOU THAT THE POWER OF DOCTOR OCTOPUS IS FAR GREATER THAN YOURS!
CAN ANYTHING THAT LIVES, DEFEAT THE MIGHTY DOCTOR OCTOPUS??
A BOOK-LENGTH SUPER-THRILLER! SPIDER-MAN FACES HIS MOST POWERFUL FOE: "DR. OCTOPUS!"
DITKO

▲ *AMAZING SPIDER-MAN #3*

**July 1963**
**Artist:** Steve Ditko

The early Spidey issues were packed with new Super Villains who would soon become iconic. Doctor Octopus, up there with the best villains of all time, made his first appearance in this issue. Ditko's cover shows the villain in shadow, adding an element of mystery to his debut.

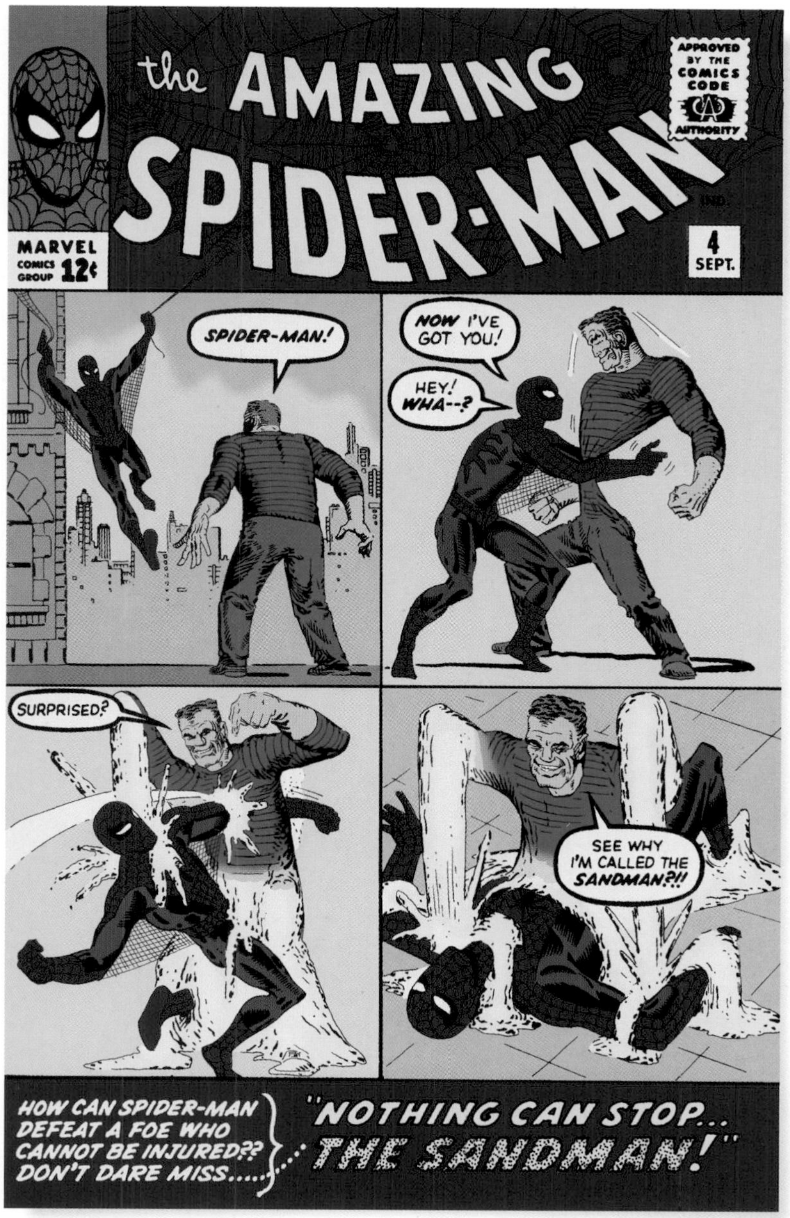
the AMAZING
SPIDER-MAN
IND.
APPROVED BY THE COMICS CODE AUTHORITY
MARVEL COMICS GROUP 12¢
4 SEPT.
SPIDER-MAN!
NOW I'VE GOT YOU!
HEY! WHA--?
SURPRISED?
SEE WHY I'M CALLED THE SANDMAN?!!
HOW CAN SPIDER-MAN DEFEAT A FOE WHO CANNOT BE INJURED?? DON'T DARE MISS.....
"NOTHING CAN STOP... THE SANDMAN!"

▲ *AMAZING SPIDER-MAN #4*

**September 1963**
**Artist:** Steve Ditko

A Ditko cover is instantly recognizable and each one a unique work of art. Ditko's use of multiple panels on this issue harkens back to his time on science fiction comics. It was a great way of introducing the Sandman to the readership—showcasing the very unusual powers of the new villain.

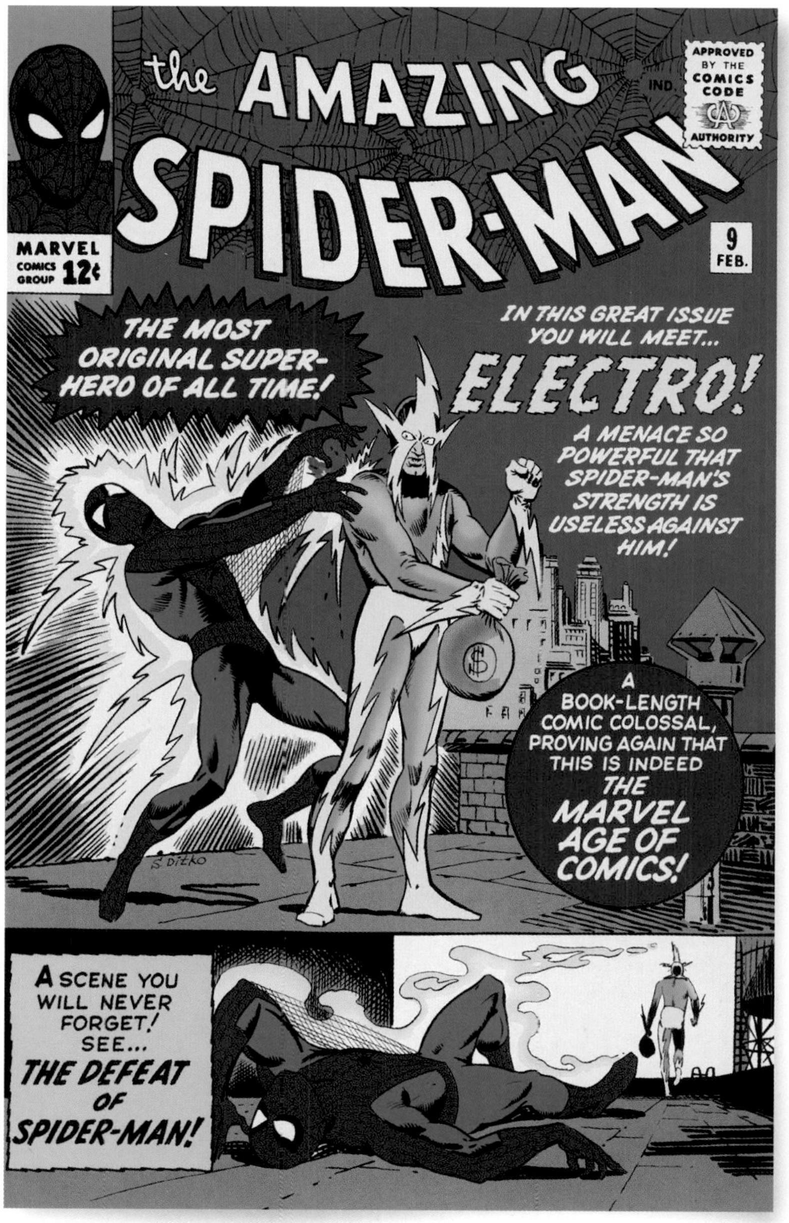
the AMAZING
SPIDER-MAN
IND.
APPROVED BY THE COMICS CODE AUTHORITY
MARVEL COMICS GROUP 12¢
9 FEB.
THE MOST ORIGINAL SUPER-HERO OF ALL TIME!
IN THIS GREAT ISSUE YOU WILL MEET...
ELECTRO!
A MENACE SO POWERFUL THAT SPIDER-MAN'S STRENGTH IS USELESS AGAINST HIM!
A BOOK-LENGTH COMIC COLOSSAL, PROVING AGAIN THAT THIS IS INDEED THE MARVEL AGE OF COMICS!
S. DITKO
A SCENE YOU WILL NEVER FORGET! SEE... THE DEFEAT OF SPIDER-MAN!

▲ *AMAZING SPIDER-MAN #9*

**February 1964**
**Artist:** Steve Ditko

Electro, another of Spider-Man's iconic foes, made his debut in this issue. Ditko's two-panel approach to the cover shows Electro in action and suggests that Spidey might have finally met his match. Electro features in the 2014 movie *Amazing Spider-Man 2*, albeit with a very different look from his comic counterpart.

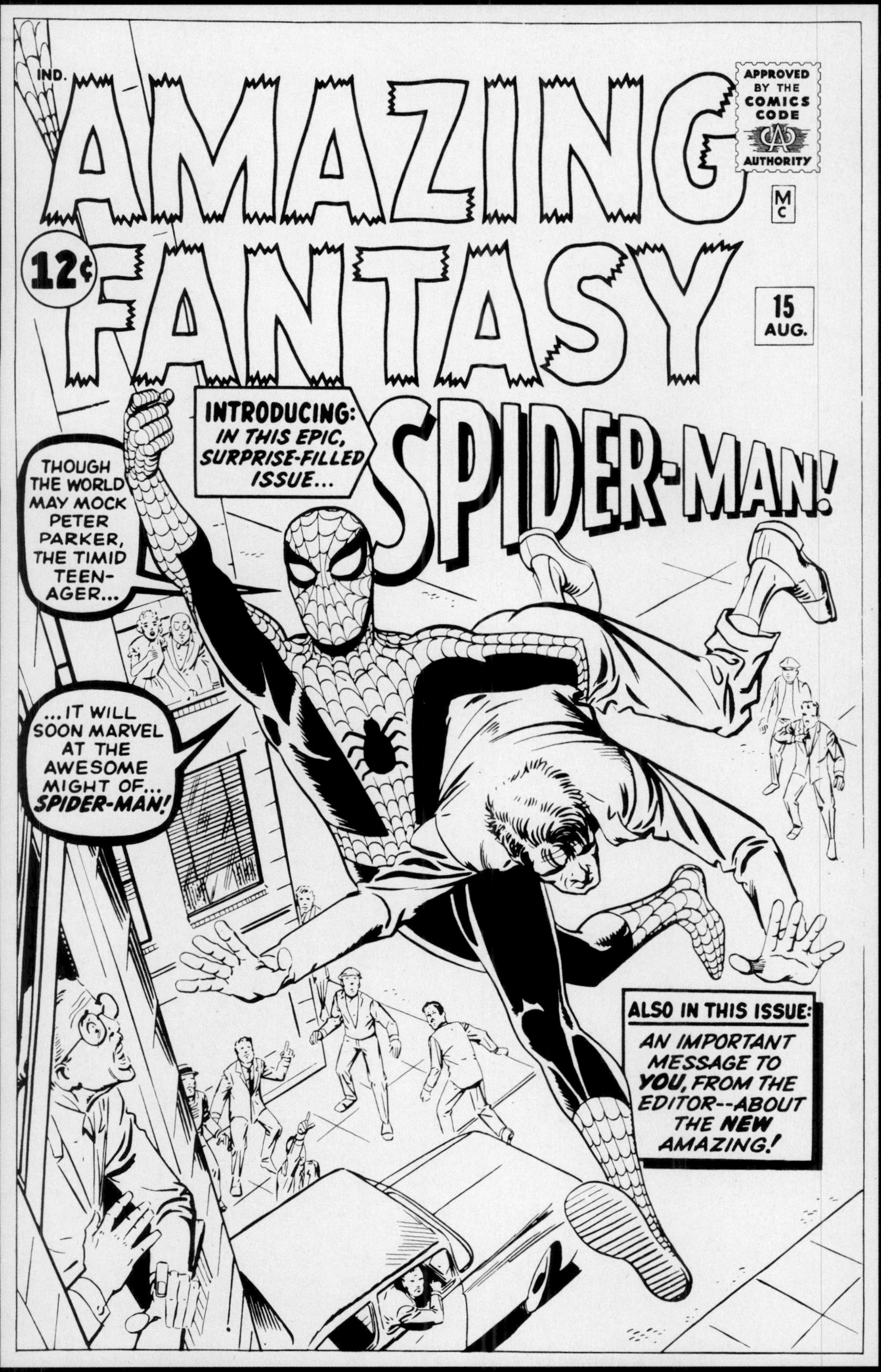
IND.
AMAZING FANTASY
APPROVED BY THE COMICS CODE AUTHORITY
MC
12¢
15 AUG.
INTRODUCING: IN THIS EPIC, SURPRISE-FILLED ISSUE...
SPIDER-MAN!
THOUGH THE WORLD MAY MOCK PETER PARKER, THE TIMID TEEN-AGER...
...IT WILL SOON MARVEL AT THE AWESOME MIGHT OF... SPIDER-MAN!
ALSO IN THIS ISSUE: AN IMPORTANT MESSAGE TO YOU, FROM THE EDITOR--ABOUT THE NEW AMAZING!

1.

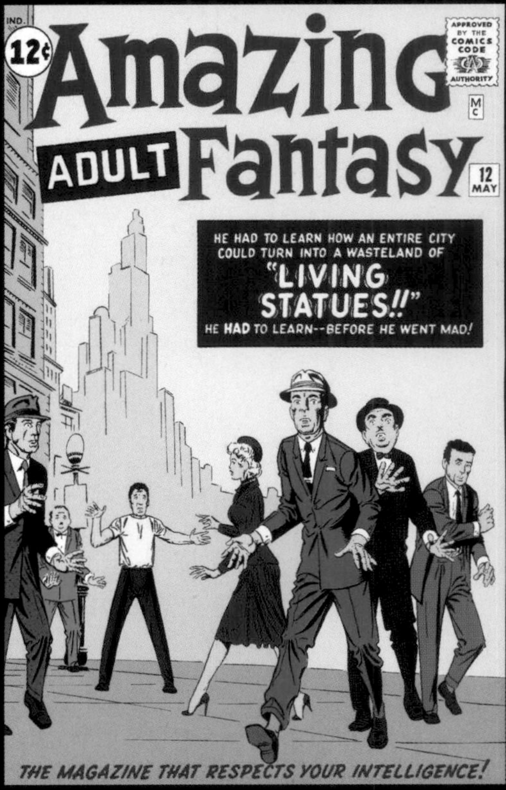
12¢
Amazing ADULT Fantasy
12 MAY
HE HAD TO LEARN HOW AN ENTIRE CITY COULD TURN INTO A WASTELAND OF "LIVING STATUES!!" HE HAD TO LEARN--BEFORE HE WENT MAD!
THE MAGAZINE THAT RESPECTS YOUR INTELLIGENCE!

2.

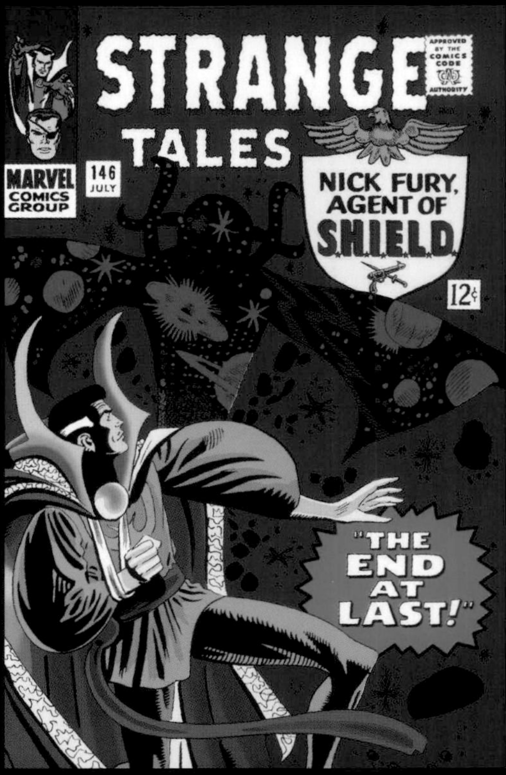
STRANGE TALES
MARVEL COMICS GROUP
146 JULY
NICK FURY, AGENT OF S.H.I.E.L.D.
12¢
"THE END AT LAST!"

3.

# STEVE DITKO

Alongside Jack Kirby and John Romita Sr., Steve Ditko was a key artist in Marvel's history, co-creating two of their greatest characters—Doctor Strange and Spider-Man. His work had a realistic noir-like quality to it—whether he was illustrating a cover or designing strange-looking characters such as the Green Goblin. Lee got Ditko on board to work on Spidey, believing Ditko's more naturalistic style would suit the teenage Super Hero better than Kirby's larger-than-life work. Ditko also brought Doctor Strange to life, creating surreal and nightmarish worlds and fantastically weird creatures. Despite quitting *Amazing Spider-Man* after only 38 issues and leaving Marvel, this visionary man's work influenced countless artists who followed.

**1. *AMAZING FANTASY* #15**

**August 1962**

Although Steve Ditko helped to create Spider-Man, this original cover for the webslinger's first appearance was never used. Instead, Jack Kirby drew a more heroic version *(see p50)*. Ditko's original art exemplifies his more realistic approach.

**2. *AMAZING ADULT FANTASY* #12**

**May 1962**

Ditko's artistic style found a home in *Amazing Adult Fantasy*, a short-lived anthology that showcased his realistic but sometimes nightmarish work. This cover highlights Ditko's skill at mixing the everyday with the bizarre.

**3. *STRANGE TALES* #146**

**July 1966**

Ditko's inventive art style came into its own depicting the adventures of Doctor Strange. This cover shows Doctor Strange facing another surreal Lee/Ditko creation—Eternity, a being made up of the fabric of existence.

**4. *AMAZING SPIDER-MAN ANNUAL* #1**

**October 1964**

During his run on *Amazing Spider-Man*, Ditko co-created many of the webslinger's greatest foes, including Doctor Octopus and the Lizard. The first *Amazing Spider-Man Annual* bought six of them together in one sinister team.

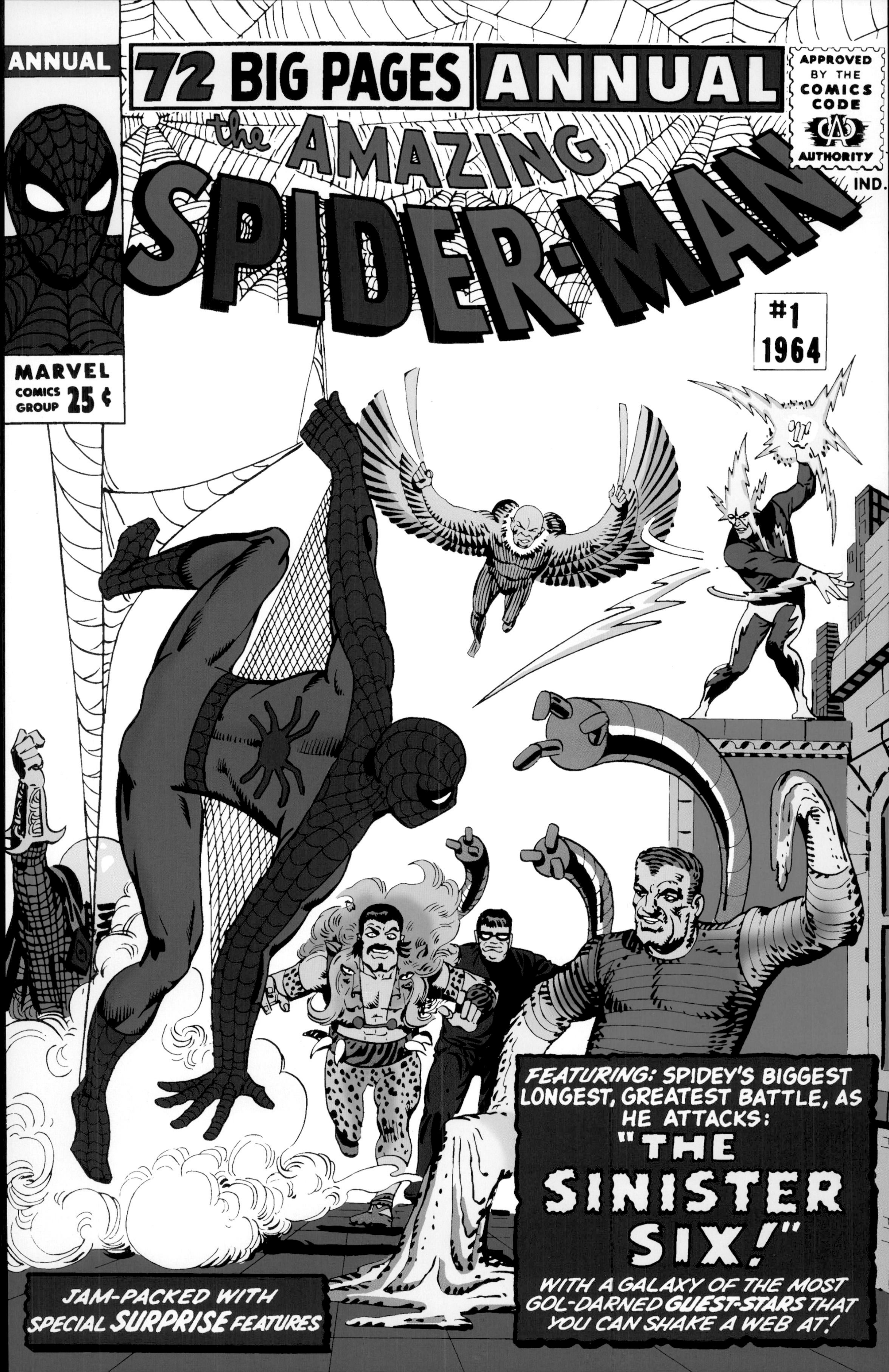
ANNUAL
72 BIG PAGES
ANNUAL
APPROVED BY THE COMICS CODE AUTHORITY
the AMAZING SPIDER-MAN
IND.
#1 1964
MARVEL COMICS GROUP 25¢
FEATURING: SPIDEY'S BIGGEST LONGEST, GREATEST BATTLE, AS HE ATTACKS:
"THE SINISTER SIX!"
WITH A GALAXY OF THE MOST GOL-DARNED GUEST-STARS THAT YOU CAN SHAKE A WEB AT!
JAM-PACKED WITH SPECIAL SURPRISE FEATURES

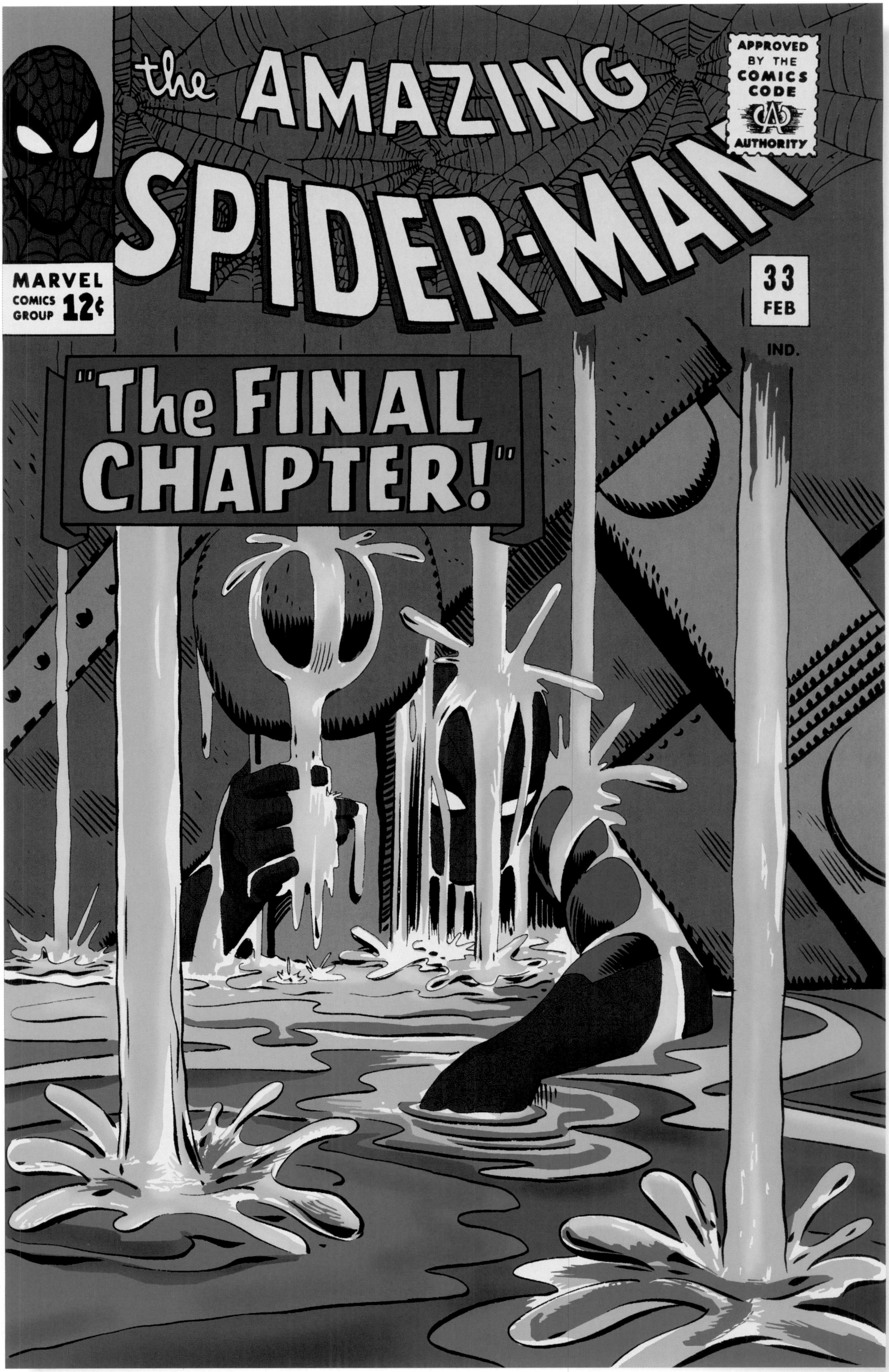
the AMAZING
SPIDER-MAN
APPROVED BY THE COMICS CODE AUTHORITY
MARVEL COMICS GROUP 12¢
33 FEB
IND.
"The FINAL CHAPTER!"

***AMAZING SPIDER-MAN* #39 ▶**

**August 1966**
**Artist:** John Romita Sr.

Following the success of Steve Ditko was a tough task, but John Romita Sr. was an inspired choice. At the time, Romita was best known for his work on romance comics, but he brought a more hip style to Spider-Man. His first cover promises readers a long-awaited revelation: Who was behind the Green Goblin's mask?

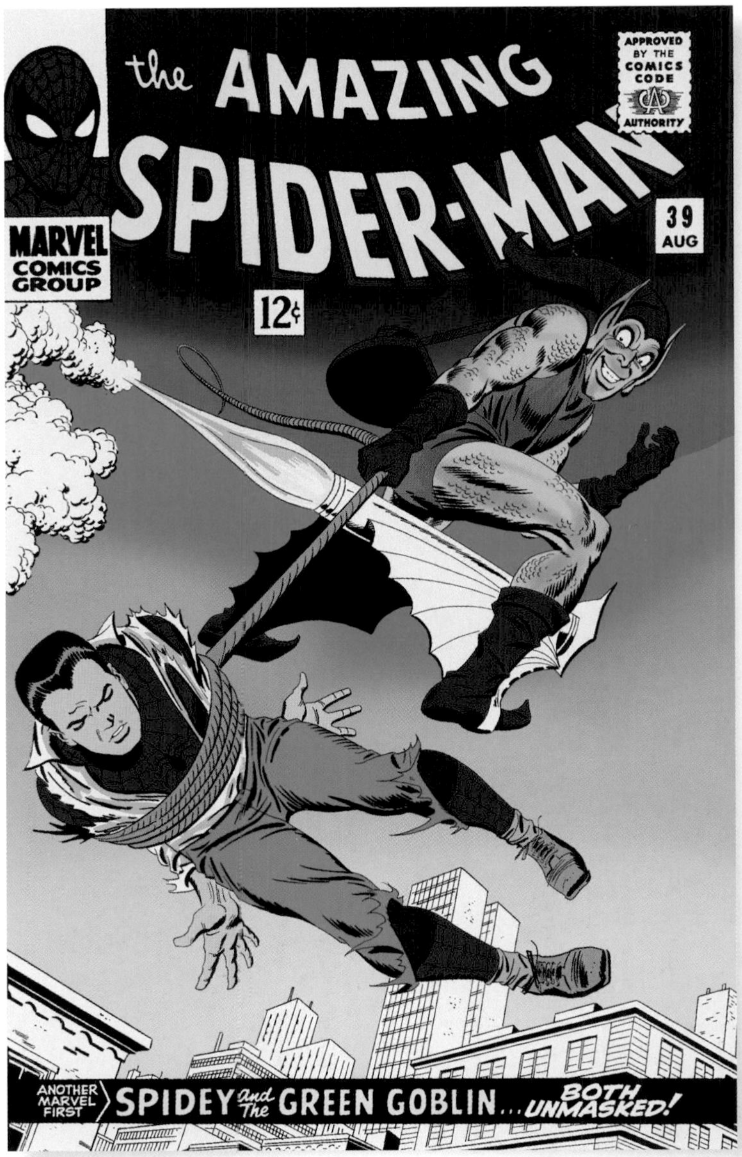
the AMAZING
SPIDER-MAN
APPROVED BY THE COMICS CODE AUTHORITY
MARVEL COMICS GROUP
39 AUG
12¢
ANOTHER MARVEL FIRST
SPIDEY and The GREEN GOBLIN... BOTH UNMASKED!

***AMAZING SPIDER-MAN* #40 ▶**

**September 1966**
**Artist:** John Romita Sr.

A companion piece to Romita's first *Amazing Spider-Man* cover, this issue saw a rage-filled Spidey taking on the Green Goblin. With Steve Ditko gone, writer Stan Lee knew he needed something special to pull the readers in. These two covers did just that. Romita's dynamic, modern style soon made Spider-Man more popular than ever.

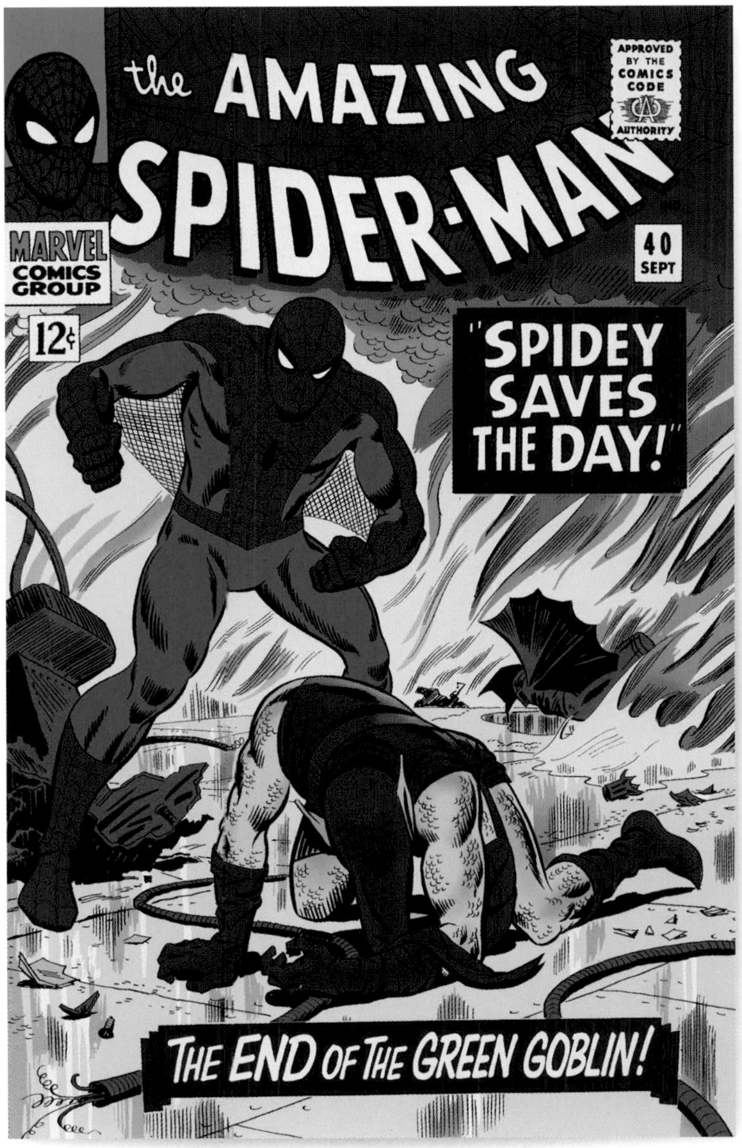
the AMAZING
SPIDER-MAN
APPROVED BY THE COMICS CODE AUTHORITY
MARVEL COMICS GROUP
40 SEPT
12¢
"SPIDEY SAVES THE DAY!"
THE END OF THE GREEN GOBLIN!

**◀ *AMAZING SPIDER-MAN* #33**

**February 1966**
**Artist:** Steve Ditko

This issue is often voted one of the best Spider-Man comics of all time. It might appear to be a simple cover, but the image of Spidey trapped under the machinery encapsulates many of Lee and Ditko's stories, in which the webslinger tries to beat overwhelming odds. The issue was one of Ditko's last, the artist leaving the title with issue #38.

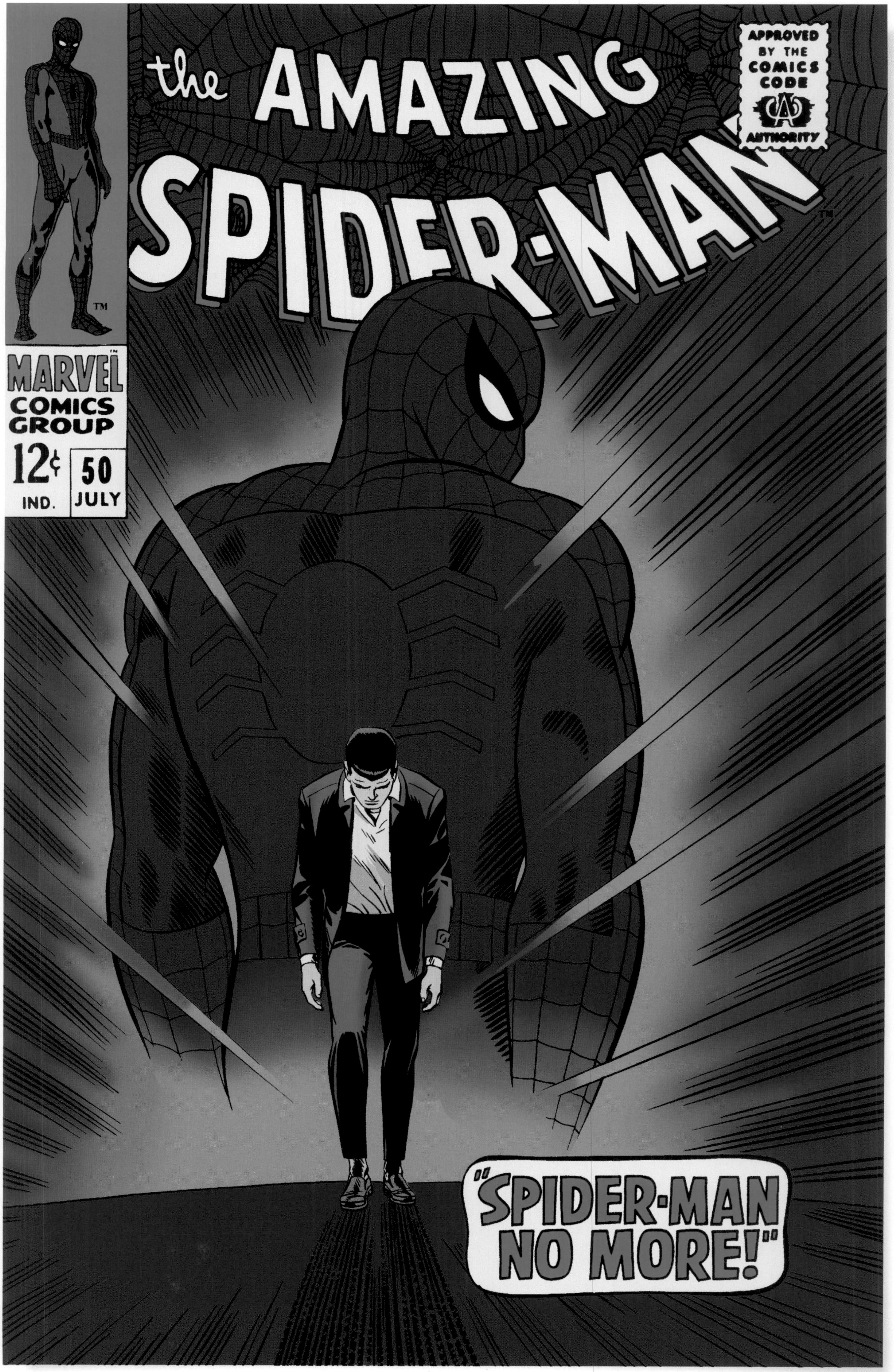
the AMAZING SPIDER-MAN
APPROVED BY THE COMICS CODE AUTHORITY
MARVEL COMICS GROUP
12¢ IND.
50 JULY
"SPIDER-MAN NO MORE!"

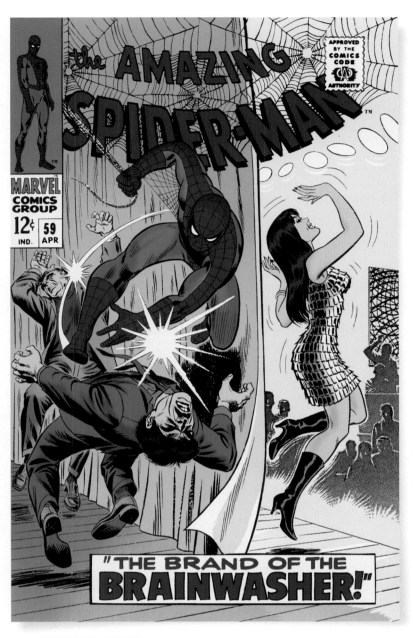

the AMAZING
SPIDER-MAN
MARVEL COMICS GROUP
12¢ 59 IND. APR
APPROVED BY THE COMICS CODE AUTHORITY
"THE BRAND OF THE BRAINWASHER!"


**▲ *AMAZING SPIDER-MAN* #59**

**April 1968**
**Artist:** John Romita Sr.

Romita's greatest addition to the Spider-Man mythos was Mary Jane Watson. She debuted on the last page of issue #42 with the classic words, "Face it, tiger... you just hit the jackpot." Mary Jane was the embodiment of the swinging 1960s, as this cover art shows—she is depicted dancing at a club that was a front for the Kingpin.

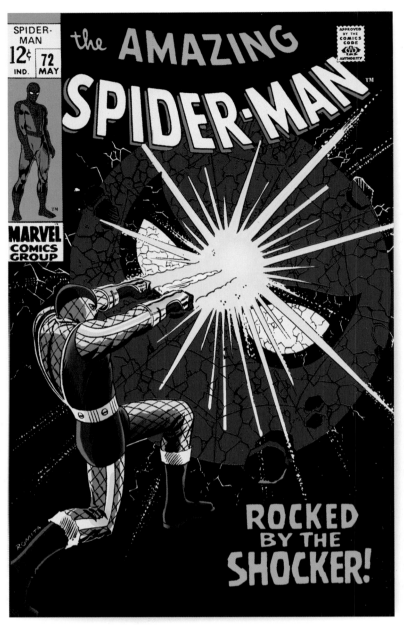

SPIDER-MAN
12¢ 72 IND. MAY
the AMAZING
SPIDER-MAN
APPROVED BY THE COMICS CODE AUTHORITY
MARVEL COMICS GROUP
ROCKED BY THE SHOCKER!


**▲ *AMAZING SPIDER-MAN* #72**

**May 1969**
**Artist:** John Romita Sr.

Some images remain strong years after their creation. This Romita masterpiece is one such cover. Spidey's spotlight is rarely used these days, but here it creates the perfect target for the Shocker. The simple, yet powerful image remains one of the strongest Spidey covers of the decade.

**◄ *AMAZING SPIDER-MAN* #50**

**July 1967**
**Artist:** John Romita Sr.

John Romita Sr. produced a number of stunning covers for Marvel and this classic *Spider-Man* cover ranks among the best. His atmospheric piece showing Peter Parker turning his back on life as a hero is still a striking image.

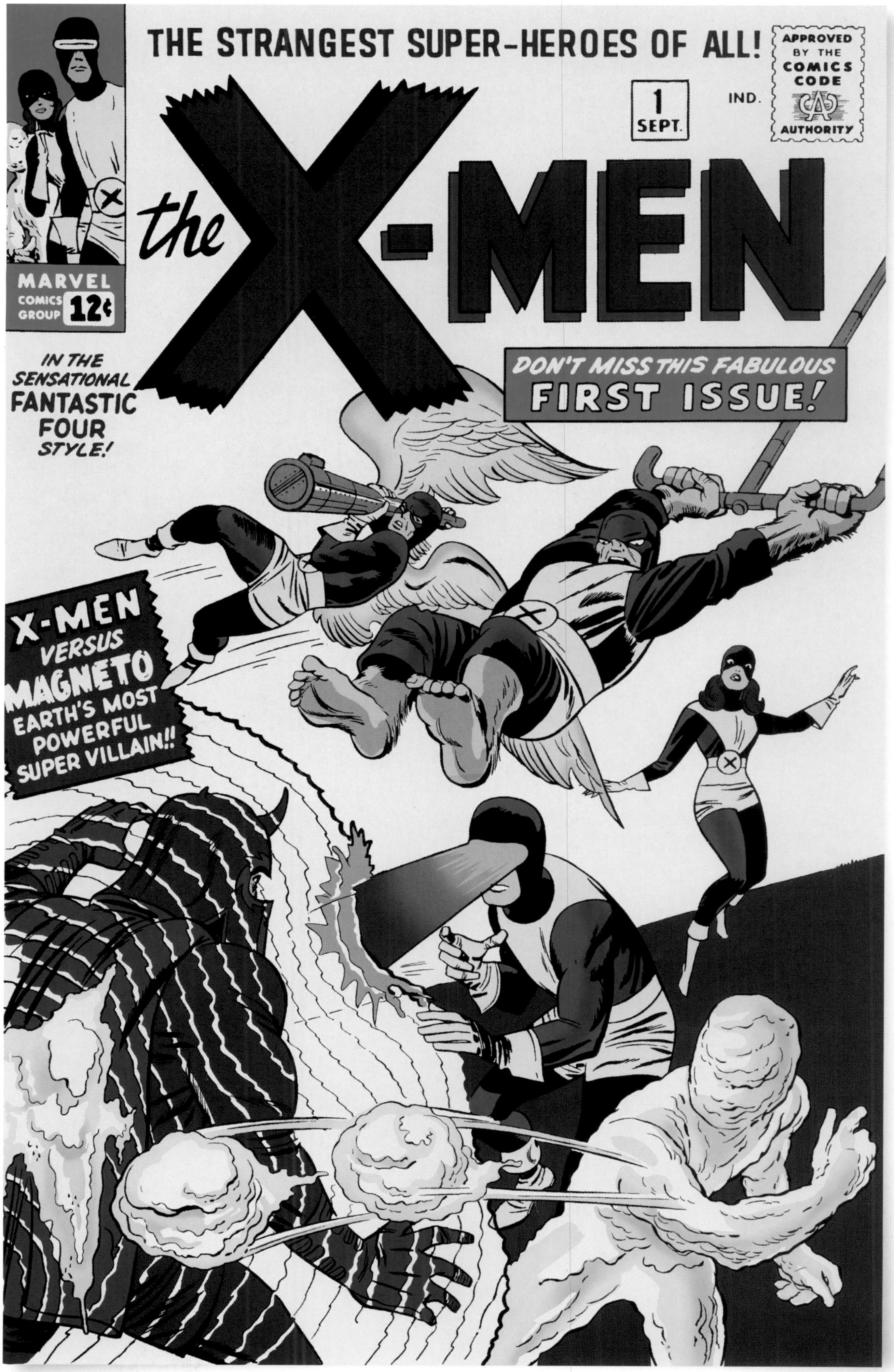
THE STRANGEST SUPER-HEROES OF ALL!
APPROVED BY THE COMICS CODE AUTHORITY
1 SEPT.
IND.
the X-MEN
MARVEL COMICS GROUP 12¢
IN THE SENSATIONAL FANTASTIC FOUR STYLE!
DON'T MISS THIS FABULOUS FIRST ISSUE!
X-MEN VERSUS MAGNETO EARTH'S MOST POWERFUL SUPER VILLAIN!!

**▲ *X-MEN* #1**

**September 1963**
**Artist:** Jack Kirby

Stan Lee and Jack Kirby came up with another unique take on the Super Hero myth with the X-Men, a group of teenage mutants who were "the strangest Super-Heroes of all." The first issue not only introduced the team, but also their enemy—Magneto. Like so much of Kirby's work at this time, it proved to be an iconic image. Jim Lee presented his own homage to the cover with his work on 1991's *X-Men* issue #1 *(see p300)*.

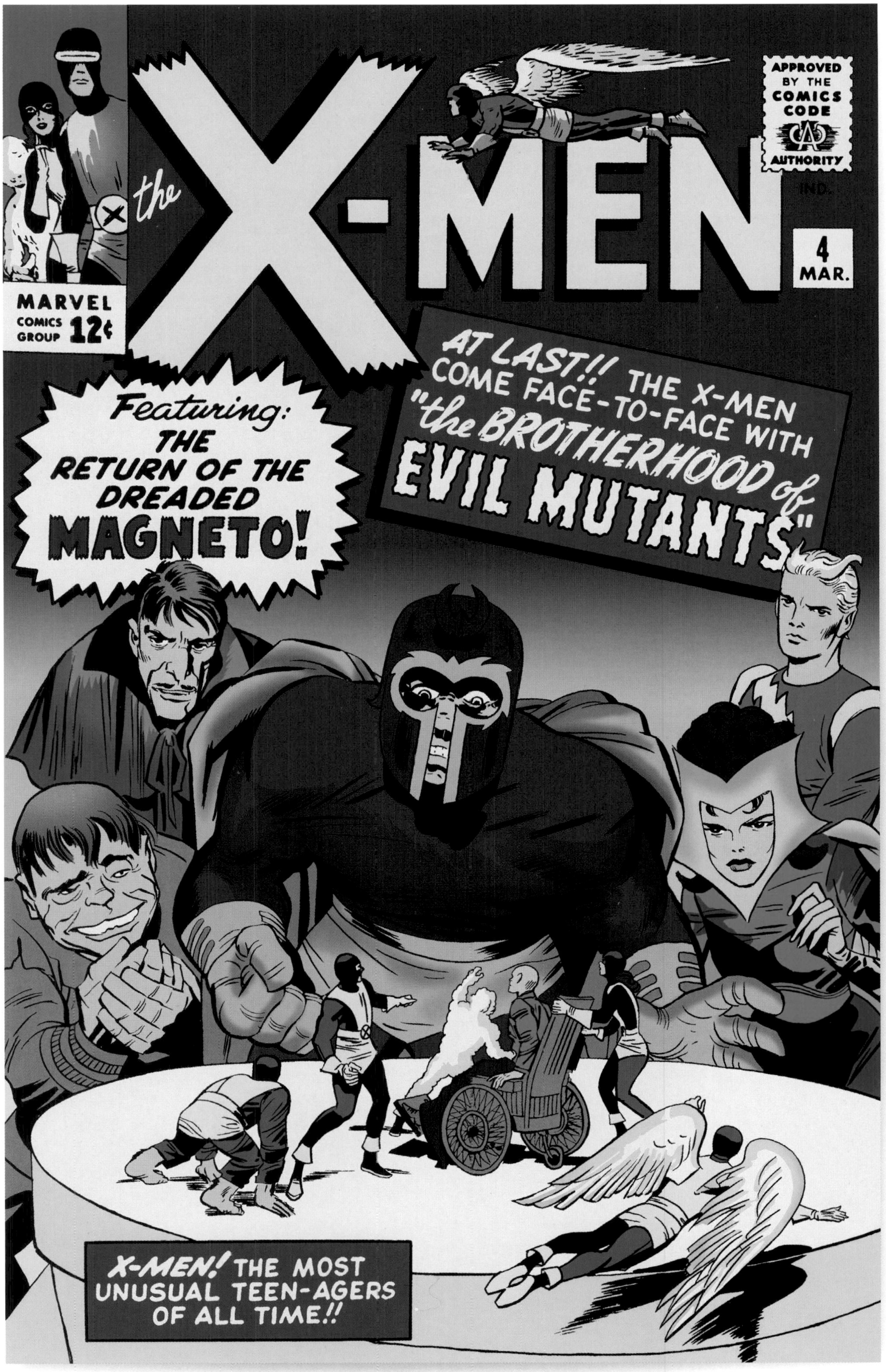
the X-MEN
APPROVED BY THE COMICS CODE AUTHORITY
IND.
4 MAR.
MARVEL COMICS GROUP 12¢
Featuring: THE RETURN OF THE DREADED MAGNETO!
AT LAST!! THE X-MEN COME FACE-TO-FACE WITH "the BROTHERHOOD of EVIL MUTANTS"
X-MEN! THE MOST UNUSUAL TEEN-AGERS OF ALL TIME!!

▲ *X-MEN #4*

**March 1964**
**Artist:** Jack Kirby

The Brotherhood of Evil Mutants graced an *X-Men* cover for the first time in this issue. Kirby's work manages to bring out the personality of each character—from the sleazy evil of Mastermind to the uncertainty of the Scarlet Witch and her brother, Quicksilver. At his villainous best, their leader Magneto dominates proceedings as he looms over the X-Men.

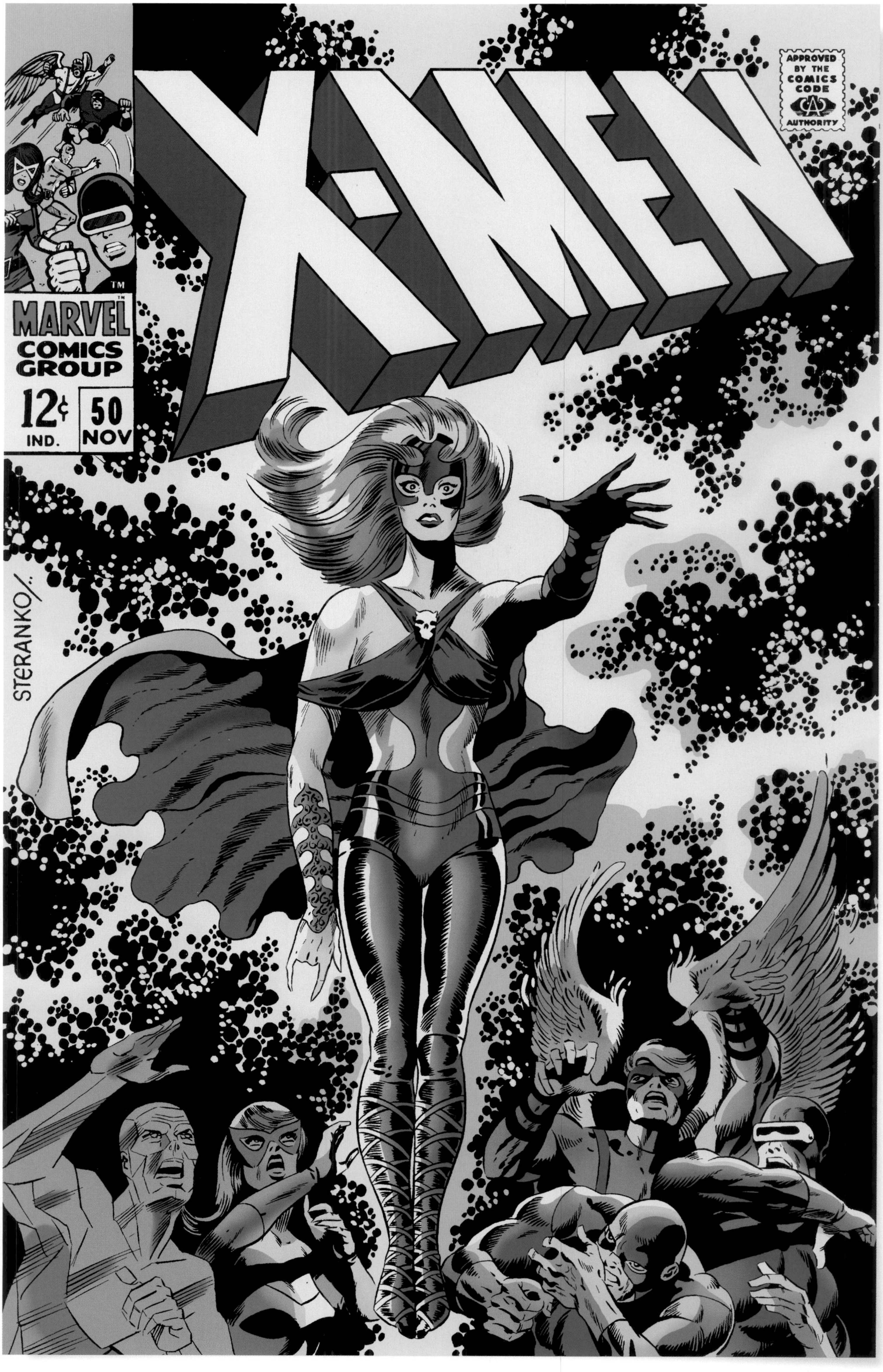
X-MEN
MARVEL
COMICS GROUP
12¢
IND.
50
NOV
APPROVED BY THE COMICS CODE AUTHORITY
STERANKO

◀ ***X-MEN* #50**

**November 1968**
**Artist:** Jim Steranko

Steranko briefly created brilliant work for *X-Men* in the late 1960s. Lorna Dane (aka Polaris) was the focus in this issue. Steranko's figure work and the eye-catching color makes this cover stand out. The energy in the backdrop also adds to the sense of power emanating from Lorna.

X-MEN
12¢ 51
IND. DEC
X-MEN
MARVEL COMICS GROUP
STERANKO

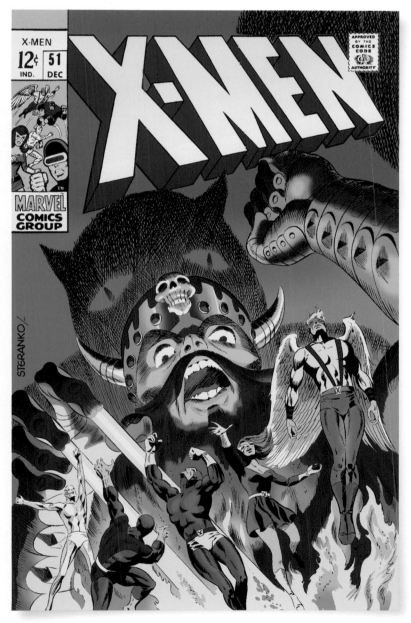

▲ ***X-MEN* #51**

**December 1968**
**Artist:** Jim Steranko

Steranko's short run on *X-Men* ended with this slightly crazy cover. The image is all about light and shadow as the X-Men learned the truth about Erik the Red, and met their old foe Magneto once again. These later issues took on a more experimental direction as Marvel tried various ways to boost sales.

X-MEN
15¢ 58
IND. JULY
X-MEN
MARVEL COMICS GROUP
ENTER... THE MAN CALLED HAVOK!

▲ ***X-MEN* #58**

**July 1969**
**Artist:** Neal Adams

Alongside Jim Steranko, Neal Adams helped redefine what comics could be in the late 1960s. Adams brought an energy and dynamic layout to his work that continues to influence artists even today. The cover for this issue shows Alex Summers as Havok for the first time. Its inspired layout and color make it ahead of its time.

X-MEN
15¢
59
IND.
AUG
APPROVED BY THE COMICS CODE AUTHORITY
X-MEN
MARVEL COMICS GROUP
THE LAST X-MAN

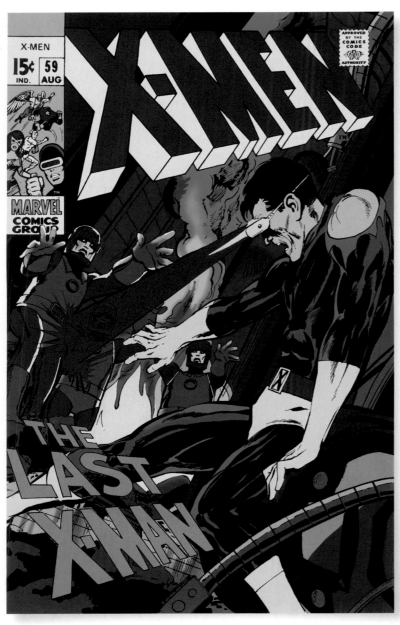

▲ *X-MEN* #59

**August 1969**
**Artist:** Neal Adams

This cover showing Cyclops surrounded by the mutant-hunting Sentinels is a brilliant example of the energy Adams puts into his work. The composition of the piece, with Cyclops in the foreground attempting to hold off his attackers, puts the viewer in the position of Cyclops, encouraging a greater empathy.

X-MEN
15¢
60
SEPT
THE STRANGEST TEENS OF ALL!
APPROVED BY THE COMICS CODE AUTHORITY
X-MEN
MARVEL COMICS GROUP
IN THE SHADOW OF... SAURON

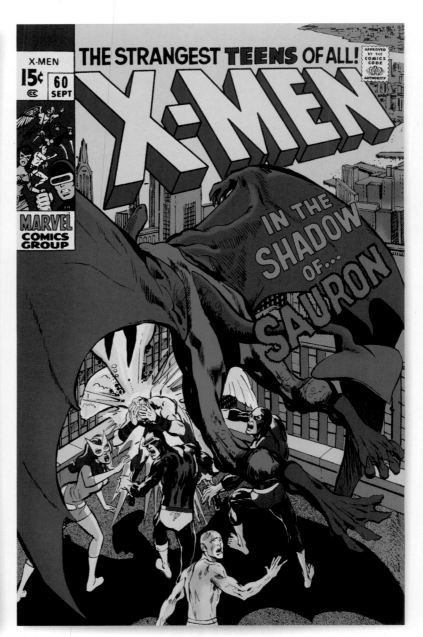

▲ *X-MEN* #60

**September 1969**
**Artist:** Neal Adams

This memorable cover by Adams introduced Sauron, one of the X-Men's strangest-looking foes. The flow and energy for which Adams' art is renowned is once again present. This issue took the X-Men to the Savage Land in a classic four-part tale.

*X-MEN* #62 ▶

**November 1969**
**Artist:** Neal Adams

One of Neal Adams' final covers on the *X-Men* was another classic, this time featuring Ka-Zar, Lord of the Savage Land, and his loyal Sabertooth tiger Zabu. The text carved into the rock echoes one of Ka-Zar's previous cover appearances on *The Incredible Hulk* issue #109 *(see p29)*.

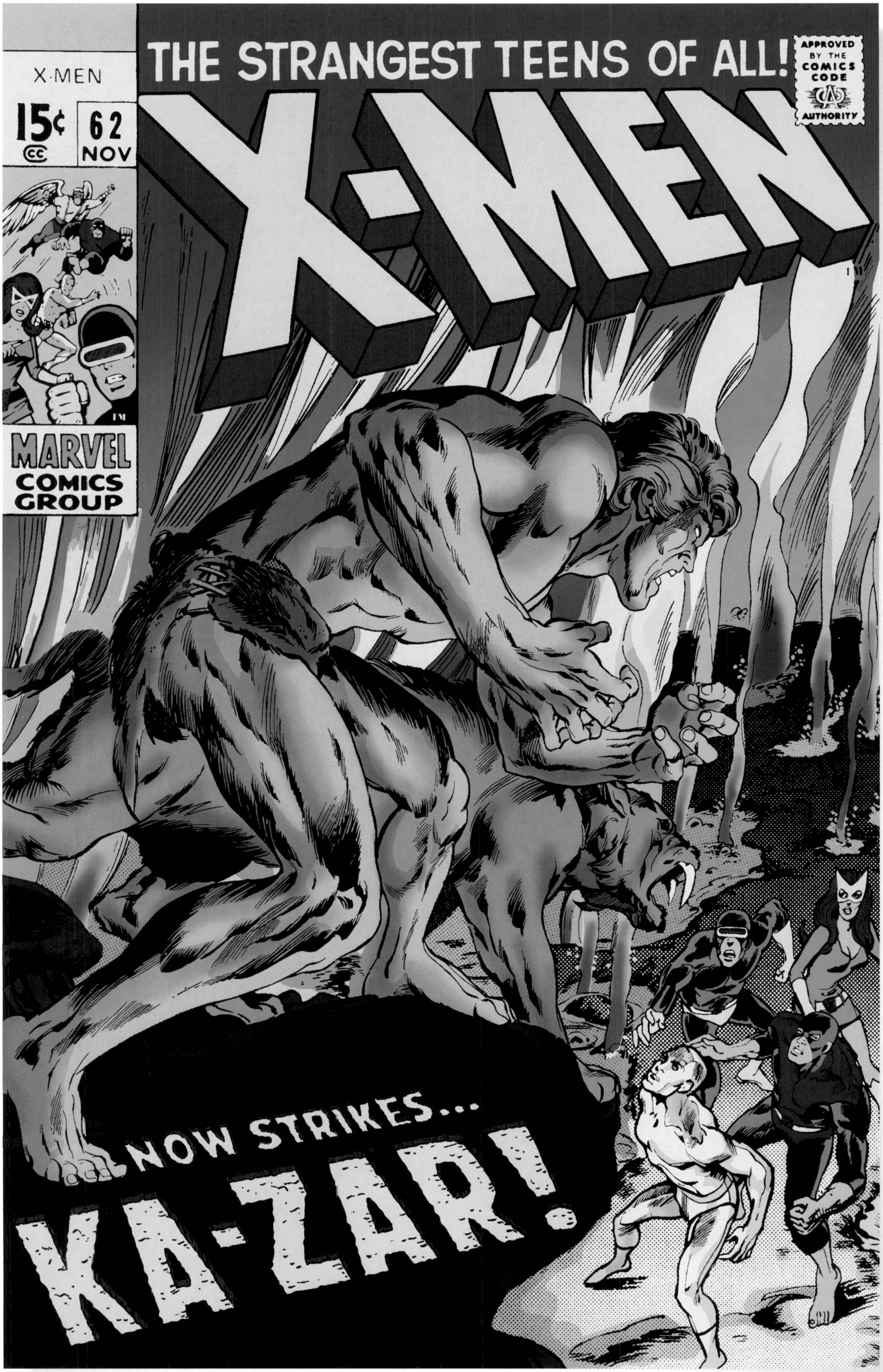
X-MEN
15¢
62
NOV
THE STRANGEST TEENS OF ALL!
APPROVED BY THE COMICS CODE AUTHORITY
X-MEN
MARVEL COMICS GROUP
NOW STRIKES...
KA-ZAR!

# THE BRONZE AGE

## 1970–1986

**THE BRONZE AGE** was a period of amazing change. A whole host of talented new artists and writers began to make their mark on the industry, and comics started to take on a more realistic approach. For Marvel, it began with *Amazing Spider-Man* issue #96 (May 1971), when they published a storyline dealing with Harry Osborn's drug addiction—without the approval of the Comics Code Authority (which acted as a censor.) This led to an updating of the code, which in turn allowed horror comics to make a comeback and for others to include more adult themes.

Artists such as Neal Adams and Jim Steranko pushed cover design in bold new directions. They were soon joined by future art legends George Pérez, John Byrne, and Frank Miller. It was also a time when comic collecting became very popular, and the increased number of comic shops meant that Marvel could start selling their books straight to specialist shops. By the end of the Bronze Age, the industry had almost changed beyond recognition.

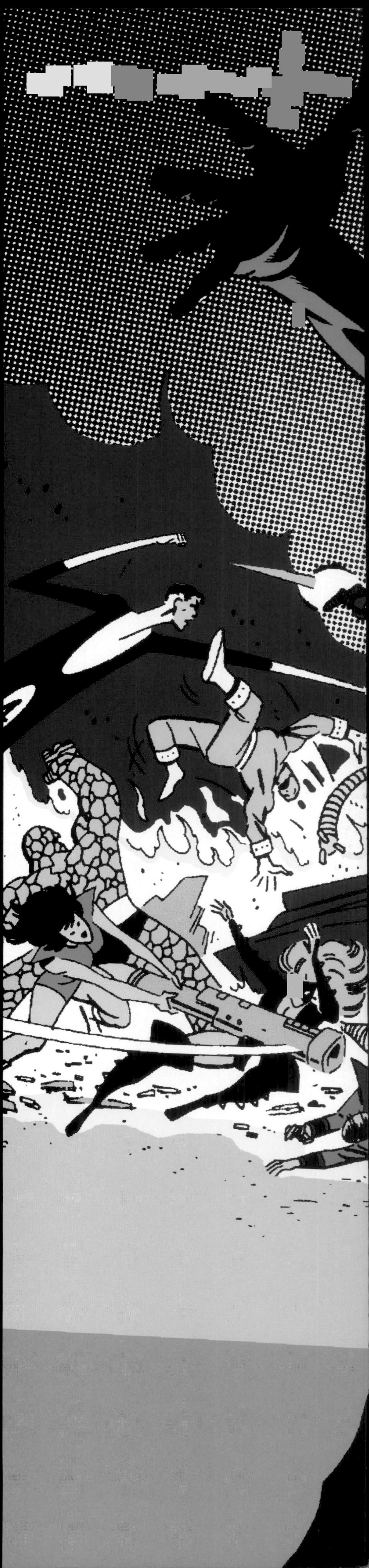

***MARVEL SUPER HEROES SECRET WARS #8*** ▶

**December 1984**
**Artist:** Mike Zeck

*(Cover shown in full on p133)*

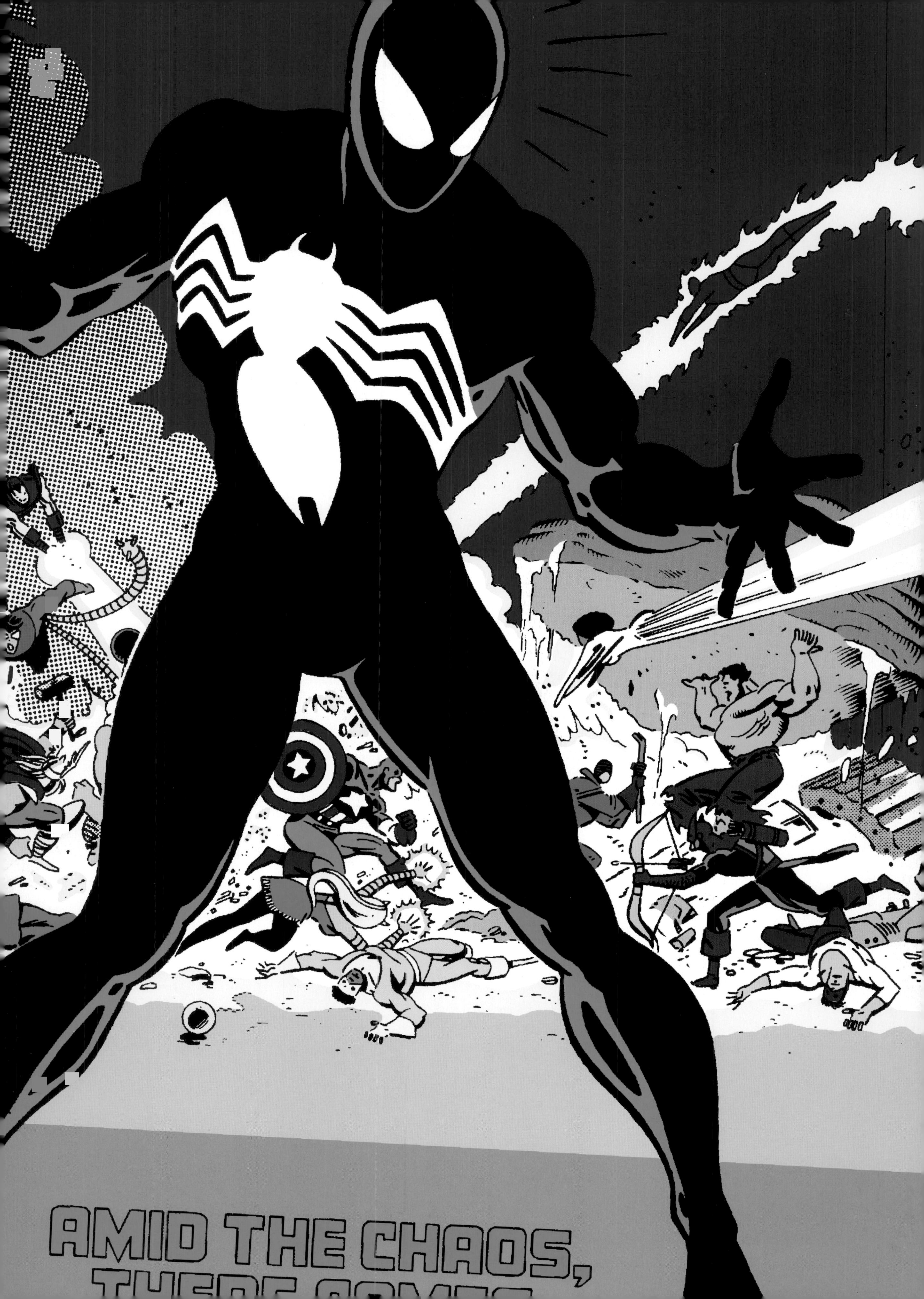
AMID THE CHAOS,

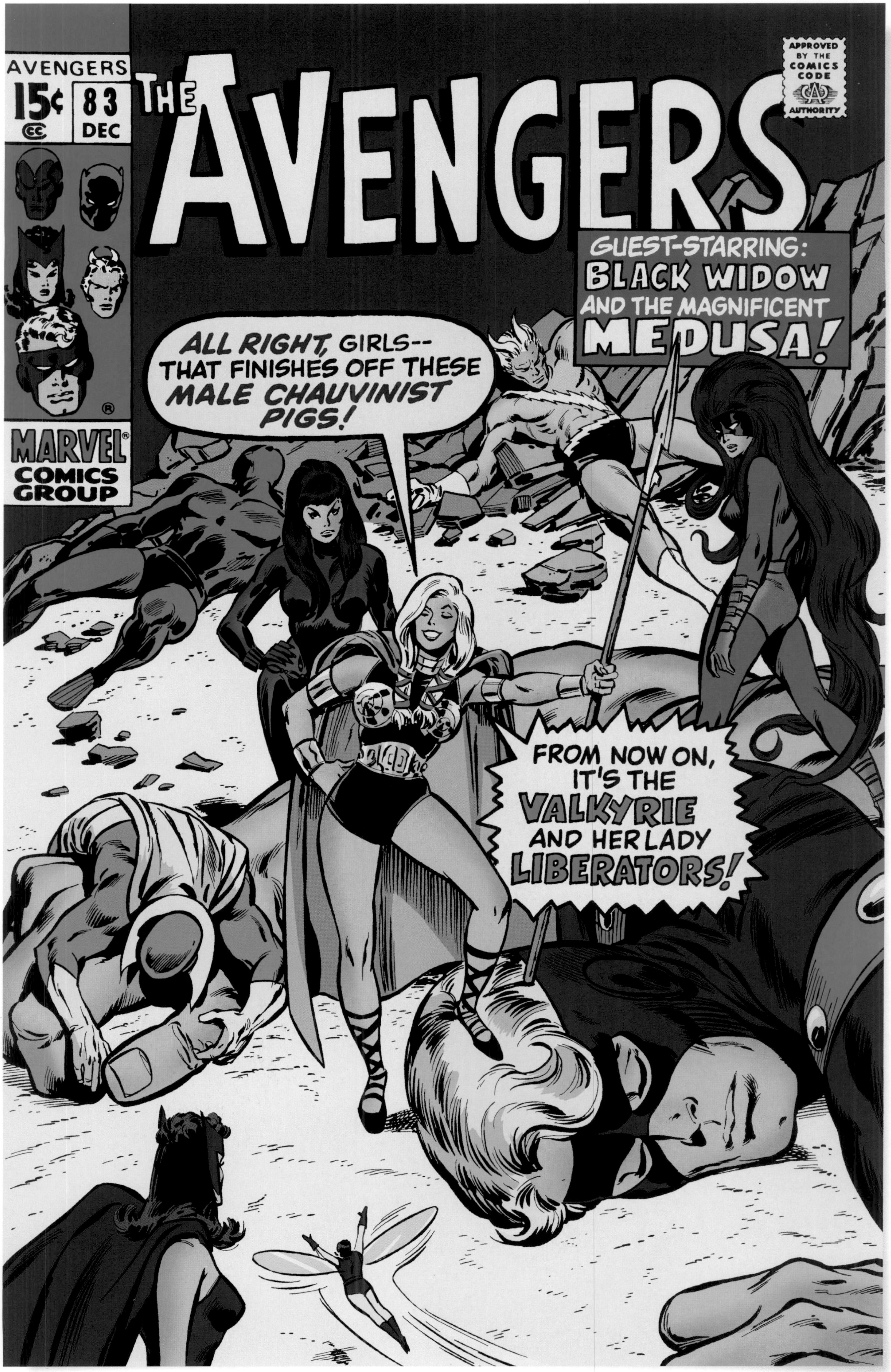
AVENGERS
15¢
83
DEC
MARVEL COMICS GROUP
THE AVENGERS
APPROVED BY THE COMICS CODE AUTHORITY
GUEST-STARRING: BLACK WIDOW AND THE MAGNIFICENT MEDUSA!
ALL RIGHT, GIRLS-- THAT FINISHES OFF THESE MALE CHAUVINIST PIGS!
FROM NOW ON, IT'S THE VALKYRIE AND HER LADY LIBERATORS!

◀ *AVENGERS* **#83**

**December 1970**
**Artist:** John Buscema

By 1970, second-wave feminism was at its peak in the US, so Marvel waded into the political waters by bringing Medusa, Scarlet Witch, Black Widow, and the Wasp together in one story. Valkyrie, a new character despite being Enchantress in disguise, stands front-and-center in this John Buscema image, having finished off the "male chauvinist pigs!"

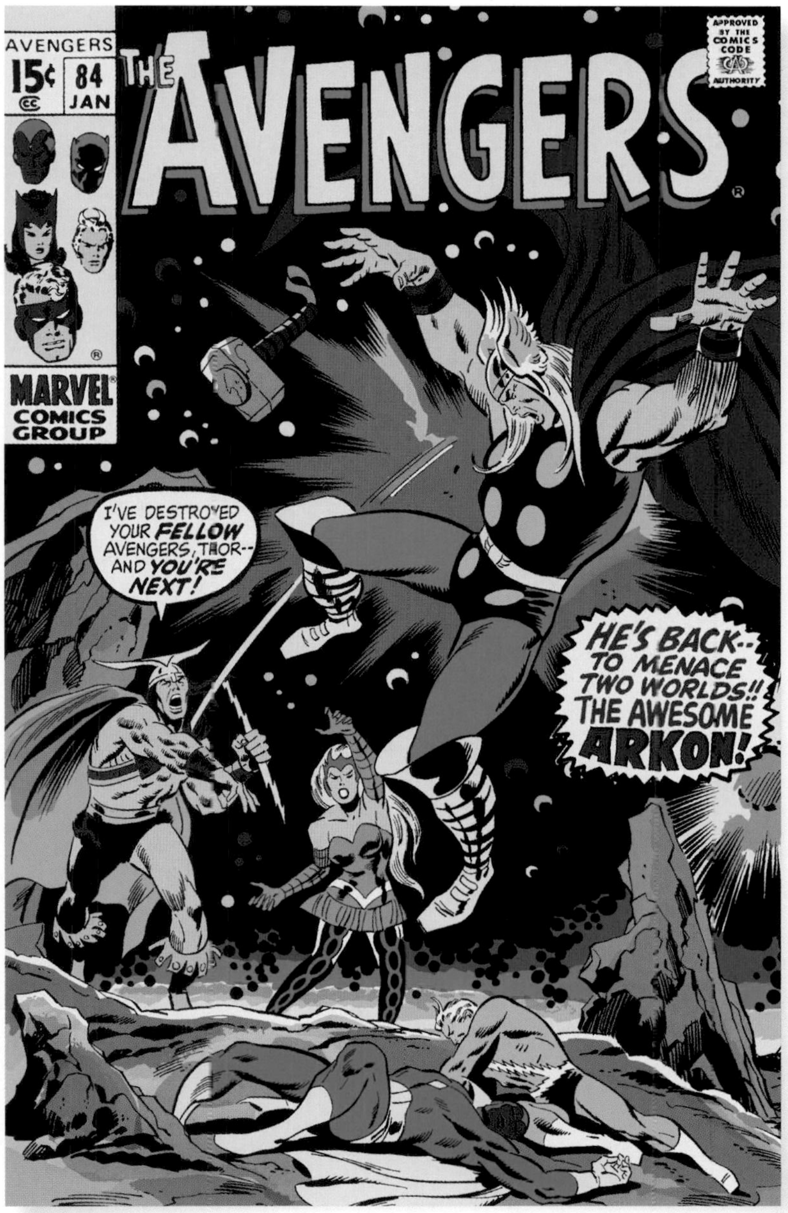
AVENGERS
15¢ 84 JAN
THE AVENGERS
MARVEL COMICS GROUP
I'VE DESTROYED YOUR FELLOW AVENGERS, THOR-- AND YOU'RE NEXT!
HE'S BACK-- TO MENACE TWO WORLDS!! THE AWESOME ARKON!

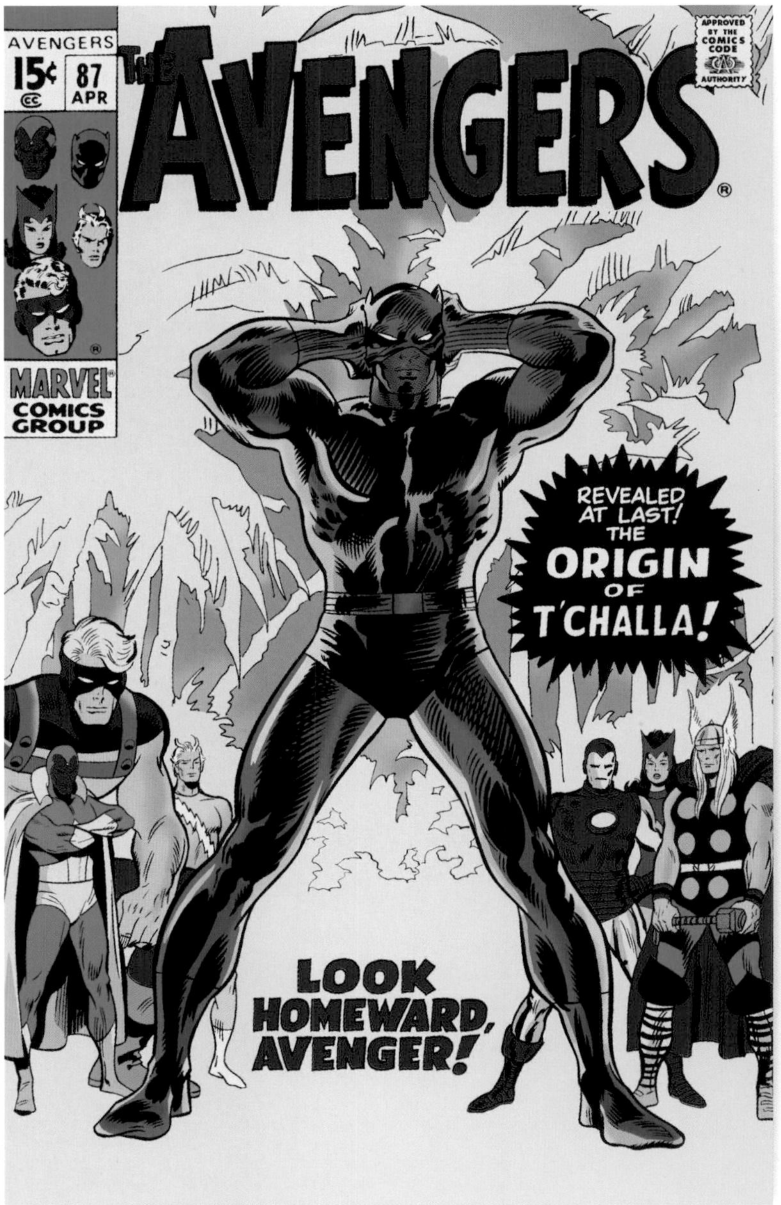
AVENGERS
15¢ 87 APR
THE AVENGERS
MARVEL COMICS GROUP
REVEALED AT LAST! THE ORIGIN OF T'CHALLA!
LOOK HOMEWARD, AVENGER!

▲ *AVENGERS* **#84**

**January 1971**
**Artist:** John Buscema

Arkon returned to plague the Avengers in this issue. Half hero, half barbarian, Arkon was just the sort of character Buscema excelled at, his style of drawing highly muscular figures bringing a real savagery to the characters. It was a technique Buscema would later bring to his work on *Conan the Barbarian*.

▲ *AVENGERS* **#87**

**April 1971**
**Artist:** John Buscema

Dominated by the powerful figure of the Black Panther, this cover was a key issue in the life of the Super Hero's alter ego, Prince T'Challa. Already a popular character from his appearances in both this title and the *Fantastic Four*, the prospect of finally learning the truth about his origins, combined with the striking cover art, enticed readers.

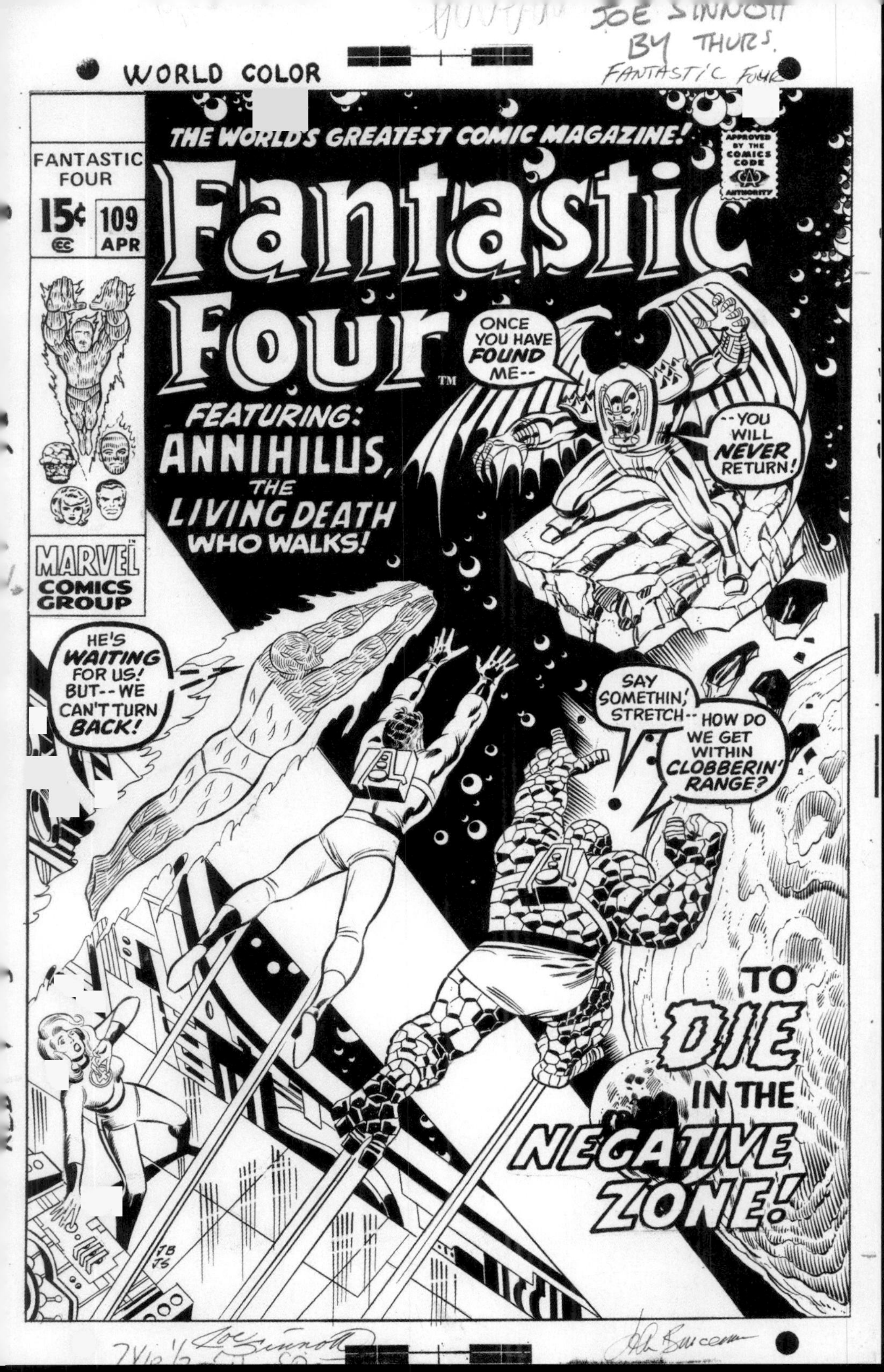
JOE SINNOTT
BY THURS.
FANTASTIC FOUR
WORLD COLOR
THE WORLD'S GREATEST COMIC MAGAZINE!
APPROVED BY THE COMICS CODE AUTHORITY
FANTASTIC FOUR
15¢ 109 APR
Fantastic Four
FEATURING: ANNIHILUS, THE LIVING DEATH WHO WALKS!
MARVEL COMICS GROUP
ONCE YOU HAVE FOUND ME--
--YOU WILL NEVER RETURN!
HE'S WAITING FOR US! BUT--WE CAN'T TURN BACK!
SAY SOMETHIN', STRETCH--
HOW DO WE GET WITHIN CLOBBERIN' RANGE?
TO DIE IN THE NEGATIVE ZONE!
1.

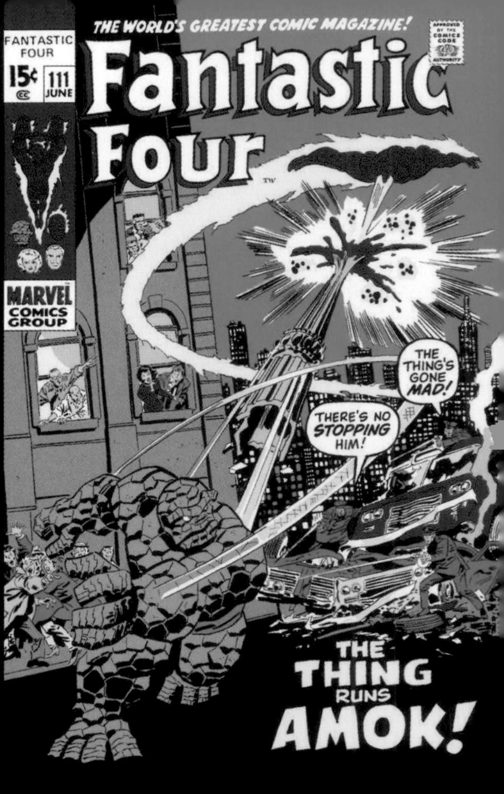
THE WORLD'S GREATEST COMIC MAGAZINE!
FANTASTIC FOUR
15¢ 111 JUNE
Fantastic Four
MARVEL COMICS GROUP
THE THING'S GONE MAD!
THERE'S NO STOPPING HIM!
THE THING RUNS AMOK!
2.

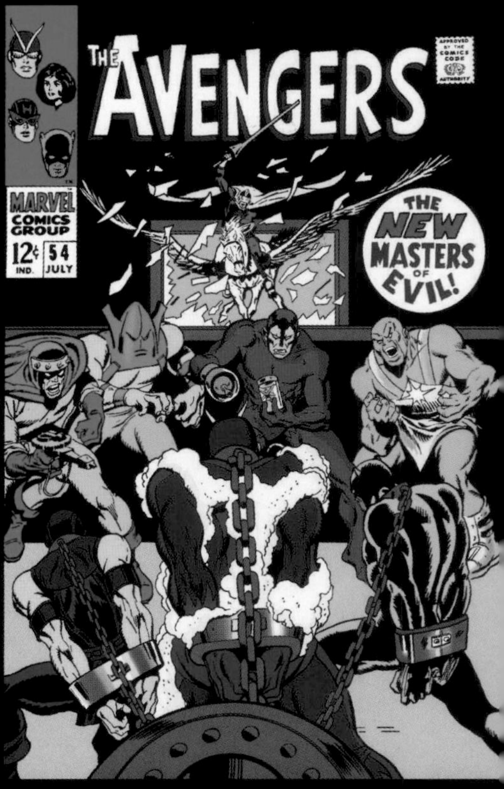
THE AVENGERS
MARVEL COMICS GROUP
12¢ IND. 54 JULY
THE NEW MASTERS OF EVIL!
3.

# JOHN BUSCEMA

Alongside Jack Kirby and John Romita Sr., John Buscema was one of Marvel's artistic founding fathers—his storytelling ability and powerful but naturalistic style influencing many of the artists who followed him. For many, he *was* Marvel, even illustrating the book *How to Draw Comics the Marvel Way*. During his long career, John illustrated just about every Marvel character and numerous covers. Some of his best-known work includes the *Avengers* and *Silver Surfer*. However, it is his decade-spanning run on *Conan the Barbarian* that best showcased his exceptional ability to draw powerful physical forms and savage action scenes. It was a facet of his artistic ability that led to John Buscema's nickname—"the Michelangelo of comics."

**1. *FANTASTIC FOUR* #109**

**April 1971**

John Buscema was a master of composition, as this piece of original art (inked by Joe Sinnott) shows. It also reflects his skill in conveying movement and action. The signatures include those of editorial as they signed off the work.

**2. *FANTASTIC FOUR* #111**

**June 1971**

Together with his exceptional figure work, John is perhaps best known for his ability to portray the raw power of muscular heroes. This dynamic cover is a good example of his style, showing the Thing clashing with his teammate the Human Torch.

**3. *AVENGERS* #54**

**July 1968**

John's vibrant and powerful art was a perfect match for the Avengers. The cover to this issue not only highlights the power he was able to instill into his characters, but also his ability to design a dramatic layout.

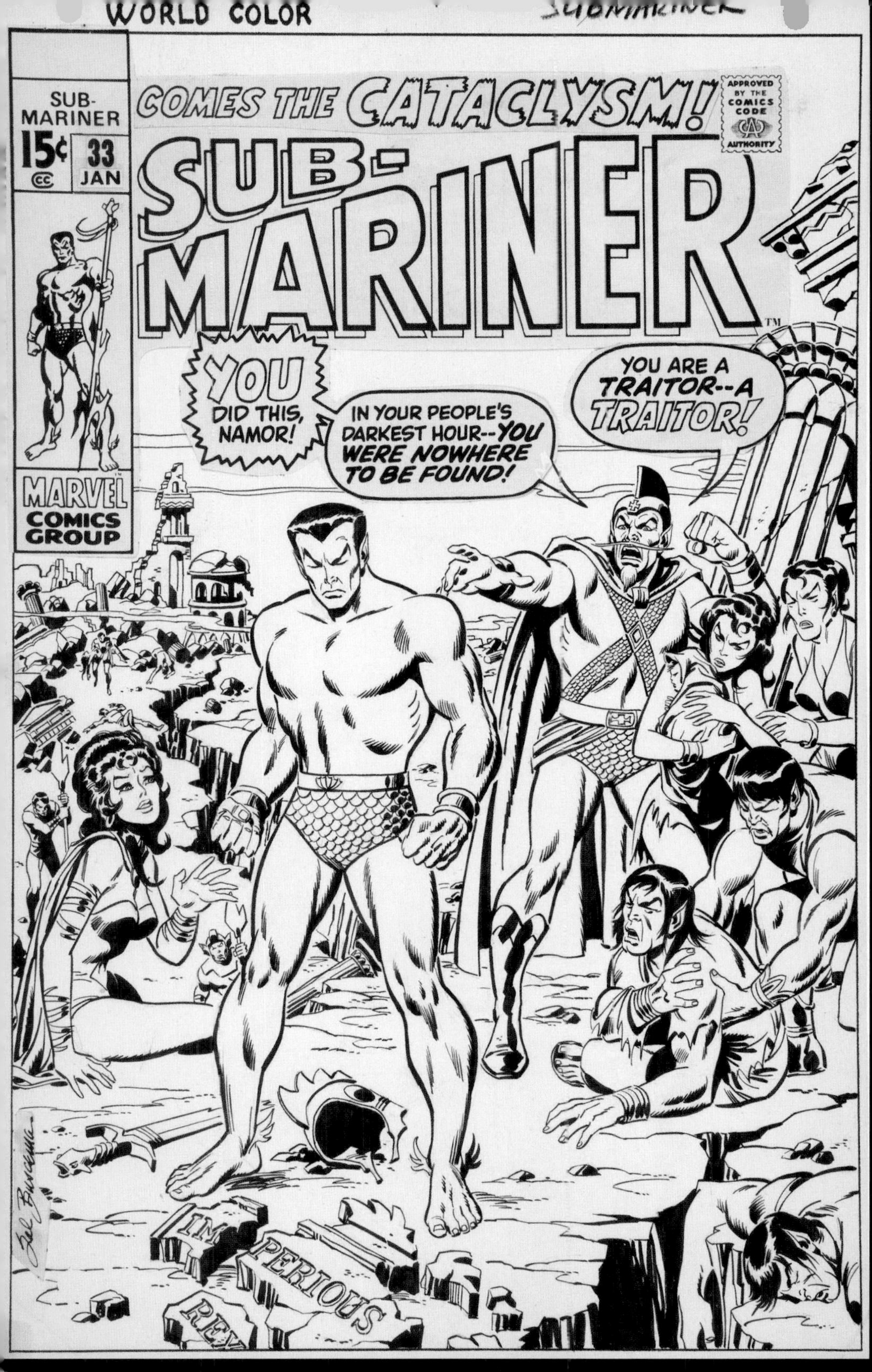

WORLD COLOR
SUB-MARINER 15¢ 33 JAN
COMES THE CATACLYSM!
APPROVED BY THE COMICS CODE AUTHORITY
SUB-MARINER
MARVEL COMICS GROUP
YOU DID THIS, NAMOR!
IN YOUR PEOPLE'S DARKEST HOUR--YOU WERE NOWHERE TO BE FOUND!
YOU ARE A TRAITOR--A TRAITOR!
IMPERIOUS REX


1.

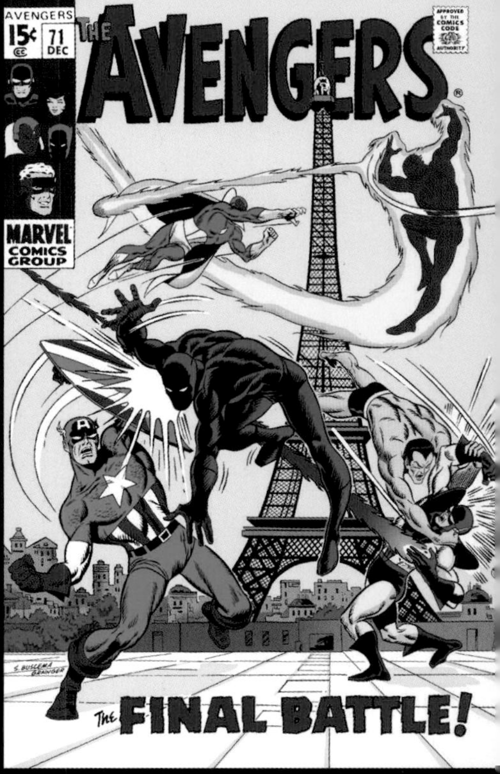

AVENGERS 15¢ 71 DEC
THE AVENGERS
APPROVED BY THE COMICS CODE AUTHORITY
MARVEL COMICS GROUP
The FINAL BATTLE!


2.

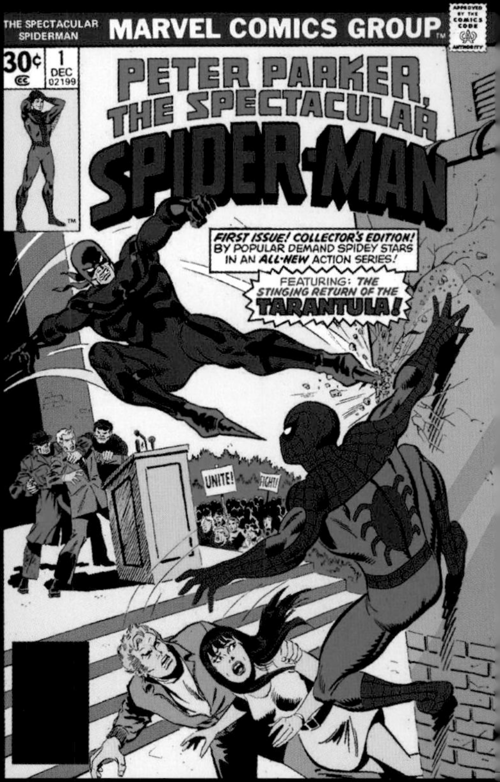

THE SPECTACULAR SPIDERMAN
MARVEL COMICS GROUP
30¢ 1 DEC 02199
PETER PARKER, THE SPECTACULAR SPIDER-MAN
FIRST ISSUE! COLLECTOR'S EDITION! BY POPULAR DEMAND SPIDEY STARS IN AN ALL-NEW ACTION SERIES!
FEATURING: THE STINGING RETURN OF THE TARANTULA!
UNITE!
FIGHT!


3.

# SAL BUSCEMA

John Buscema's brother Sal originally wanted to be an inker ather than a penciller, but he quickly became one of Marvel's nost prolific artists. He pencilled many of their best-selling itles and created a number of striking covers. Sal illustrated all of Marvel's most famous heroes and villains during his ong career and enjoyed critically acclaimed runs on the *Avengers*, *Hulk*, and *Captain America*. He is best known for his 10-year run on *Spectacular Spider-Man*, during which he llustrated some of the webslinger's greatest epics, including he "Clone Saga." Sal's loose, energetic style coupled with his fast-paced storytelling (hailed by many as the best in he business) was perfectly suited to illustrating Spidey's

**1. *SUB-MARINER* #33**

**January 1971**

This Sal Buscema cover (original cover art shown here) is full of tension. Sal artfully conveyed the anger and regret felt by the Sub-Mariner on learning of a huge disaster that had struck Atlantis during his absence from his undersea kingdom.

**2. *AVENGERS* #71**

**December 1969**

This energetic fight scene showing the Avengers fighting the Invaders in World War II is a perfect example of Sal's smooth but action-packed style. Sal could put a real sense of

**3. *PETER PARKER, THE SPECTACULAR SPIDER-MAN* #1**

**December 1976**

Sal was the original artist on *The Spectacular Spider-Man* and illustrated over 100 issues of the title. The cover to the first issue is a dramatic one, showing the evil Tarantula mid-air during an attack on Spidey. It is a fine example of Sal's ability to illustrate movement and fast-paced action.

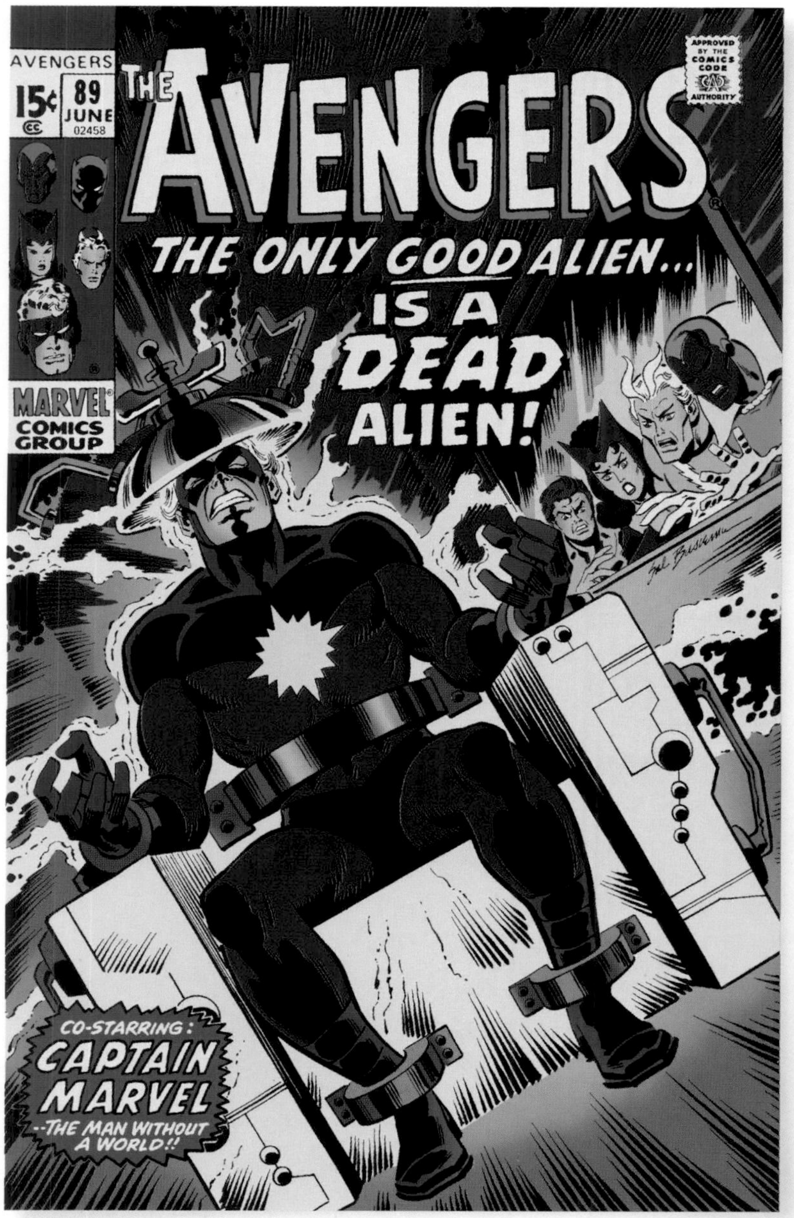
AVENGERS
15¢
89
JUNE
02458
THE AVENGERS
THE ONLY GOOD ALIEN... IS A DEAD ALIEN!
MARVEL COMICS GROUP
CO-STARRING: CAPTAIN MARVEL --THE MAN WITHOUT A WORLD!!

▲ *AVENGERS* #89

**June 1971**
**Artist:** Sal Buscema

John Buscema's kid brother, Sal, finally hit the big time in his own right with this stunning work, and he aimed to shock. This cover also marked the start of the Kree/Skrull war storyline. It was not only one of the first multipart epics to feature in the *Avengers*, but was also widely regarded as one of the most exciting and compelling story arcs of its time.

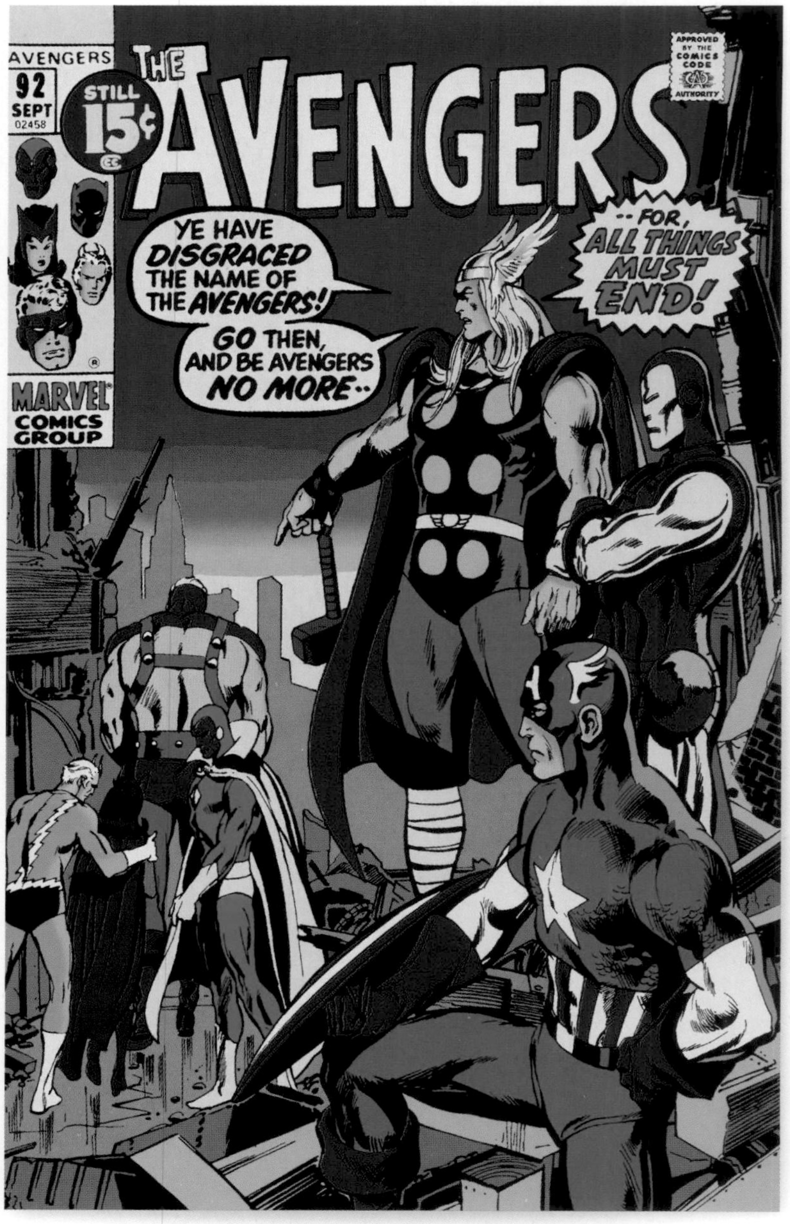
AVENGERS
92
SEPT
02458
STILL 15¢
THE AVENGERS
YE HAVE DISGRACED THE NAME OF THE AVENGERS!
GO THEN, AND BE AVENGERS NO MORE..
--FOR, ALL THINGS MUST END!
MARVEL COMICS GROUP

▲ *AVENGERS* #92

**September 1971**
**Artist:** Neal Adams

The Kree/Skrull war continued with a twist as the Avengers turned on their own team members. Neal Adam's image of Captain America, Thor, and Iron Man disbanding the team makes a striking cover. However, fans didn't need to mourn for long—all was not as it seemed, and the three Avengers were later revealed to be shape-changing Skrulls.

*AVENGERS* #118 ▶

**December 1973**
**Artist:** Unknown & John Romita Sr.

The Avengers/Defenders war was the first major crossover between the two teams, and John Romita Sr. produced an action-packed scene for the conclusion. It was rare to show this many heroes on a cover, which made its impact even more dramatic. The cover shows the architects of the war—the evil Loki and the dread Dormammu—on the verge of defeating both teams, using the powerful Evil Eye.

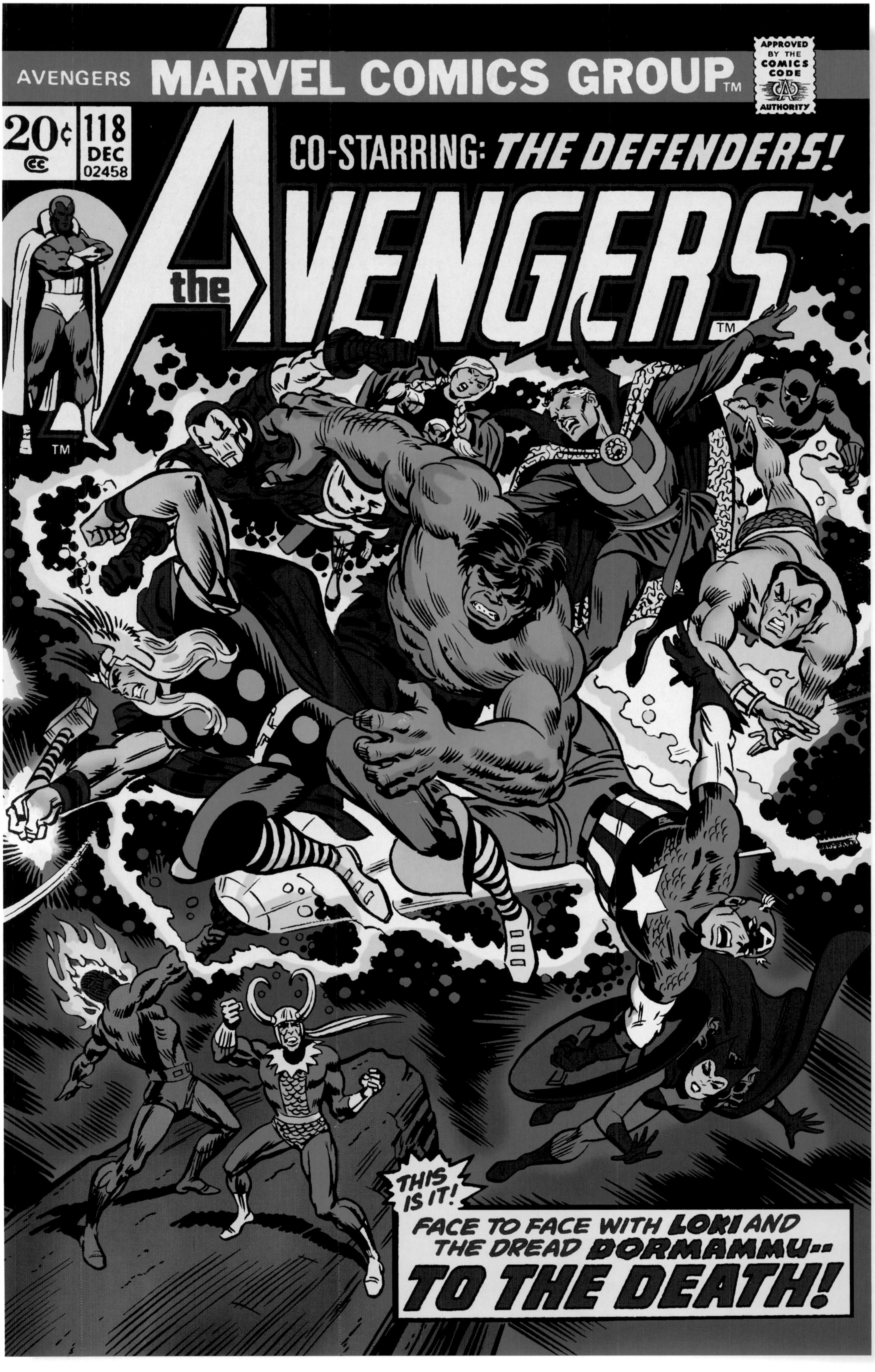
AVENGERS
MARVEL COMICS GROUP
APPROVED BY THE COMICS CODE AUTHORITY
20¢
118 DEC 02458
CO-STARRING: THE DEFENDERS!
THE AVENGERS
THIS IS IT!
FACE TO FACE WITH LOKI AND THE DREAD DORMAMMU--
TO THE DEATH!

***AVENGERS* #201 ▶**

**November 1980**
**Artist:** George Pérez

Marvel has always had fun with their heroes—it's one of the company's main selling points. This Pérez cover proved the perfect foil for the series of hard-hitting storylines that had preceded it. The image of Jarvis, the Avengers' long-suffering butler, taking control provided a welcome shot of humor to the book: Thor might have wielded a mystical hammer, but Jarvis had a vacuum cleaner!

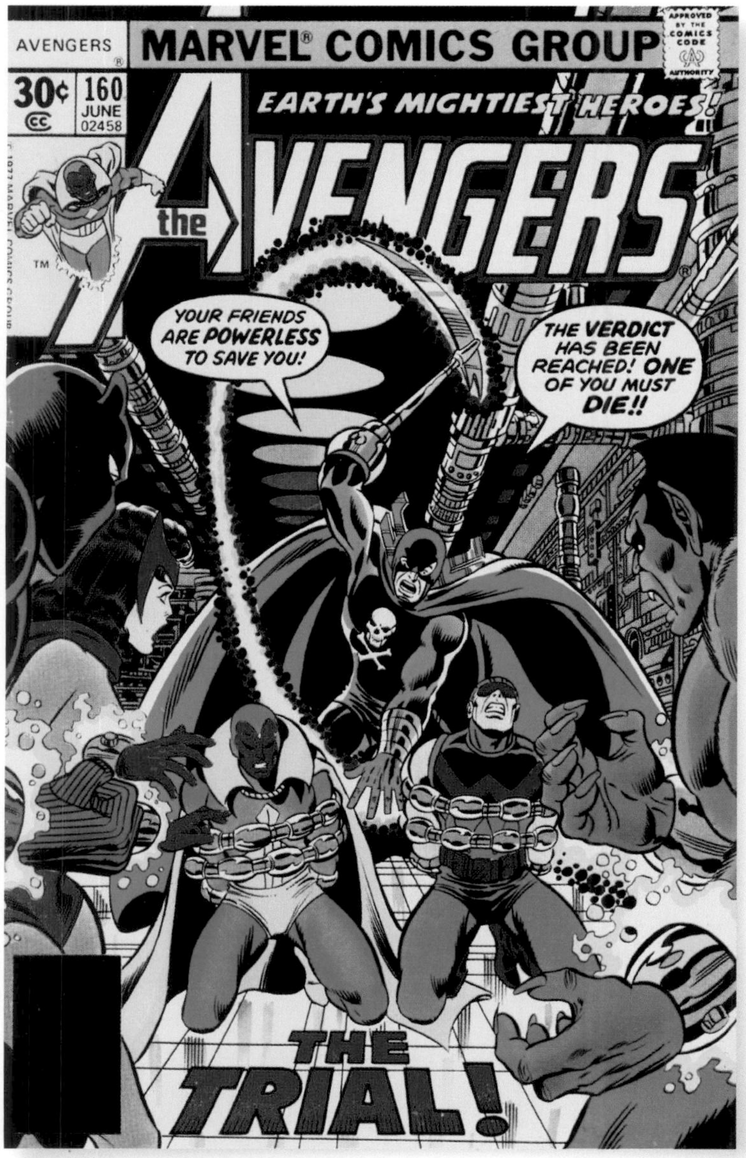
AVENGERS
MARVEL COMICS GROUP
30¢ 160 JUNE 02458
EARTH'S MIGHTIEST HEROES!
the AVENGERS
YOUR FRIENDS ARE POWERLESS TO SAVE YOU!
THE VERDICT HAS BEEN REACHED! ONE OF YOU MUST DIE!!
THE TRIAL!

**◀ *AVENGERS* #160**

**June 1977**
**Artist:** George Pérez

George Pérez quickly became one of Marvel's leading artists after joining them in the 1970s, and he has been an undisputed star of the comic world ever since. Pérez had a long history with *Avengers* (issue #141 was his first) and produced countless covers regarded as modern-day classics by fans and critics alike—including this early example, showing the Grim Reaper looming over Wonder Man and the Vision.

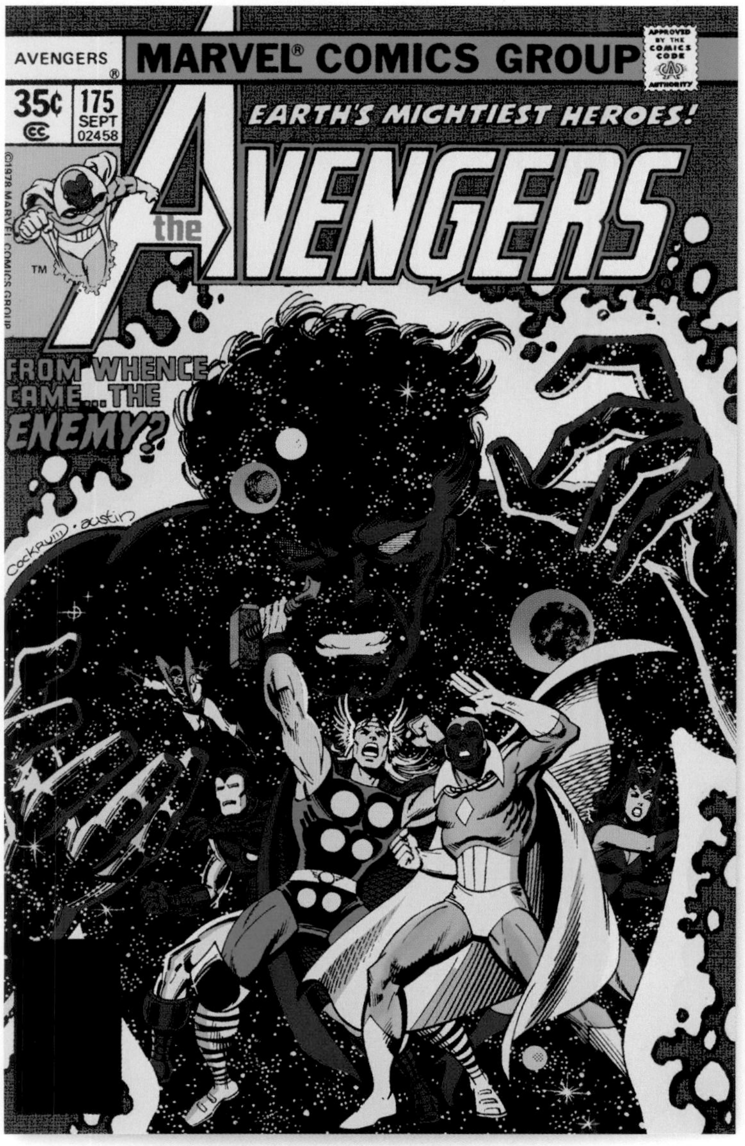
AVENGERS
MARVEL COMICS GROUP
35¢ 175 SEPT 02458
EARTH'S MIGHTIEST HEROES!
the AVENGERS
FROM WHENCE CAME... THE ENEMY?

**◀ *AVENGERS* #175**

**September 1978**
**Artist:** Dave Cockrum

The "Kovac" Saga is regarded as an all-time great, and this dramatic cover by Dave Cockrum encapsulated the cosmic story perfectly. The time-traveling Kovac came from the future, gained God-like abilities, and became one with the universe. He had the power to destroy not only the Avengers, but also the whole world.

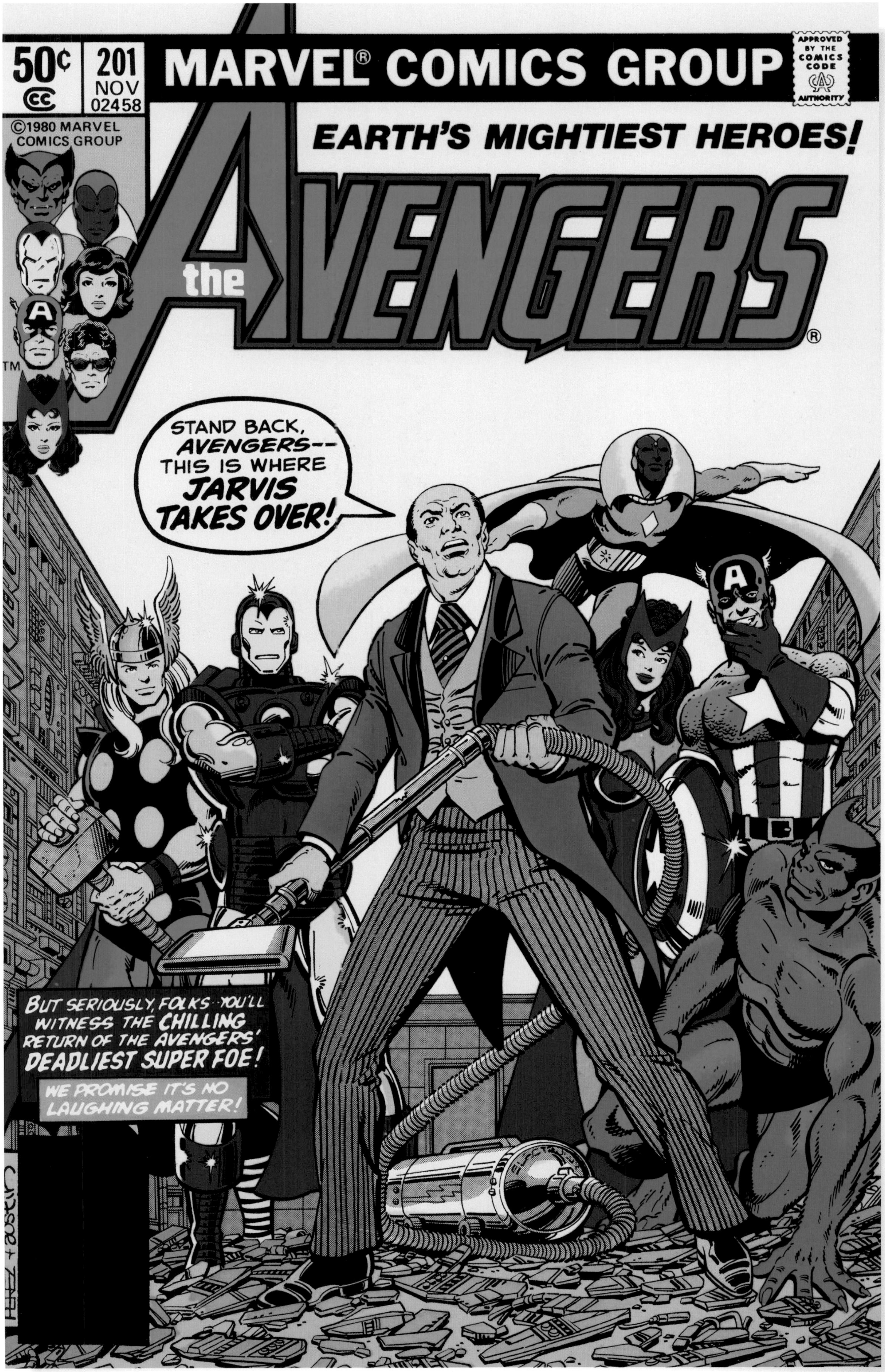
50¢
201
NOV
02458
MARVEL® COMICS GROUP
APPROVED BY THE COMICS CODE AUTHORITY
©1980 MARVEL COMICS GROUP
EARTH'S MIGHTIEST HEROES!
the AVENGERS®
STAND BACK, AVENGERS-- THIS IS WHERE JARVIS TAKES OVER!
BUT SERIOUSLY, FOLKS--YOU'LL WITNESS THE CHILLING RETURN OF THE AVENGERS' DEADLIEST SUPER FOE!
WE PROMISE IT'S NO LAUGHING MATTER!

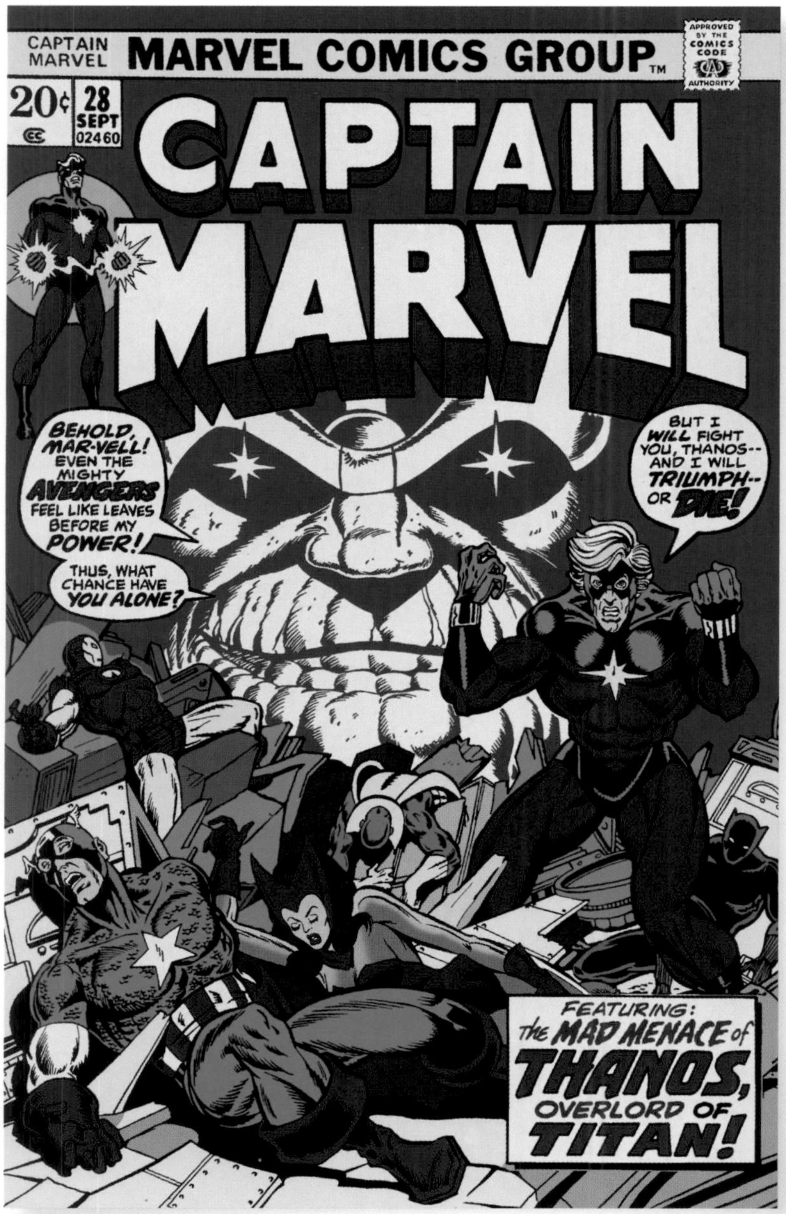
CAPTAIN MARVEL
MARVEL COMICS GROUP
20¢ 28 SEPT 02460
CAPTAIN MARVEL
BEHOLD, MAR-VELL! EVEN THE MIGHTY AVENGERS FEEL LIKE LEAVES BEFORE MY POWER!
THUS, WHAT CHANCE HAVE YOU ALONE?
BUT I WILL FIGHT YOU, THANOS-- AND I WILL TRIUMPH-- OR DIE!
FEATURING: The MAD MENACE of THANOS, OVERLORD OF TITAN!

▲ *CAPTAIN MARVEL* #28

**September 1973**
**Artist:** Jim Starlin

With the Avengers defeated, Jim Starlin's cover presented Captain Marvel as the only hero left to stop the evil Titan Thanos' plans. Thanos appeared on a cover for the first time with this issue and would go on to be one of the greatest villains in the Marvel Universe, even appearing in the post-credits epilogue of *The Avengers* movie of 2012.

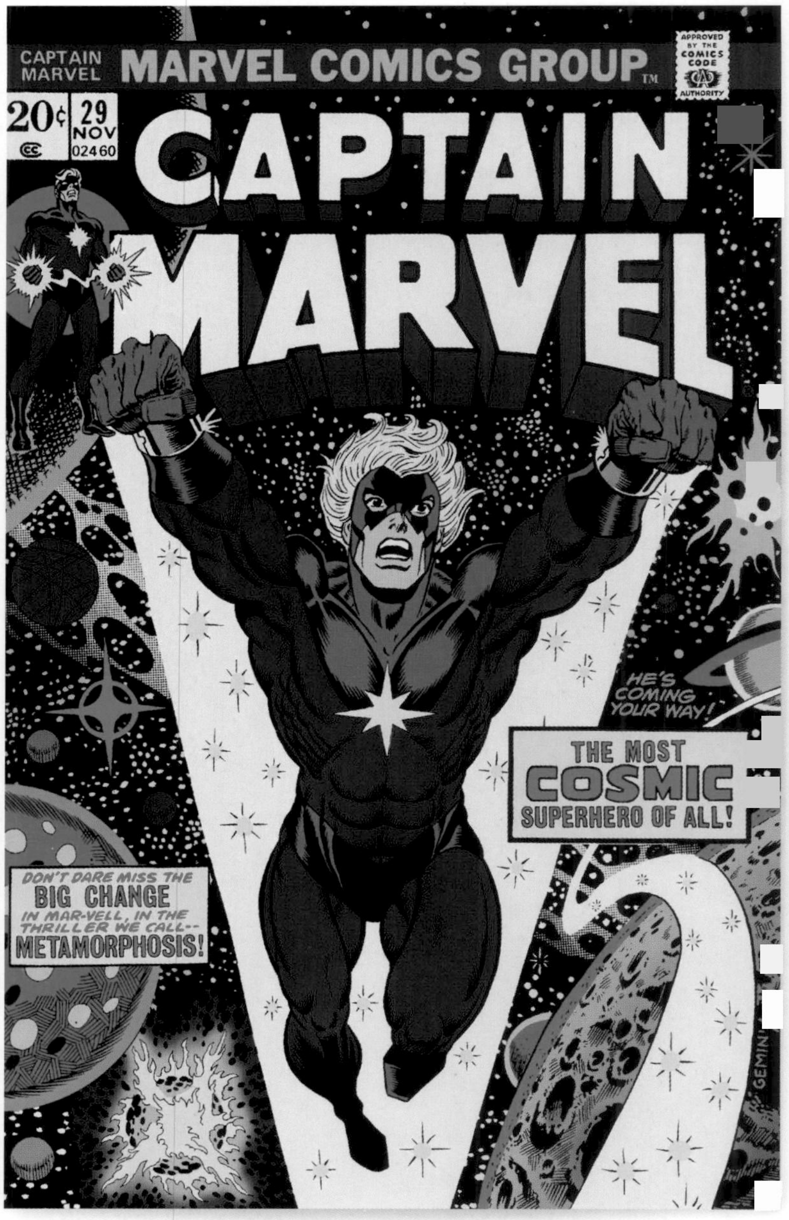
CAPTAIN MARVEL
MARVEL COMICS GROUP
20¢ 29 NOV 02460
CAPTAIN MARVEL
HE'S COMING YOUR WAY!
THE MOST COSMIC SUPERHERO OF ALL!
DON'T DARE MISS THE BIG CHANGE IN MAR-VELL, IN THE THRILLER WE CALL-- METAMORPHOSIS!

▲ *CAPTAIN MARVEL* #29

**November 1973**
**Artist:** Jim Starlin

Jim Starlin built his reputation as a writer and artist on *Captain Marvel* before going on to be one of the best-known artists in the business. Starlin was renowned for his intergalactic stories, and this early *Captain Marvel* cover epitomizes his style—a powerful central figure in a rather brilliant cosmic setting.

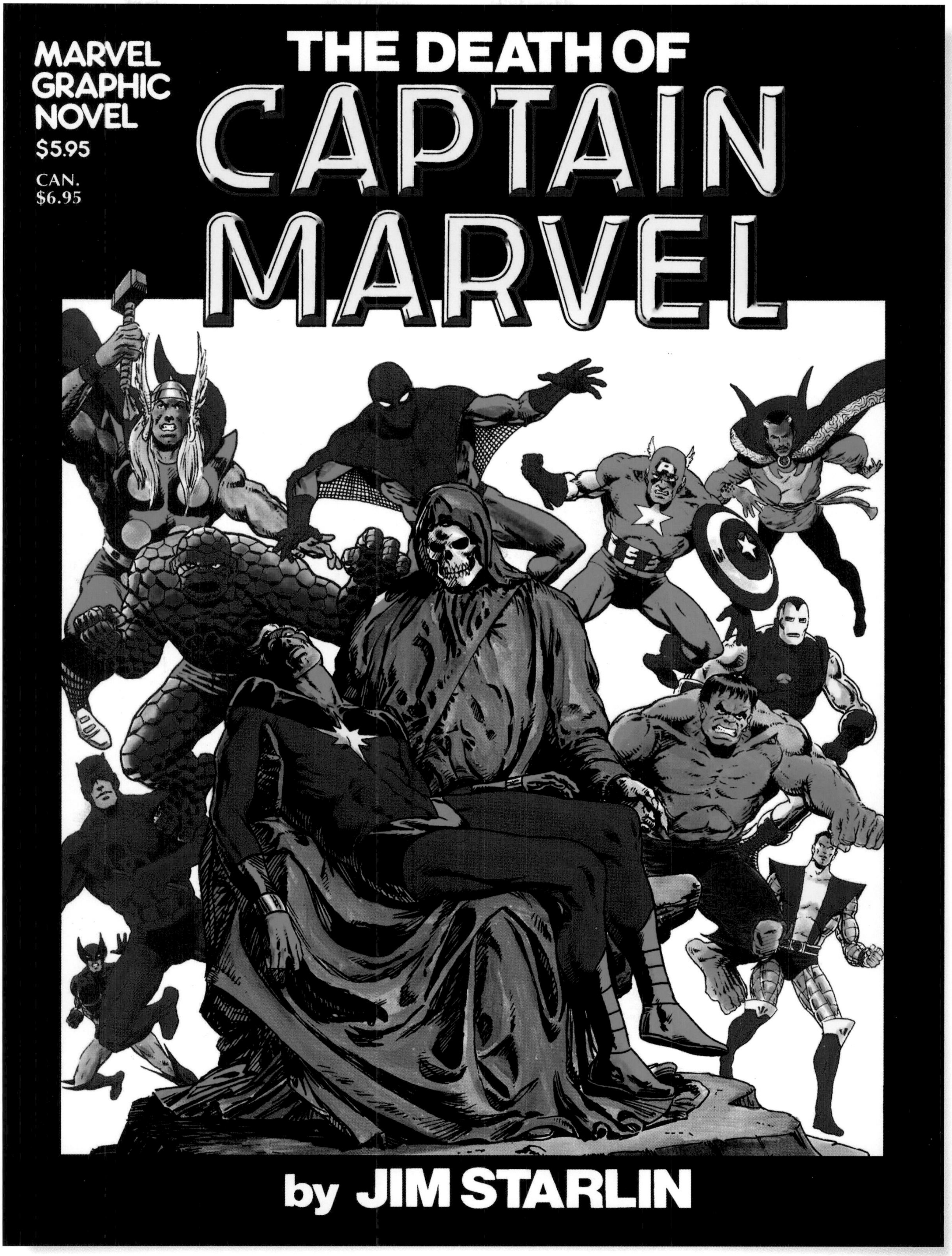
MARVEL GRAPHIC NOVEL
$5.95
CAN. $6.95
THE DEATH OF CAPTAIN MARVEL
by JIM STARLIN

▲ *MARVEL GRAPHIC NOVEL 1: THE DEATH OF CAPTAIN MARVEL*

**April 1982**
**Artist:** Jim Starlin

When Marvel laurched a graphic novel line, they needed something special to start the series. This epic tale was just the thing, with Jim Starlin writing and illustrating the final Captain Marvel story and doing the unthinkable—killing a major character in tragic and realistic circumstances. The cover is an atmospheric masterpiece, reflecting the intensity of the story.

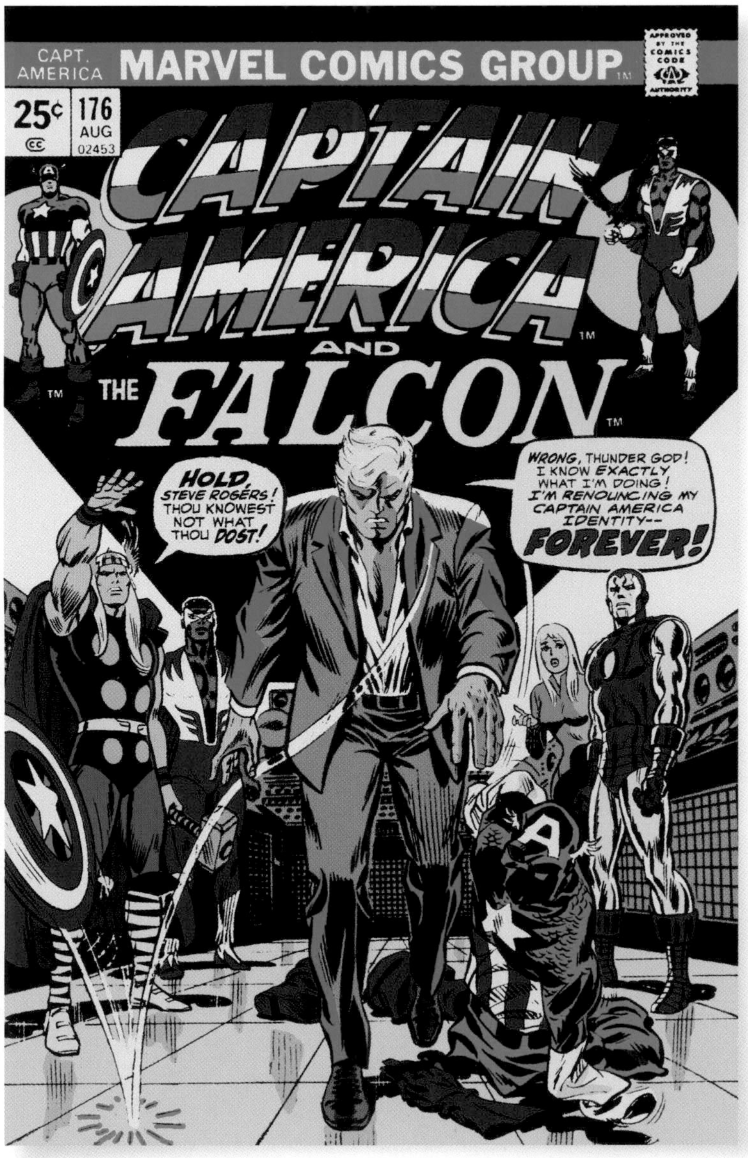
CAPT. AMERICA
MARVEL COMICS GROUP
25¢ 176 AUG 02453
CAPTAIN AMERICA AND THE FALCON
HOLD STEVE ROGERS! THOU KNOWEST NOT WHAT THOU DOST!
WRONG, THUNDER GOD! I KNOW EXACTLY WHAT I'M DOING! I'M RENOUNCING MY CAPTAIN AMERICA IDENTITY-- FOREVER!

◀ *CAPTAIN AMERICA* #176

**August 1974**
**Artist:** John Romita Sr.

The Watergate Affair touched even Marvel's heroes. This Romita cover reflects the post-Watergate soul-searching of many Americans. It features Steve Rogers turning his back on his role as Captain America. He felt betrayed after learning a "high-ranking political official" (the President) was the leader of the evil Secret Empire.

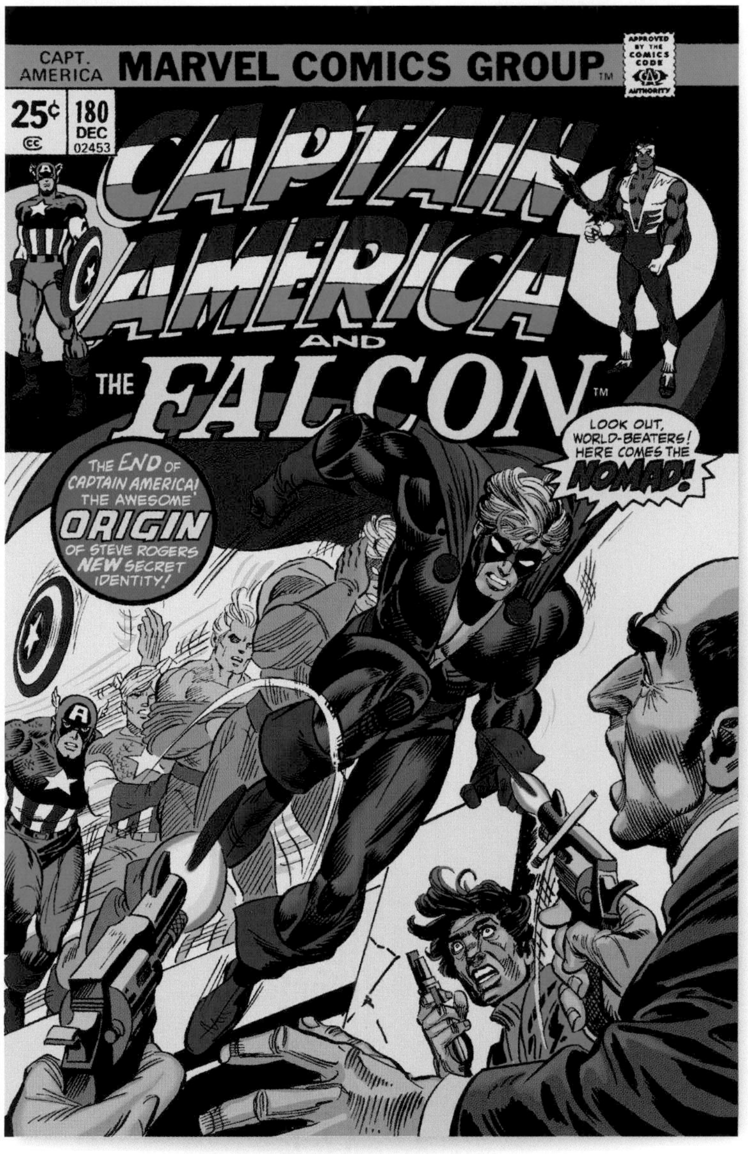
CAPT. AMERICA
MARVEL COMICS GROUP
25¢ 180 DEC 02453
CAPTAIN AMERICA AND THE FALCON
THE END OF CAPTAIN AMERICA! THE AWESOME ORIGIN OF STEVE ROGERS NEW SECRET IDENTITY!
LOOK OUT, WORLD-BEATERS! HERE COMES THE NOMAD!

◀ *CAPTAIN AMERICA* #180

**December 1974**
**Artist:** Gil Kane

Captain America's soul-searching continued as he took on a new identity—Nomad, the man without a country. The cover is by Gil Kane, a Marvel veteran who produced many of the company's most famous covers. Kane's dynamic art style is used to full effect here, as the reader sees Steve Rogers leap into his new role.

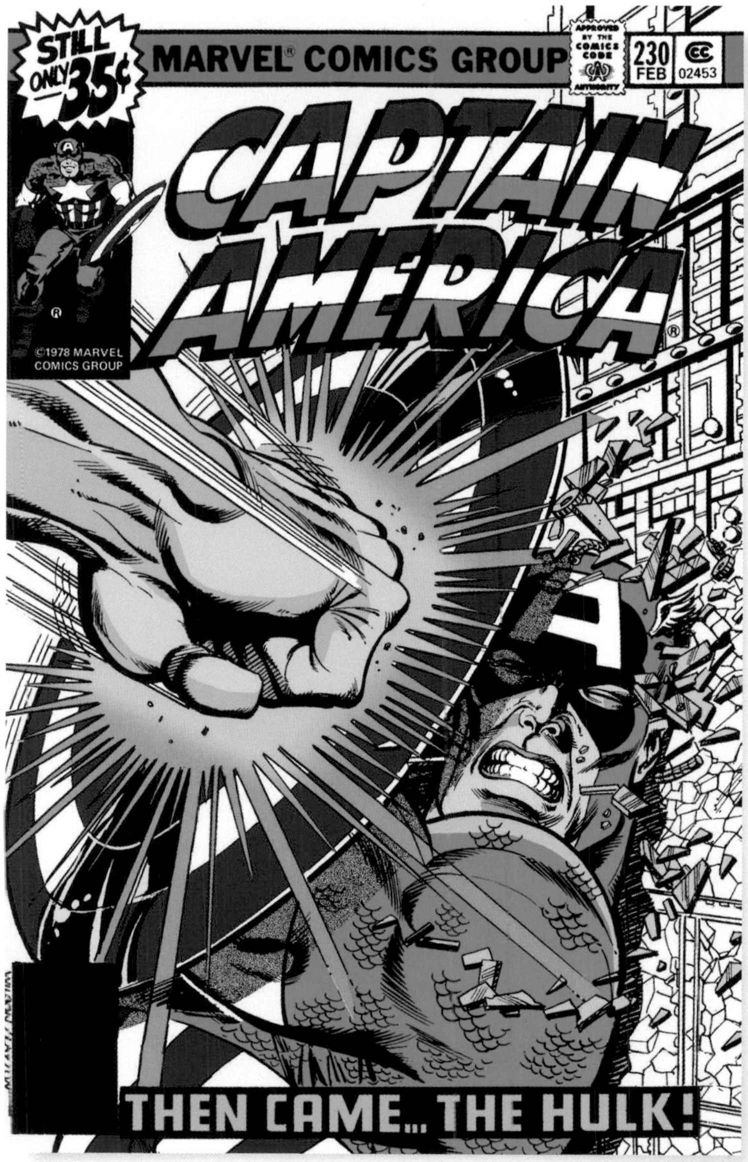
STILL ONLY 35¢
MARVEL COMICS GROUP
230 FEB 02453
CAPTAIN AMERICA
©1978 MARVEL COMICS GROUP
THEN CAME... THE HULK!

◀ *CAPTAIN AMERICA* #230

**February 1979**
**Artist:** Ron Wilson

This powerful cover was illustrated by Ron Wilson, an artist most often associated with the Thing (he was the main artist on *Marvel-Two-in-One* and the Thing's first self-titled solo series). Wilson was used to drawing monstrously strong heroes, and here he manages to portray terrifying strength in a single punch. The reader can almost feel the impact of the Hulk's attack.

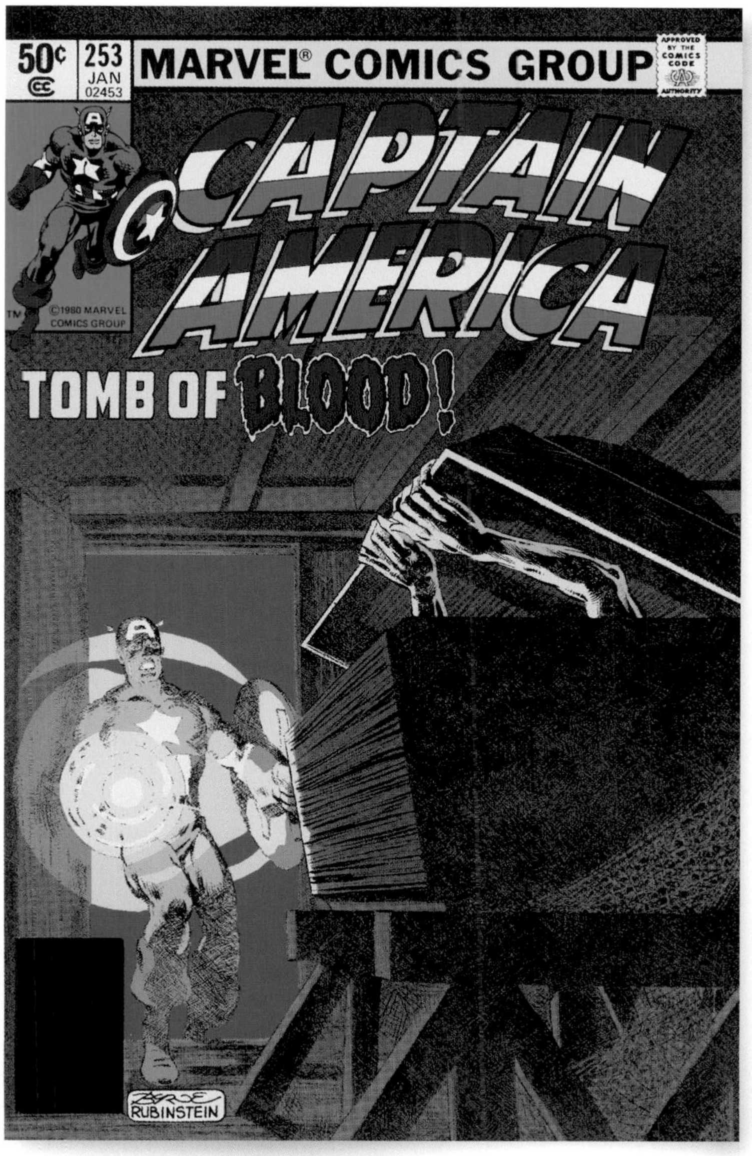
50¢ 253 JAN 02453
MARVEL COMICS GROUP
CAPTAIN AMERICA
©1980 MARVEL COMICS GROUP
TOMB OF BLOOD!
RUBINSTEIN

◀ *CAPTAIN AMERICA* #253

**January 1981**
**Artist:** John Byrne

John Byrne's spooky, atmospheric cover was influenced by some of the horror comics of the pre-Marvel era. This issue saw the return of Baron Blood, a British vampire who had backed the Axis Powers during World War II. Byrne's careful use of light and shadow was a sign of his increasing confidence as an artist.

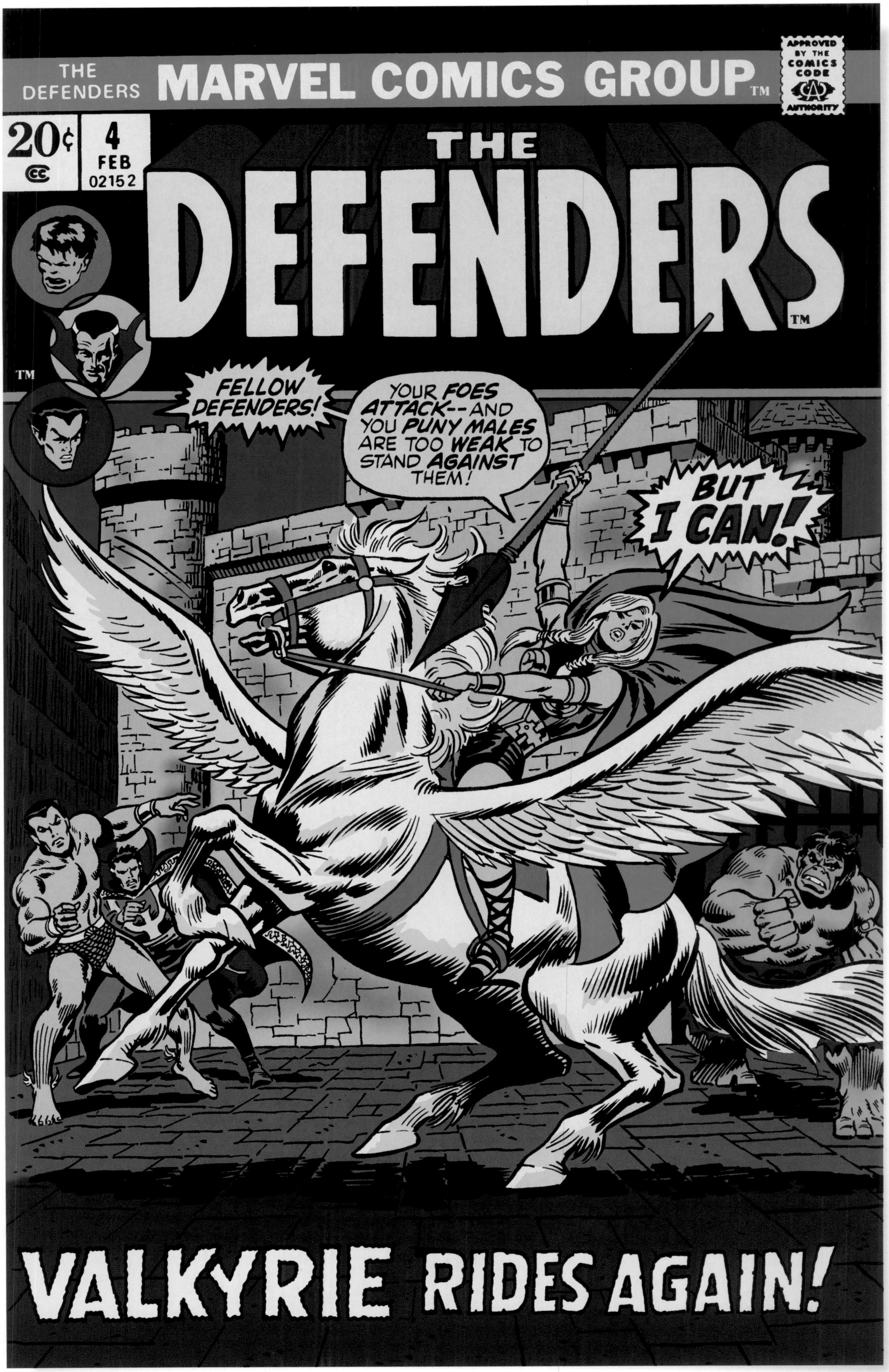
THE DEFENDERS
MARVEL COMICS GROUP™
APPROVED BY THE COMICS CODE AUTHORITY
20¢
4 FEB 02152
THE DEFENDERS™
FELLOW DEFENDERS!
YOUR FOES ATTACK-- AND YOU PUNY MALES ARE TOO WEAK TO STAND AGAINST THEM!
BUT I CAN!
VALKYRIE RIDES AGAIN!

◀ ***DEFENDERS* #4**

**February 1973**
**Artists:** Jim Starlin and John Buscema

Valkyrie made a dramatic return in this issue, riding the Black Knight's old horse. This time she had a new human host, a woman named Barbara Norris, and she was at the forefront of feminism, declaring that if the puny males couldn't defeat the bad guys, then she would. This version of Valkyrie became a mainstay of the *Defenders* and remained with the team for several years.

OCT # 49 50¢
MARVEL COMICS GROUP
DOCTOR STRANGE
MASTER OF THE MYSTIC ARTS

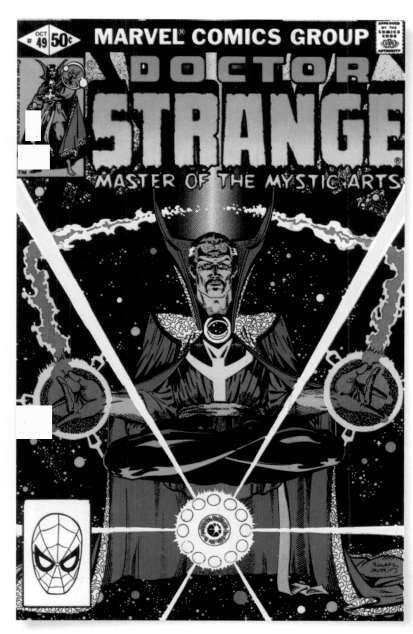

▲ ***DOCTOR STRANGE* #49**

**October 1981**
**Artist:** Marshall Rogers

Artist Marshall Rogers and writer Roger Stern had already worked together for a while before they brought their magic to Marvel's Sorcerer Supreme. Rogers excelled at stylish, otherworldly imagery and this cover shows off his amazing artwork perfectly.

MARVEL COMICS GROUP
WIN A Columbia TEN-SPEED FORMULA 10 RACER!
DETAILS INSIDE
FEB 60¢ UK 20p #51
DOCTOR STRANGE
A MATTER OF TIME...
...WITH SGT. FURY AND THE HOWLING COMMANDOS!

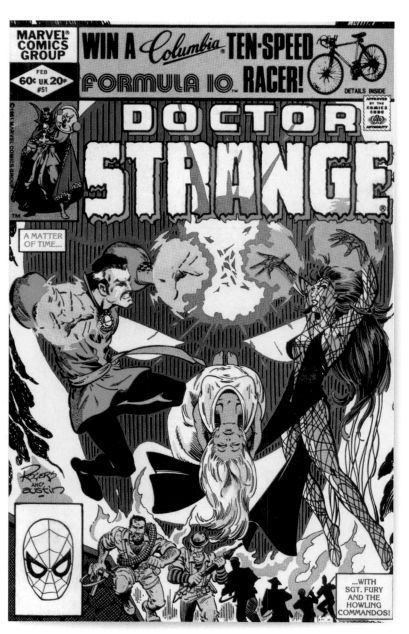

▲ ***DOCTOR STRANGE* #51**

**February 1982**
**Artist:** Marshall Rogers

This second example of Rogers' work on *Doctor Strange* shows how well he conveyed action. Mystical battles were always a visual treat in *Doctor Strange* stories, ever since the days when Steve Ditko first illustrated the character. Rogers was one of the few who could match the sense of unreality that Ditko brought to his early tales.

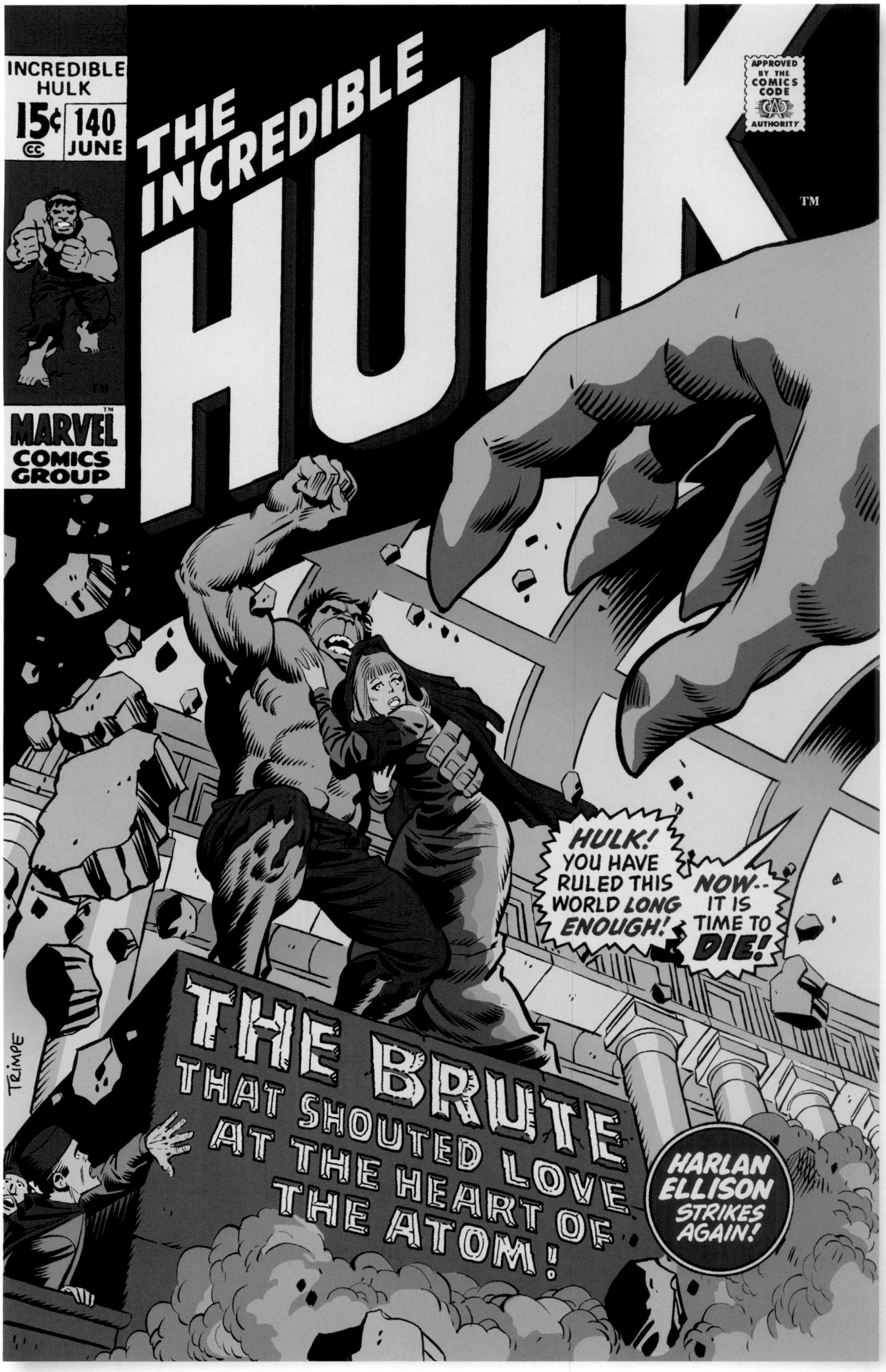
INCREDIBLE HULK
15¢ 140 JUNE
THE INCREDIBLE HULK
APPROVED BY THE COMICS CODE AUTHORITY
MARVEL COMICS GROUP
HULK! YOU HAVE RULED THIS WORLD LONG ENOUGH!
NOW-- IT IS TIME TO DIE!
THE BRUTE THAT SHOUTED LOVE AT THE HEART OF THE ATOM!
HARLAN ELLISON STRIKES AGAIN!
TRIMPE

▲ *INCREDIBLE HULK* #140

**June 1971**
**Artist:** Herb Trimpe

This Herb Trimpe classic was the cover to one of the greatest Hulk stories of all time, where the Hulk was shrunk into a microscopic world. Here he retained Bruce Banner's intelligence, was hailed as a hero, found true love with Jarella, and was about to live happily ever after—before it all went horribly wrong. The dynamic cover reflects a key moment in the story's heart-breaking climax, when the Hulk was seized and taken back to Earth.

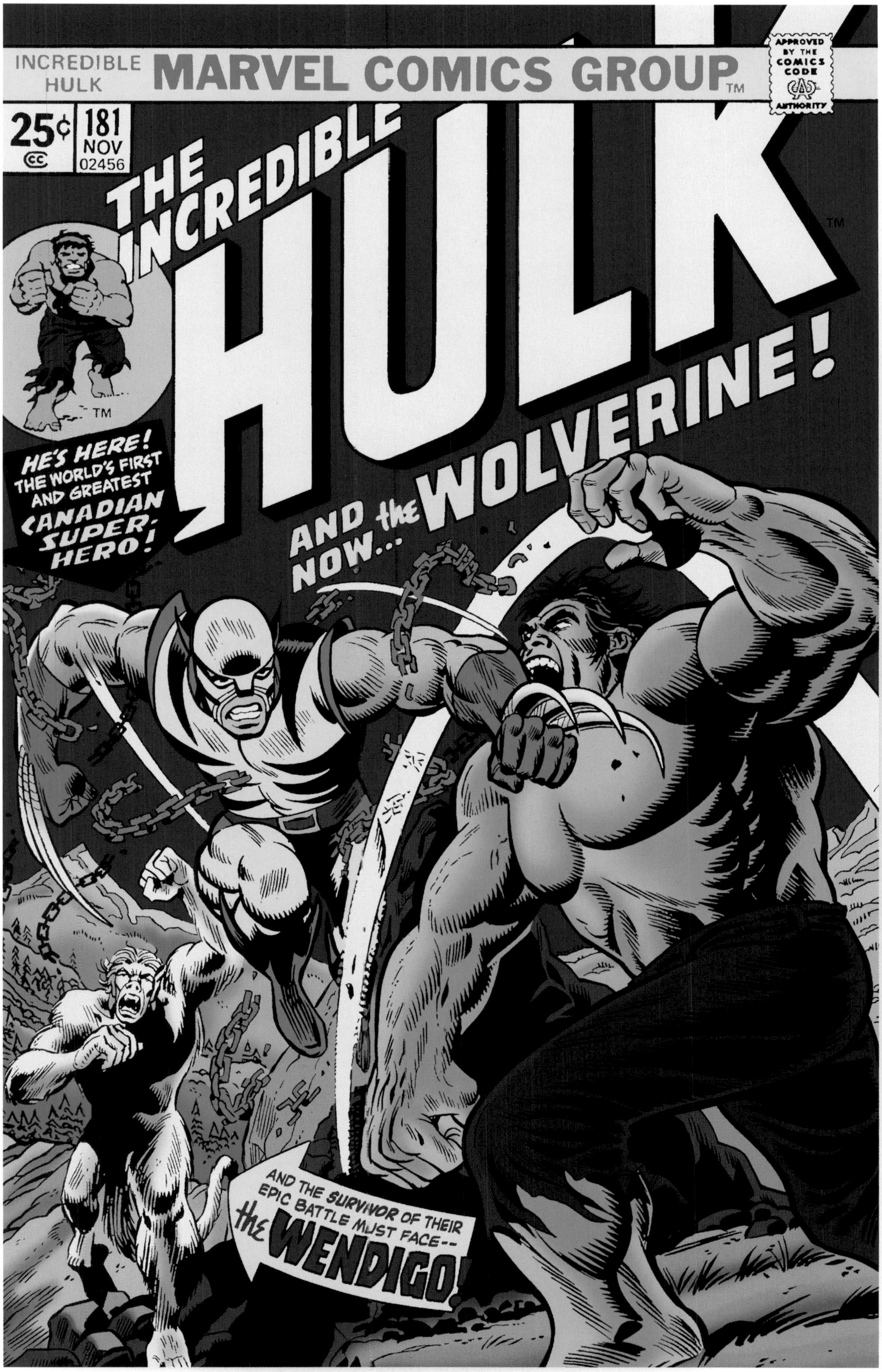
INCREDIBLE HULK
MARVEL COMICS GROUP
APPROVED BY THE COMICS CODE AUTHORITY
25¢
181 NOV
02456
THE INCREDIBLE HULK
HE'S HERE! THE WORLD'S FIRST AND GREATEST CANADIAN SUPER-HERO!
AND NOW... the WOLVERINE!
AND THE SURVIVOR OF THEIR EPIC BATTLE MUST FACE-- the WENDIGO!

▲ *INCREDIBLE HULK* #181

**November 1974**
**Artist:** Herb Trimpe

"And now...the Wolverine!" It's hard to believe such a simple tagline could signal the introduction of a hero who would become one of Marvel's most popular characters. Trimpe's cover is packed with action as the Canadian mutant clashes with the Hulk. Wolverine later achieved fame as part of the *New X-Men*, and his smackdowns with the Hulk became one of the most anticipated clashes in the Marvel Universe.

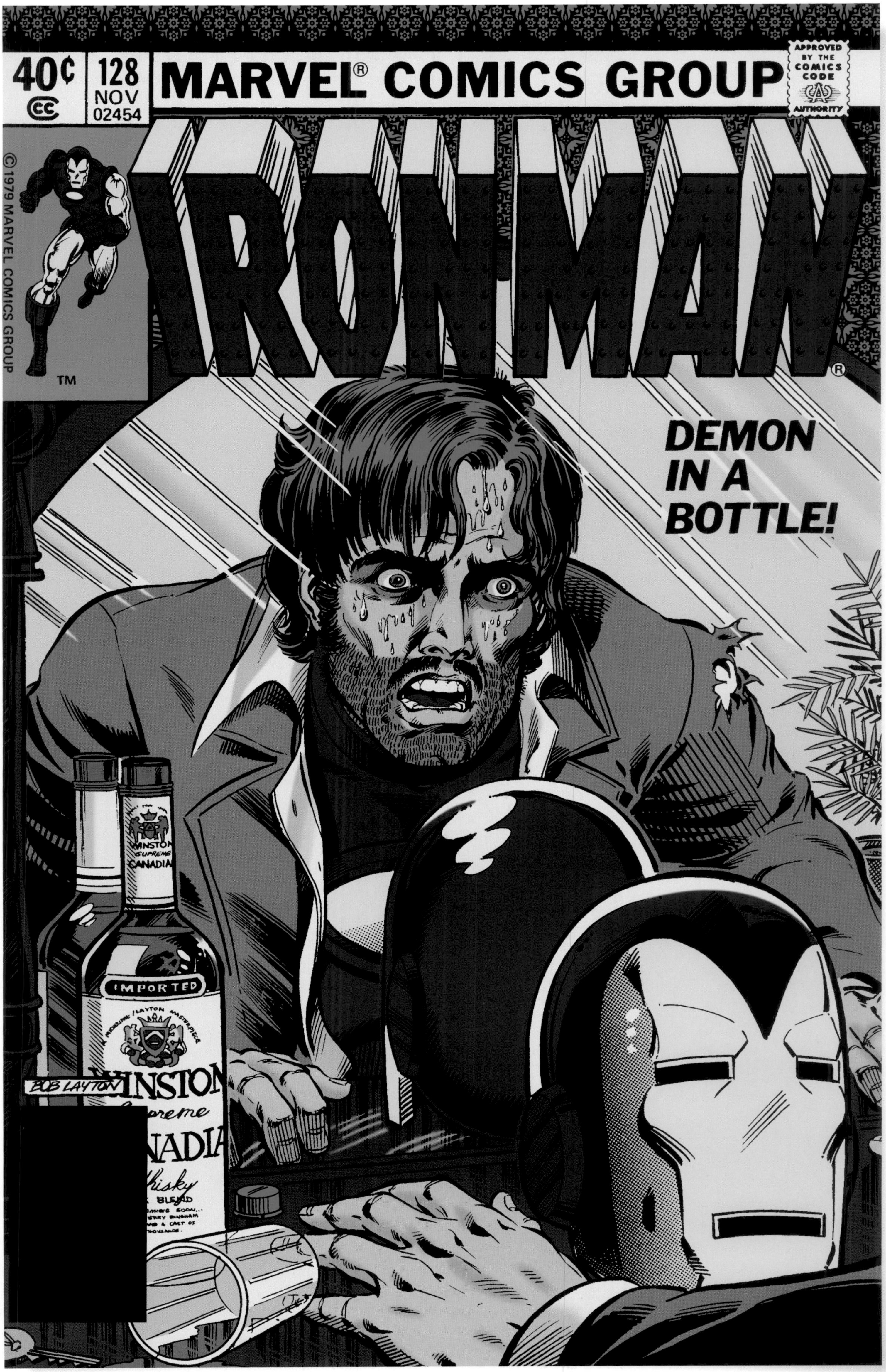
40¢
128
NOV
02454
MARVEL® COMICS GROUP
APPROVED BY THE COMICS CODE AUTHORITY
© 1979 MARVEL COMICS GROUP
IRON MAN®
TM
DEMON IN A BOTTLE!
BOB LAYTON
IMPORTED

◀ ***IRON MAN* #128**

**November 1979**
**Artist:** Bob Layton

Often hailed as one of the greatest Marvel stories of all time, the "Demon in a Bottle!" storyline dealt with Tony Stark's alcoholism. It was a shockingly realistic story and needed a tough, hard-hitting cover. Bob Layton produced another exceptional piece—one often voted high on countdowns of *Iron Man's* best. The look of pain and horror on Stark's face, with the Iron Man helmet staring at him, is a haunting image.

50¢
142
JAN
02454
MARVEL COMICS GROUP
©1980 MARVEL COMICS GROUP
IRON MAN
SEE: THE GOLDEN AVENGER'S ALL-NEW
ARMOR
DESIGNED FOR
OUTER SPACE ACTION!

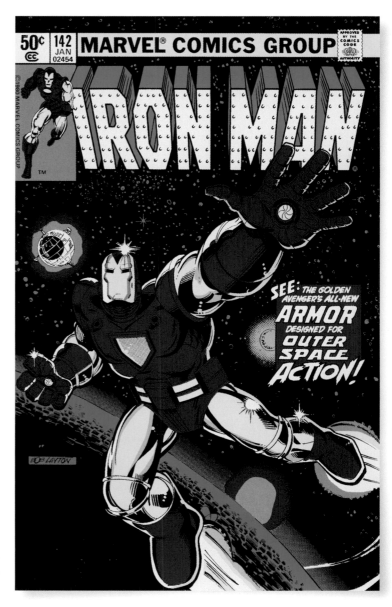

***IRON MAN* #142** ▶

**January 1981**
**Artist:** Bob Layton

These days Iron Man has countless armored suits at his disposal, but back in 1981 a change of armor was still a relatively new thing for the hero. This made Bob Layton's cover featuring a new space-faring armor all the more special.

60¢
170
MAY
02454
MARVEL COMICS GROUP
THE INVINCIBLE
IRON MAN
AN IRON MAN
YOU'VE NEVER
SEEN BEFORE!

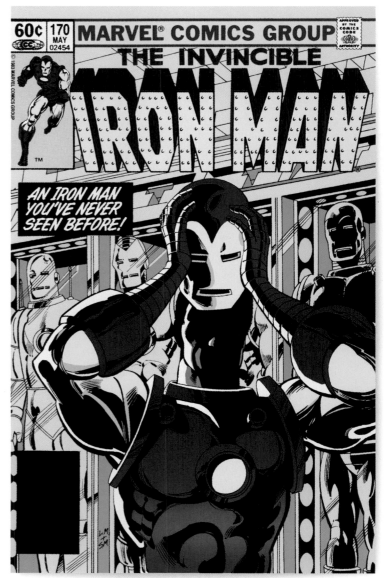

***IRON MAN* #170** ▶

**May 1983**
**Artist:** Luke McDonnell

Jim Rhodes was revealed as the new Iron Man in this issue while Tony Stark relapsed into alcoholism. The prospect of a new Iron Man isn't only highlighted in the shadowy figure of Rhodes donning the helmet, but also in the array of previous armors in the background.

***DEVIL DINOSAUR* #1** ▶

**April 1978**
**Artist:** Jack Kirby

*Devil Dinosaur* saw Kirby at his most inventive. The series lasted only nine issues, but Devil Dinosaur and his simian ally Moon-Boy remain cult favorites. The pair originally adventured on a prehistoric Earth, although this was later retconned to a parallel Earth. The cover to the first issue is from Kirby's second spell at Marvel, and is considered to be one of his best.

BLACK PANTHER
MARVEL COMICS GROUP
30¢
1 JAN 02685
FIRST ISSUE! THE ALL-NEW, ALL-EXCITING
BLACK PANTHER
HE'S BACK! AS ONLY JACK KIRBY CAN DO IT!
THEY SEARCHED FOR IT! THEY FOUGHT--AND EVEN KILLED FOR IT! WHAT WAS IT?
KING SOLOMON'S FROG!

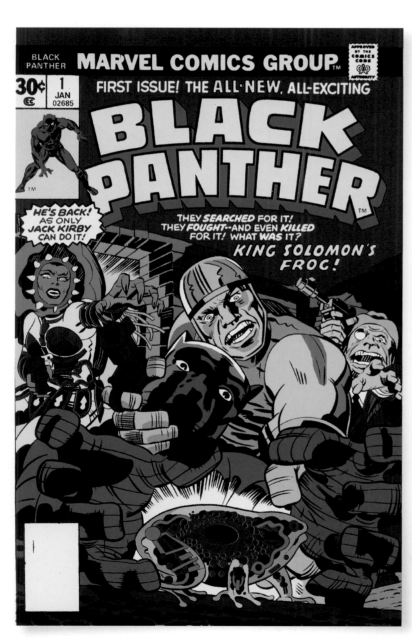

▲ ***BLACK PANTHER* #1**

**January 1977**
**Artist:** Jack Kirby

More than a decade after first apearing in *Fantasic Four* issue #52, the Black Panther finally got his own series. Jack Kirby, having returned to Marvel in the mid'70s, helped launch *Black Panther*. Kirby's powerhouse style brought real energy to the debut issue, which features the kind of strange but dazzling cover at which Kirby excelled.

THE ETERNALS
MARVEL COMICS GROUP
30¢
10 APR 02334
©1977 MARVEL COMICS GROUP
WHEN GODS WALK THE EARTH!
THE ETERNALS
THE CITY THAT DIED TWICE!
DOOM THREATENS THE DOMAIN OF THE DEVIANTS!

▲ ***ETERNALS* #10**

**April 1977**
**Artist:** Jack Kirby

*Eternals* was the most important title Kirby masterminded during his return to Marvel. It showed the artist at his cosmic best, as seen on this cover with its terrifying and powerful imagery. The characters he introduced in the short-lived series—especially the all-powerful Celestials—remain a vital part of the Marvel Universe.

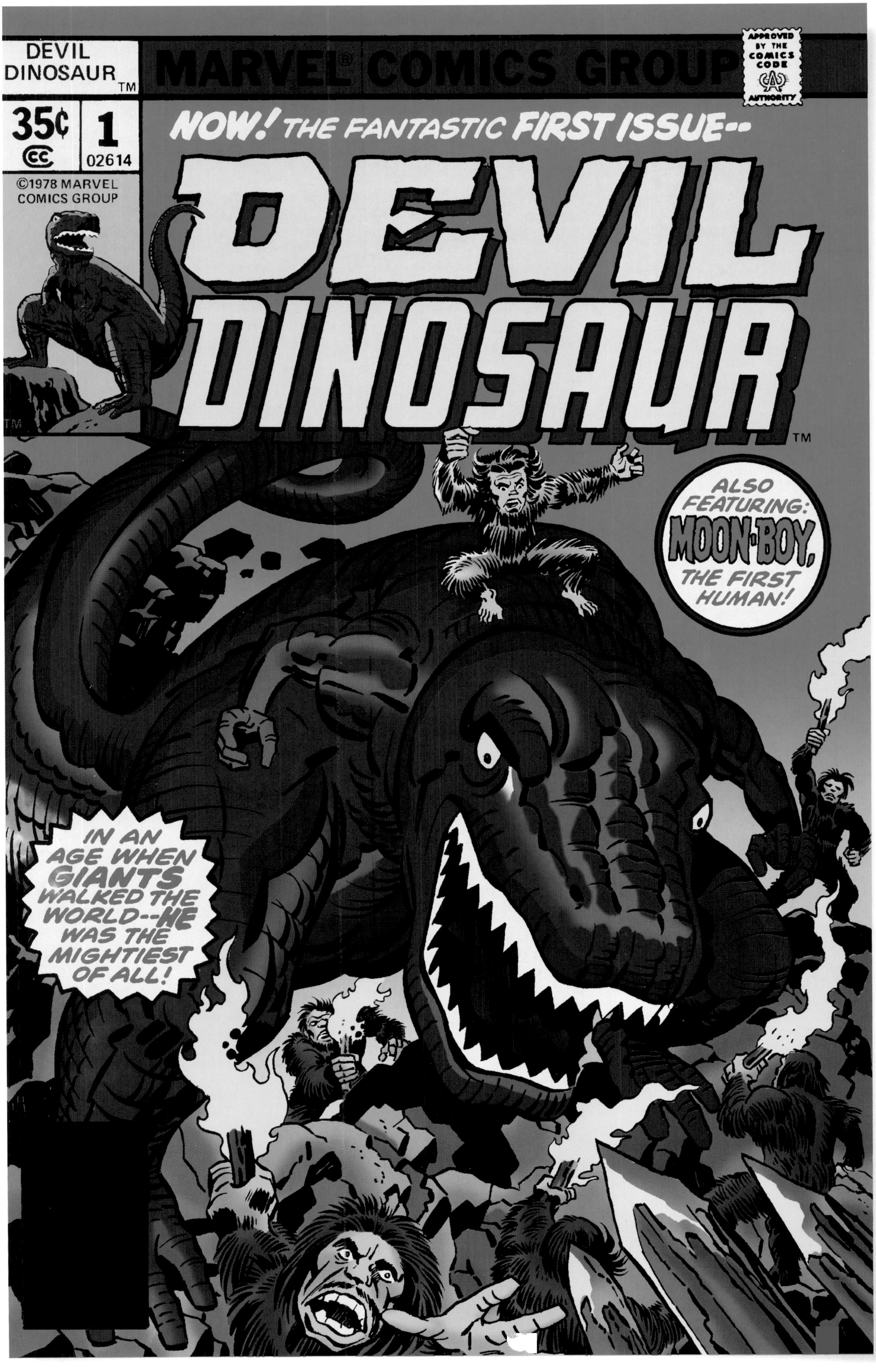
DEVIL DINOSAUR TM
MARVEL® COMICS GROUP
APPROVED BY THE COMICS CODE AUTHORITY
35¢
1
02614
©1978 MARVEL COMICS GROUP
NOW! THE FANTASTIC FIRST ISSUE--
DEVIL DINOSAUR TM
ALSO FEATURING: MOON-BOY, THE FIRST HUMAN!
IN AN AGE WHEN GIANTS WALKED THE WORLD--HE WAS THE MIGHTIEST OF ALL!

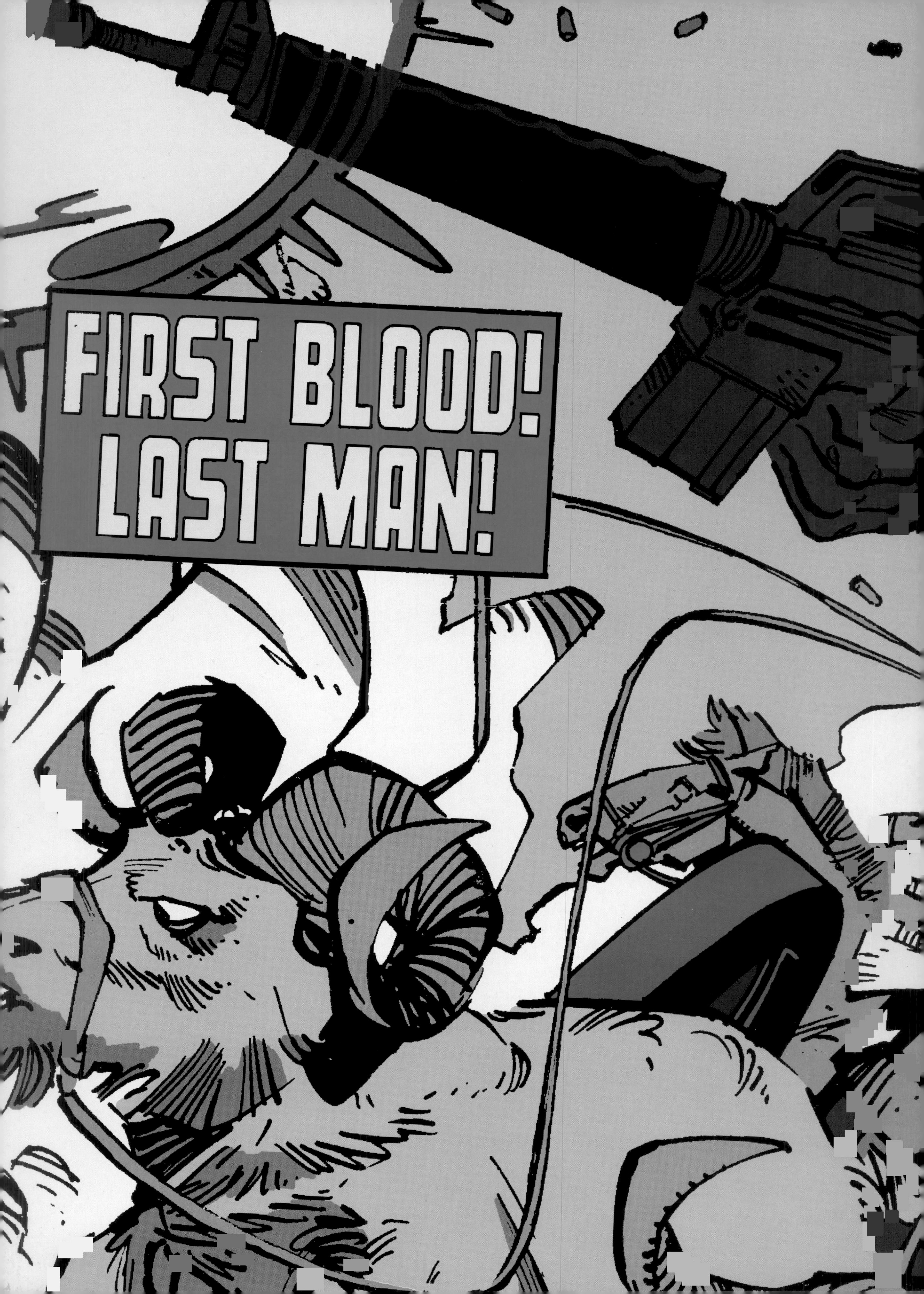
FIRST BLOOD! LAST MAN!

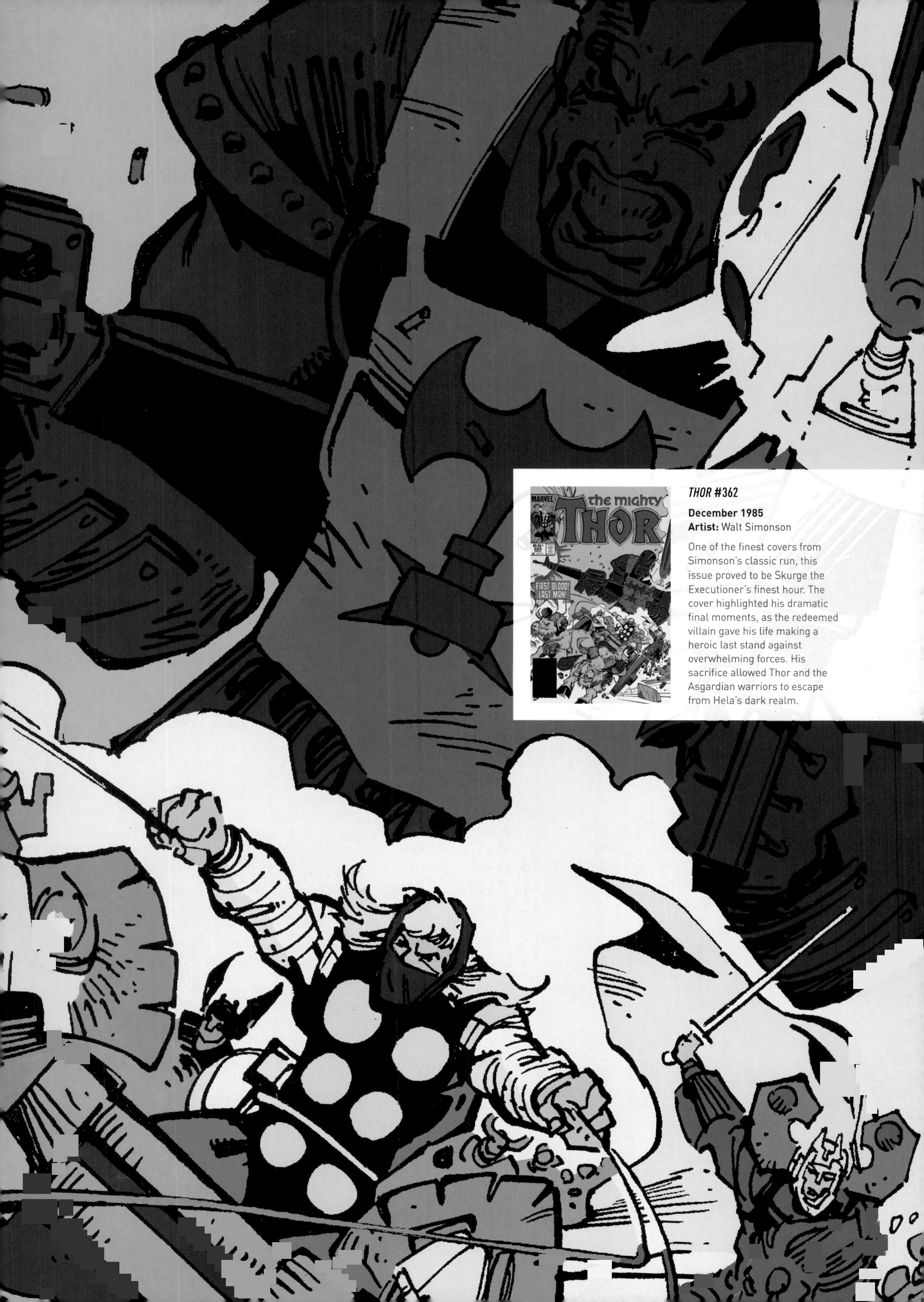
MARVEL
the mighty
THOR
FIRST BLOOD! LAST MAN!

*THOR* #362

**December 1985**
**Artist:** Walt Simonson

One of the finest covers from Simonson's classic run, this issue proved to be Skurge the Executioner's finest hour. The cover highlighted his dramatic final moments, as the redeemed villain gave his life making a heroic last stand against overwhelming forces. His sacrifice allowed Thor and the Asgardian warriors to escape from Hela's dark realm.

MARVEL COMICS GROUP
60¢ 239 FEB 02462
WIN A Columbia TEN-SPEED FORMULA 10 RACER!
DETAILS INSIDE
THE WORLD'S GREATEST COMIC MAGAZINE!
Fantastic Four
HOLOCAUST IN THE DESERT!
PLUS: THE MOST UNEXPECTED GUEST-STAR OF ALL TIME!

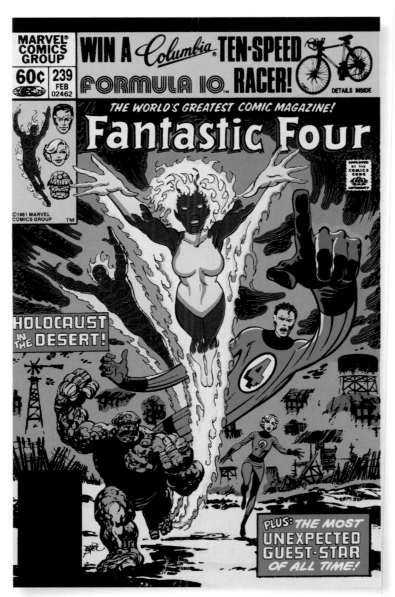

◀ *FANTASTIC FOUR* #239

**February 1982**
**Artist:** John Byrne

A second Human Torch took to the skies in this issue as Johnny Storm's girlfriend Frankie Raye briefly joined him as another fiery hero. Byrne's cover has Frankie central to the image. The tagline of "the most unexpected guest-star of all time!" is no lie, as the Thing's Aunt Petunia makes her first appearance.

60¢ 249 DEC 02462
MARVEL COMICS GROUP
THE WORLD'S GREATEST COMIC MAGAZINE!
Fantastic Four
"MAN AND SUPER-MAN!"

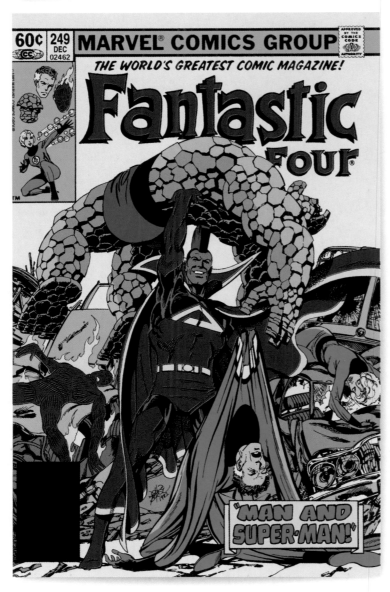

◀ *FANTASTIC FOUR* #249

**December 1982**
**Artist:** John Byrne

The Gladiator had first been seen in the pages of the *X-Men*, but he took on the Fantastic Four in this issue. Writer and artist John Byrne illustrated a dramatic cover showing the alien Super Hero standing triumphantly amidst a defeated FF.

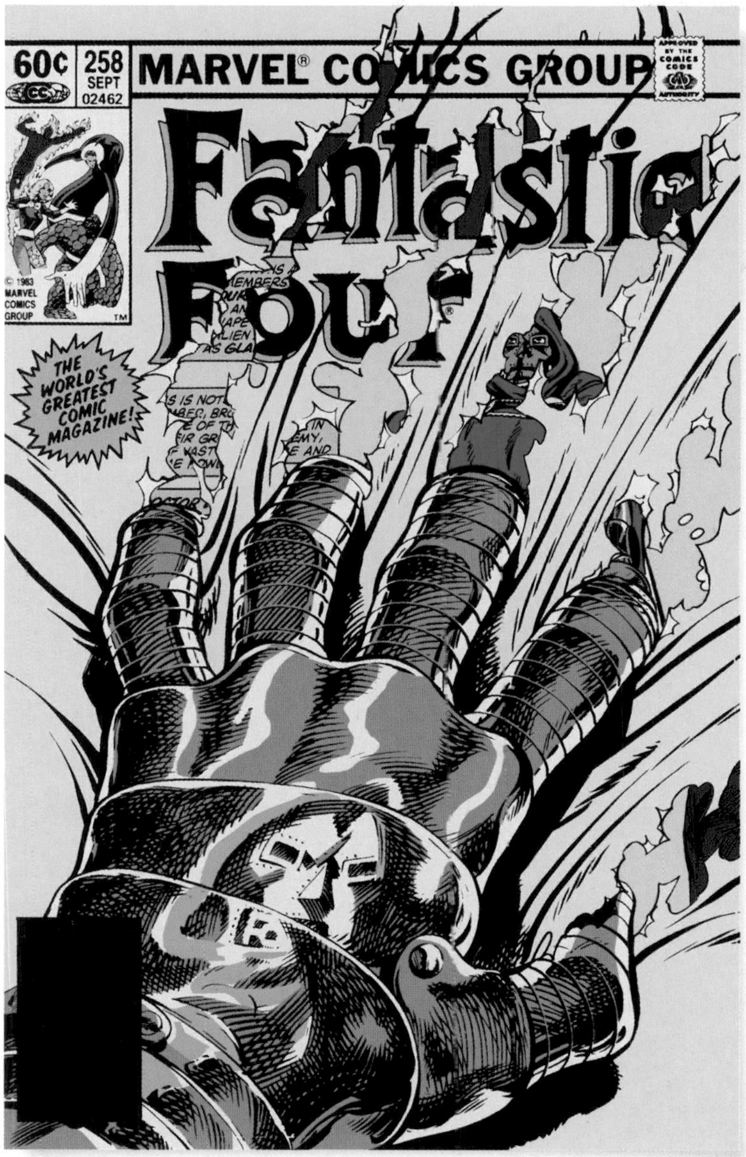
60¢
258
SEPT
02462
MARVEL COMICS GROUP
Fantastic Four
THE WORLD'S GREATEST COMIC MAGAZINE!

◄ *FANTASTIC FOUR* **#258**

**September 1983**
**Artists:** John Byrne

John Byrne's covers often used strange angles or interesting images to make an effective cover. For this one he chose simplicity and power, and he made the villain the focus of the issue. Doom's armored hand (with his face reflected in it) tearing through the cover is a warning as to what was happening inside.

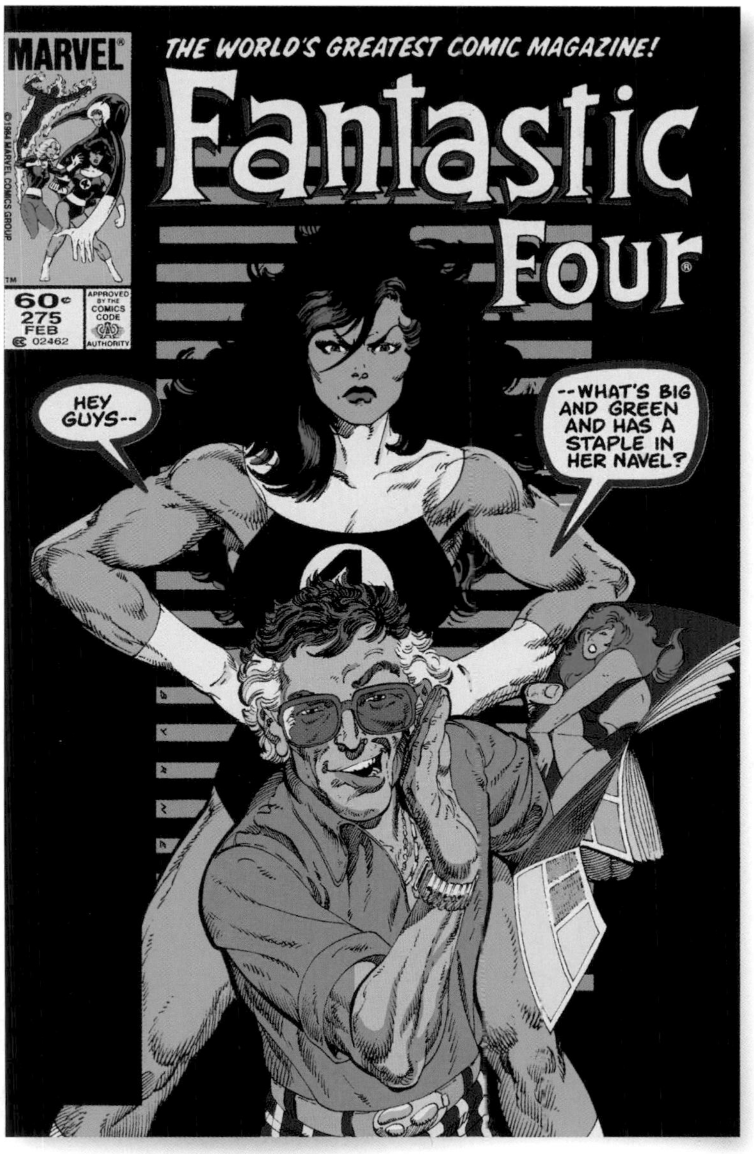
MARVEL
THE WORLD'S GREATEST COMIC MAGAZINE!
Fantastic Four
60¢
275
FEB
02462
HEY GUYS--
--WHAT'S BIG AND GREEN AND HAS A STAPLE IN HER NAVEL?

◄ *FANTASTIC FOUR* **#275**

**February 1985**
**Artist:** John Byrne

John Byrne showed his humorous side again with this issue, which features an editor who bears a strong resemblance to Marvel's own Stan Lee. The editor in the story, T.J. Vance, was threatening to print provocative photos of the She-Hulk—a problem that Bruce Banner's alter ego never had to deal with.

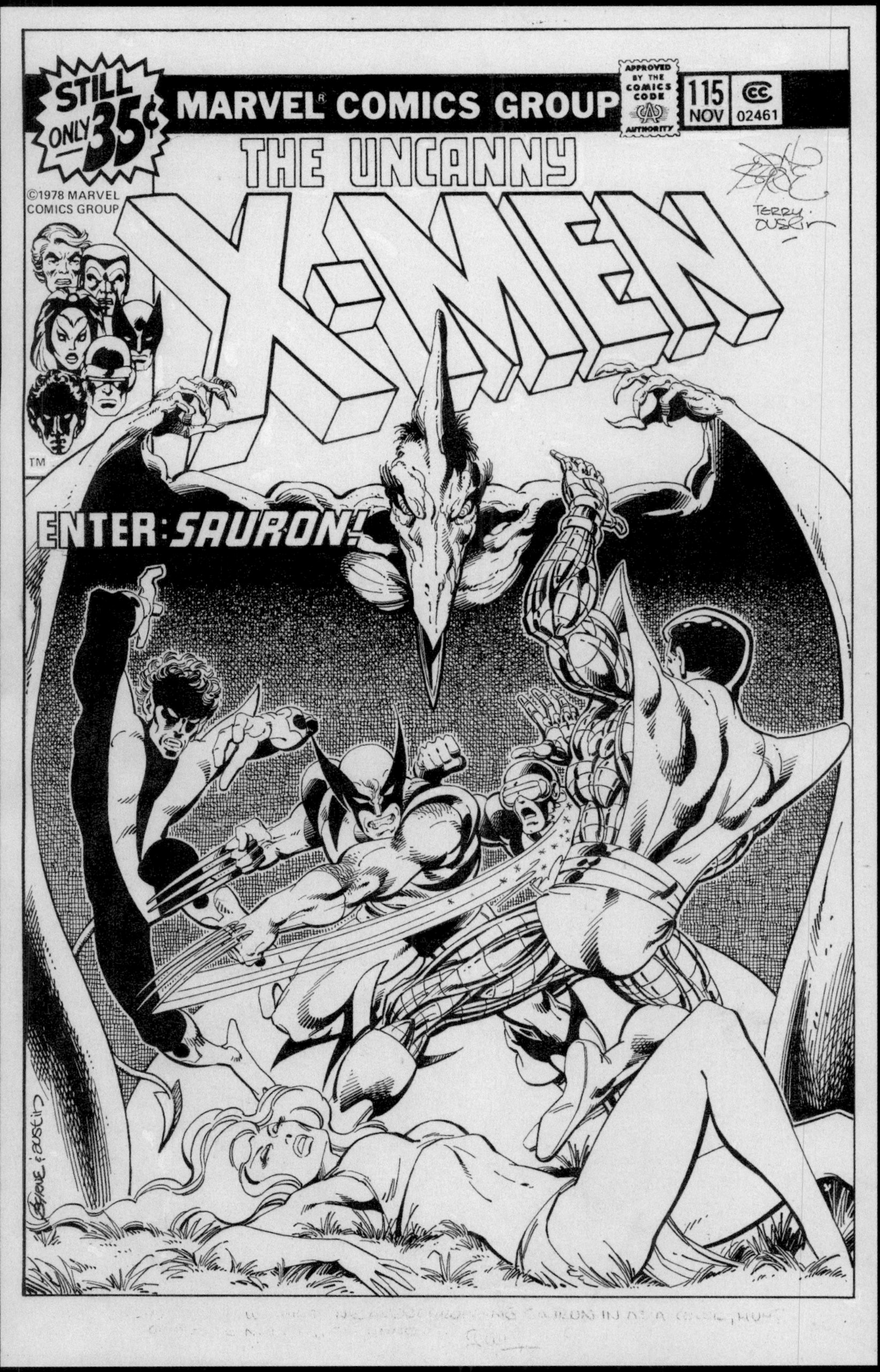
STILL ONLY 35¢
MARVEL COMICS GROUP
115 NOV
THE UNCANNY
X-MEN
ENTER: SAURON!

1.

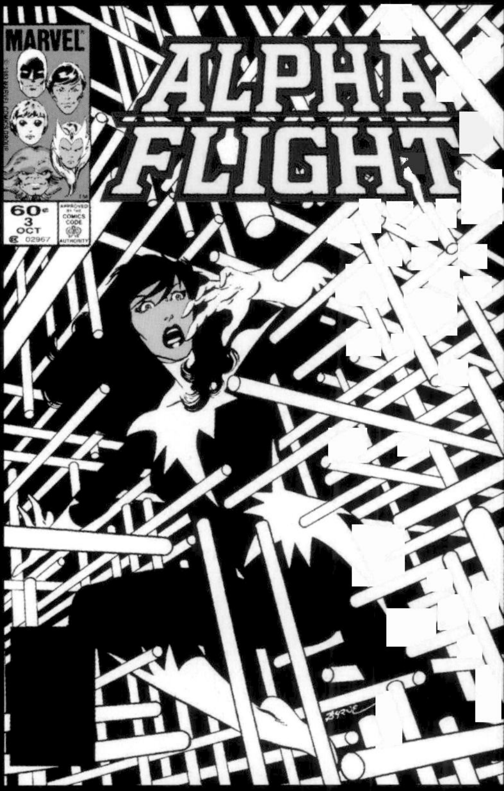
MARVEL
ALPHA FLIGHT

2.

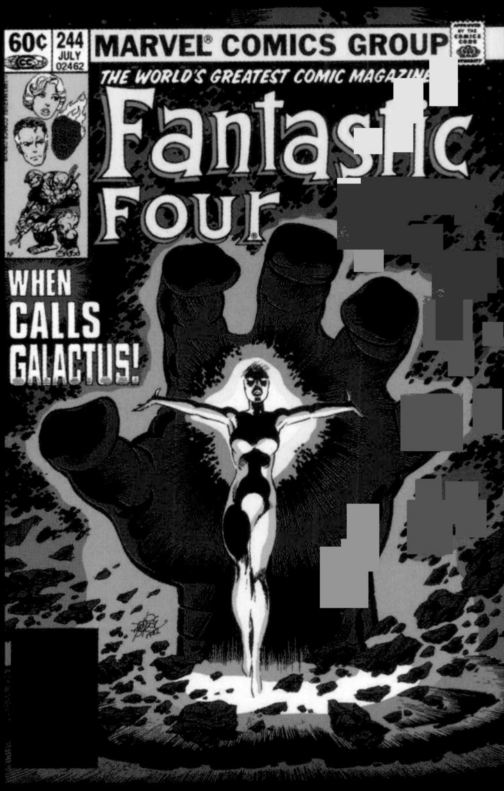
MARVEL COMICS GROUP
WHEN
CALLS
GALACTUS!

3.

# JOHN BYRNE

Not only is John Byrne the artist behind some of Marvel's greatest comics and covers, he was also responsible for the rise in prominence of Wolverine. When Byrne joined writer Chris Claremont on the fledgling "All-New All-Different" *X-Men* in 1977, he persuaded the writer to give fellow Canadian Wolverine a greater role in the team. Byrne's interpretation of Wolverine made him one of Marvel's most popular heroes. Byrne is also renowned for his work on *Fantastic Four*; he brought a sense of adventure to the series not seen since the days of Lee and Kirby. His exceptional storytelling ability, coupled with a highly graphic but naturalistic style, has influenced a number of artists, including Bryan Hitch and Todd McFarlane.

### 1. *UNCANNY X-MEN* #115

**November 1978**

One of John Byrne's early *Uncanny X-Men* covers (original art shown here) highlights the increased role Wolverine played thanks to Byrne's involvement. Byrne was a master of composition, creating an action-packed cover depicting Wolverine controlled by Sauron.

### 2. *ALPHA FLIGHT* #3

**October 1983**

Byrne was not scared to play with the graphic form. At a time when many artists took a conservative approach to cover design, Byrne explored new directions, such as this stark—and striking—use of black and white.

### 3. *FANTASTIC FOUR* #244

**July 1982**

Byrne created a series of exceptional covers during his five-year run on *Fantastic Four*. In this powerful image of Frankie Raye being transformed into a herald of Galactus, Byrne instilled a real sense of the cosmic energy at work.

### 4. *UNCANNY X-MEN* #142

**February 1981**

This shocking cover sh[illegible]g Wolverine being killed [illegible] Sentinel from "Days of Future Pas[illegible] displayed Byrne's skill as a master [illegible] layout. It is a brutal but eye-catching image of futuristic versions of Wolverine and Storm.

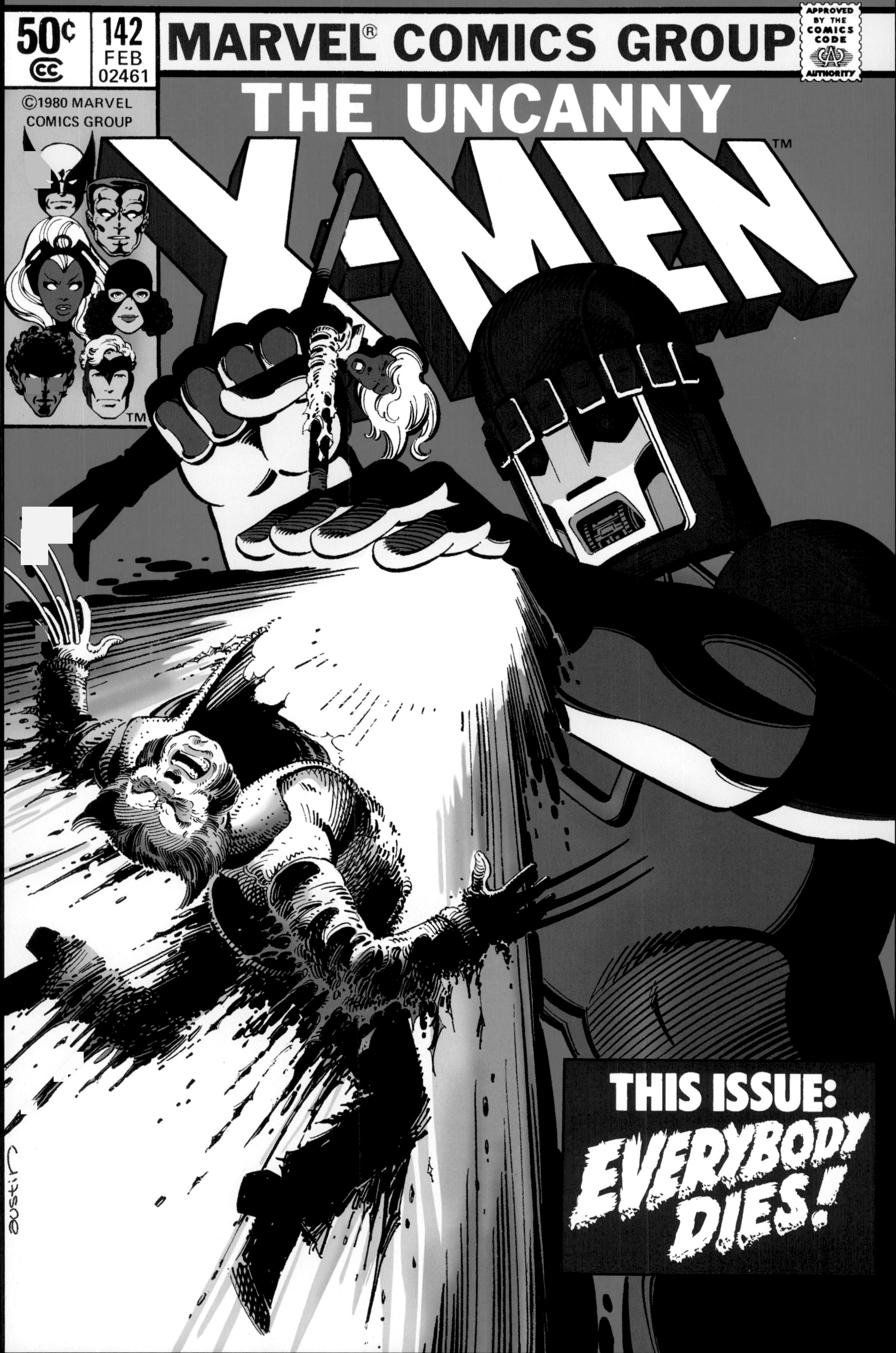

50¢
CC
142
FEB
02461
MARVEL® COMICS GROUP
APPROVED BY THE COMICS CODE CA AUTHORITY
©1980 MARVEL COMICS GROUP
THE UNCANNY
X-MEN™
THIS ISSUE:
EVERYBODY DIES!
austin

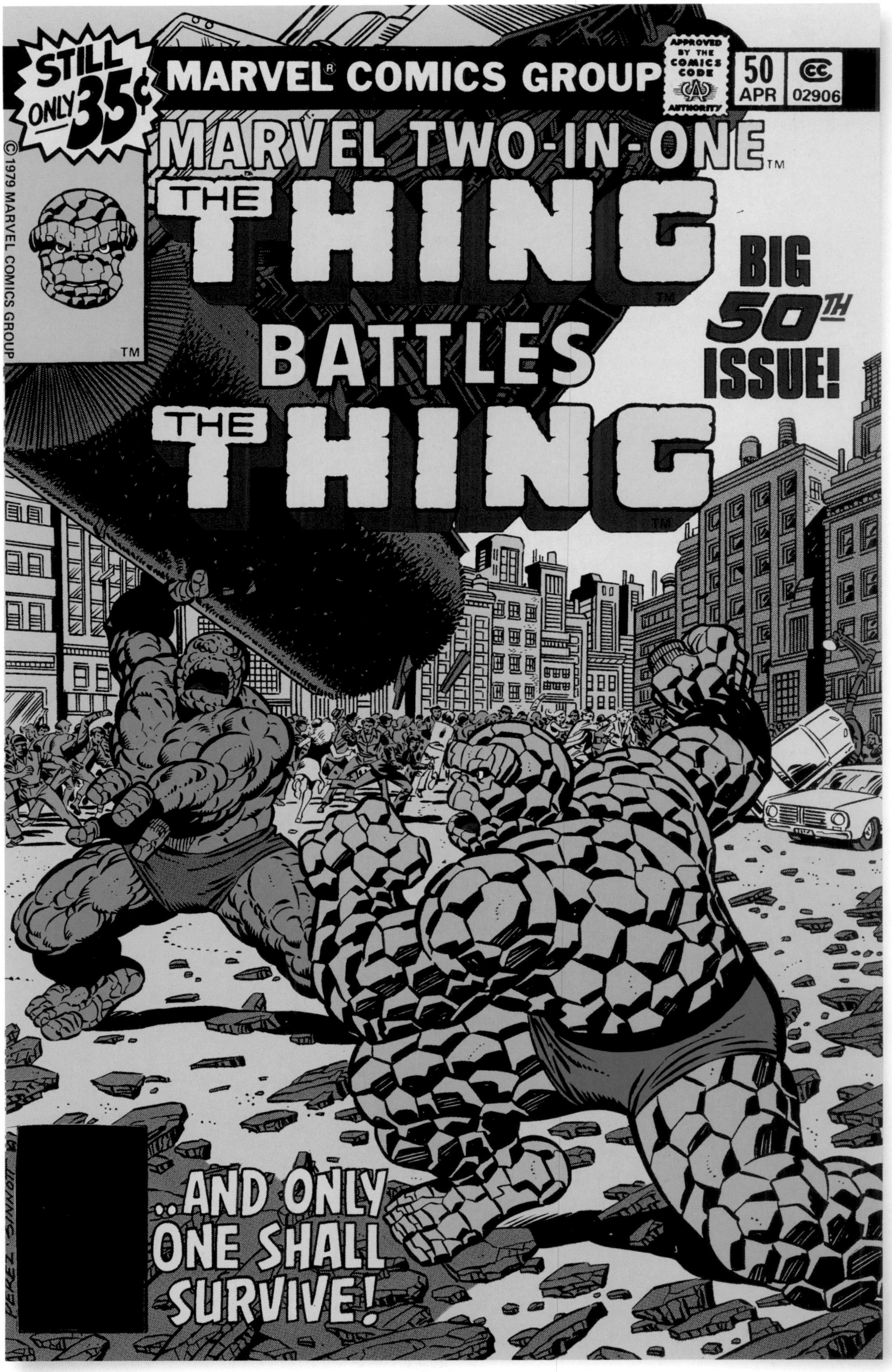
STILL ONLY 35¢
MARVEL® COMICS GROUP
APPROVED BY THE COMICS CODE AUTHORITY
50 APR
CC 02906
©1979 MARVEL COMICS GROUP
MARVEL TWO-IN-ONE™
THE THING™
BATTLES
THE THING™
BIG 50TH ISSUE!
..AND ONLY ONE SHALL SURVIVE!

▲ *MARVEL TWO-IN-ONE* #50

**April 1979**
**Artist:** George Pérez

George Pérez handled the cover art for this epic that was written and illustrated by John Byrne. The cover shows the key scene of the issue as the modern-day Thing traveled back in time in an attempt to cure himself of his mutation. He ends up facing, and fighting, his younger and more monstrous self. The tagline told the truth—it was a meeting only one Thing would survive.

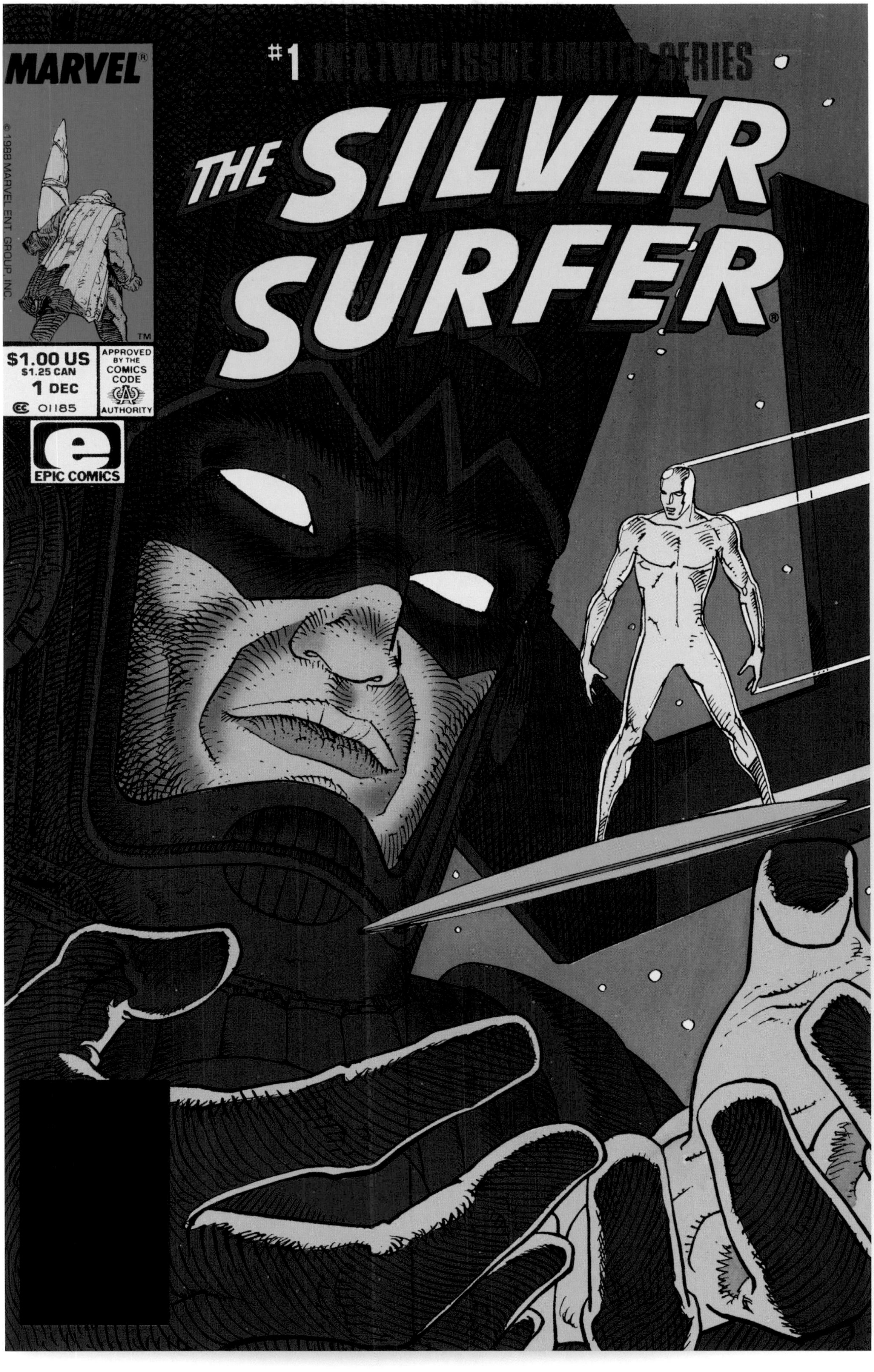
MARVEL
#1 IN A TWO-ISSUE LIMITED SERIES
THE SILVER SURFER
© 1988 MARVEL ENT. GROUP, INC.
$1.00 US
$1.25 CAN
1 DEC
APPROVED BY THE COMICS CODE AUTHORITY
EPIC COMICS

▲ *SILVER SURFER* #1

**December 1988**
**Artist:** Moebius

In the world of comics, artists don't come much bigger than Moebius. An award-winning part of the European comic scene, Moebius teamed up with writer Stan Lee to create the two-issue story "Parable." Moebius produced a truly godlike Galactus and brought out the alien-outsider in the Silver Surfer, the subtle colors adding to the grandeur of the scene. The series went on to win an Eisner Award.

STILL ONLY 35¢
MARVEL® COMICS GROUP
158 MAY
02459
©1979 MARVEL COMICS GROUP
DAREDEVIL

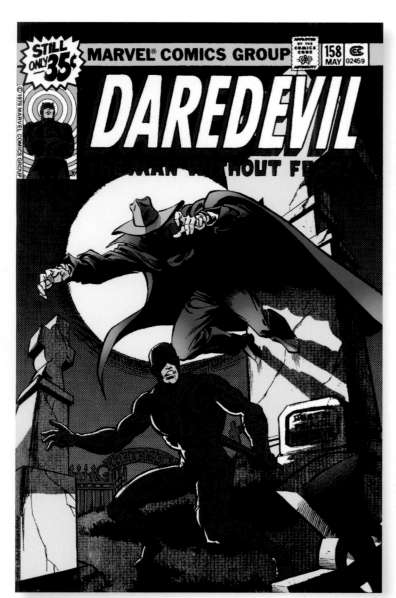

◀ *DAREDEVIL* **#158**

**May 1979**
**Artist:** Frank Miller

For his first *Daredevil* cover, Frank Miller held back slightly from the action-packed noir style that would soon make *Daredevil* one of the most popular comics of the decade. Miller grew in confidence while working on this series, quickly becoming one of the medium's top creators.

75¢
14
1980
02921
MARVEL® COMICS GROUP
KING-SIZE ANNUAL!
©1980 MARVEL COMICS GROUP
SPIDER-MAN
SPIDEY and DOCTOR STRANGE versus DOCTOR DOOM and the DREAD DORMAMMU. 'nuff said!

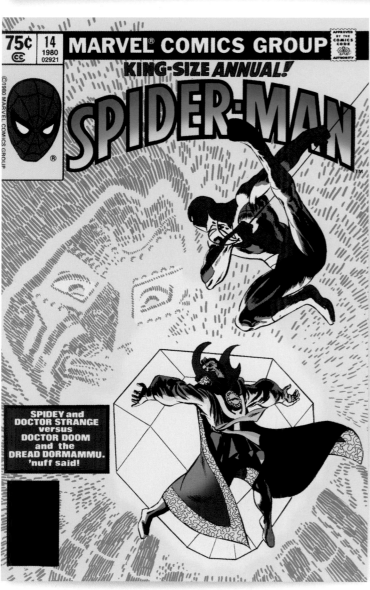

◀ *AMAZING SPIDER-MAN ANNUAL* **#14**

**October 1980**
**Artist:** Frank Miller

Frank Miller worked on covers for Marvel before becoming a writer and artist on the interiors. This cover is a clear example of his early style, displaying a bold use of color and shadow. It also highlights Miller's ability to infuse a powerful sense of movement and energy to his art.

*DAREDEVIL* **#168** ▶

**January 1981**
**Artist:** Frank Miller

The cover of this issue helped Frank Miller put his mark on *Daredevil*. As well as writing and illustrating the issue, Miller introduced Elektra, a new character who was the lost love of Matt Murdock's life and a deadly assassin. It became one of the most popular Marvel stories of all time. Unfortunately, however, Elektra's name was spelled incorrectly on the cover.

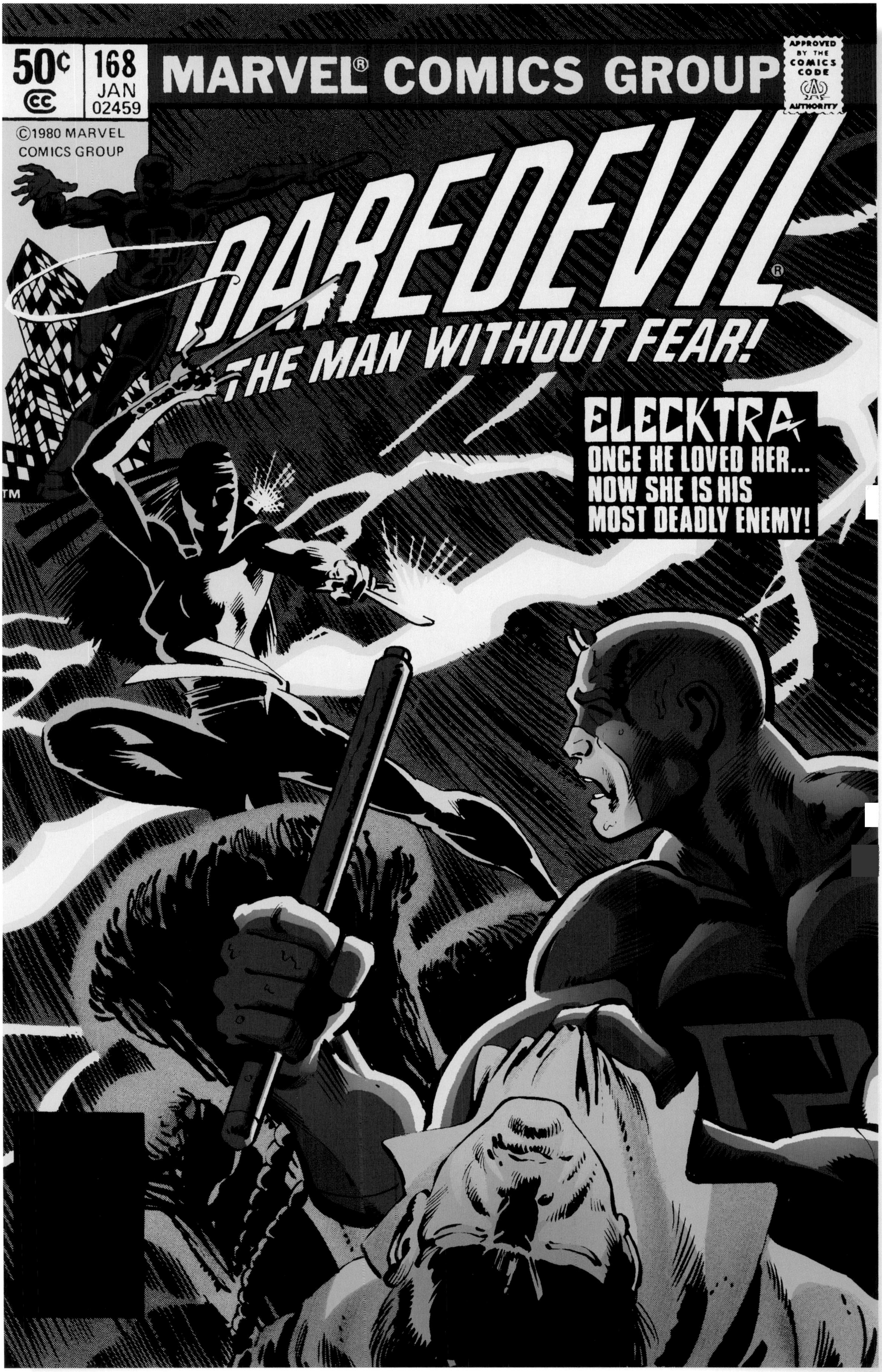
50¢
168
JAN
02459
MARVEL® COMICS GROUP
APPROVED BY THE COMICS CODE AUTHORITY
©1980 MARVEL COMICS GROUP
DAREDEVIL®
THE MAN WITHOUT FEAR!
ELECKTRA
ONCE HE LOVED HER...
NOW SHE IS HIS
MOST DEADLY ENEMY!

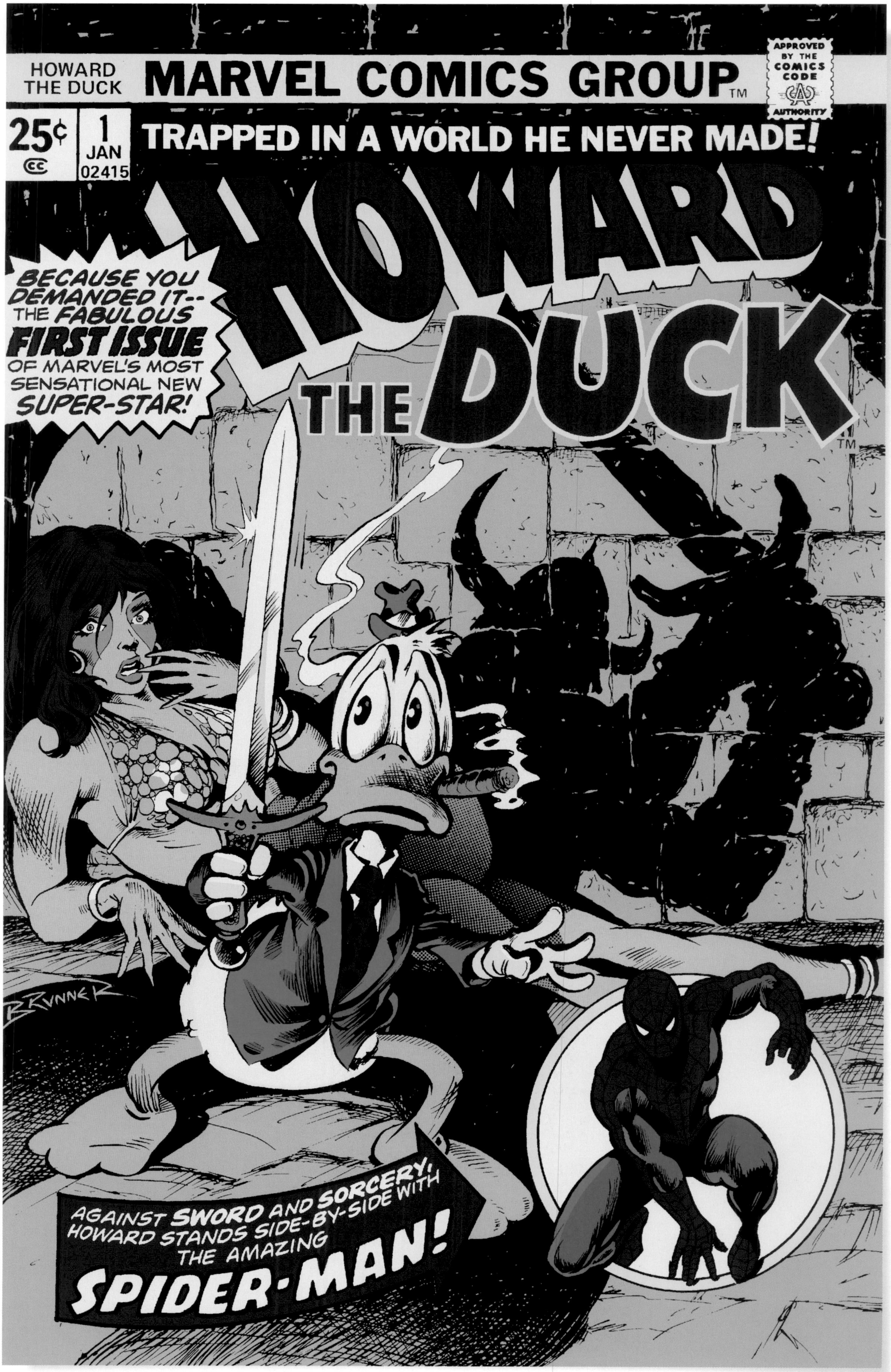

HOWARD THE DUCK
MARVEL COMICS GROUP
APPROVED BY THE COMICS CODE AUTHORITY
25¢
1 JAN 02415
TRAPPED IN A WORLD HE NEVER MADE!
HOWARD THE DUCK
BECAUSE YOU DEMANDED IT-- THE FABULOUS FIRST ISSUE OF MARVEL'S MOST SENSATIONAL NEW SUPER-STAR!
BRUNNER
AGAINST SWORD AND SORCERY, HOWARD STANDS SIDE-BY-SIDE WITH THE AMAZING SPIDER-MAN!

◀ ***HOWARD THE DUCK* #1**

**January 1976**
**Artist:** Frank Brunner

Sword and Sorcery meet satire on this cover, as Howard the Duck gained his own series. The sight of Howard, sword in hand and with a heroine right out of a Robert E. Howard story behind him, firmly established that this duck's adventures were not going to be the normal Super-Hero fare. Howard soon became a cult star thanks to writer Steve Gerber's intelligent and funny scripts, combined with some great art from the likes of Frank Brunner and Gene Colan.

HOWARD THE DUCK
MARVEL COMICS GROUP
APPROVED BY THE COMICS CODE AUTHORITY
30¢ 8 JAN 02415
TRAPPED IN A WORLD HE NEVER MADE!
HOWARD THE DUCK
FINAL
Carter Yells Fowl
Assassination Attempt Defended By Gunman
"Thought He Was In Season," Explains Prisoner

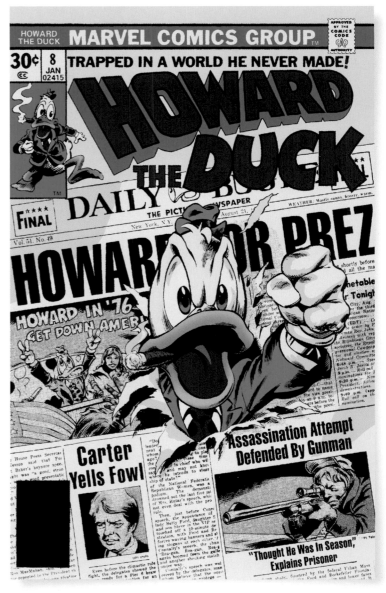

***HOWARD THE DUCK* #8** ▶

**January 1977**
**Artist:** Gene Colan

Not many comic book characters get to run for high office, but Howard the Duck did just that when he decided to take on the establishment. This excellent Gene Colan cover saw Howard announce he was running for President in '76, the headlines behind already hinting at the political satire to come.

HOWARD THE DUCK
MARVEL COMICS GROUP
APPROVED BY THE COMICS CODE AUTHORITY
30¢ 12 MAY 02415
TRAPPED IN A WORLD HE NEVER MADE!
©1977 MARVEL COMICS GROUP
HOWARD THE DUCK
REMEMBER THE GOOD OLD DAYS, HOWARD?
THE WORLD WAS YOUNG...
BEFORE THEY PUT YOU AWAY...?
LOVE WAS IN BLOOM...
AND YOU HAD A MIND INSTEAD OF...
"DUCK'S HEAD SOUP!"

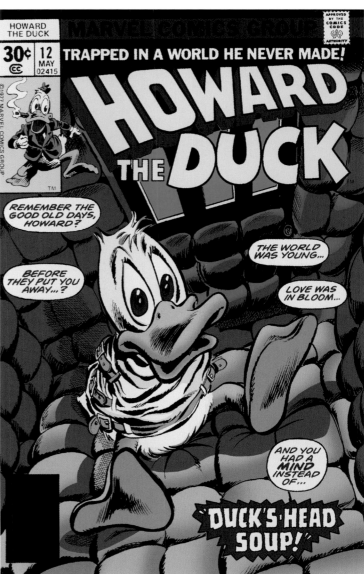

***HOWARD THE DUCK* #12** ▶

**May 1977**
**Artist:** Gene Colan

Another snappy Gene Colan cover shows Howard the Duck in a dangerous plight—locked inside an asylum. The story inside the issue was equally strange, as Howard investigated the goings-on at Sauerbraten County Medical Facility. It ended with a surprise appearance by the rock band Kiss!

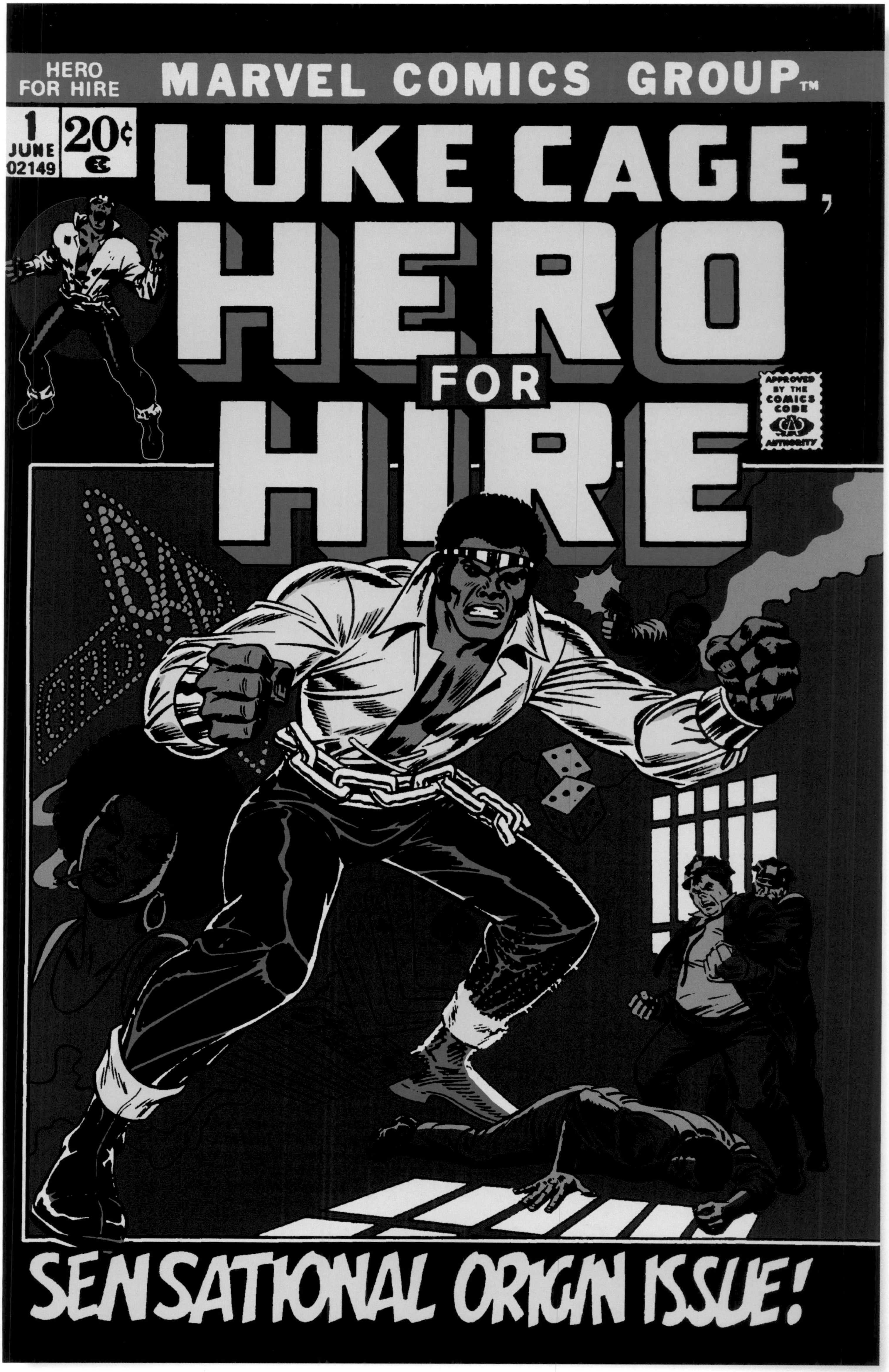
HERO FOR HIRE
MARVEL COMICS GROUP™
1 JUNE 02149
20¢
LUKE CAGE,
HERO FOR HIRE
APPROVED BY THE COMICS CODE AUTHORITY
SENSATIONAL ORIGIN ISSUE!

◀ ***LUKE CAGE, HERO FOR HIRE* #1**

**June 1972**
**Artist:** George Tuska

Blaxploitation movies were hugely popular in the early 1970s and Marvel added their own comic-book take on the genre with *Luke Cage, Hero for Hire*. Luke was one of the first African-American Super Heroes to star in his own comic, as Marvel again pushed back barriers with their titles. The cover is more like a movie poster than a regular comic cover, showing key scenes from the issue and Luke's troubled past.

IRON FIST
MARVEL COMICS GROUP
30¢ 14 AUG 02176
KUNG FU ACTION IN THE MIGHTY MARVEL MANNER!
IRON FIST
WHITE SNOW.. WHITE DOOM!
YOU'RE SNOW-BLIND, HERO! YOUR FLAMING FIST MEANS NOTHING NOW!
INTRODUCING! THE SAVAGERY OF SABRE-TOOTH!

▲ ***IRON FIST* #14**

**August 1977**
**Artist:** Dave Cockrum

A big cultural trend in the early 1970s was the martial arts craze, following the release of Bruce Lee's movie *Enter the Dragon*. One of Marvel's unique takes on the genre was *Iron Fist*. This classic cover isn't just an accomplished work of comic cover art though—it also marks the first appearance of the character Sabretooth.

POWERMAN
MARVEL COMICS GROUP
35¢ 50 02149
BEGINNING: A NEW ERA OF GREATNESS!
POWER MAN AND IRON FIST
FANTASTIC 50TH ISSUE!
NOW! THE MOST UNLIKELY TEAM OF ALL IN THE MOST UNBEATABLE ADVENTURES EVER!

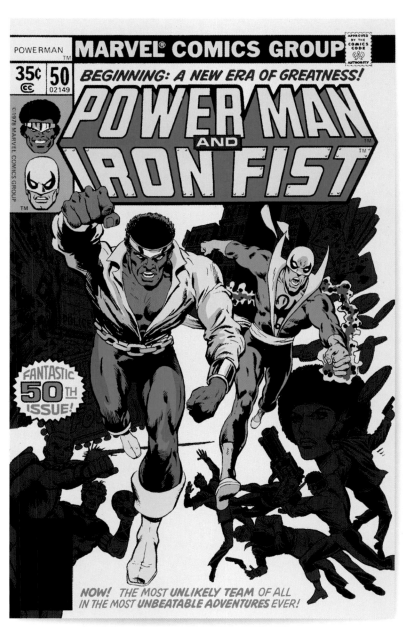

▲ ***POWER MAN AND IRON FIST* #50**

**April 1978**
**Artist:** Dave Cockrum

*Iron Fist* and *Luke Cage: Power Man* (*Luke Cage, Hero for Hire* had been renamed) became one title with this issue and one of the best-loved comics of the time. Dave Cockrum's cool cover montage has echoes of Luke's first issue and perfectly suits the heroes' realistic street-level adventures.

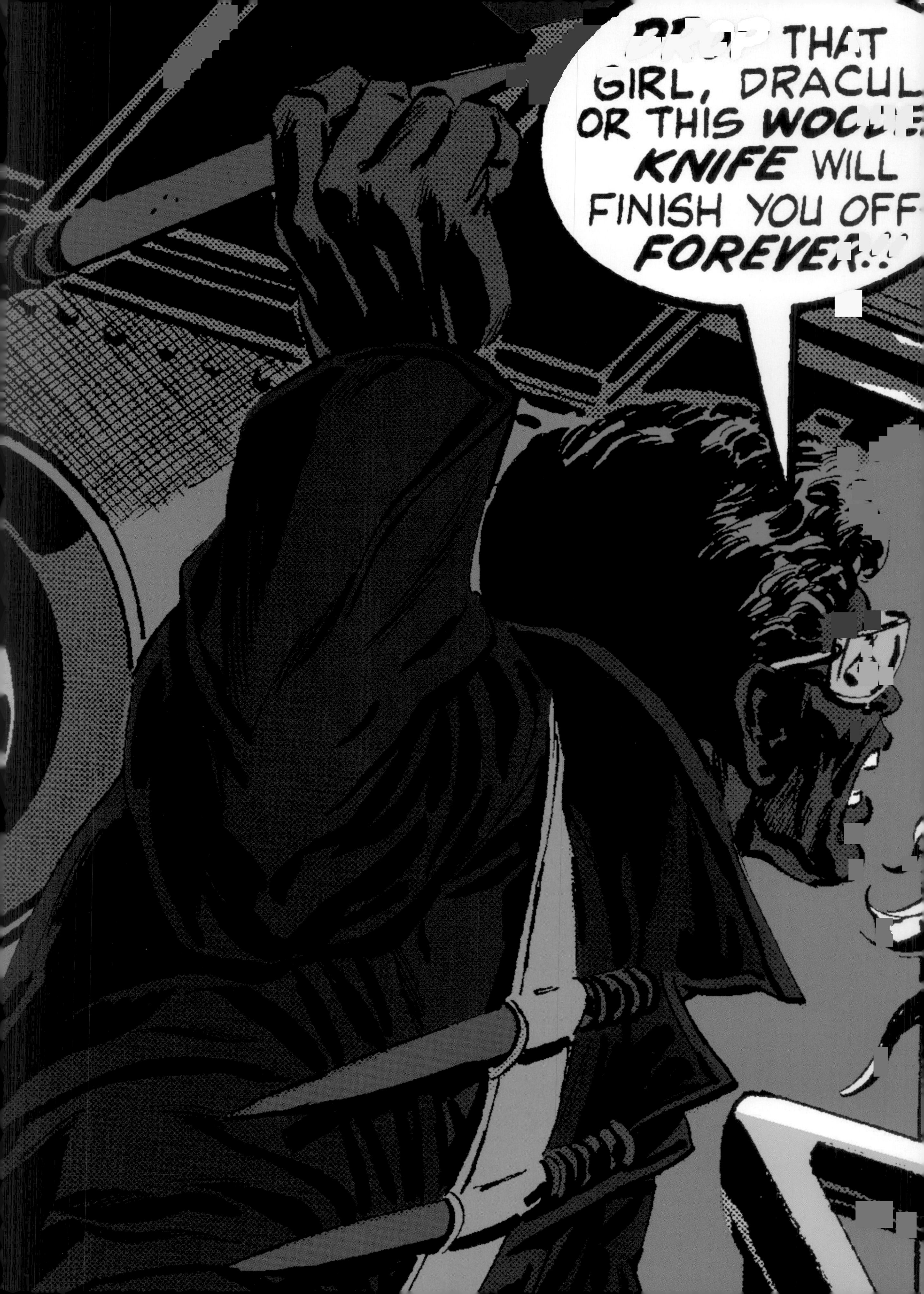
THAT GIRL, DRACUL OR THIS WOO KNIFE WILL FINISH YOU OFF FOREVER

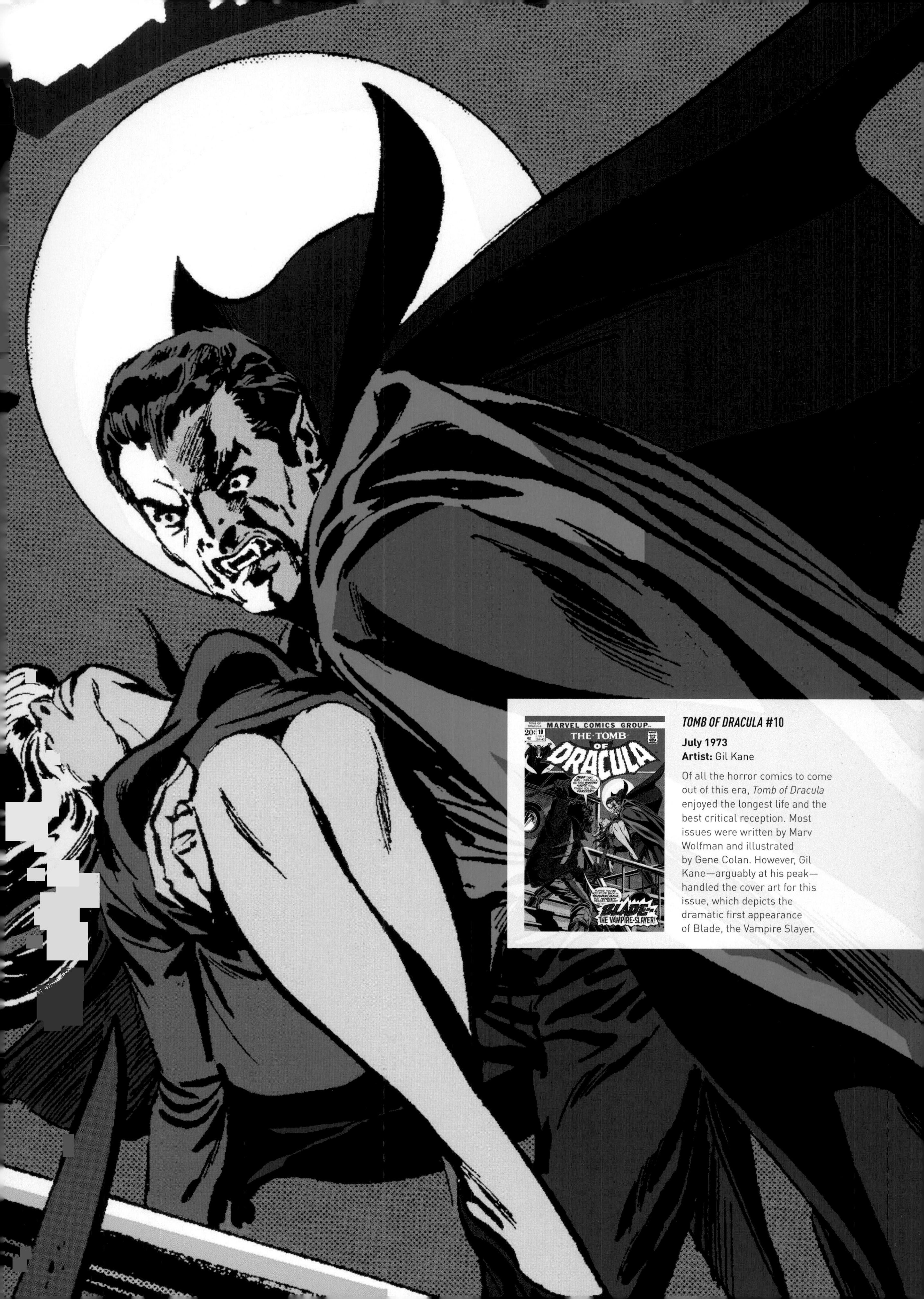
MARVEL COMICS GROUP
THE TOMB OF DRACULA
BLADE—THE VAMPIRE-SLAYER!

*TOMB OF DRACULA* #10

**July 1973**
**Artist:** Gil Kane

Of all the horror comics to come out of this era, *Tomb of Dracula* enjoyed the longest life and the best critical reception. Most issues were written by Marv Wolfman and illustrated by Gene Colan. However, Gil Kane—arguably at his peak—handled the cover art for this issue, which depicts the dramatic first appearance of Blade, the Vampire Slayer.

MARVEL SPOTLIGHT
MARVEL COMICS GROUP
25¢ 2 FEB 02120
MARVEL SPOTLIGHT ON...
WEREWOLF BY NIGHT
THE MOON.. IT'S SO FULL --SO BRIGHT--
AND-- I'M STARTING TO CHANGE AGAIN--
--TURNING INTO--
NIGHT OF FULL MOON--NIGHT OF FEAR!

▲ ***MARVEL SPOTLIGHT* #2**

**February 1972**
**Artist:** Neal Adams

When the Comics Code Authority began to relax its guidelines to allow horror comics once more, Marvel wasted little time in turning its attention to horror-related heroes. Jack Russell, aka the Werewolf by Night, was one of the first, with Neal Adams depicting Jack's painful transformation into the werewolf in a multi-frame cover image.

MARVEL SPOTLIGHT
MARVEL COMICS GROUP
20¢ 5 AUG 02120
MARVEL SPOTLIGHT ON...
GHOST RIDER
IS HE ALIVE.. OR DEAD?
A LEGEND IS BORN!
THE MOST SUPERNATURAL SUPERHERO OF ALL!

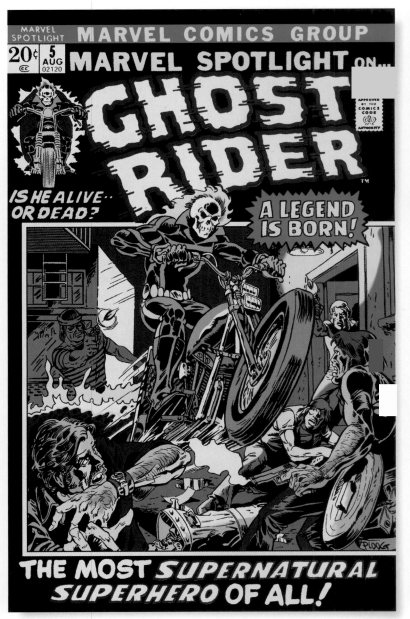

▲ ***MARVEL SPOTLIGHT* #5**

**August 1972**
**Artist:** Mike Ploog

Ghost Rider—perhaps one of Marvel's coolest looking heroes—made his debut this issue, courtesy of artist Mike Ploog and writer Gary Friedrich, aided and abetted by editor Roy Thomas. Ploog's action-packed cover illustration introduced the character's famous motorcycle and helped to establish the debutant as "The most Supernatural Super Hero of all!"

***ADVENTURE INTO FEAR* #11** ▶

**December 1972**
**Artist:** Neal Adams

This atmospheric Neal Adams cover shows an early appearance of the monstrous Man-Thing. The creature had first appeared in *Savage Tales* issue #1 (May 1971), but soon gained his own full-color series. The Adams cover reflects how, since the relaxation of the Comics Code, Marvel were able to feature mystical elements such as the pentagram.

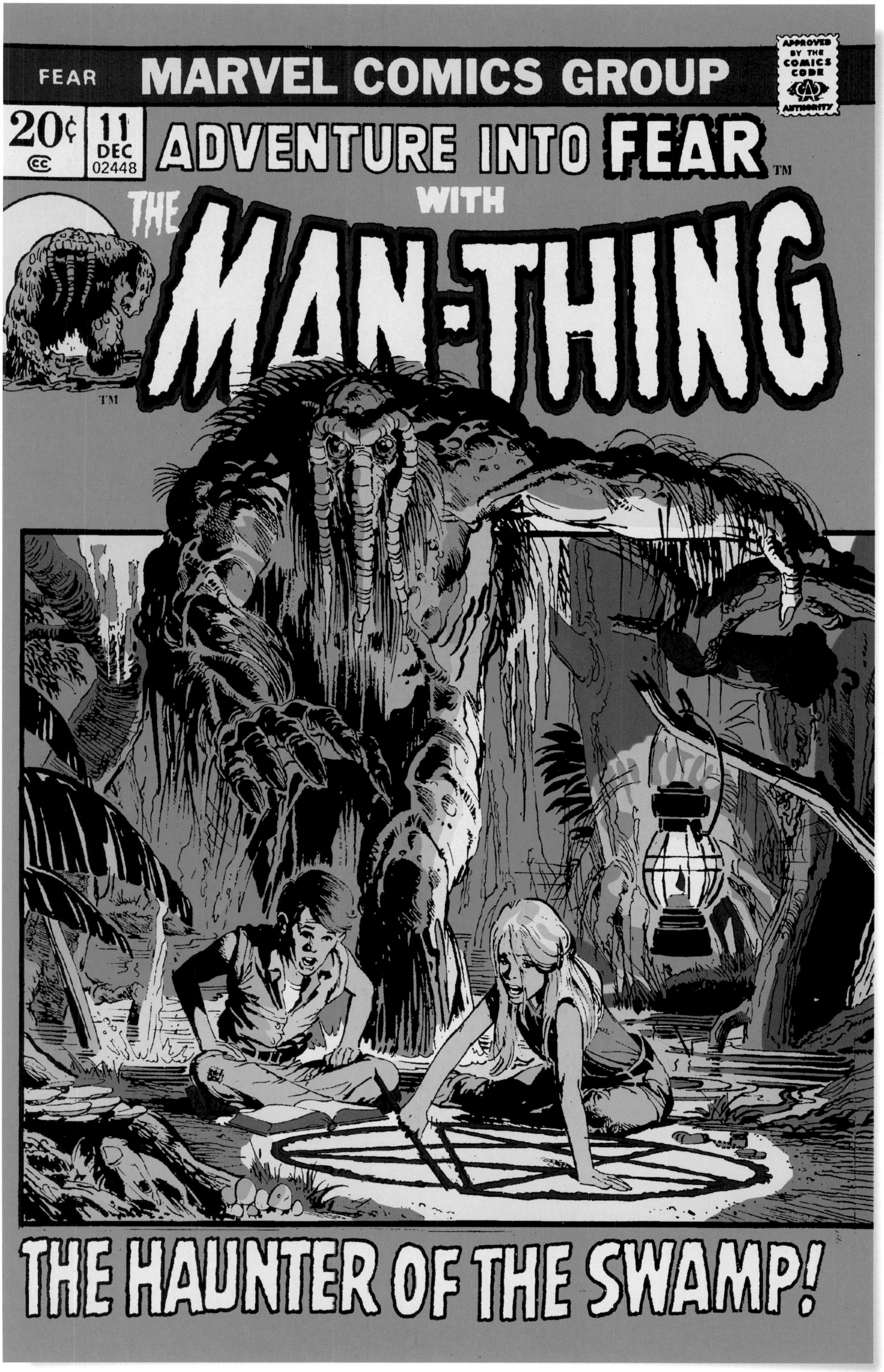
FEAR
MARVEL COMICS GROUP
APPROVED BY THE COMICS CODE AUTHORITY
20¢
11 DEC 02448
ADVENTURE INTO FEAR
WITH
THE MAN-THING
THE HAUNTER OF THE SWAMP!

WORLD SCREAMIERE! FANTASTIC, FEAR-FILLED FIRST ISSUE!
02189
TALES OF THE ZOMBIE
MARVEL MONSTER GROUP 75¢ No.1
HE LIVES! HE STRIKES! NO GRAVE CAN HOLD HIM!
NIGHT OF THE WALKING DEAD
PHOTOS! FEATURES! ILLUSTRATED TERROR TALES FROM THE UNHOLY HAUNT OF
VOODOO
AND
BLACK MAGIC
BORIS
EXTRA BONUS: THE THING FROM THE BOG

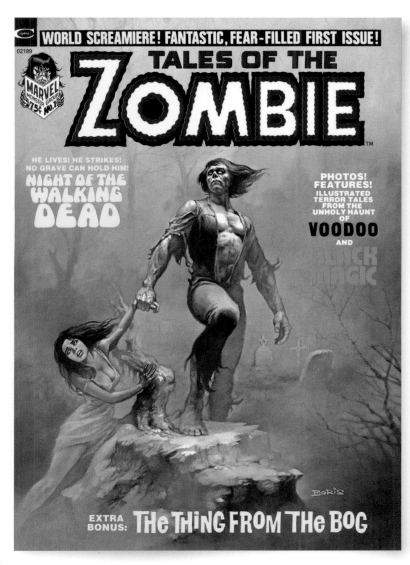

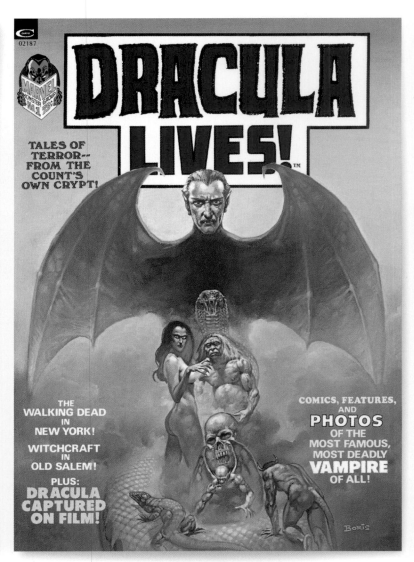

▲ *TALES OF THE ZOMBIE* #1

**July 1973**
**Artist:** Boris Vallejo

Marvel created a new magazine line that didn't come under the scrutiny of the Comics Code Authority. Cover artist Boris Vallejo was one of the best fantasy artists in the business, combining horror and sensuality to great effect, as demonstrated here with his depiction of Simon Garth, the Zombie.

02187
MARVEL MONSTER GROUP No.1 75¢
DRACULA LIVES!
TALES OF TERROR-- FROM THE COUNT'S OWN CRYPT!
THE WALKING DEAD IN NEW YORK!
WITCHCRAFT IN OLD SALEM!
PLUS: DRACULA CAPTURED ON FILM!
COMICS, FEATURES, AND PHOTOS OF THE MOST FAMOUS, MOST DEADLY VAMPIRE OF ALL!
BORIS

▲ *DRACULA LIVES* #1

**August 1973**
**Artist:** Boris Vallejo

The greatest vampire of all gained his own magazine shortly after the successful launch of *Tomb of Dracula* in the previous month. Boris Vallejo's stunning painted artwork graced the cover. The more adult-oriented content—indicated by the sophisticated painterly covers—proved to be a big hit for Marvel.

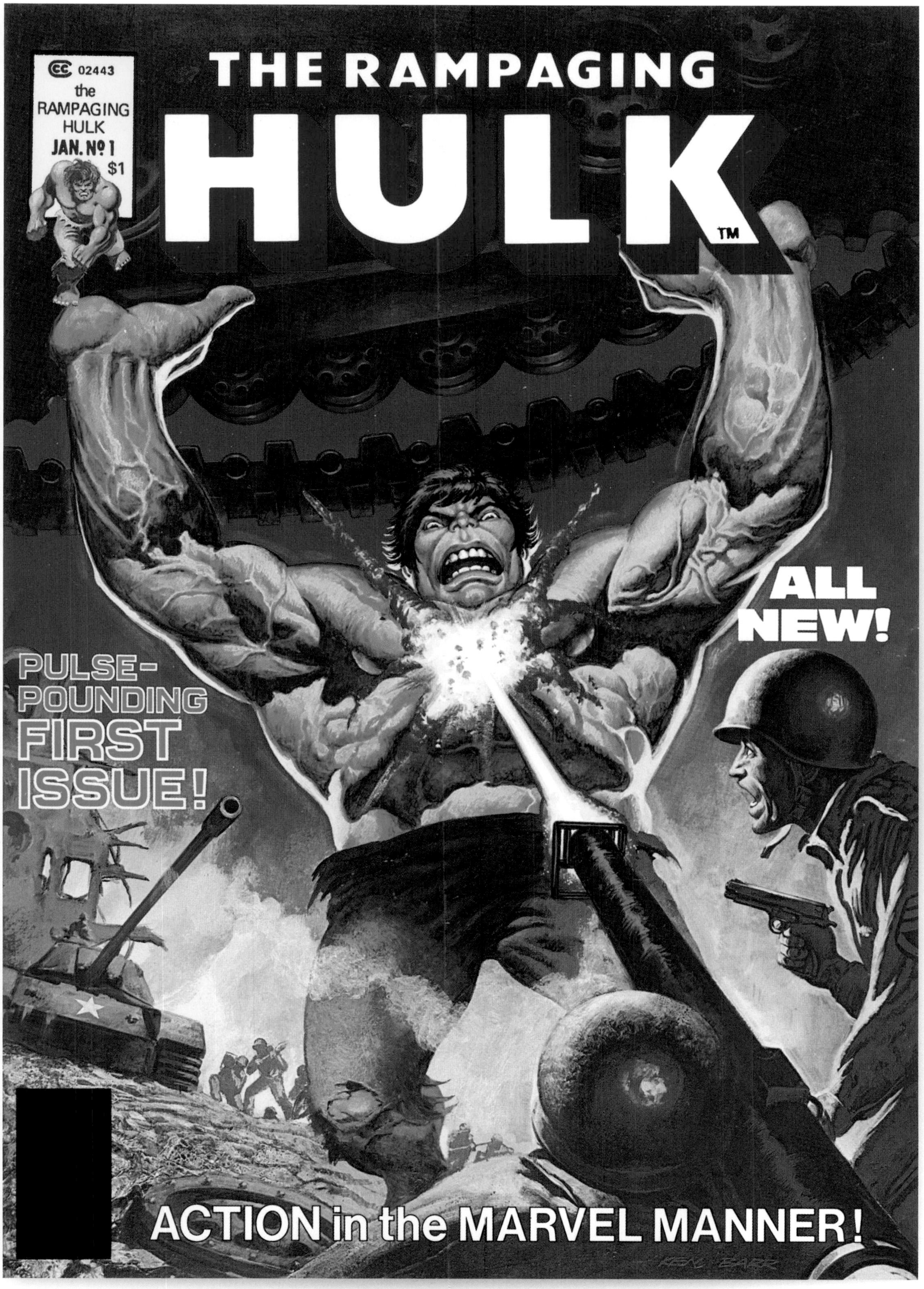
02443
the
RAMPAGING
HULK
JAN. Nº 1
$1
THE RAMPAGING
HULK
TM
ALL NEW!
PULSE-POUNDING FIRST ISSUE!
ACTION in the MARVEL MANNER!

▲ ***RAMPAGING HULK*** **#1**

**January 1977**
**Artist:** Ken Barr

Marvel also gave some of their Super Heroes the magazine treatment. The Hulk was one of the first to make the transition, and the fantastic painted cover by Ken Barr makes the green Goliath look more realistic and menacing than ever, with him staring angrily out at the reader as well as the soldiers in the foreground. The title was an anthology, featuring harder-edged, more adult stories than those in the regular comic books.

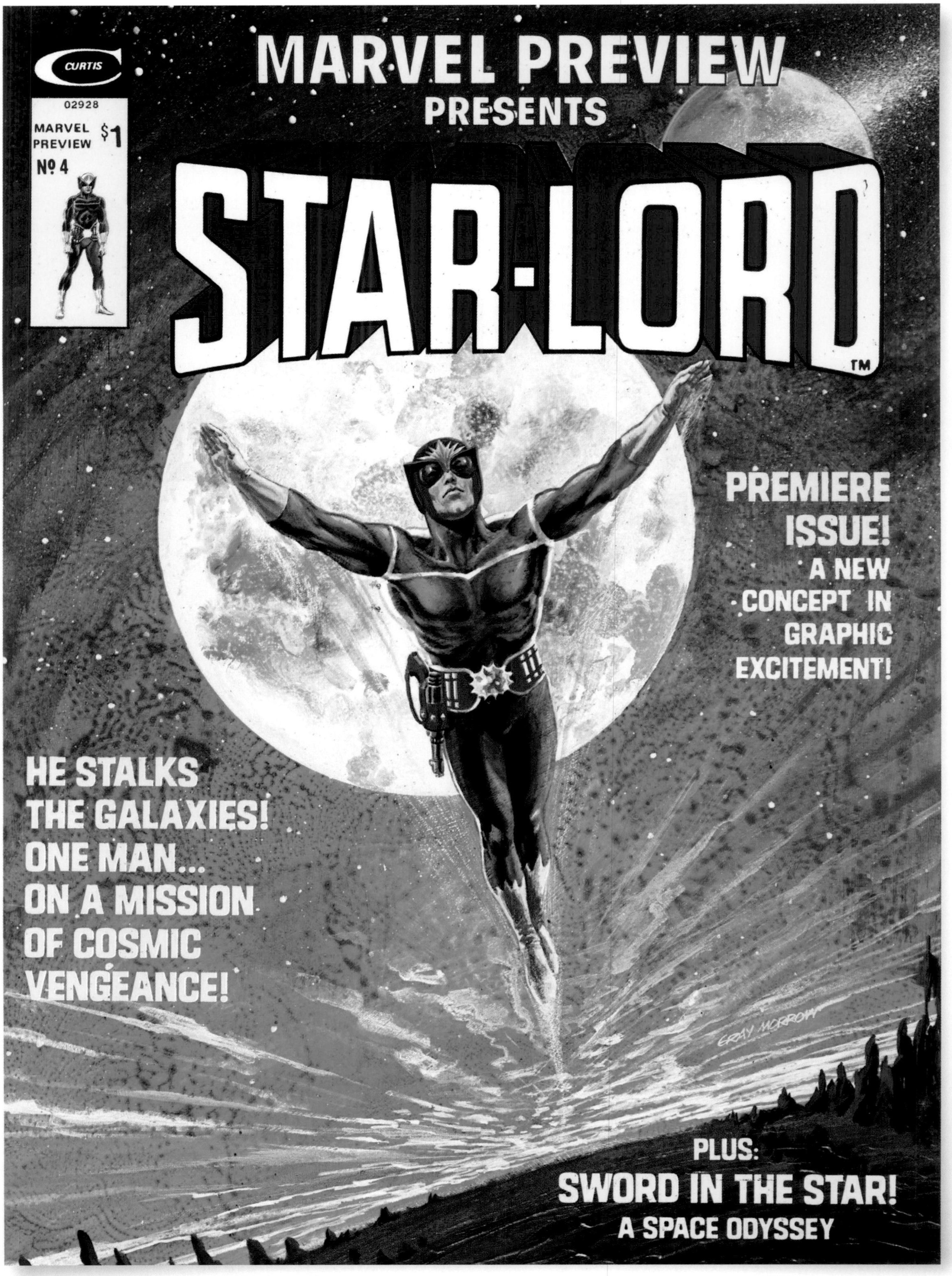
CURTIS
02928
MARVEL PREVIEW
$1
Nº 4
MARVEL PREVIEW
PRESENTS
STAR-LORD
TM
PREMIERE ISSUE!
A NEW CONCEPT IN GRAPHIC EXCITEMENT!
HE STALKS THE GALAXIES!
ONE MAN... ON A MISSION OF COSMIC VENGEANCE!
GRAY MORROW
PLUS:
SWORD IN THE STAR!
A SPACE ODYSSEY

▲ *MARVEL PREVIEW #4*

**January 1976**
**Artist:** Gray Morrow

Star-Lord started out a solo adventurer but would later be the leader of a new incarnation of the Guardians of the Galaxy. This issue was his first appearance, revealing just how he ended up in space. The painterly style of Gray Morrow's cover was heavily influenced by his other job— illustrating paperback book covers.

***AMAZING ADVENTURES* #18 ▶**

**May 1973**

**Artist:** John Romita Sr.

Marvel created an action-packed, comic book follow-up to H.G. Wells' novel *War of the Worlds*, with John Romita Sr. producing a futuristic cover for the debut issue. It shows the hero, Killraven, in a post-apocalyptic landscape ravaged by Martian war-machines.

AMAZING ADVENTURES
MARVEL COMICS GROUP
20¢
18 MAY 02487
AMAZING ADVENTURES FEATURING
WAR OF THE WORLDS
BASED ON CONCEPTS CREATED IN THE PROPHETIC NOVEL BY H.G. WELLS!
THE POWER-PACKED PREMIERE OF A STARTLING NEW SERIES!
THEY CALL HIM-- KILLRAVEN!

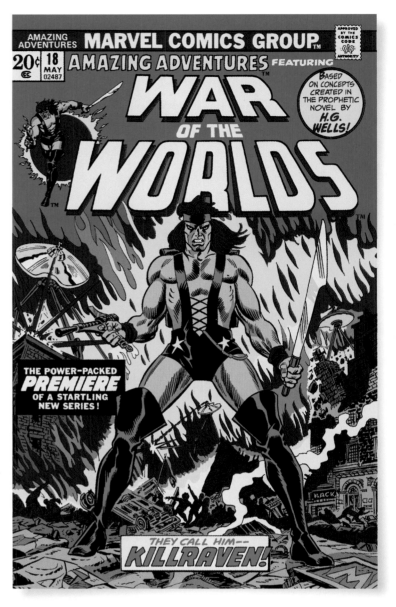

***MARVEL PRESENTS* #3 ▶**

**February 1976**

**Artist:** John Romita Sr.

Decades before a new incarnation of the Guardians of the Galaxy took to the big screen, the original team enjoyed futuristic adventures. The Guardians first appeared in *Marvel Super Heroes* issue #18 in 1969. They remained the stars of *Marvel Presents* until the series finished with issue #12, and John Romita Sr. producing one of the most striking early covers.

MARVEL PRESENTS
MARVEL COMICS GROUP
25¢
3 FEB 02113
MARVEL PRESENTS:
GUARDIANS OF THE GALAXY
NOW IN THEIR OWN BRAND-NEW SERIES AT LAST!
FEATURING-- THE POWER OF STARHAWK!
UNIVERSE-SPANNING ACTION IN THE SPECTACULAR MARVEL MANNER!

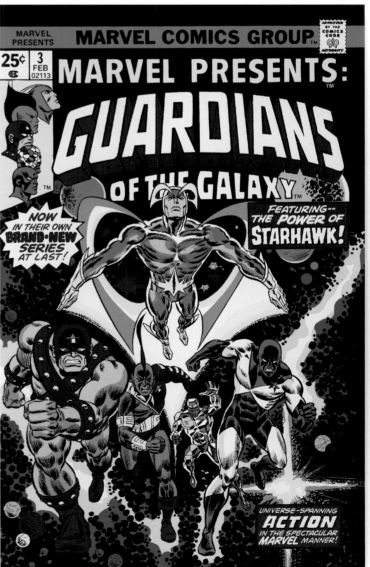

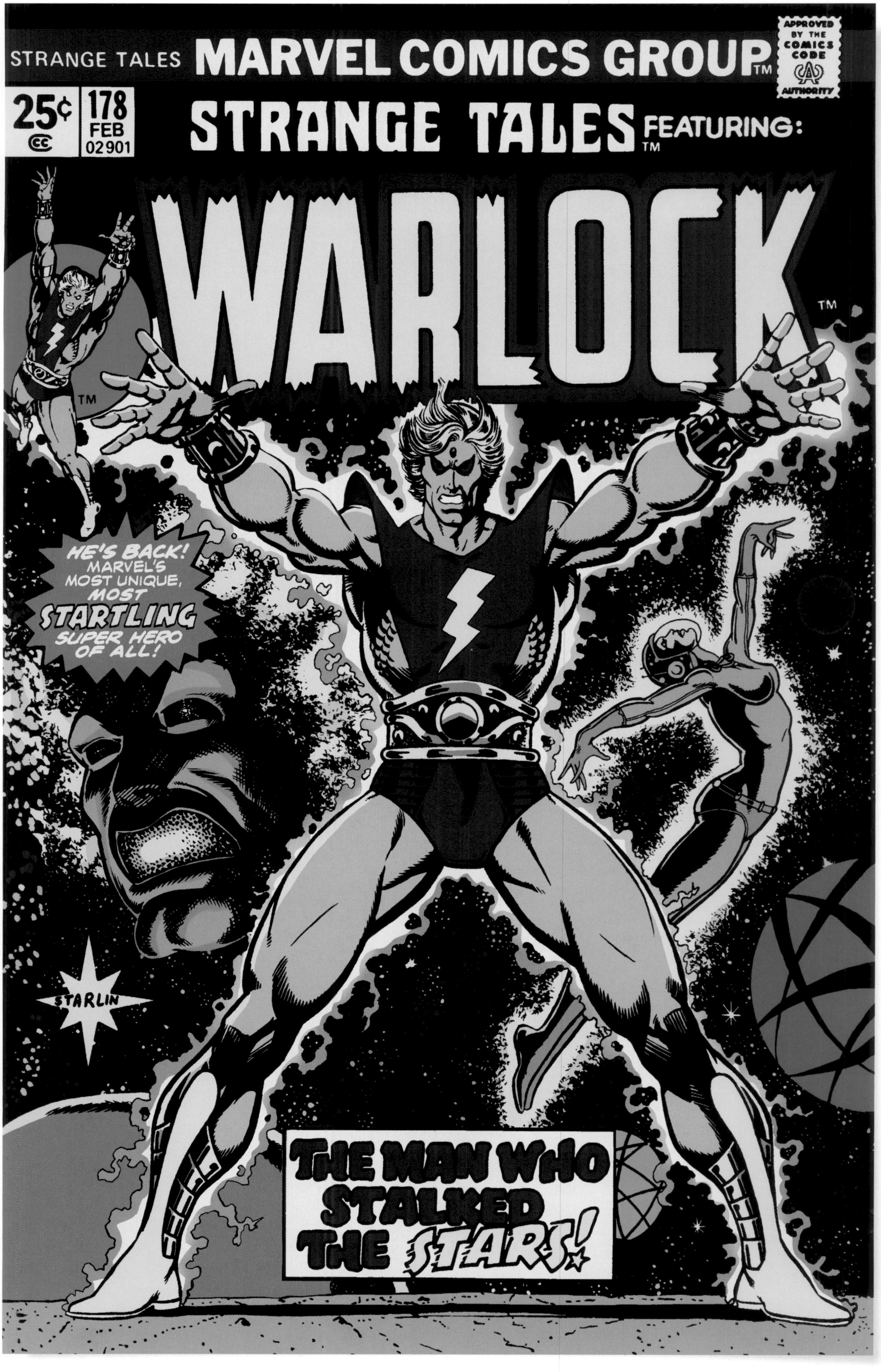
STRANGE TALES MARVEL COMICS GROUP
APPROVED BY THE COMICS CODE AUTHORITY
25¢ 178 FEB 02901
STRANGE TALES FEATURING:
WARLOCK
HE'S BACK! MARVEL'S MOST UNIQUE, MOST STARTLING SUPER HERO OF ALL!
STARLIN
THE MAN WHO STALKED THE STARS!

***WARLOCK* #11** ▶

**February 1976**
**Artist:** Jim Starlin

Jim Starlin's *Warlock* picked up pace in this issue as the intricate, star-spanning tale continued. The cover, showing Adam Warlock looking at his own corpse, reflected a key moment in the series and one of the great time-travel stories in Marvel history.

WARLOCK
MARVEL COMICS GROUP
25¢
11 FEB 02153
WARLOCK
HERE IT IS!
The STRANGE DEATH of ADAM WARLOCK!

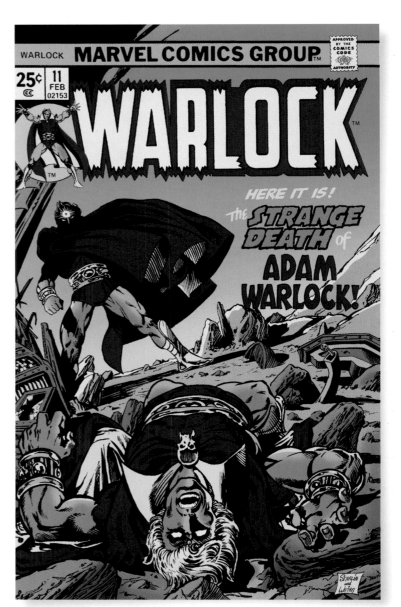

***WARLOCK* #15** ▶

**November 1976**
**Artist:** Jim Starlin

Adam Warlock's series ended with this issue and one of Jim Starlin's best covers. The cover featured some of Starlin's other creations—including the green-skinned Gamora and the Mad God Thanos, whose head dominates the left-hand side of the cover. His cruel expression radiates pure evil.

WARLOCK
MARVEL COMICS GROUP
30¢
15 NOV. 02153
WARLOCK
UNLEASHED··AT LAST!

◀ ***STRANGE TALES* #178**

**February 1975**
**Artist:** Jim Starlin

Jim Starlin's run of Adam Warlock stories was years ahead of its time. He was one of the first Marvel creators to successfully work as a writer and artist. Starlin's first *Warlock* cover is filled with the cosmic energy his work is renowned for. The character proved so popular that he retained his own series with Jim Starlin's *Warlock* issue #9 coming out two years after the previous issue.

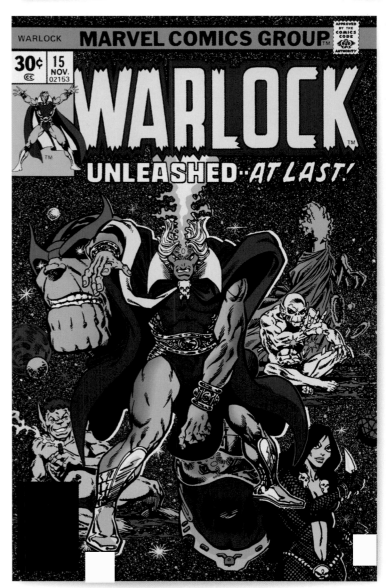

# *NOVA* #12

**August 1977**

**Artist:** John Buscema

Before the computer age, cover creation was a far more hands-on job. In the case of *Nova* issue #12, artist John Buscema would have started the process with a rough layout showing character placement in conjunction with the logo (1). Once that had been approved by Marvel's Art Editor, he would then move on to more detailed pencils (2, 3), before passing the art on to an inker—in this case, Frank Giacoia—to add black line to his pencils (4). Editorial would then make a high-quality copy of the artwork—complete with logo and text added—for a colorist to finish the work. The completed work (5) would then be approved by Marvel's editorial, before it was sent to the printers with the rest of the issue.

1. Sketch
2. Pencil
3. Pencil
4. Inked pencil
5. Final cover

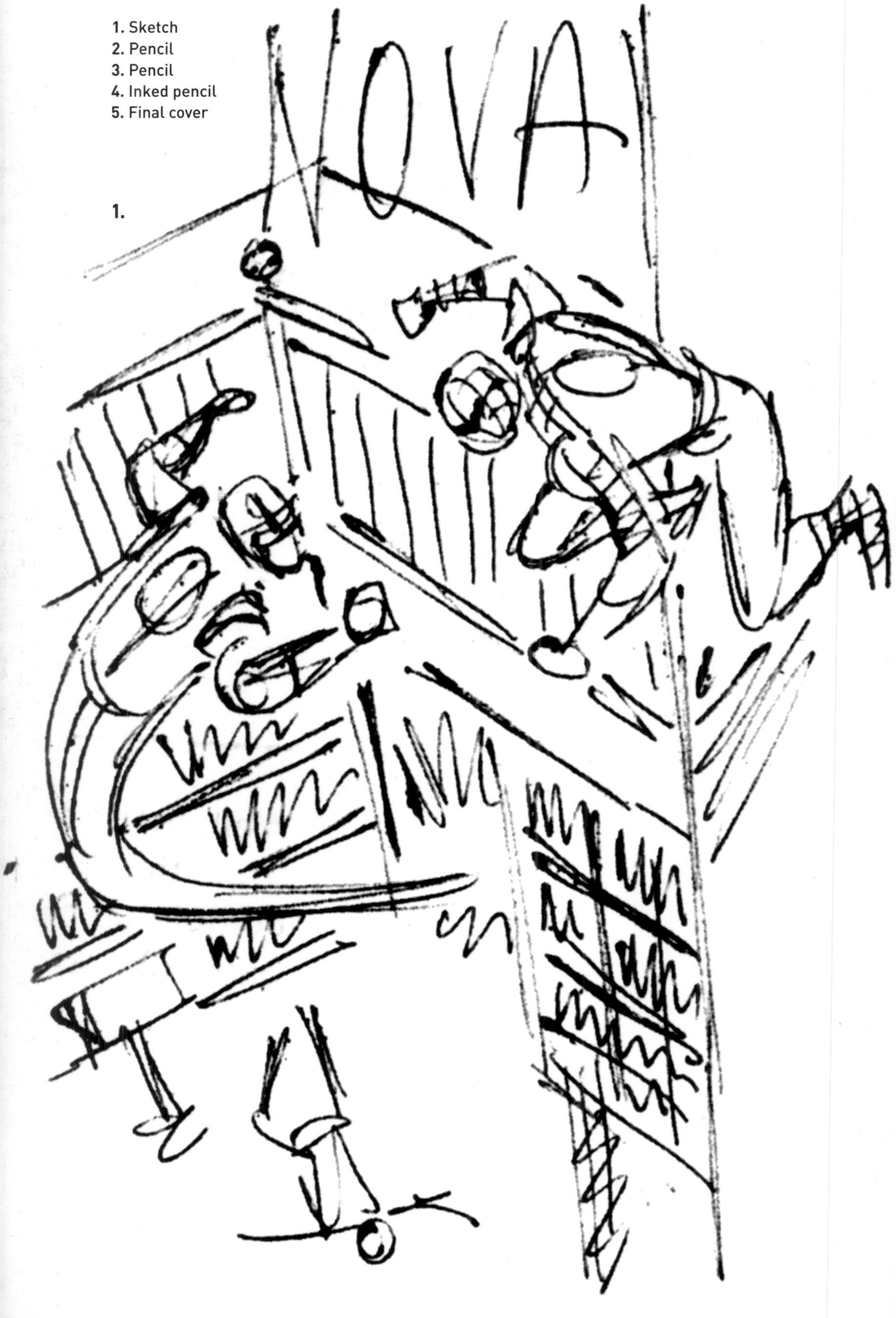
NOVA

1.

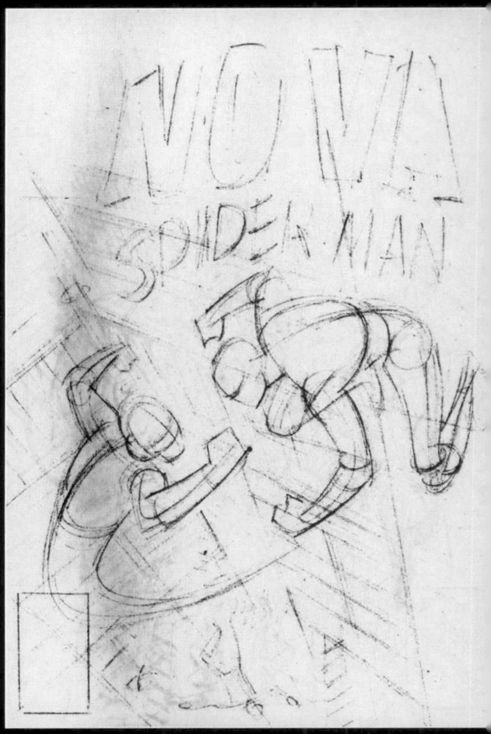
NOVA
SPIDER-MAN

2.

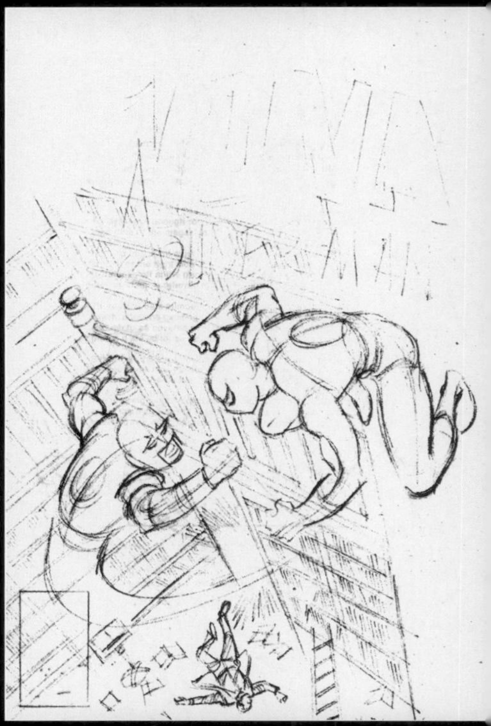

3.

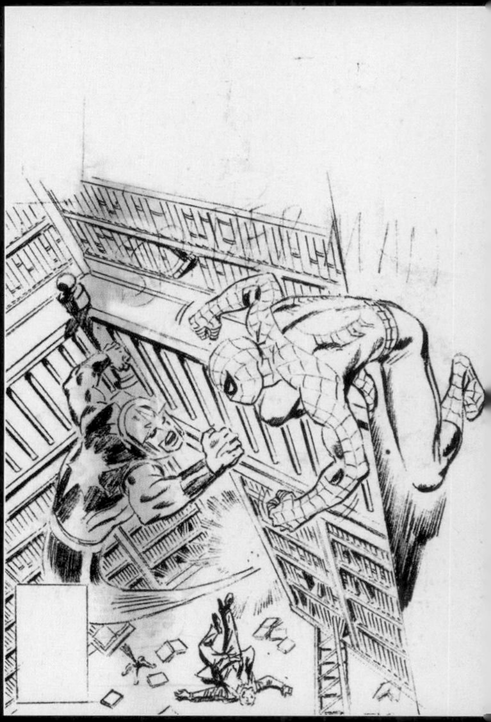

4.

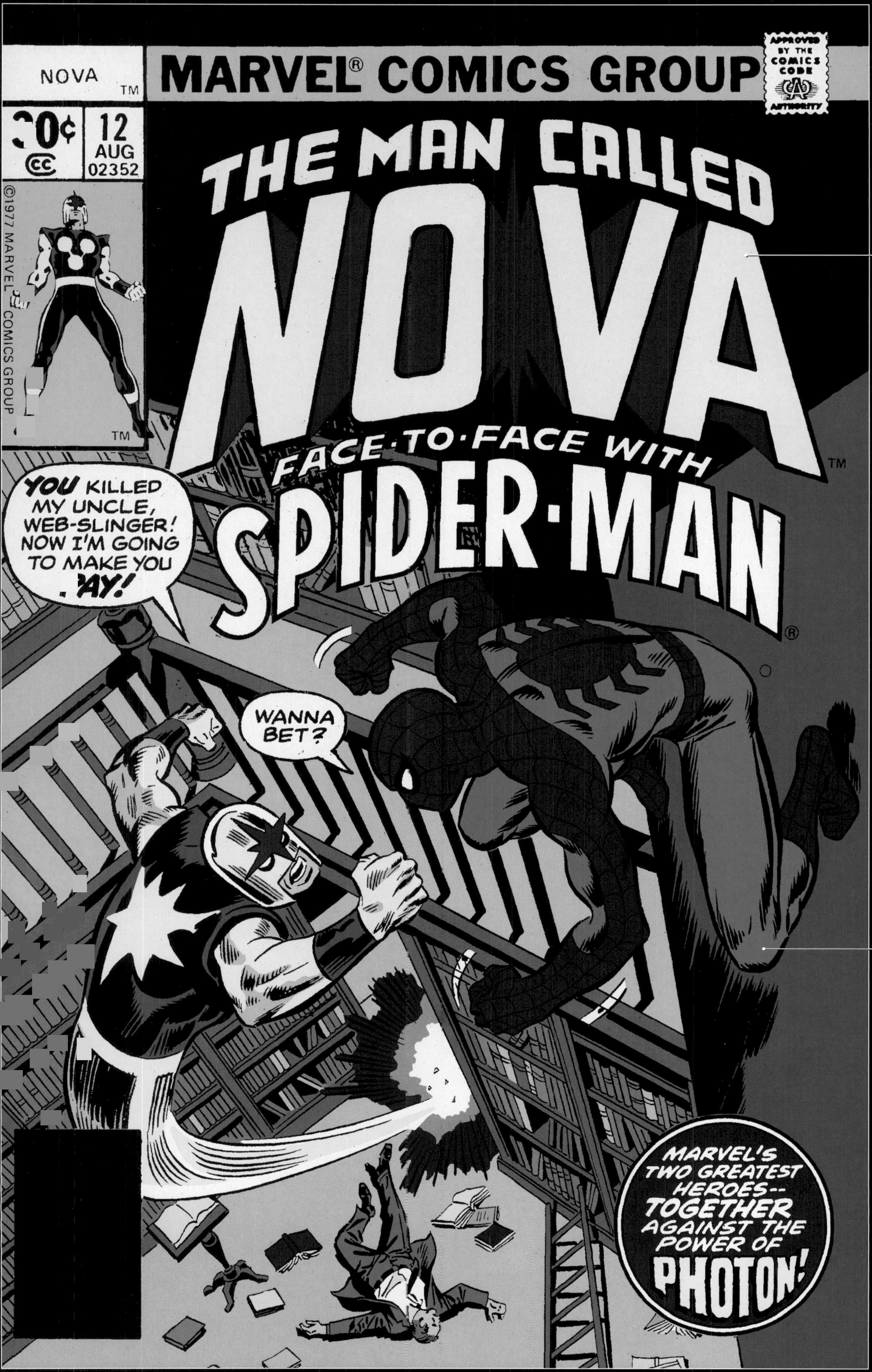
NOVA
TM
MARVEL® COMICS GROUP
APPROVED BY THE COMICS CODE AUTHORITY
0¢
12
AUG
02352
©1977 MARVEL COMICS GROUP
TM
THE MAN CALLED
NOVA
FACE·TO·FACE WITH
SPIDER·MAN
TM
®
YOU KILLED MY UNCLE, WEB-SLINGER! NOW I'M GOING TO MAKE YOU AY!
WANNA BET?
MARVEL'S TWO GREATEST HEROES-- TOGETHER AGAINST THE POWER OF PHOTON!

Marvel used their own group of specialist letterers and designers to create logos and add text to the covers.

Covers often showed fight scenes. Action always helped sell comics—especially if it was two popular characters clashing.

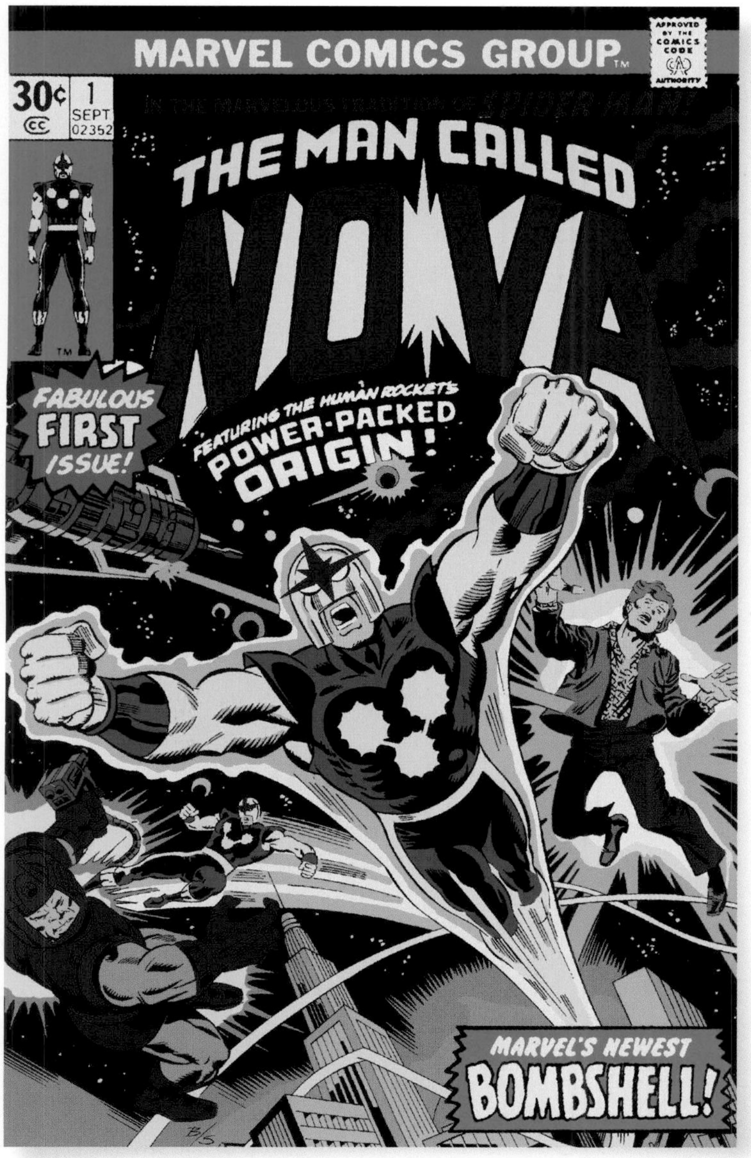
MARVEL COMICS GROUP
30¢ 1 SEPT 02352
THE MAN CALLED NOVA
FABULOUS FIRST ISSUE!
FEATURING THE HUMAN ROCKET'S POWER-PACKED ORIGIN!
MARVEL'S NEWEST BOMBSHELL!

◀ *NOVA* #1

**September 1976**
**Artist:** Rich Buckler

Marvel released a number of new titles in the mid-1970s and *Nova* proved to be one of the most popular. Rich Buckler's cover showcases Nova's origin as the star-spanning cosmic hero. The top strap highlights the fact that Marvel were trying to create another teenage Super Hero in the tradition of Spider-Man.

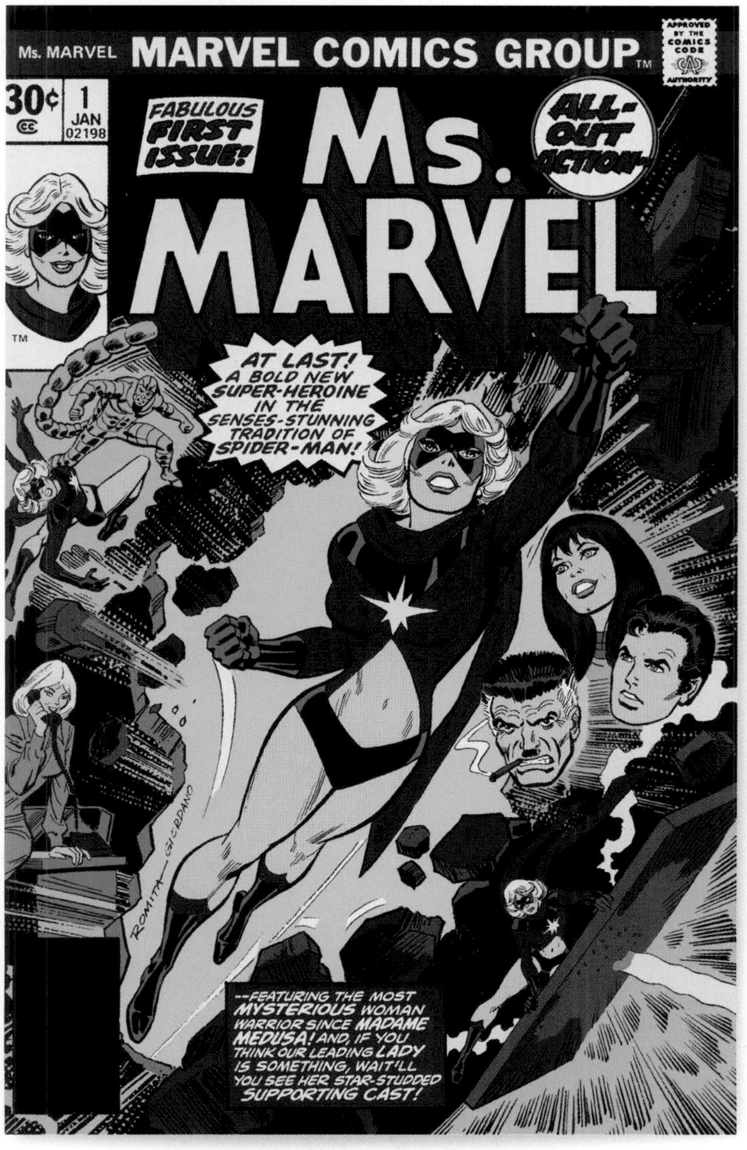
Ms. MARVEL
MARVEL COMICS GROUP
30¢ 1 JAN 02198
FABULOUS FIRST ISSUE!
Ms. MARVEL
ALL-OUT ACTION
AT LAST! A BOLD NEW SUPER-HEROINE IN THE SENSES-STUNNING TRADITION OF SPIDER-MAN!
--FEATURING THE MOST MYSTERIOUS WOMAN WARRIOR SINCE MADAME MEDUSA! AND, IF YOU THINK OUR LEADING LADY IS SOMETHING, WAIT'LL YOU SEE HER STAR-STUDDED SUPPORTING CAST!

◀ *MS. MARVEL* #1

**January 1977**
**Artist:** John Romita Sr.

Carol Danvers was revealed as Ms. Marvel, a new female Super Hero, in this issue. In the early 1970s, female Super Heroes were still relatively few—something Marvel tried to change with Ms. Marvel and Spider-Woman. This classy cover was the perfect montage to attract new readers to the title.

*MACHINE MAN* #1–4 ▶

**October 1984–January 1985**
**Artist:** Barry Windsor-Smith

Barry Windsor-Smith originally made his name as the artist on *Conan the Barbarian*. His return to Marvel in the 1980s resulted in a great series of covers. These four covers show the Machine Man's growth during the story (which was set in the year 2020) and the fact that he was literally rebuilt, having been found on a scrap heap. It was a tale that saw the hero grow from being little more than a broken android into a true machine man.

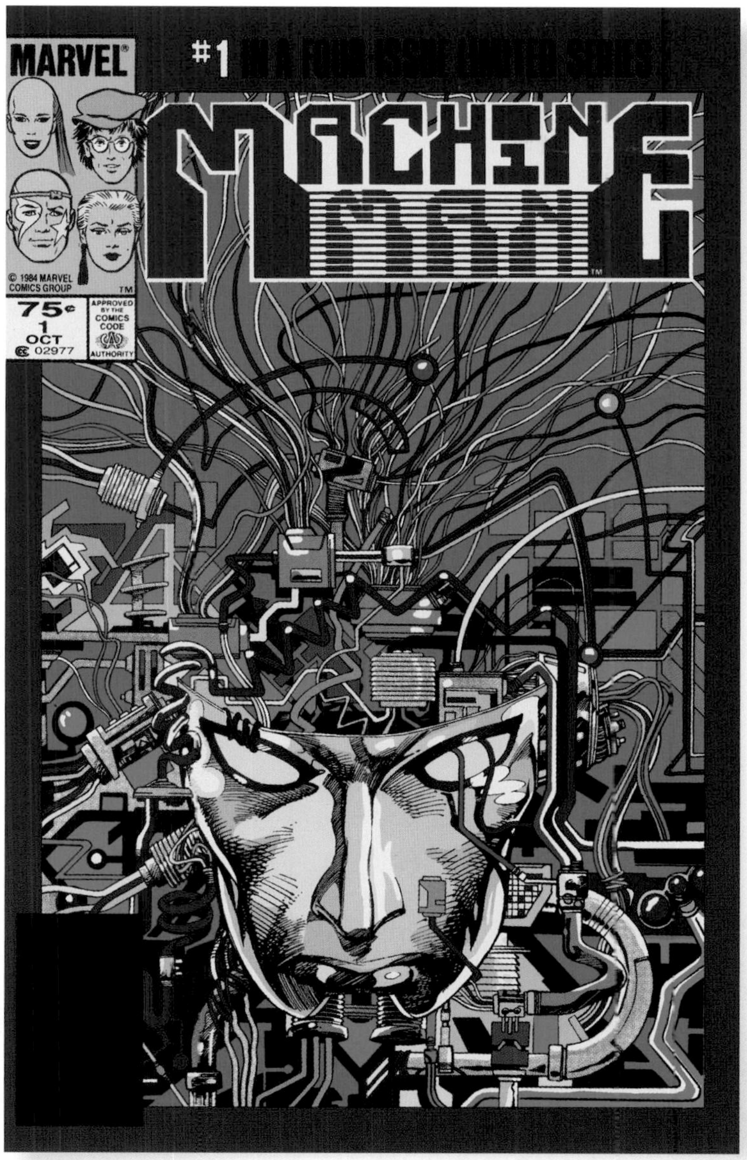
MARVEL
#1 IN A FOUR-ISSUE LIMITED SERIES
MACHINE MAN
© 1984 MARVEL COMICS GROUP
75¢ 1 OCT
APPROVED BY THE COMICS CODE AUTHORITY

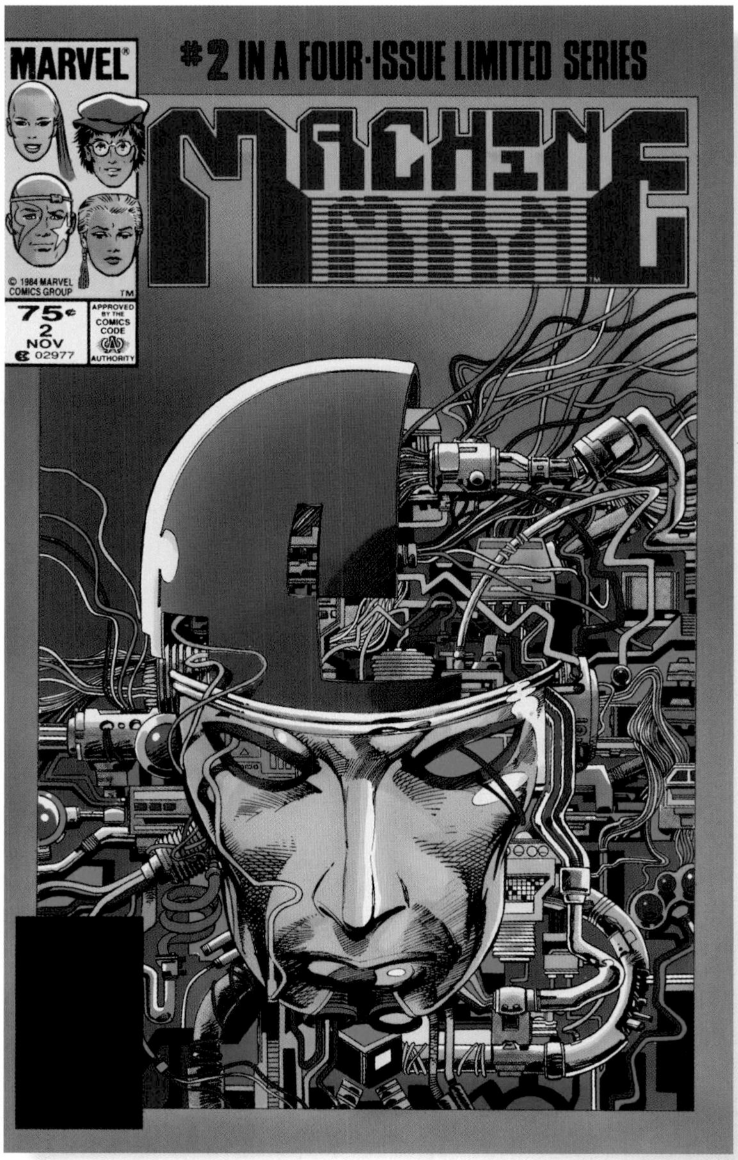
MARVEL
#2 IN A FOUR-ISSUE LIMITED SERIES
MACHINE MAN
© 1984 MARVEL COMICS GROUP
75¢ 2 NOV
APPROVED BY THE COMICS CODE AUTHORITY

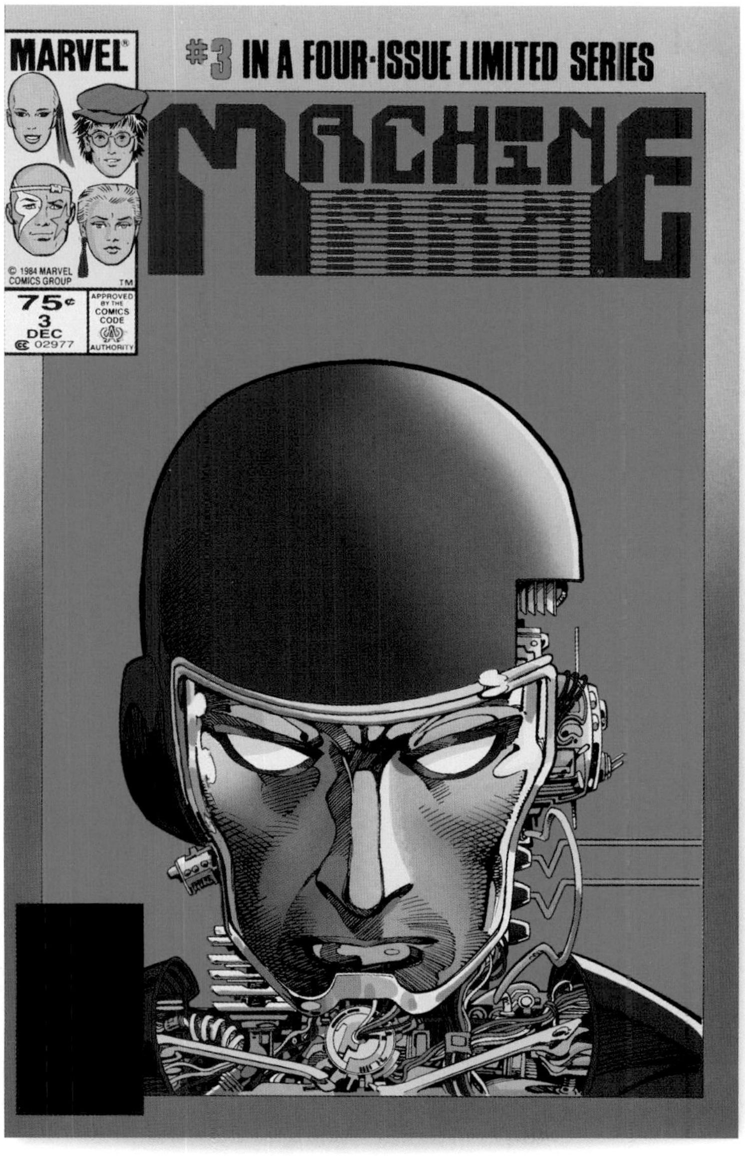
MARVEL
#3 IN A FOUR-ISSUE LIMITED SERIES
MACHINE MAN
© 1984 MARVEL COMICS GROUP
75¢ 3 DEC
APPROVED BY THE COMICS CODE AUTHORITY

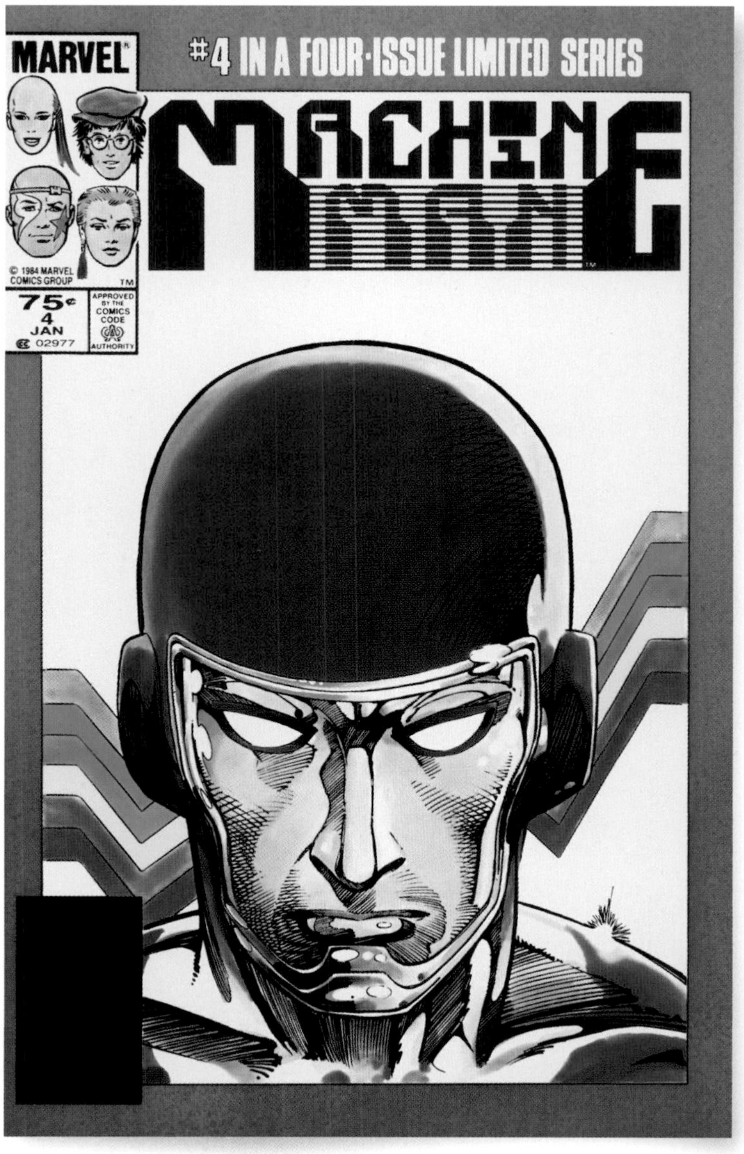
MARVEL
#4 IN A FOUR-ISSUE LIMITED SERIES
MACHINE MAN
© 1984 MARVEL COMICS GROUP
75¢ 4 JAN
APPROVED BY THE COMICS CODE AUTHORITY

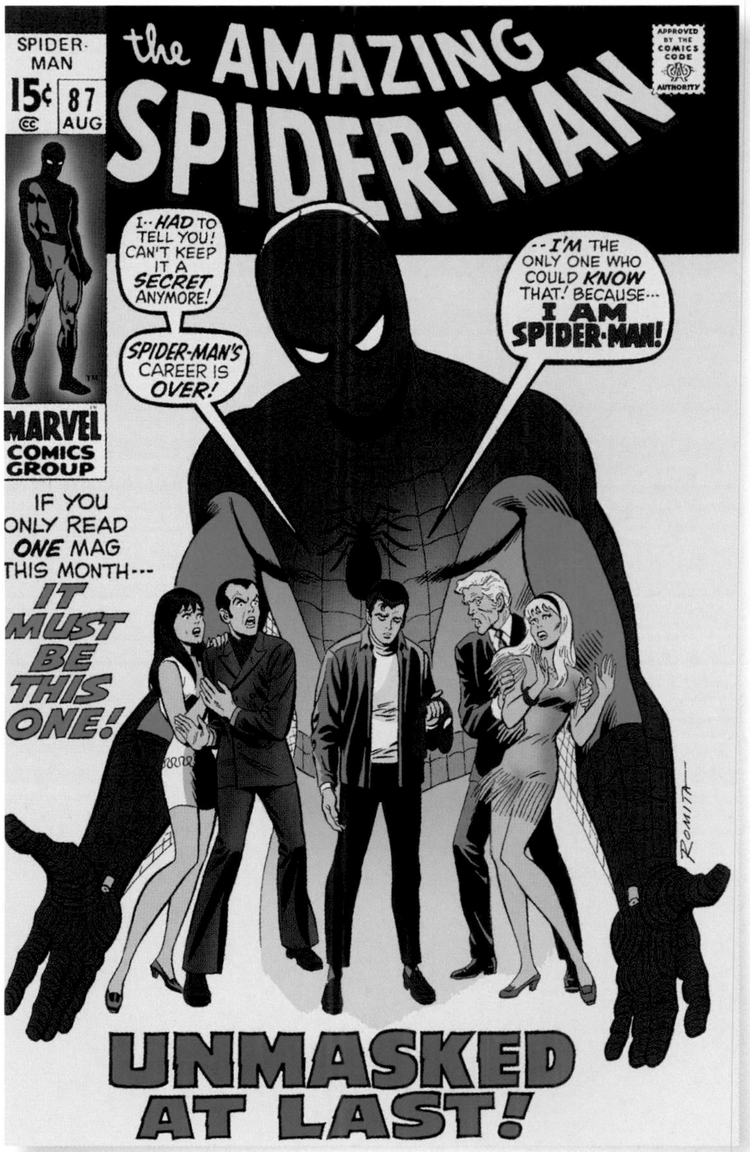
SPIDER-MAN
15¢ 87 AUG
the AMAZING SPIDER-MAN
I--HAD TO TELL YOU! CAN'T KEEP IT A SECRET ANYMORE!
SPIDER-MAN'S CAREER IS OVER!
--I'M THE ONLY ONE WHO COULD KNOW THAT! BECAUSE--- I AM SPIDER-MAN!
MARVEL COMICS GROUP
IF YOU ONLY READ ONE MAG THIS MONTH--- IT MUST BE THIS ONE!
UNMASKED AT LAST!

◀ ***AMAZING SPIDER-MAN* #87**

**August 1970**
**Artist:** John Romita Sr.

Soap-opera drama has always been a big part of Spider-Man's success—and this cover has that in spades. With Romita as artist, Spidey had become Marvel's most popular character. This issue showcases Romita's talent for combining drama with super heroics, as Peter reveals his true identity to his friends.

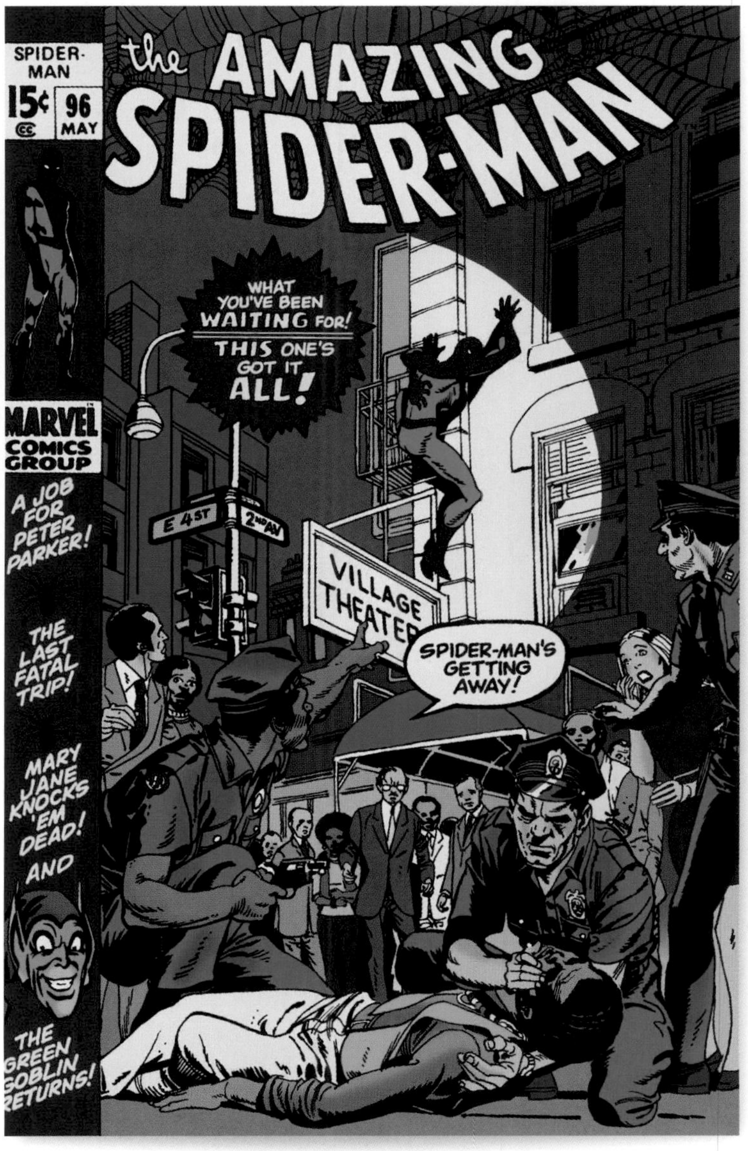
SPIDER-MAN
15¢ 96 MAY
the AMAZING SPIDER-MAN
WHAT YOU'VE BEEN WAITING FOR! THIS ONE'S GOT IT ALL!
MARVEL COMICS GROUP
A JOB FOR PETER PARKER!
THE LAST FATAL TRIP!
MARY JANE KNOCKS 'EM DEAD!
AND THE GREEN GOBLIN RETURNS!
VILLAGE THEATER
SPIDER-MAN'S GETTING AWAY!

◀ ***AMAZING SPIDER-MAN* #96**

**May 1971**
**Artist:** Gil Kane

In this classic Gil Kane piece, Marvel pushed the boundaries of the medium—this time by dealing with the subject of drug abuse. The Comics Code Authority refused to give this issue its seal of approval, but Marvel published it anyway, using Harry Osborn's addiction to highlight the dangers of drug use.

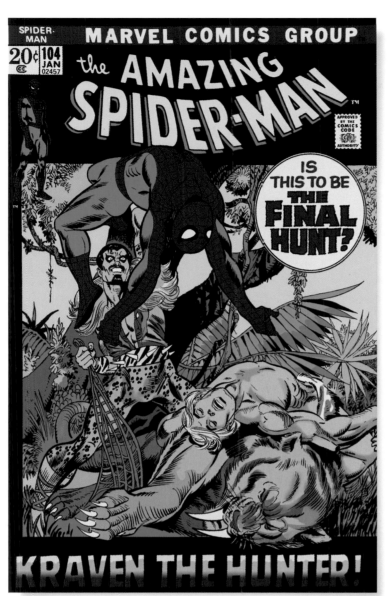

SPIDER-MAN
MARVEL COMICS GROUP
20¢ 104 JAN 02457
the AMAZING SPIDER-MAN
APPROVED BY THE COMICS CODE AUTHORITY
IS THIS TO BE THE FINAL HUNT?
KRAVEN THE HUNTER!

◀ *AMAZING SPIDER-MAN* #104

**January 1972**
**Artist:** Gil Kane

Gil Kane demonstrated a real flair for design in his work, as this Spider-Man and Kraven cover shows. Indeed, it was Kane who was responsible for the boxed-off-image layout of many of the covers produced in this era, during which he was the company's leading artist.

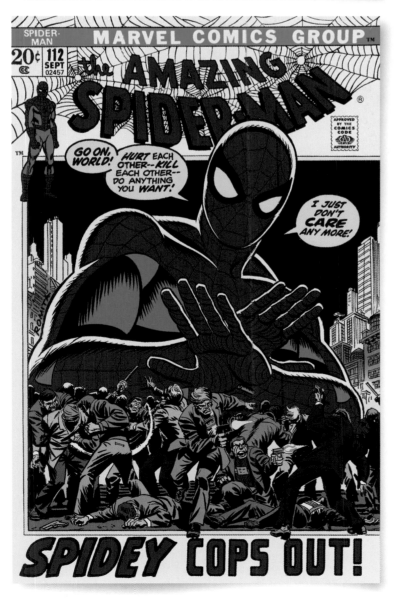

SPIDER-MAN
MARVEL COMICS GROUP
20¢ 112 SEPT 02457
the AMAZING SPIDER-MAN
APPROVED BY THE COMICS CODE AUTHORITY
GO ON, WORLD!
HURT EACH OTHER--KILL EACH OTHER--DO ANYTHING YOU WANT!
I JUST DON'T CARE ANY MORE!
SPIDEY COPS OUT!

◀ *AMAZING SPIDER-MAN* #112

**September 1972**
**Artist:** John Romita Sr.

This classic Romita cover shows the webslinger turning his back on his heroic duties, as rioters create havoc on the streets of New York (reflecting the period of civil unrest in the '70s).
The real reason for Spidey's malaise however, was revealed inside the comic: concern for his Aunt May's health, in the first part of a powerful story.

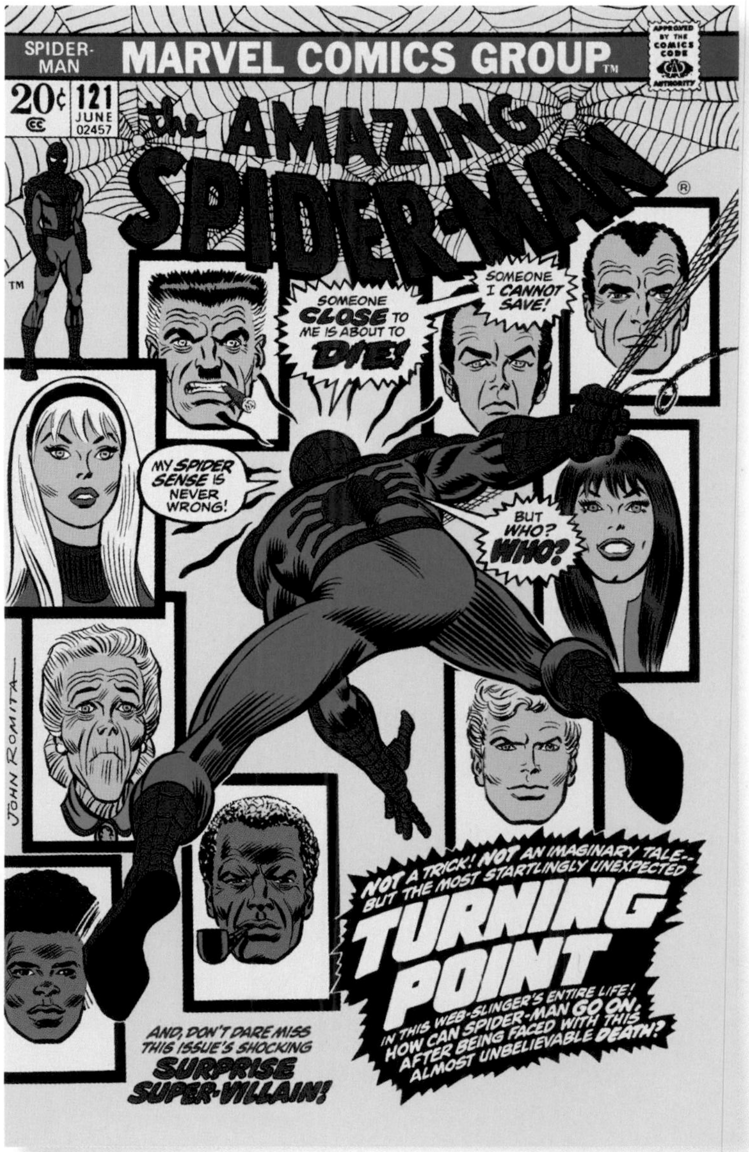
SPIDER-MAN
MARVEL COMICS GROUP
20¢ 121 JUNE 02457
the AMAZING SPIDER-MAN
SOMEONE CLOSE TO ME IS ABOUT TO DIE!
SOMEONE I CANNOT SAVE!
MY SPIDER SENSE IS NEVER WRONG!
BUT WHO? WHO?
JOHN ROMITA
NOT A TRICK! NOT AN IMAGINARY TALE-- BUT THE MOST STARTLINGLY UNEXPECTED
TURNING POINT
IN THIS WEB-SLINGER'S ENTIRE LIFE! HOW CAN SPIDER-MAN GO ON, AFTER BEING FACED WITH THIS ALMOST UNBELIEVABLE DEATH?
AND, DON'T DARE MISS THIS ISSUE'S SHOCKING SURPRISE SUPER-VILLAIN!

◀ ***AMAZING SPIDER-MAN* #121**

**June 1973**
**Artist:** John Romita Sr.

John Romita Sr.'s cover was designed to tantalize fans: Someone Spidey knew was going to die, but who would it be? The somewhat shocking answer was Gwen Stacy, thrown to her doom by the Green Goblin. This issue, and the one that followed it, signified a change not only in Spidey's life but also in Marvel's comics. If Gwen Stacy, one of the most popular supporting characters in the Marvel Universe, could be killed, it meant that no one was safe.

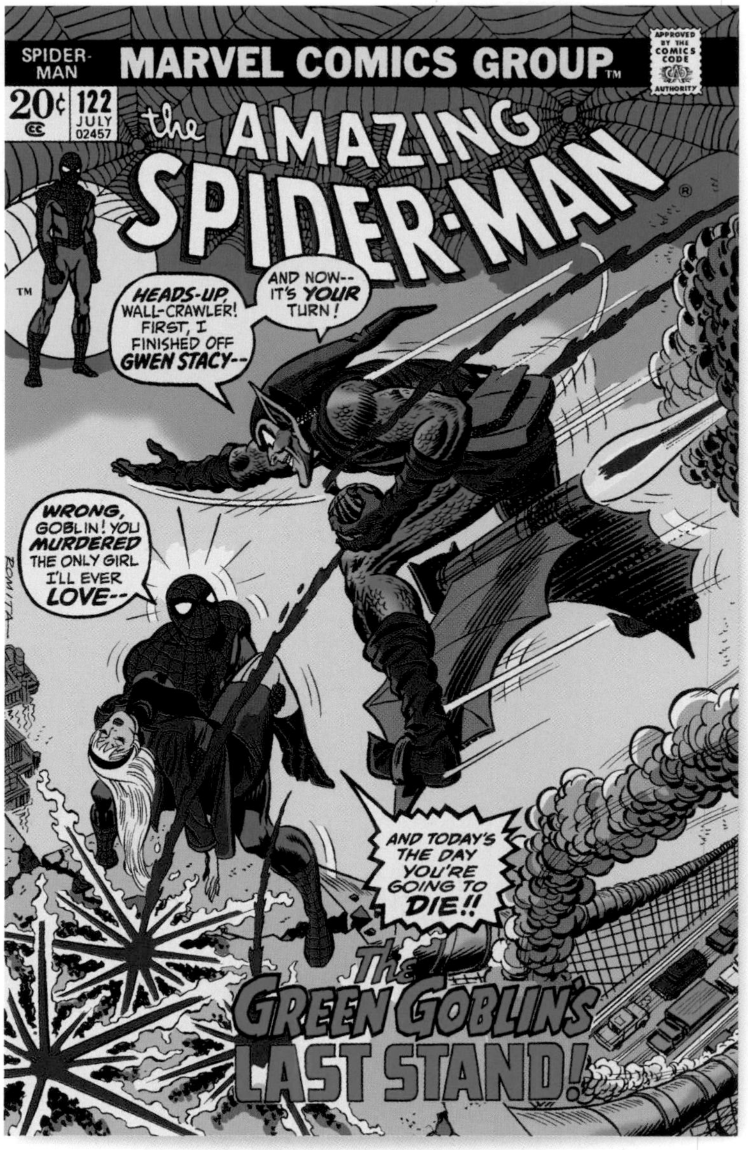
SPIDER-MAN
MARVEL COMICS GROUP
20¢ 122 JULY 02457
the AMAZING SPIDER-MAN
HEADS-UP, WALL-CRAWLER! FIRST, I FINISHED OFF GWEN STACY--
AND NOW-- IT'S YOUR TURN!
WRONG, GOBLIN! YOU MURDERED THE ONLY GIRL I'LL EVER LOVE--
AND TODAY'S THE DAY YOU'RE GOING TO DIE!!
The GREEN GOBLIN'S LAST STAND!

◀ ***AMAZING SPIDER-MAN* #122**

**July 1973**
**Artist:** John Romita Sr.

The powerful cover image of the webslinger carrying Gwen Stacy's body made this issue a must-have for Spidey fans. As the grief-stricken hero declares that her killer will pay, the cover seemed to promise the vengeance they wanted, too. Although Romita produced another outstanding cover, it was Gil Kane who got to draw the story, which appeared to show another death—this time, the Green Goblin's.

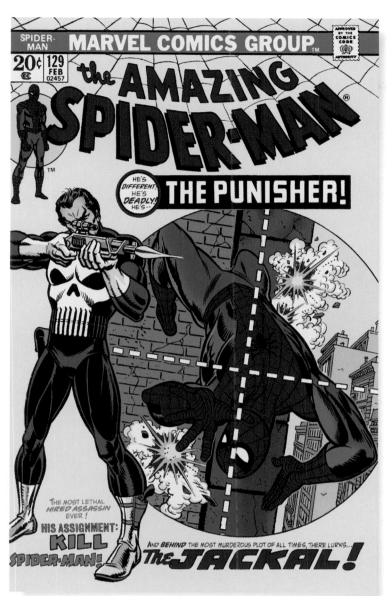

SPIDER-MAN
MARVEL COMICS GROUP
20¢ 129 FEB 02457
the AMAZING SPIDER-MAN
HE'S DIFFERENT! HE'S DEADLY! HE'S--
THE PUNISHER!
THE MOST LETHAL HIRED ASSASSIN EVER!
HIS ASSIGNMENT: KILL SPIDER-MAN!
AND BEHIND THE MOST MURDEROUS PLOT OF ALL TIMES, THERE LURKS...
The JACKAL!

◀ ***AMAZING SPIDER-MAN* #129**

**February 1974**
**Artist:** Gil Kane

The Punisher made his debut this issue, with Gil Kane providing an amazing cover of Spidey caught in the vigilante's crosshairs. John Romita Sr. inked Kane's cover, while Ross Andru illustrated the interior. The Punisher started out as a villain, but over the years he slowly became more of an anti-hero—and one of Marvel's most popular characters. In this issue, the Punisher was manipulated by the Jackal into believing that Spider-Man was a criminal.

SPIDER-MAN
MARVEL COMICS GROUP
20¢ 131 APR 02457
the AMAZING SPIDER-MAN
NO! THIS WEDDING WILL NOT TAKE PLACE!
AUNT MAY --MARRYING DOCTOR OCTOPUS? THAT'S JUST THE START-- OF THE GREATEST ACTION ISH EVER!
BUT IT WILL, WALL-CRAWLER-- OVER YOUR DEAD BODY!
WITH THIS RING, I THEE-- WEB?

◀ ***AMAZING SPIDER-MAN* #131**

**April 1974**
**Artist:** Gil Kane

This might well be the weirdest Spider-Man cover of all time—and one of the strangest stories. Gil Kane handled the cover art showing Doctor Octopus about to marry Peter Parker's Aunt May. It was crazy, but true. However, it was a marriage of convenience for Doc Ock—the villain only wanted to get his arms on an island May had inherited, which just happened to house a nuclear power plant.

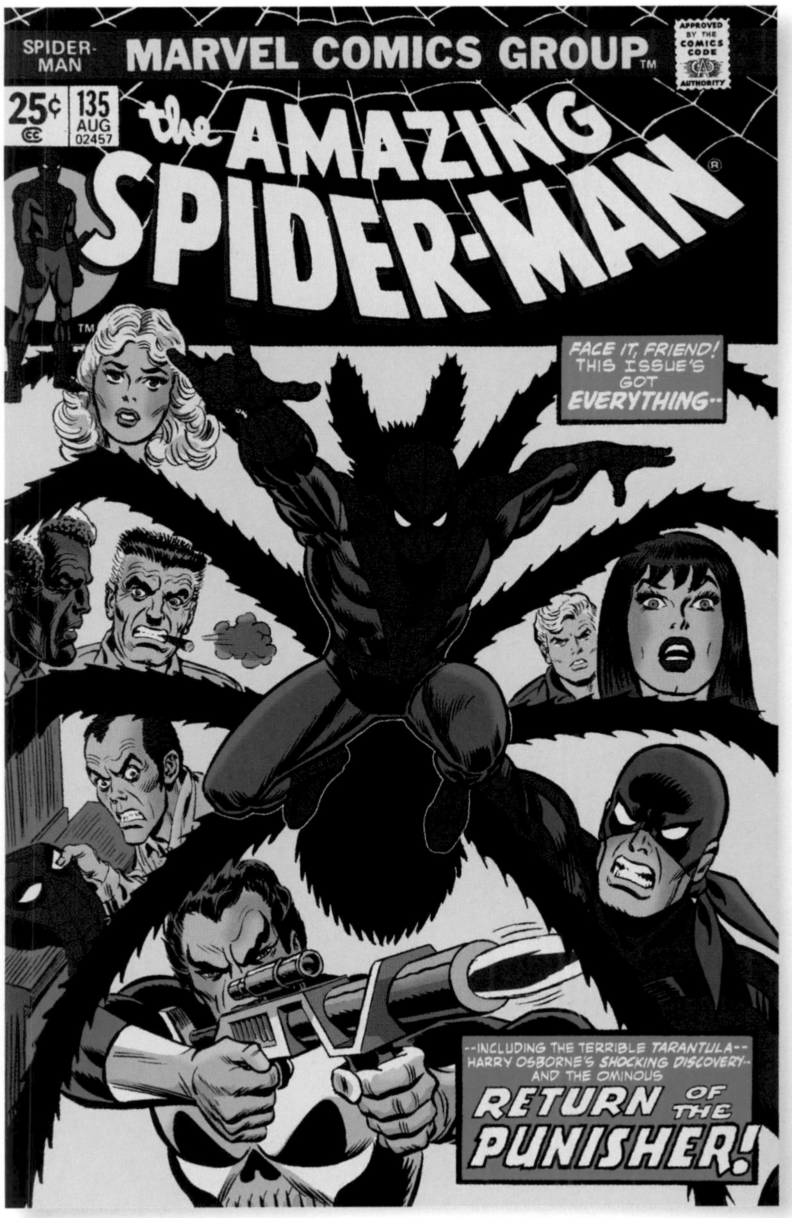
SPIDER-MAN
MARVEL COMICS GROUP
25¢ 135 AUG 02457
the AMAZING SPIDER-MAN
FACE IT, FRIEND! THIS ISSUE'S GOT EVERYTHING--
--INCLUDING THE TERRIBLE TARANTULA-- HARRY OSBORNE'S SHOCKING DISCOVERY-- AND THE OMINOUS
RETURN OF THE PUNISHER!

▲ ***AMAZING SPIDER-MAN* #135**

**August 1974**
**Artist:** John Romita Sr.

The shadowy image of a tarantula is used to nice effect on this cover, separating the quick-fire images that reflect the key moments in the story—including the return of the Punisher. The art conveys the soap-opera-style drama of Spidey's adventures and also the uniqueness of his enemies.

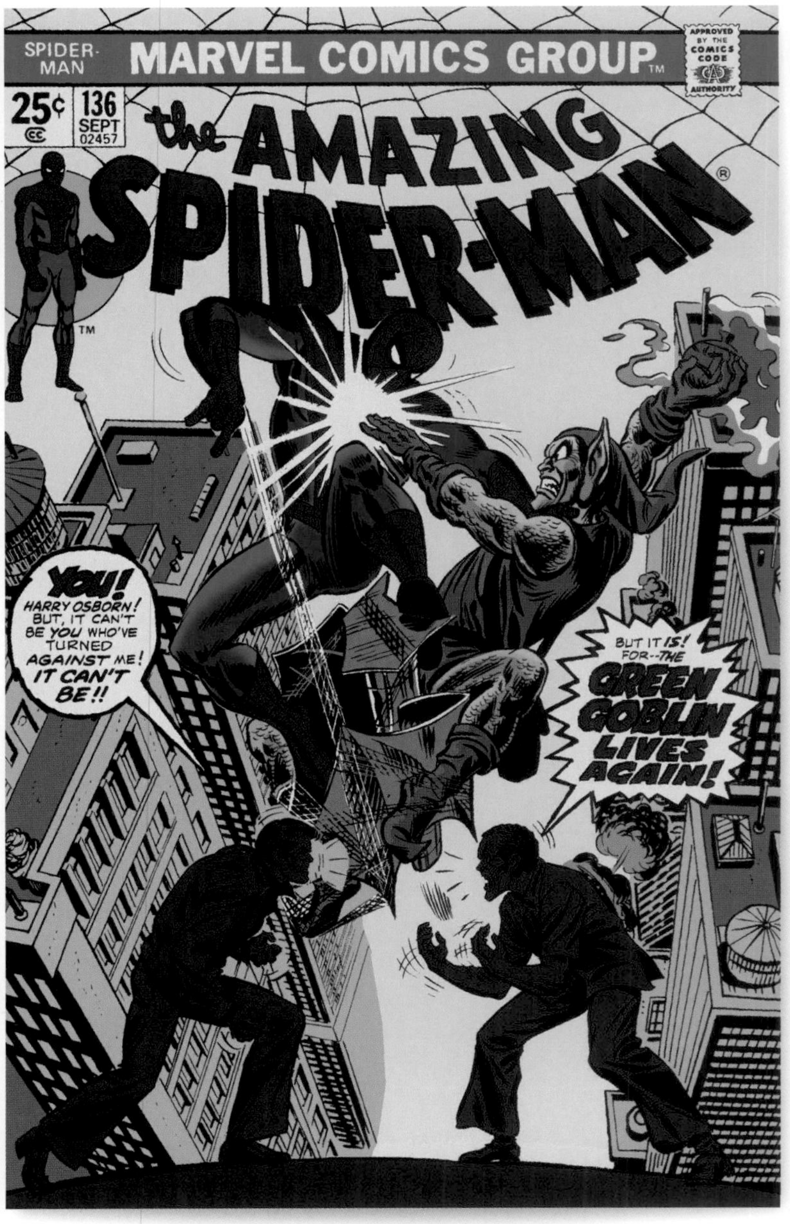
SPIDER-MAN
MARVEL COMICS GROUP
25¢ 136 SEPT 02457
the AMAZING SPIDER-MAN
YOU! HARRY OSBORN! BUT, IT CAN'T BE YOU WHO'VE TURNED AGAINST ME! IT CAN'T BE!!
BUT IT IS! FOR--THE GREEN GOBLIN LIVES AGAIN!

▲ ***AMAZING SPIDER-MAN* #136**

**September 1974**
**Artist:** John Romita Sr.

With its excellent use of coloring and layout, this John Romita masterpiece shows Harry Osborn in the role of the Green Goblin for the first time, pitting him against his closest friend, Peter Parker. The use of both friends in their civilian identities below their alter egos highlights the tense action of the issue.

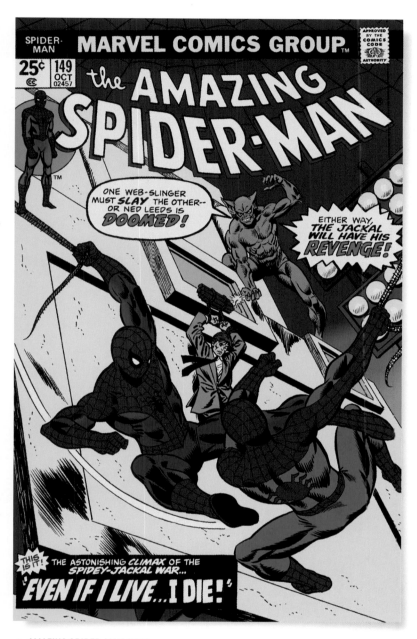

SPIDER-MAN
MARVEL COMICS GROUP
25¢ 149 OCT 02457
the AMAZING SPIDER-MAN
ONE WEB-SLINGER MUST SLAY THE OTHER-- OR NED LEEDS IS DOOMED!
EITHER WAY, THE JACKAL WILL HAVE HIS REVENGE!
THIS IS IT! THE ASTONISHING CLIMAX OF THE SPIDEY-JACKAL WAR...
'EVEN IF I LIVE...I DIE!'

▲ *AMAZING SPIDER-MAN* #149

**October 1975**
**Artist:** Gil Kane

What Spidey fan could resist buying this now classic issue after seeing its stunning Gil Kane cover? The webslinger met his match in this issue—literally. He was forced to fight his own clone—with the winner still not sure whether he was the real Spider-Man or just a copy.

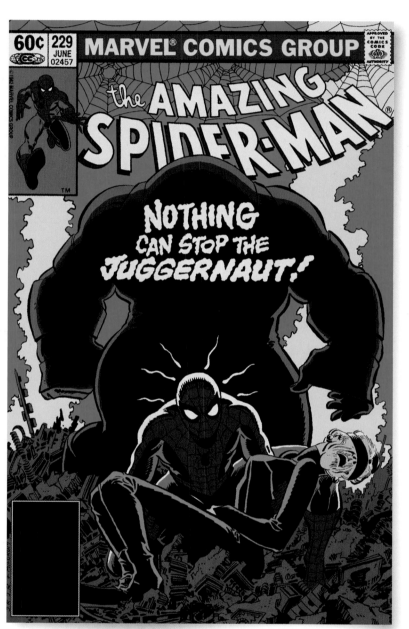

60¢ 229 JUNE 02457
MARVEL® COMICS GROUP
the AMAZING SPIDER-MAN
NOTHING CAN STOP THE JUGGERNAUT!

▲ *AMAZING SPIDER-MAN* #229

**June 1982**
**Artist:** John Romita Jr.

This is often voted one of the all-time great Spider-Man stories. Writer Roger Stern and artist John Romita Jr. teamed up to pit Spidey against the Juggernaut. The cover proves the younger Romita had all the skills of his father when it came to creating brilliant, eye-catching covers.

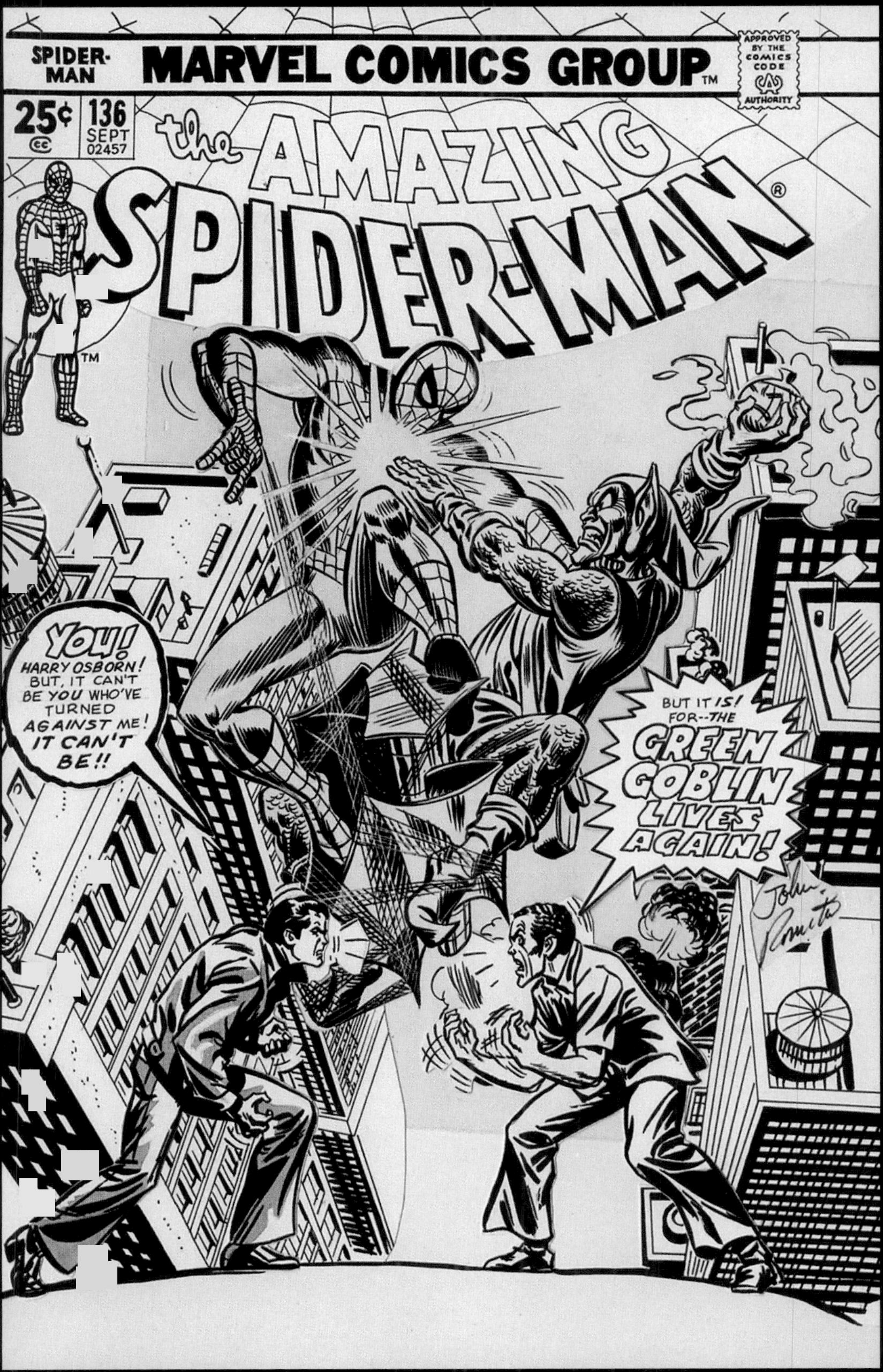
SPIDER-MAN
MARVEL COMICS GROUP
APPROVED BY THE COMICS CODE AUTHORITY
25¢ 136 SEPT 02457
the AMAZING SPIDER-MAN
YOU! HARRY OSBORN! BUT, IT CAN'T BE YOU WHO'VE TURNED AGAINST ME! IT CAN'T BE!!
BUT IT IS! FOR--THE GREEN GOBLIN LIVES AGAIN!
John Romita

1.

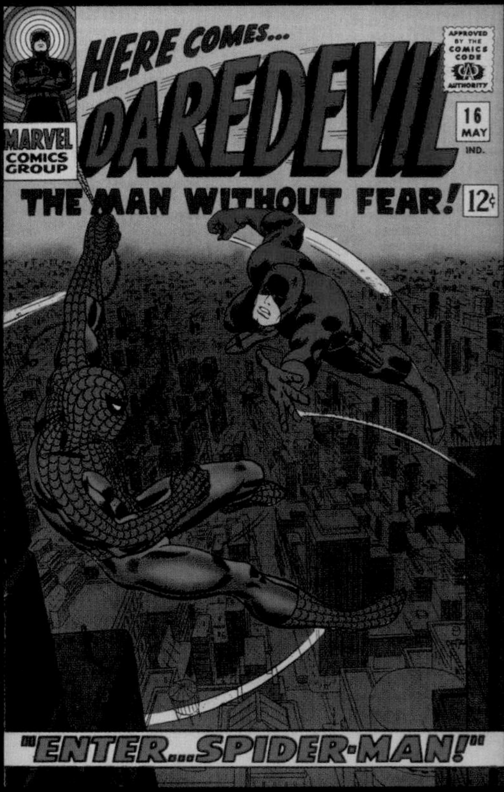
HERE COMES... DAREDEVIL
MARVEL COMICS GROUP
16 MAY
THE MAN WITHOUT FEAR! 12¢
"ENTER...SPIDER-MAN!"

2.

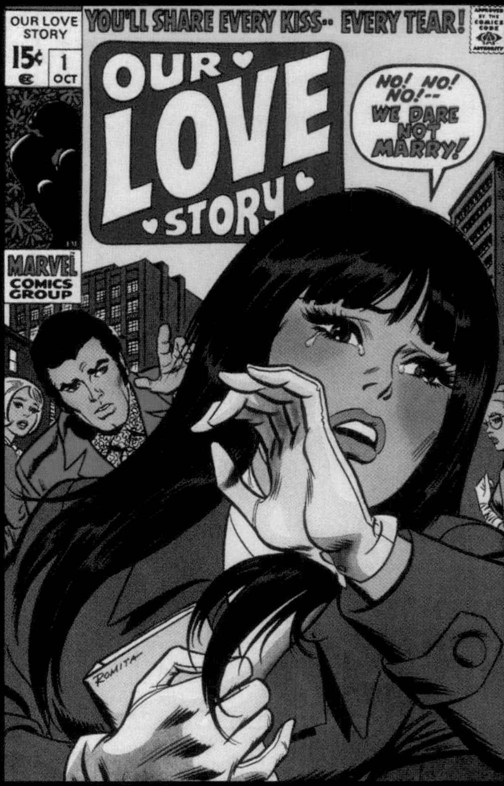
OUR LOVE STORY 15¢ 1 OCT
YOU'LL SHARE EVERY KISS-- EVERY TEAR!
OUR LOVE STORY
NO! NO! NO!-- WE DARE NOT MARRY!
MARVEL COMICS GROUP
ROMITA

3.

# JOHN ROMITA SR.

John Romita Sr. is one of the most important artists ever to grace Marvel's hallowed halls. Not only did his clear, stylish artwork make Spider-Man a household name, but his role as Marvel's Art Editor led him to help visualize a vast swath of Marvel heroes—including Wolverine, the Punisher, and Luke Cage—and produce some of the company's most iconic covers. Before he started on Spider-Man, Romita had mostly drawn romance titles for DC Comics. He brought this style (good-looking characters created with a clean line) over to his Super-Hero work. Taking over *Amazing Spider-Man* from Steve Ditko, Romita naturally made all of the characters better looking, and also created Spidey's girlfriend, Mary Jane Watson. The comic soon became Marvel's best-selling title.

**1. *AMAZING SPIDER-MAN* #136**

**September 1974**

This black-and-white cover mock-up is a great example of Romita's fine talents as a draftsman. Romita skillfully conveys the anger in the figures of Peter and Harry, while the dramatic layout adds a real sense of danger to the scene.

**2. *DAREDEVIL* #16**

**May 1966**

Stan Lee used this cover as a test piece to see if Romita could handle illustrating the webslinger. The motion of the two heroes clashing on the cover, and the stunning interior work, proved to Lee that Romita was the perfect choice to follow Ditko.

**3. *OUR LOVE STORY* #1**

**October 1969**

Romita had cut his teeth on romance comics and continued to illustrate the occasional issue while working for Marvel. As this cover shows, Romita was a master of conveying emotion, as well as making his characters both attractive and realistic.

**4. *AMAZING SPIDER-MAN* #123**

**August 1973**

During his stint as Marvel's Art Editor, Romita helped create a number of heroes, including Luke Cage. The new character soon guest-starred in *Amazing Spider-Man*, and Romita combined perspective and action to create a dramatic cover.

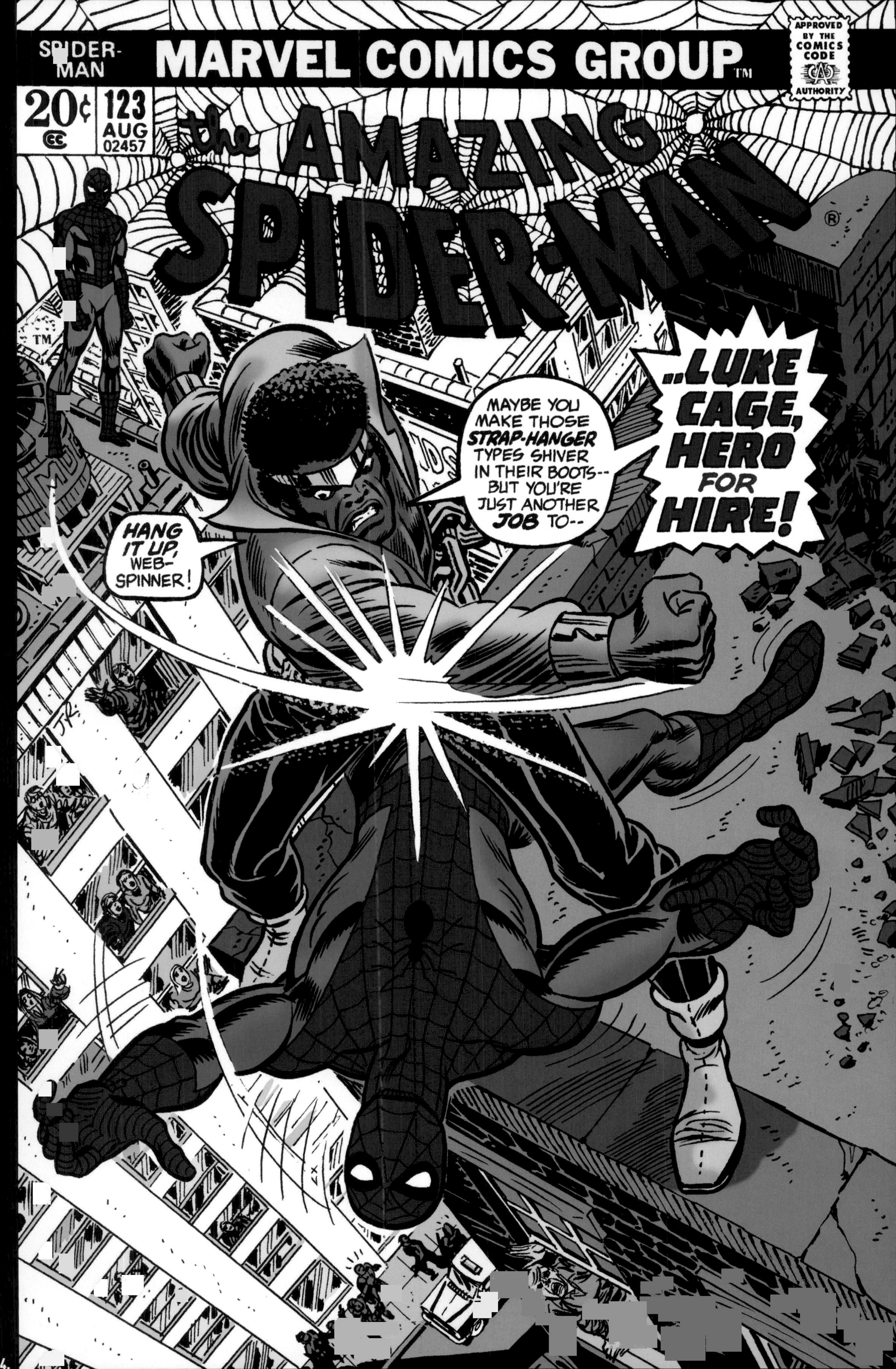
SPIDER-MAN
MARVEL COMICS GROUP
APPROVED BY THE COMICS CODE AUTHORITY
20¢
123
AUG
02457
the AMAZING SPIDER-MAN
HANG IT UP, WEB-SPINNER!
MAYBE YOU MAKE THOSE STRAP-HANGER TYPES SHIVER IN THEIR BOOTS-- BUT YOU'RE JUST ANOTHER JOB TO--
..LUKE CAGE, HERO FOR HIRE!

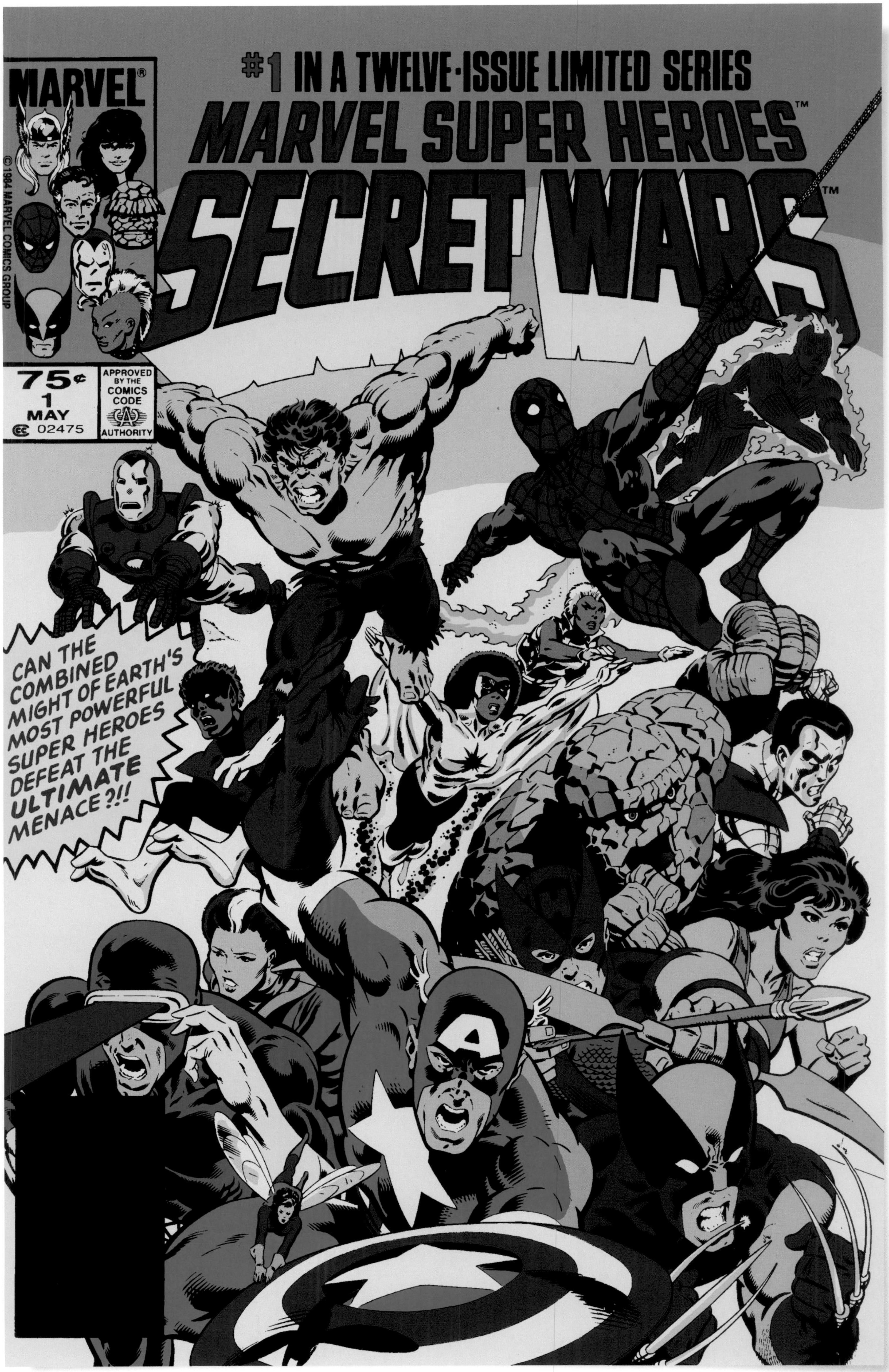
MARVEL®
© 1984 MARVEL COMICS GROUP
75¢
1
MAY
02475
APPROVED BY THE COMICS CODE AUTHORITY
#1 IN A TWELVE-ISSUE LIMITED SERIES
MARVEL SUPER HEROES™
SECRET WARS™
CAN THE COMBINED MIGHT OF EARTH'S MOST POWERFUL SUPER HEROES DEFEAT THE ULTIMATE MENACE?!!

***AMAZING SPIDER-MAN* #252 ▶**

**May 1984**
**Artist:** Ron Frenz

Frenz's striking image was a homage to Jack Kirby's original *Amazing Fantasy* issue #15 cover *(see p50)*. This Spidey issue came out the same month as the *Secret Wars* series, and it tantalized fans by showing Spider-Man in a new black costume, leaving them hungry to find out how he came to be wearing it.

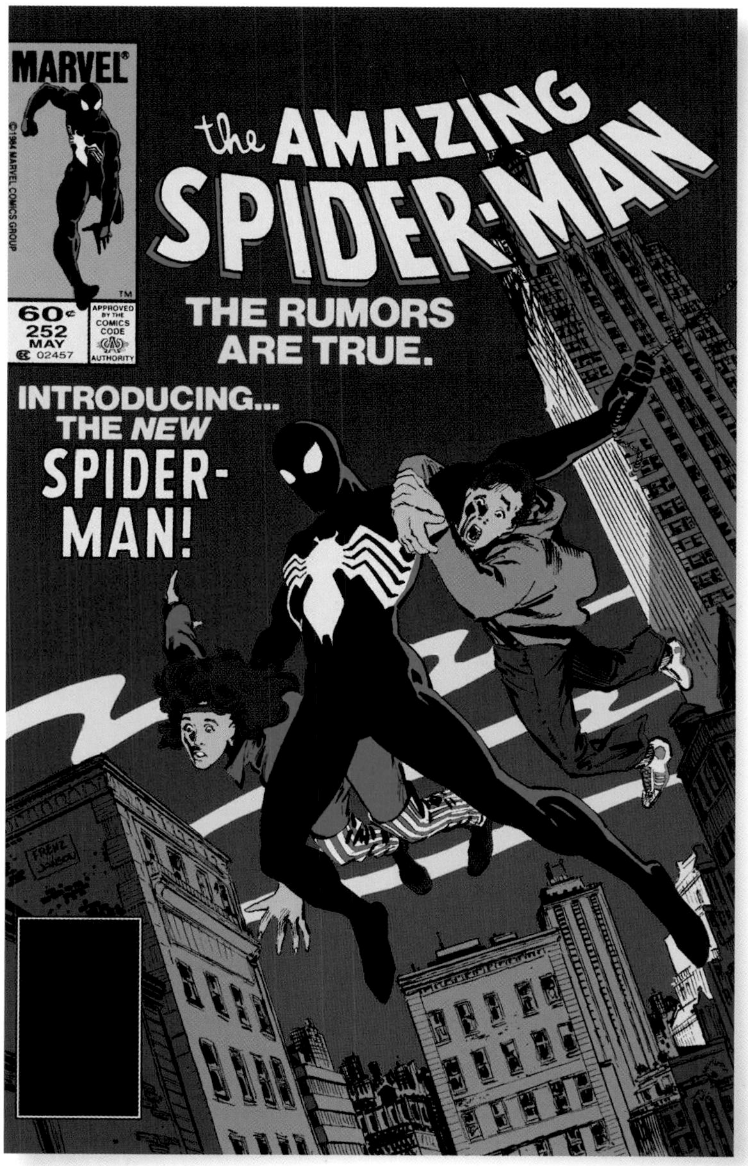
MARVEL
the AMAZING SPIDER-MAN
60¢ 252 MAY
THE RUMORS ARE TRUE.
INTRODUCING... THE NEW SPIDER-MAN!

***MARVEL SUPER HEROES SECRET WARS* #8 ▶**

**December 1984**
**Artist:** Mike Zeck

Readers had to wait until issue #8 of *Secret Wars* to learn about Spidey's new costume and how he got it. Mike Zeck's cover not only showed the webslinger dressed in black, but also hinted at the devastation caused by the wars.

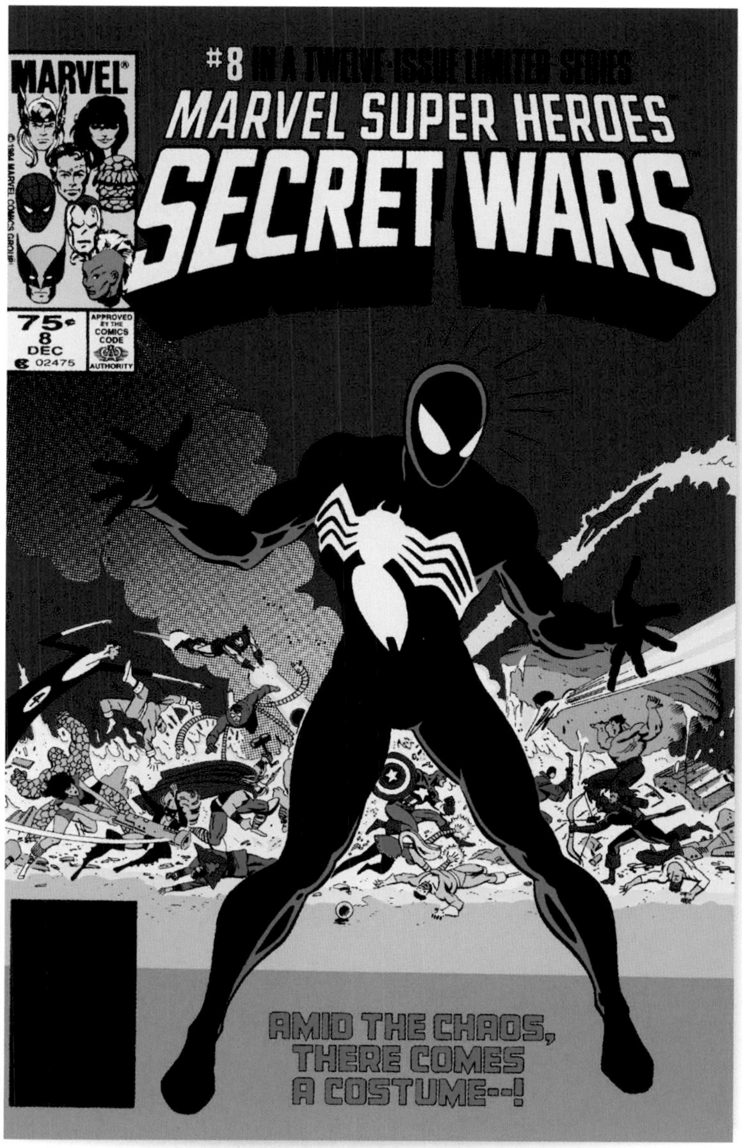
#8 IN A TWELVE-ISSUE LIMITED SERIES
MARVEL
MARVEL SUPER HEROES
SECRET WARS
75¢ 8 DEC
AMID THE CHAOS, THERE COMES A COSTUME--!

**◀ *MARVEL SUPER HEROES SECRET WARS* #1**

**May 1984**
**Artist:** Mike Zeck

It was the biggest crossover series of the decade as Marvel's great heroes were transported to the distant planet of Battleworld to fight their greatest enemies. The cover was by Mike Zeck, who also illustrated the 12-part series. It was the first epic to bring together so many characters in such a long series, and Zeck's artistic expertise truly brings the exciting cast to life in this piece.

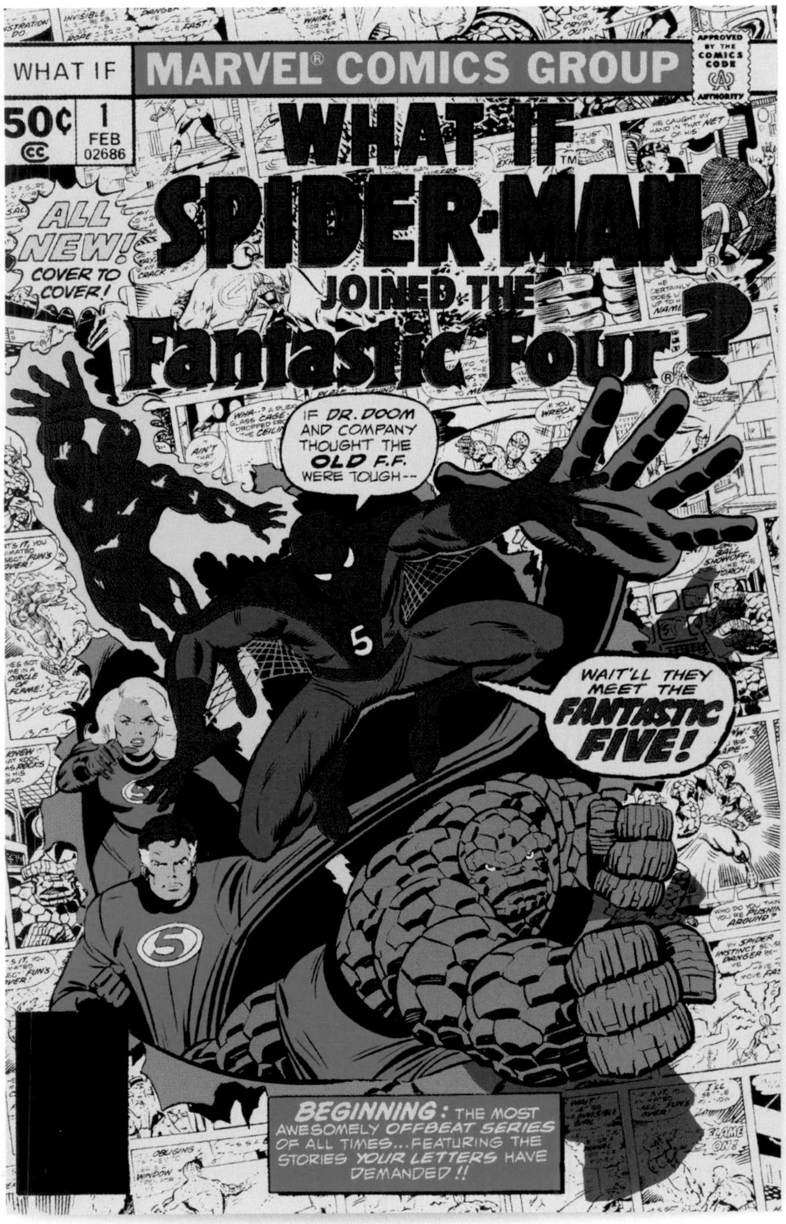
WHAT IF
MARVEL® COMICS GROUP
50¢ 1 FEB 02686
WHAT IF SPIDER-MAN JOINED THE Fantastic Four?
ALL NEW! COVER TO COVER!
IF DR. DOOM AND COMPANY THOUGHT THE OLD F.F. WERE TOUGH--
WAIT'LL THEY MEET THE FANTASTIC FIVE!
BEGINNING: THE MOST AWESOMELY OFFBEAT SERIES OF ALL TIMES...FEATURING THE STORIES YOUR LETTERS HAVE DEMANDED!!

▲ ***WHAT IF?* #1**

**February 1977**
**Artist:** Jim Craig

The *What If?* series was a simple but brilliant concept. It introduced readers to parallel Earths where some of Marvel's most important storylines had decidedly different outcomes. Jim Craig's cover showing Spidey as part of the Fantastic Five was an intriguing concept—and a great way to start the series.

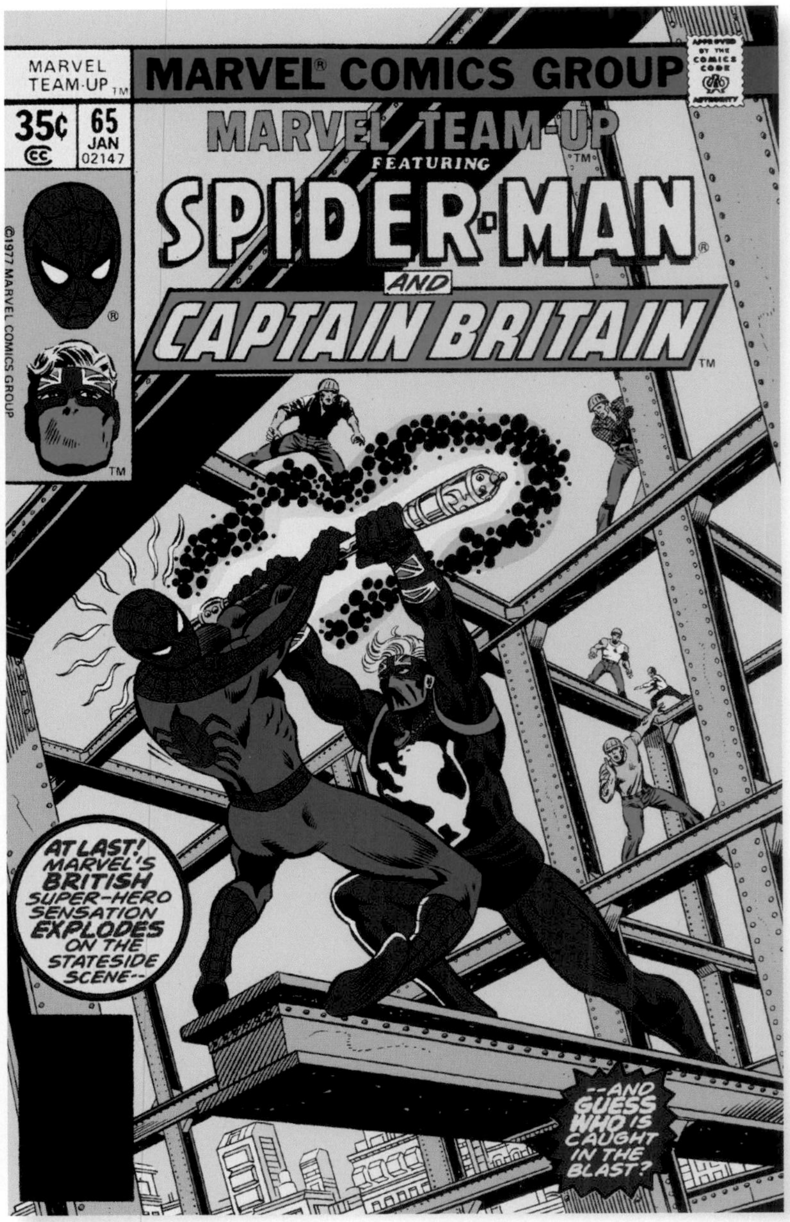
MARVEL TEAM-UP
MARVEL® COMICS GROUP
35¢ 65 JAN 02147
MARVEL TEAM-UP FEATURING
SPIDER-MAN AND CAPTAIN BRITAIN
©1977 MARVEL COMICS GROUP
AT LAST! MARVEL'S BRITISH SUPER-HERO SENSATION EXPLODES ON THE STATESIDE SCENE--
--AND GUESS WHO IS CAUGHT IN THE BLAST?

▲ ***MARVEL TEAM-UP* #65**

**January 1978**
**Artist:** George Pérez

Captain Britain made his first US appearance in this issue, alongside Spider-Man. George Pérez produced an exciting cover to introduce the hero to a new audience. Captain Britain's appearance led to a traditional comic-book misunderstanding with the two heroes coming to blows before teaming up to stop their true enemy, Arcade.

***MARVEL FANFARE* #6** ▶

**January 1983**
**Artist:** P. Craig Russell

*Marvel Fanfare* was a prestige-format Marvel comic that showcased the work of the very best artists. Even by the high standards of the series, this P. Craig Russell cover of the Scarlet Witch and Spider-Man is something special. Russell has only produced a limited amount of comic-book work, but his contributions have been outstanding.

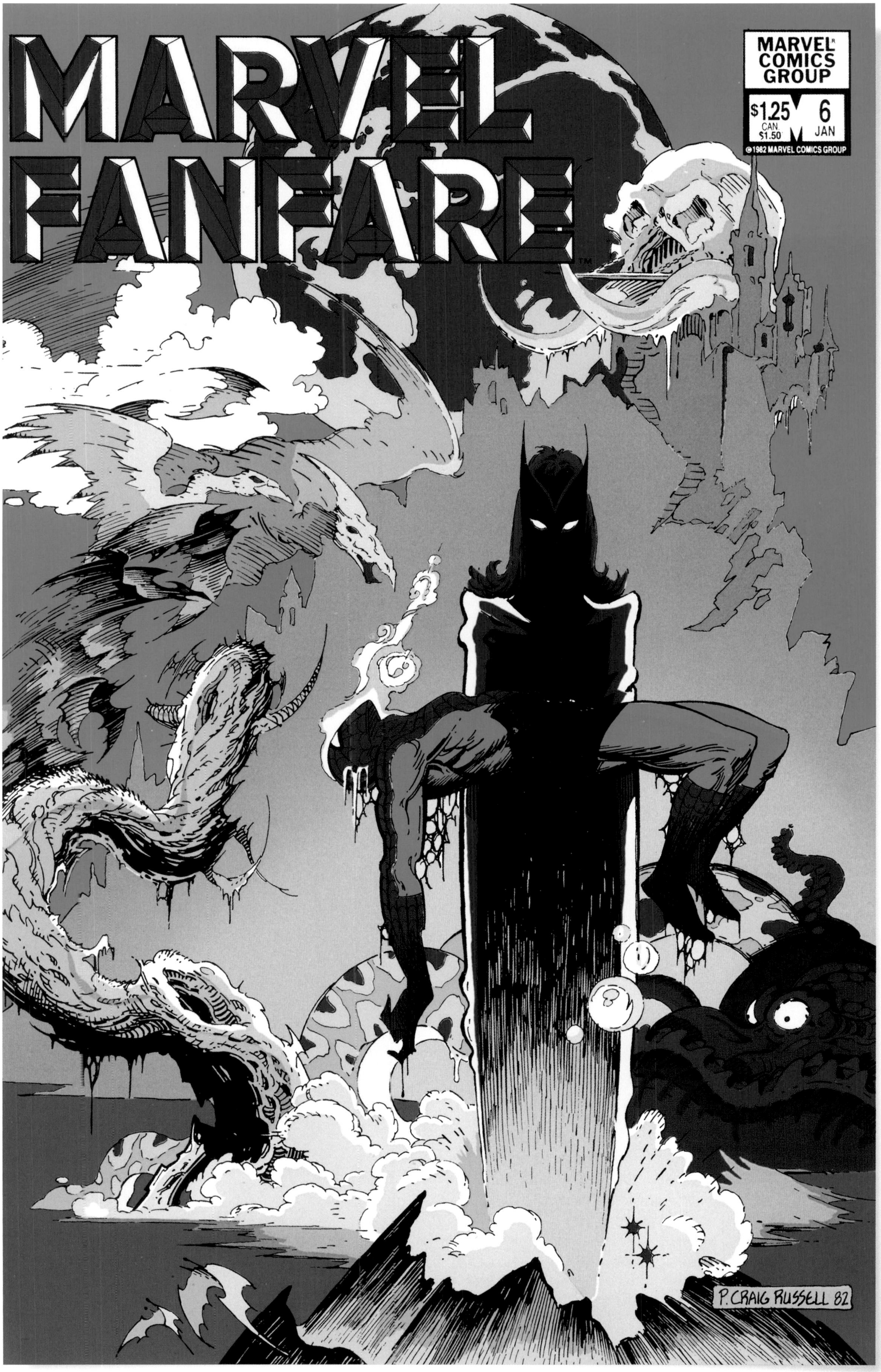
MARVEL FANFARE
MARVEL COMICS GROUP
$1.25 CAN $1.50
6 JAN
©1982 MARVEL COMICS GROUP
P. CRAIG RUSSELL 82

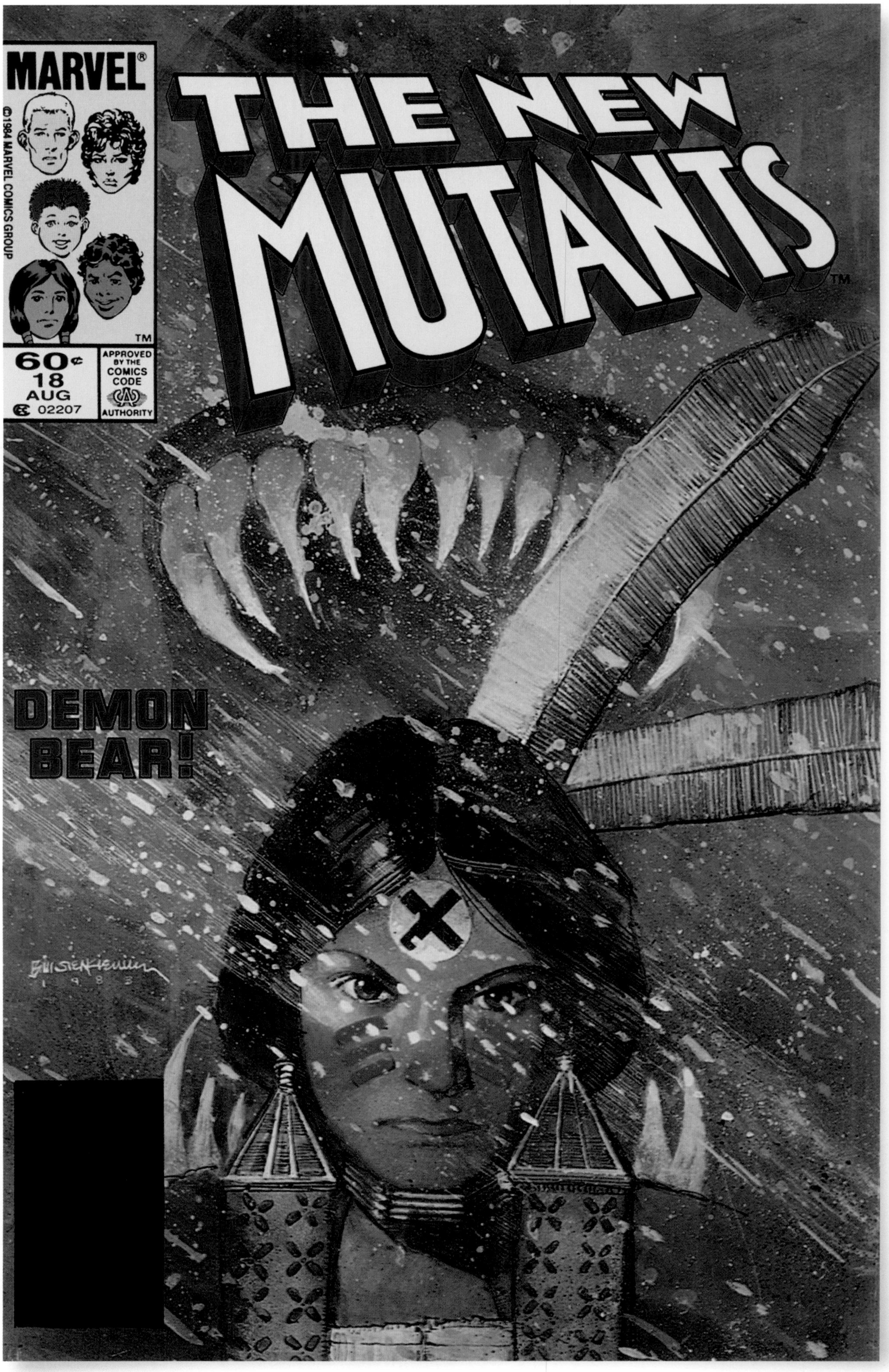
MARVEL
©1984 MARVEL COMICS GROUP
THE NEW MUTANTS
60¢
18
AUG
02207
APPROVED BY THE COMICS CODE AUTHORITY
DEMON BEAR!

▲ ***THE NEW MUTANTS* #18**

**August 1984**
**Artist:** Bill Sienkiewicz

One of the most-loved eras of *The New Mutants* started when Bill Sienkiewicz joined writer Chris Claremont on the book. Sienkiewicz had already been working for Marvel for several years, but it was during his work on *The New Mutants* that he really developed his famous expressionistic style. The cover of his first issue signified the start of the classic "Demon Bear" saga and focused on Dani Moonstar (aka Mirage), with help from Sienkiewicz's haunting portrait.

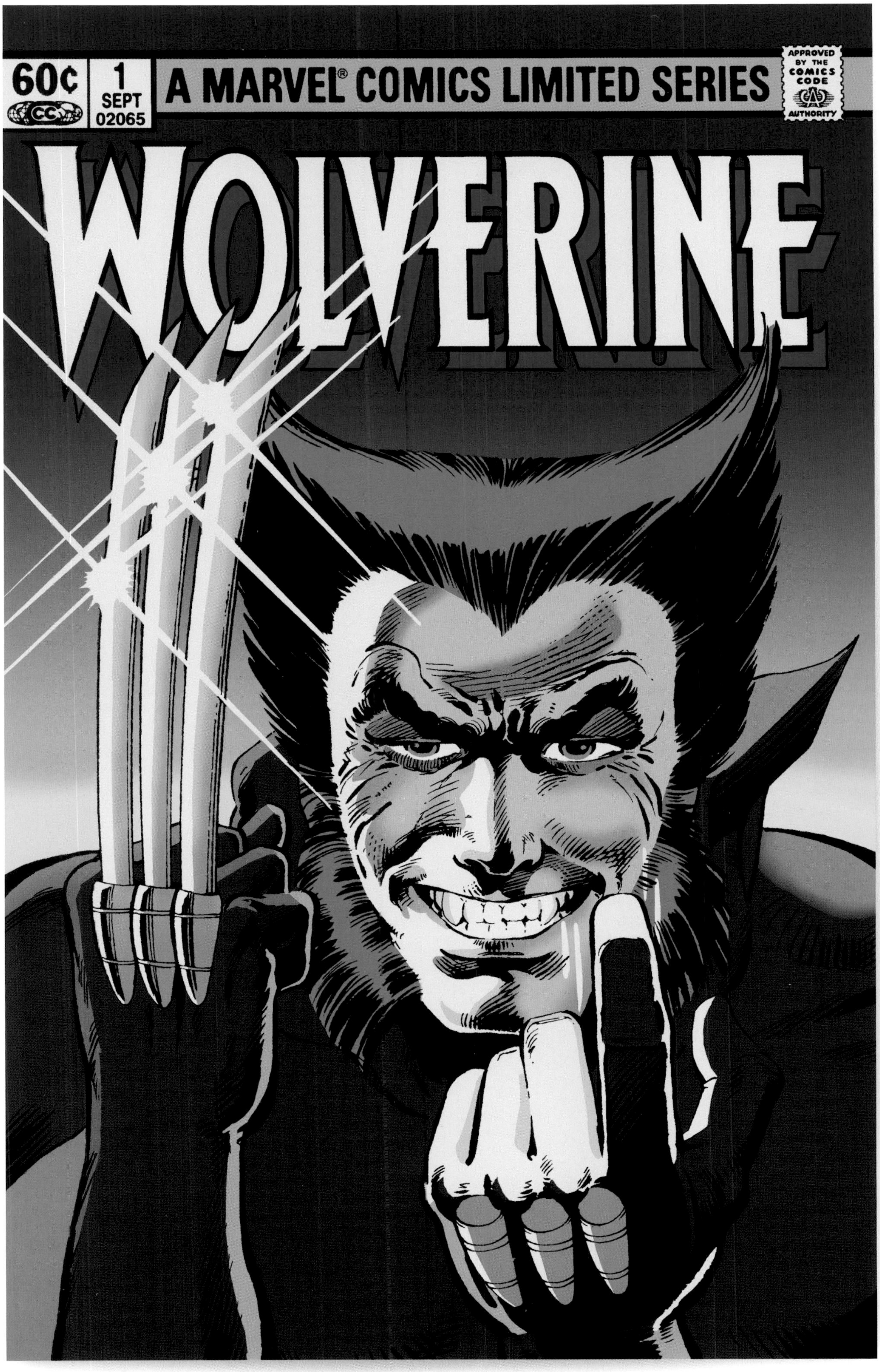
60¢
1
SEPT
02065
A MARVEL® COMICS LIMITED SERIES
APPROVED BY THE COMICS CODE AUTHORITY
WOLVERINE

▲ *WOLVERINE* #1

**September 1982**
**Artist:** Frank Miller

Wolverine's first long-awaited series saw one of Marvel's hottest artists, Frank Miller, team with writer Chris Claremont. Miller's love of Japanese manga and film was reflected in the storyline, while his cover art showcases his exceptional ability to add a sense of realism to the toughest of characters.

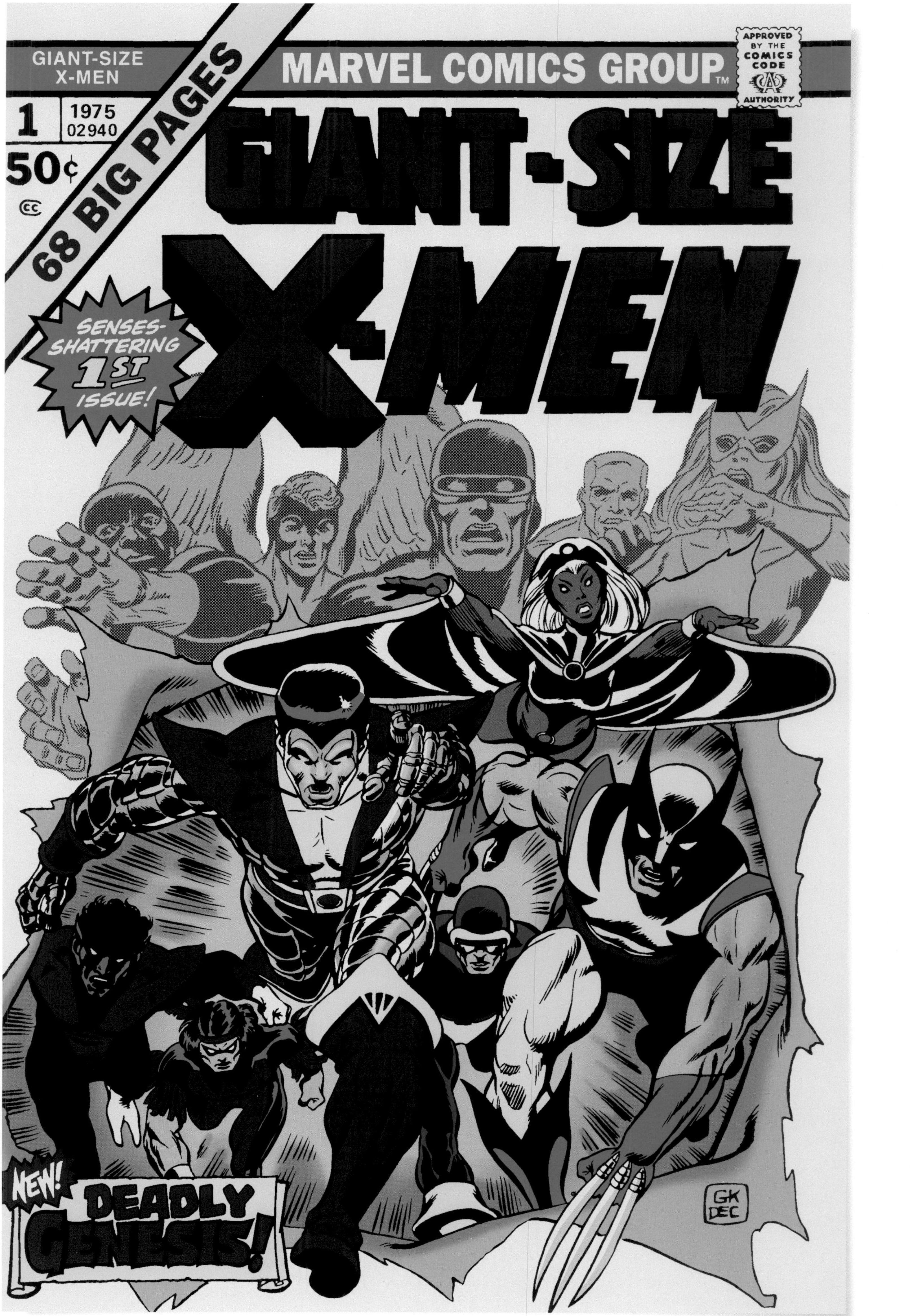
GIANT-SIZE X-MEN
MARVEL COMICS GROUP
APPROVED BY THE COMICS CODE AUTHORITY
1
1975
02940
50¢
68 BIG PAGES
GIANT-SIZE X-MEN
SENSES-SHATTERING 1ST ISSUE!
NEW! DEADLY GENESIS!
GK DEC

### ◀ *GIANT-SIZE X-MEN* #1

**May 1975**
**Artists:** Gil Kane and Dave Cockrum

Few comics have changed the very nature of a company the way the new, more international X-Men title changed Marvel. Thanks to the new team's success, the X-Men didn't just become a comic series, but an entire franchise—and it all began with this bumper issue and one spectacular, and much copied, cover. Gil Kane's stylish and striking cover (inked by the new team's co-creator, Dave Cockrum) shows the all-new X-Men bursting out, as the old team look on in shock.

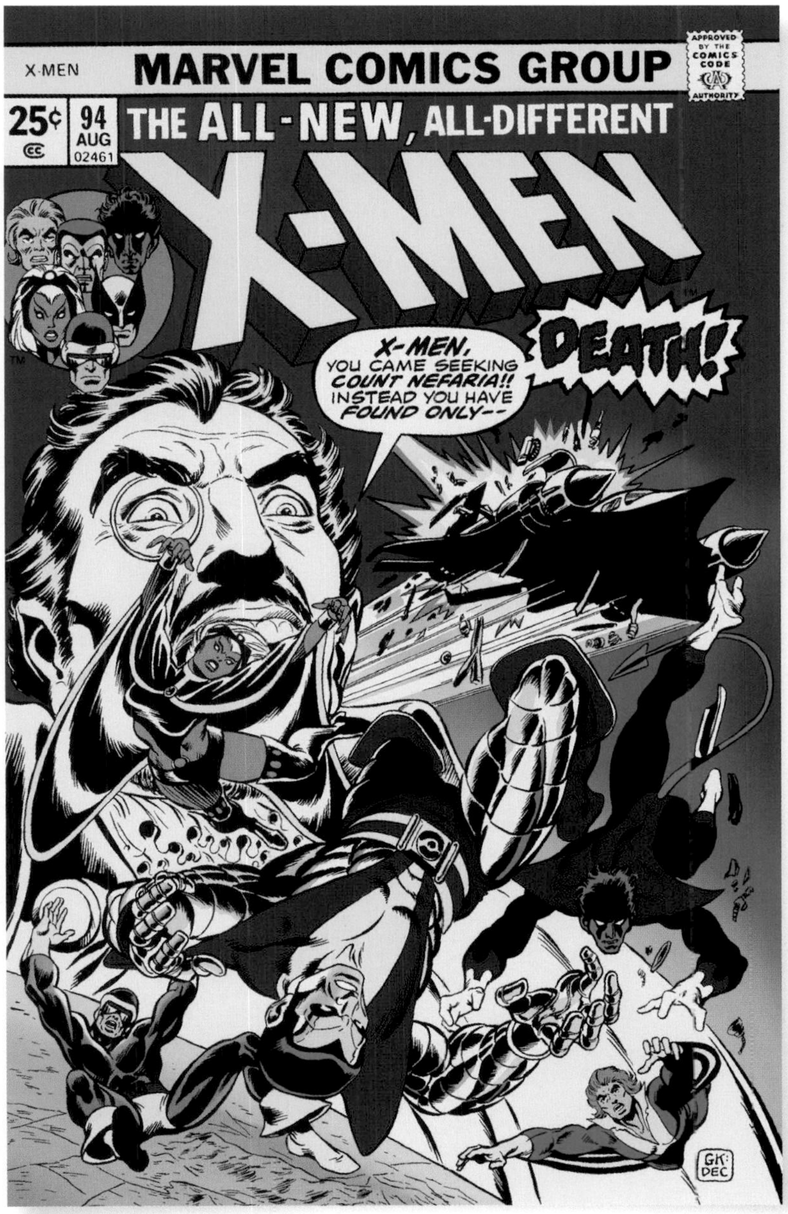
X-MEN
MARVEL COMICS GROUP
APPROVED BY THE COMICS CODE AUTHORITY
25¢ 94 AUG 02461
THE ALL-NEW, ALL-DIFFERENT
X-MEN
X-MEN, YOU CAME SEEKING COUNT NEFARIA!! INSTEAD YOU HAVE FOUND ONLY--
DEATH!
GK/DEC

### ▲ *X-MEN* #94

**August 1975**
**Artists:** Gil Kane and Dave Cockrum

Following the success of *Giant-Size X-Men*, the team's regular book was started up again, continuing the numbering from the previous incarnation of the team. Dave Cockrum and Gil Kane again joined forces to create a dramatic cover showing the villainous Count Nefaria sending the mutant team to their doom. Writer Chris Claremont also joined on this issue.

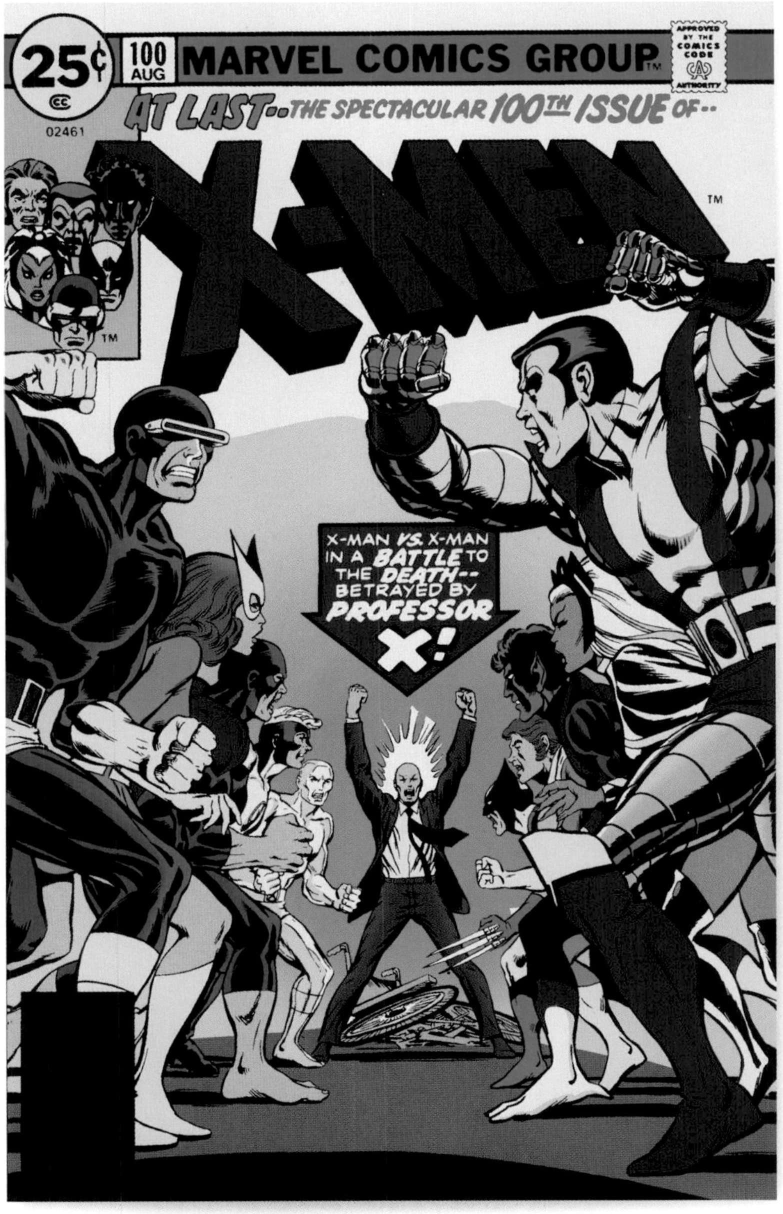
25¢ 100 AUG 02461
MARVEL COMICS GROUP
APPROVED BY THE COMICS CODE AUTHORITY
AT LAST--THE SPECTACULAR 100TH ISSUE OF--
X-MEN
X-MAN VS. X-MAN IN A BATTLE TO THE DEATH-- BETRAYED BY PROFESSOR X!

### ▲ *X-MEN* #100

**August 1976**
**Artist:** Dave Cockrum

The cover of this centenary issue shows the original X-Men team facing off against their successors. Writer Chris Claremont was starting to come into his own after six issues. The cover demonstrates how, alongside Dave Cockrum (and later John Byrne), Claremont was developing and expanding the X-Men universe.

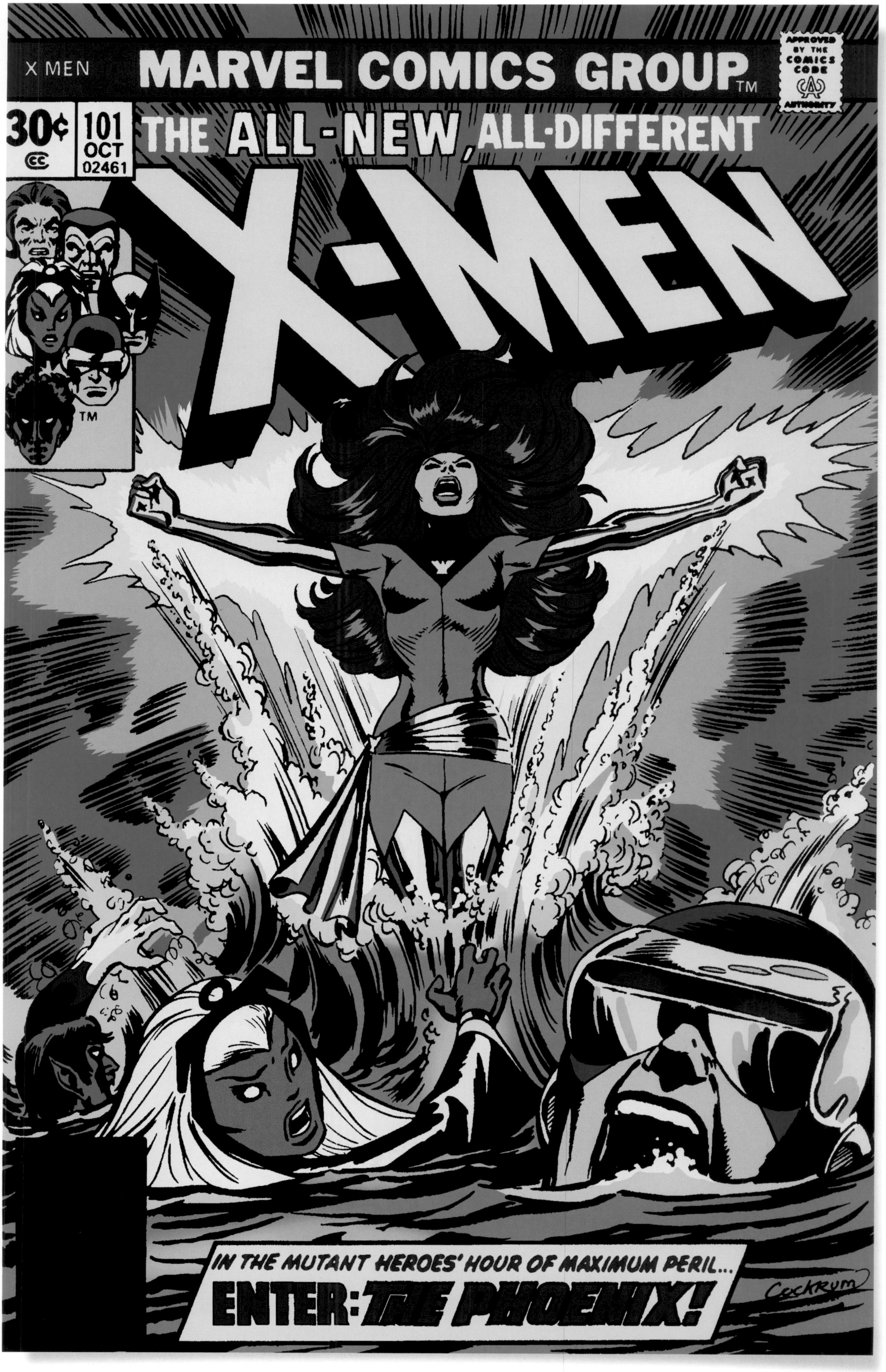
X MEN
MARVEL COMICS GROUP
APPROVED BY THE COMICS CODE AUTHORITY
30¢
101 OCT 02461
THE ALL-NEW, ALL-DIFFERENT
X-MEN
IN THE MUTANT HEROES' HOUR OF MAXIMUM PERIL...
ENTER: THE PHOENIX!
COCKRUM

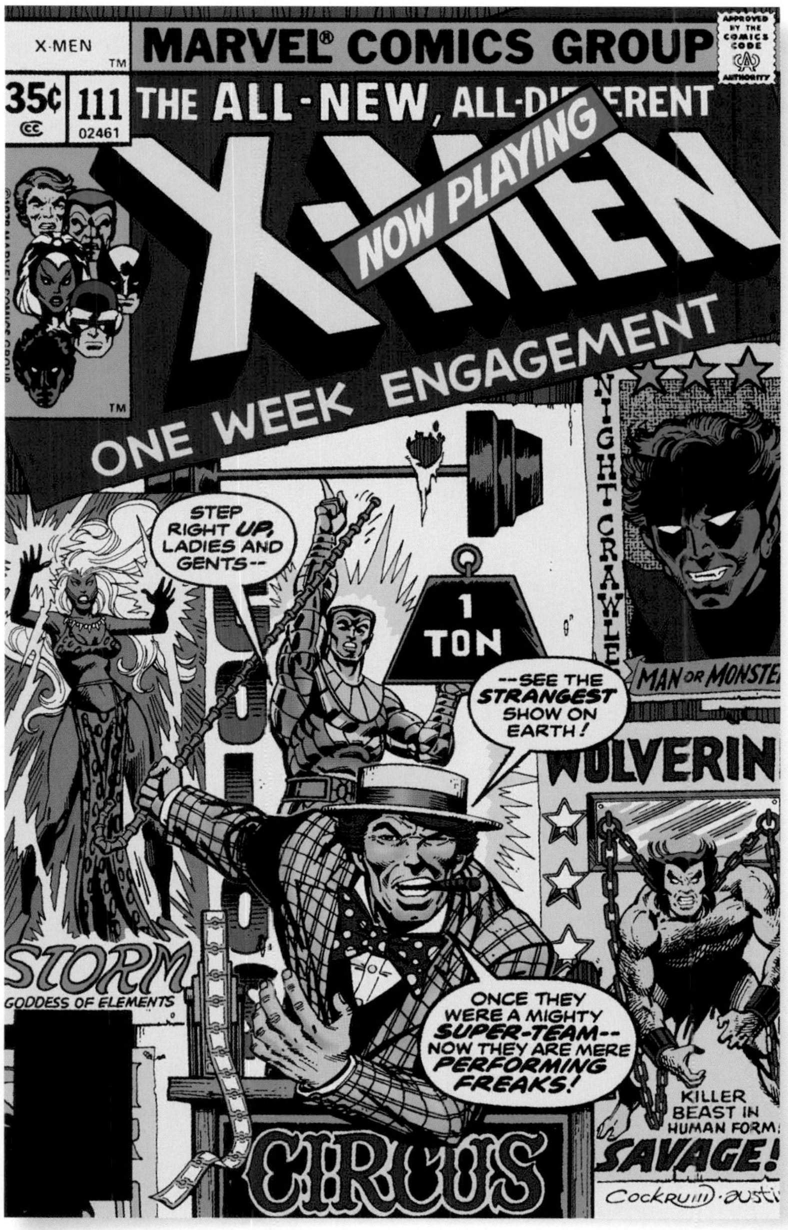
X-MEN
MARVEL® COMICS GROUP
35¢
111
02461
X-MEN
NOW PLAYING
ONE WEEK ENGAGEMENT
STEP RIGHT UP, LADIES AND GENTS--
1 TON
--SEE THE STRANGEST SHOW ON EARTH!
NIGHTCRAWLER
MAN OR MONSTER
WOLVERIN
STORM
GODDESS OF ELEMENTS
ONCE THEY WERE A MIGHTY SUPER-TEAM-- NOW THEY ARE MERE PERFORMING FREAKS!
KILLER BEAST IN HUMAN FORM:
SAVAGE!
CIRCUS

▲ *X-MEN* #111

**June 1978**
**Artist:** Dave Cockrum

While the new *X-Men* comic was proving successful, it was only when penciller John Byrne joined the book (with issue #108) that the series became the publishing juggernaut that it is today. Dave Cockrum continued to contribute some outstanding covers for the team though, including this one, showing the X-Men trapped in a mysterious circus freak-show.

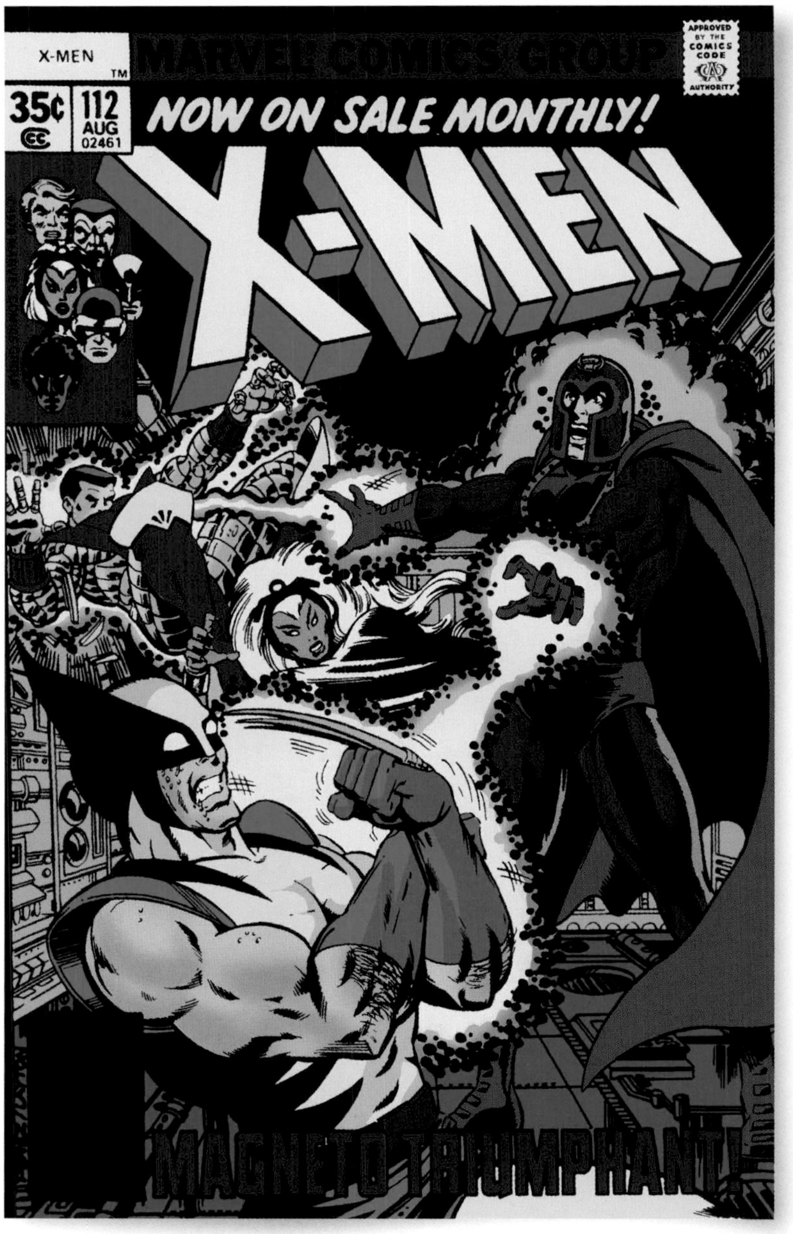
X-MEN
MARVEL COMICS GROUP
35¢
112
AUG
02461
NOW ON SALE MONTHLY!
X-MEN
MAGNETO TRIUMPHANT!

▲ *X-MEN* #112

**August 1982**
**Artists:** Dave Cockrum and George Pérez

Dave Cockrum and George Pérez worked together to create this tense cover, while John Byrne handled the interior art. Byrne also suggested to writer Chris Claremont that Wolverine could be given a larger role in the team. So on the cover, Wolverine takes center stage—but his Adamantium skeleton proved all too easy for Magneto to control.

◀ *X-MEN* #101

**October 1976**
**Artist:** Dave Cockrum

With the new X-Men team edgier than the previous incarnation, it was time to give Jean Grey (Marvel Girl) a makeover. When Jean Grey died and came back as Phoenix, it not only inspired one of the most striking *X-Men* covers of all time, but it also created a character who would take the lead in many of Marvel's best-loved X-Men-related epics. In many ways, this cover signifies when the "All-New, All-Different" X-Men really started to come into their own.

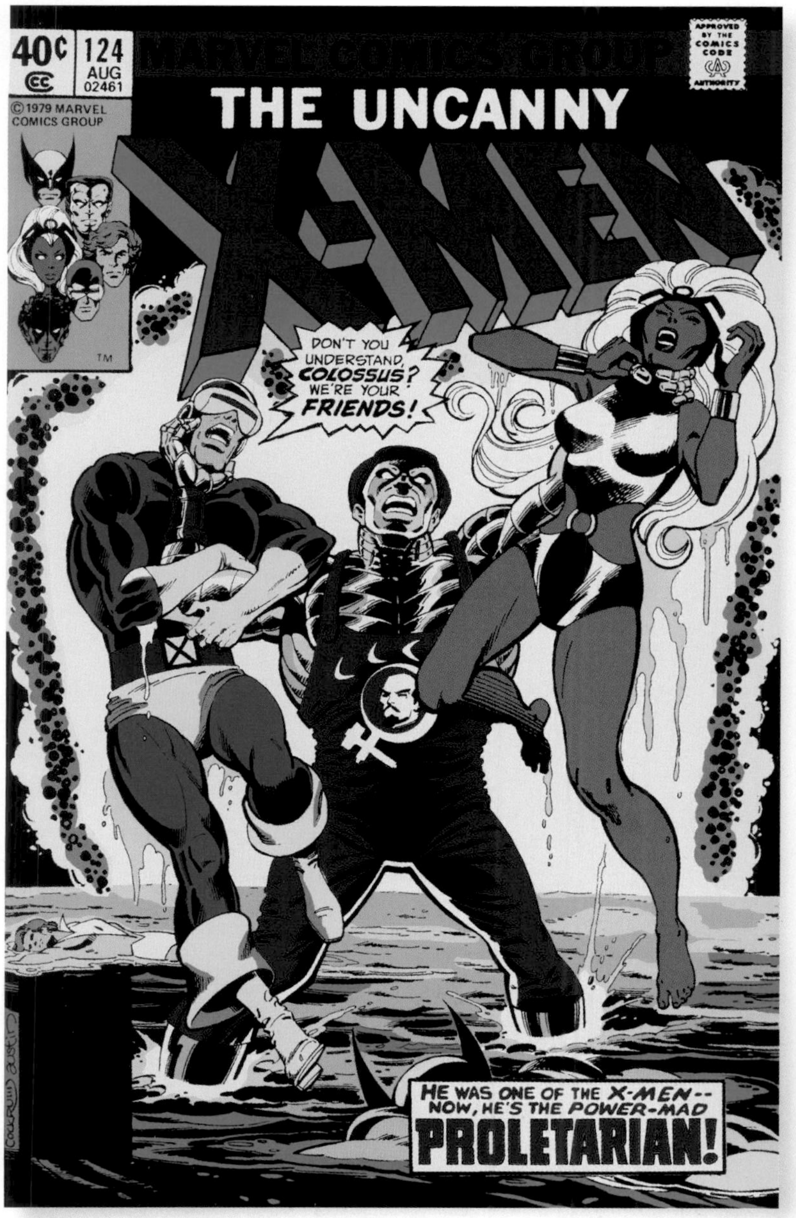
40¢
124
AUG
02461
MARVEL COMICS GROUP
APPROVED BY THE COMICS CODE AUTHORITY
©1979 MARVEL COMICS GROUP
THE UNCANNY
X-MEN
DON'T YOU UNDERSTAND, COLOSSUS? WE'RE YOUR FRIENDS!
HE WAS ONE OF THE X-MEN-- NOW, HE'S THE POWER-MAD
PROLETARIAN!

▲ *UNCANNY X-MEN* #124

**August 1979**
**Artist:** Dave Cockrum

Marvel had added "Uncanny" to the title from issue #114. This issue explored Colossus' Soviet background when he was brainwashed by the villain Arcade into believing he was a Russian hero called the Proletarian rather than a member of the X-Men. In a world in the midst of the Cold War, the image of Colossus in Soviet insignia was powerful and topical.

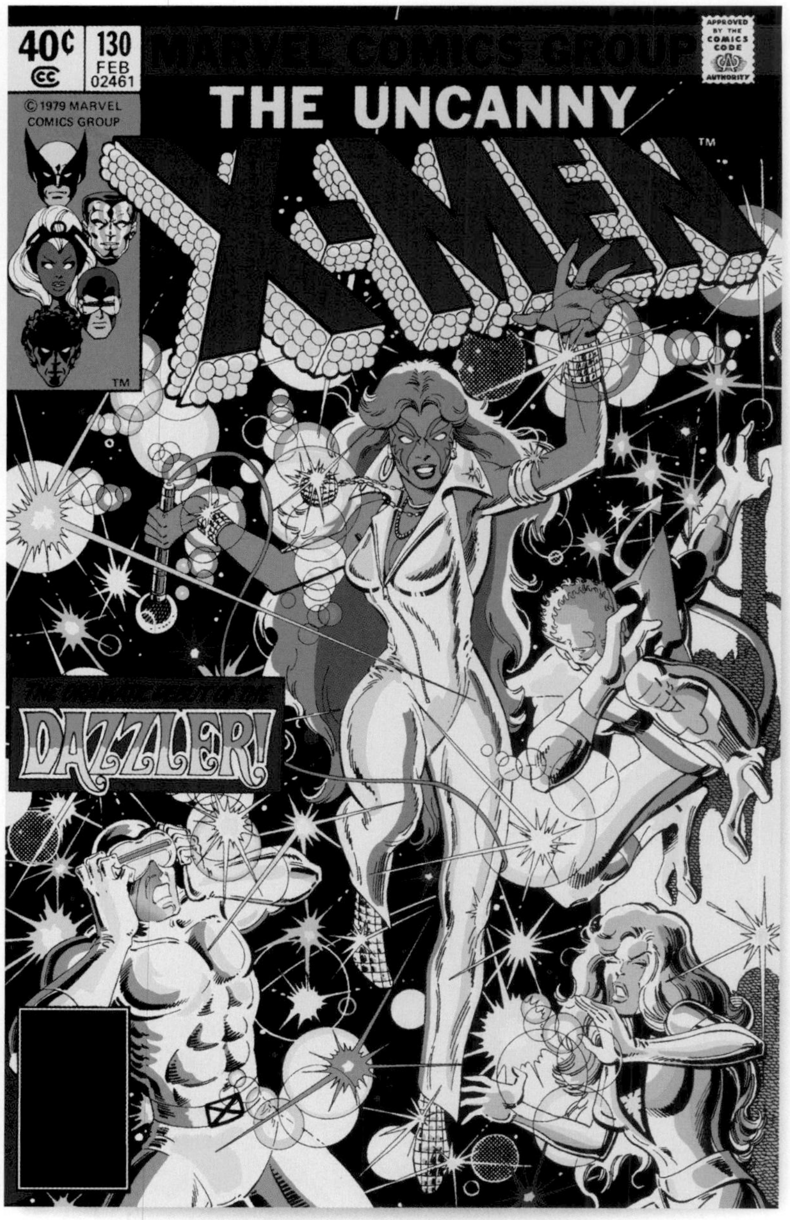
40¢
130
FEB
02461
MARVEL COMICS GROUP
APPROVED BY THE COMICS CODE AUTHORITY
©1979 MARVEL COMICS GROUP
THE UNCANNY
X-MEN
DAZZLER!

▲ *UNCANNY X-MEN* #130

**February 1980**
**Artist:** John Romita Jr.

Dazzler had originally been conceived as part of a multimedia cross-promotion between Marvel and Casablanca Records. The record company planned to launch the career of a singer that they would name Dazzler just as Marvel produced a comic about her. However, ultimately the singer only came to exist in the world of *X-Men* comics. The cover of Dazzler's debut appearance is a mash-up of X-Men and disco, with disco lights even added to the logo.

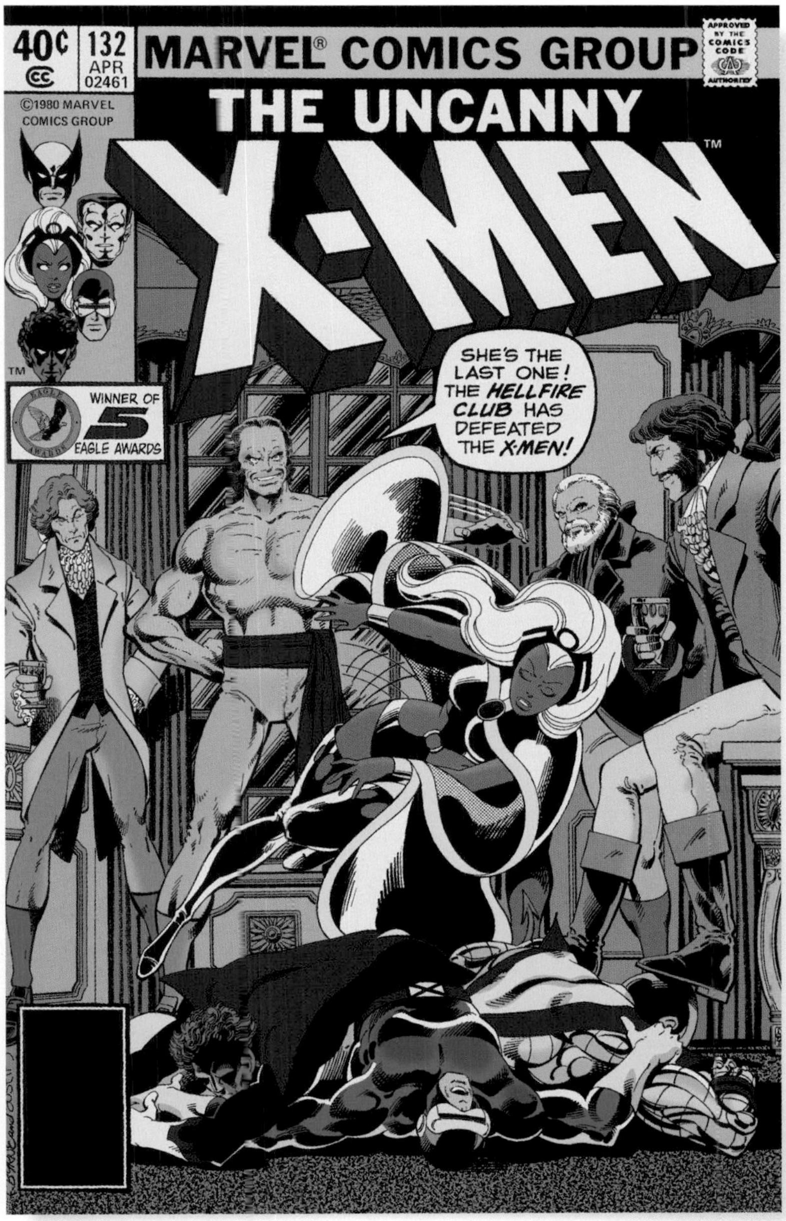
40¢ 132 APR 02461
MARVEL® COMICS GROUP
©1980 MARVEL COMICS GROUP
THE UNCANNY
X-MEN
WINNER OF 5 EAGLE AWARDS
SHE'S THE LAST ONE! THE HELLFIRE CLUB HAS DEFEATED THE X-MEN!

▲ *UNCANNY X-MEN* #132

**April 1980**
**Artist:** John Byrne

The "Hellfire Club" saga remains one of the most important stories in the X-Men's history. This cover highlights the unique-looking villains of the Hellfire Club (a social club with a slightly sinister agenda), the like of which had never been seen in a Marvel comic before. By this point *Uncanny X-Men* was winning awards and going from strength to strength each month.

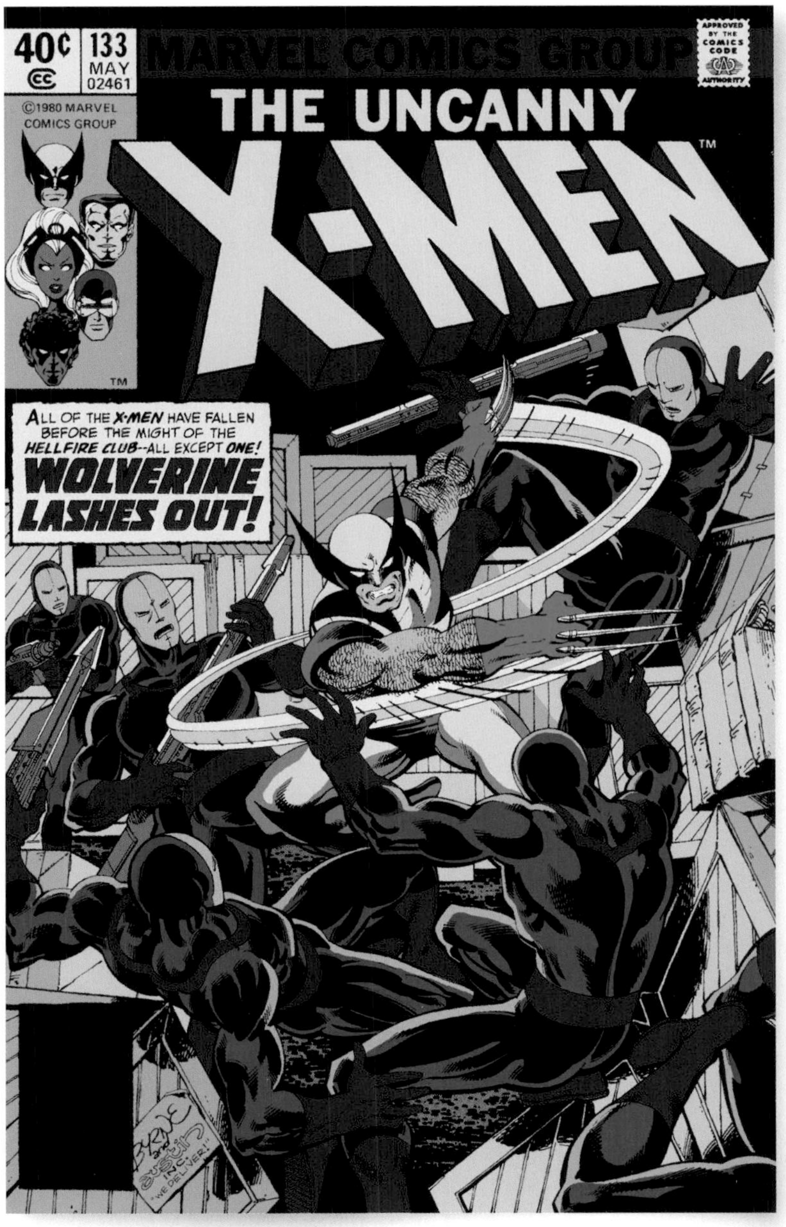
40¢ 133 MAY 02461
MARVEL COMICS GROUP
©1980 MARVEL COMICS GROUP
THE UNCANNY
X-MEN
ALL OF THE X-MEN HAVE FALLEN BEFORE THE MIGHT OF THE HELLFIRE CLUB--ALL EXCEPT ONE!
WOLVERINE LASHES OUT!

▲ *UNCANNY X-MEN* #133

**May 1980**
**Artist:** John Byrne

Wolverine had gradually become the most popular mutant Super Hero during Claremont and Byrne's run, but this was the issue in which he really cut loose. The image, showing Wolverine taking on the Hellfire Club's security, was the first time the hero had the cover to himself. It certainly wouldn't be the last.

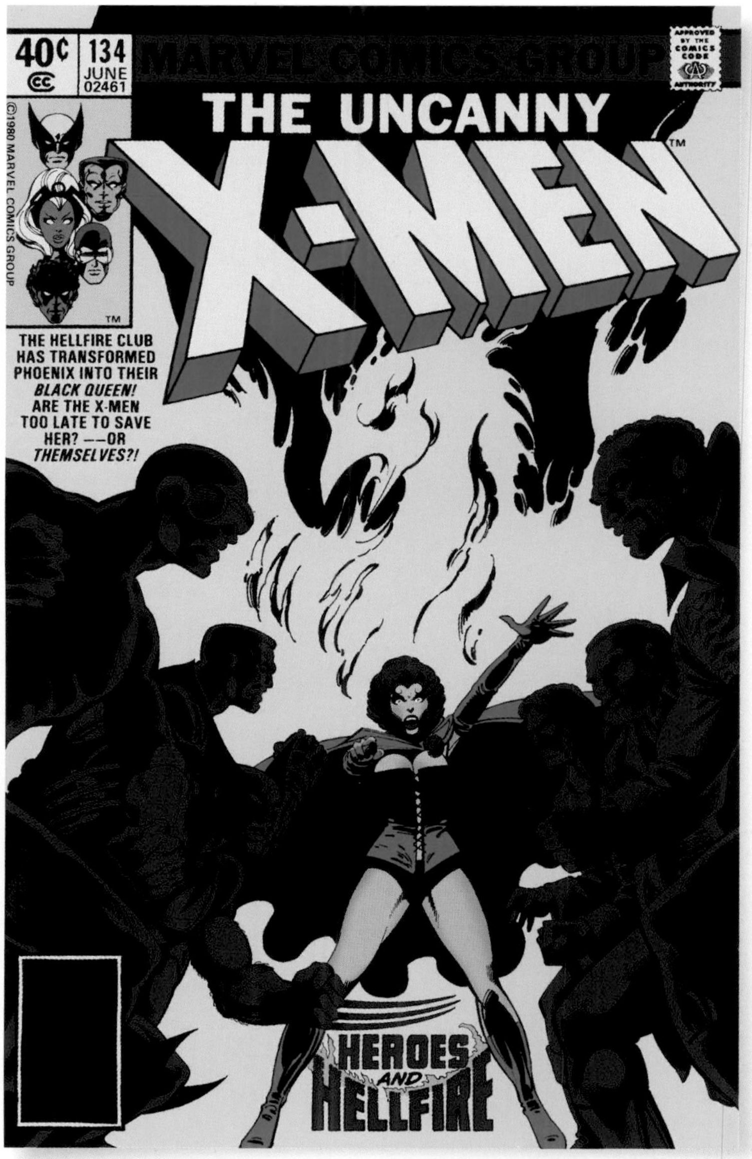
40¢
134
JUNE
02461
MARVEL COMICS GROUP
THE UNCANNY
X-MEN
©1980 MARVEL COMICS GROUP
THE HELLFIRE CLUB HAS TRANSFORMED PHOENIX INTO THEIR *BLACK QUEEN!* ARE THE X-MEN TOO LATE TO SAVE HER? --OR *THEMSELVES?!*
HEROES AND HELLFIRE

**◀ *UNCANNY X-MEN* #134**

**June 1980**
**Artist:** John Byrne

When Jean Grey gives in to the darkside, she is remade by the Hellfire Club as their Black Queen. She takes center stage on this cover, surrounded by the Phoenix flame. The drama intensified in this issue, and the cover is all about dramatic color—the powerful red and yellow reflecting the fiery danger the X-Men team faced.

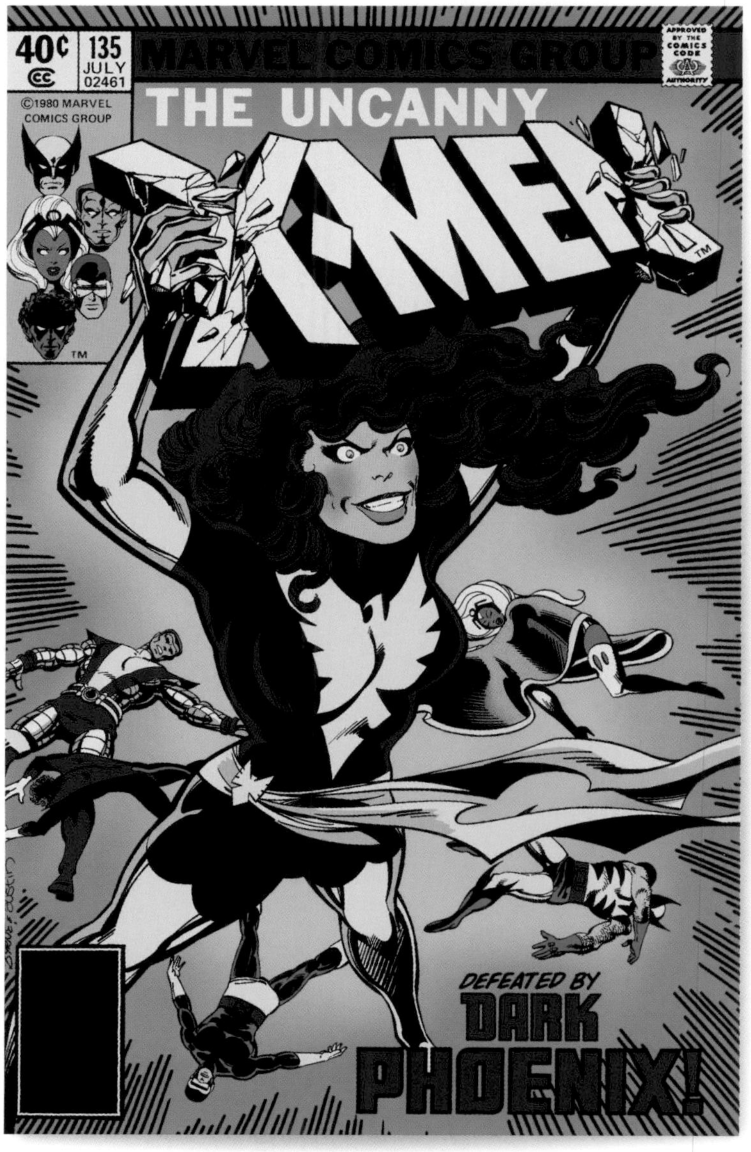
40¢
135
JULY
02461
©1980 MARVEL COMICS GROUP
MARVEL COMICS GROUP
THE UNCANNY
X-MEN
DEFEATED BY
DARK PHOENIX!

**◀ *UNCANNY X-MEN* #135**

**July 1980**
**Artist:** John Byrne

Jean Grey's fall continued in this issue with the hero becoming Dark Phoenix. The powerful cover shows a supercharged and insane-looking Jean crushing the X-Men logo, clearly signifying how she was hell-bent on destroying everything in her path. It was a sign of the drama within, as the X-Men had to face one of their own who had now become their deadliest enemy.

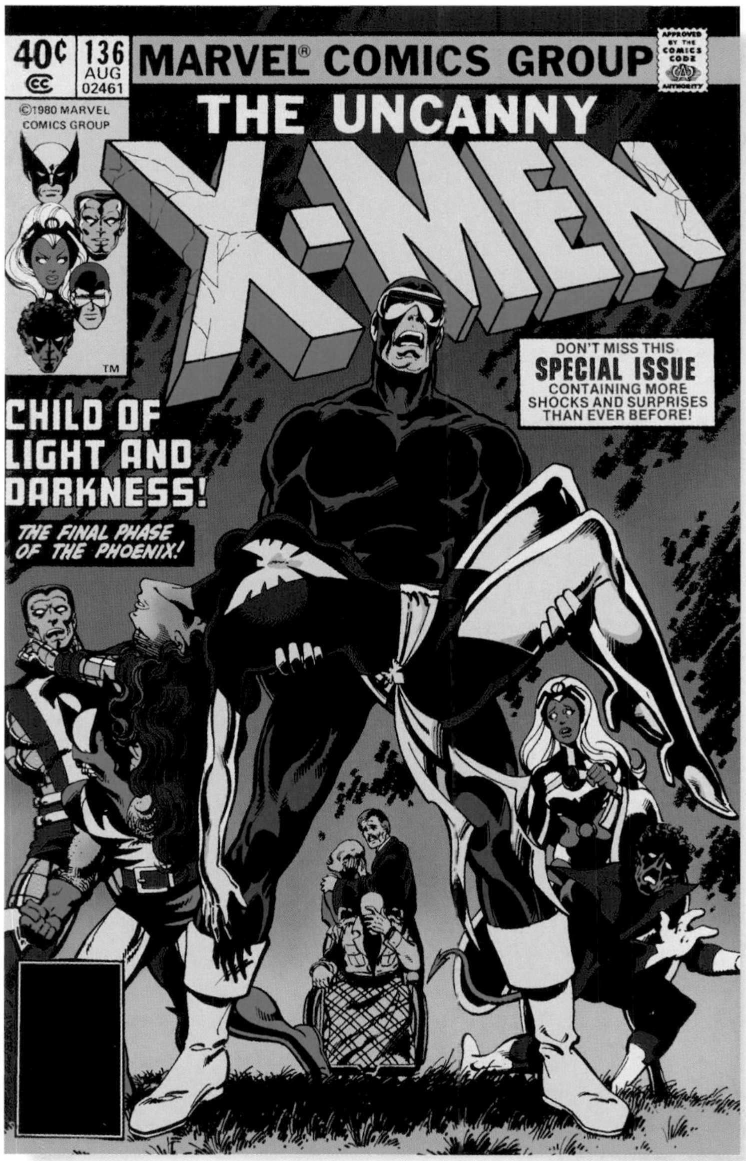
40¢ 136 AUG 02461
MARVEL COMICS GROUP
©1980 MARVEL COMICS GROUP
THE UNCANNY
X-MEN
DON'T MISS THIS SPECIAL ISSUE CONTAINING MORE SHOCKS AND SURPRISES THAN EVER BEFORE!
CHILD OF LIGHT AND DARKNESS!
THE FINAL PHASE OF THE PHOENIX!

◄ *UNCANNY X-MEN* #136

**August 1980**
**Artist:** John Byrne

The "Dark Phoenix" saga reached its penultimate chapter this issue with an emotional cover. The image of Cyclops holding what seems to be the corpse of Jean Grey in his arms (she is in fact, unconscious) is an exceptionally powerful one, as is Cyclops' agonized expression. While the main pose has been used before, this is one of the most famous instances of its use.

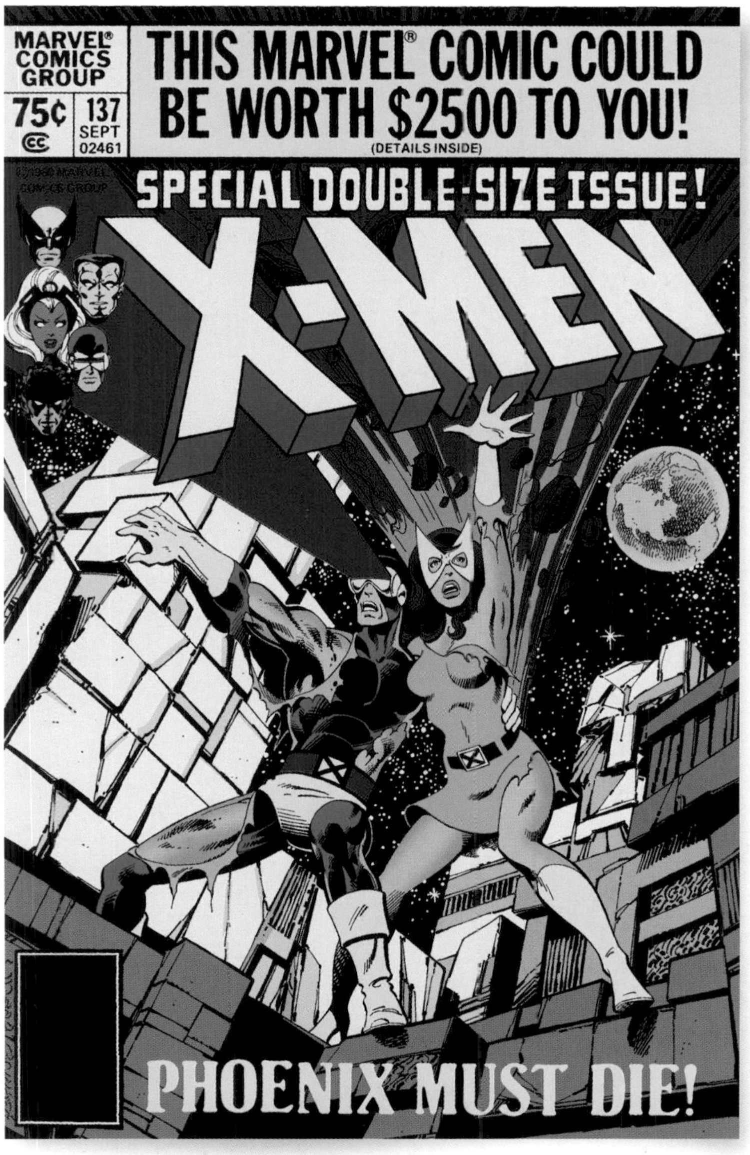
MARVEL COMICS GROUP
75¢ 137 SEPT 02461
THIS MARVEL COMIC COULD BE WORTH $2500 TO YOU!
(DETAILS INSIDE)
SPECIAL DOUBLE-SIZE ISSUE!
X-MEN
PHOENIX MUST DIE!

◄ *UNCANNY X-MEN* #137

**September 1980**
**Artist:** John Byrne

The tagline says it all: "Phoenix Must Die!" The "Dark Phoenix" saga came to its tragic conclusion in this special double-size issue as the X-Men and Jean Grey fought for her life. The iconic image of Cyclops and Jean Grey (in her original Marvel Girl costume) making a last stand remains burned into every X-Men fan's memory.

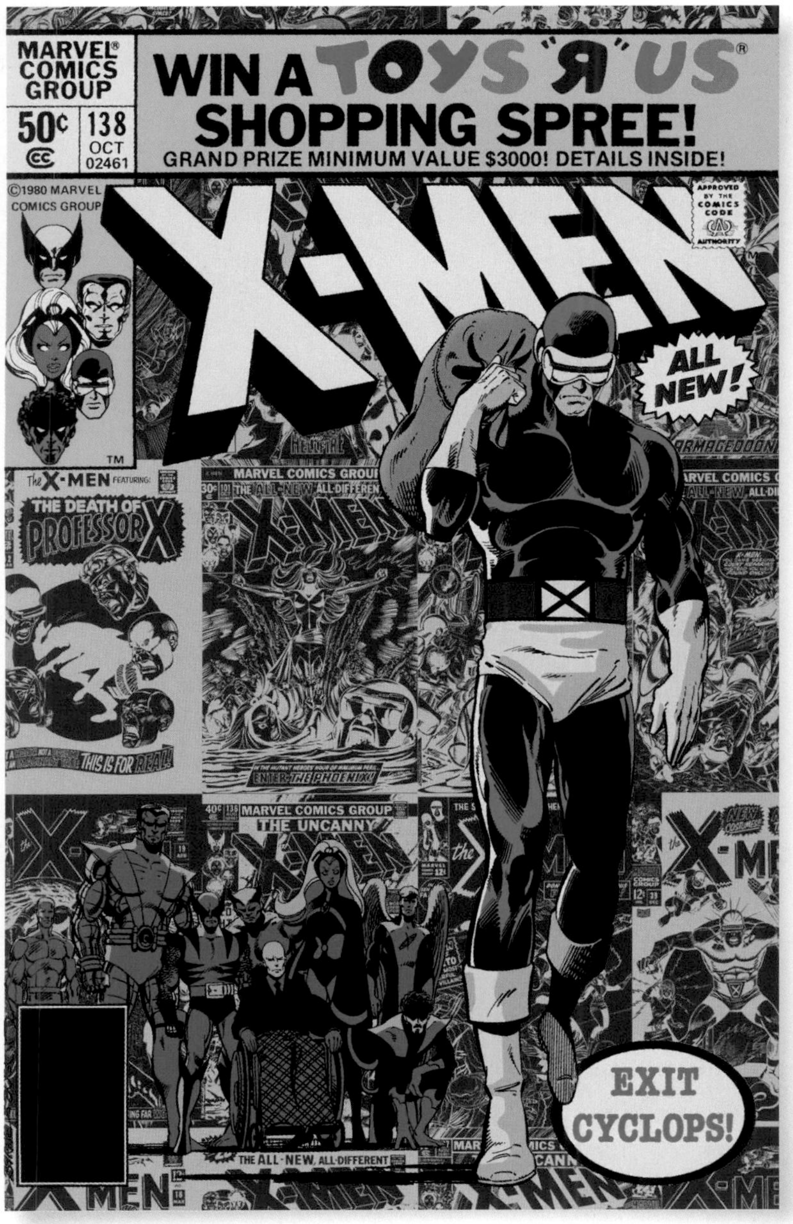
MARVEL® COMICS GROUP
50¢ 138 OCT 02461
WIN A TOYS "R" US SHOPPING SPREE!
GRAND PRIZE MINIMUM VALUE $3000! DETAILS INSIDE!
©1980 MARVEL COMICS GROUP
X-MEN
ALL NEW!
EXIT CYCLOPS!

▲ *X-MEN* #138

**October 1980**
**Artist:** John Byrne

John Byrne's run as *X-Men* artist produced many classic covers and stories, but this simple cover remains a highlight. A fitting epilogue to the "Dark Phoenix" saga, it featured Cyclops quitting the team as he tried to come to terms with the death of Jean Grey. Byrne's layout has been used many times since, while the backdrop of old covers illustrated Cyclops' long history with the team.

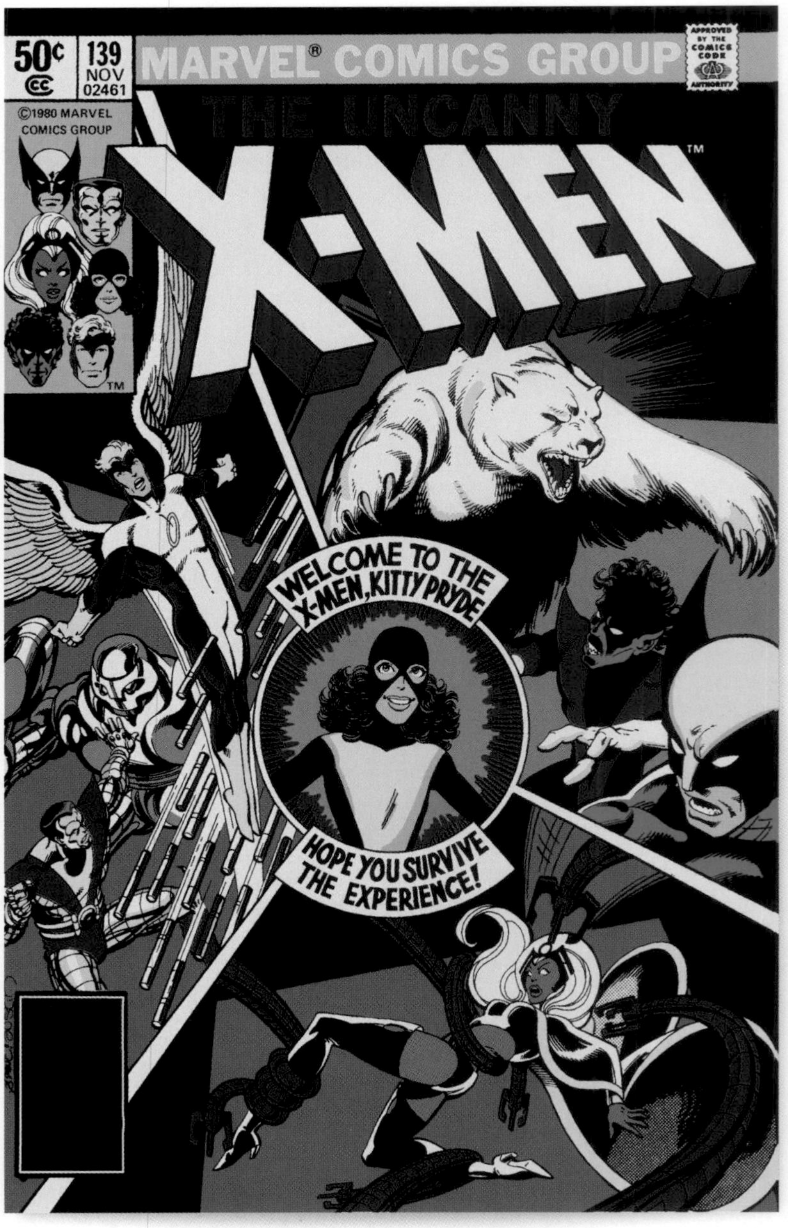
50¢ 139 NOV 02461
MARVEL® COMICS GROUP
©1980 MARVEL COMICS GROUP
THE UNCANNY
X-MEN
WELCOME TO THE X-MEN, KITTY PRYDE
HOPE YOU SURVIVE THE EXPERIENCE!

▲ *UNCANNY X-MEN* #139

**November 1980**
**Artist:** John Byrne

After the grim trauma of the "Dark Phoenix" saga, it was time to shake things up at Xavier's Mansion. Kitty Pryde was just the person to add some fresh, new blood to the team. This cover, showing the teenage Kitty surrounded by the X-Men in peril, heralded a time of change for the title.

*UNCANNY X-MEN* #141 ▶

**January 1981**
**Artist:** John Byrne

Even by the high standards of John Byrne, the cover to the first part of the classic story "Days of Future Past" is something special. The image of a desperate and aged Wolverine next to a grown-up Kate Pryde is a startling one, especially with the list of dead or captured X-Men behind them. It is a cover that has often been copied, but never bettered.

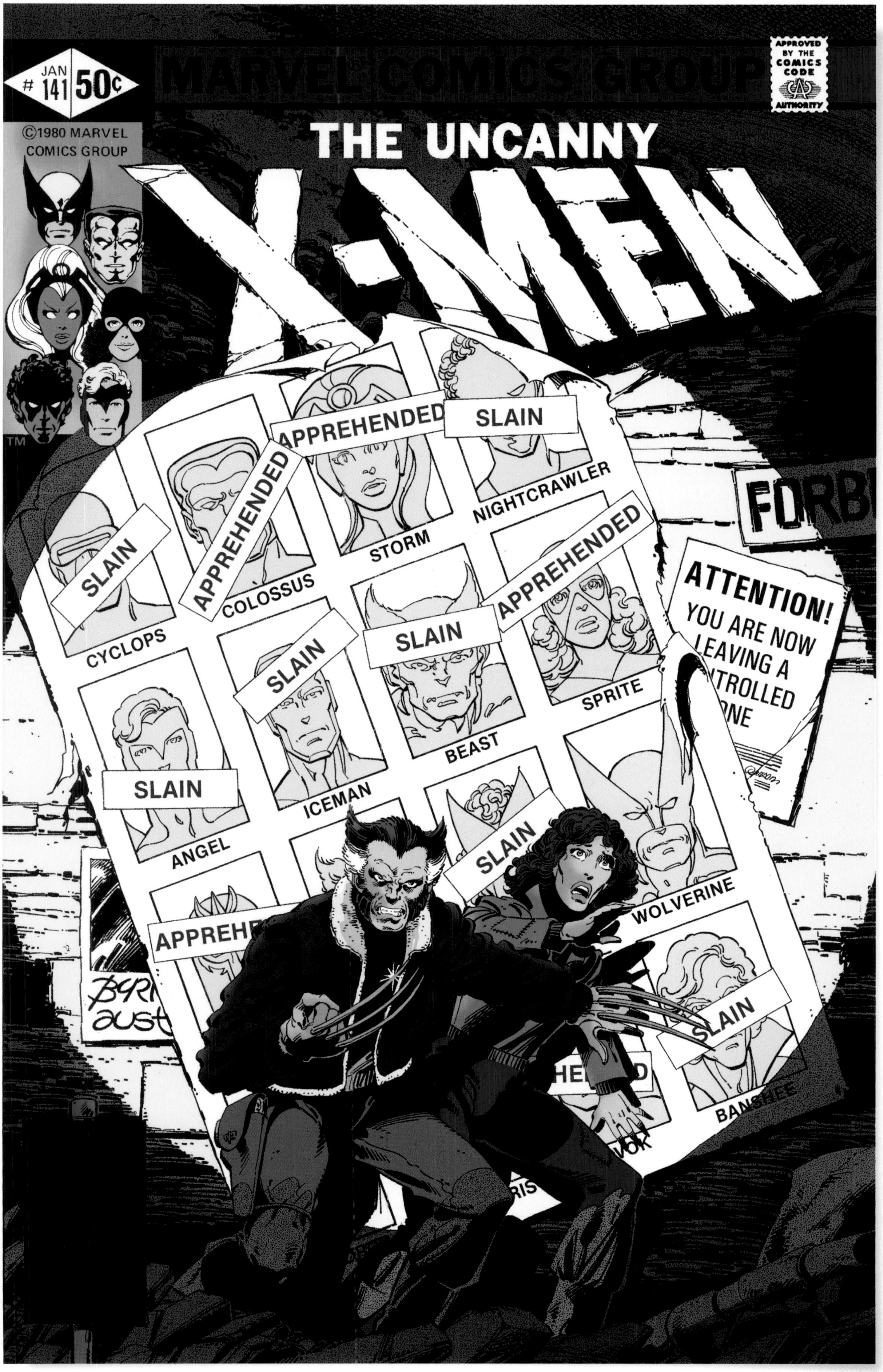

# JAN 141 50¢
MARVEL COMICS GROUP
APPROVED BY THE COMICS CODE AUTHORITY
©1980 MARVEL COMICS GROUP
THE UNCANNY
X-MEN
TM
SLAIN
CYCLOPS
APPREHENDED
COLOSSUS
APPREHENDED
STORM
SLAIN
NIGHTCRAWLER
SLAIN
ICEMAN
SLAIN
BEAST
APPREHENDED
SPRITE
SLAIN
ANGEL
SLAIN
WOLVERINE
APPREHE
SLAIN
BANSHEE
FORB
ATTENTION!
YOU ARE NOW LEAVING A

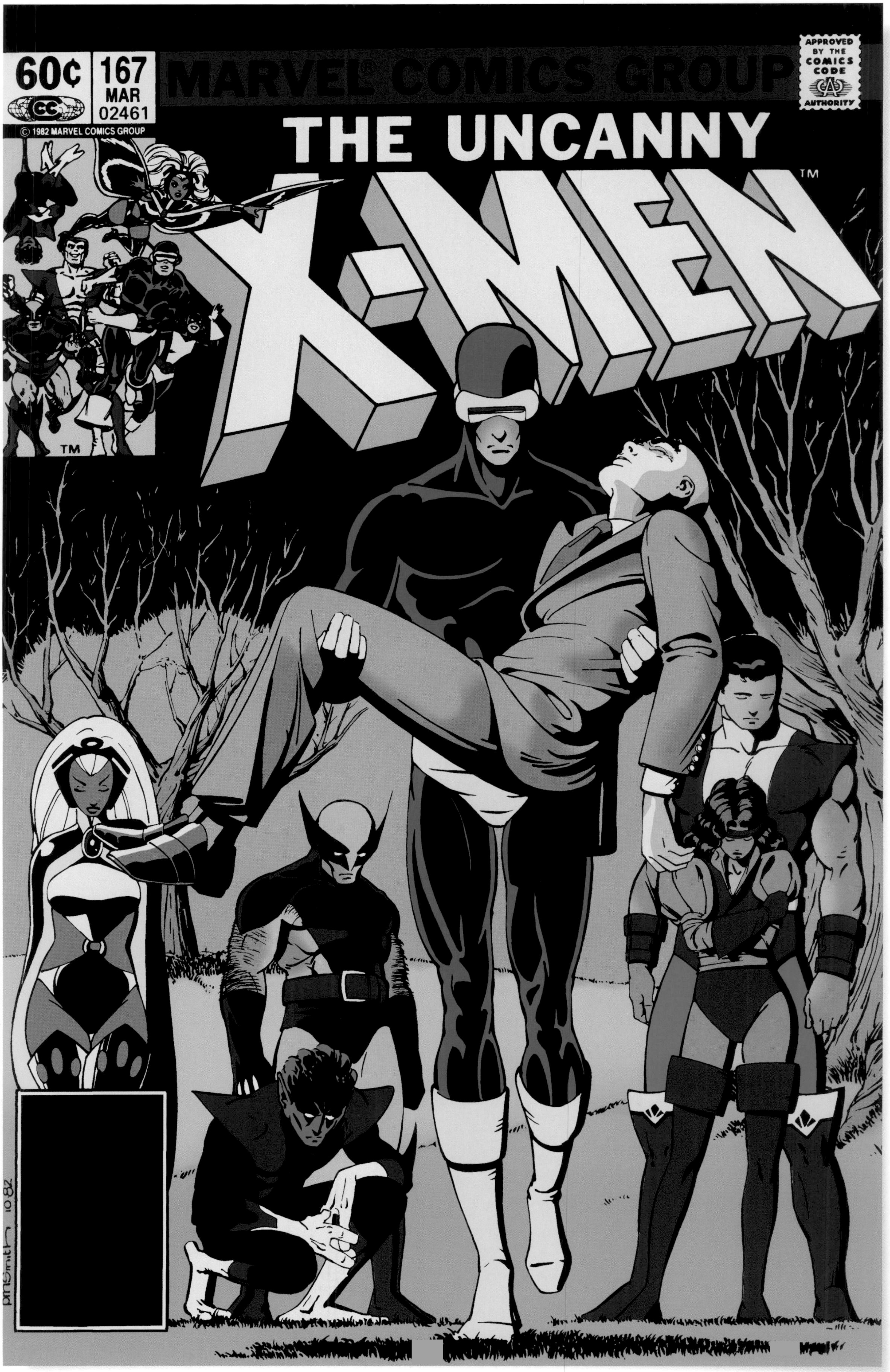
60¢
167
MAR
02461
© 1982 MARVEL COMICS GROUP
MARVEL® COMICS GROUP
APPROVED BY THE COMICS CODE AUTHORITY
THE UNCANNY
X-MEN
TM
pmSmith 10 82

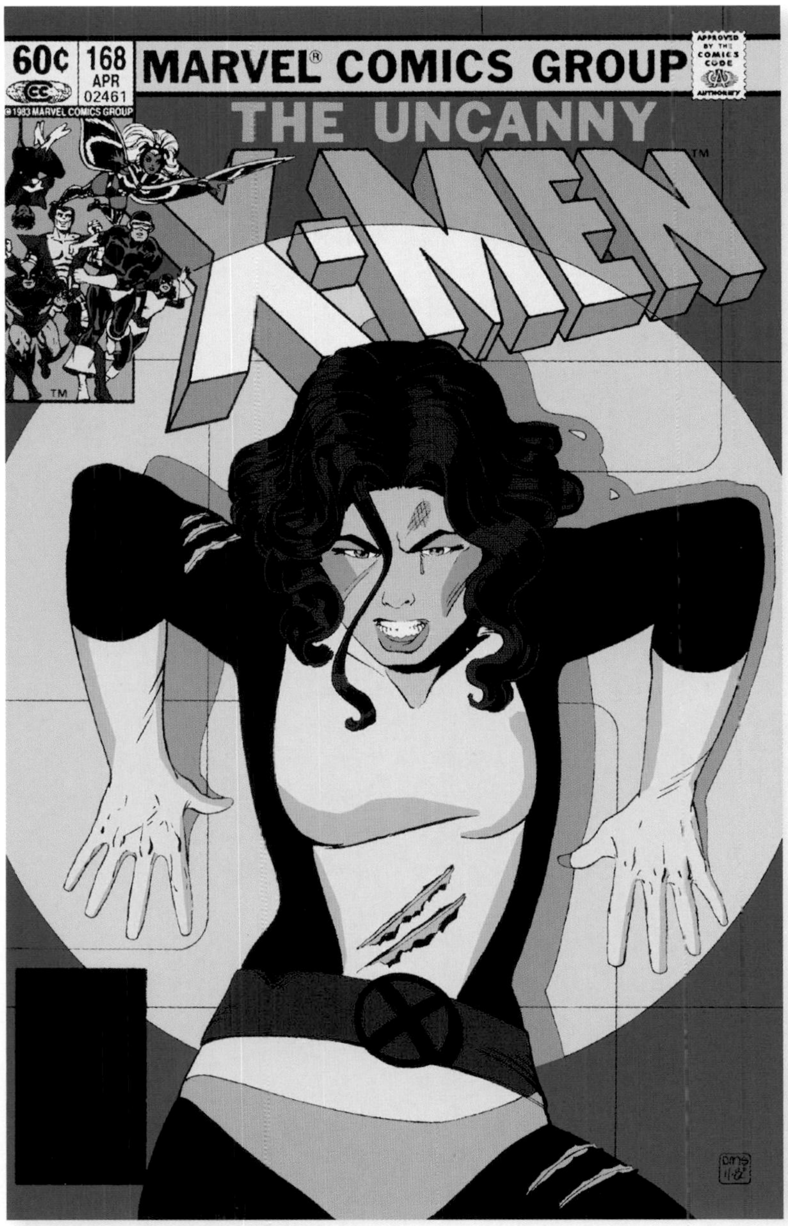
60¢
168
APR
02461
MARVEL® COMICS GROUP
THE UNCANNY
X-MEN

▲ ***UNCANNY X-MEN* #168**

**April 1983**
**Artist:** Paul Smith

Kitty Pryde was the standout star of Paul Smith's run on *Uncanny X-Men*. This cover is a compelling character study of Kitty, and the story "Professor Xavier is a Jerk" was a favorite of movie maker Joss Whedon, who later referenced it during his stint as a writer on *Astonishing X-Men* between 2004 and 2008.

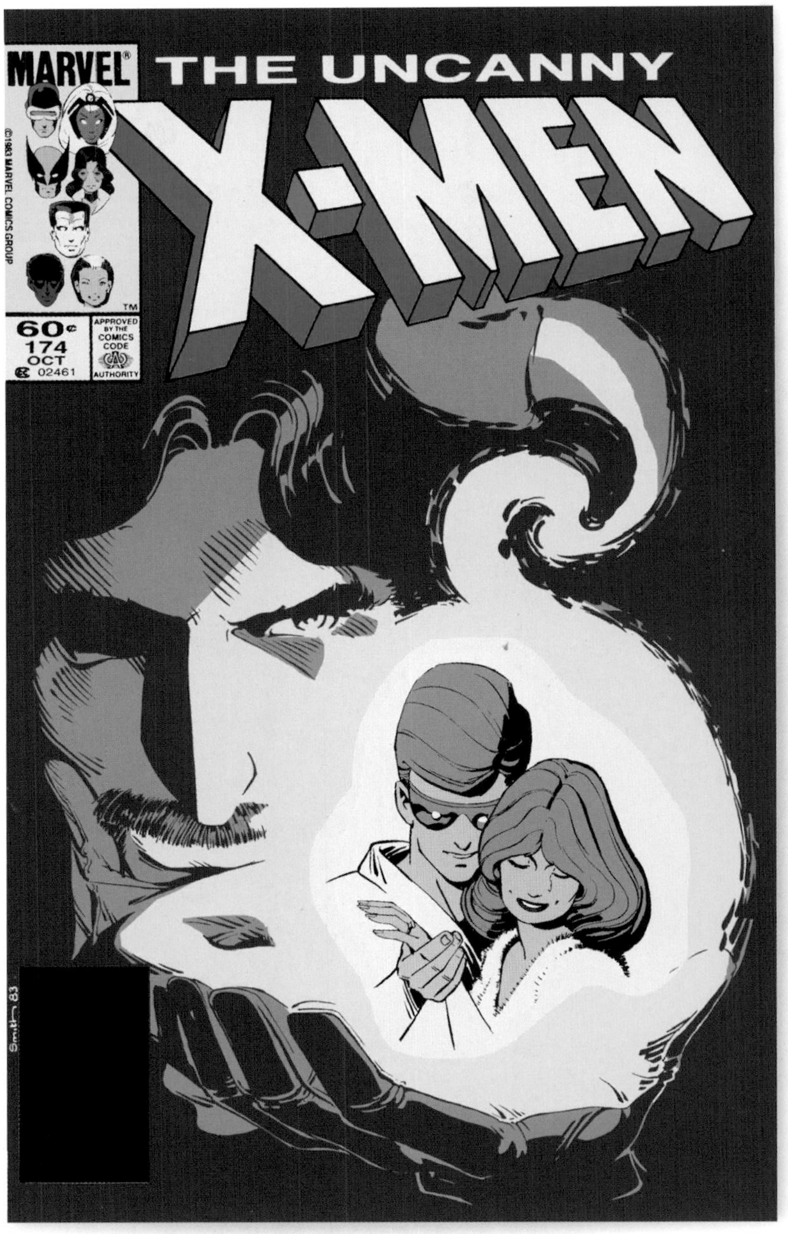
MARVEL®
THE UNCANNY
X-MEN
60¢
174
OCT
02461

▲ ***UNCANNY X-MEN* #174**

**October 1983**
**Artist:** Paul Smith

Paul Smith's penultimate cover on *Uncanny X-Men* is a work of real beauty. It also harks back to the "Dark Phoenix" saga, as it shows Mastermind watching Cyclops and his new love Madelyne Pryor—who bore an uncanny likeness to his dead wife Jean Grey. The story had a real cliffhanger too, as Madelyne herself apparently became the new Dark Phoenix.

◀ ***UNCANNY X-MEN* #167**

**March 1983**
**Artist:** Paul Smith

It took someone special to live up to the high standards John Byrne had set on *Uncanny X-Men*. Luckily artist Paul Smith was more than able for the job, and working with writer Chris Claremont, they created a short run on the title that many fans consider a series best. The cover for this issue sees Cyclops holding Professor X's corpse (an echo of the image on *X-Men* issue #136). Professor X is not dead though—he has just been taken over by the alien Brood.

***X-MEN ANNUAL* #9** ▶

**December 1985**
**Artist:** Arthur Adams

Arthur Adams burst onto the comic-book scene illustrating *Longshot*. A true stylist, Adams has always been famous for the painstaking detail he puts into his art. His work on the *Uncanny X-Men Annual* saw Storm taken to Asgard to become the new "Goddess of Thunder," her new Asgardian look gracing the stunning cover.

MARVEL
#1 IN A SIX-ISSUE LIMITED SERIES
LONGSHOT
75¢ 1 SEPT

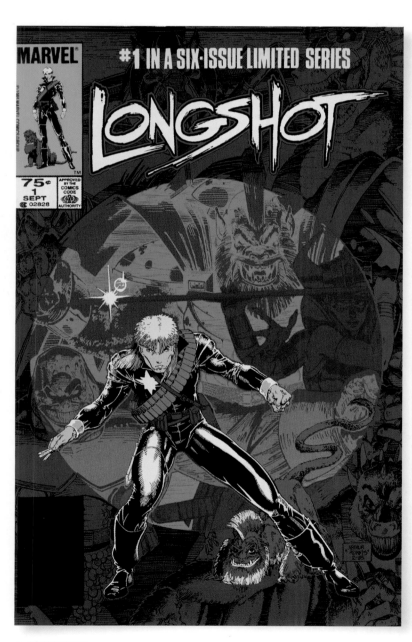

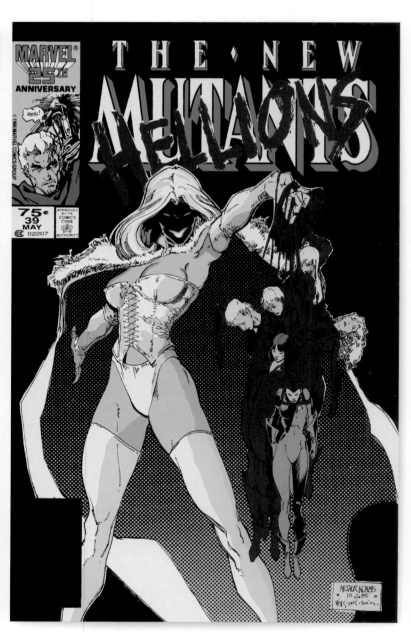

▲ ***LONGSHOT* #1**

**September 1985**
**Artist:** Arthur Adams

Adams' pencil work is exquisite and highly detailed, and this cover was a stunning start by the artist who quickly became one of the biggest names in the business. *Longshot* was Adams' first published work for Marvel. Written by Ann Nocenti, issue #1 introduced a number of characters—Longshot included—who would eventually become part of the X-Men mythos.

MARVEL
25th ANNIVERSARY
THE NEW MUTANTS
HELLIONS
75¢ 39 MAY

▲ ***THE NEW MUTANTS* #39**

**May 1986**
**Artist:** Arthur Adams

Adams' work soon started gracing other covers, too. His portrait of a villainous Emma Frost holding up the corpses of the New Mutants is particularly striking thanks to his detailed line work. The story itself saw the New Mutants become part of the Hellions at Emma Frost's Massachusetts Academy—hence their name spray painted over the title logo.

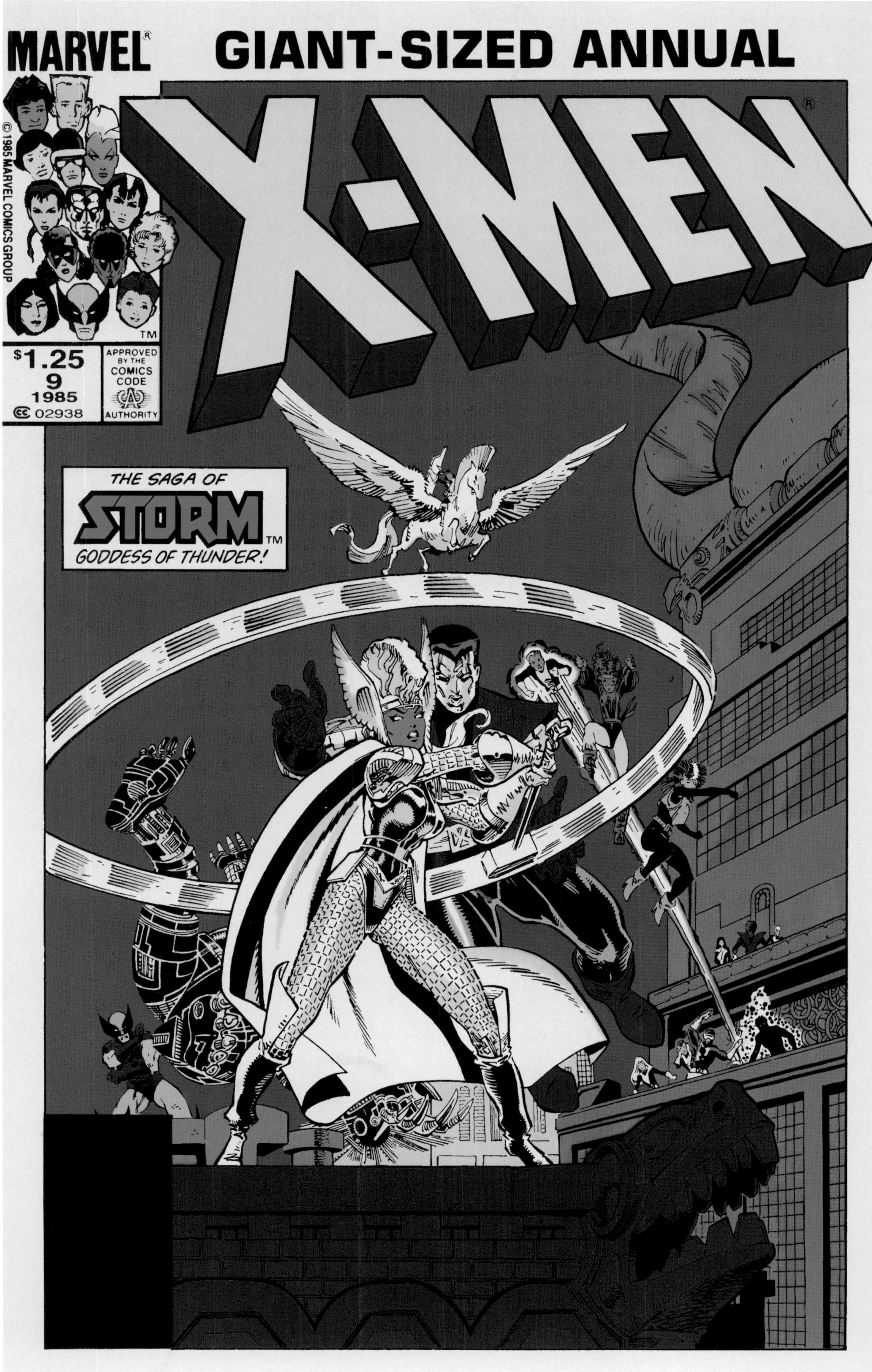
MARVEL
GIANT-SIZED ANNUAL
X-MEN
© 1985 MARVEL COMICS GROUP
$1.25
9
1985
APPROVED BY THE COMICS CODE AUTHORITY
THE SAGA OF
STORM
GODDESS OF THUNDER!

# THE MODERN AGE

## 1986–

THE MID-1980s SAW a change in storytelling. Led by creators such as Alan Moore and Frank Miller, writers and artists started to explore darker, more adult themes in their comics. Alongside this, creator-owned comics came to the fore through the rise of publishers such as Image, Dark Horse, and Marvel's own Epic and Icon Imprints. This period also saw the rise of the X-Men. By the 1990s Marvel's mutants were not only a part of a best-selling comic, but also a huge franchise, with countless X-Men-related books in print.

A whole new generation of artists also burst onto the comic-book scene. Jim Lee, Marc Silvestri, Alan Davis, Carlos Pacheco, David Aja, and others started to push the boundaries of the art forward once again, creating some amazing covers along the way. By the 21st century, comics were becoming increasingly part of mainstream culture, with many top movies in Hollywood being based on Marvel heroes. The rise of digital publishing also gave readers a new way of reading comics. Publishing was changing, and Marvel was at the forefront of that change.

*THE NEW AVENGERS* #1 ▶

**January 2005**
**Artist:** David Finch

*(Cover shown in full on p162)*

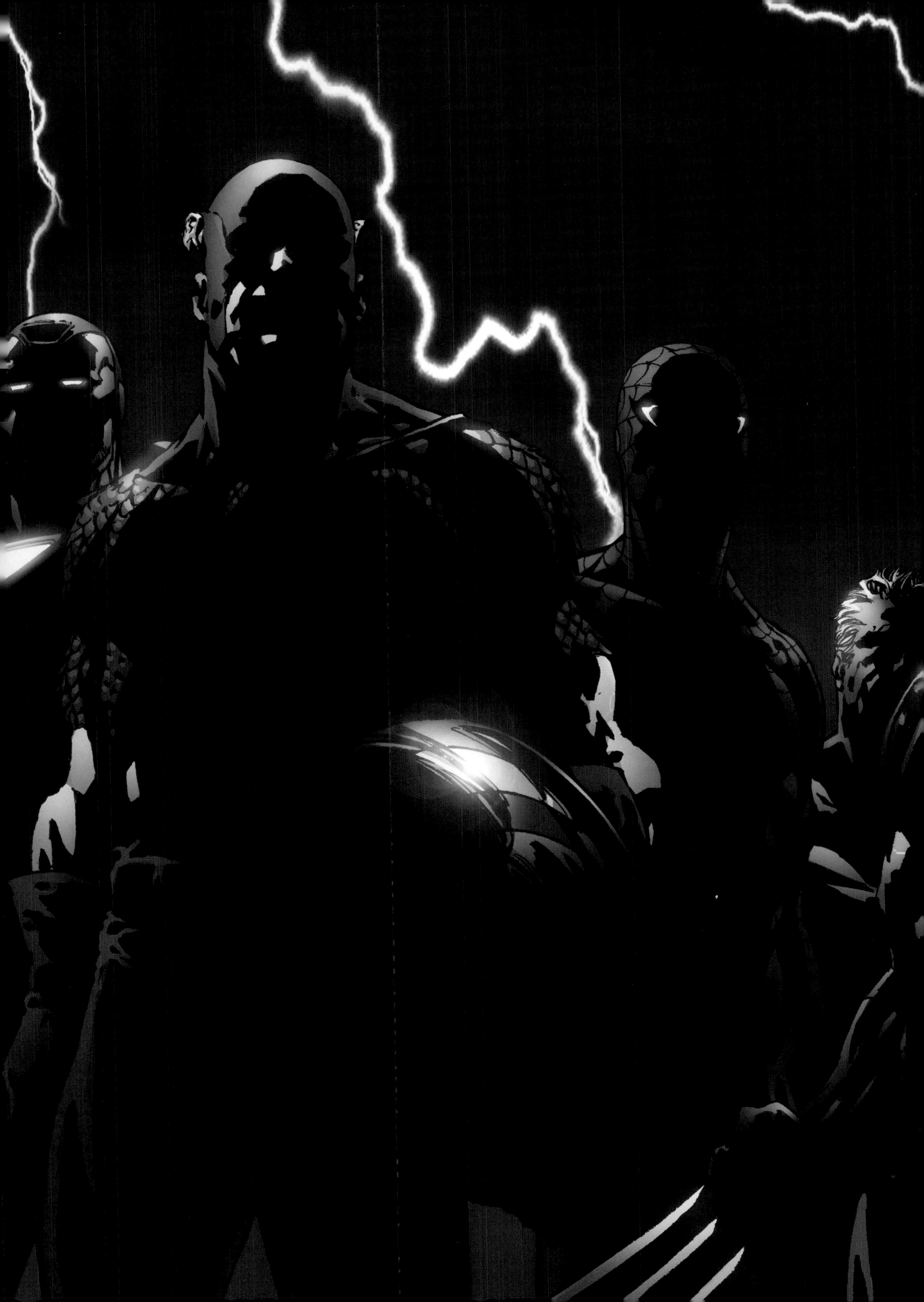

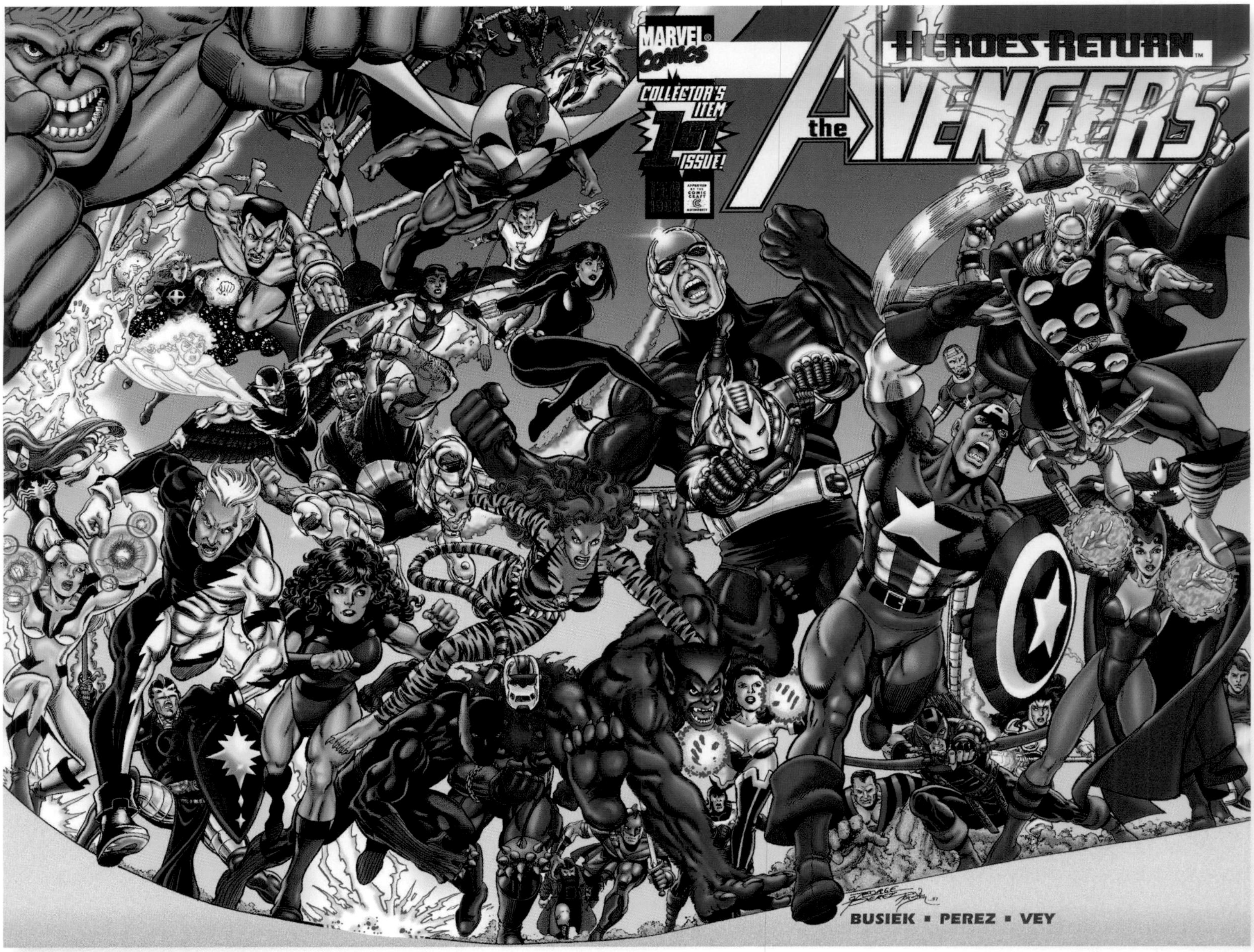
MARVEL COMICS
COLLECTOR'S ITEM
1ST ISSUE!
HEROES RETURN
the AVENGERS
BUSIEK • PEREZ • VEY

▲ *AVENGERS* #1

**February 1998**
**Artist:** George Pérez

When *Avengers* was relaunched in 1998, Marvel put two of its best at the helm—writer Kurt Busiek and artist George Pérez. The latter produced a stunning cover for the debut issue (shown here in full), featuring a host of potential Avengers bursting out of the cover. Pérez had originally made his name illustrating the title in the 1970s, but he produced some of his best work on the new series.

*AVENGERS* #2 ▶

**March 1998**
**Artist:** George Pérez

George Pérez got to draw numerous Avengers once again for the second cover of the relaunched comic—but this time with a twist. The evil Morgan le Fay had altered reality into an Arthurian world, transforming the heroes into feudal versions of themselves. This made for a very unusual cover image.

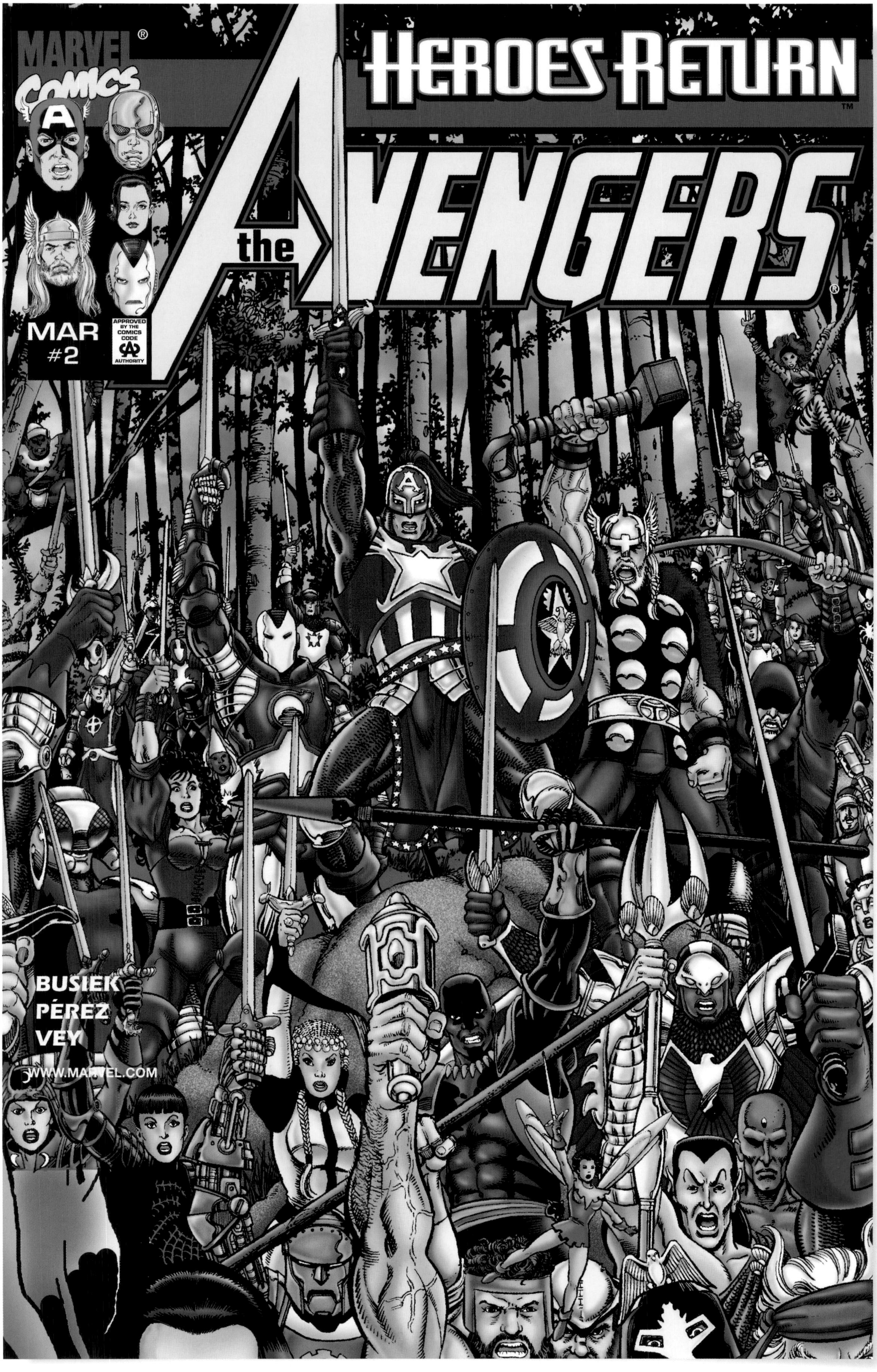
MARVEL COMICS
HEROES RETURN
the AVENGERS
MAR #2
APPROVED BY THE COMICS CODE AUTHORITY
BUSIEK
PÉREZ
VEY
WWW.MARVEL.COM

***AVENGERS* #503 ▶**

**December 2004**
**Artist:** David Finch

David Finch produced a dark and thoughtful cover for the final part of the "Avengers Disassembled" epic, which saw the Avengers destroyed from within by an insane Scarlet Witch. The sight of Captain America surrounded by his friends' weaponry suggested that even more Avengers could die.

AVENGERS
FOREVER
BUSIEK
PACHECO
MERINO
HOT TUNA
#1
OF 12
DEC
MARVEL COMICS

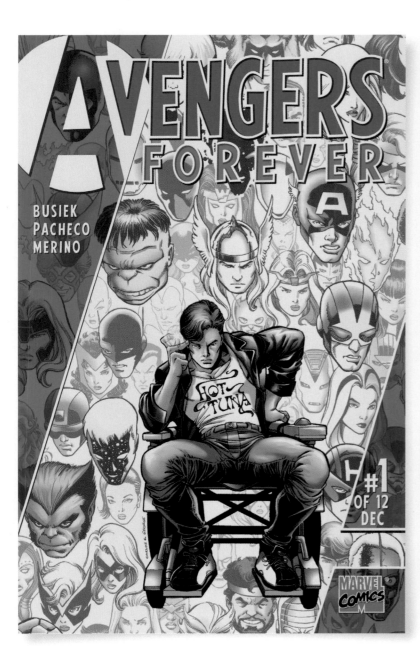

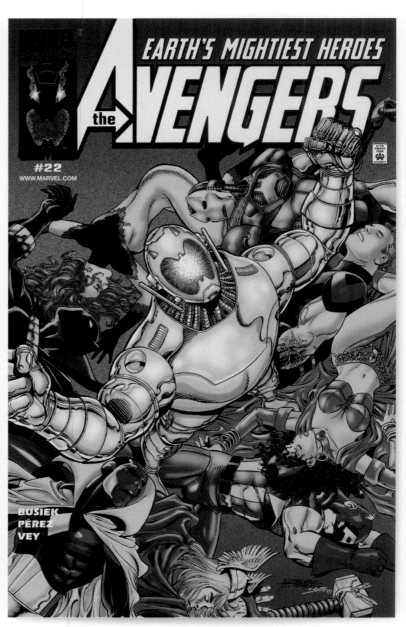

▲ ***AVENGERS FOREVER* #1**

**December 1998**
**Artist:** Carlos Pacheco

*Avengers Forever* was Kurt Busiek's complex, 12-part epic that brought together Avengers from across the timeline. The first issue's cover, by Carlos Pacheco, is a simple, but effective image featuring Rick Jones, the Hulk's old sidekick, contemplating a new line-up of the Avengers.

EARTH'S MIGHTIEST HEROES
the AVENGERS
#22
WWW.MARVEL.COM
BUSIEK
PÉREZ
VEY

▲ ***AVENGERS* #22**

**November 1999**
**Artist:** George Pérez

Ultron, a robot created by Dr. Hank Pym in *Avengers* issue #55 (August 1968), has always been one of the team's deadliest enemies. This cover by George Pérez is one of the most menacing Ultron covers to date, showing the ferocious robot standing victorious over the defeated heroes.

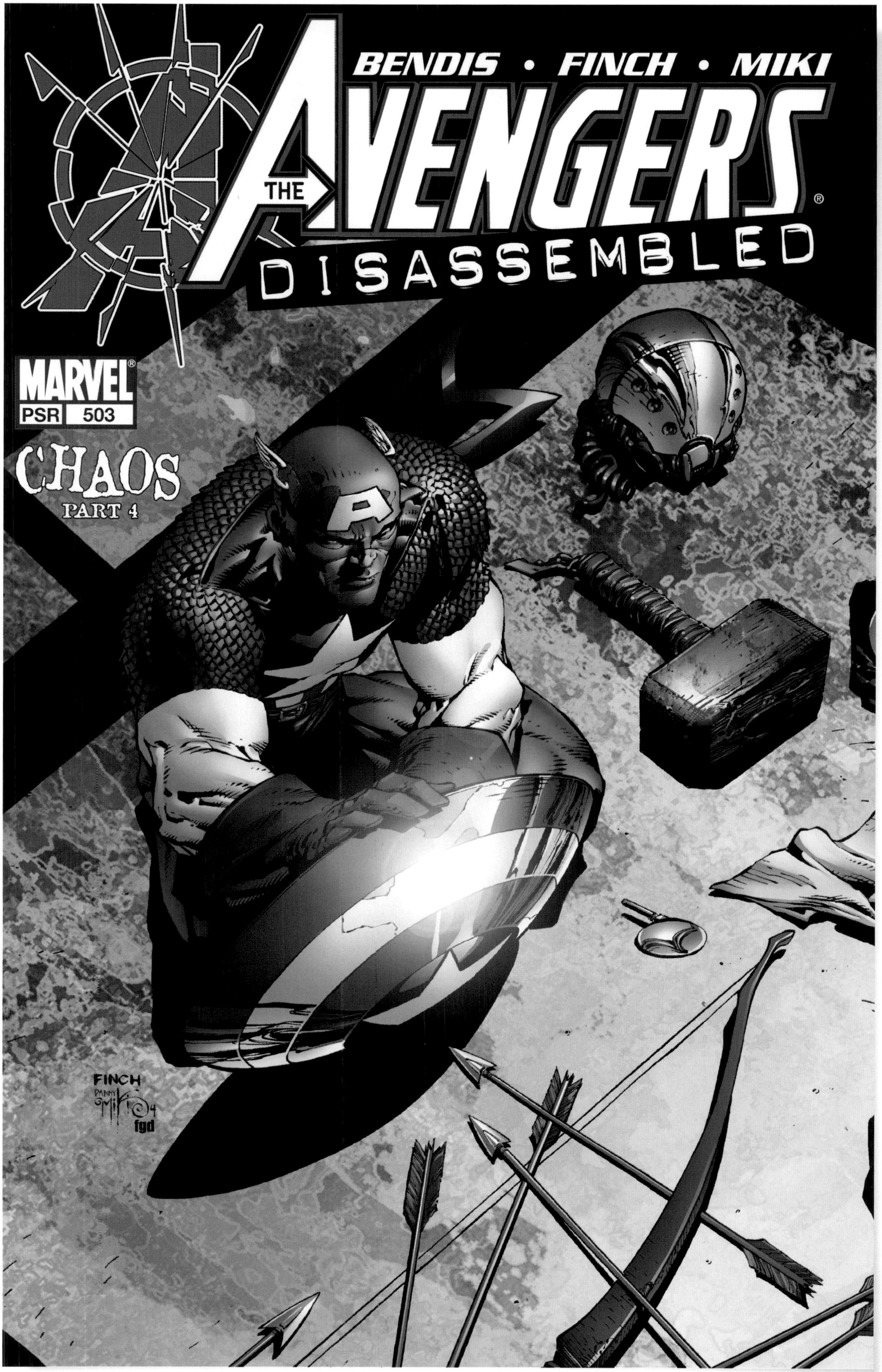
BENDIS · FINCH · MIKI
THE AVENGERS
DISASSEMBLED
MARVEL
PSR 503
CHAOS
PART 4
FINCH
fgd

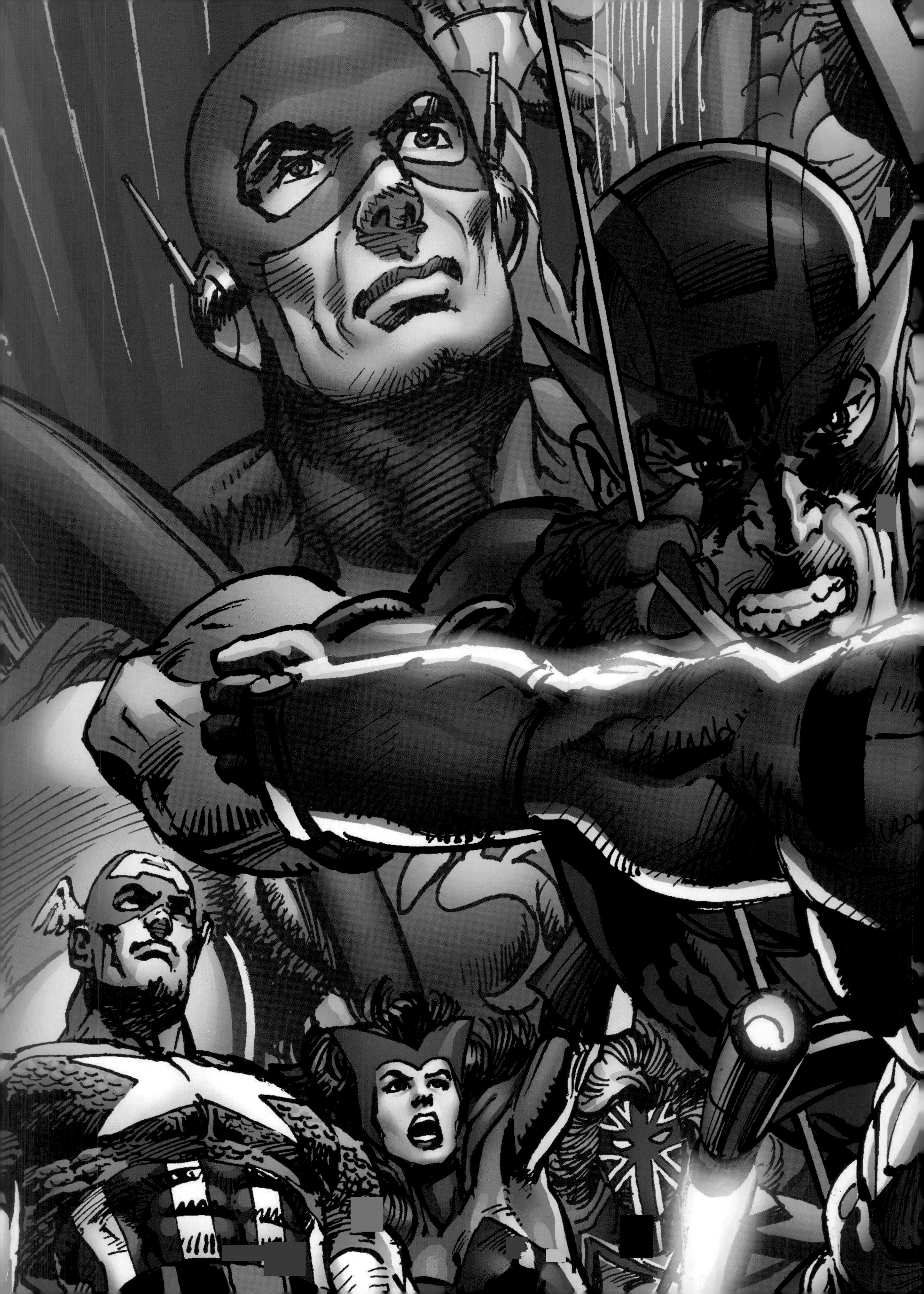

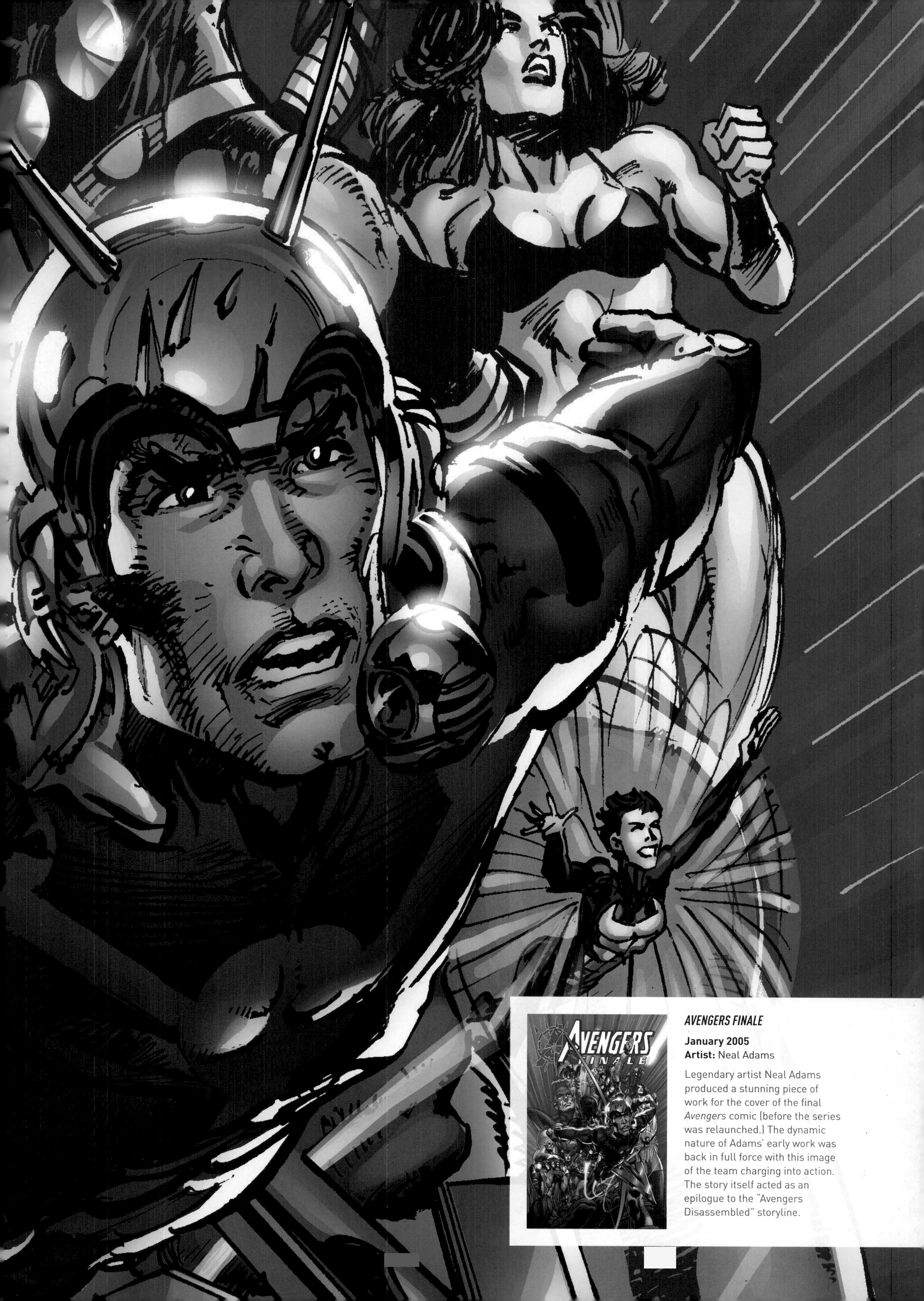
AVENGERS
FINALE

***AVENGERS FINALE***

**January 2005**
**Artist:** Neal Adams

Legendary artist Neal Adams produced a stunning piece of work for the cover of the final *Avengers* comic (before the series was relaunched.) The dynamic nature of Adams' early work was back in full force with this image of the team charging into action. The story itself acted as an epilogue to the "Avengers Disassembled" storyline.

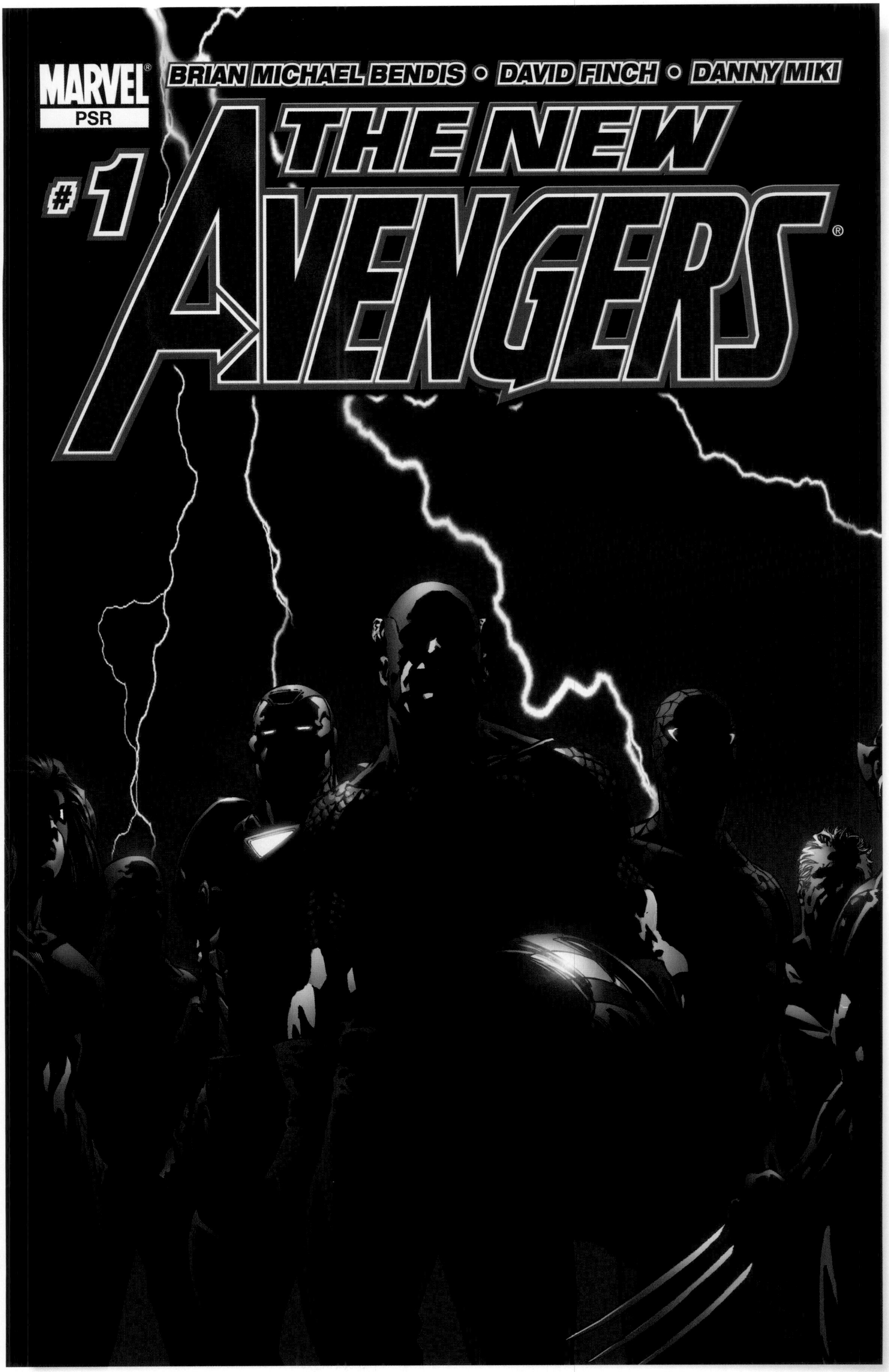
MARVEL
PSR
BRIAN MICHAEL BENDIS • DAVID FINCH • DANNY MIKI
#1
THE NEW
AVENGERS

MARVEL
PSR 2
BENDIS
FINCH
MIKI
D'ARMATA
THE NEW AVENGERS

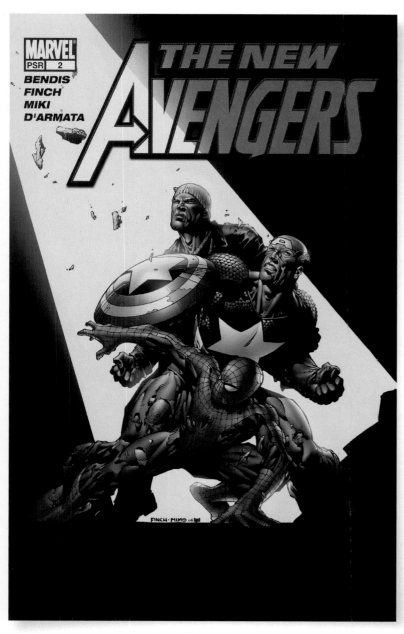

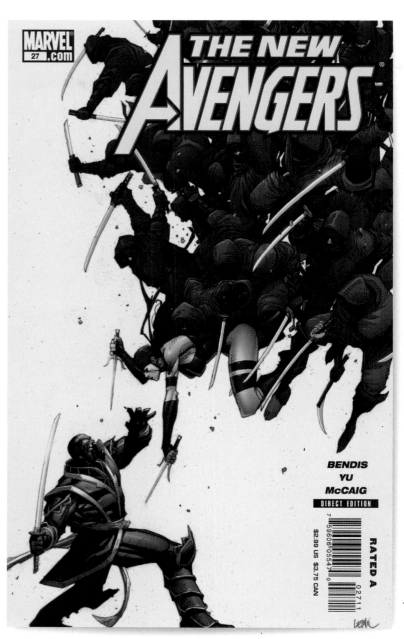

▲ *THE NEW AVENGERS* #2

**February 2005**
**Artist:** David Finch

With Spider-Man now a member of the Avengers, he soon became a regular on the covers. The second issue is another dramatic and tense-looking work from Finch. The image reflects the main story, as the heroes joined forces in an attempt to stop a mass breakout from the Super Villain penitentiary known as the Raft.

MARVEL
27 .com
THE NEW AVENGERS
BENDIS
YU
McCAIG
DIRECT EDITION
RATED A
$2.99 US $3.75 CAN

▲ *THE NEW AVENGERS* #27

**April 2007**
**Artist:** Leinil Francis Yu

Leinil Francis Yu produced this stylish cover during his brief run as artist on *The New Avengers*. His striking image shows new hero Ronin (Clint Barton taking over the role from Echo) facing off against an overwhelming horde of ninja assassins led by Elektra.

◀ *THE NEW AVENGERS* #1

**January 2005**
**Artist:** David Finch

This was the book that made the Avengers one of Marvel's bestsellers, and created an entire franchise, with various Avengers-related titles spinning off its success. The cover for issue #1 is darker and moodier than those of the previous title, and Finch instills a real sense of heroic power and mystery into the characters by showing them in half-shadow.

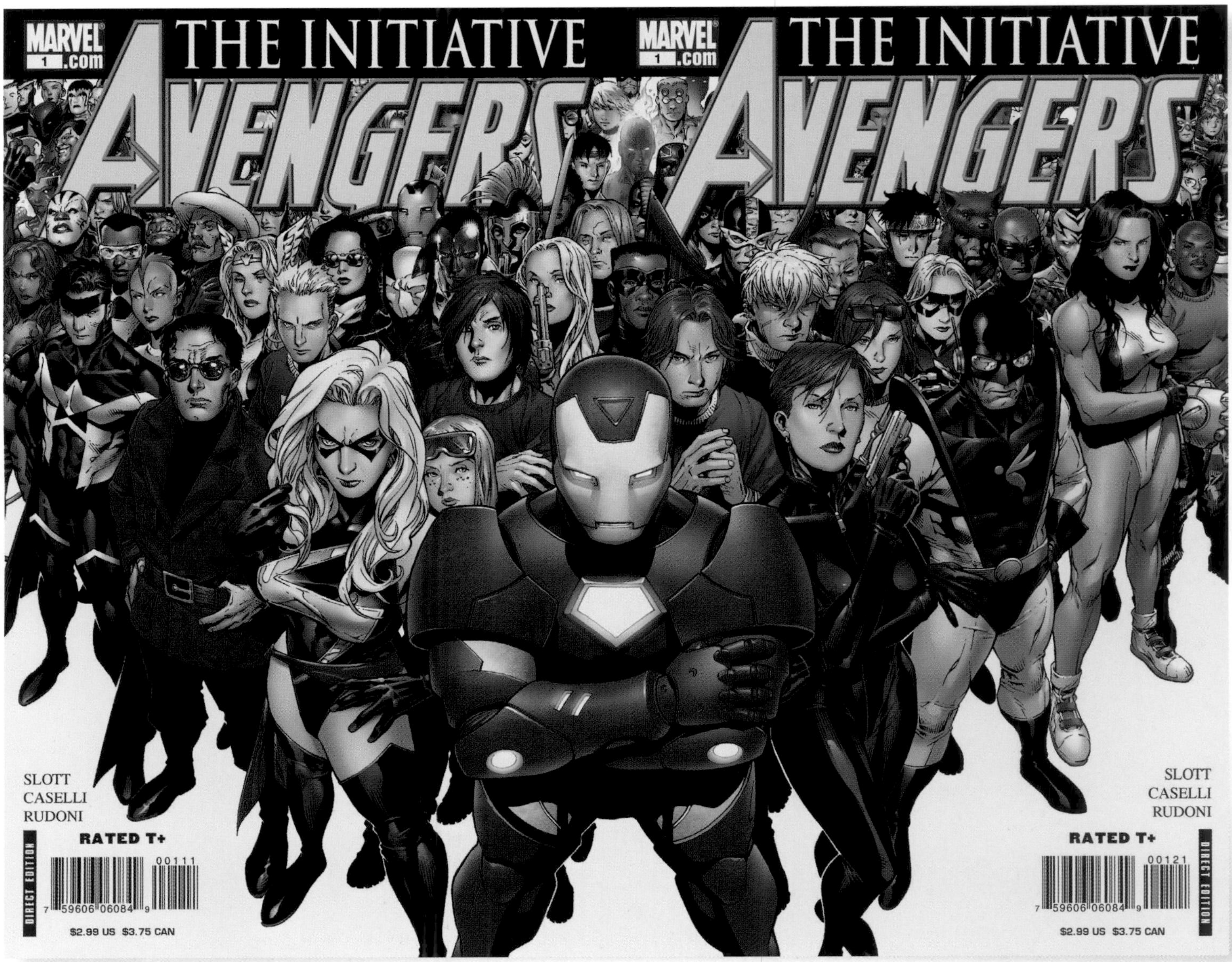
MARVEL
1 .com
THE INITIATIVE
AVENGERS
MARVEL
1 .com
THE INITIATIVE
AVENGERS
SLOTT
CASELLI
RUDONI
RATED T+
DIRECT EDITION
$2.99 US $3.75 CAN
SLOTT
CASELLI
RUDONI
RATED T+
DIRECT EDITION
$2.99 US $3.75 CAN

▲ ***AVENGERS: THE INITIATIVE* #1**

**June 2007**
**Artist:** Jim Cheung

Jim Cheung produced the art for a unique cover—or rather two covers—that could be put together to reveal one big image of the Avengers Initiative. Following on from the Civil War, which split Marvel's Super-Hero community in two, the new series focused on young heroes as they trained to be potential Avengers.

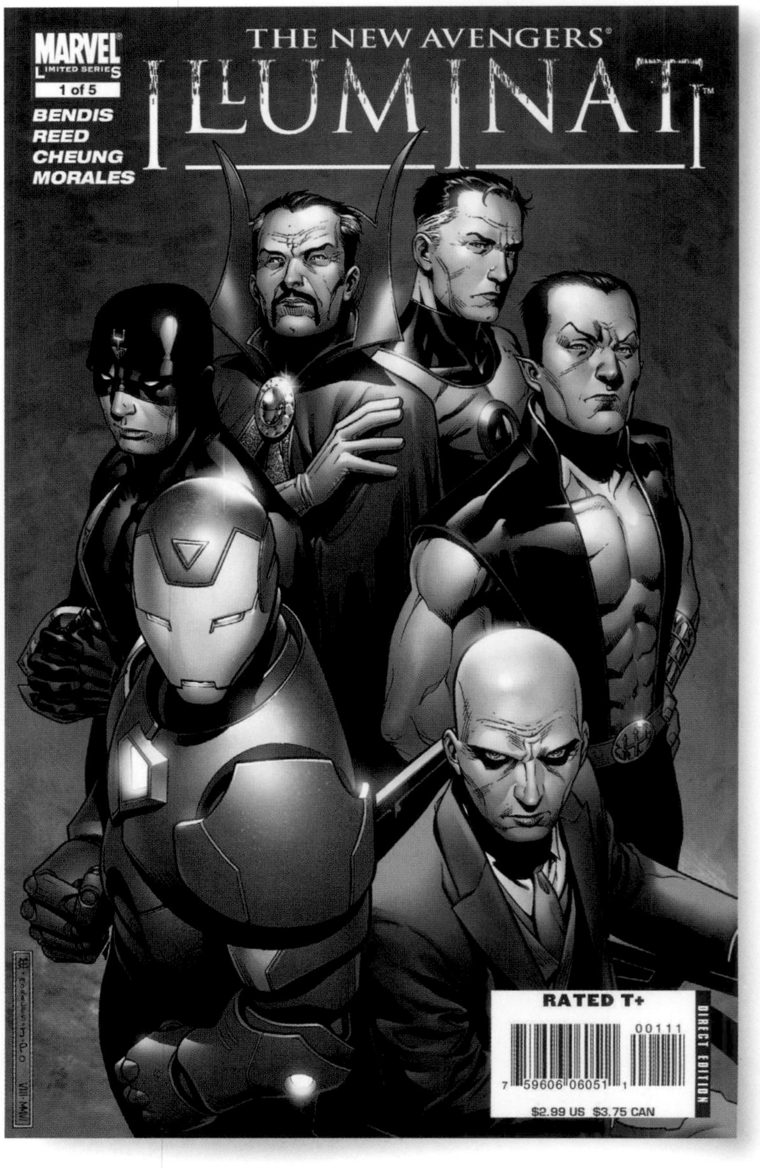
MARVEL
LIMITED SERIES
1 of 5
THE NEW AVENGERS
ILLUMINATI
BENDIS
REED
CHEUNG
MORALES
RATED T+
DIRECT EDITION
$2.99 US $3.75 CAN

***THE NEW AVENGERS: ILLUMINATI* #1** ▶

**February 2007**
**Artist:** Jim Cheung

One of the most shocking revelations writer Brian Michael Bendis introduced to the Avengers was that six of Marvel's most respected heroes had formed a secret group—the Illuminati. Jim Cheung illustrated the series, his first cover bringing the heroes together in an atmospheric work that hints at the group's hidden affiliation.

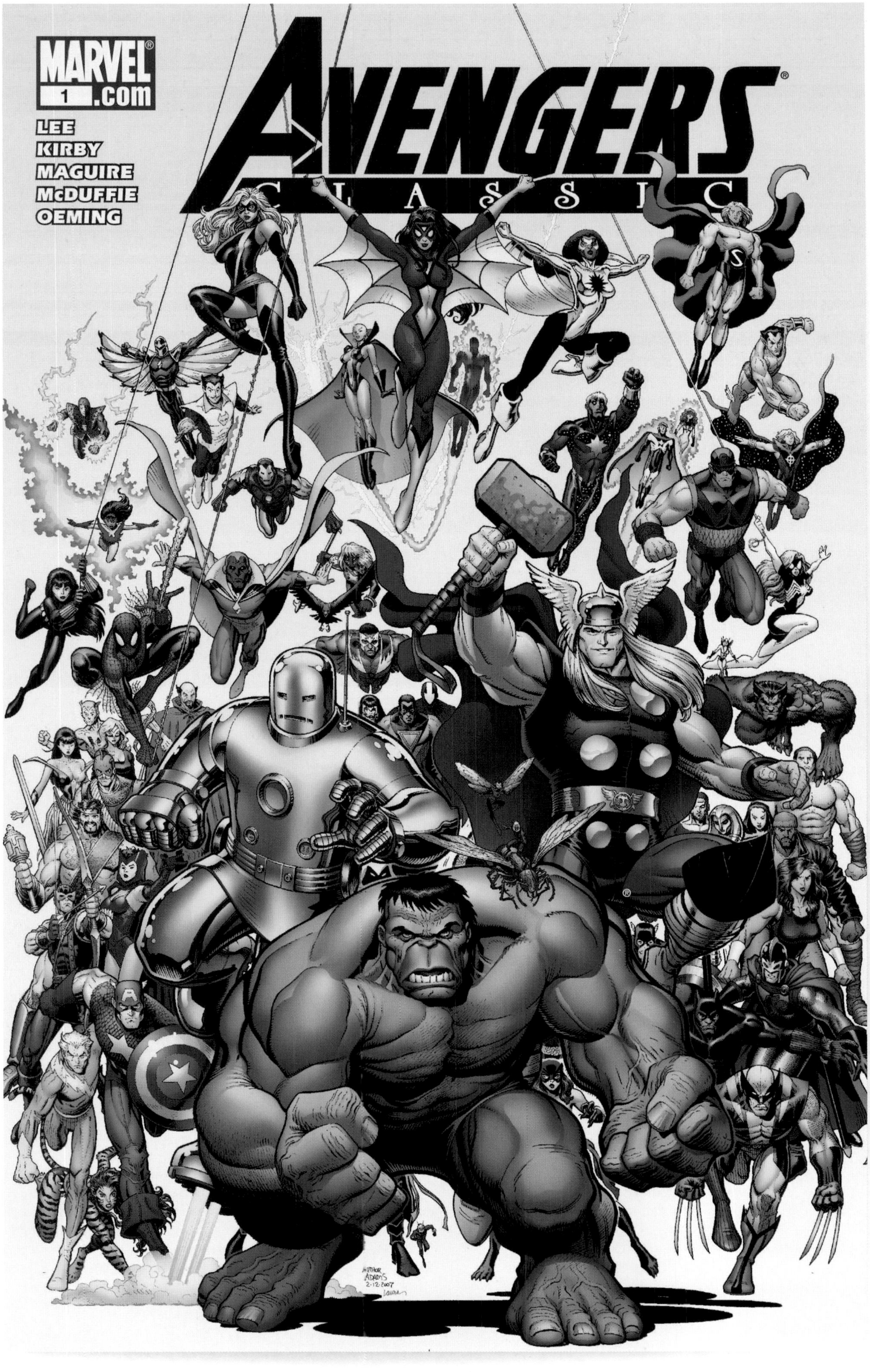
MARVEL
1 .com
LEE
KIRBY
MAGUIRE
McDUFFIE
OEMING
AVENGERS
CLASSIC

▲ ***AVENGERS CLASSIC* #1**

**August 2007**
**Artist:** Art Adams

Art Adams created a stunning piece of work for the debut issue of *Avengers Classic*, a series that reprinted Avengers tales from their first issue (with some modern material added). Adams manages to incorporate just about every hero who had ever been an Avenger for his cover. It was interesting to see Adams' artistic take on the original team, including Iron Man, Thor, and the Hulk.

***AVENGERS VS X-MEN* #1 ▶**

**June 2012**
**Artist:** Jim Cheung

When it was decided to pit the Avengers against the X-Men, Marvel knew they would need an A-list artist for this crossover event. Jim Cheung had broken into the world of comics as a teenager via Marvel UK and has gone on to become one of the industry's top artists. He provided the cover art for *Avengers vs. X-Men* (or *AVX*), showing both teams on the verge of war in a stunning piece of work.

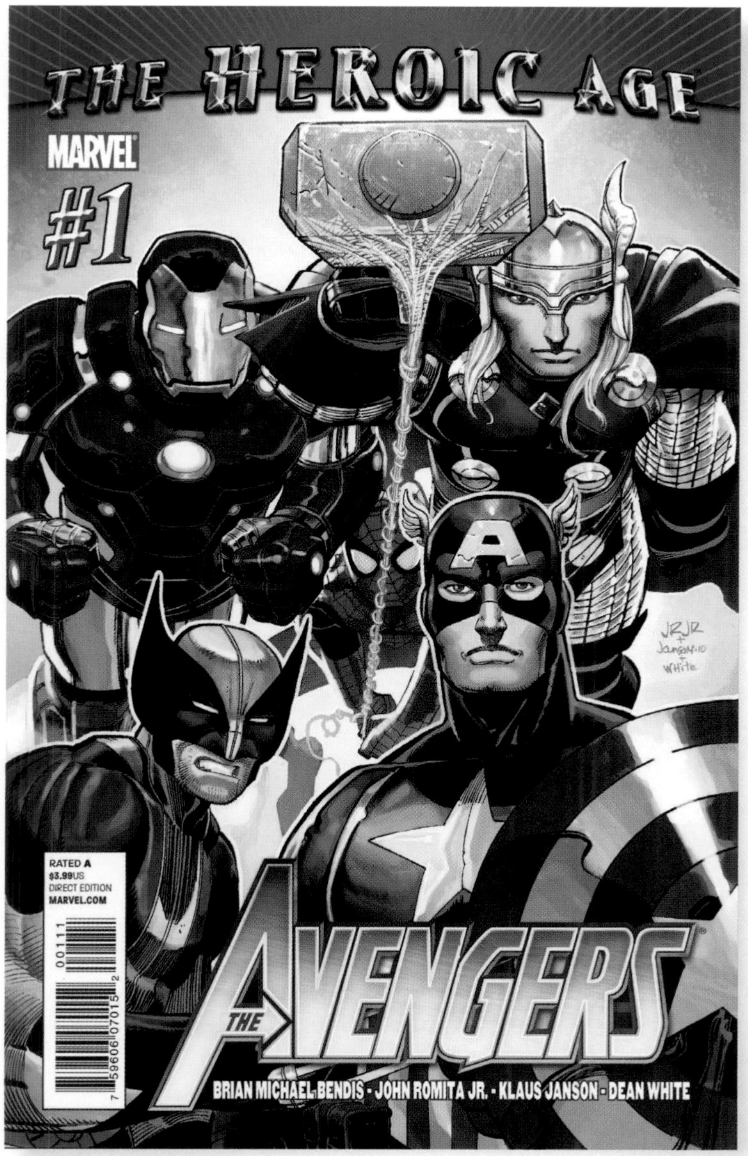
THE HEROIC AGE
MARVEL
#1
RATED A
$3.99US
DIRECT EDITION
MARVEL.COM
THE AVENGERS
BRIAN MICHAEL BENDIS · JOHN ROMITA JR. · KLAUS JANSON · DEAN WHITE

**◀ *AVENGERS* #1**

**July 2010**
**Artist:** John Romita Jr.

The *Avengers* was relaunched following the end of the "Dark Reign," a period in Marvel continuity during which the unstable Norman Osborn gained political control of America's heroes. Steve Rogers, Osborn's more honorable successor, formed several new Avengers teams. Romita Jr.'s cover reflects the nobility of the main team and was the defining image of the new "Heroic Age."

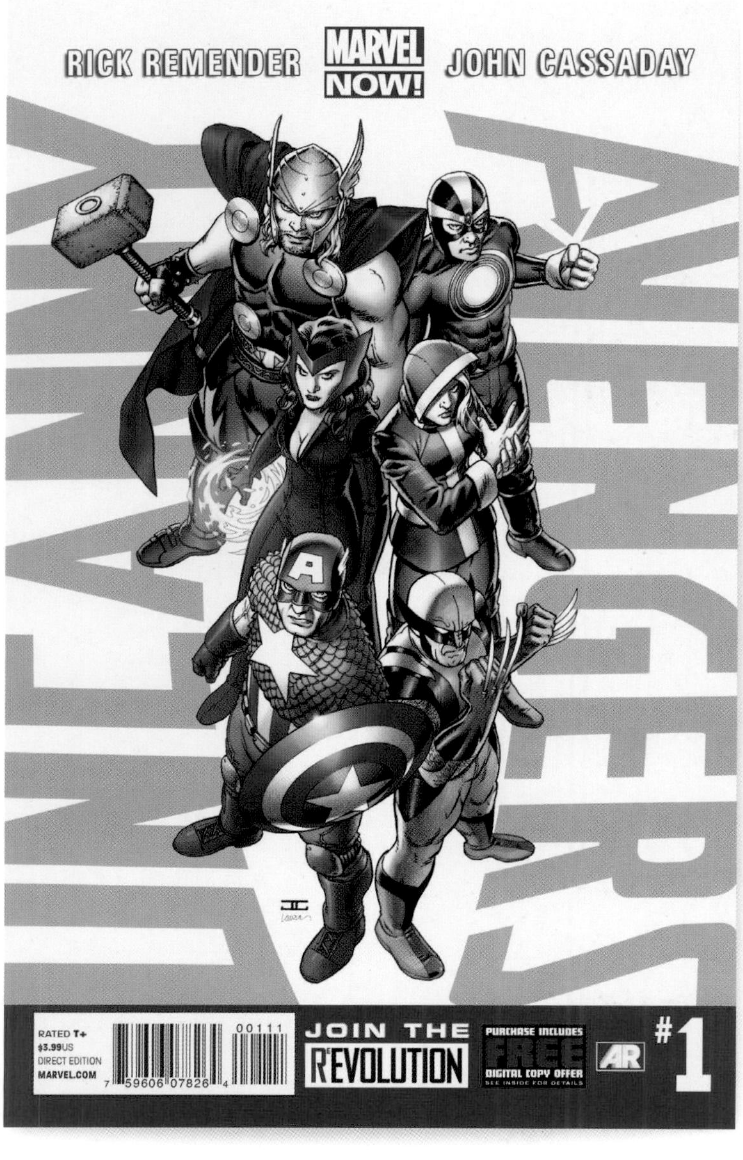
RICK REMENDER
MARVEL NOW!
JOHN CASSADAY
UNCANNY AVENGERS
RATED T+
$3.99US
DIRECT EDITION
MARVEL.COM
JOIN THE REVOLUTION
PURCHASE INCLUDES FREE DIGITAL COPY OFFER
AR
#1

**◀ *UNCANNY AVENGERS* #1**

**December 2012**
**Artist:** John Cassaday

Combining both the X-Men and Avengers into one team was a simple yet brilliant idea. John Cassaday, who had become one of the biggest names in the business by this time, illustrated the cover for the debut issue. Cassaday showcased the line-up and even incorporated the logo into his work, using it to separate the X-Men and Avengers.

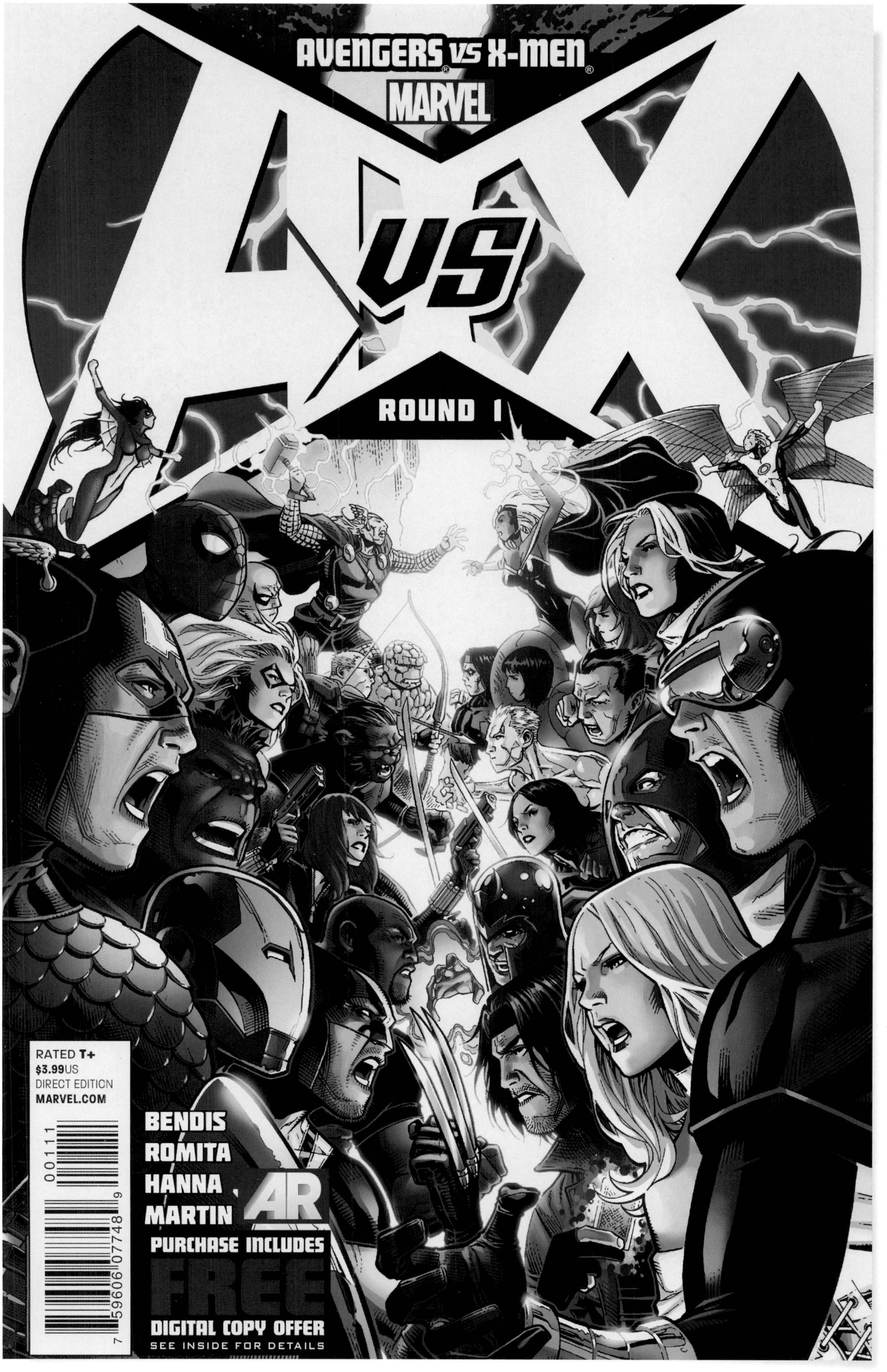
AVENGERS VS X-MEN
MARVEL
A VS X
ROUND 1
RATED T+
$3.99US
DIRECT EDITION
MARVEL.COM
BENDIS
ROMITA
HANNA
MARTIN
AR
PURCHASE INCLUDES
FREE
DIGITAL COPY OFFER
SEE INSIDE FOR DETAILS

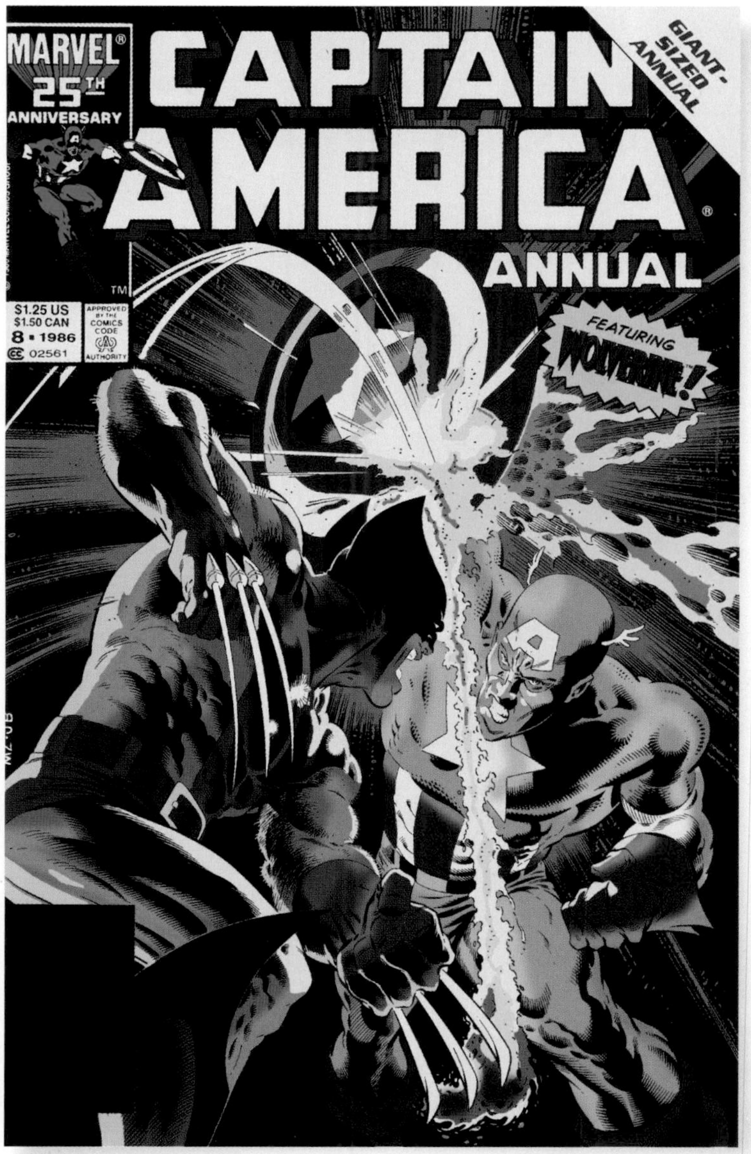
MARVEL
25TH ANNIVERSARY
CAPTAIN AMERICA
GIANT-SIZED ANNUAL
ANNUAL
$1.25 US
$1.50 CAN
8 • 1986
FEATURING WOLVERINE!

◀ *CAPTAIN AMERICA ANNUAL* **#8**

**September 1986**
**Artist:** Mike Zeck

By the mid-1980s, Wolverine was firmly established as one of Marvel's favorite heroes, and an appearance by him on a cover would usually lead to an increase in sales. This was one of the most spectacular Wolverine covers outside of his own title. Mike Zeck's dynamic style gives the piece a dangerous energy fit for a Super Hero of Wolverine's standing.

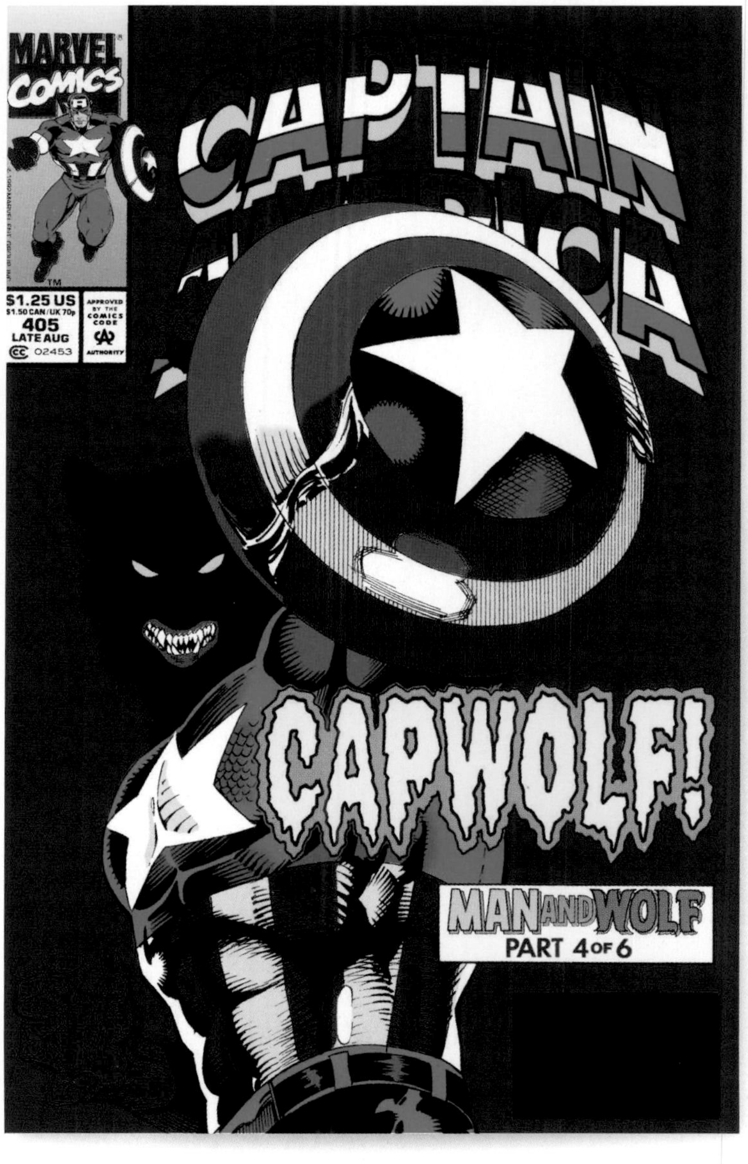
MARVEL COMICS
CAPTAIN AMERICA
$1.25 US
405
LATE AUG
CAPWOLF!
MAN AND WOLF
PART 4 OF 6

◀ *CAPTAIN AMERICA* **#405**

**August 1992**
**Artist:** Rik Levins

One of the strangest *Captain America* adventures saw Steve Rogers become a werewolf called "Capwolf." The Rik Levins cover has a simple layout, but the image of Capwolf is a striking and strangely intriguing one, typical of the title's experimental stories during the mid-90s.

MARVEL
UNIVERSE
OCTOBER
1995
Captain America

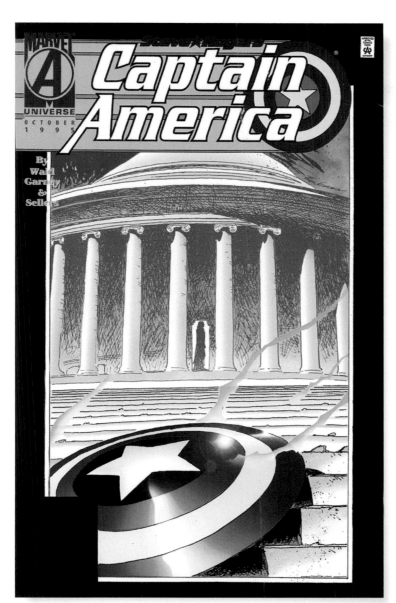

◀ *CAPTAIN AMERICA* #444

**October 1995**
**Artist:** Ron Garney

Writer Mark Waid and artist Ron Garney provided what many consider to be the best *Captain America* stories of the decade. Garney's covers were both stylish and eye-catching—and this one is a fine example. The discarded shield outside the White House hints at Cap's meeting with the President, and his eventual exile.

COMICS
CAPTAIN AMERICA
MAY '96 451
Captain America
MAN WITHOUT A COUNTRY

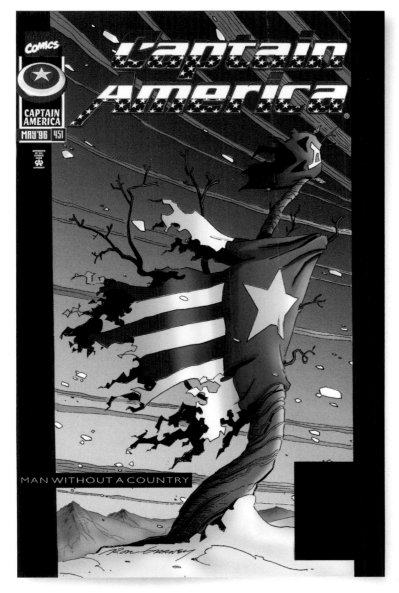

◀ *CAPTAIN AMERICA* #451

**May 1996**
**Artist:** Ron Garney

Ron Garney's stark cover reflected Steve Rogers taking up a new costume in this issue—one without the familiar stars and stripes emblazoned on it (seen here seemingly discarded and blowing in the wind). The striking image also obliquely refers to Cap's exile beyond US soil.

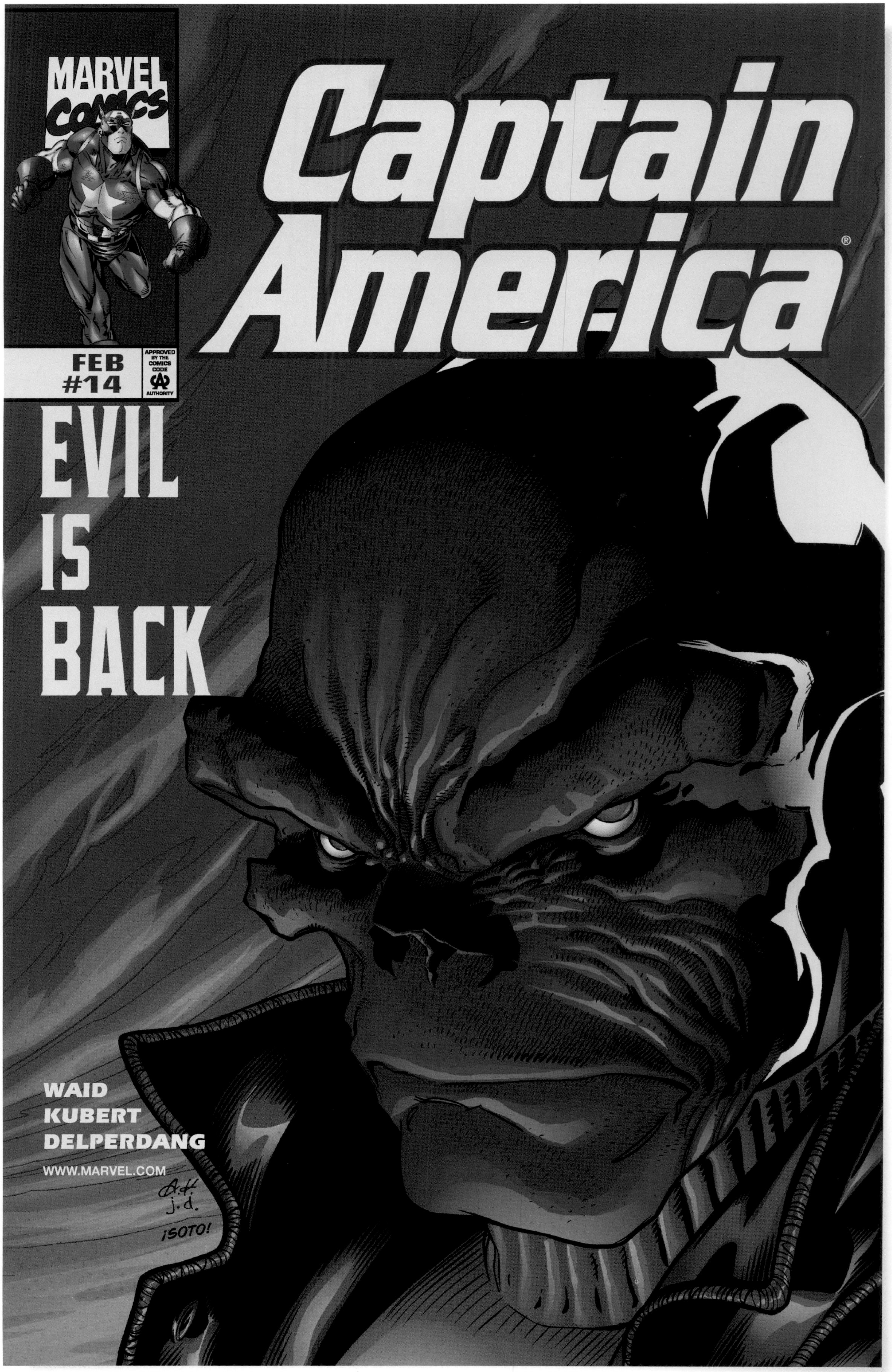
MARVEL COMICS
Captain America®
FEB #14
APPROVED BY THE COMICS CODE AUTHORITY
EVIL IS BACK
WAID
KUBERT
DELPERDANG
WWW.MARVEL.COM
¡SOTO!

◀ *CAPTAIN AMERICA* #14

**February 1999**
**Artist:** Andy Kubert

Andy Kubert's terrifying portrait of the Red Skull made this Cap cover one of the most iconic of the decade. Writer Mark Waid's first run on *Captain America* had been cut short when the title was outsourced for a year to creators from publisher Image Comics. However, when the title returned, Marvel brought Waid back and relaunched the series from a new issue #1. It proved to be a huge success.

MARVEL COMICS
Captain America
#32
WWW.MARVEL.COM
JURGENS
ORDWAY

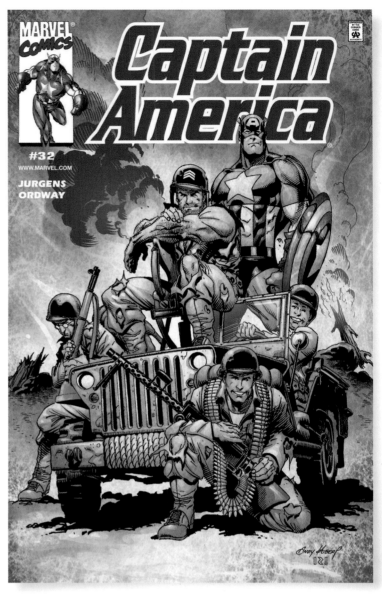

*CAPTAIN AMERICA* #32 ▶

**August 2000**
**Artist:** Andy Kubert

Andy Kubert got to draw Nick Fury and his Howling Commandos for this classic Captain America cover. Kubert's father, the legendary artist Joe Kubert, had made his name illustrating Sergeant Rock for DC Comics, and Andy's image has definite echoes of his father's work.

CAPTAIN AMERICA
JOHN NEY RIEBER
JOHN CASSADAY
1
MARVEL PG

*CAPTAIN AMERICA* #1 ▶

**June 2002**
**Artist:** John Cassaday

The after-effects of the real-life 9/11 terrorist attacks that had taken place the previous year were felt in this issue as Cap was sent to the Middle East to find those responsible. Cassaday's stunning cover is über-patriotic and militaristic, reflecting a country—and indeed a world—trying to come to terms with the attacks.

MARVEL
PSR
ED BRUBAKER · STEVE EPTING
#1
CAPTAIN
AMERICA
OUT OF
TIME
PART 1

MARVEL
PSR 6
BRUBAKER
EPTING
D'ARMATA
CAPTAIN
AMERICA
OUT OF
TIME
PART 6

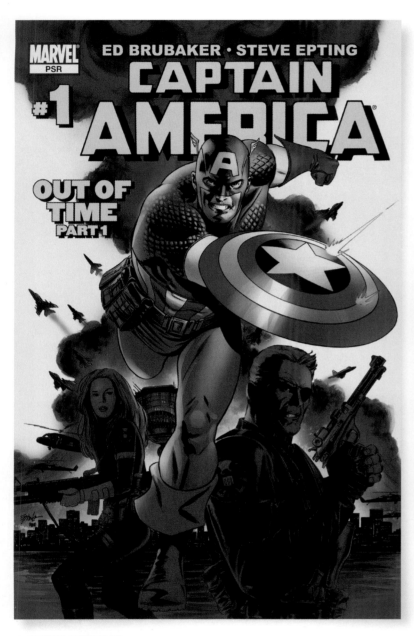

▲ *CAPTAIN AMERICA* #1

**January 2005**
**Artist:** Steve Epting

Writer Ed Brubaker and artist Steve Epting created one of the all-time great *Captain America* sagas, "Out of Time." Epting's covers were exceptional montages, resembling high-end movie posters. This cover highlights a change in storytelling style, as Cap's adventures became more like a top-class spy-thriller than a traditional Super-Hero adventure.

▲ *CAPTAIN AMERICA* #6

**June 2005**
**Artist:** Steve Epting

Ed Brubaker's story gave a new twist to Bucky Barnes' role as Cap's old sidekick, making him a deadly assassin rather than teenage poster boy. Epting's cover for this issue focuses on Cap's exploits in World War II. It is another movie-style montage, the stark red Nazi flags providing a sinister backdrop.

MARVEL
11 .com
CAPTAIN AMERICA
BRUBAKER
EPTING
PERKINS
D'ARMATA
THE WINTER SOLDIER
PART 3

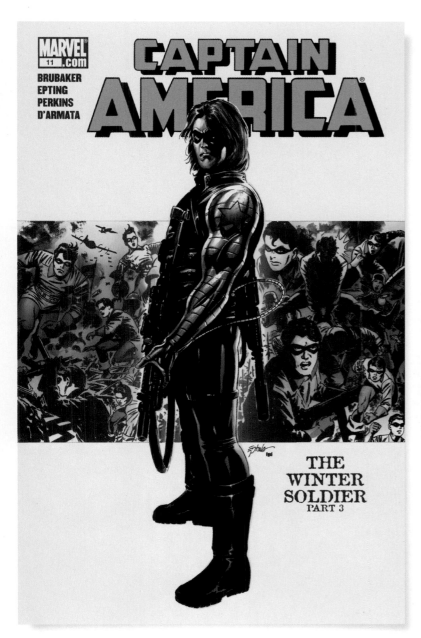

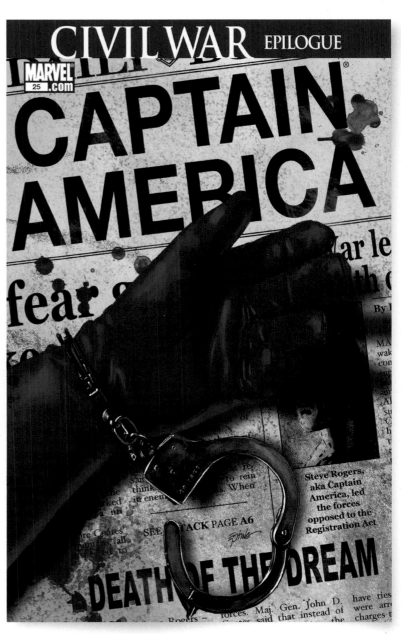

▲ *CAPTAIN AMERICA* #11

**November 2005**
**Artist:** Steve Epting

"The Winter Soldier" (Bucky Barnes, who had become a Soviet assassin since his days as Cap's sidekick) is the main focus on this issue's cover, with a montage of Bucky's war-time exploits behind him. The character and story was the inspiration for 2014's second *Captain America* movie.

CIVIL WAR EPILOGUE
MARVEL
25 .com
CAPTAIN AMERICA
Steve Rogers, aka Captain America, led the forces opposed to the Registration Act
DREAM

▲ *CAPTAIN AMERICA* #25

**April 2007**
**Artist:** Ed McGuinness

Ed McGuinness' simple but emotionally charged cover illustrated a story that made headlines across the world—the assassination of Captain America. The headlines on the background image echo famous assassinations of real-life American heroes, making the cover all the more emotively powerful.

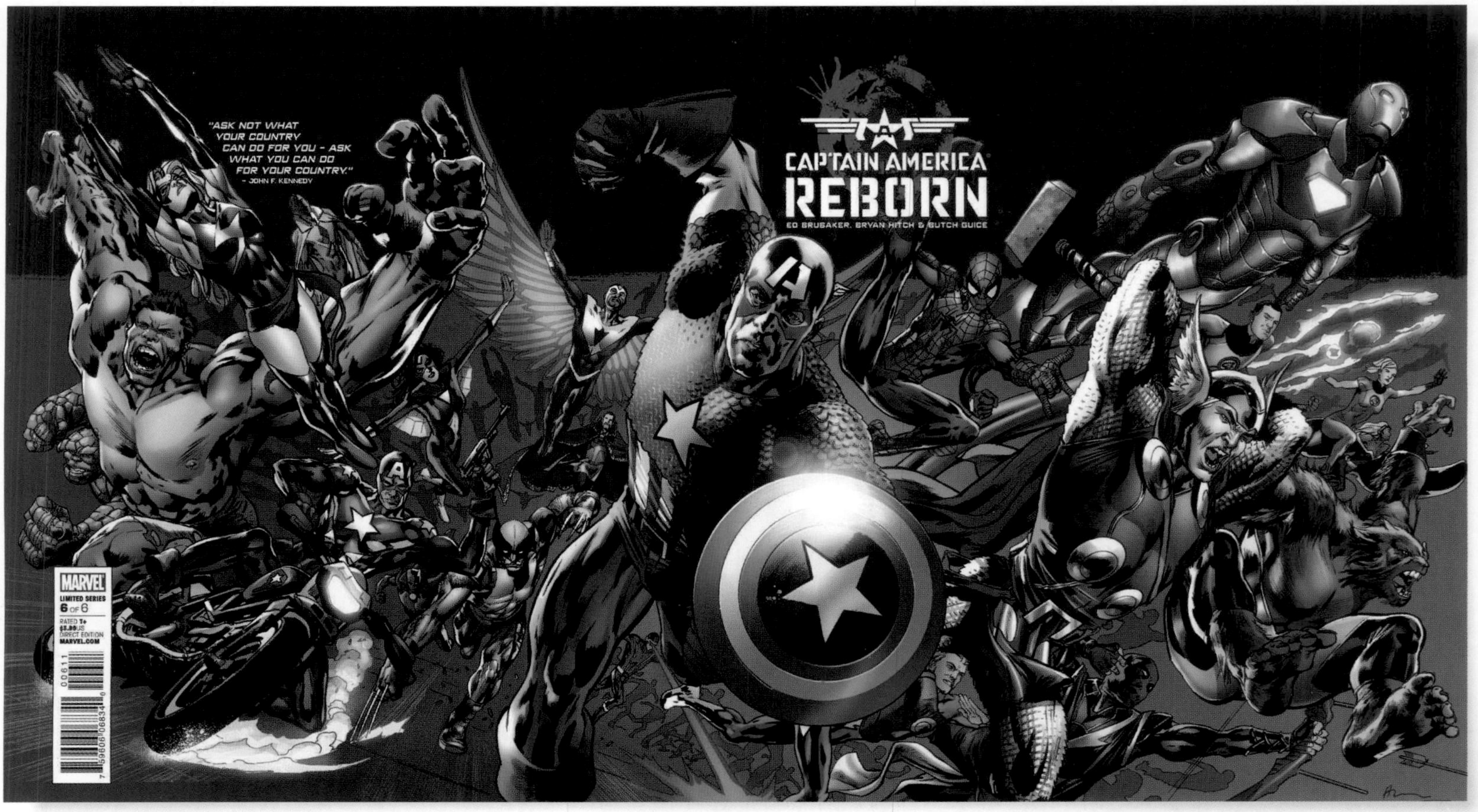
"ASK NOT WHAT YOUR COUNTRY CAN DO FOR YOU - ASK WHAT YOU CAN DO FOR YOUR COUNTRY."
- JOHN F. KENNEDY
CAPTAIN AMERICA
REBORN
MARVEL
LIMITED SERIES
6 OF 6

▲ *CAPTAIN AMERICA REBORN #6*

**March 2010**
**Artist:** Bryan Hitch

Bryan Hitch is one of the most talented artists in the business and provided a stunning wraparound cover for the final issue of the series that had revealed Steve Rogers was still alive, but lost in time. Hitch's art is as bombastic as the final chapter's action-packed conclusion. It also shows the original Captain America taking his rightful place at the forefront of Marvel's heroes.

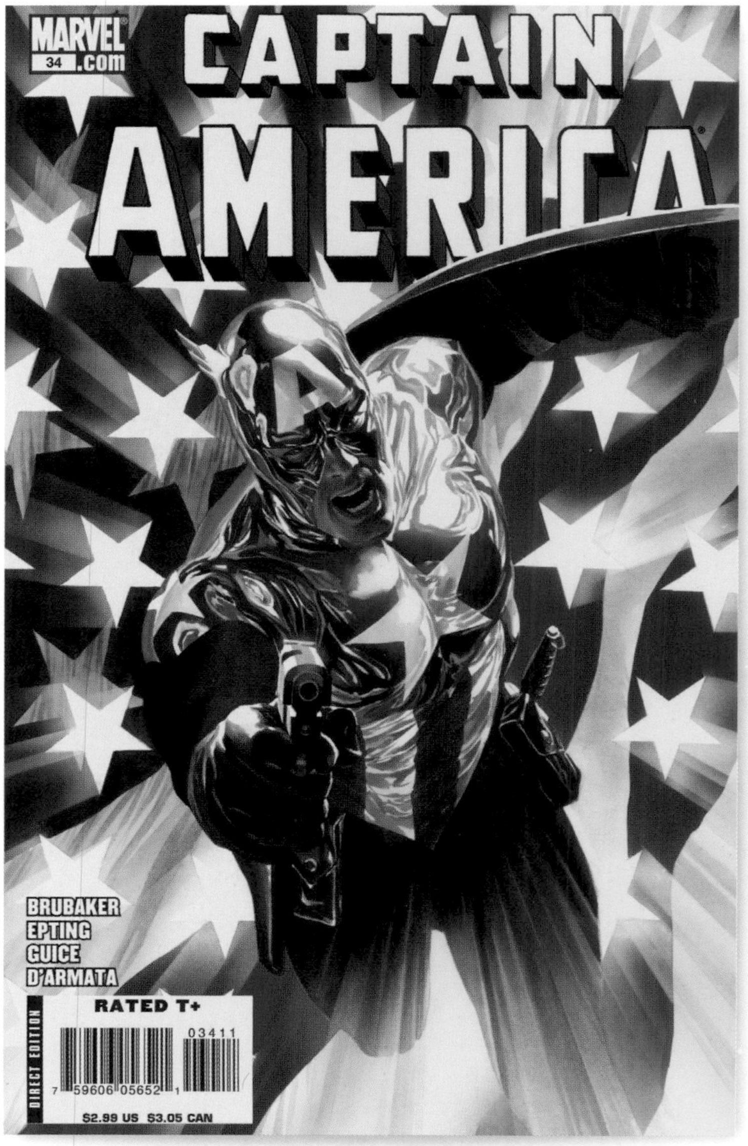
MARVEL
34 .com
CAPTAIN
AMERICA
BRUBAKER
EPTING
GUICE
D'ARMATA
RATED T+
DIRECT EDITION
$2.99 US $3.05 CAN

*CAPTAIN AMERICA #34* ▶

**March 2008**
**Artist:** Alex Ross

When Bucky Barnes took on the role of Captain America from the seemingly dead Steve Rogers it was always going to be a big deal. Alex Ross produced a stunning painted cover showing the new Captain America—complete with a brand new costume. Bucky had been the Winter Soldier, a deadly assassin, and continued to use guns as Captain America. It was the portrayal of Cap with a gun that shocked many readers.

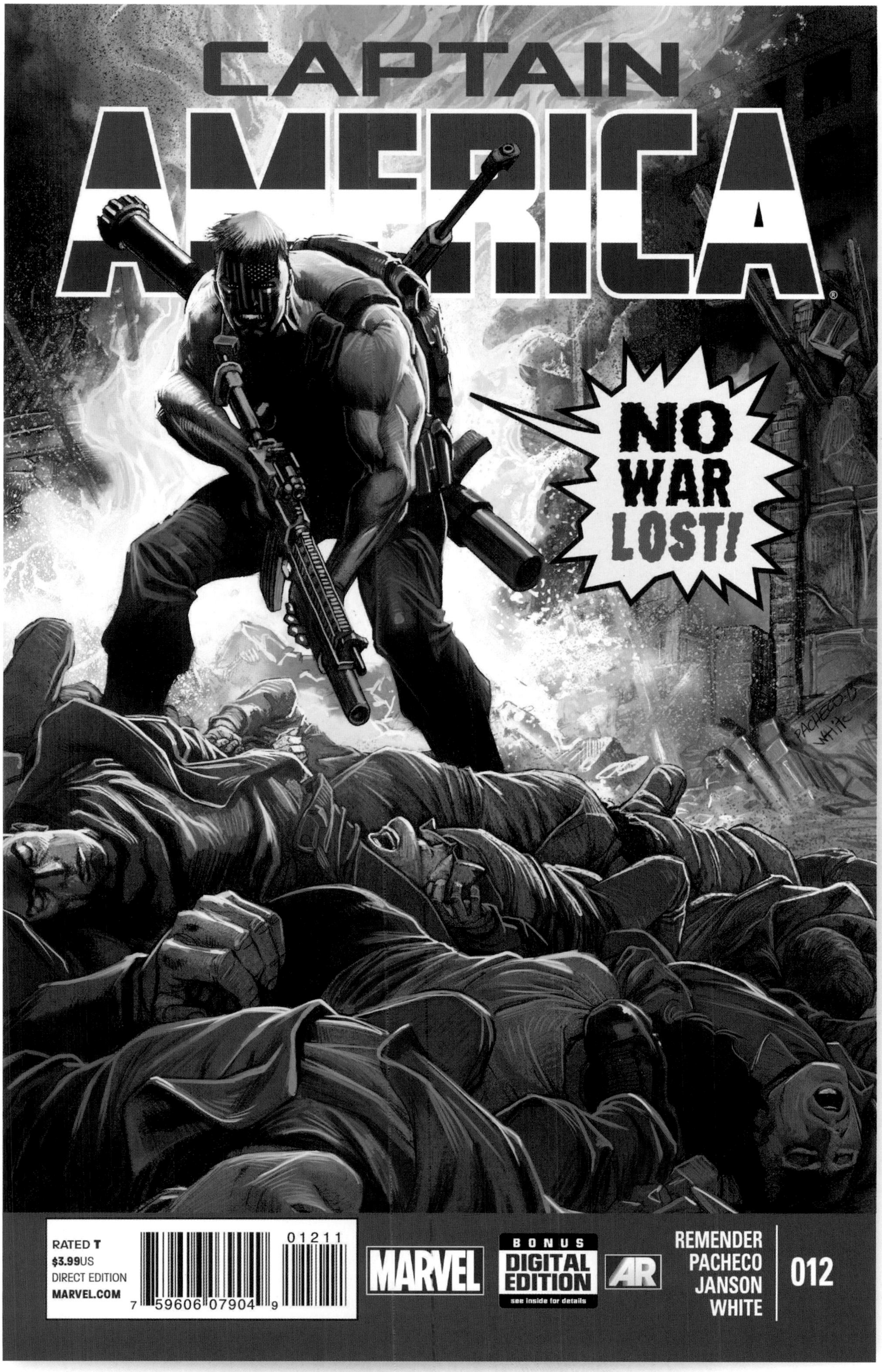
CAPTAIN AMERICA
NO WAR LOST!
RATED T
$3.99US
DIRECT EDITION
MARVEL.COM
MARVEL
BONUS DIGITAL EDITION
see inside for details
AR
REMENDER
PACHECO
JANSON
WHITE
012

▲ *CAPTAIN AMERICA* #12

**December 2013**
**Artist:** Carlos Pacheco

Crazed war-veteran and failed Super Soldier Nuke had first been seen in the classic *Daredevil* issue #232 (July 1986) and had seldom been used since the end of that story. He was, however, center stage in this story, and never looked as menacing as he does on Carlos Pacheco's powerful cover, which shows him standing over the bodies of his victims.

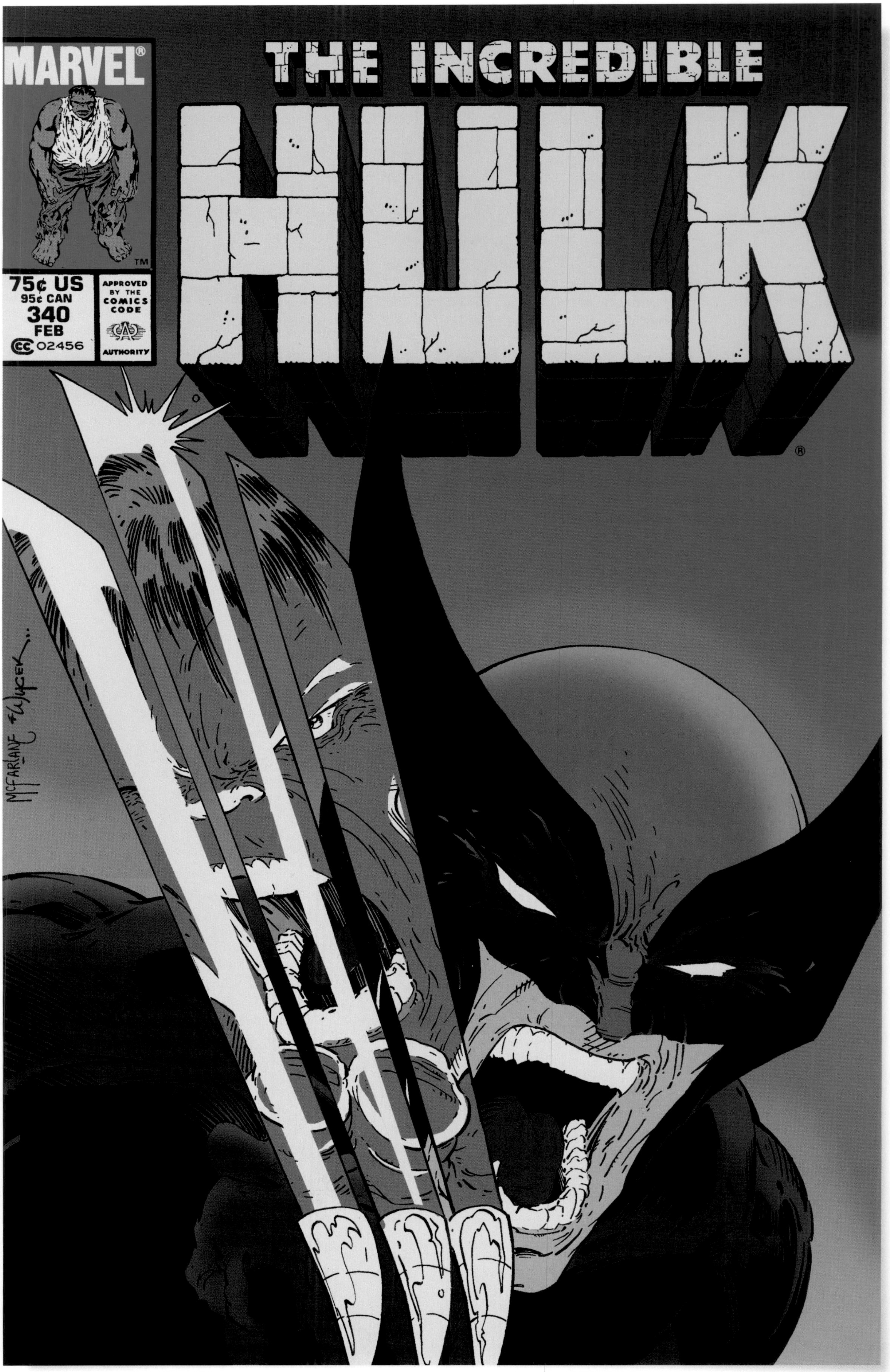
MARVEL
THE INCREDIBLE
HULK
75¢ US
95¢ CAN
340
FEB
02456
APPROVED BY THE COMICS CODE AUTHORITY

MARVEL
THE INCREDIBLE
HULK
75¢ US
95¢ CAN
333
JULY
APPROVED BY THE COMICS CODE AUTHORITY

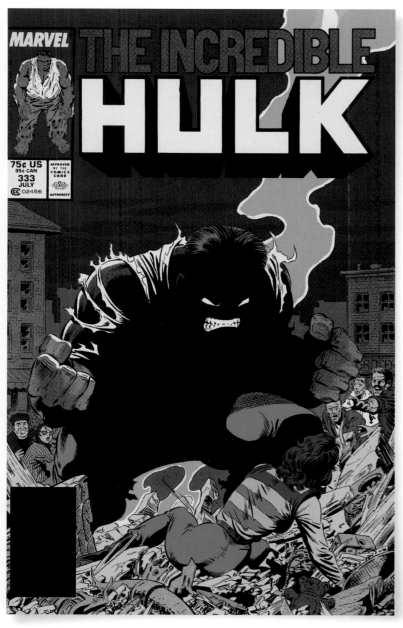

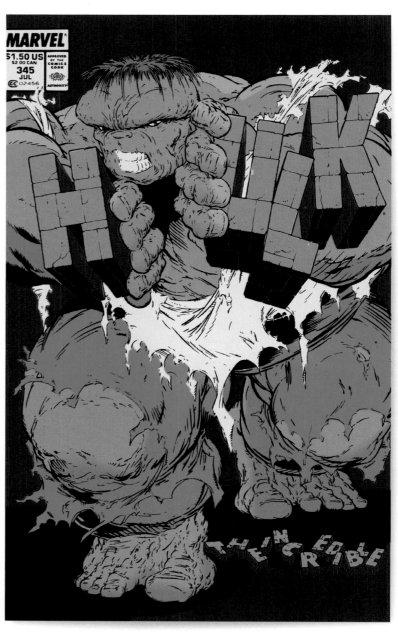

▲ *INCREDIBLE HULK* #333

**July 1987**
**Artist:** Steve Geiger

The Hulk had rarely looked as angry as he did on this cover, illustrated by Steve Geiger. Bruce Banner had just learned shocking secrets of his past. The trauma he felt was transferred to his monstrous alter ego, which Geiger brilliantly reflects in his depiction of a glowering Hulk.

MARVEL
$1.50 US
$2.00 CAN
345
JUL
APPROVED BY THE COMICS CODE AUTHORITY
HULK
THE INCREDIBLE

▲ *INCREDIBLE HULK* #345

**July 1988**
**Artist:** Todd McFarlane

Todd McFarlane frequently reinvented (or simply broke) the rules of cover design in order to create an eye-catching image. This cover is a classic example—McFarlane made the logo part of the cover artwork, so he could have the gray, enraged Hulk smashing it up.

◀ *INCREDIBLE HULK* #340

**February 1988**
**Artist:** Todd McFarlane

Todd McFarlane's work on the Hulk (with writer Peter David) revitalized the hero and propelled McFarlane to the big league. This classic cover is a shining example of what made his run so popular. Since Wolverine's first appearance in *Incredible Hulk* issue #181 in November 1974 (after a cameo in issue #180), Hulk-Wolverine fights have always been a big deal. This artwork, with the gray Hulk cleverly reflected in Wolverine's claws, showcases one of the best.

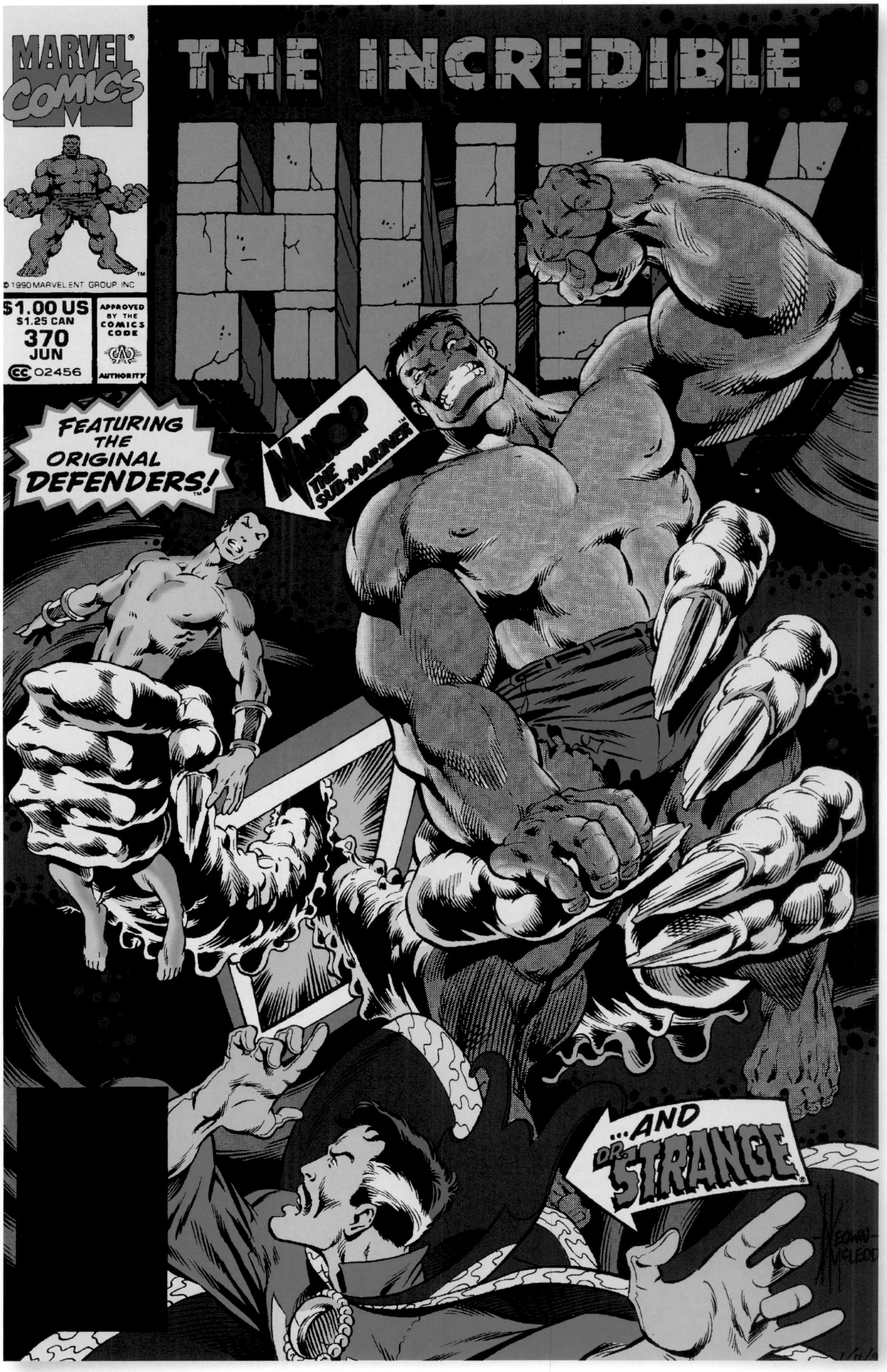
MARVEL COMICS
THE INCREDIBLE HULK
© 1990 MARVEL ENT. GROUP, INC.
$1.00 US
$1.25 CAN
370
JUN
APPROVED BY THE COMICS CODE AUTHORITY
02456
FEATURING THE ORIGINAL DEFENDERS!
NAMOR THE SUB-MARINER
...AND DR. STRANGE
KEOWN-McLEOD

▲ ***INCREDIBLE HULK* #370**

**June 1990**
**Artist:** Dale Keown

Dale Keown followed Todd McFarlane as artist on *Incredible Hulk* and, working with writer Peter David, created what is considered by fans to be one of the title's best runs. Keown also produced a number of fantastic covers, including this one, which brings the original Defenders together for the first time in years.

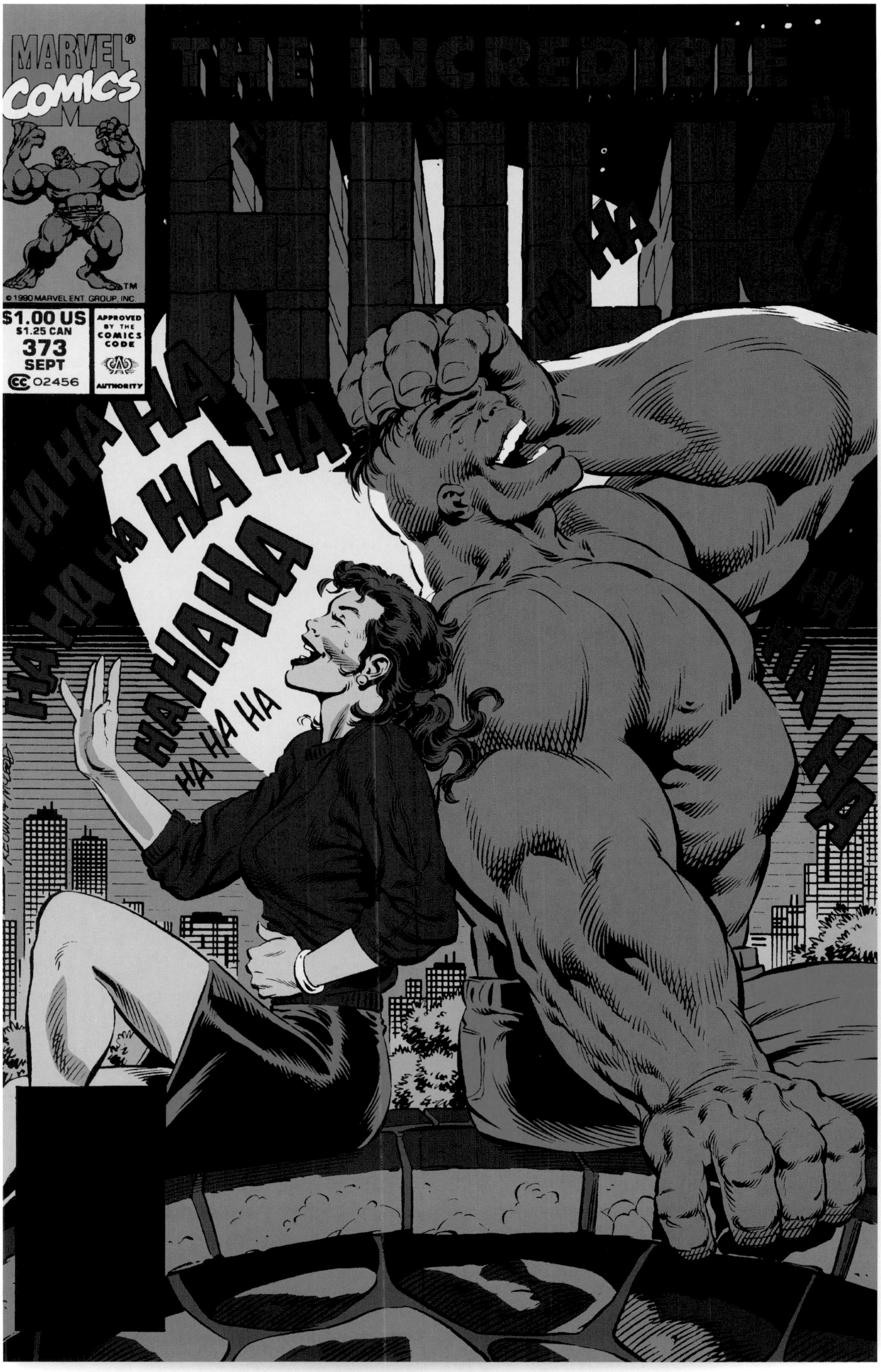
MARVEL COMICS
THE INCREDIBLE HULK
©1990 MARVEL ENT. GROUP, INC.
$1.00 US
$1.25 CAN
373
SEPT
02456
APPROVED BY THE COMICS CODE AUTHORITY
HA HA HA
HA HA HA HA
HA HA HA HA HA
HA HA HA
HA HA HA
HA HA HA

▲ *INCREDIBLE HULK* #373

**September 1990**
**Artist:** Dale Keown

Peter David remains one of the best writers to chronicle the Hulk's adventures, bringing a sense of humanity to the character. This classic cover by Keown, featuring the Hulk and Betty Ross (Bruce Banner's main love interest) sharing a few laughs, best exemplifies that aspect of David and Keown's time on the title.

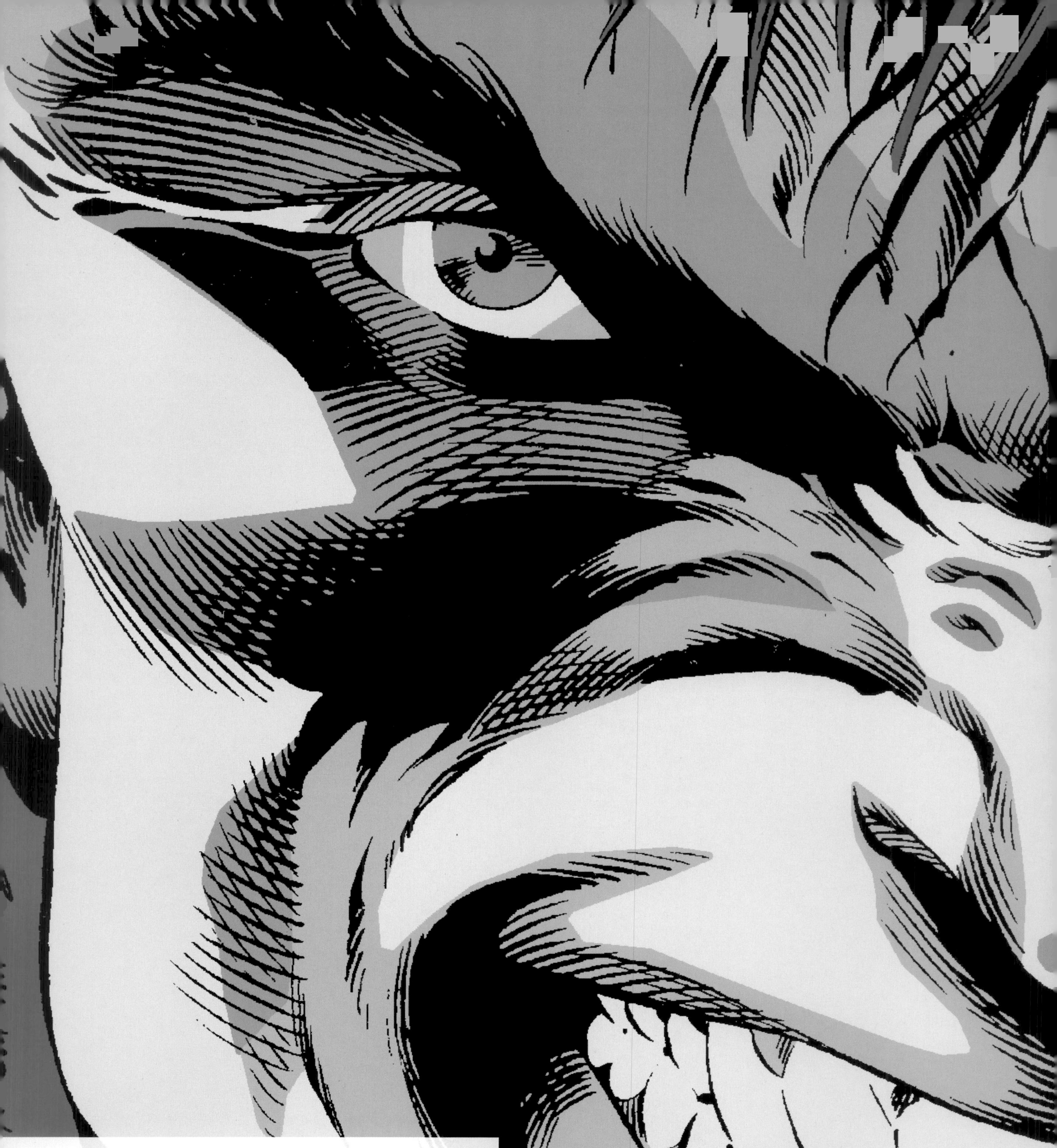

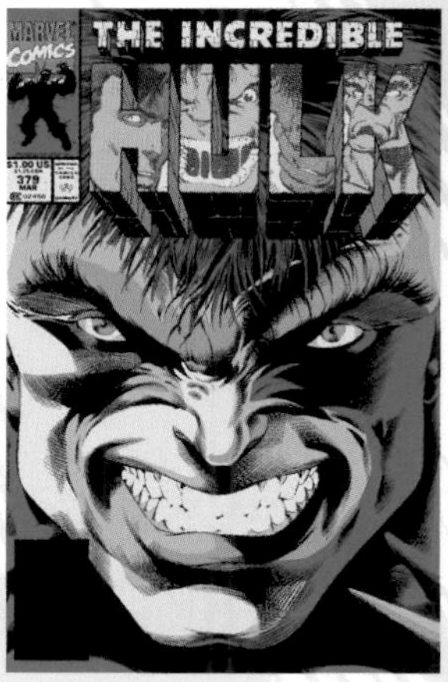
MARVEL COMICS
THE INCREDIBLE
HULK

*INCREDIBLE HULK* #379 ▶

**March 1991**
**Artist:** Dale Keown

One of the standout covers from Keown's run on *Incredible Hulk*, this issue marked the start of a new Hulk "persona," as Bruce Banner's intellect and the Hulk's physical form became one. The change was reflected in the title logo, which showed glimpses of previous incarnations of the Hulk. Keown's portrayal was about a mixture of power and intellect, the new Hulk managing to be both more human and more dangerous.

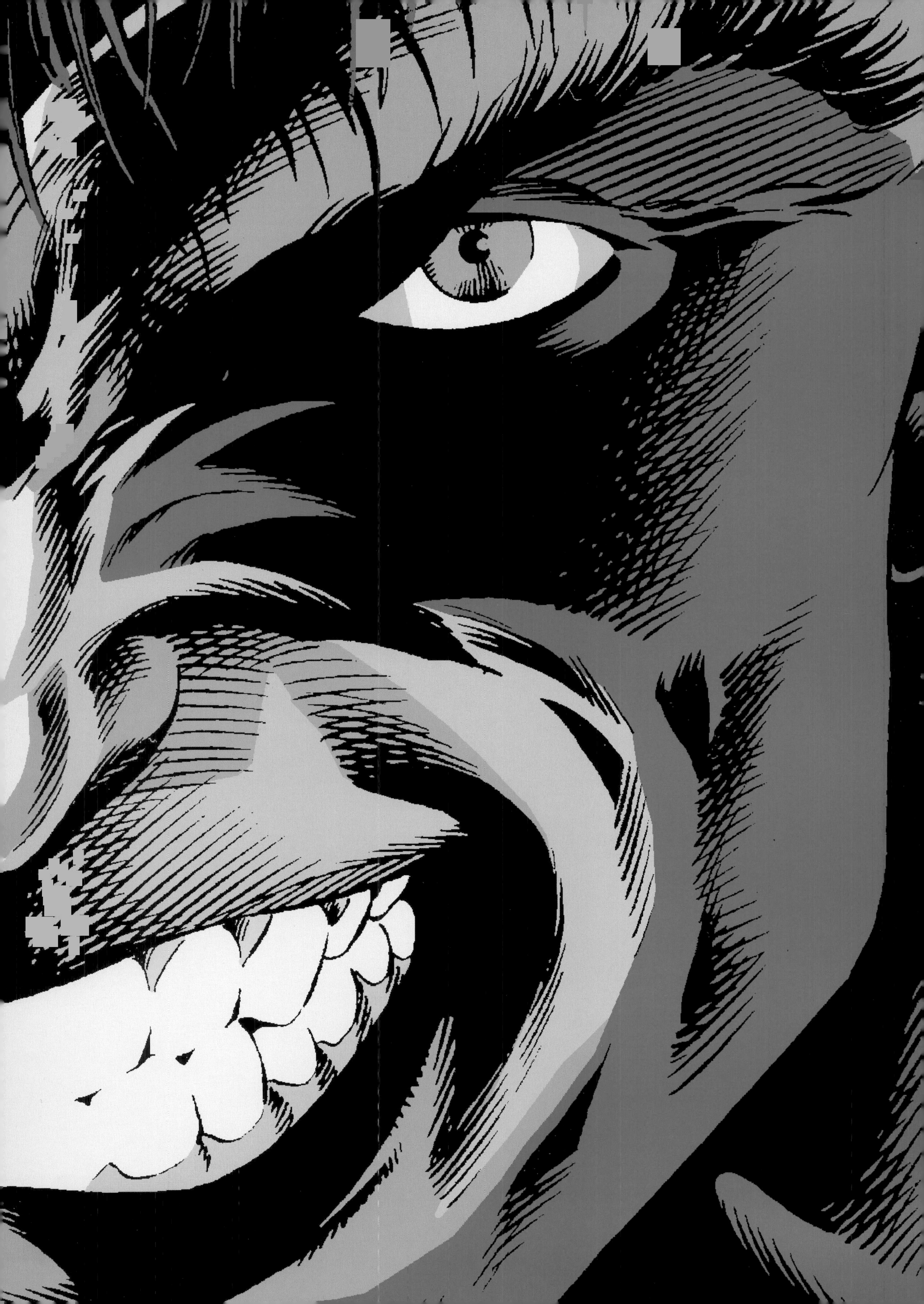

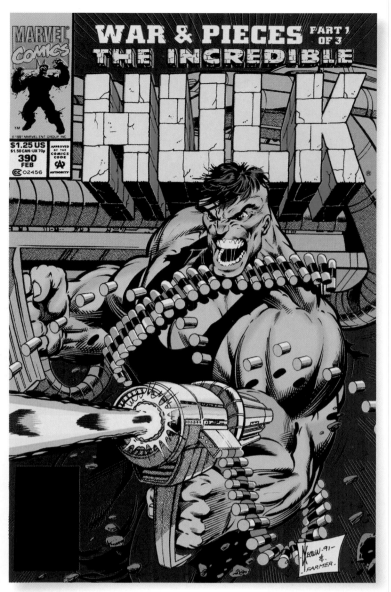

MARVEL COMICS
WAR & PIECES PART 1 OF 3
THE INCREDIBLE HULK
$1.25 US
390
FEB

◀ ***INCREDIBLE HULK* #390**

**February 1992**
**Artist:** Dale Keown

Guns were big business in the 1990s. At times, it seemed like every hero was suddenly carrying really big, over-the-top weaponry. The new incarnation of the Hulk also got in on the action with this issue when he became involved in a Middle-Eastern conflict. The sight of the Hulk at war was a new and shocking image.

MARVEL COMICS
THE INCREDIBLE HULK
$1.25 US
395
JULY

◀ ***INCREDIBLE HULK* #395**

**July 1992**
**Artist:** Dale Keown

The Punisher became very popular in the late 1980s and early 1990s, and he guest-starred in a number of Marvel titles. Keown's image of the vigilante, reflected in the glasses of a mean-looking Hulk, suggested that this was going to be a deadly confrontation. The story saw the Hulk return to Las Vegas to avenge the death of a friend.

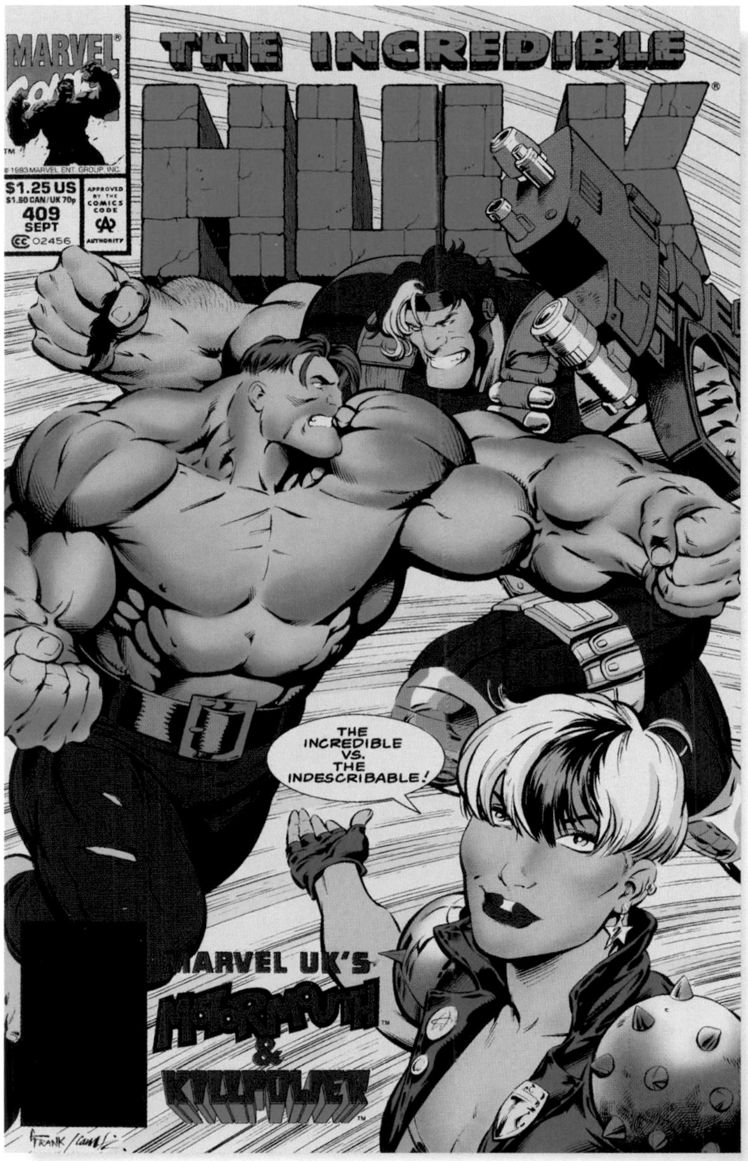
MARVEL COMICS
THE INCREDIBLE HULK
$1.25 US
409
SEPT
THE INCREDIBLE VS. THE INDESCRIBABLE!
MARVEL UK'S

### ◀ *INCREDIBLE HULK* #409

**September 1993**
**Artist:** Gary Frank

In this issue, British-born artist Gary Frank got to illustrate the characters with whom he had made his name—Motormouth and Killpower. These characters had been created by Marvel UK and illustrated by Frank before he succeeded Dale Keown on *Incredible Hulk*. It was one of the few occasions when Marvel UK characters appeared on the cover of a mainstream US title.

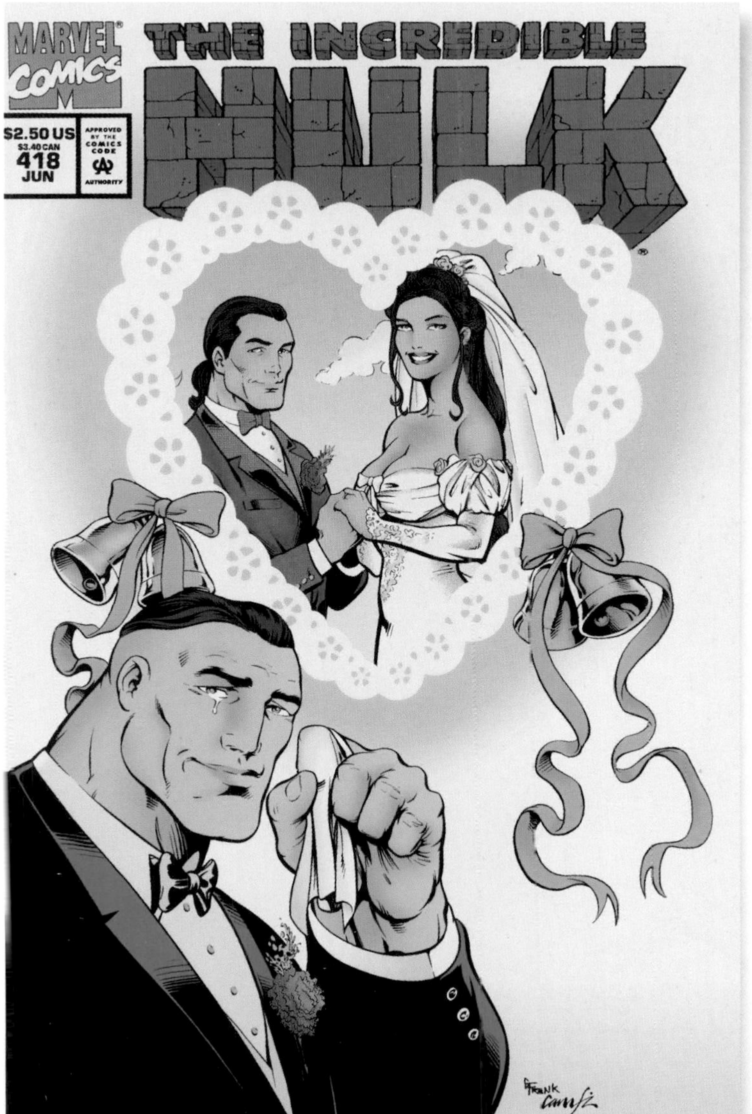
MARVEL COMICS
THE INCREDIBLE HULK
$2.50 US
$3.40 CAN
418
JUN

### ◀ *INCREDIBLE HULK* #418

**June 1994**
**Artist:** Gary Frank

Rick Jones married his girlfriend Marlo in this issue that came with a die-cut cover. The early 1990s saw many special-treatment covers. Just about anything and everything was tried, from die-cuts to foil. Such covers added a whole new element of design to the books. Lifting the die-cut cover of *Incredible Hulk* issue #418 reveals the guests at Rick and Marlo's wedding.

MARVEL COMICS
THE INCREDIBLE
HULK
426
FEB
DELUXE

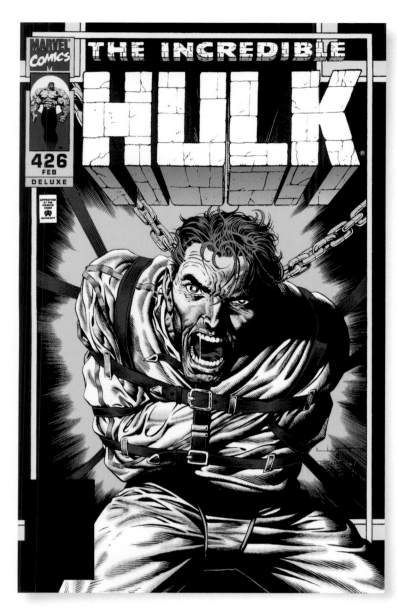

◀ *INCREDIBLE HULK* #426

**February 1995**
**Artist:** Liam Sharp

Liam Sharp produced this startling cover during his short run on *Incredible Hulk*. Sharp's close-up of a straightjacketed Banner screaming out at the reader hinted at the shock inside the issue, as Hulk's ferocious consciousness dominated Banner's comparatively puny frame.

MARVEL
PSR 60
JONES
DEODATO JR
HULK
DIRECT EDITION
$2.25 US $3.75 CAN
SPLIT DECISIONS 1 OF 5

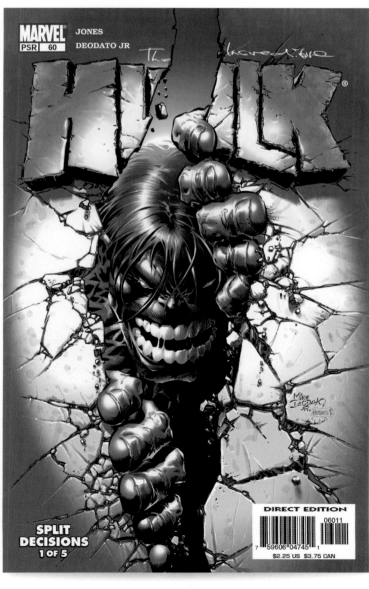

◀ *INCREDIBLE HULK* #60

**November 2003**
**Artist:** Mike Deodato Jr.

The Hulk's second volume took the green-skinned beast back to his roots as a vicious monster fueled by anger. Artist Mike Deodato Jr. gave this new, brutal incarnation a sense of raw power, showcased on the cover. Deodato experimented with the design and layout to create a memorable image of an enraged Hulk breaking through a wall—and the title logo.

*INCREDIBLE HULK* #94 ▶

**June 2006**
**Artist:** José Ladrönn

Writer Greg Pak created one of the best Hulk stories of the decade with his "Planet Hulk" saga. The third part's cover, drawn by José Ladrönn, was later used for the story's graphic novel collection. It shows the Hulk in his new role as a gladiator in an alien arena. The image gave the character a dramatic new visual twist, and this latest incarnation proved extremely popular.

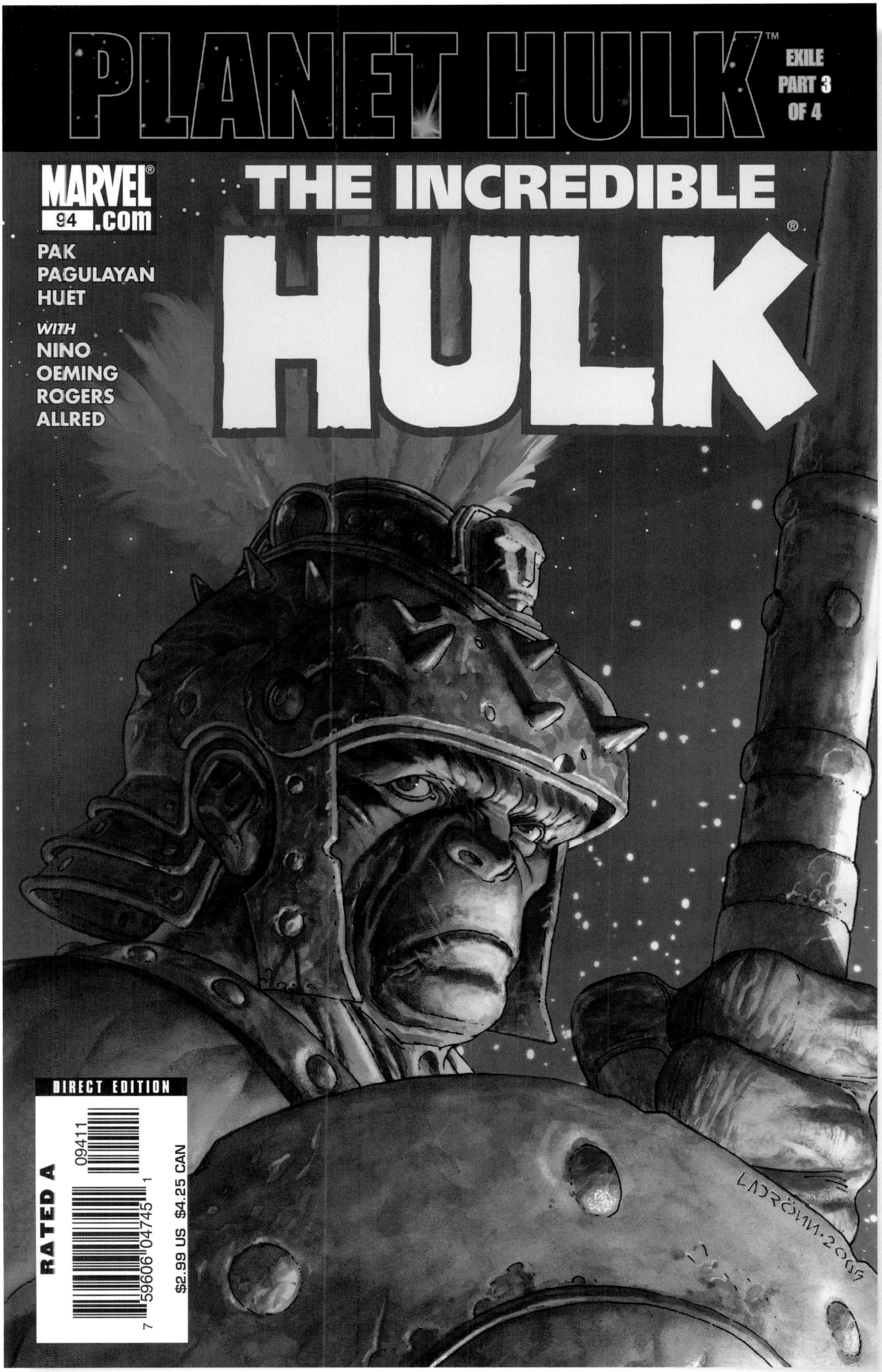
PLANET HULK™
EXILE
PART 3
OF 4
MARVEL®
94 .com
THE INCREDIBLE
HULK®
PAK
PAGULAYAN
HUET
WITH
NINO
OEMING
ROGERS
ALLRED
DIRECT EDITION
RATED A
$2.99 US $4.25 CAN
LADRÖNN·2005

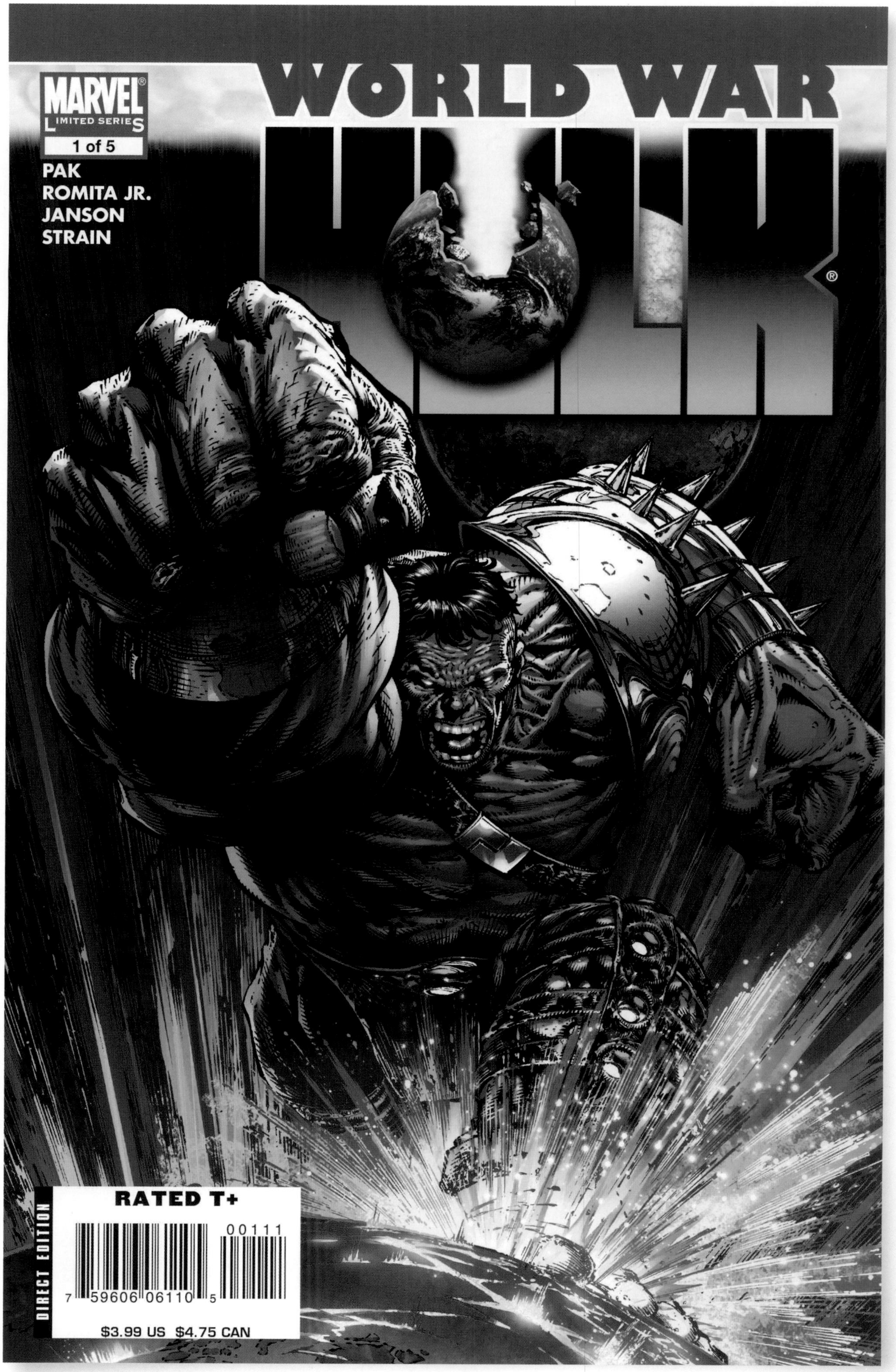
WORLD WAR
HULK
MARVEL
LIMITED SERIES
1 of 5
PAK
ROMITA JR.
JANSON
STRAIN
RATED T+
DIRECT EDITION
$3.99 US $4.75 CAN

▲ *WORLD WAR HULK* #1

**August 2007**
**Artist:** David Finch

The Hulk was returning to Earth to seek revenge on the so-called heroes who had exiled him into space and—he believed—destroyed his adopted planet. David Finch's powerful cover illustration shows a Hulk that is more barbarian than monster, a terrifying creature filled with rage. It left readers wondering just what would happen when he reached Earth...

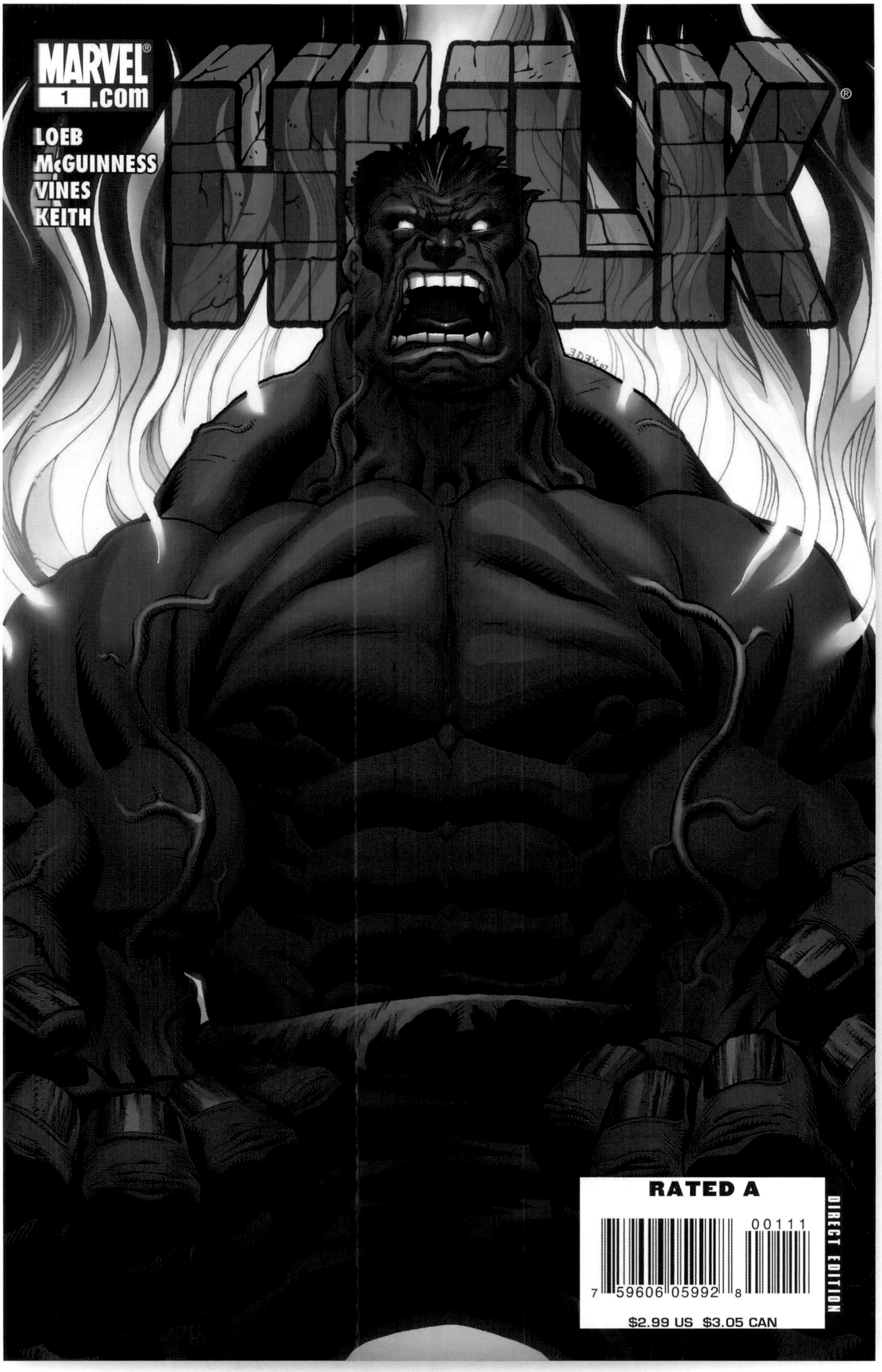
MARVEL
1 .com
HULK
LOEB
McGUINNESS
VINES
KEITH
RATED A
DIRECT EDITION
$2.99 US $3.05 CAN

▲ *HULK* #1

**January 2008**
**Artist:** Ed McGuinness

Ed McGuinness was the perfect choice to create a new incarnation of the Hulk: His art is always larger than life, and he specializes in portraying muscular characters. McGuinness helped to create a memorable first issue cover image; the change of color (and creation of this new Hulk, later revealed to be none other than Thunderbolt Ross) ensured that readers were desperate to find out what had happened to the green-skinned behemoth.

JEPH LOEB • ED McGUINNESS • DEXTER VINES
HULK
MARVEL
11 .com
RATED A
DIRECT EDITION
$3.99 US
WWW.MARVEL.COM

JEPH LOEB • ED McGUINNESS • DEXTER VINES
HULK
MARVEL
VARIANT
EDITION
11
RATED A
DIRECT EDITION
$3.99 US
WWW.MARVEL.COM

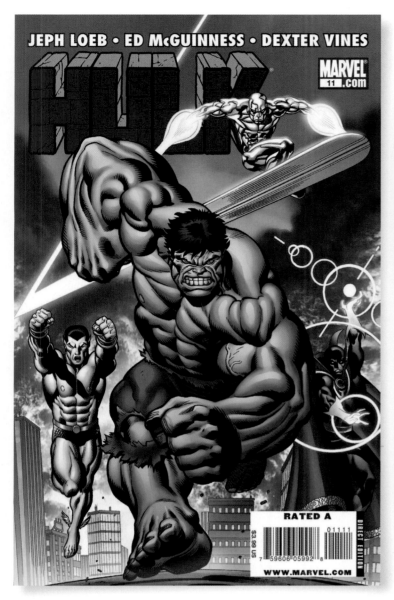

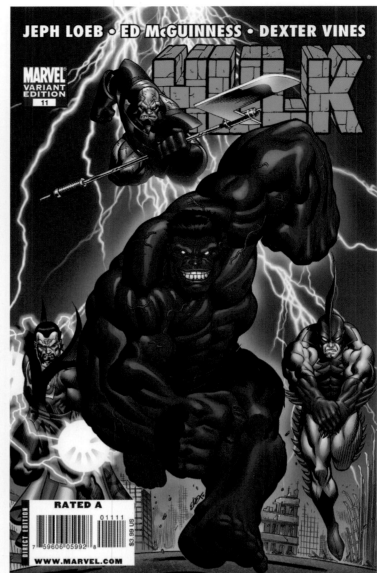

▲ *HULK* #11

**April 2009**
**Artist:** Ed McGuinness

Cover variants proved to be big news in the 2000s, and the second part of the "Defenders/Offenders War" story showed how alternative covers could be used to complement the main one. In this case the original cover shows the green Hulk and the Defenders while the variant shows the Red Hulk and the Offenders in a mirrored pose, providing a dramatic contrast between the two groups.

*HULK & THING: HARD KNOCKS* #1–4 ▶

**November 2005–February 2006**
**Artist:** Jae Lee

Artist Jae Lee created beautiful covers for this four-part series about the long rivalry between the Hulk and the Thing. The story, written by Bruce Jones, depicted the Hulk and the Thing talking over their old fights before coming to blows once again. Lee's close-up covers look like stills from the fight and also proved to be four of the most dramatic covers to feature the two heroes.

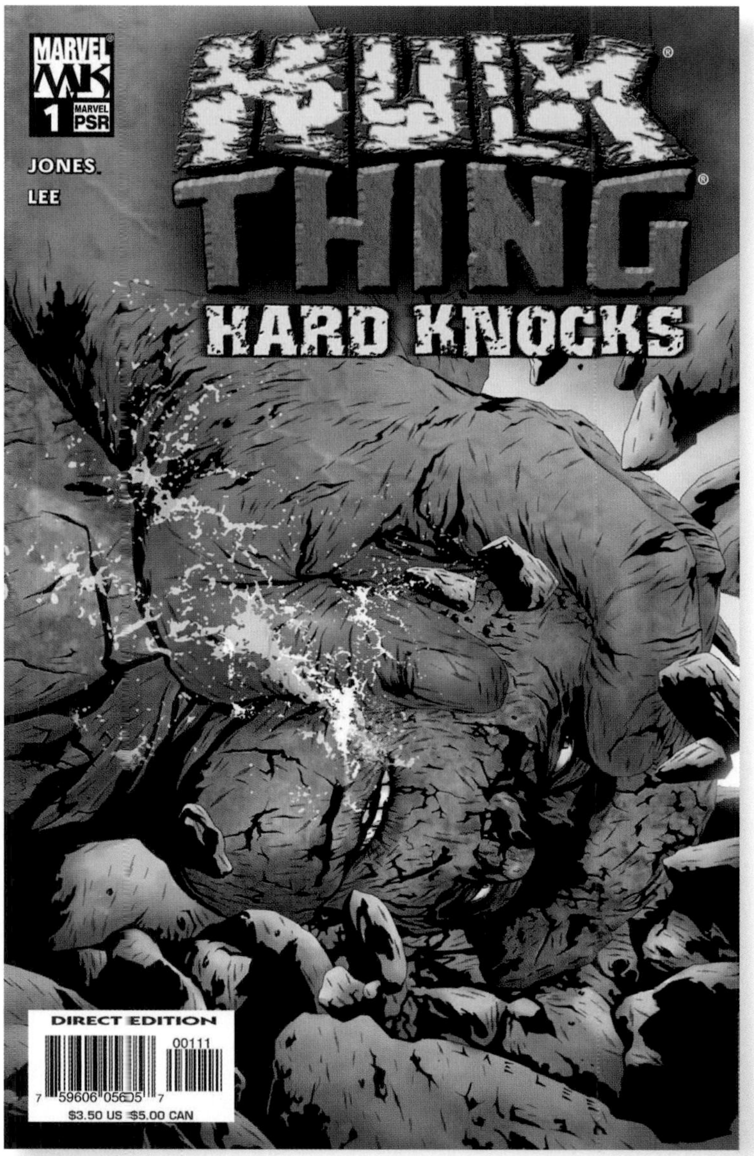
MARVEL
1
HULK
THING
HARD KNOCKS
JONES
LEE
DIRECT EDITION
$3.50 US $5.00 CAN

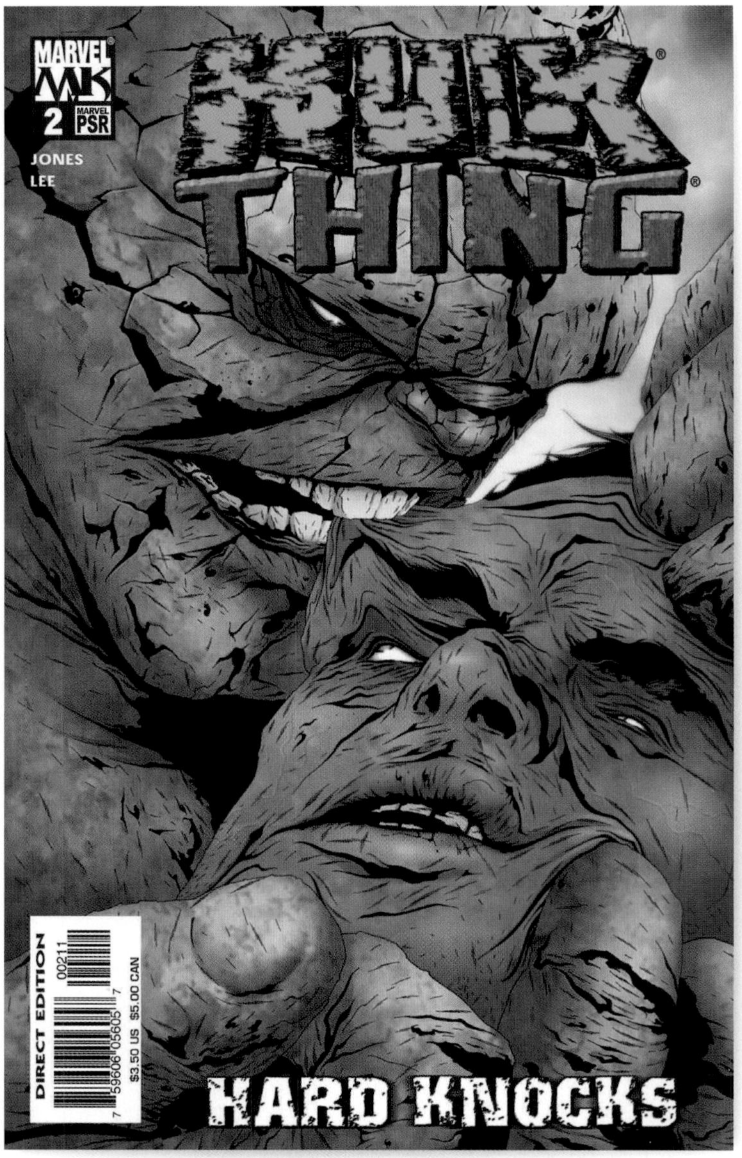
MARVEL
2
HULK
THING
JONES
LEE
HARD KNOCKS
DIRECT EDITION
$3.50 US $5.00 CAN

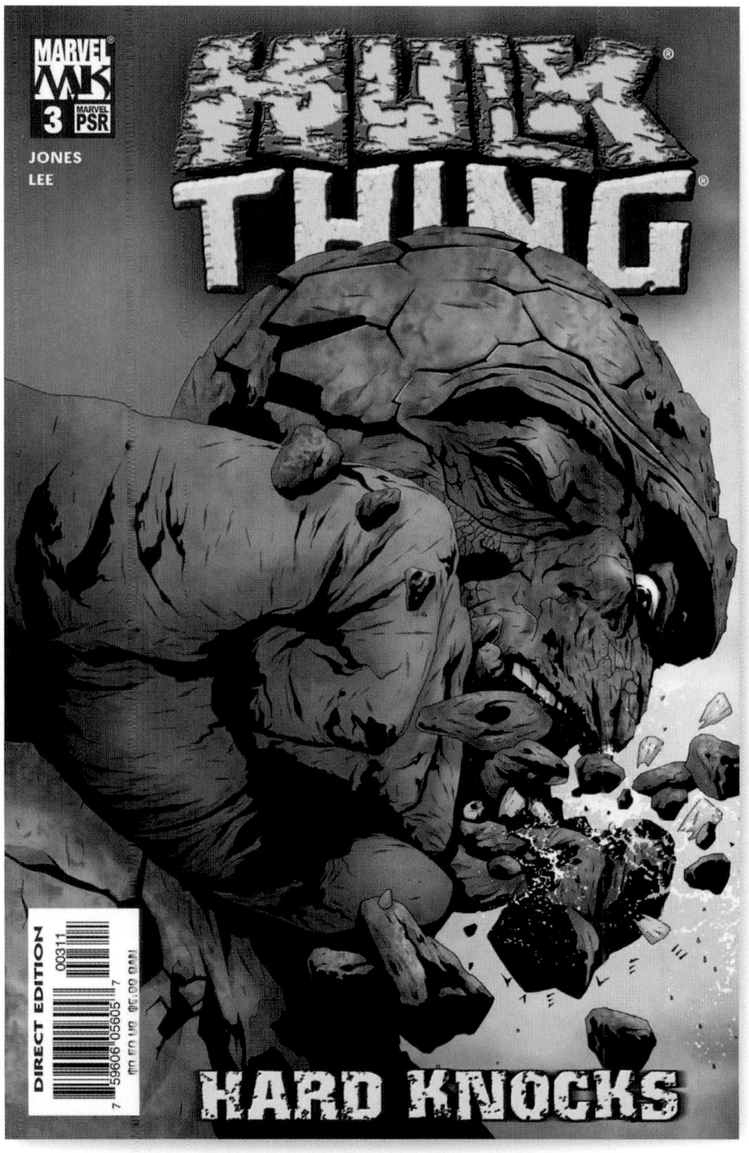
MARVEL
3
HULK
THING
JONES
LEE
HARD KNOCKS
DIRECT EDITION

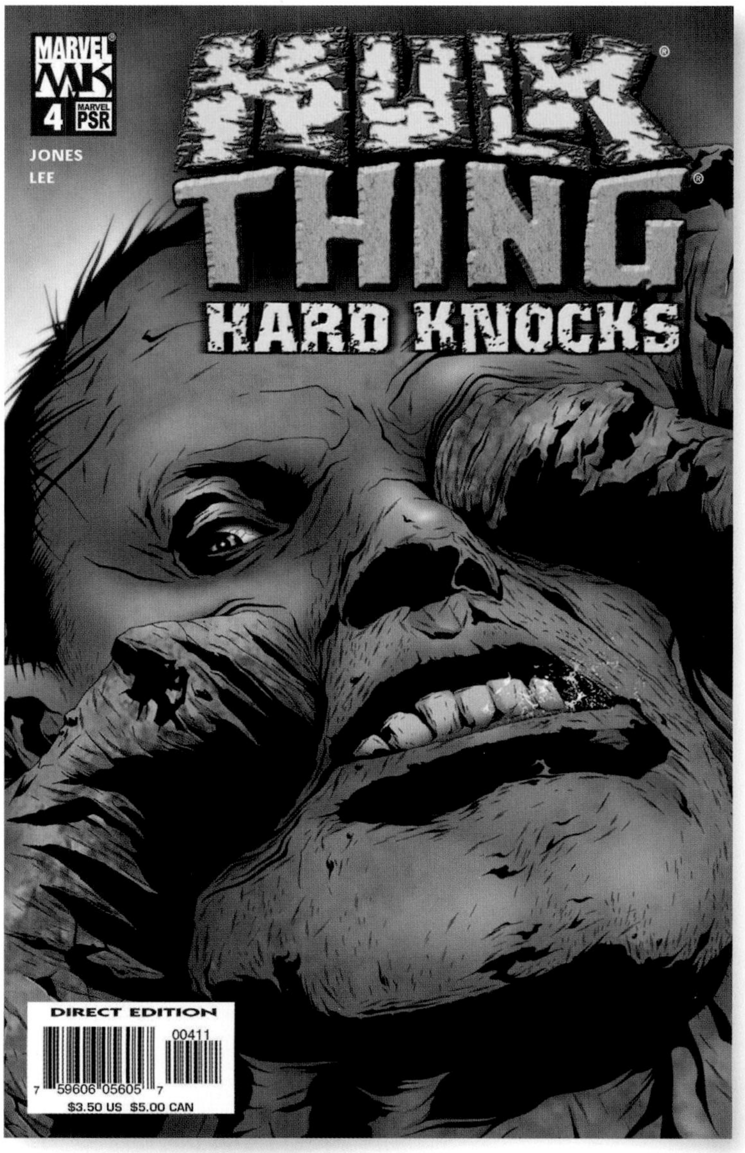
MARVEL
4
HULK
THING
HARD KNOCKS
JONES
LEE
DIRECT EDITION
$3.50 US $5.00 CAN

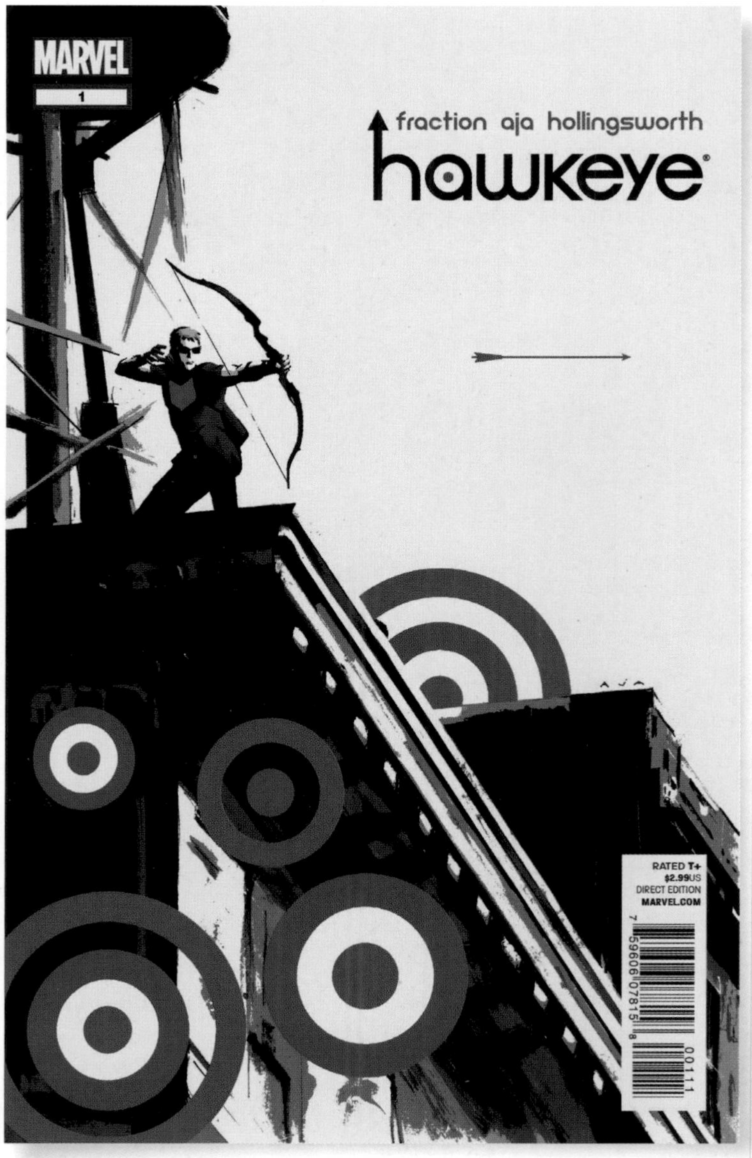
MARVEL
1
fraction aja hollingsworth
hawkeye
RATED T+
$2.99US
DIRECT EDITION
MARVEL.COM

**◀ *HAWKEYE* #1**

**October 2012**
**Artist:** David Aja

Marvel's covers became increasingly stylized in the 2010s as artists pushed the boundaries of design. Writer Matt Fraction and artist David Aja produced one of the most adventurous Marvel comics in decades with *Hawkeye*. Each issue had a fabulous slick cover, and this debut issue set the standard for what was to follow. Aja eventually won a prestigious Eisner award for his work on this series.

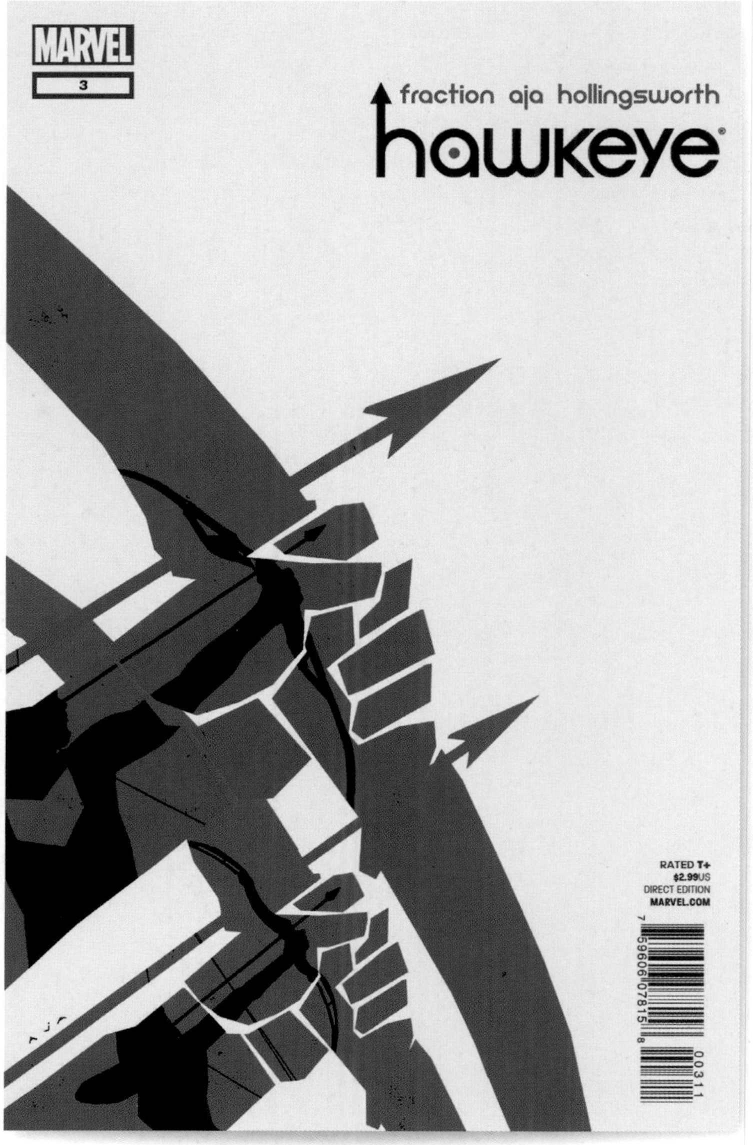
MARVEL
3
fraction aja hollingsworth
hawkeye
RATED T+
$2.99US
DIRECT EDITION
MARVEL.COM

**◀ *HAWKEYE* #3**

**December 2012**
**Artist:** David Aja

David Aja's art, coupled with Matt Fraction's stories, led to the new *Hawkeye* series gaining rave reviews. Aja's third cover shows the weapons of two Hawkeyes—Clint Barton and Kate Bishop (Hawkeye of the *Young Avengers*). The image uses the same black, white, and purple color scheme of the early covers, which gave the book a distinctive look and set it apart from its competition.

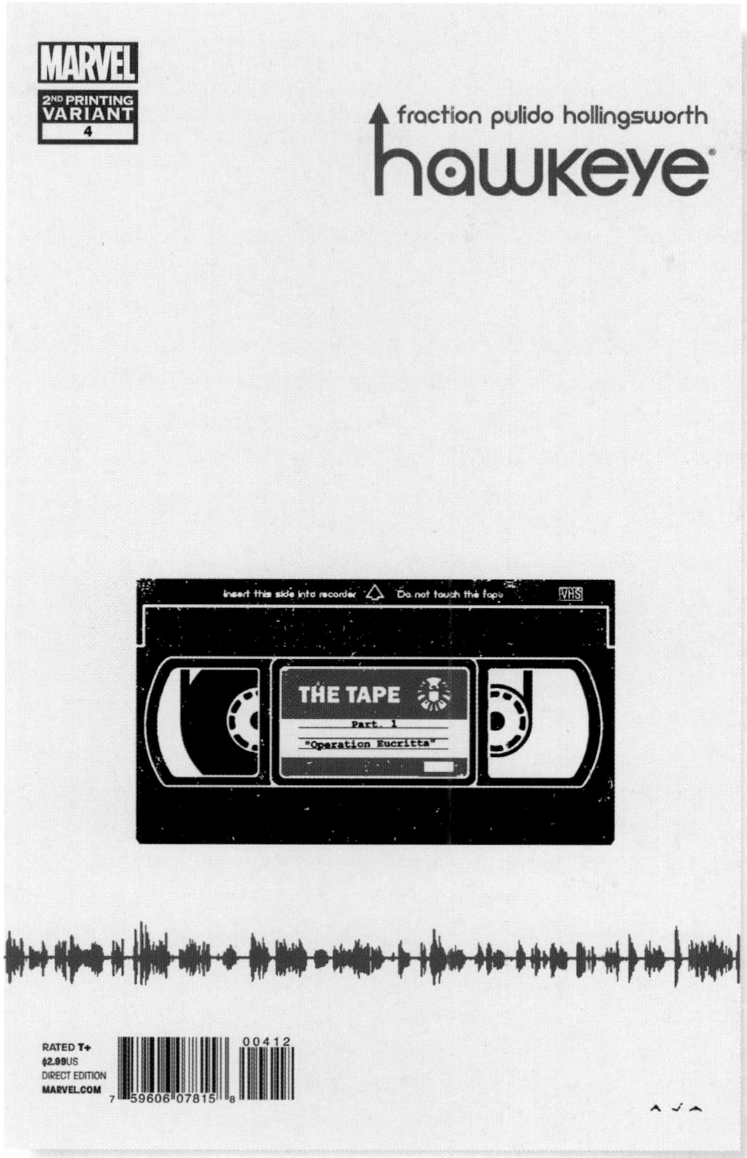
MARVEL
2ND PRINTING VARIANT
4
fraction pulido hollingsworth
hawkeye
THE TAPE
Part 1
"Operation Eucritta"
RATED T+
$2.99US
DIRECT EDITION
MARVEL.COM

◀ *HAWKEYE* **#4**

**January 2013**
**Artist:** David Aja

Issues #4 and #5 of *Hawkeye* are both fine examples of David Aja's stylistic and intelligent covers. The two-part story was called "The Tape" and involved Hawkeye trying to recover a politically sensitive video tape. The first part, in extreme contrast to most other Marvel Comics covers, simply shows a VHS cassette with sound waves below it, and lots of white space. It is enigmatic in its simplicity.

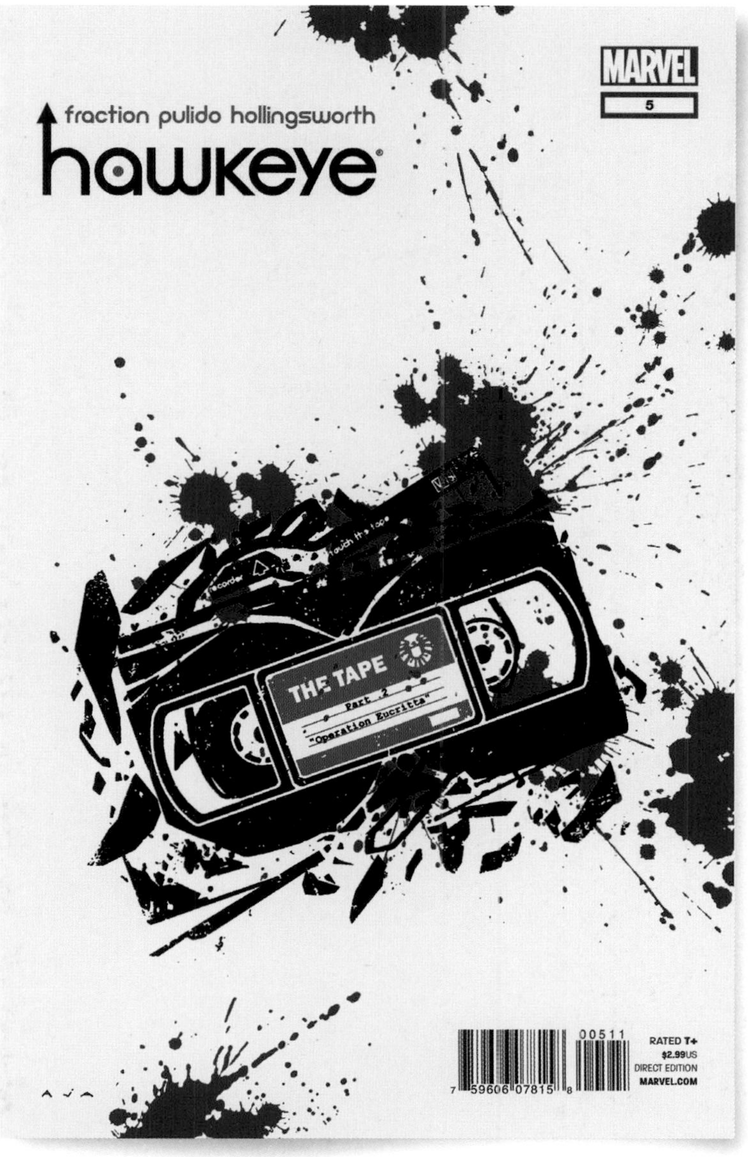
MARVEL
5
fraction pulido hollingsworth
hawkeye
THE TAPE
Part 2
"Operation Eucritta"
RATED T+
$2.99US
DIRECT EDITION
MARVEL.COM

◀ *HAWKEYE* **#5**

**February 2013**
**Artist:** David Aja

The cover for the second part of "The Tape" was a dramatic and grisly contrast to that of part one. The blood splatters also signified the end of the "purple" cover phase. In a medium that usually employs action-packed, detailed covers, Aja's designs for *Hawkeye* were truly a breath of fresh air.

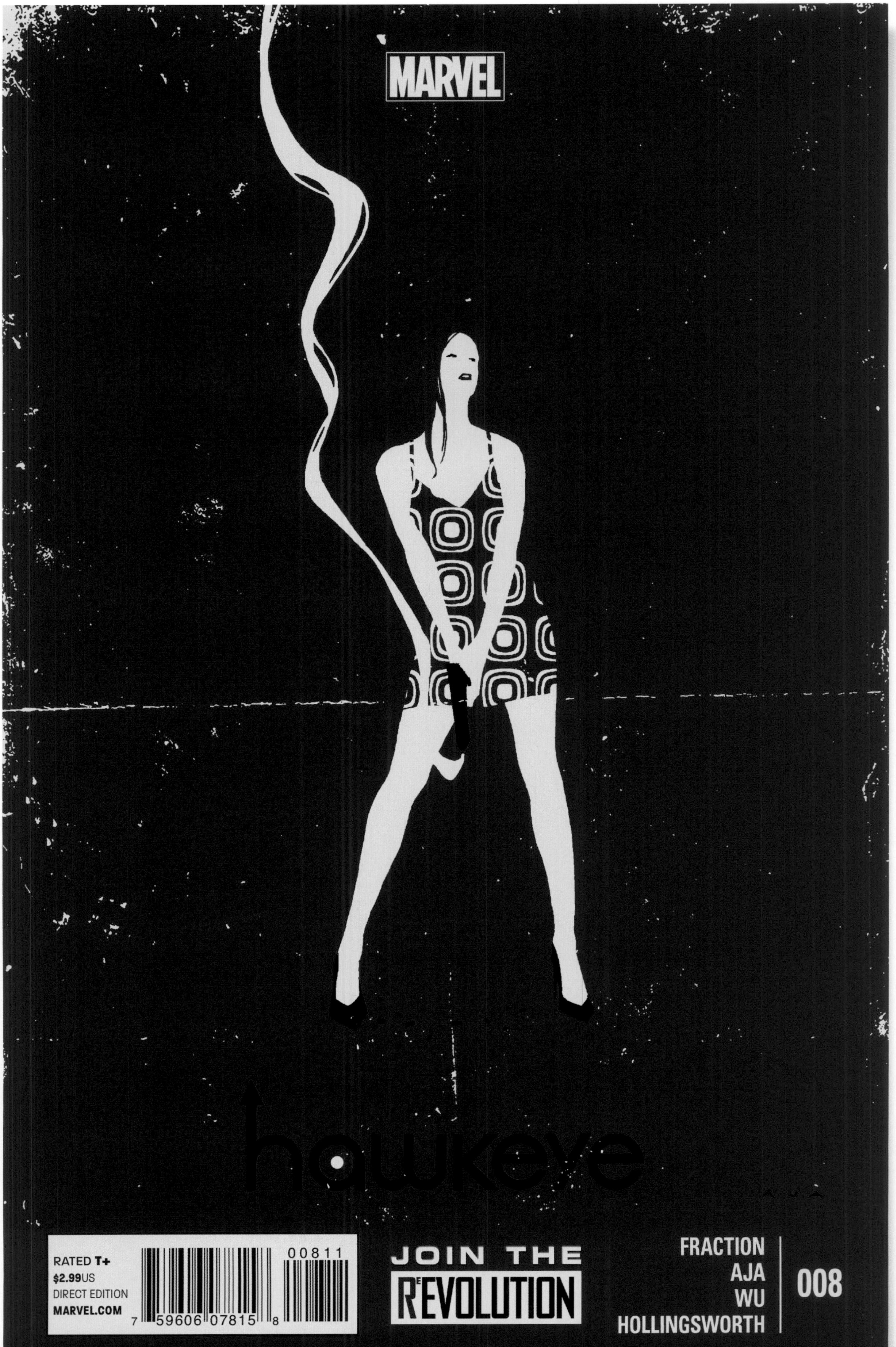
MARVEL
hawkeye
RATED T+
$2.99US
DIRECT EDITION
MARVEL.COM
JOIN THE
REVOLUTION
FRACTION
AJA
WU
HOLLINGSWORTH
008

***HAWKEYE* #9 ▶**

**May 2013**
**Artist:** David Aja

This cover focuses on another Hawkeye, Kate Bishop. The young archer was becoming far more than a supporting character in the series, and this issue focused on her adventures rather than those of Clint Barton. Aja shows a keen sense for design on the cover, playing with both the logo and the brand to create a special cover image of Kate Bishop.

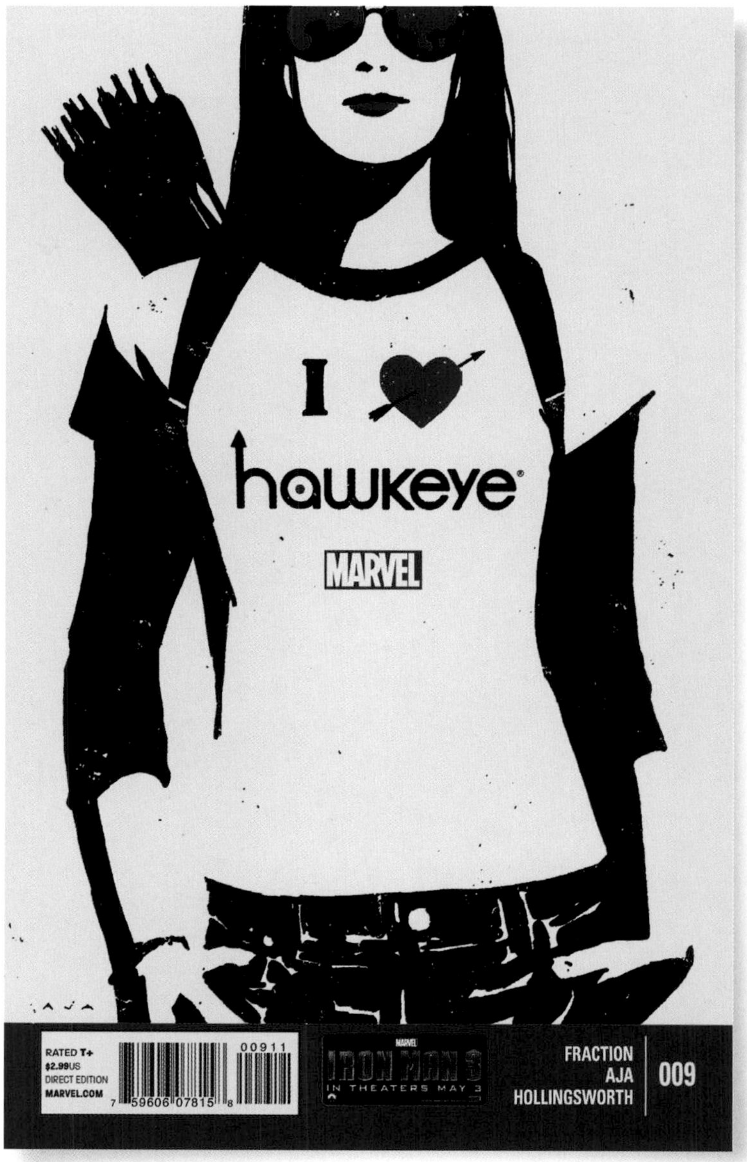
I ♥
hawkeye
MARVEL
RATED T+
$2.99US
DIRECT EDITION
MARVEL.COM
IRON MAN 3
IN THEATERS MAY 3
FRACTION
AJA
HOLLINGSWORTH
009

***HAWKEYE* #11 ▶**

**July 2013**
**Artist:** David Aja

Pizza Dog takes center stage on the cover of one of the most inventive issues of *Hawkeye*. The image, showing the bloody pawprints left by Hawkeye's dog, reflects the fact that the whole issue is told from the dog's perspective. It was a unique cover for a unique series.

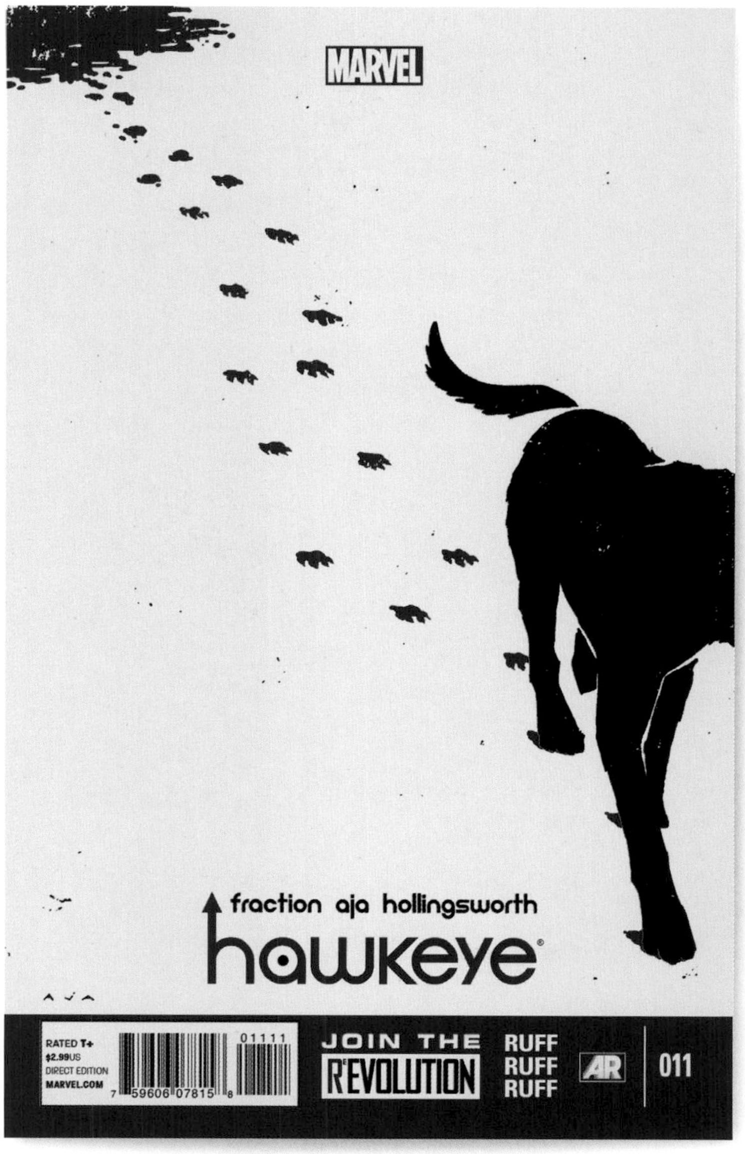
MARVEL
fraction aja hollingsworth
hawkeye
RATED T+
$2.99US
DIRECT EDITION
MARVEL.COM
JOIN THE
REVOLUTION
RUFF
RUFF
RUFF
AR
011

**◀ *HAWKEYE* #8**

**April 2013**
**Artist:** David Aja

While most comic-book covers often utilize bright visuals, few use one color in such a dominant way as this "Valentine special" issue of *Hawkeye*. The central image of Cherry (one of Clint Barton's many ex-girlfriends) on a blood-red background really conveys a feeling of violence and danger. With such bold use of color and imagery, artist David Aja pushed the boundaries of design in ways not seen since the days of Jim Steranko.

MARVEL
IRON MAN
75¢ US
95¢ CAN
232
JUL

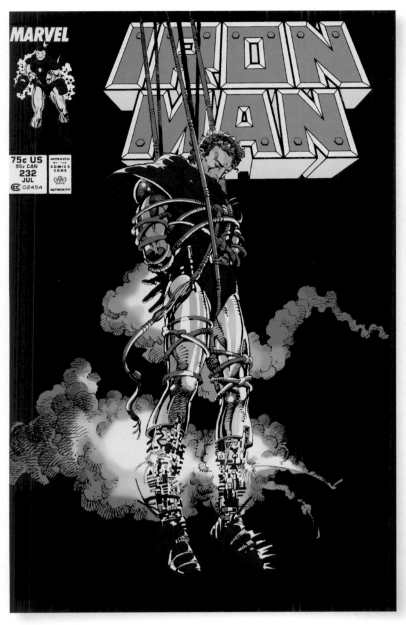

▲ *IRON MAN* #232

**July 1988**
**Artist:** Barry Windsor-Smith

The "Armor Wars" epic—in which Tony Stark tried to reclaim stolen Stark technology—ended with this epilogue. Barry Windsor-Smith created a beautiful, but disturbing cover, which shows Tony Stark's corpse-like body suspended from cables, hinting at the nightmarish story inside.

MARVEL
ARMOR WARS II
IRON MAN
$1.00 US
$1.25 CAN
262
NOV

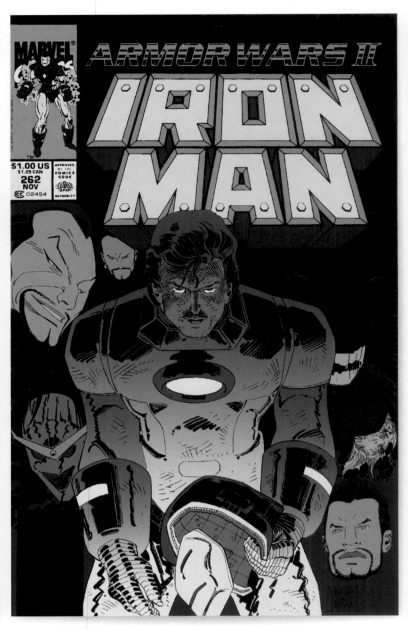

▲ *IRON MAN* #262

**November 1990**
**Artist:** John Romita Jr.

The follow-up to "Armor Wars" continued in this issue behind a stunning John Romita Jr. cover. The cover art reflected the turmoil that Stark was undergoing, as the villainous Kearson DeWitt took control of his nervous system, literally manipulating Stark's every move, while others prepared to make their own moves against the hero.

*IRON MAN* #282 ▶

**July 1992**
**Artist:** Kevin Hopgood

British-born artist Kevin Hopgood introduced the character War Machine to the Iron Man universe in this issue. The comic had never seen armor quite like the War Machine's. The militaristic design and gray coloring of the armor made this an impactful cover. The artist had fun with typography by having War Machine's name as graffiti over the Iron Man title.

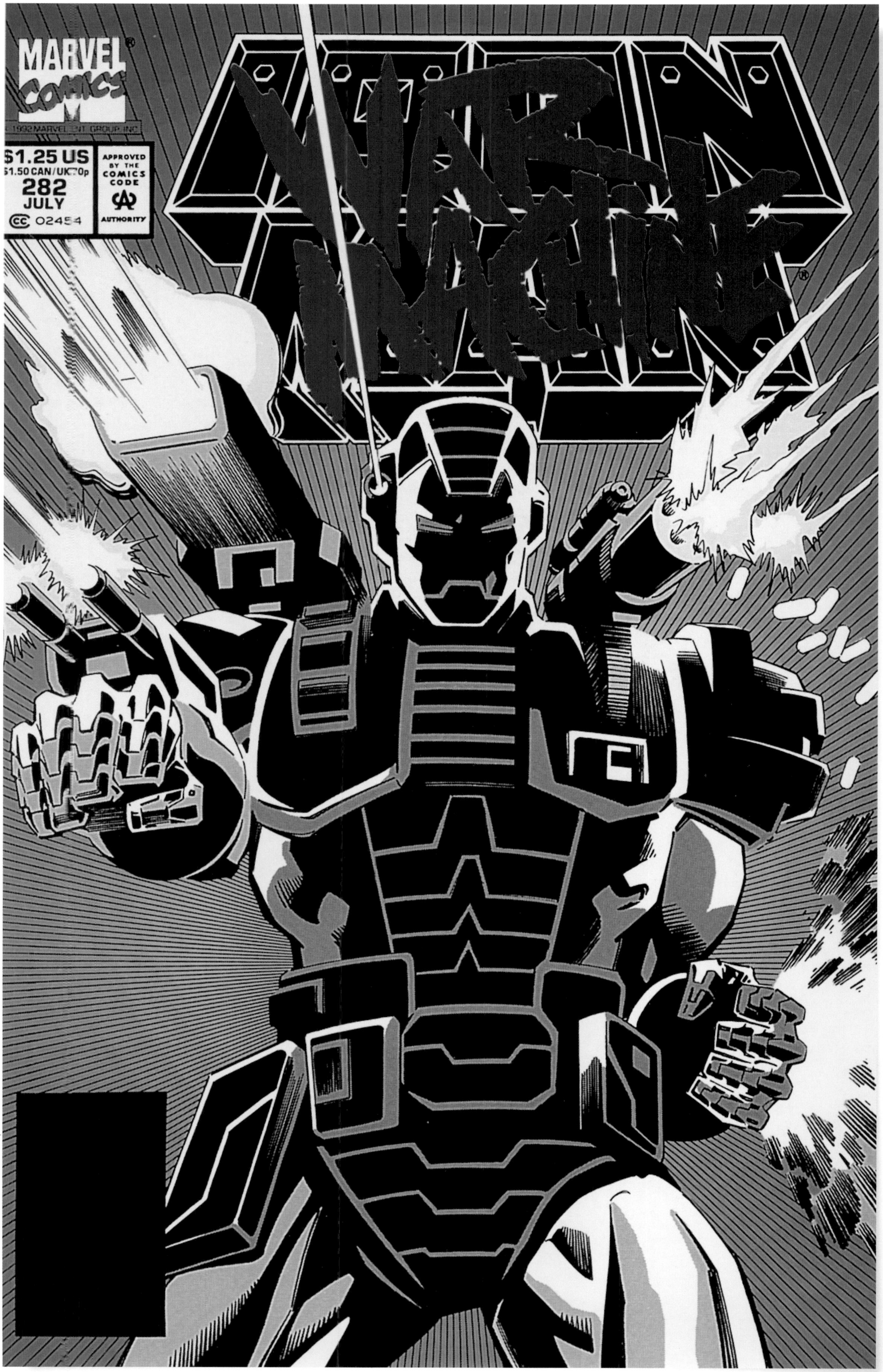
MARVEL
COMICS
$1.25 US
282
JULY
APPROVED BY THE COMICS CODE AUTHORITY
WAR MACHINE

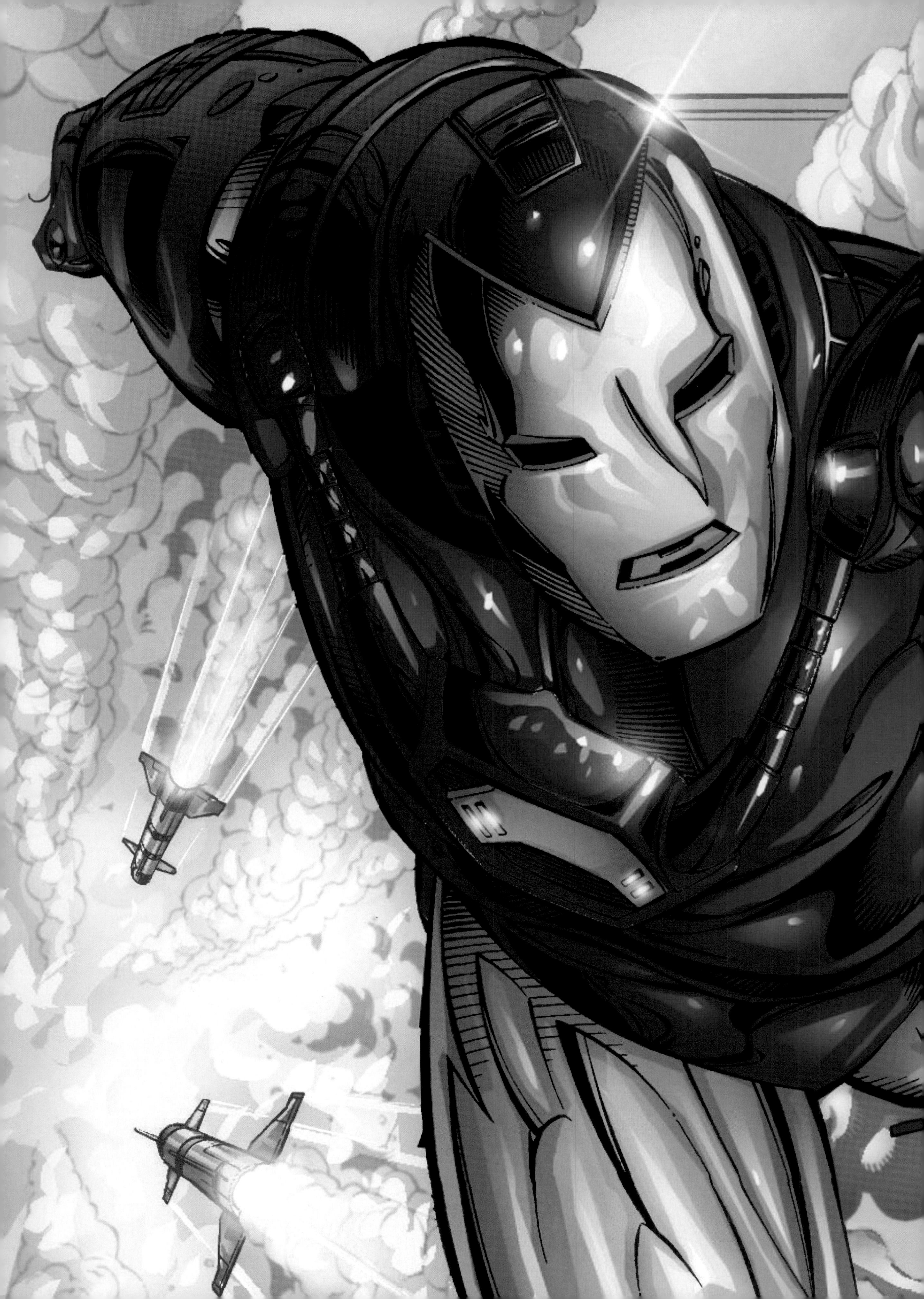

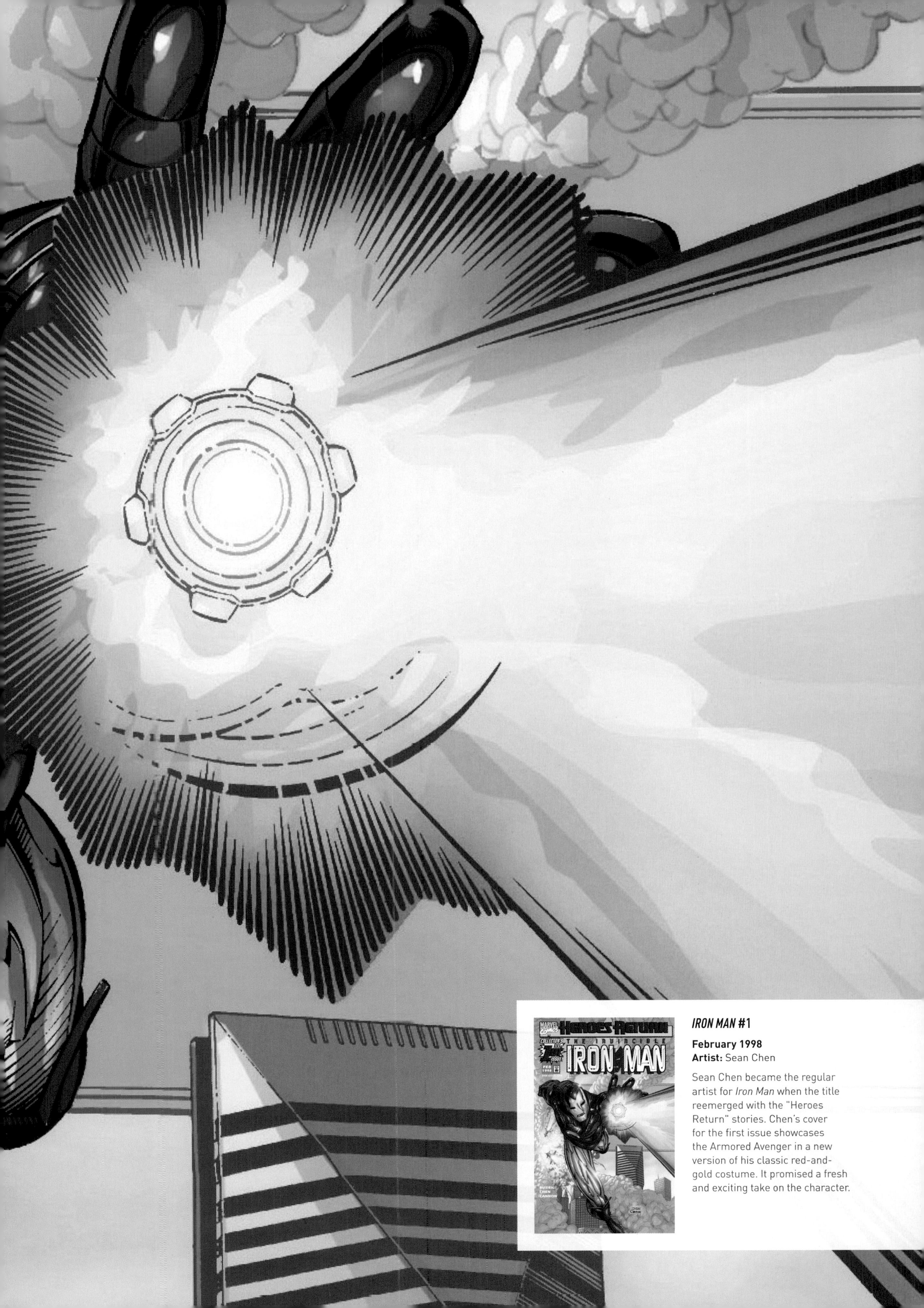


HEROES RETURN
THE INVINCIBLE
IRON MAN

*IRON MAN* #1

**February 1998**
**Artist:** Sean Chen

Sean Chen became the regular artist for *Iron Man* when the title reemerged with the "Heroes Return" stories. Chen's cover for the first issue showcases the Armored Avenger in a new version of his classic red-and-gold costume. It promised a fresh and exciting take on the character.

MARVEL COMICS
THE INVINCIBLE
IRON MAN
#29
WWW.MARVEL.COM

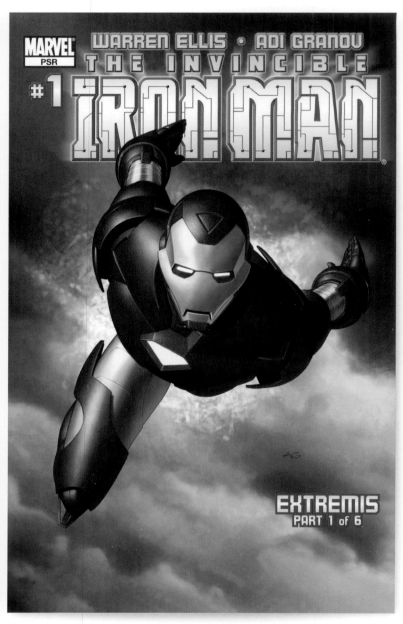

▲ *IRON MAN* #29

**June 2000**
**Artist:** Joe Quesada

Future Marvel Editor-in-Chief Joe Quesada created this story about Iron Man's latest armor becoming sentient and turning against its creator. Quesada also provided the cover for his story—his dramatic image instills the sentient armor with a suitably menacing feel as it gripped one of Stark's old helmets.

MARVEL PSR
WARREN ELLIS • ADI GRANOV
THE INVINCIBLE
#1 IRON MAN
EXTREMIS
PART 1 of 6

▲ *IRON MAN* #1

**January 2005**
**Artist:** Adi Granov

Writer Warren Ellis and artist Adi Granov teamed up to relaunch *Iron Man*, creating a story that would later provide the inspiration for the third *Iron Man* movie. Granov created a striking incarnation of the hero, his realistic take on the Armored Avenger staring straight out at the reader from the cover.

MARVEL
8 .com
THE INVINCIBLE
IRON MAN
KNAUF
ZIRCHER
HANNA
EXECUTE
PROGRAM
PART 2 of 6

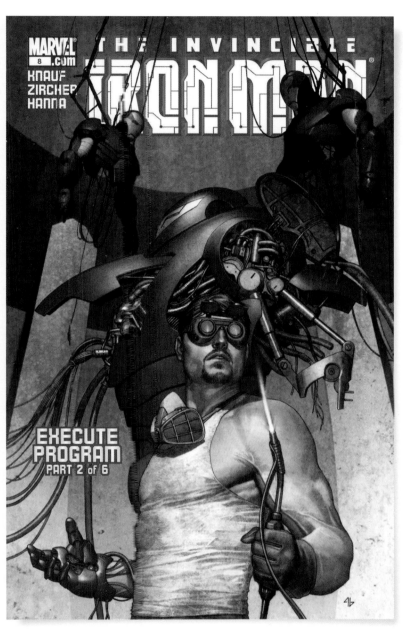

▲ ***IRON MAN* #8**

**July 2006**
**Artist:** Adi Granov

Adi Granov's stylish run on *Iron Man* continued with a cover focusing on Tony Stark in inventor mode. Granov also worked as an artist for the first *Iron Man* movie, and elements of his version of Tony Stark on this cover clearly influenced the movie incarnation.

MARVEL
15 .com
THE INITIATIVE
KNAUF
DE LA TORRE
SIBAL
WHITE
IRON MAN
DIRECTOR OF S.H.I.E.L.D.

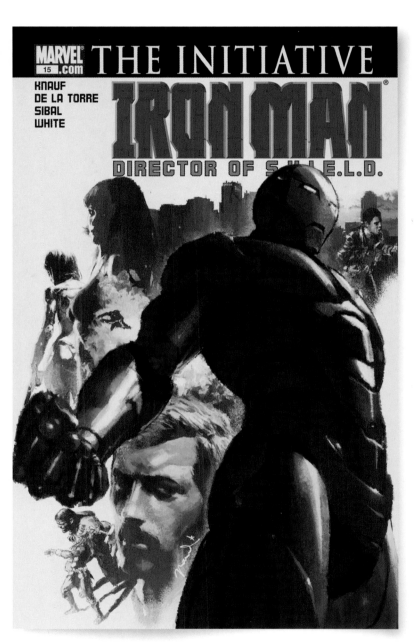

▲ ***IRON MAN: DIRECTOR OF S.H.I.E.L.D.* #15**

**April 2007**
**Artists:** Gerald Parel and Adi Granov

This explosive cover heralded a new direction for Iron Man's adventures as his alter ego, Tony Stark, became head of S.H.I.E.L.D. Stark's adventures had always been more realistic than many other heroes, and this cover reflects his new dual role as hero and super spy.

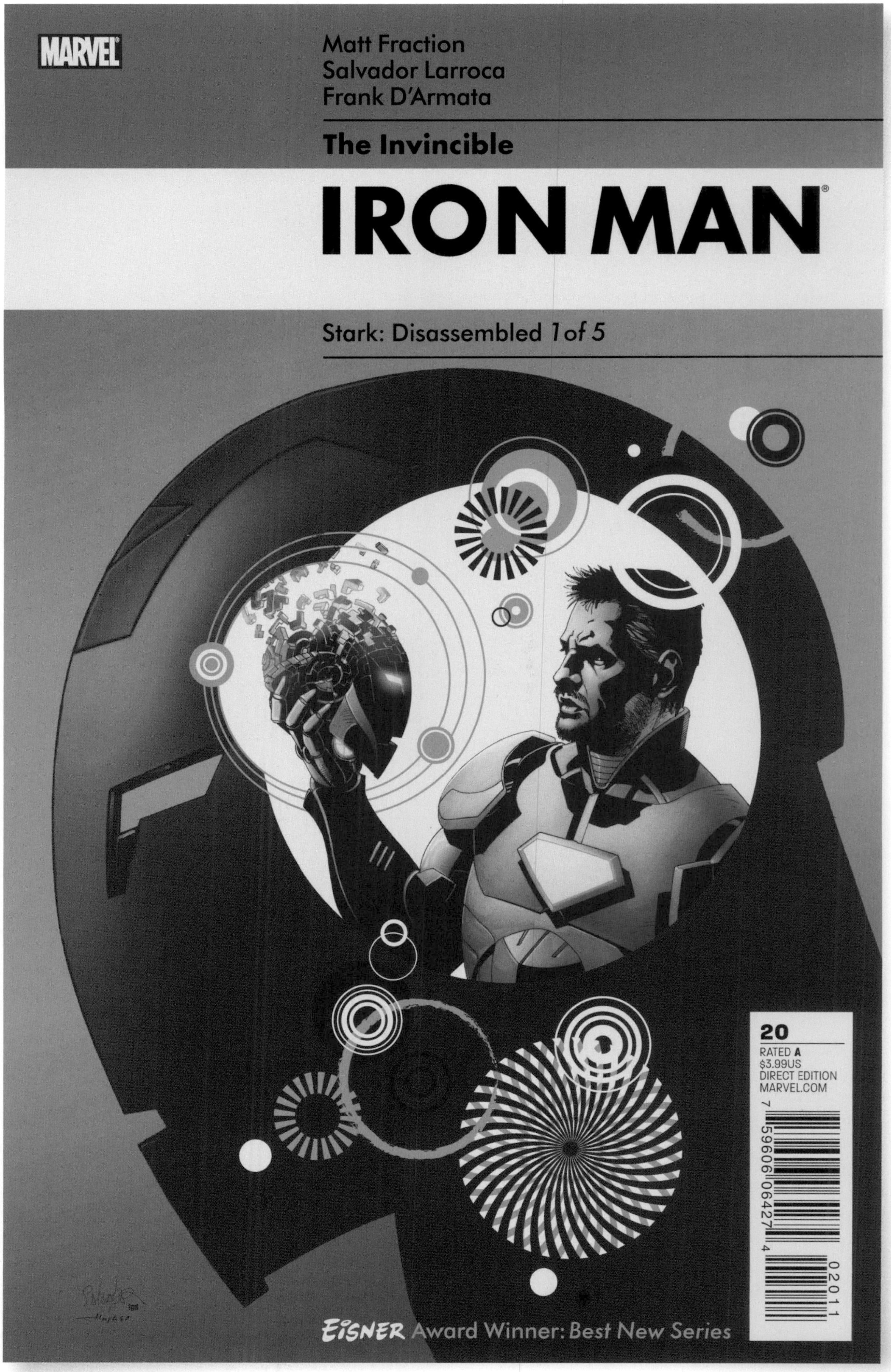
MARVEL
Matt Fraction
Salvador Larroca
Frank D'Armata
The Invincible
IRON MAN
Stark: Disassembled 1 of 5
20
RATED A
$3.99US
DIRECT EDITION
MARVEL.COM
EISNER Award Winner: Best New Series

▲ ***INVINCIBLE IRON MAN* #20**

**January 2010**
**Artist:** Salvador Larroca

This slightly surreal cover perfectly captured a turning point in the life of Tony Stark and Iron Man as the hero struggled to reboot his mind after he had wiped it to stop Norman Osborn from learning his secrets. All five parts of this storyline reflected Stark's inner struggle. This first part showcased Stark's concern that he would never regain his lost knowledge.

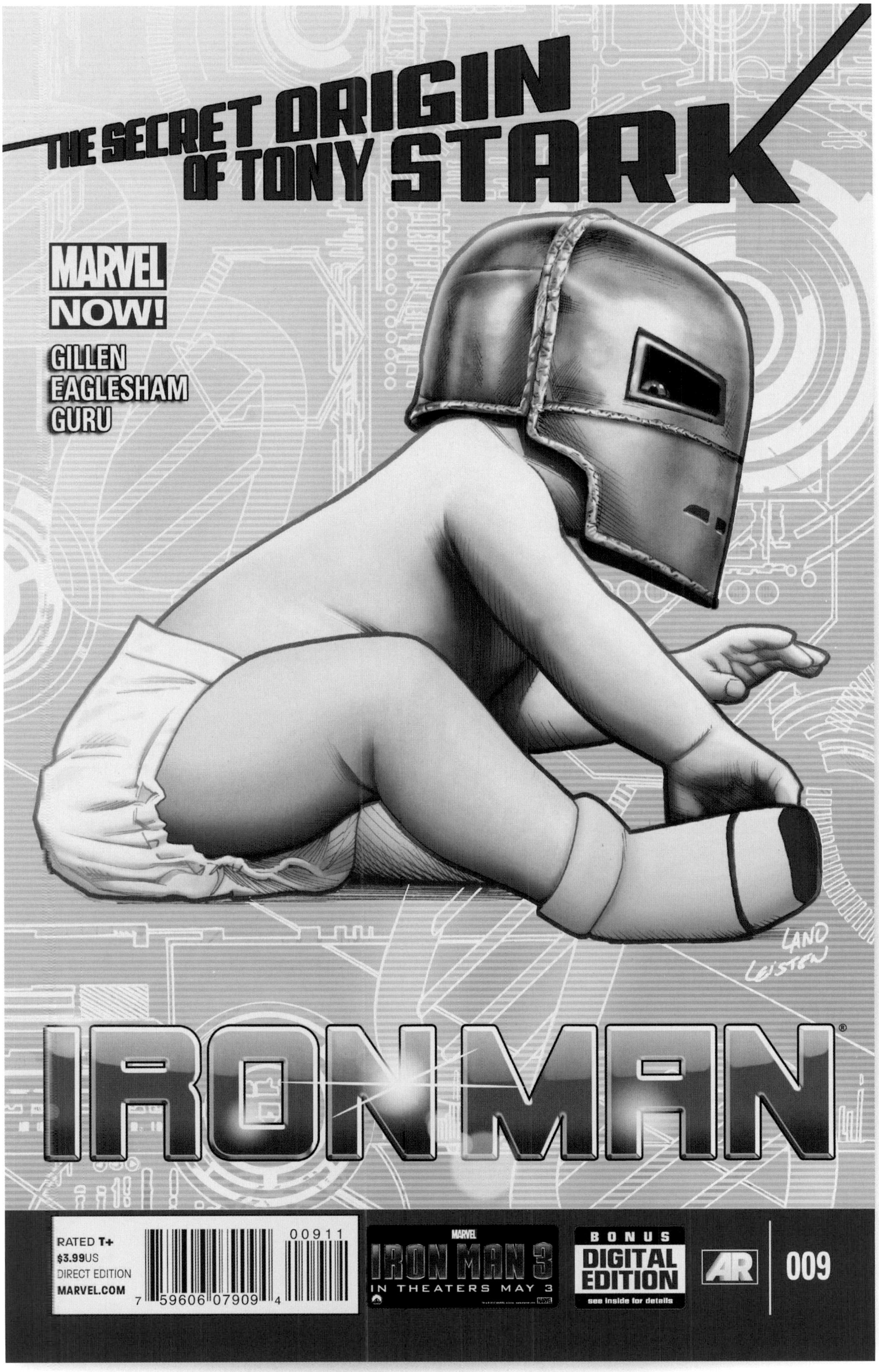
THE SECRET ORIGIN OF TONY STARK
MARVEL NOW!
GILLEN
EAGLESHAM
GURU
LAND
LEISTEN
IRON MAN
RATED T+
$3.99US
DIRECT EDITION
MARVEL.COM
00911
7 59606 07909 4
MARVEL
IRON MAN 3
IN THEATERS MAY 3
BONUS
DIGITAL EDITION
see inside for details
AR
009

▲ ***IRON MAN* #9**

**June 2013**
**Artist:** Greg Land

Few covers can claim to be truly original, but this Greg Land piece, showing an infant Tony Stark, managed it. It signalled the start of one of the most shocking *Iron Man* stories of all time, as writer Kieron Gillen's story seemed to suggest alien intervention leading up to Stark's birth—only to reveal that Tony had been adopted and that the Stark's natural son, Arno, was still alive.

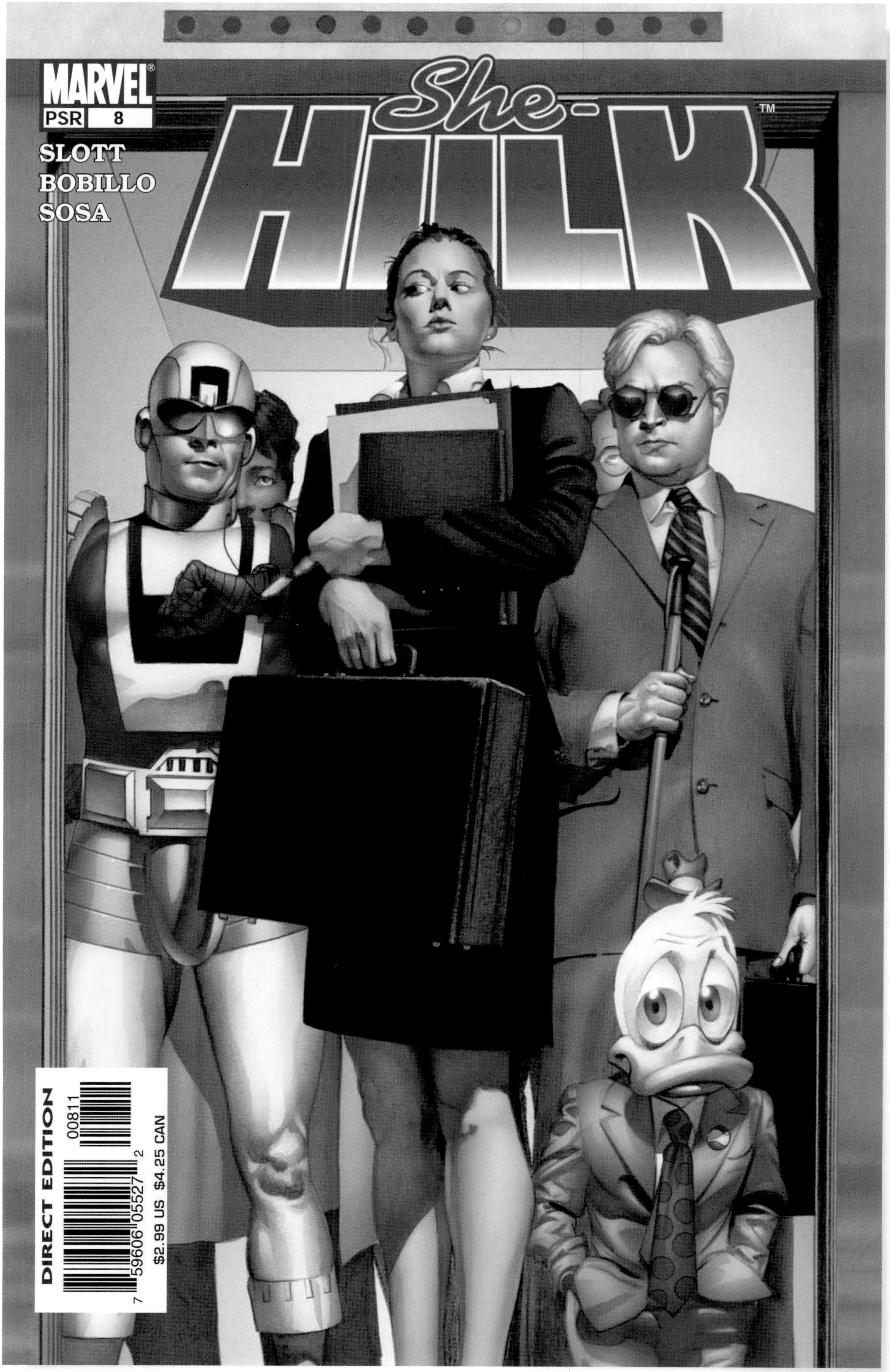
MARVEL
PSR 8
She-HULK
SLOTT
BOBILLO
SOSA
DIRECT EDITION
$2.99 US $4.25 CAN

◀ ***SHE-HULK* #8**

**December 2004**
**Artist:** Mike Mayhew

Under writer Dan Slott, She-Hulk enjoyed one of her most creative—and humorous—runs. These aspects are both exemplified in this Mike Mayhew cover, showcasing She-Hulk's office life. With cameos by Matt Murdock (Daredevil) and Howard the Duck, it artfully mixes the mundane with the chaotic in the Marvel universe.

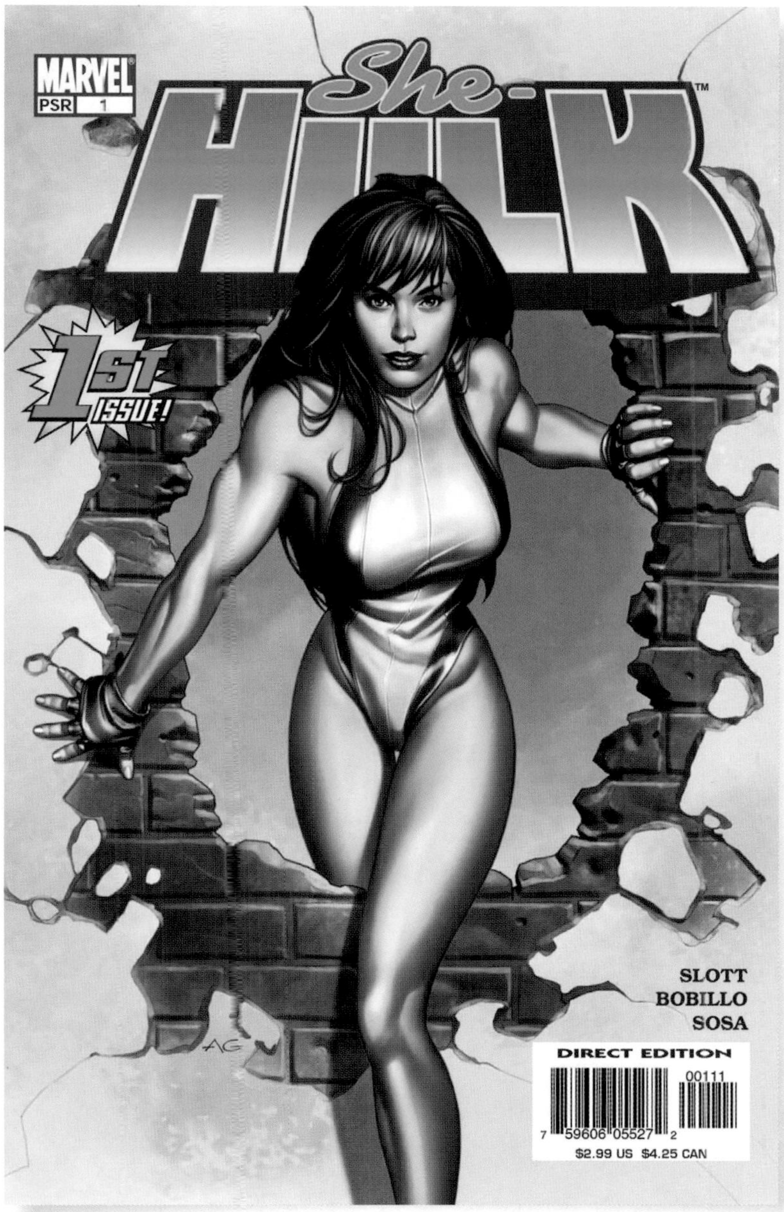
MARVEL
PSR 1
She-
HULK
1ST ISSUE!
SLOTT
BOBILLO
SOSA
DIRECT EDITION
$2.99 US $4.25 CAN

▲ ***SHE-HULK* #1**

**May 2004**
**Artist:** Adi Granov

Writer Dan Slott created some excellent stories during his time on the title, each one behind a stunning cover. On the debut cover to the hero's new series, Adi Granov manages to portray both the power and beauty of She-Hulk in this issue. In fact, this became one of the most frequently seen images of the character.

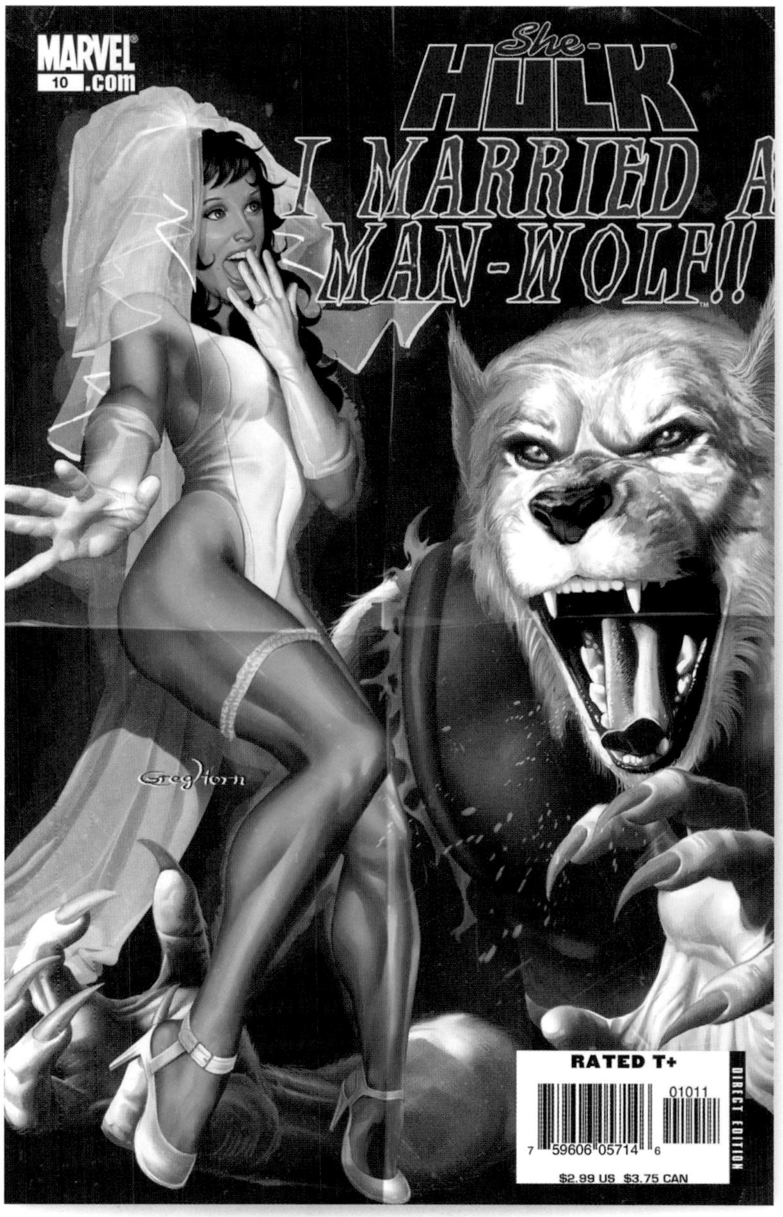
MARVEL
10 .com
She-
HULK
I MARRIED A
MAN-WOLF!!
RATED T+
DIRECT EDITION
$2.99 US $3.75 CAN

▲ ***SHE-HULK* #10**

**October 2006**
**Artist:** Greg Horn

Dan Slott's *She-Hulk* was relaunched in 2005. The new series continued the title's tradition of great covers, and one of the favorites was this Greg Horn piece depicting the hero's relationship with John Jameson, a.k.a. the Man-Wolf. The pulpy 1950's horror-movie look of the cover was an accurate reflection of the comic's knowing humor.

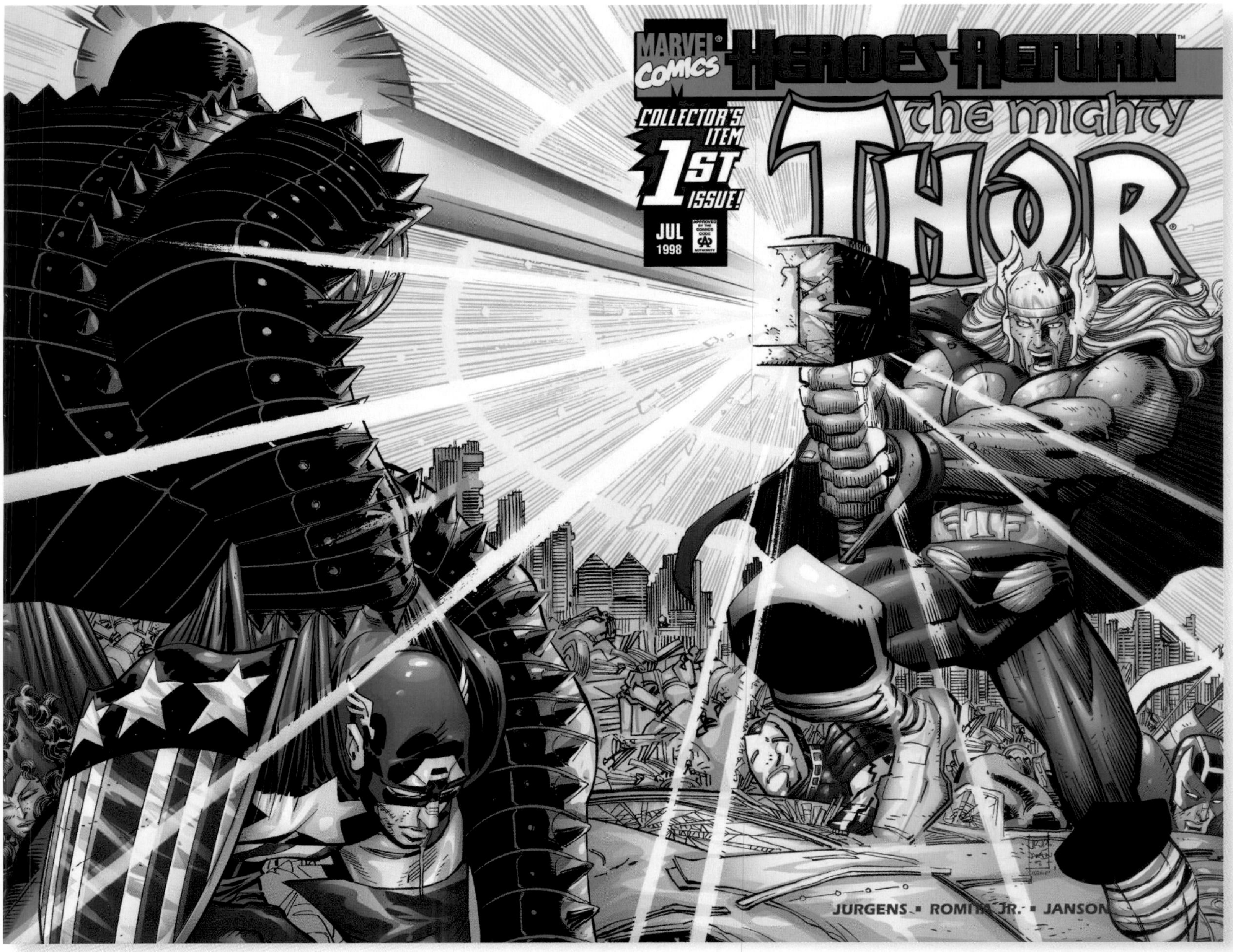
MARVEL COMICS
HEROES RETURN
COLLECTOR'S ITEM
1ST ISSUE!
JUL 1998
the mighty
THOR
JURGENS • ROMITA JR. • JANSON

▲ *THOR* #1

**July 1998**
**Artist:** John Romita Jr.

When Thor's own series was relaunched following the end of the "Heroes Reborn" saga, John Romita Jr. was brought in as the artist. His powerful style was the perfect match for Thor, who has rarely looked as godlike as he does on this stunning wraparound cover.

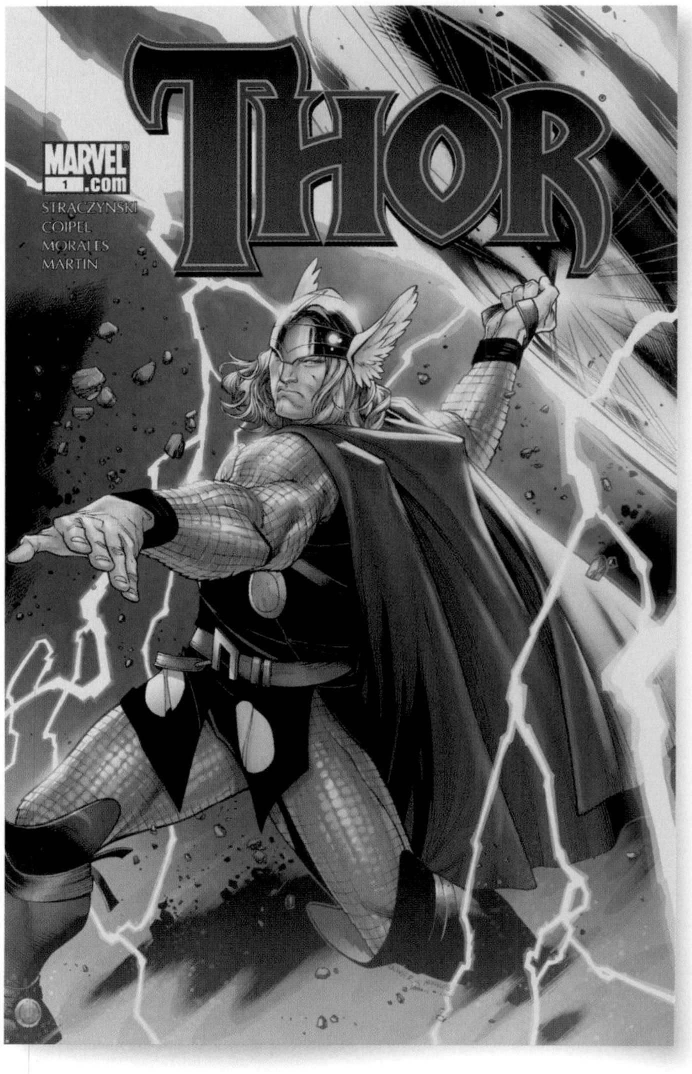
THOR
MARVEL
1 .com
STRACZYNSKI
COIPEL
MORALES
MARTIN

*THOR* #1 ▶

**September 2007**
**Artist:** Olivier Coipel

The first new *Thor* comic since 2004 needed to feature something special on the cover. Artist Olivier Coipel's interpretation of the powerful God of Thunder shows a new, darker look for Thor than had been seen previously.

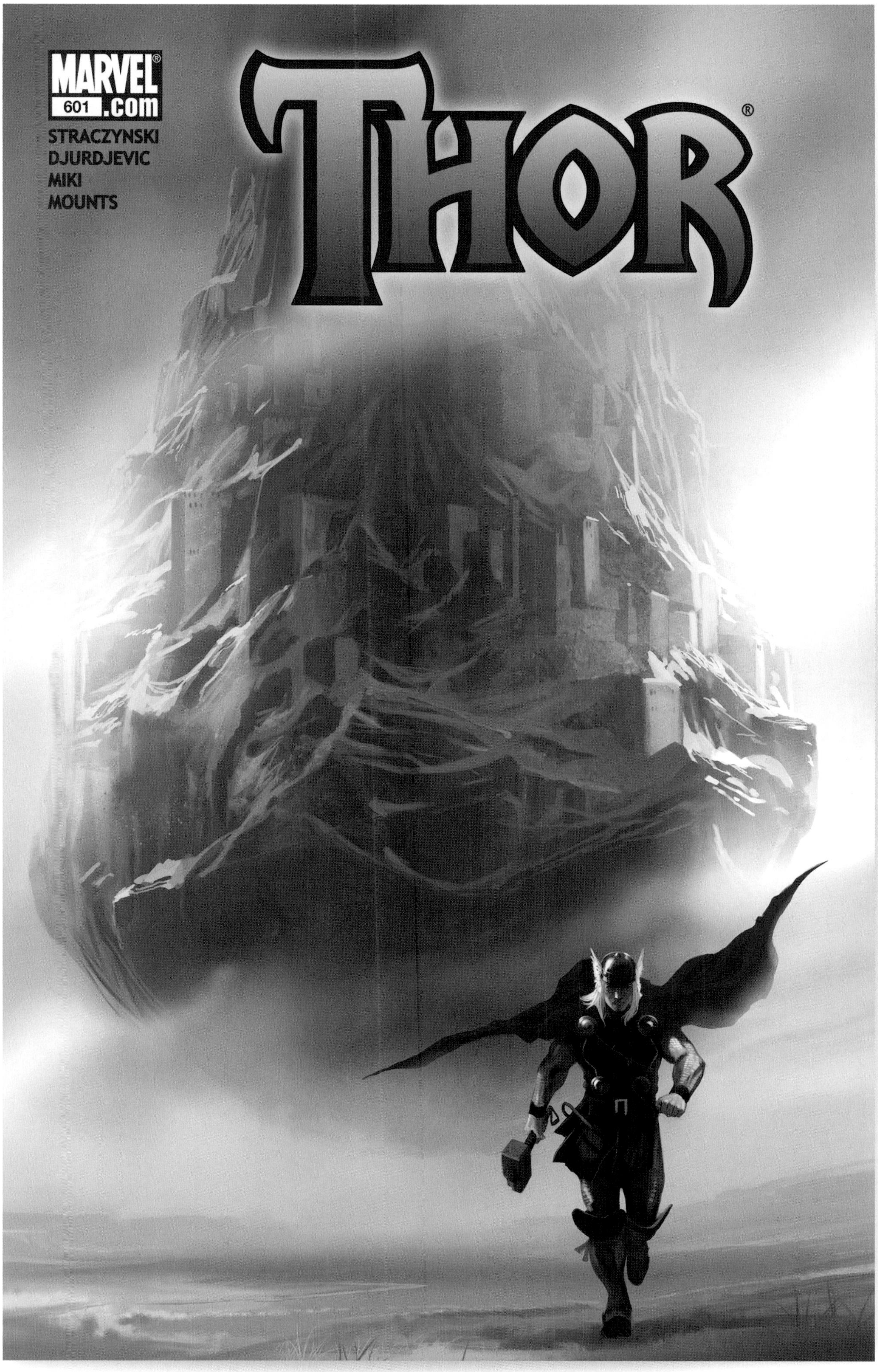
MARVEL
601 .com
STRACZYNSKI
DJURDJEVIC
MIKI
MOUNTS
THOR®

▲*THOR* **#601**

**June 2009**
**Artist:** Marko Djurdjevic

This issue boasts one of the most beautiful covers in *Thor*'s history, and one of the greatest modern interpretations of Thor's home, Asgard. Marko Djurdjevic captured Thor's anger and melancholy at being exiled from Asgard in one moody, expressionistic piece. This art style had a big influence on the first *Thor* movie (2011).

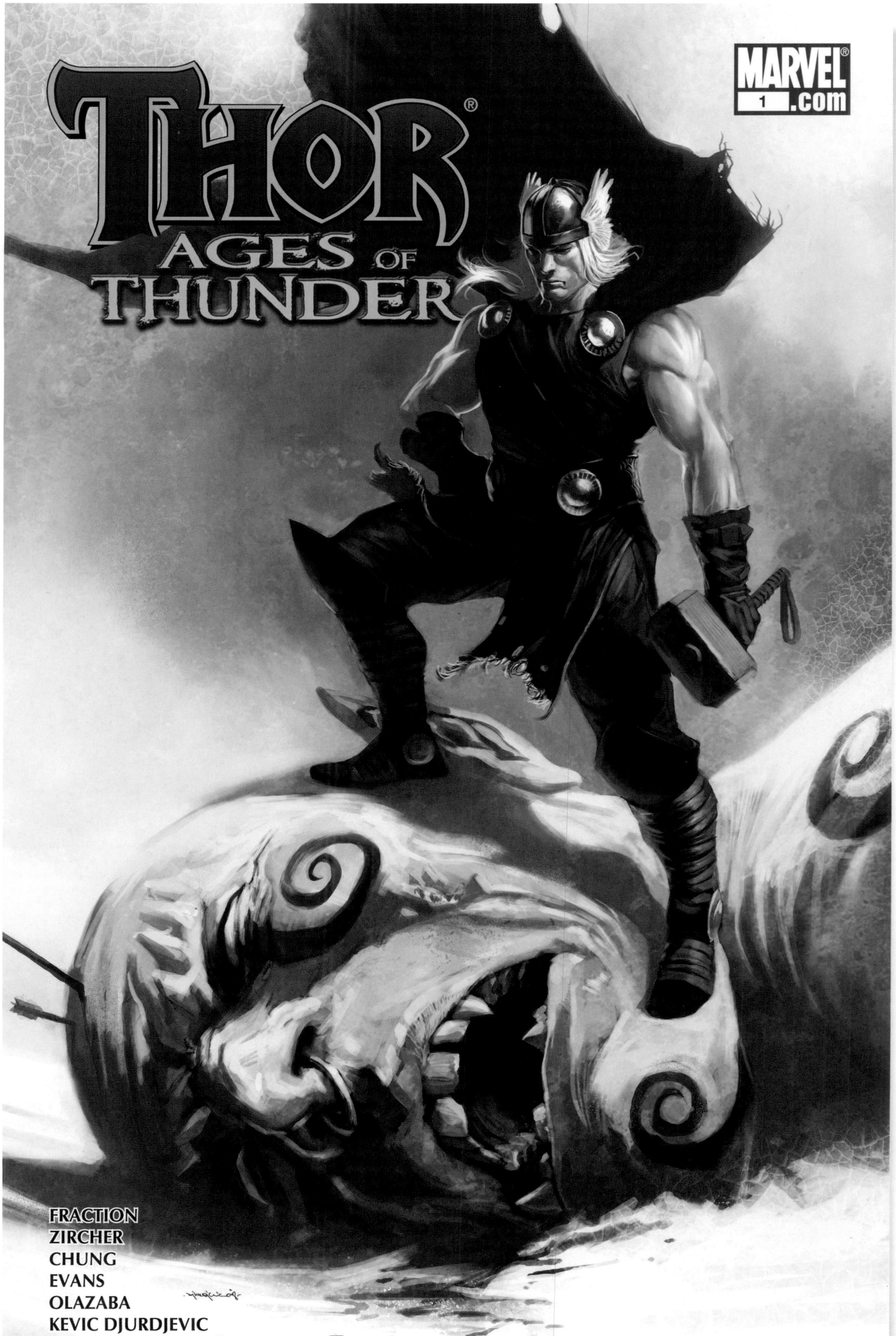
MARVEL
1 .com
THOR
AGES OF THUNDER
FRACTION
ZIRCHER
CHUNG
EVANS
OLAZABA
KEVIC DJURDJEVIC

MARVEL
PSR+ 1
LOKI
RODI
RIBIC
DIRECT EDITION
$3.50 US $5.00 CAN

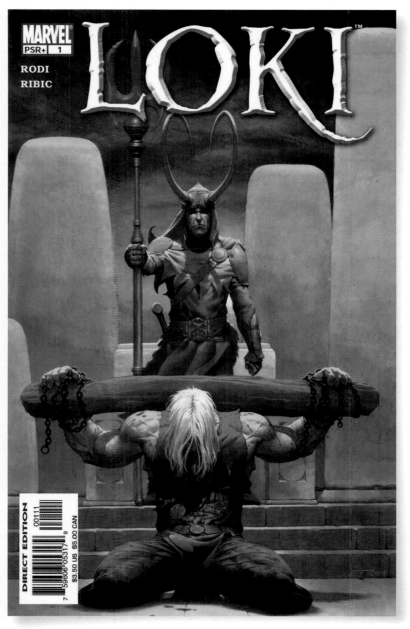

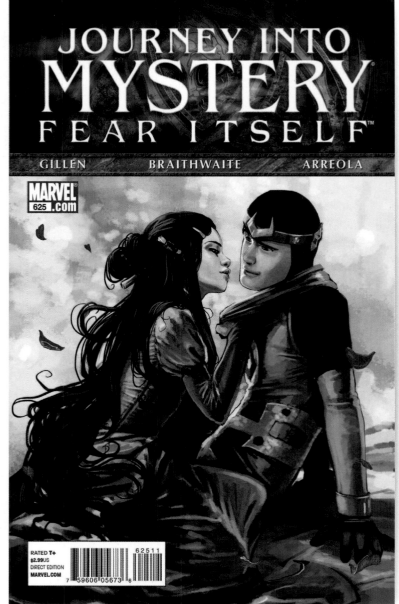

▲ *LOKI* #1

**September 2004**
**Artist:** Esad Ribic

Thor's evil adopted brother, Loki, gained his very own miniseries, with Esad Ribic creating beautifully painted covers for all four issues. Each one showcased Loki's troubled relationship with the Thunder God. The first, showing Loki looming menacingly over his captured brother, set the scene for the Loki-centric series.

JOURNEY INTO
MYSTERY
FEAR ITSELF
GILLEN
BRAITHWAITE
ARREOLA
MARVEL
625 .com
RATED T+
$2.99US
DIRECT EDITION
MARVEL.COM

▲ *JOURNEY INTO MYSTERY* #625

**September 2011**
**Artist:** Stephanie Hans

Stephanie Hans' romantic-looking cover belies writer Kieron Gillen's dark and ultimately tragic fantasy told within. Far from being a romantic tale, issue #625 told the story of a young Loki attempting to save the world from the Serpent, an ancient Asgardian God of Fear.

◀ *THOR: AGES OF THUNDER* #1

**June 2008**
**Artist:** Marko Djurdjevic

*Thor: Ages of Thunder* recounted tales of Thor's Asgardian adventures. Artist Marko Djurdjevic created a suitably mythic-looking cover for this one-off issue, showing the Thunder God standing triumphantly on a defeated Frost Giant. Other one-shots telling more tales of Thor's Asgardian life soon followed, each with a highly detailed Djurdjevic cover.

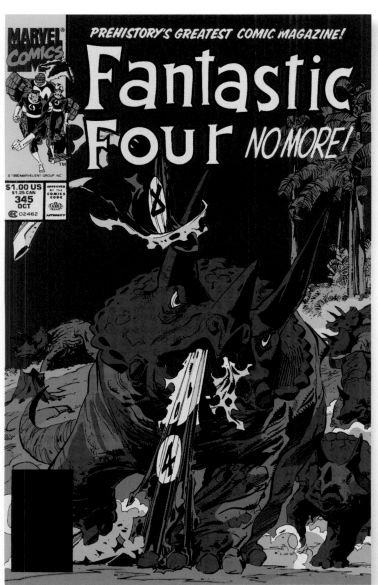

***FANTASTIC FOUR* #348 ▶**

**January 1991**
**Artist:** Art Adams

This issue's cover (and the story inside) brought together four of Marvel's most popular heroes of the time—Ghost Rider, the Hulk, Spider-Man, and Wolverine—into an all-new *Fantastic Four*. Add artist Art Adams producing some of his finest work, and you have a classic *Fantastic Four* cover. The heroes joined forces to rescue the original team, who had been captured by a rogue Skrull.

MARVEL COMICS
PREHISTORY'S GREATEST COMIC MAGAZINE!
Fantastic Four
NO MORE!
$1.00 US $1.25 CAN 345 OCT

**◀ *FANTASTIC FOUR* #345**

**October 1990**
**Artist:** Walt Simonson

Could the Fantastic Four really be dead? That was the question raised by the image of a triceratops with torn FF costumes hanging out of its mouth. The strapline was changed from the usual "World's Greatest Comic Magazine" to "Prehistory's Greatest Comic Magazine" to reflect the time-travel nature of the story as Simonson's inventive run on the title continued.

MARVEL COMICS
THE WORLD'S MOST COLLECTABLE COMIC MAGAZINE!
Fantastic Four
$1.00 US $1.25 CAN 349 FEB
FEATURING THE WORLD'S MOST EXPLOITATIVE CAMEO!

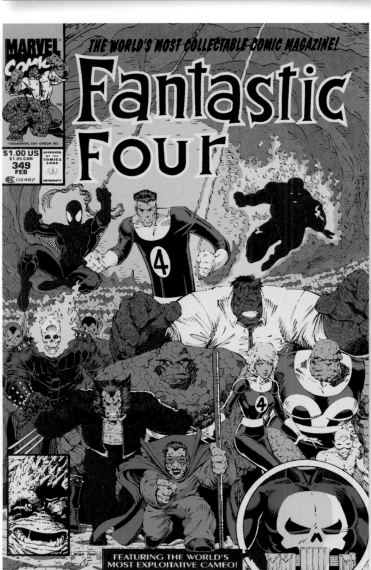

**◀ *FANTASTIC FOUR* #349**

**February 1991**
**Artist:** Art Adams

Art Adams produced another outstanding piece of work for this cover, lining the original Fantastic Four up alongside a new team that had formed to save them following their capture in the previous issue. The sight of all the heroes together, alongside the Mole Man, marching out towards the reader resulted in an eye-catching cover.

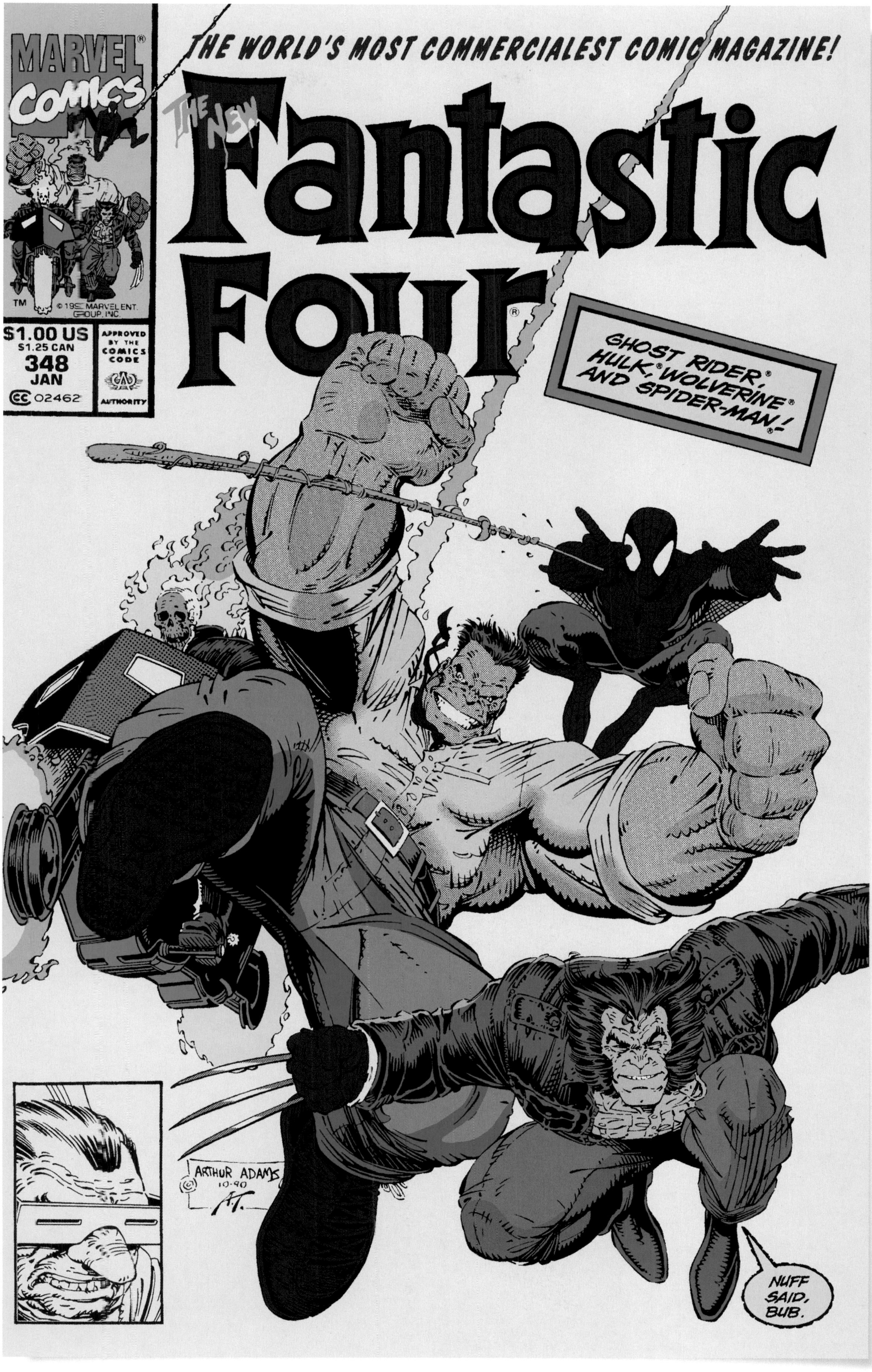
MARVEL COMICS
THE WORLD'S MOST COMMERCIALEST COMIC MAGAZINE!
THE NEW Fantastic Four
$1.00 US
$1.25 CAN
348
JAN
APPROVED BY THE COMICS CODE AUTHORITY
GHOST RIDER, HULK, WOLVERINE AND SPIDER-MAN!
ARTHUR ADAMS 10-90
NUFF SAID, BUB.

GIANT-SIZED 350TH ISSUE SPECTACULAR!
MARVEL COMICS
Fantastic Four
AIN'T NOTHING LIKE THE REAL THING!
$1.50 US
350
MAR
50 YEARS
CAPTAIN AMERICA
1941 – 1991

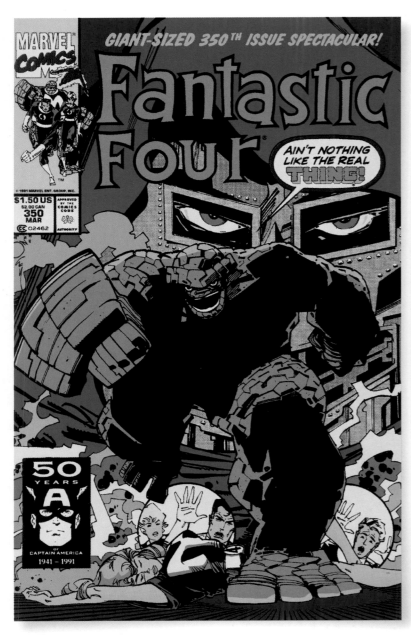

▲ ***FANTASTIC FOUR* #350**

**March 1991**
**Artist:** Walt Simonson

"Ain't nothing like the real Thing!" Ben Grimm's word balloon said it all on this anniversary issue cover—the founding member of the Fantastic Four was once again transformed into the FF's powerhouse. Simonson's image of the Thing standing over girlfriend Sharon Ventura, with Doctor Doom looming large in the background, suggested that this was going to be another epic clash between the FF and their archenemy.

MARVEL COMICS
THE WORLD'S GREATEST COMIC MAGAZINE!
Fantastic Four
NOV.'96 1
JIM LEE
BRANDON CHOI
SCOTT WILLIAMS

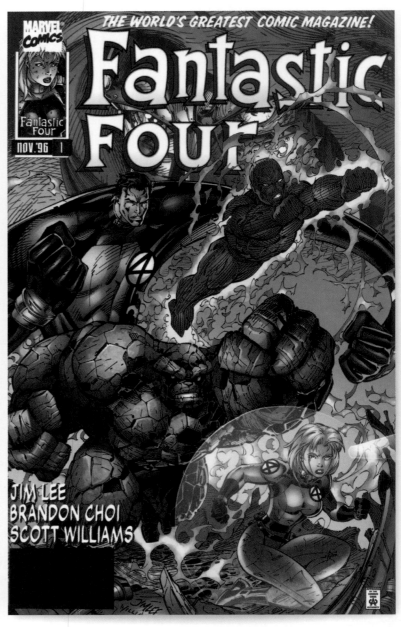

▲ ***FANTASTIC FOUR* #1**

**November 1996**
**Artist:** Jim Lee

In 1996, four of Marvel's biggest titles were taken over by creators from rival publisher Image Comics and relaunched as part of the "Heroes Reborn" imprint. Jim Lee was the biggest name in comics at the time and he took on the *Fantastic Four*, updating their origin and giving the art a sleek, modern-day feel, as can be seen on the first issue. It brought the bestselling, artistic energy of Image Comics—and especially Jim Lee—to the FF.

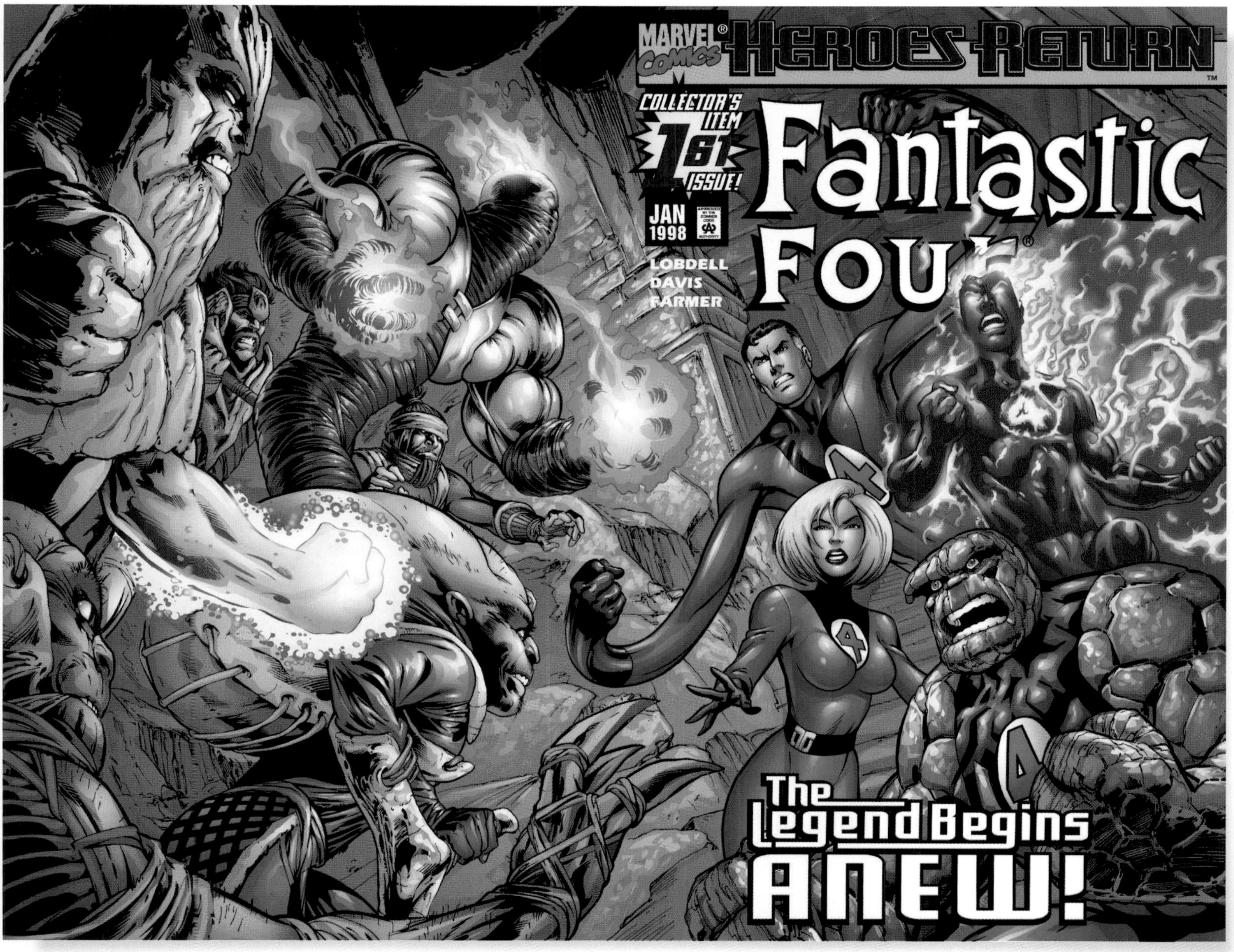
MARVEL COMICS
HEROES RETURN
COLLECTOR'S ITEM
1st ISSUE!
JAN 1998
LOBDELL
DAVIS
FARMER
Fantastic Four
The Legend Begins
ANEW!

▲ *FANTASTIC FOUR* #1

**January 1998**
**Artist:** Alan Davis

Marvel's "Heroes Return" branding saw the company bring top creators to their major titles as they returned to Marvel after a year of being produced by Image Comics. Alan Davis' style was perfect for the *Fantastic Four*, as he brought a vitality and spirit of adventure to Marvel's First Family, as exemplified by his first cover.

MARVEL
PG 60 489
MARK WAID
MIKE WIERINGO
KARL KESEL
FANTASTIC FOUR
WORLD'S CHEAPEST
ONLY
9¢
COMIC MAGAZINE

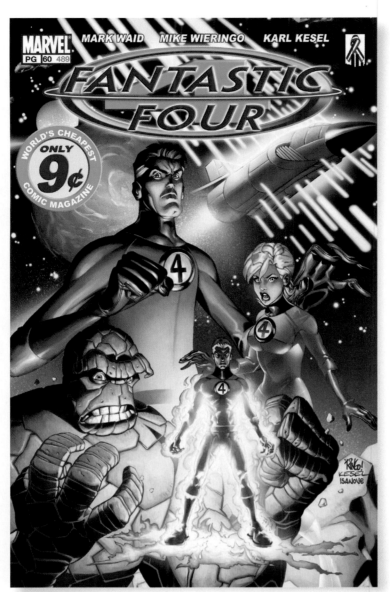

◄ *FANTASTIC FOUR* #60

**October 2002**
**Artist:** Mike Wieringo

Mike Wieringo's cover art for the *Fantastic Four* conveyed a sense of wonder that only the best FF artists brought to the title, while Mark Waid's scripts ensured a series of great stories. Such was Marvel's confidence in this new creative duo that they released the issue for only 9 cents.

MARVEL
61
WAID
WIERINGO
KESEL
FANTASTIC FOUR

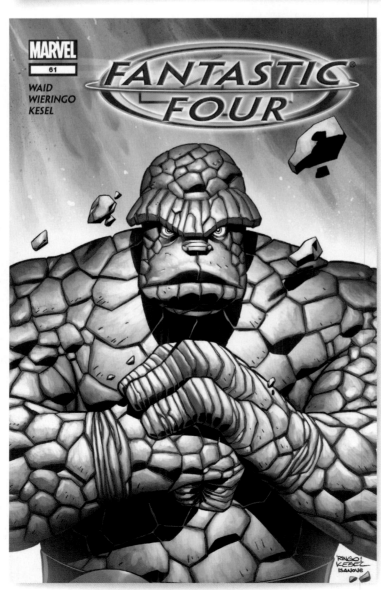

◄ *FANTASTIC FOUR* #61

**November 2002**
**Artist:** Mike Wieringo

The Thing was perhaps the most human of Marvel's monstrous heroes, and artist Mike Wieringo's interpretation manages to encapsulate this theme perfectly. He evokes not only The Thing's amazing strength, but also his inner nobility.

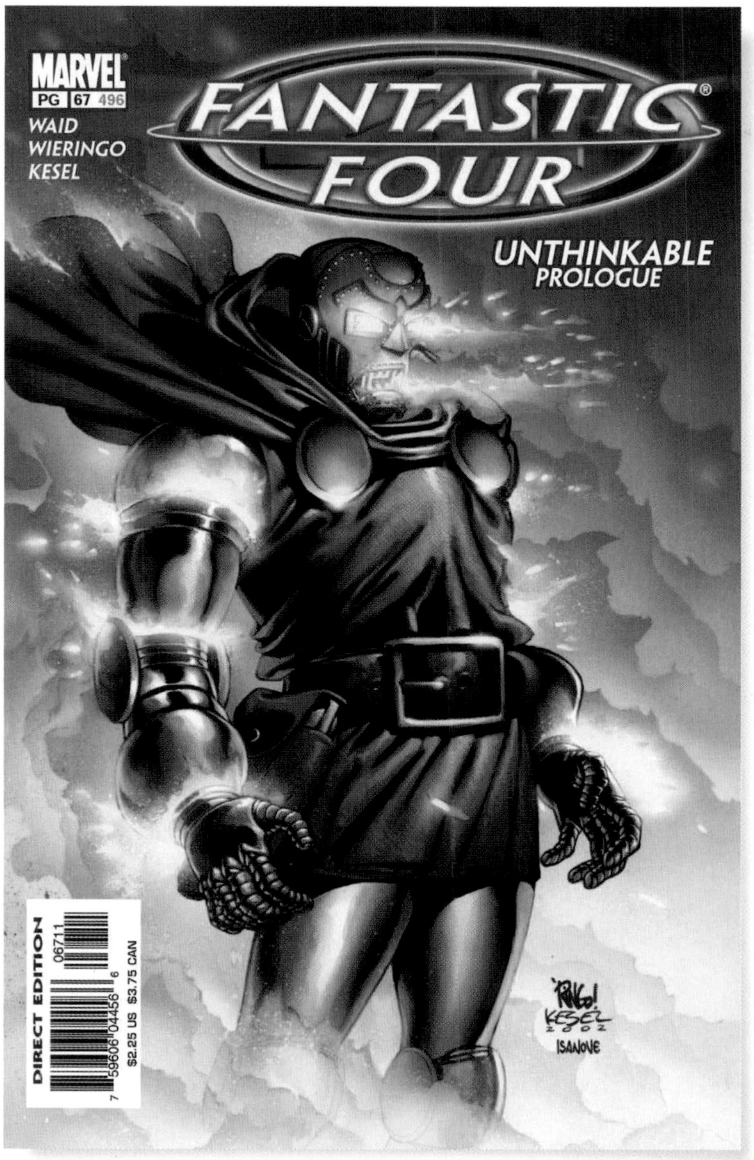
MARVEL
PG 67 496
WAID
WIERINGO
KESEL
FANTASTIC FOUR
UNTHINKABLE
PROLOGUE
DIRECT EDITION
$2.25 US $3.75 CAN

◀ *FANTASTIC FOUR* **#67**

**May 2003**
**Artist:** Mike Wieringo

This issue was a prologue to "Unthinkable," a highlight of Mark Waid and Mike Wieringo's time working on the *Fantastic Four*. Wieringo's striking cover portrays a powerful and despotic Doctor Doom burning with energy gained through selling the soul of his true love to demons.

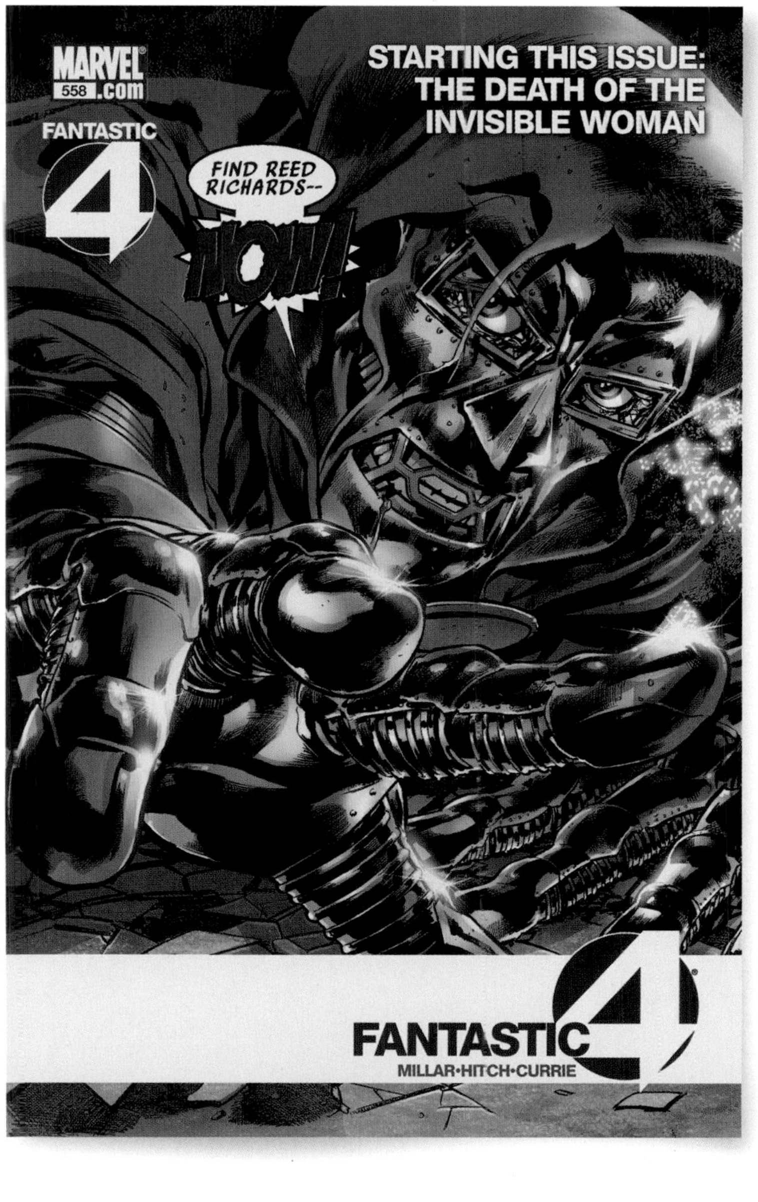
MARVEL
558 .com
FANTASTIC 4
STARTING THIS ISSUE: THE DEATH OF THE INVISIBLE WOMAN
FIND REED RICHARDS--
NOW!
FANTASTIC 4
MILLAR•HITCH•CURRIE

◀ *FANTASTIC FOUR* **#558**

**August 2008**
**Artist:** Bryan Hitch

Doctor Doom has been the subject of many great covers, but Bryan Hitch's startling close-up of Latveria's dictator presented a new aspect to the character. It is one of the only times Doom has looked scared on a cover, making the reader instantly want to find out exactly what, or who, Doom feared so much.

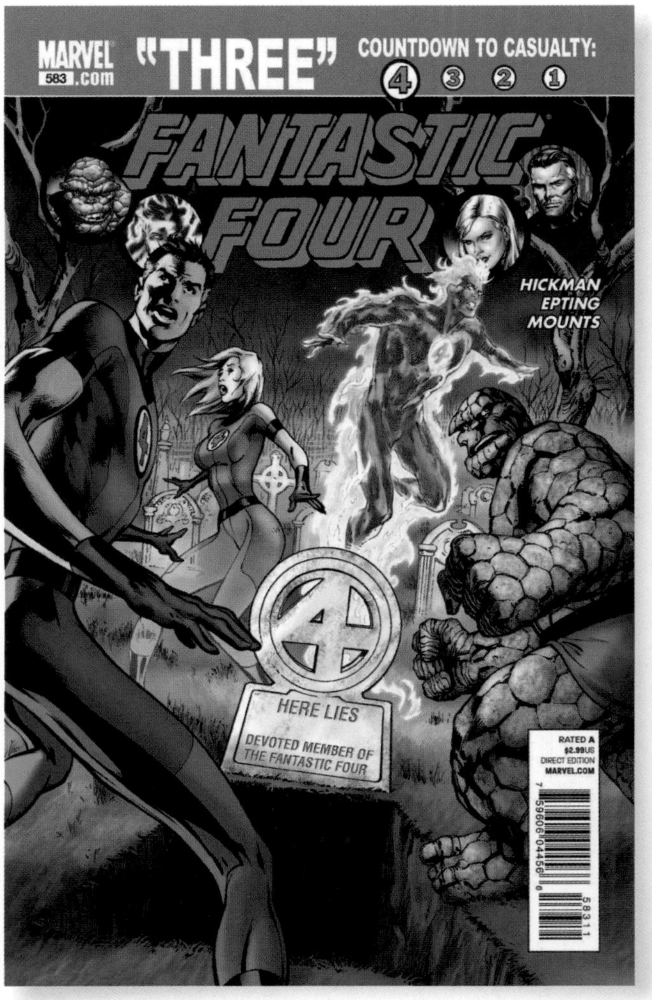
MARVEL
583 .com
"THREE"
COUNTDOWN TO CASUALTY:
4 3 2 1
FANTASTIC FOUR
HICKMAN
EPTING
MOUNTS
HERE LIES
DEVOTED MEMBER OF
THE FANTASTIC FOUR
RATED A
$2.99US
DIRECT EDITION
MARVEL.COM

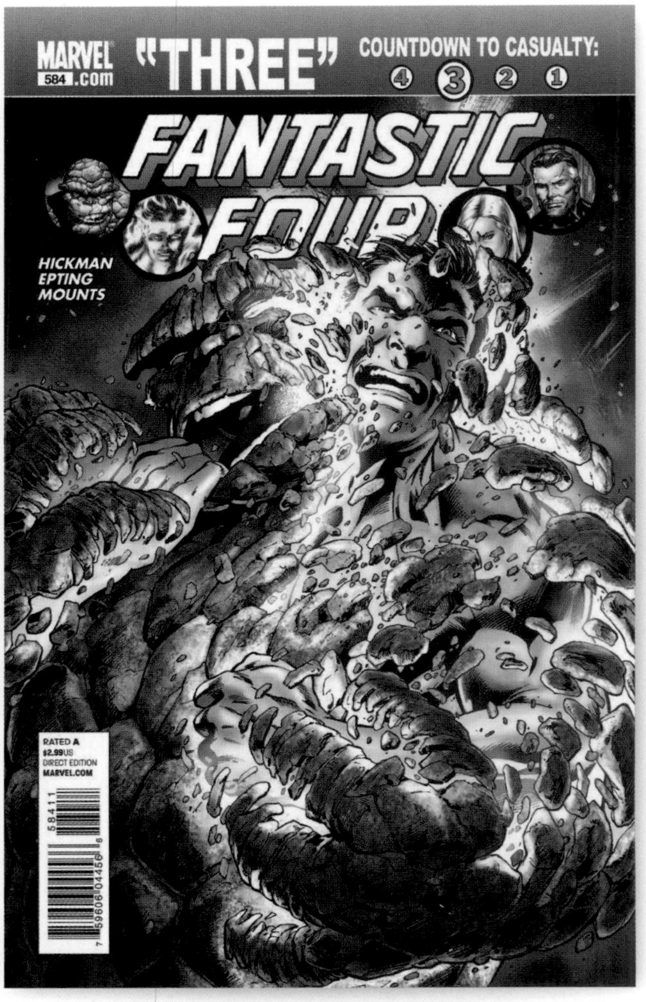
MARVEL
584 .com
"THREE"
COUNTDOWN TO CASUALTY:
4 3 2 1
FANTASTIC FOUR
HICKMAN
EPTING
MOUNTS
RATED A
$2.99US
DIRECT EDITION
MARVEL.COM

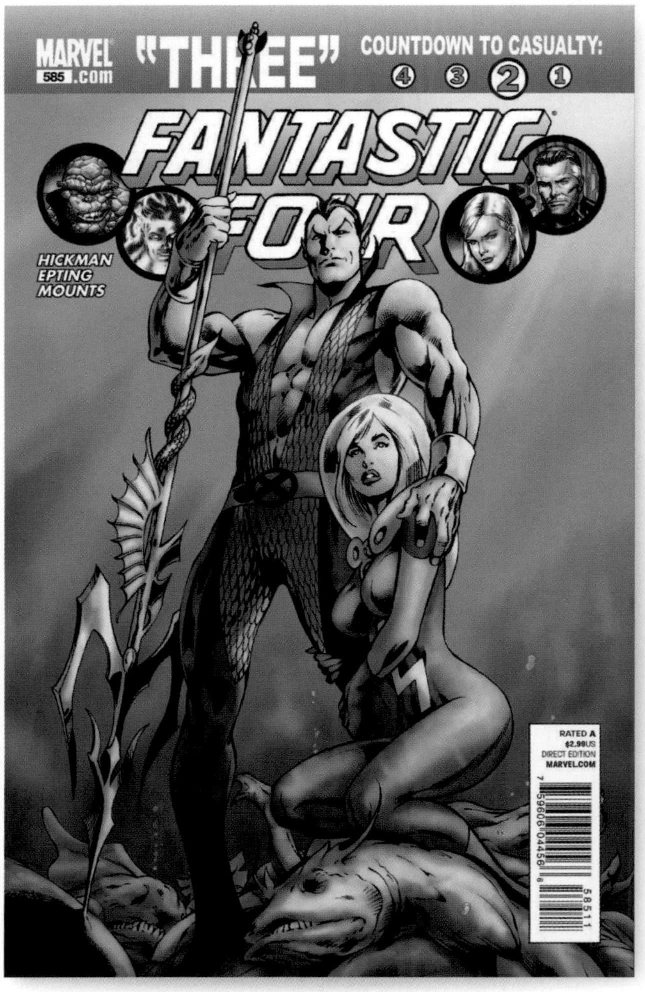
MARVEL
585 .com
"THREE"
COUNTDOWN TO CASUALTY:
4 3 2 1
FANTASTIC FOUR
HICKMAN
EPTING
MOUNTS
RATED A
$2.99US
DIRECT EDITION
MARVEL.COM

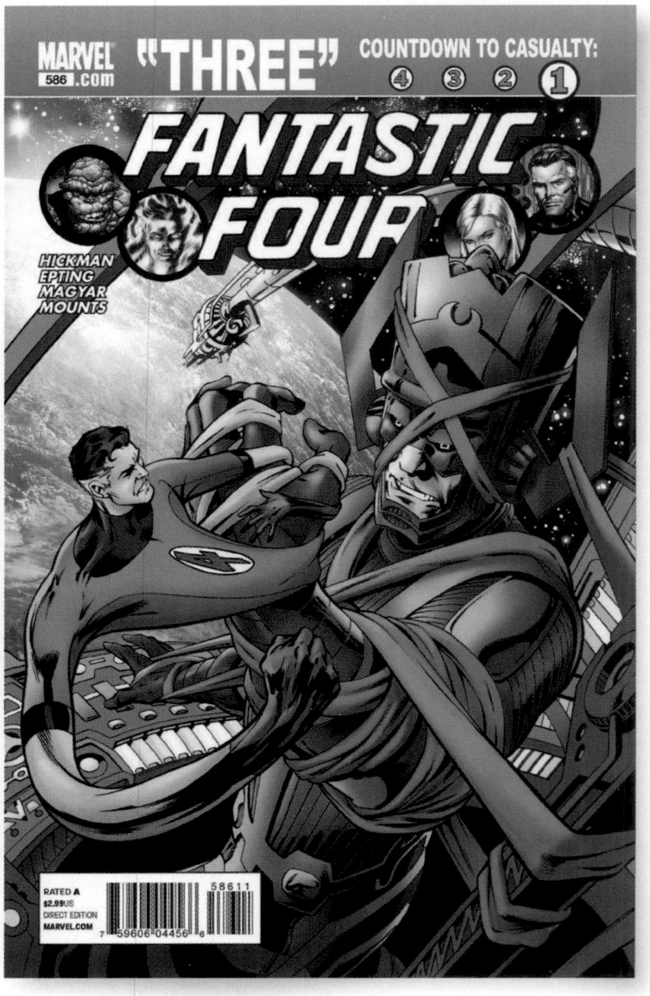
MARVEL
586 .com
"THREE"
COUNTDOWN TO CASUALTY:
4 3 2 1
FANTASTIC FOUR
HICKMAN
EPTING
MAGYAR
MOUNTS
RATED A
$2.99US
DIRECT EDITION
MARVEL.COM

▲ *FANTASTIC FOUR* #583–586

**November 2010–February 2011**
**Artist:** Alan Davis

The strapline on each of these four issues gave an ominous "Countdown to Casualty," as the Fantastic Four approached a time when one of them would die. Issue #583 depicts the team standing around an empty grave, while the following issues show Ben, Sue, and Reed in strange—and possibly deadly—situations. Writer Jonathan Hickman's critically acclaimed run on the FF was nearing a key moment, and, tellingly, the hero who did not get a cover of his own was the one destined to die—the Human Torch.

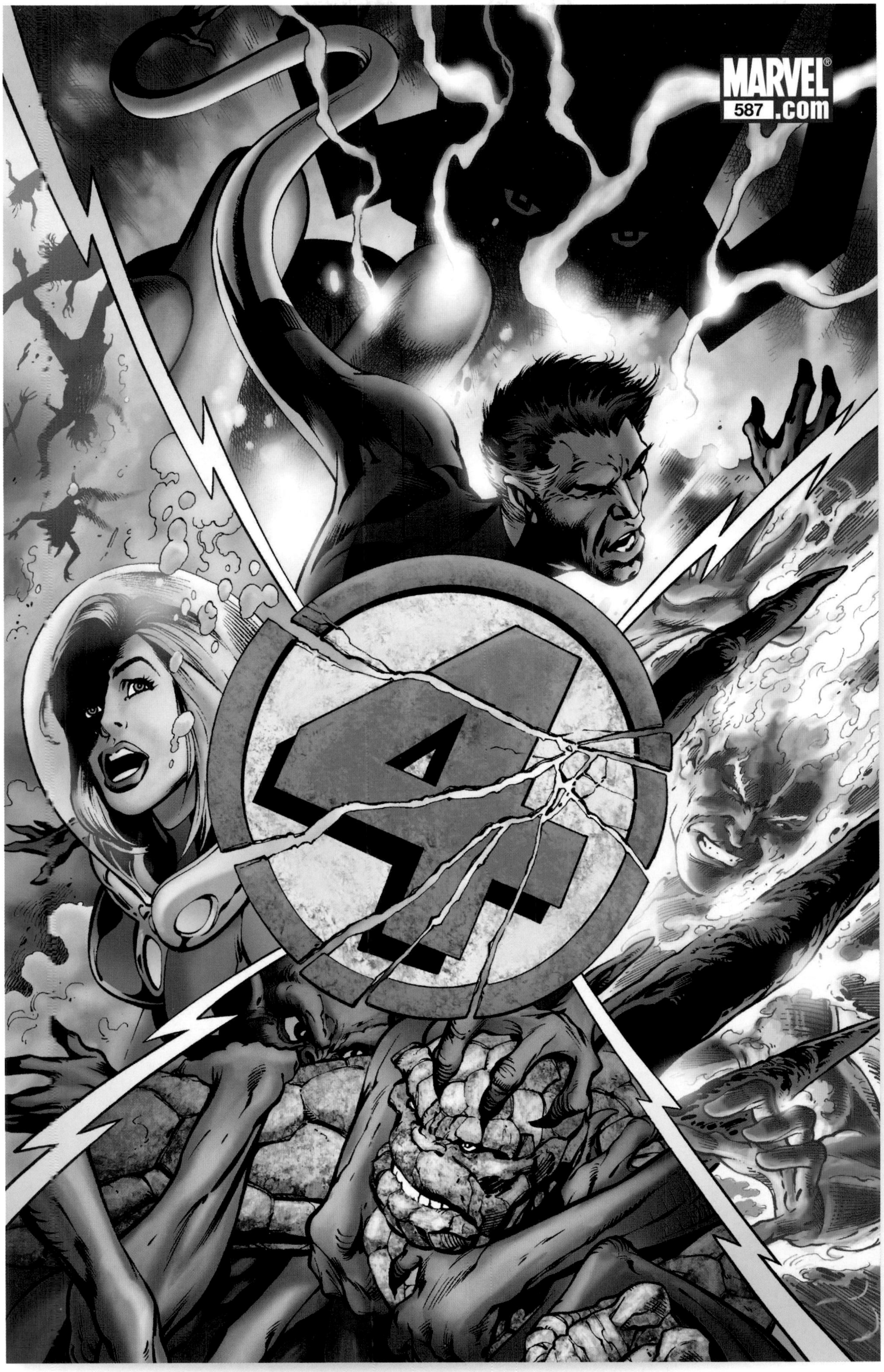
MARVEL
587 .com

▲ *FANTASTIC FOUR* #587

**March 2011**
**Artist:** Alan Davis

Alan Davis' dramatic cover image for the fifth installment of the "Three" story arc depicts each member of the Fantastic Four in deadly peril, arranged around an ominously cracked 4 insignia. The result was one of the most tense covers in the FF's long history. To further increase the tension, the issue came in a black sealed bag emblazoned with a 3 insignia.

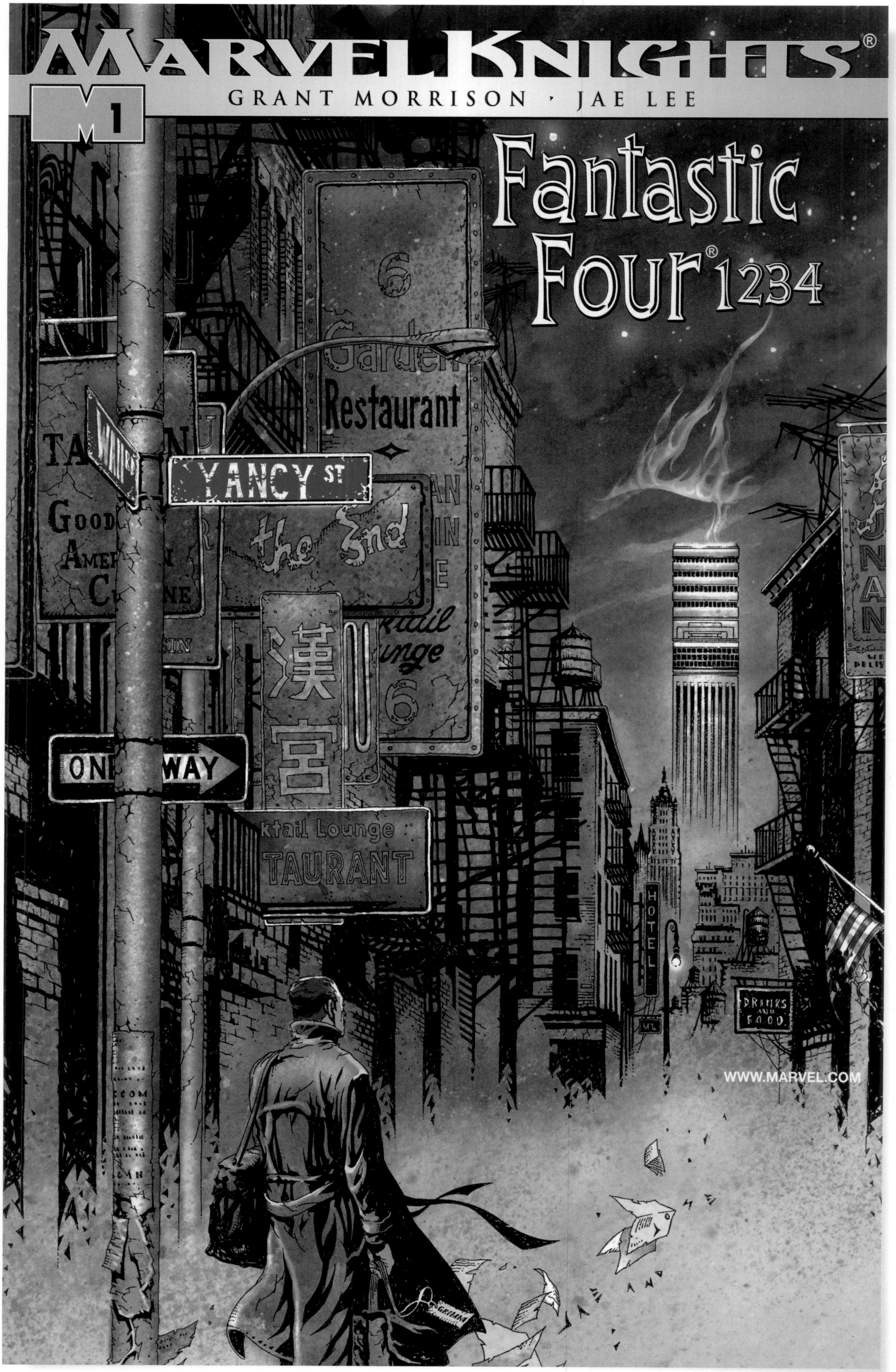
MARVEL KNIGHTS®
M 1
GRANT MORRISON · JAE LEE
Fantastic Four® 1234
Restaurant
YANCY ST
the End
漢
宮
ONE WAY
ktail Lounge
TAURANT
HOTEL
DRINKS AND FOOD
WWW.MARVEL.COM

◀ ***FANTASTIC FOUR 1234* #1**

**October 2001**
**Artist:** Jae Lee

Working with writer Grant Morrison, Jae Lee brought his unique vision to the Fantastic Four on a four-part miniseries, which focused on the bonds that united the team. Lee's illustration of Yancy Street, once home to Ben Grimm, established the dark, moody tone of the series. As Ben desperately tried to alter his own past so that he never became the Thing, evil Doctor Doom was masterminding the team's destruction.

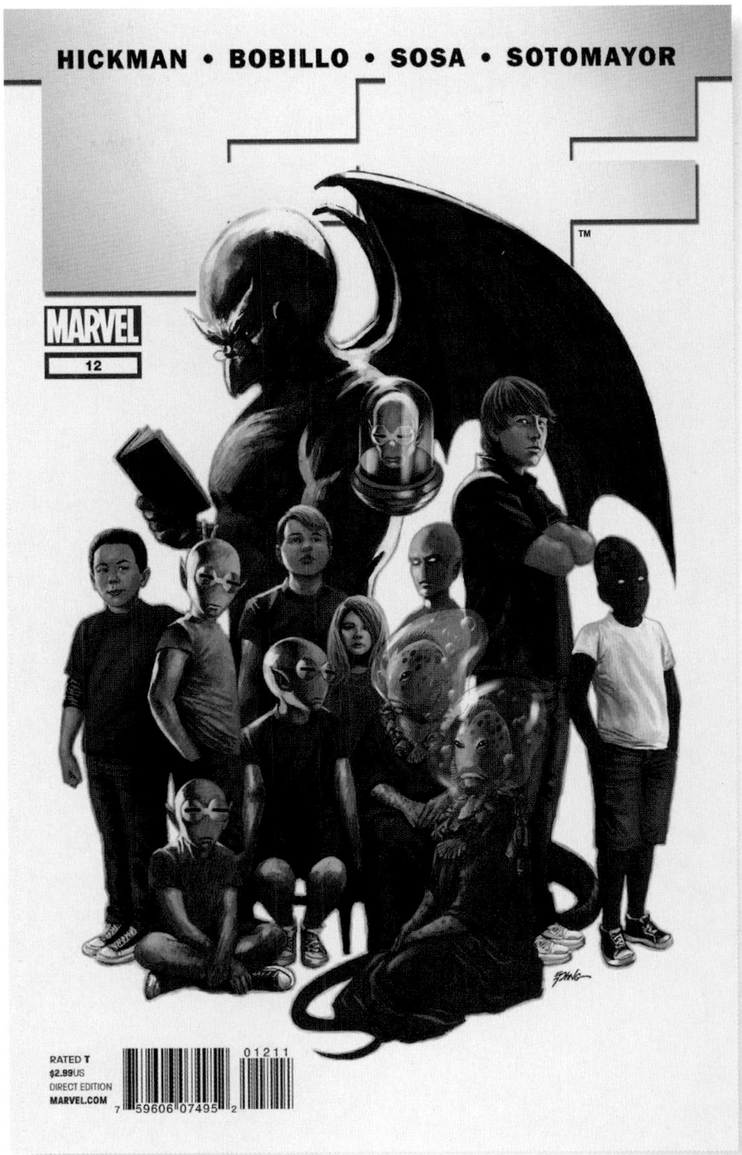
HICKMAN • BOBILLO • SOSA • SOTOMAYOR
MARVEL
12
RATED T
$2.99US
DIRECT EDITION
MARVEL.COM

***FF* #12** ▶

**January 2012**
**Artist:** Steve Epting

The FF—or Future Foundation—replaced the Fantastic Four both as a team and a comic in the 2010s. The FF was actually an organization for young, gifted minds, founded by Mr. Fantastic. Epting's simple cover shines the spotlight on these great young characters (and a reformed, intelligent Dragon Man), and brought a fresh energy to the book.

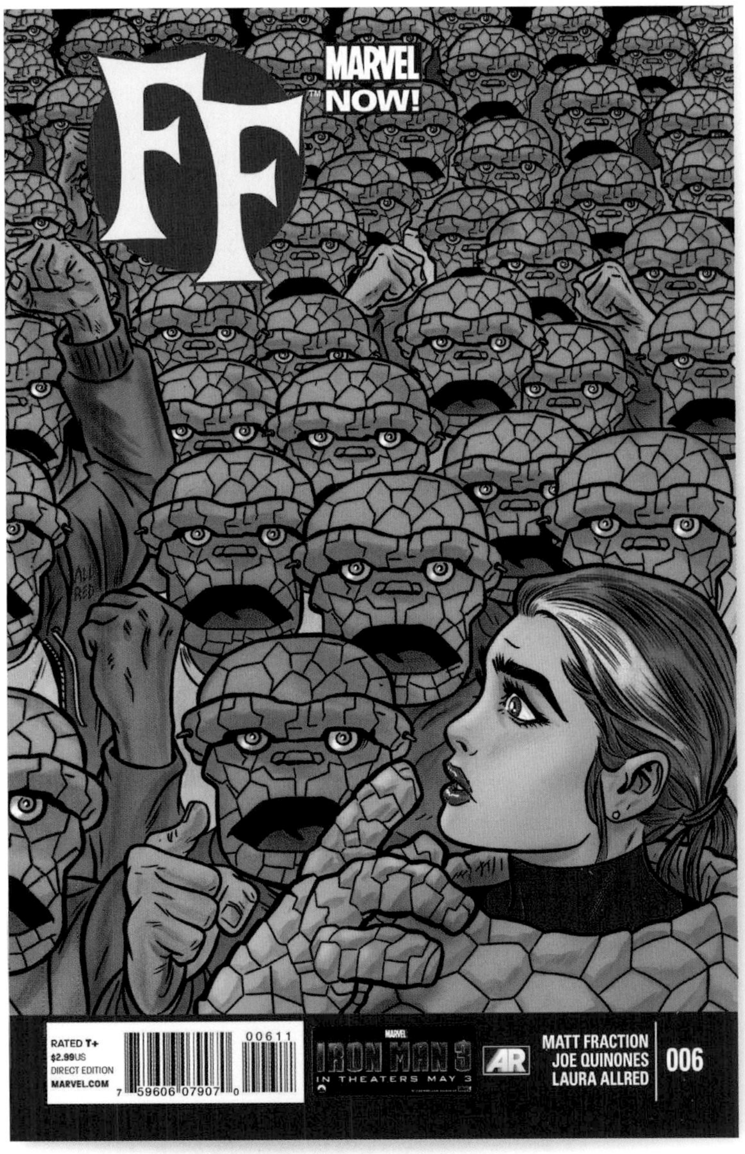
FF
MARVEL NOW!
RATED T+
$2.99US
DIRECT EDITION
MARVEL.COM
IRON MAN 3
IN THEATERS MAY 3
MATT FRACTION
JOE QUINONES
LAURA ALLRED
006

***FF* #6** ▶

**June 2013**
**Artist:** Mike Allred

The FF gained a second volume, written by Matt Fraction and illustrated by Mike Allred. The new series was strange, funny, and sometimes bizarre—as exemplified by this crazy cover showing new FF member Darla Deering (aka Miss Thing) being stalked by a masked Yancy Street Gang, who resented her taking on the role of the Thing.

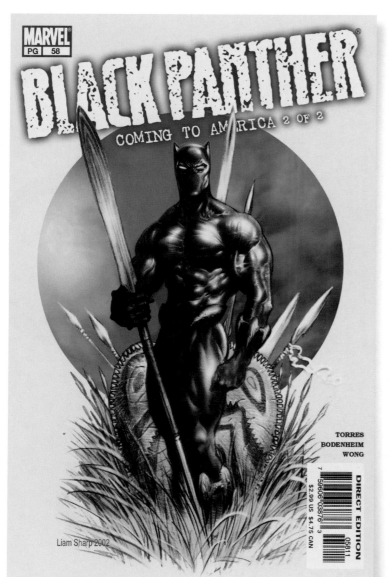

***BLACK PANTHER* #11** ▶

**February 2006**
**Artist:** Mike Deodato Jr.

Comic fans always love team-ups and this issue had one of the coolest. Black Panther joined forces with the Falcon, Shang Chi, and Luke Cage to take on Shang Chi's estranged father Han (a criminal mastermind). Deodato's cover brought all the main players together in one stylish image that also reflected the villain's Asian powerbase.

MARVEL
PG 58
BLACK PANTHER
COMING TO AMERICA 2 OF 2
TORRES
BODENHEIM
WONG
DIRECT EDITION
$2.99 US $4.75 CAN
Liam Sharp 2002

◀ ***BLACK PANTHER* #58**

**June 2003**
**Artist:** Liam Sharp

The Black Panther was one of Marvel's first African heroes and Liam Sharp used the Panther's African background to add some beautiful design elements to his cover. The bright African sun helps to frame the Panther and gives the image an almost mythical element.

MARVEL
525
BLACK PANTHER
THE MOST DANGEROUS MAN ALIVE!
RATED T+
$2.99US
DIRECT EDITION
MARVEL.COM
THE KINGPIN OF WAKANDA
LISS•MARTINBROUGH•SERRANO

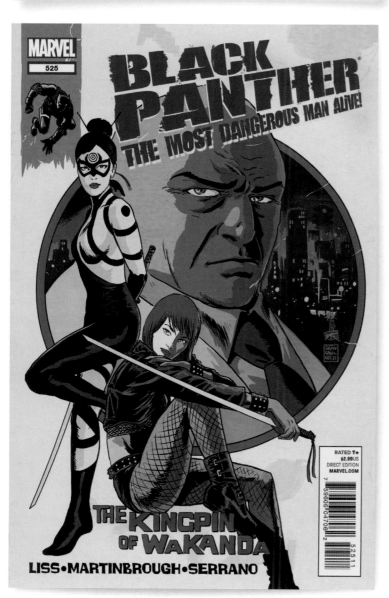

◀ ***BLACK PANTHER: THE MOST DANGEROUS MAN ALIVE* #525**

**January 2012**
**Artist:** Francesco Francavilla

When Black Panther took over Daredevil's title from issue #513, the new series produced a number of adventurous cover designs. The covers that Francavilla produced for "The Most Dangerous Man Alive" story-arc had a real pulp-fiction detective-story look, right down to the faded colors. The cover featured the Panther's latest adversary, the Kingpin.

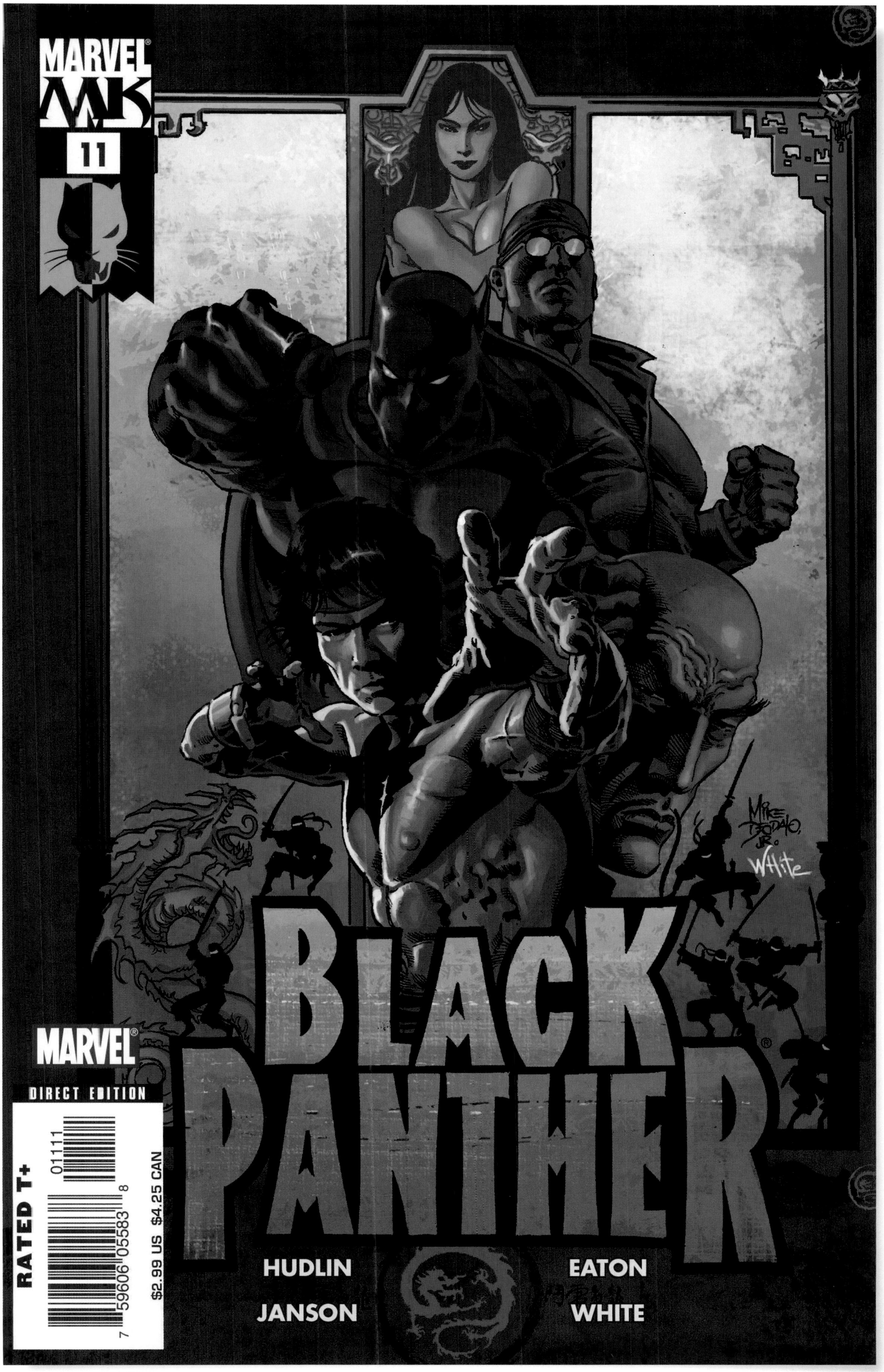
MARVEL
MK
11
MARVEL
DIRECT EDITION
RATED T+
$2.99 US $4.25 CAN
BLACK PANTHER
HUDLIN
EATON
JANSON
WHITE

# *BLACK PANTHER* #1

**April 2005**

**Artist:** John Romita Jr.

For the creation of the *Black Panther* issue #1 cover, John Romita Jr. started the process the traditional way, creating a number of rough character poses (1) before moving onto pencils. Once these were approved, the finished pencils (2) were inked by the legendary Klaus Janson (3) before passing on to Dean White for coloring (4). White colored the cover on computer, but gave it a natural, painterly feel to reflect the subject of the piece. The finished art was then sent digitally to Marvel, whose design team added the Marvel branding, before turning the cover into a high-resolution format ready for print (5). With the advent of direct sales to comic shops, covers are now produced months in advance of the final comic-book art, so that they can be used for advanced promotion.

1. Sketch
2. Pencil
3. Ink
4. Color
5. Final cover

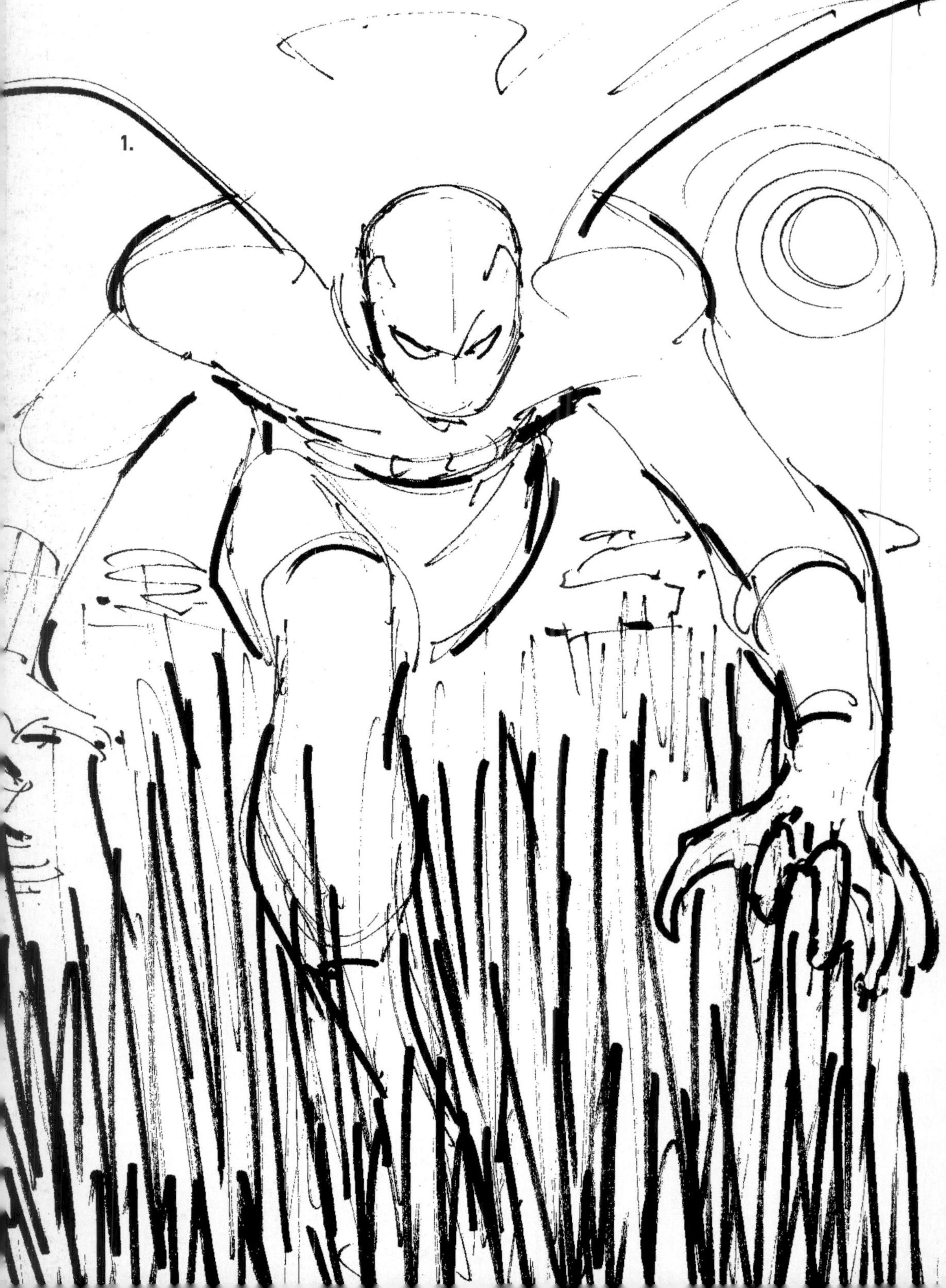

1.

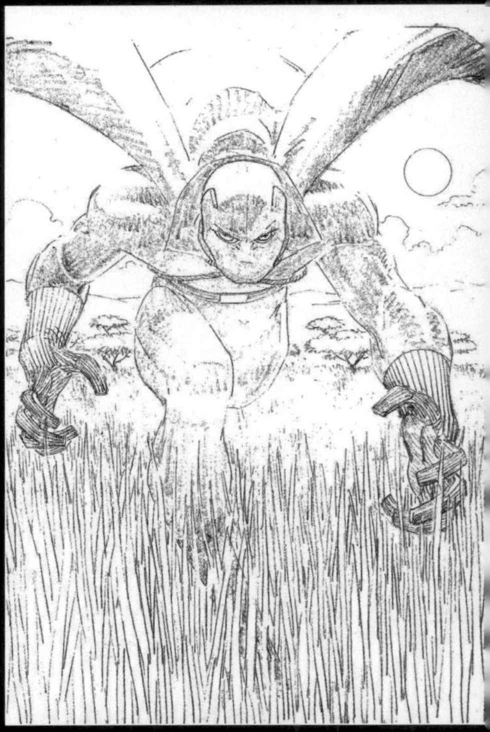

2.

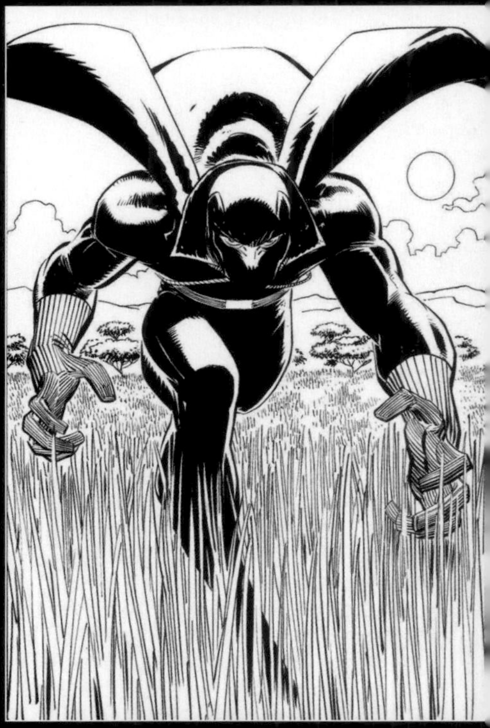

3.

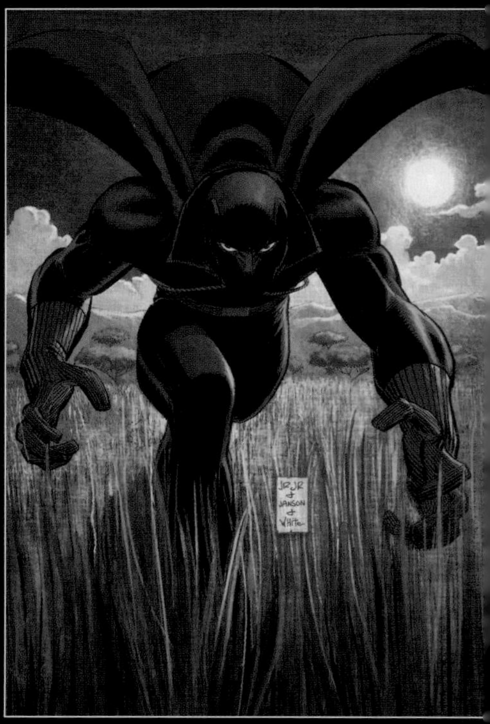

4.

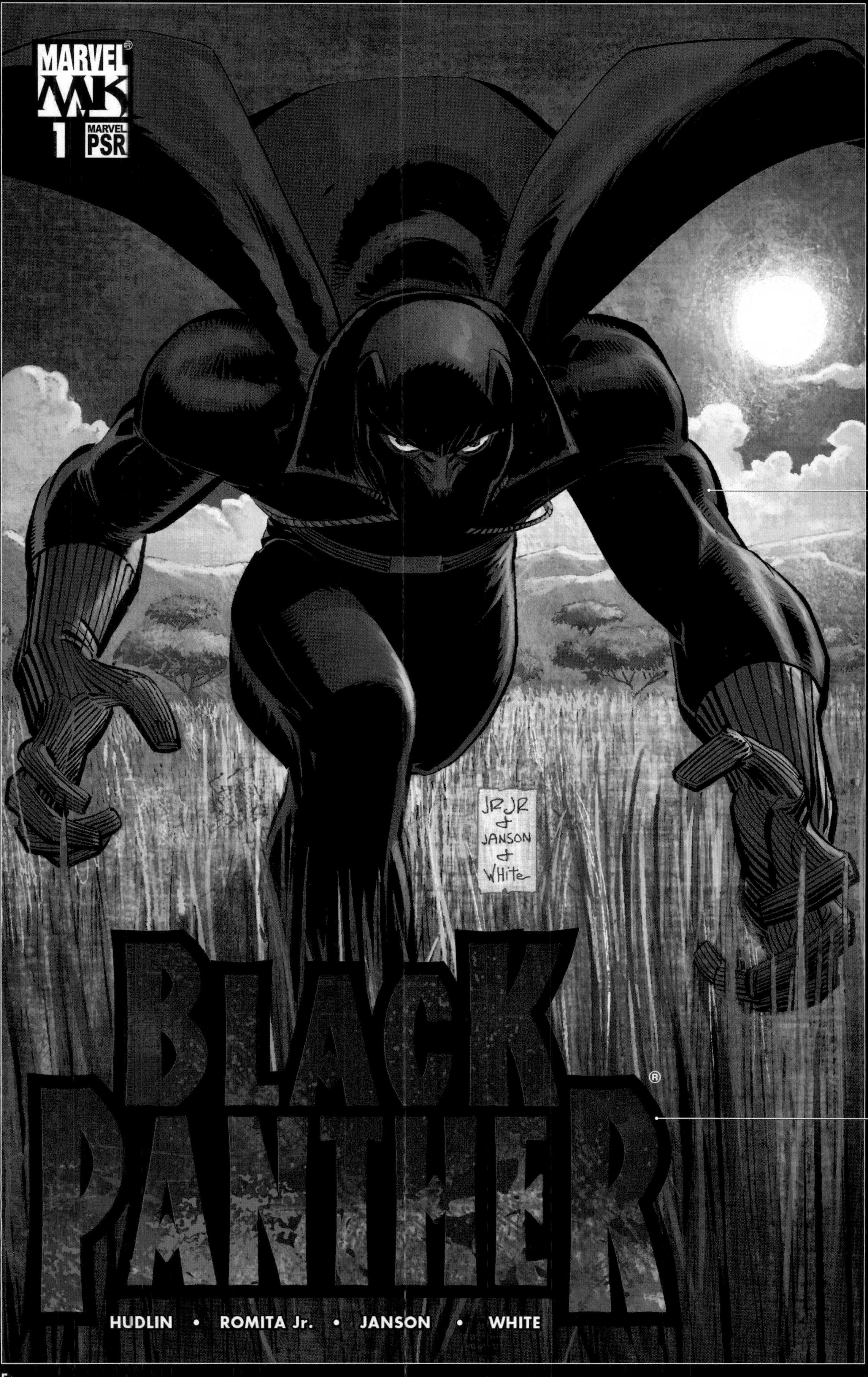
MARVEL
1
MARVEL PSR
JRJR & JANSON & WHITE
BLACK PANTHER
HUDLIN • ROMITA Jr. • JANSON • WHITE

Romita's pose for the Black Panther portrayed the hero as a hunter. He also reinstated the cloak to the hero's costume.

The Black Panther logo was updated for the new series, with subtle textures that reflect the story's African setting.

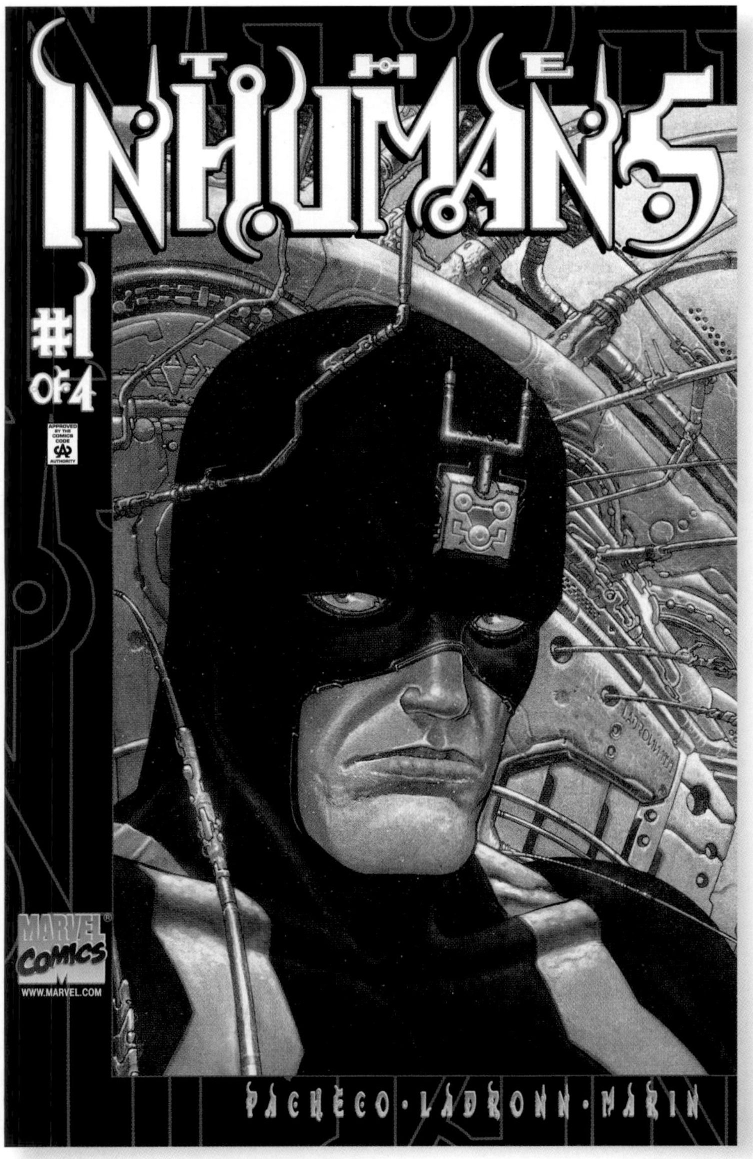
THE INHUMANS
#1 OF 4
MARVEL COMICS
WWW.MARVEL.COM
PACHECO · LADRONN · MARIN

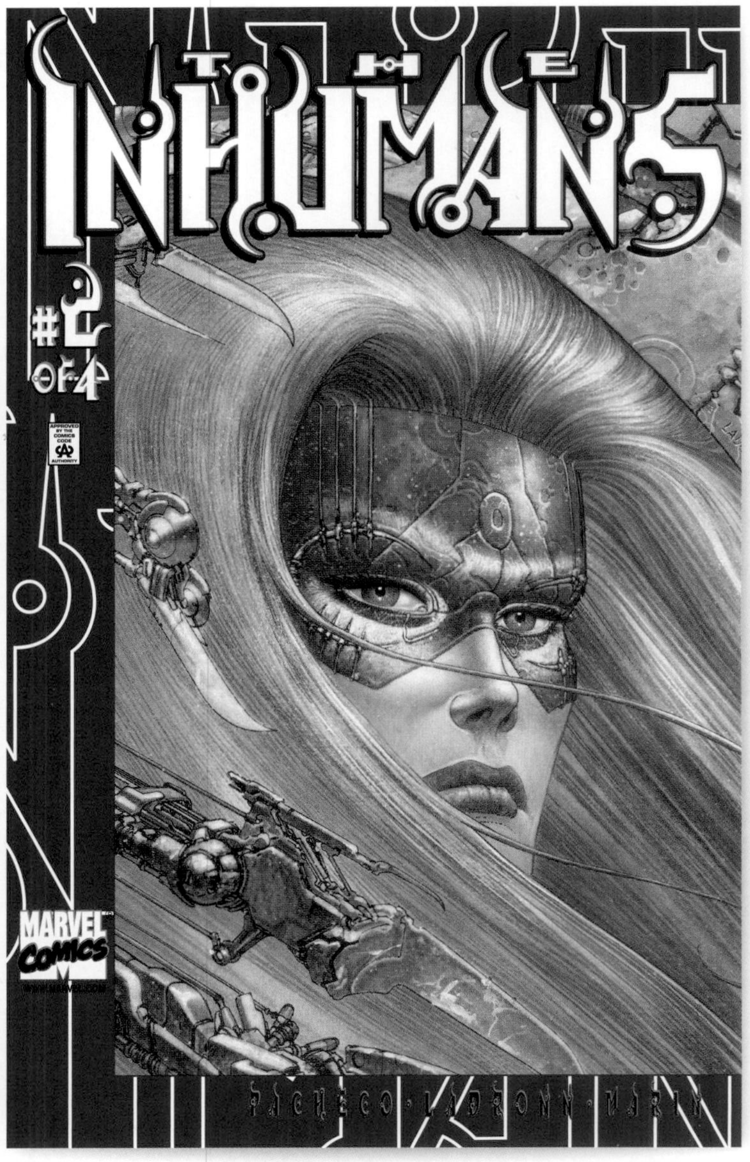
THE INHUMANS
#2 OF 4
MARVEL COMICS
PACHECO · LADRONN · MARIN

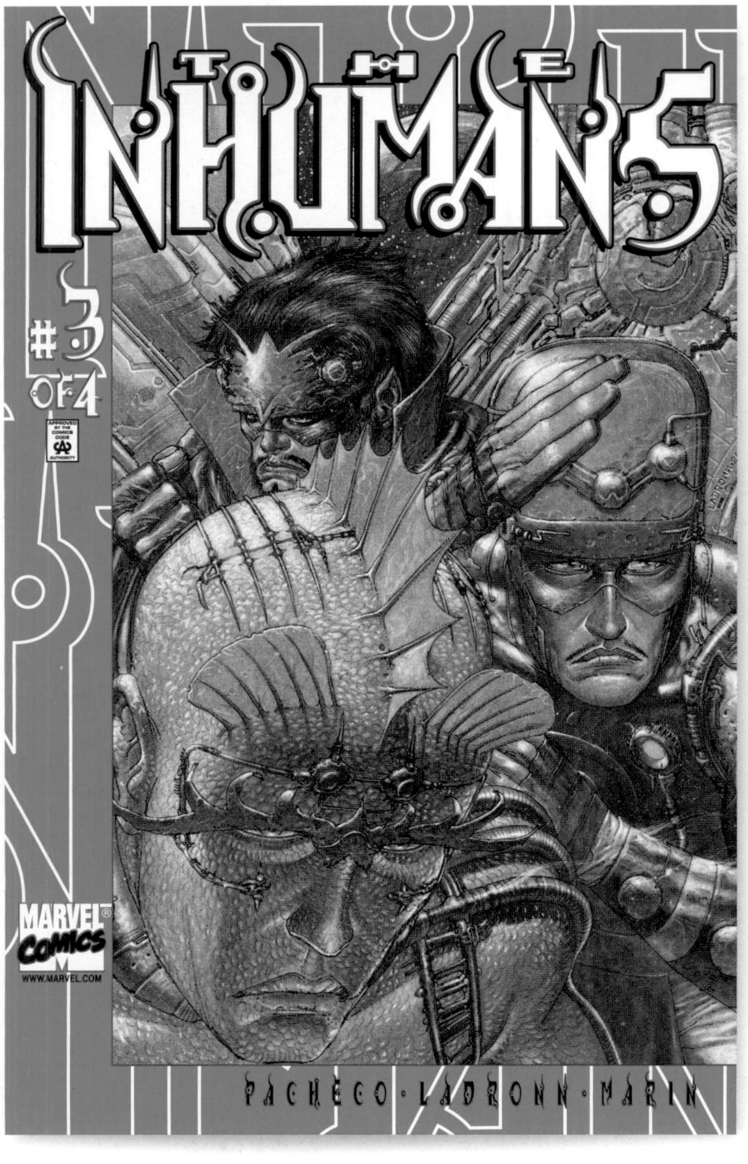
THE INHUMANS
#3 OF 4
MARVEL COMICS
WWW.MARVEL.COM
PACHECO · LADRONN · MARIN

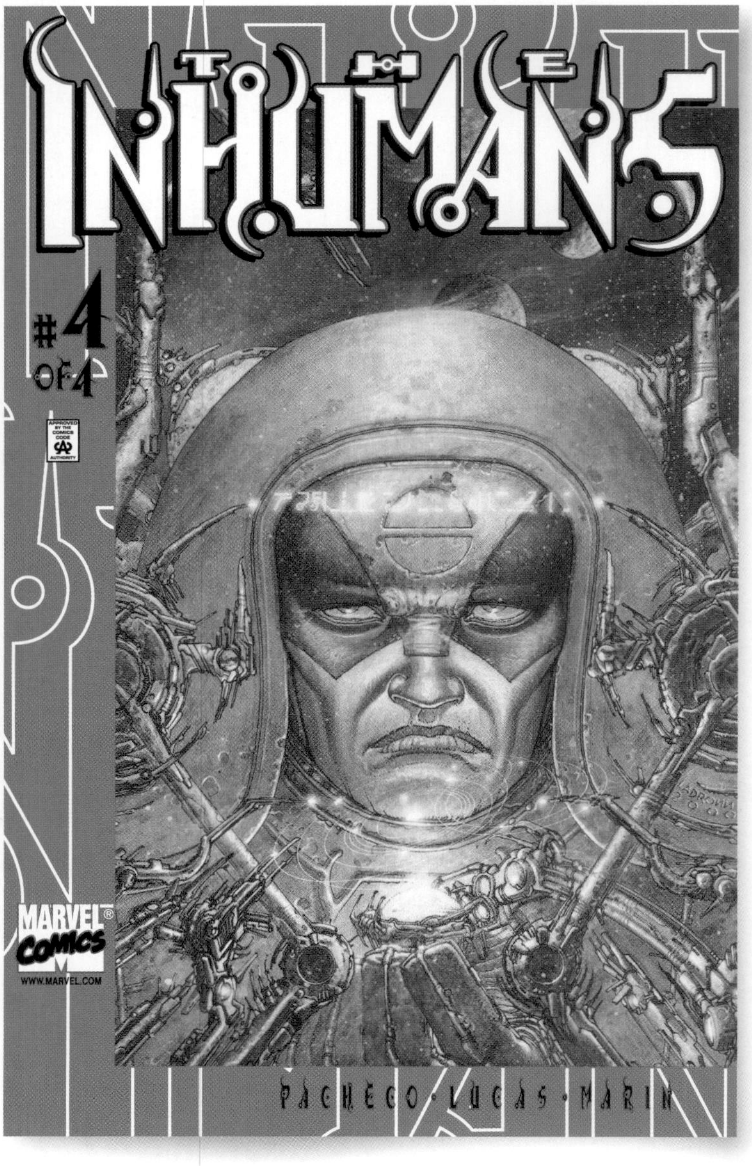
THE INHUMANS
#4 OF 4
MARVEL COMICS
WWW.MARVEL.COM
PACHECO · LUCAS · MARIN

***INHUMANS* #1 ▶**

**November 1998**
**Artist:** Jae Lee

The cover of the first issue of this 12-part series is a powerful one. It portrays the Inhuman royal family with their king, Black Bolt, in the forefront, flanked by his wife Medusa and his closest allies. The Inhumans look both regal and alien, thanks to Lee's dark and stylish work.

MARVEL
KNIGHTS
NOV
#1
WWW.MARVEL.COM
JENKINS
LEE
INHUMANS

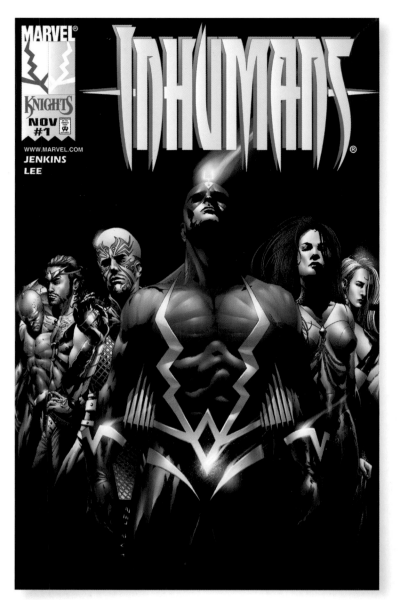

***INHUMAN* #1 ▶**

**April 2014**
**Artist:** Joe Madureira

Top artist Joe Madureira returned to Marvel to illustrate Inhuman. The cover shows the Inhumans covertly living side-by-side with humanity. They were Inhumans who—like the title's hero, Dante – had no knowledge of their true genetic origins until exposure to the Inhumans' Terrigen Mists brought out their Inhuman abilities. This issue marks the increased importance of the Inhumans in the wider Marvel Universe.

INHUMAN
#1
CHARLES SOULE JOE MADUREIRA MARTE GRACIA
MARVEL'S
LATEST EPIC
BEGINS HERE!
ALL-NEW MARVEL NOW!
001

**◀ *THE INHUMANS* #1–4**

**June–October 2000**
**Artist:** José Ladrönn

The third volume of *The Inhumans* was a four-part miniseries, written by Rafael Marin and illustrated by José Ladrönn. Each cover reflects the alien nature of the Inhumans' origins (a focal point of the series, with a close-up of one or two of the main Inhumans—Black Bolt, Medusa, and Karnak and Triton. Issue #4 featured the Inhumans' enemy Ronan the Accuser.

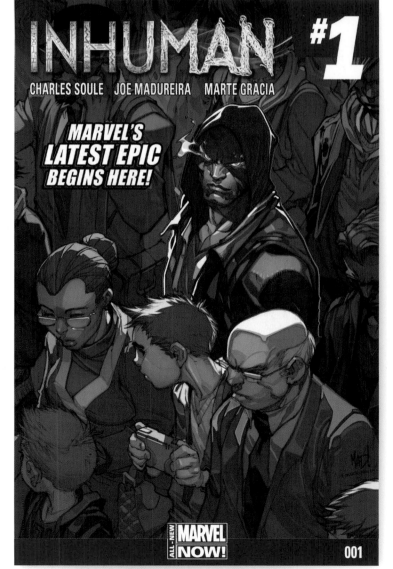

MARVELS
BOOK ONE OF FOUR

MARVELS
BOOK TWO OF FOUR
DEVILS

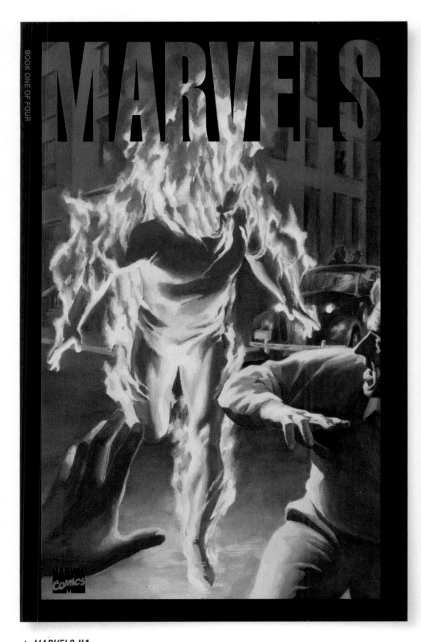

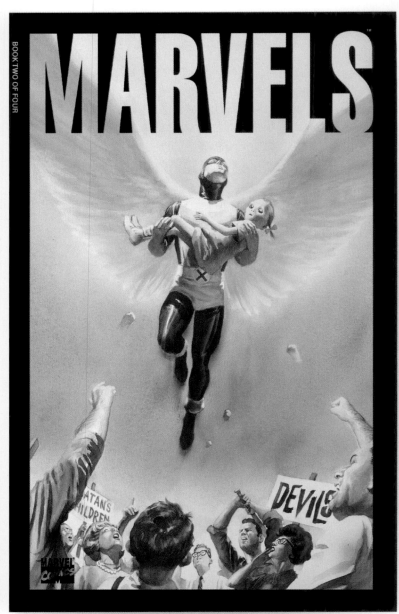

▲ ***MARVELS* #1**

**January 1994**
**Artist:** Alex Ross

Every now and again, an artist bursts onto the comic scene and changes the very nature of the business. Alex Ross did just that with the launch of *Marvels*, widely considered to be the best miniseries of the decade. The painted cover image was based on the classic version of the first Human Torch from *Marvel Comics issue* #1 *(see p10)*.

▲ ***MARVELS* #2**

**February 1994**
**Artist:** Alex Ross

Each issue of *Marvels* dealt with a different era of Marvel history, with Kurt Busiek's brilliant scripts giving Alex Ross a chance to shine. The second issue concentrated on the early days of Marvel's modern heroes. Ross' painted cover depicts the rise of the X-Men, with a beautiful version of Angel escaping a baying mob.

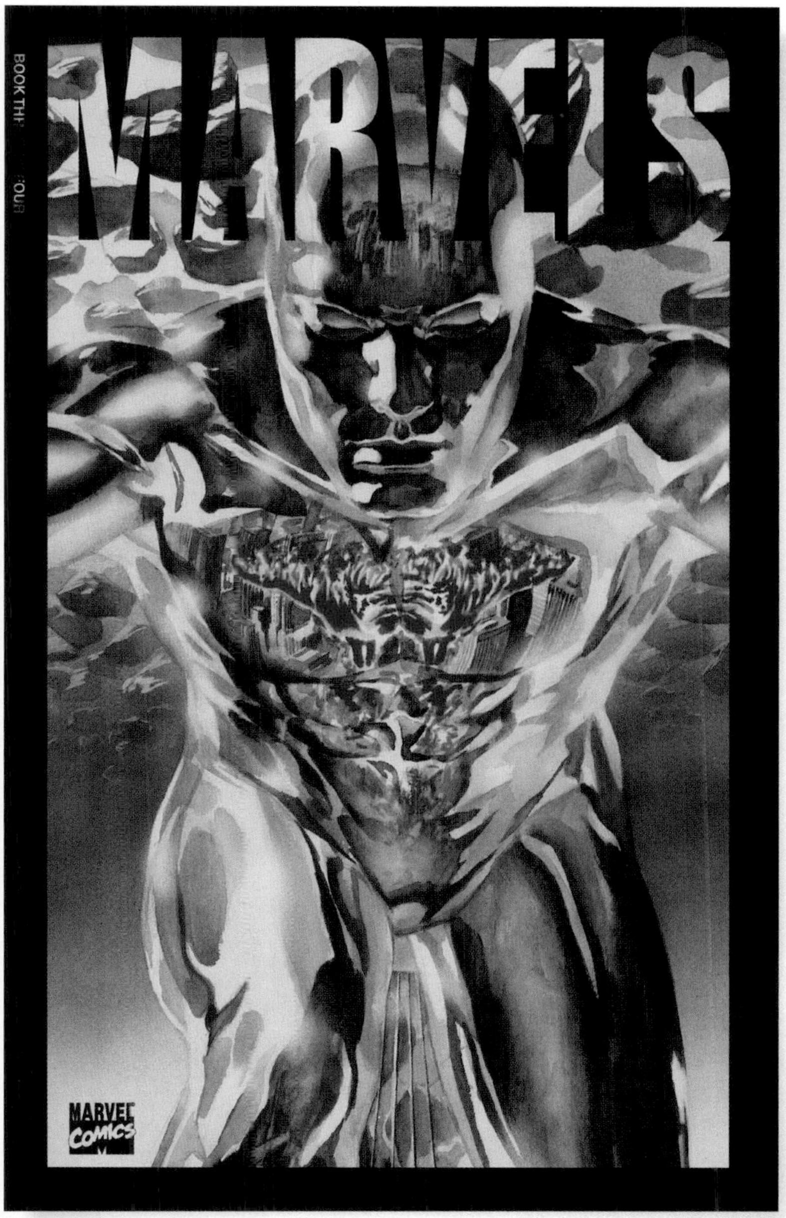
MARVELS
MARVEL COMICS

▲ *MARVELS* #3

**March 1994**
**Artist:** Alex Ross

The third book in the *Marvels* series focused on the arrival of Galactus (originally told in the classic *Fantastic Four* issue #48 of 1966). For the cover, Ross painted a striking portrayal of Galactus' herald, the Silver Surfer, with the Fantastic Four's Human Torch and the city of Manhattan reflecting off his alien skin.

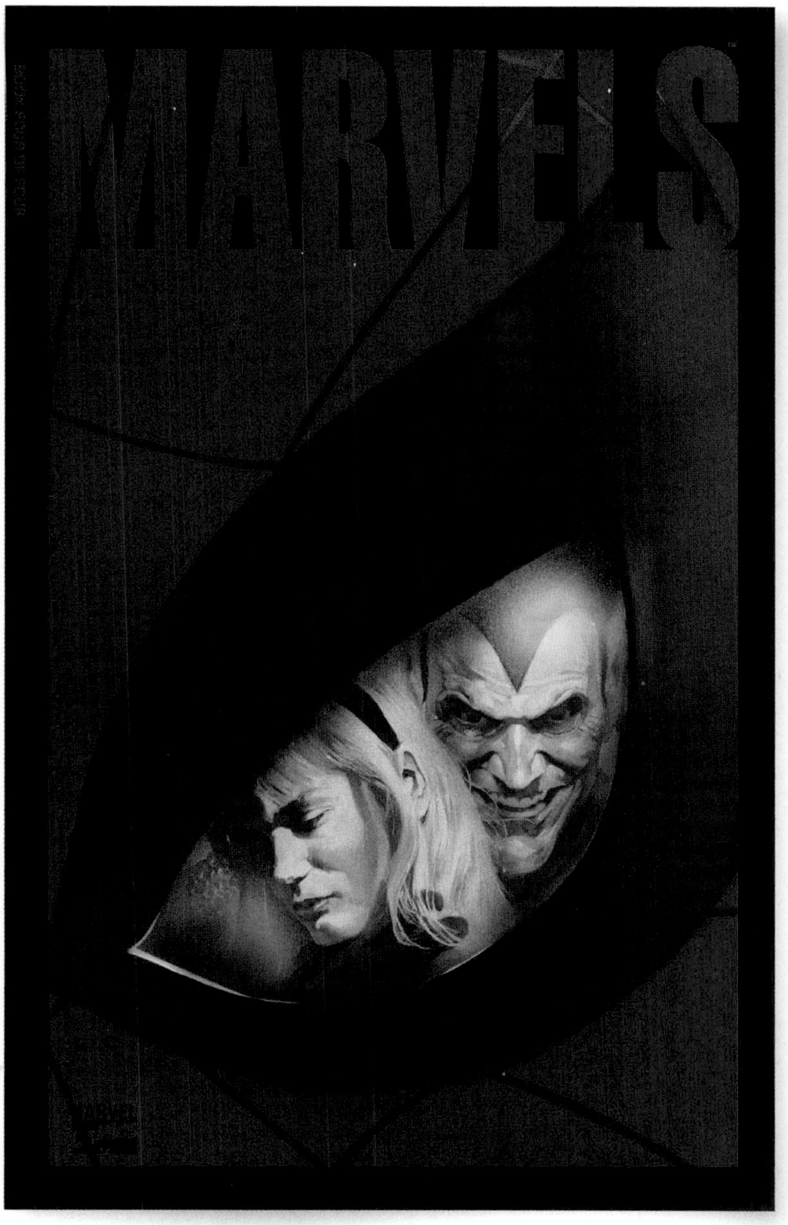
MARVELS

▲ *MARVELS* #4

**April 1994**
**Artist:** Alex Ross

The conclusion of *Marvels* centered around one of the company's greatest (and most tragic) stories—the death of Gwen Stacy. Many consider this to be the best cover of the series, with its portrayal of the Green Goblin and Gwen as seen in the reflection of Spider-Man's eyepiece.

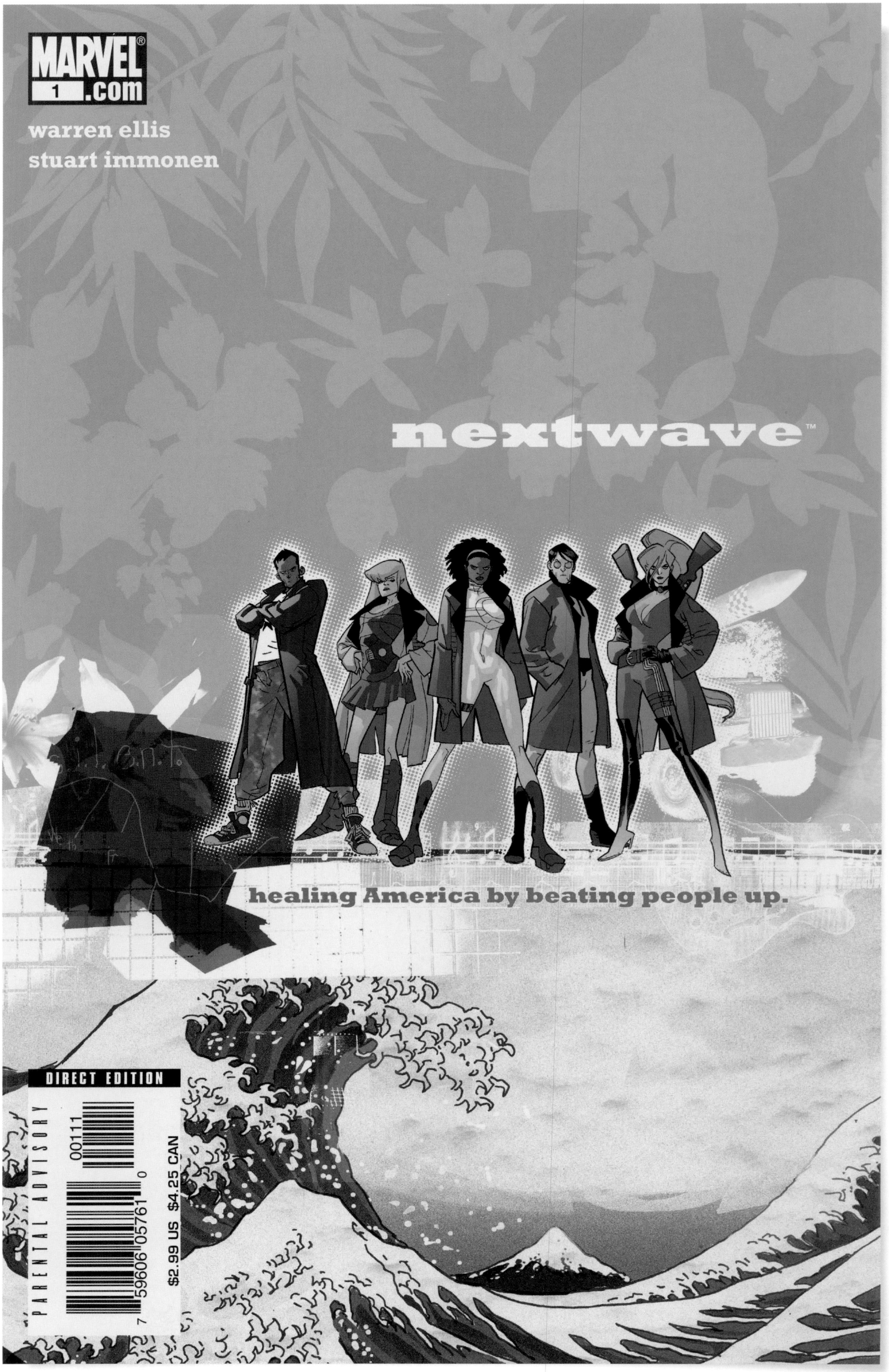
MARVEL
1 .com
warren ellis
stuart immonen
nextwave™
healing America by beating people up.
DIRECT EDITION
PARENTAL ADVISORY
$2.99 US $4.25 CAN

### ◀ *NEXTWAVE: AGENTS OF H.A.T.E.* #1

**March 2006**
**Artist:** Stuart Immonen

With *Nextwave*, writer Warren Ellis and artist Stuart Immonen created a series that both celebrated and mocked the Super-Hero genre. The cover to its debut issue firmly established that the title was different from regular Marvel books. The stylish design mixes an image of *The Great Wave off Kanagawa* by Japanese painter Hokusai with the superteam, topped off by the book's satirical tagline, "healing America by beating people up."

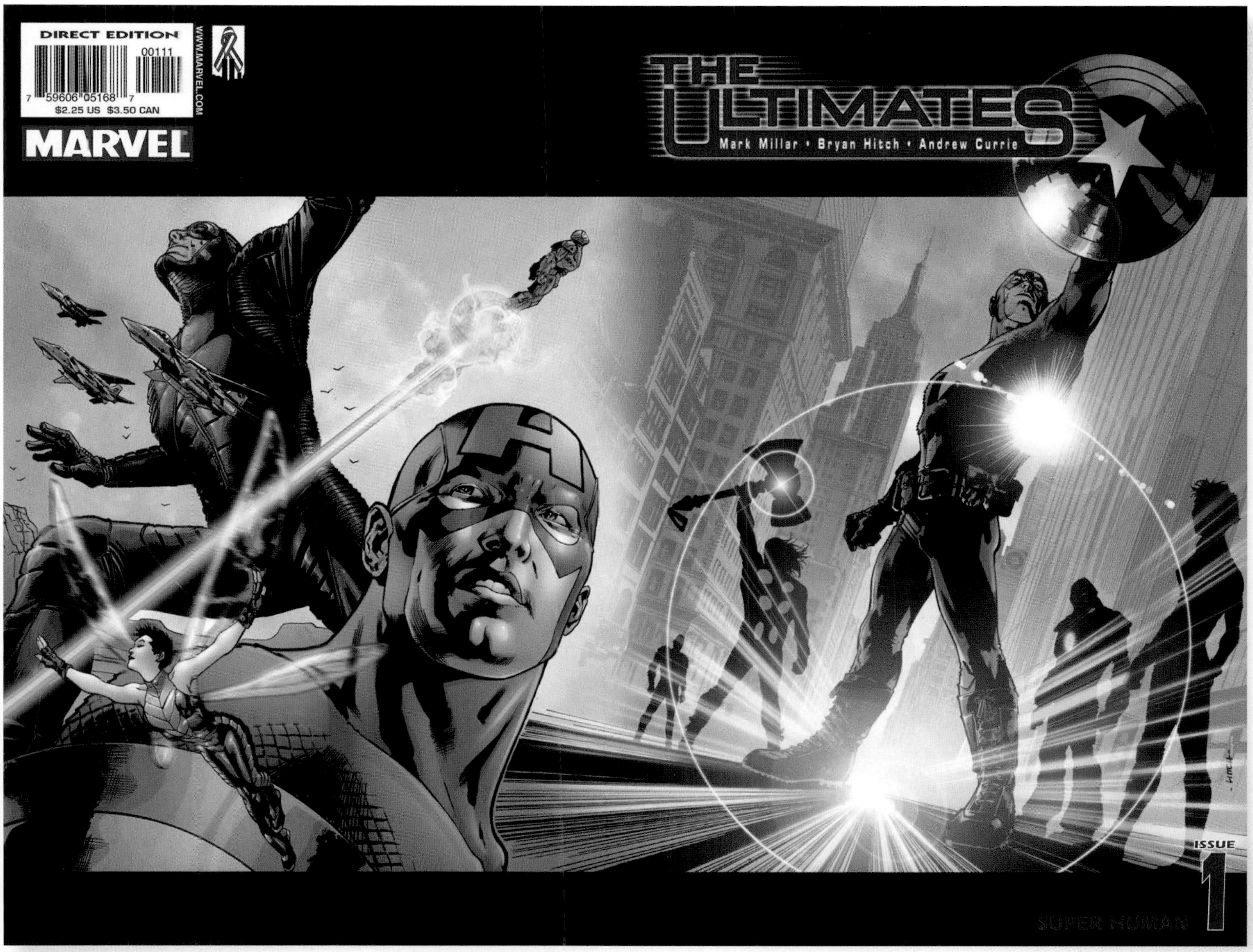
DIRECT EDITION
$2.25 US $3.50 CAN
WWW.MARVEL.COM
MARVEL
THE ULTIMATES
Mark Millar • Bryan Hitch • Andrew Currie
ISSUE
1
SUPER HUMAN

### ▲ *THE ULTIMATES* #1

**March 2002**
**Artist:** Bryan Hitch

One of the most important Marvel comics of the 2000s, *The Ultimates* was a reimagined version of the Avengers, set in Marvel's new "Ultimate Universe." Bryan Hitch's cover for the debut issue emphasized the role of Captain America and the first issue focused almost entirely on Cap in World War II. Writer Mark Millar and artist Bryan Hitch created a masterful series, influencing many of the Marvel movies that followed, especially Marvel's *The Avengers* (2012).

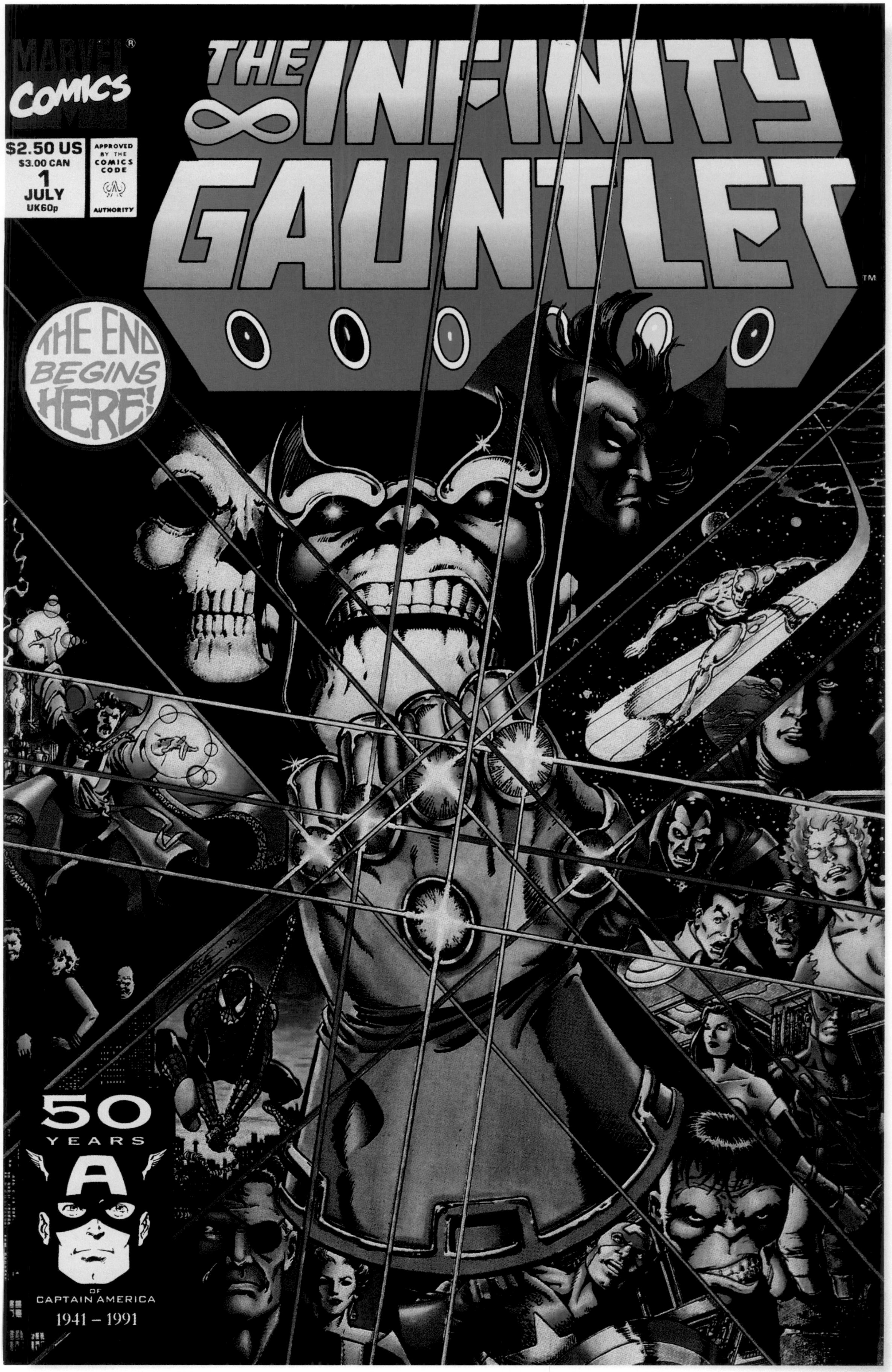
MARVEL COMICS
THE INFINITY GAUNTLET
$2.50 US
$3.00 CAN
1
JULY
UK60p
APPROVED BY THE COMICS CODE AUTHORITY
THE END BEGINS HERE!
50 YEARS OF CAPTAIN AMERICA
1941 – 1991

**WHOSE SIDE...**
**...ARE YOU ON?**

THE MARVEL UNIVERSE IS CHANGING. IN
THE WAKE OF A TRAGEDY, CAPITOL HILL
PROPOSES THE SUPER HERO REGISTRATION
ACT, REQUIRING ALL COSTUMED HEROES
TO UNMASK THEMSELVES BEFORE THE
GOVERNMENT. DIVIDED, THE NATION'S
GREATEST CHAMPIONS MUST EACH DECIDE
HOW TO REACT—A DECISION THAT WILL
ALTER THE COURSE OF THEIR LIVES FOREVER!

MARK MILLAR

STEVE MCNIVEN

DEXTER VINES

MORRY HOLLOWELL

**CIVIL WAR**
A MARVEL COMICS® EVENT IN SEVEN PARTS

**MARVEL**
RATED T+
DIRECT EDITION
00111
7 59606 05921 8
$3.99 US  $5.75 CAN

1

*CIVIL WAR #1* ▲

**July 2006**
**Artist:** Steve McNiven

Marvel created a new design style for the
launch of *Civil War*, the company's 2006
saga that made headlines across the
world. Steve McNiven's striking cover for
the first issue hints at the drama to come,
while the white border and careful
placement of text revealed the increasing
role that design was playing in Marvel's
covers as they sought new ways to
make their comics stand out.

◄ *THE INFINITY GAUNTLET #1*

**July 1991**
**Artist:** George Pérez

Award-winning artist George Pérez was
at the helm for *The Infinity Gauntlet*, one
of Marvel's first comic-book blockbusters.
Pérez's stunning cover for the first issue
displays a host of Marvel's Super Heroes
around the central image of Thanos. The
cover established the star-spanning nature
of the series, with heroes such as Silver
Surfer and the Hulk caught up in Thanos'
attempt to impress Death by wiping out
half of the universe.

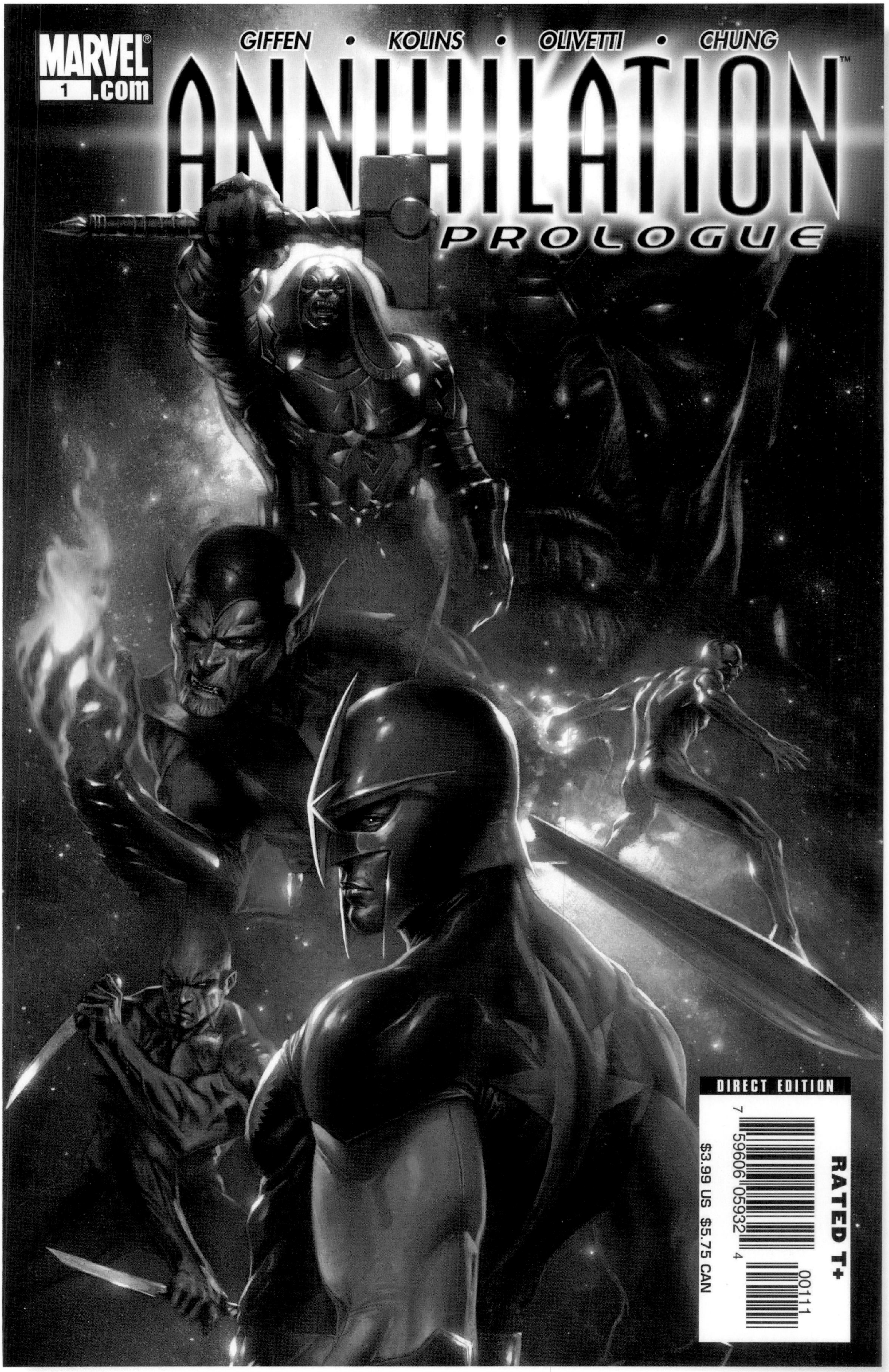
MARVEL
1 .com
GIFFEN • KOLINS • OLIVETTI • CHUNG
ANNIHILATION
PROLOGUE
DIRECT EDITION
RATED T+
$3.99 US $5.75 CAN

DIRECT EDITION
GIFFEN • DiVITO • VILLARI
ANNIHILATION
MARVEL
LIMITED SERIES
1 of 6
RATED A
$2.99 US $3.75 CAN

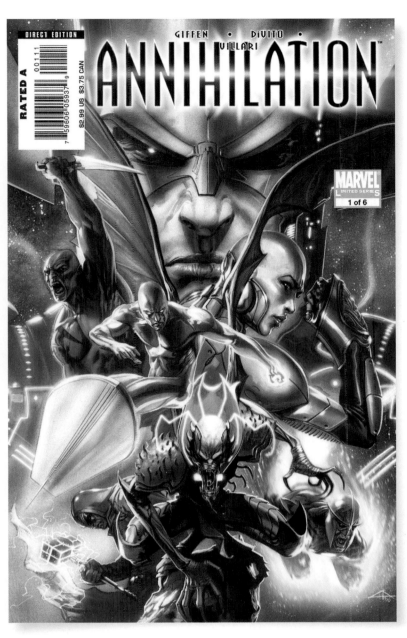

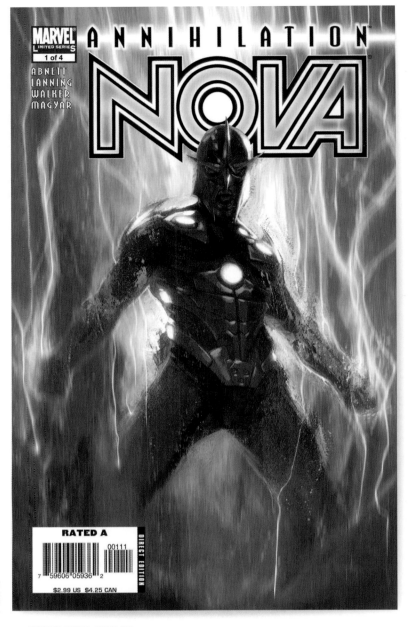

▲ *ANNIHILATION* #1

**October 2006**
**Artist:** Gabriele Dell'Otto

The Annihilation event continued with another Gabriele Dell'Otto painted cover featuring some of Marvel's most powerful heroes and villains. With Annihilus at the center of the image and the face of Galactus looming large in the background, the first issue cover firmly established that this was an event on a truly cosmic scale.

MARVEL
LIMITED SERIES
1 of 4
ANNIHILATION
ABNETT
LANNING
WALKER
MAGYAR
NOVA
RATED A
DIRECT EDITION
$2.99 US $4.25 CAN

▲ *ANNIHILATION: NOVA* #1

**June 2006**
**Artist:** Gabriele Dell'Otto

*Nova* was relaunched in 2006 as part of the Annihilation event. Gabriele Dell'Otto's dramatic cover of Nova standing alone reflected the hero's new role as the only survivor of the Nova Corps, following its destruction by the Annihilation Wave (a vast alien army led by Annihilus).

◄ *ANNIHILATION: PROLOGUE* #1

**May 2006**
**Artist:** Gabriele Dell'Otto

*Annihilation* was the series that made Marvel's cosmic heroes popular again, as they starred in one vast intergalactic war story. Each issue in the multi-part epic had amazing painted covers that were more like those found on science fiction novels than comics. Gabriele Dell'Otto set the standard high with this movie-poster style montage, heralding the start of the epic.

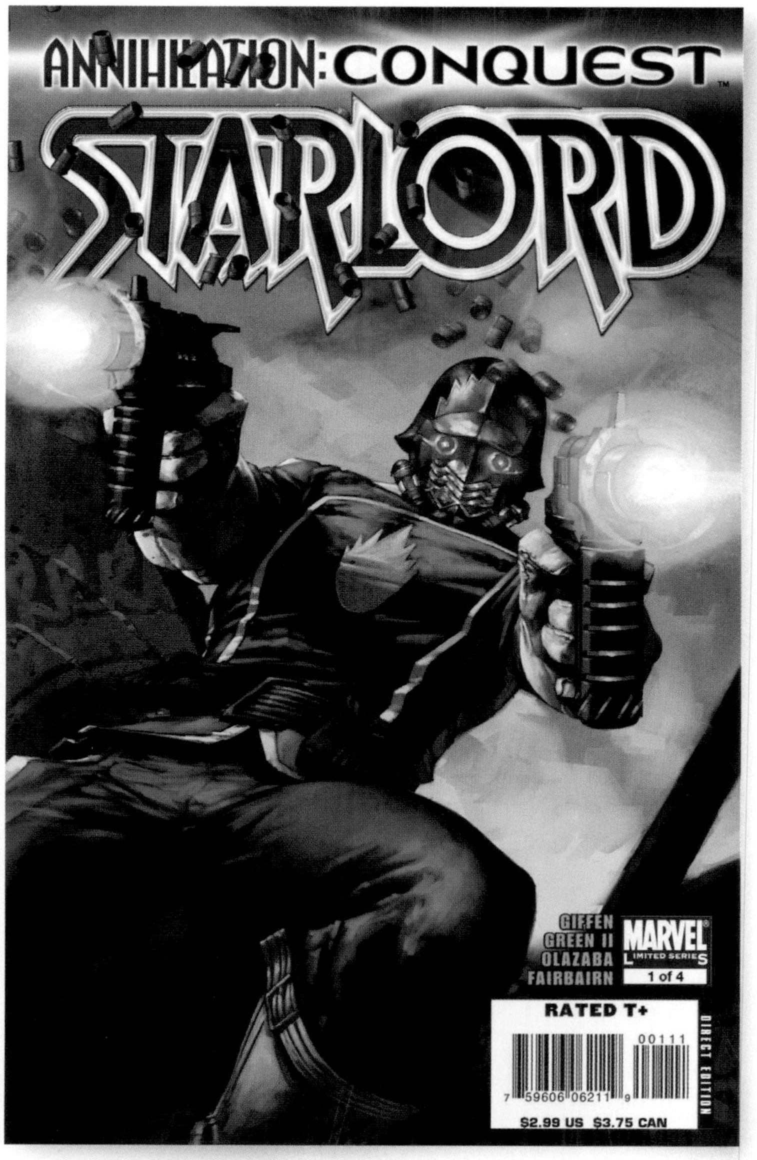
ANNIHILATION: CONQUEST
STARLORD
GIFFEN
GREEN II
OLAZABA
FAIRBAIRN
MARVEL
LIMITED SERIES
1 of 4
RATED T+
DIRECT EDITION
$2.99 US $3.75 CAN

◄ ***ANNIHILATION: CONQUEST—STARLORD* #1**

**September 2007**
**Artist:** Nic Klein

The success of *Annihilation* led to a follow-up, *Annihilation: Conquest*, which saw Marvel's cosmic heroes facing a new threat—the Phalanx. The series had started with a prologue that led into several miniseries, including one featuring Starlord. Artist Nic Klein created an action-packed pose for the first cover, depicting the hero blasting his guns out at the reader.

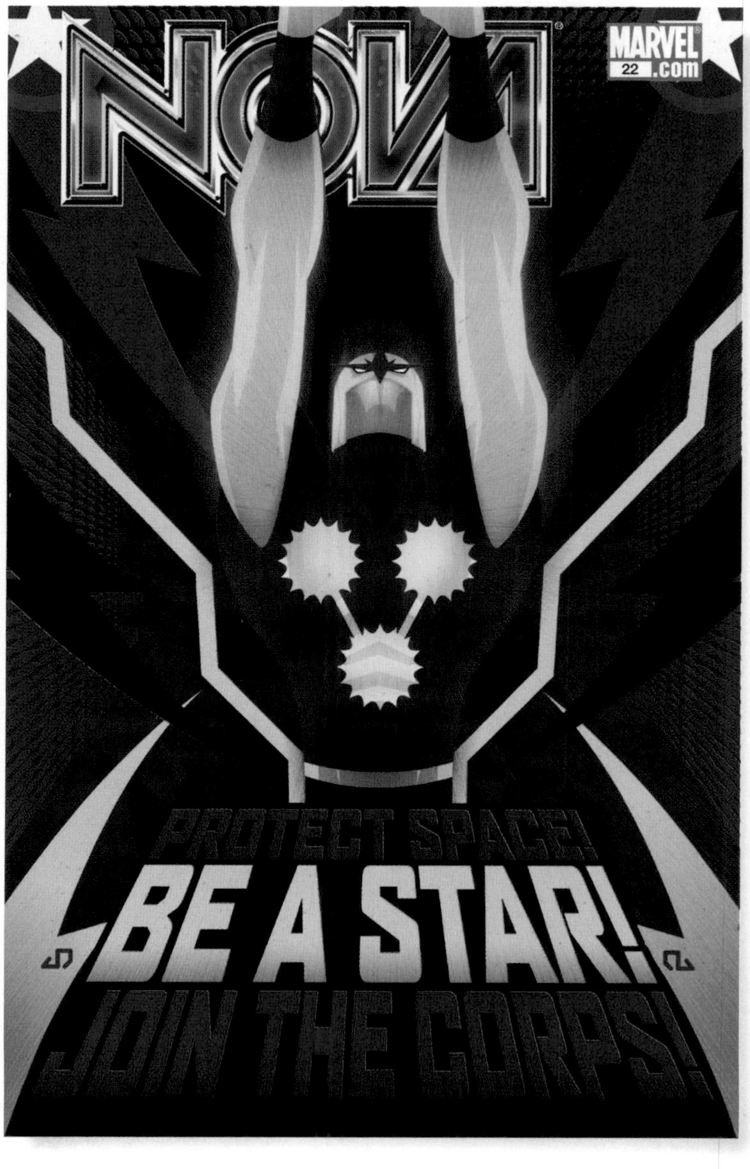
NOVA
MARVEL
22 .com
PROTECT SPACE!
BE A STAR!
JOIN THE CORPS!

◄ ***NOVA* #22**

**April 2009**
**Artist:** Juan Doe

Writers Andy Lanning and Dan Abnett re-established *Nova* as one of Marvel's greatest cosmic heroes and—by this issue—left the hero close to death after his powers had been stripped from him by the alien entity Worldmind. This issue heralded the return of the Nova Corps, with Juan Doe turning the cover into a stylish recruitment poster for the new corps.

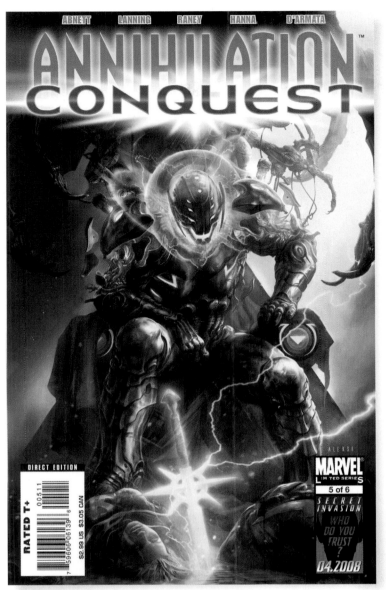

ABNETT LANNING RANEY HANNA D'ARMATA
ANNIHILATION
CONQUEST
DIRECT EDITION
RATED T+
$2.99 US $3.05 CAN
MARVEL
LIMITED SERIES
5 of 6
SECRET INVASION
WHO DO YOU TRUST ?
04.2008

◀ *ANNIHILATION: CONQUEST* **#5**

**May 2008**
**Artist:** Aleksi Briclot

As *Annihilation: Conquest* continued its run, this cover revealed the true bad guy of the series—leader of the Phalanx, Ultron. Aleksi Briclot's image of the Avengers' old enemy sitting astride a throne was one of the most powerful interpretations of the villain. The series also featured the characters who would become the new Guardians of the Galaxy.

ABNETT LANNING RANEY HANNA D'ARMATA
ANNIHILATION
CONQUEST
MARVEL
LIMITED SERIES
6 of 6
RATED T+
DIRECT EDITION
$3.99 US $4.05 CAN

◀ *ANNIHILATION: CONQUEST* **#6**

**June 2008**
**Artist:** Aleksi Briclot

Some of Marvel's greatest cosmic heroes appeared together for this final part of *Annihilation: Conquest*. Briclot's cover, with its dramatic use of color and lighting, gives the reader the sense that the heroes, led by Adam Warlock, are about to face their greatest battle yet against Ultron and the Phalanx.

***GUARDIANS OF THE GALAXY* #7 ▶**

**November 2013**
**Artist:** Sara Pichelli

Artist Sara Pichelli perfectly captured the chaotic swagger and the bold attitude of the new group of guardians on this cover. The illustration shows the mismatched heroes in an art style that set the group apart from existing teams of Super Heroes.

MARVEL
1 .com
1ST ISSUE
ABNETT LANNING PELLETIER MAGYAR FAIRBAIRN
GUARDIANS OF THE GALAXY

**◀ *GUARDIANS OF THE GALAXY* #1**

**July 2008**
**Artist:** Clint Langley

Andy Lanning and Dan Abnett masterminded a modern-day relaunch for *Guardians of the Galaxy*. The new guardians were a disparate group of alien heroes. Chris Langley's cover quickly established the fast-paced style of the new series, and created a look that would carry the team to the big screen in 2014.

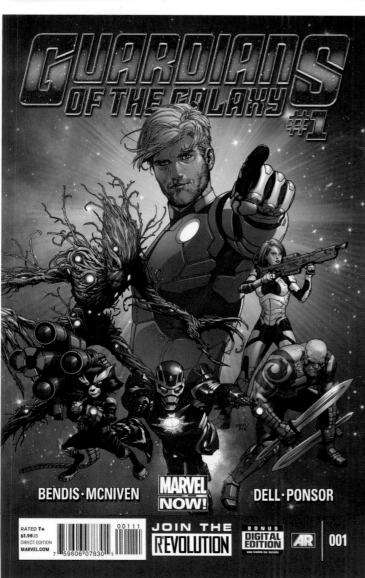

GUARDIANS OF THE GALAXY
#1
BENDIS·MCNIVEN
MARVEL NOW!
DELL·PONSOR
RATED T+
$3.99US
DIRECT EDITION
MARVEL.COM
JOIN THE REVOLUTION
BONUS DIGITAL EDITION
AR
001

**◀ *GUARDIANS OF THE GALAXY* #1**

**May 2013**
**Artist:** Steve McNiven

*Guardians of the Galaxy* was relaunched again as part of 2013's Marvel Now! branding. Artist Steve McNiven used a team shot on the cover to introduce the heroes, featuring Star-Lord front and center. This new series boosted the groups' standing in the Marvel Universe to coincide with the release of the *Guardians of the Galaxy* movie in 2014.

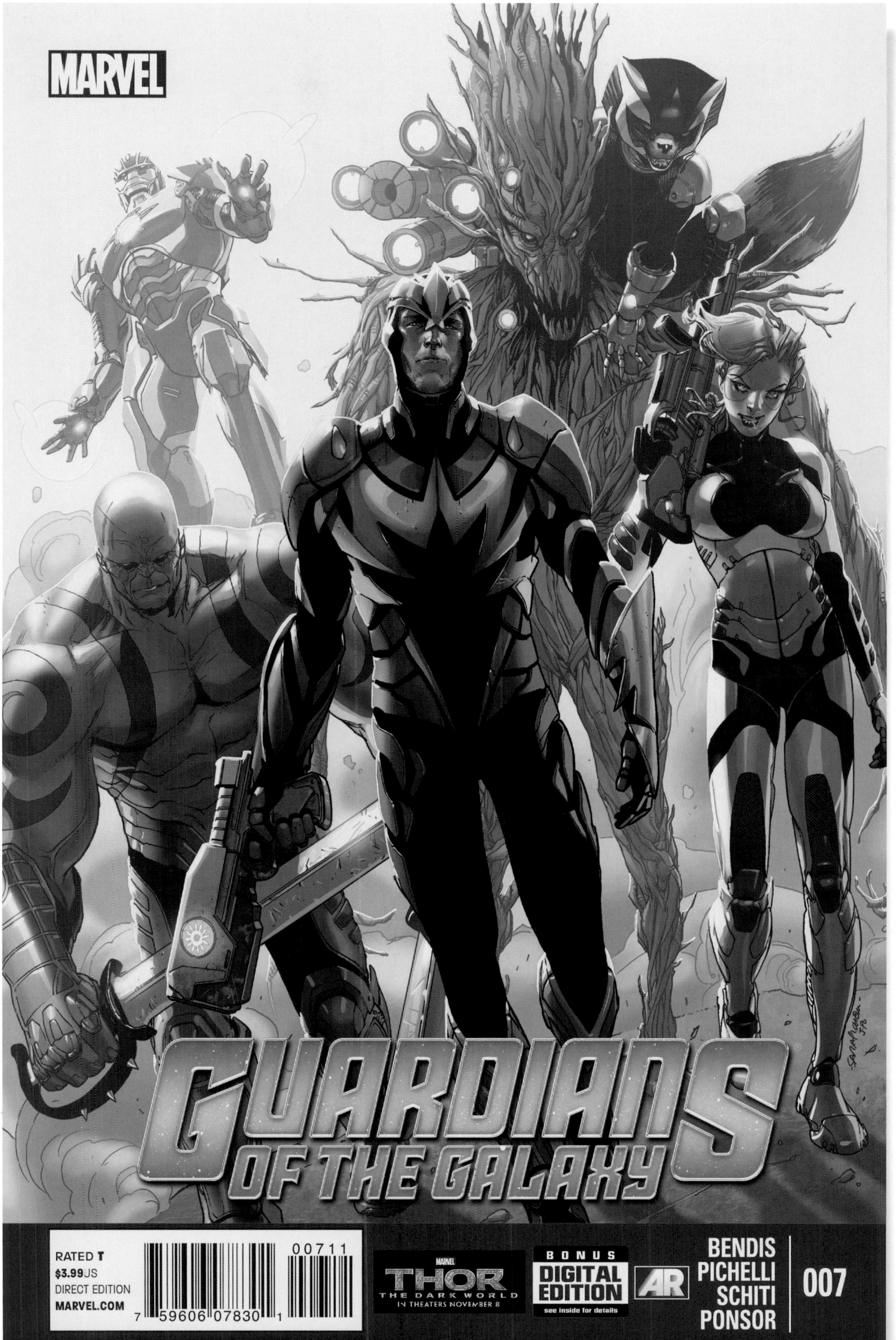
MARVEL
GUARDIANS OF THE GALAXY
RATED T
$3.99US
DIRECT EDITION
MARVEL.COM
THOR THE DARK WORLD
IN THEATERS NOVEMBER 8
BONUS DIGITAL EDITION
see inside for details
AR
BENDIS
PICHELLI
SCHITI
PONSOR
007

MARVEL
LIMITED SERIES
1 of 8
SECRET INVASION
BENDIS
YU
MORALES
MARTIN

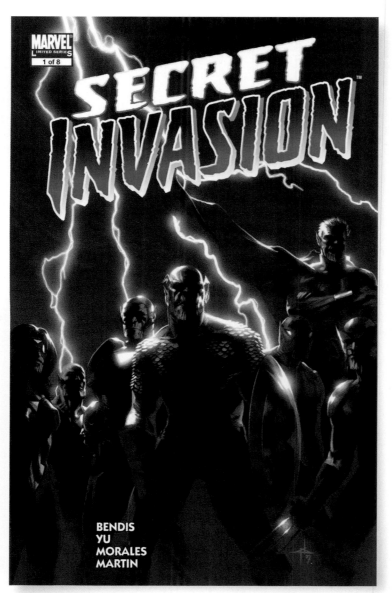

◀ *SECRET INVASION* #1

**June 2008**
**Artist:** Gabriele Dell'Otto

Marvel's big event of 2008 saw Earth invaded by shape-changing Skrulls. Gabriele Dell'Otto's cover for the first issue depicts humanity's greatest heroes in shadow, the Skrull outlines of their faces just visible. It was a clear message that no hero could be trusted and, as far as this storyline was concerned, anyone could be a Skrull.

THE SECRET INVASION
MS. MARVEL
MARVEL
25 .com
REED
MELO
BENES
SOTOMAYOR
RATED T+
DIRECT EDITION
$3.99 US $4.05 CAN

◀ *MS. MARVEL* #25

**May 2008**
**Artist:** Greg Horn

The Skrull "Secret Invasion" spread beyond the central series, with various Marvel titles featuring Skrull-themed covers. Greg Horn's painting of a Skrull Ms. Marvel hints that the title's lead character might be an alien—a fact that was central to the storyline as those closest to the heroine started to doubt her.

SECRET INVASION
MARVEL
15 .com
THE MIGHTY AVENGERS
DIRECT EDITION
RATED A
$2.99 US $3.05 CAN

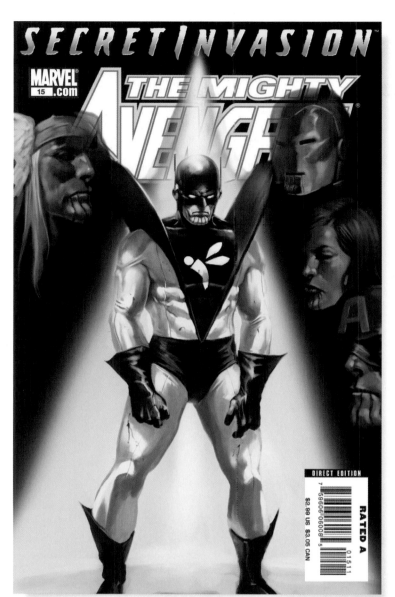

◄ *MIGHTY AVENGERS* #15

**August 2008**
**Artist:** Marko Djurdjevic

As the "Secret Invasion" continued, some heroes found out that they had been Skrulls all along—and in some cases, never even realized it. One of the biggest shocks was the revelation that Yellowjacket was a Skrull. Djurdjevic's cover shows that not only was Yellowjacket a Skrull, but he was one who had started to enjoy his life as an Avenger too much and was replaced by his Skrull masters. It also acted as a homage to *Avengers* issue #213 (November 1981), in terms of the layout and character poses.

SECRET INVASION
ABNETT LANNING PELLETIER MAGYAR GURU
GUARDIANS OF THE
RATED T+
DIRECT EDITION
$2.99 US $3.05 CAN
MARVEL
4 .com

◄ *GUARDIANS OF THE GALAXY* #4

**October 2008**
**Artist:** Clint Langley

The "Secret Invasion" of Earth was now in full force and soon even Marvel's star-spanning heroes were affected by it. Covers such as this one, by artist Clint Langley, helped to convey one of the main ideas of "Secret Invasion"—that behind their masks any hero could be a Skrull, even an interplanetary one such as Star-Lord.

MARVEL
LIMITED SERIES
1 of 5
KIRKMAN
PHILLIPS
CHUNG
MARVEL
ZOMBIES
RATED T+
DIRECT EDITION
$2.99 US $4.25 CAN

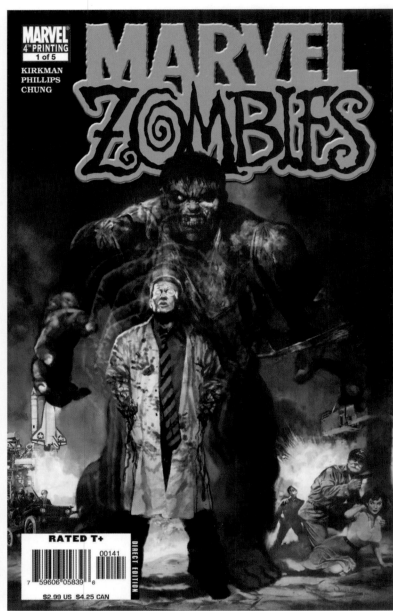

▲ *MARVEL ZOMBIES* #1

**February 2006**
**Artist:** Arthur Suydam

Arthur Suydam's zombified paintings of classic Marvel covers were a big reason for the success of *Marvel Zombies* (a title written by *The Walking Dead* creator Robert Kirkman). The original cover of the first issue in the series was a homage to *Amazing Fantasy* issue #15 (August 1962; *see p50*) and the first appearance of Spider-Man.

MARVEL
4TH PRINTING
1 of 5
KIRKMAN
PHILLIPS
CHUNG
MARVEL
ZOMBIES
RATED T+
DIRECT EDITION
$2.99 US $4.25 CAN

▲ *MARVEL ZOMBIES* #1 (FOURTH PRINTING VARIANT)

**April 2006**
**Artist:** Arthur Suydam

Cover variants became increasingly popular in the 2000s, with avid collectors seeking out every version of a cover. This fourth printing of *Marvel Zombies* issue #1 featured a homage to *Incredible Hulk* issue #1 (May 1962; *see p28*). A zombie Hulk was one of the standout characters of the series, his stomach bloated with the friends he had eaten.

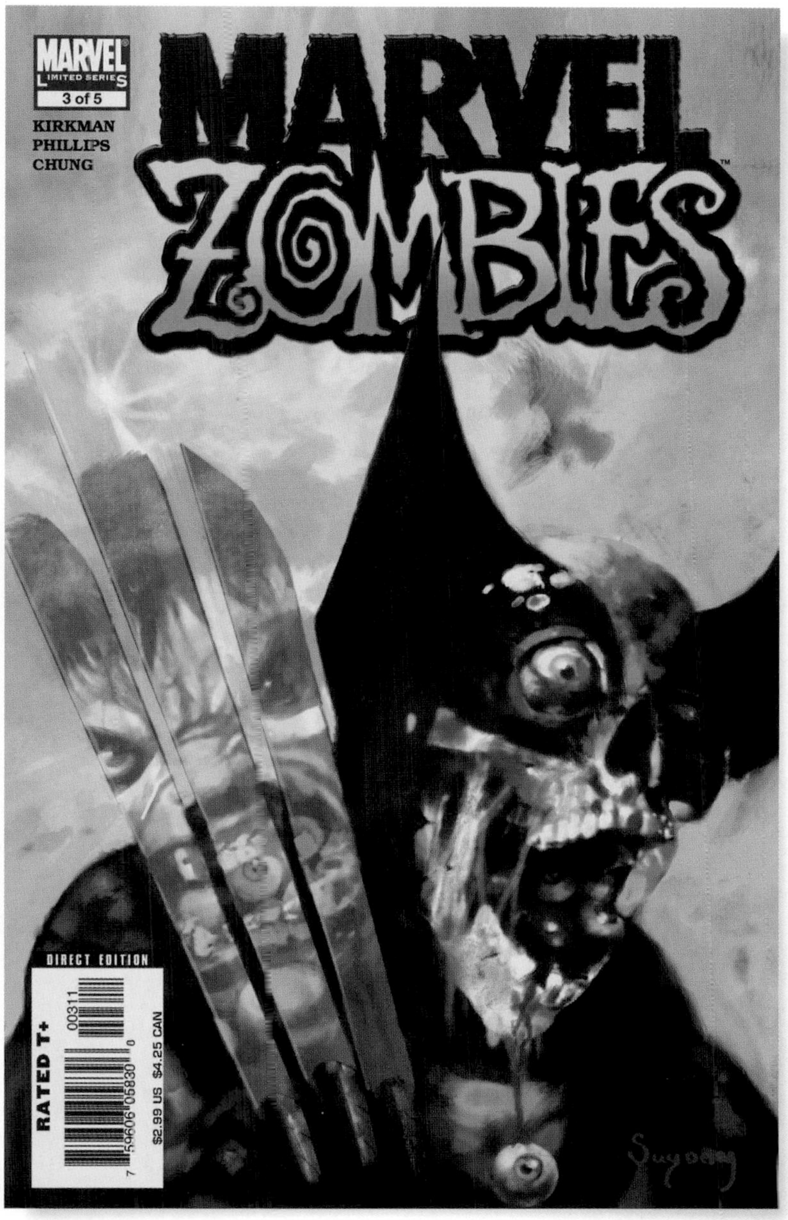
MARVEL LIMITED SERIES
3 of 5
KIRKMAN
PHILLIPS
CHUNG
MARVEL ZOMBIES
DIRECT EDITION
RATED T+
$2.99 US $4.25 CAN

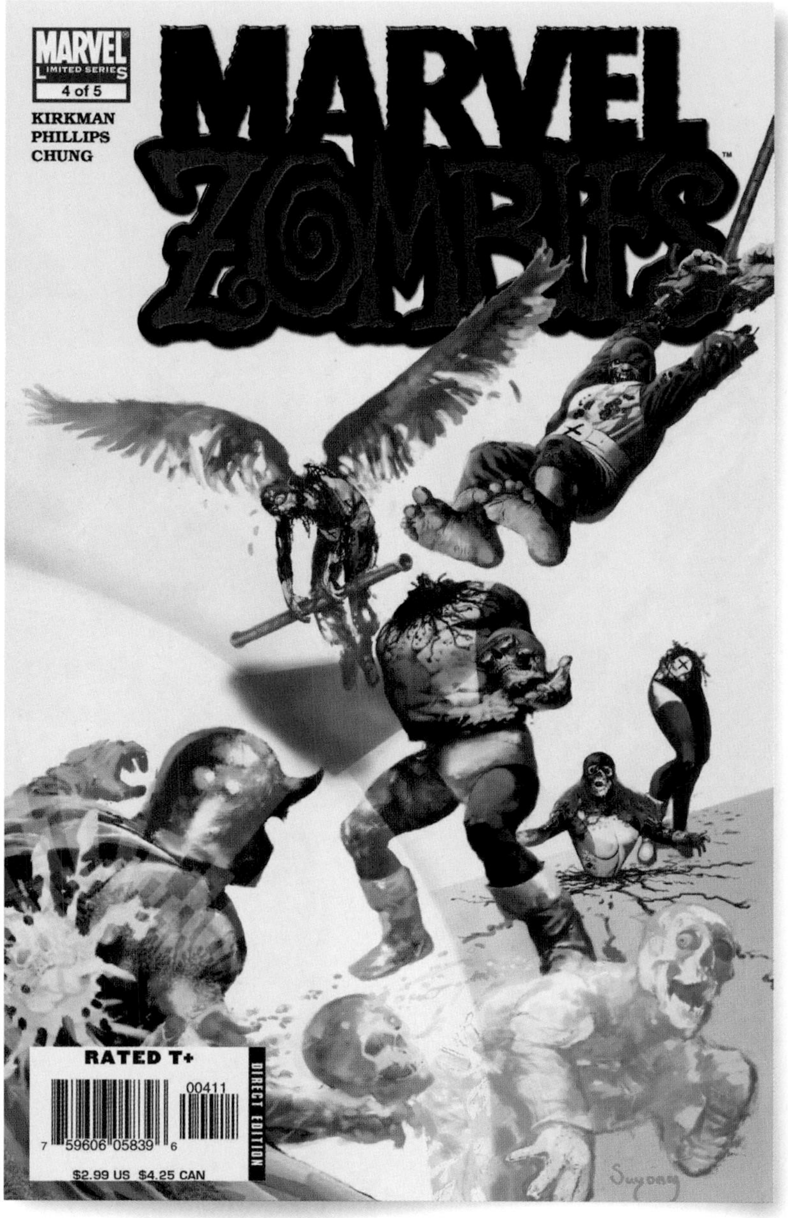
MARVEL LIMITED SERIES
4 of 5
KIRKMAN
PHILLIPS
CHUNG
MARVEL ZOMBIES
RATED T+
DIRECT EDITION
$2.99 US $4.25 CAN

▲ ***MARVEL ZOMBIES* #3**

**April 2006**
**Artist:** Arthur Suydam

This *Marvel Zombies* cover was another homage, this time to Todd McFarlane's classic *Incredible Hulk* issue #340 (February 1988; *see p178*). Additions such as the bloody eyeballs in Wolverine's mouth conveyed the setting of this story—a world filled with zombie Super Heroes—and are also what made Suydam's work so very eye-catching.

▲ ***MARVEL ZOMBIES* #4**

**May 2006**
**Artist:** Arthur Suydam

This homage to *The X-Men* issue #1 (September 1963; *see p60*)—with a grisly Cyclops holding his own severed head in his arms and Beast's arms falling off—is a perfect example of the humor that made *Marvel Zombies* a smash hit. Suydam's zombies lived on long after the series, appearing as variants on many other Marvel titles.

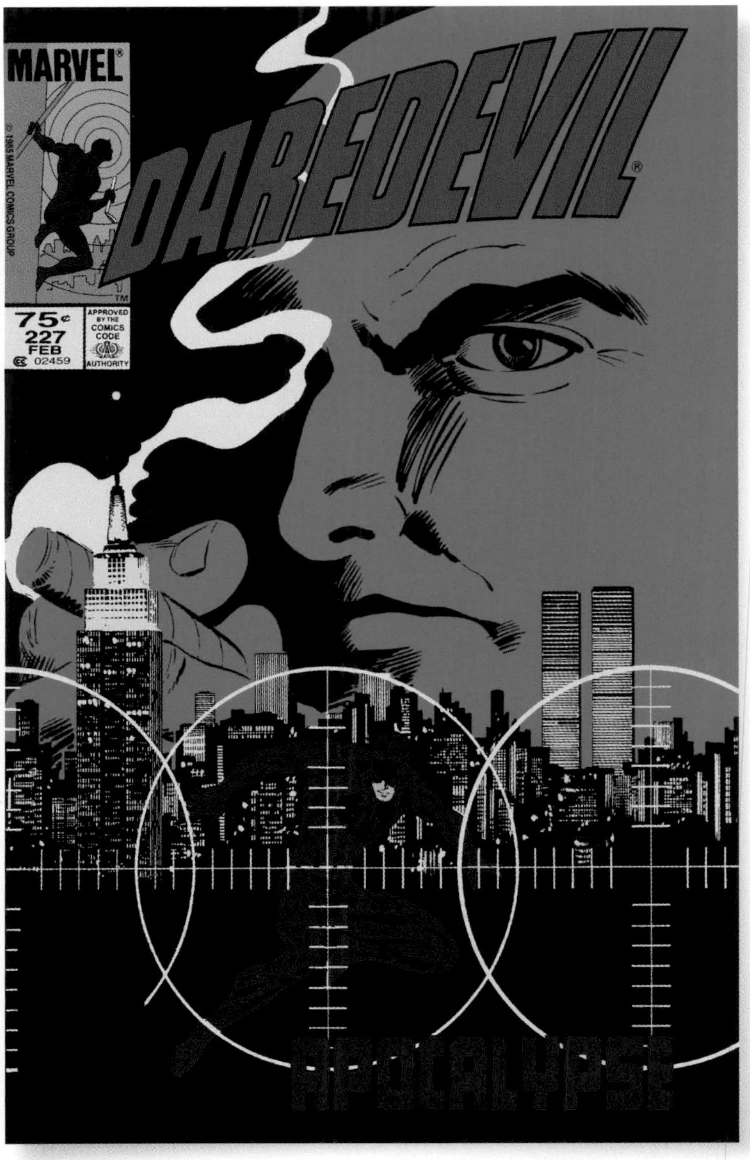
MARVEL
© 1985 MARVEL COMICS GROUP
75¢
227
FEB
02459
APPROVED BY THE COMICS CODE AUTHORITY
DAREDEVIL
APOCALYPSE

◀ ***DAREDEVIL* #227**

**February 1986**
**Artist:** David Mazzucchelli

After a three-year absence, comic-book megastar Frank Miller returned to *Daredevil* as a writer to mastermind one of the hero's greatest stories. Known as "Born Again," the story arc saw the Kingpin learn Daredevil's secret identity, and then set out to ruin him. David Mazzucchelli produced stunning art for both the cover and the story.

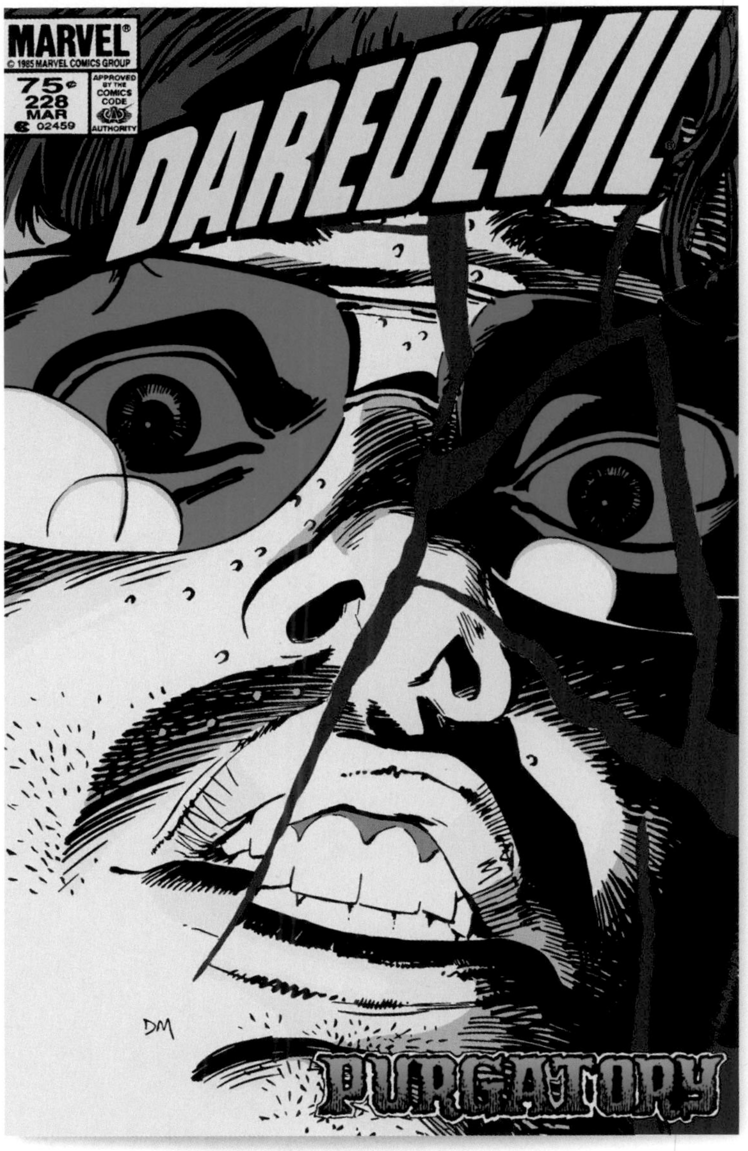
MARVEL
© 1985 MARVEL COMICS GROUP
75¢
228
MAR
02459
APPROVED BY THE COMICS CODE AUTHORITY
DAREDEVIL
DM
PURGATORY

◀ ***DAREDEVIL* #228**

**March 1986**
**Artist:** David Mazzucchelli

Each cover of the "Born Again" saga had a religiously themed tagline. "Purgatory" was the perfect summation of Daredevil's suffering in this dark issue. The cover image reflects the chaotic, terrified state of Matt Murdock's mind, the cracks revealing how close to insanity the hero is as a result of the Kingpin tearing apart his life.

MARVEL
25TH
ANNIVERSARY
DAREDEVIL
BORN AGAIN
75¢
230
MAY
MAZZUCCHELLI

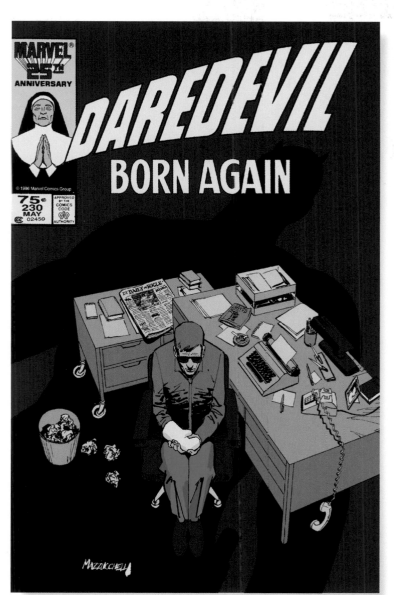

◀ *DAREDEVIL* #230

**May 1986**
**Artist:** David Mazzucchelli

This key issue in the "Born Again" saga featured reporter Ben Urich on the cover. Daredevil's shadow looms over Urich as he tries to come to terms with death threats caused by his connection to the hero. The saga saw most of the main characters going through their own personal hells to be born again as better people.

MARVEL
25TH
ANNIVERSARY
DAREDEVIL
75¢
232
JULY
MAZZUCCHELLI
GOD AND COUNTRY

◀ *DAREDEVIL* #232

**July 1986**
**Artist:** David Mazzucchelli

Mazzucchelli's penultimate cover for the "Born Again" saga saw the debut of Nuke, a villainous product of the secret Super Soldier program that had created Captain America. As Nuke's tattooed face peers over at Daredevil on the cover, the story's religious themes were given a military twist in the cover line, "God and Country."

MARVEL
DOUBLE-SIZED ISSUE!
DAREDEVIL
THE MAN WITHOUT FEAR!
$1.25 US
$1.75 CAN
252
MAR
APPROVED BY THE COMICS CODE AUTHORITY

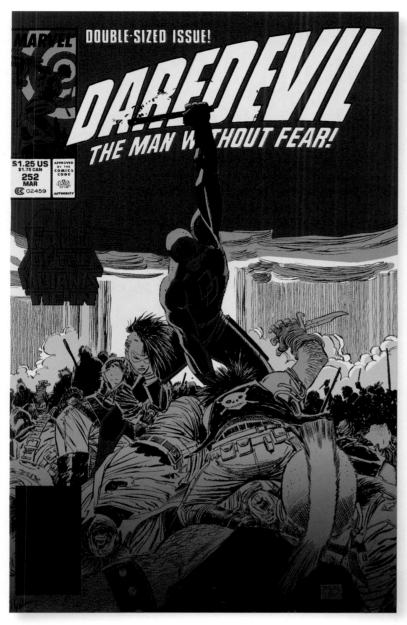

▲ *DAREDEVIL* #252

**March 1988**
**Artist:** John Romita Jr.

John Romita Jr. created this powerful cover for a "Fall of the Mutants" crossover issue of *Daredevil*, featuring the Man Without Fear trying to maintain order and stop the bad guys during a blackout. Working with writer Ann Nocenti, Romita Jr. created a well-respected run on the title. The cover beautifully demonstrates his maturing art style.

MARVEL
Merry Christmas
DAREDEVIL
75¢ US
95¢ CAN
253
APR
APPROVED BY THE COMICS CODE AUTHORITY

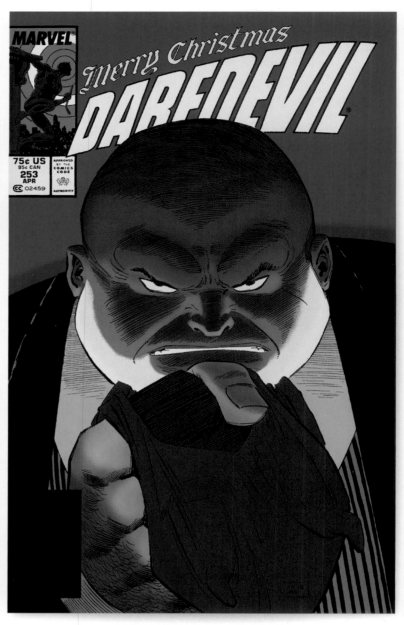

▲ *DAREDEVIL* #253

**April 1988**
**Artist:** John Romita Jr.

Romita Jr. gave Kingpin a real sense of power and menace on this cover, a Christmas-themed issue of *Daredevil* that seemed lacking any seasonal cheer. Romita Jr.'s interpretation of the character caught the eye of Frank Miller, who would go on to work closely with Romita Jr. five years later on the *Daredevil: The Man Without Fear* series.

*DAREDEVIL* #1 ▶

**November 1988**
**Artist:** Joe Quesada

When Daredevil was given to Joe Quesada's Marvel Knights imprint to relaunch, Marvel's future boss took on the artistic chores himself, illustrating filmmaker Kevin Smith's challenging story. Quesada created some stunning covers for the series, starting with this acrobatic image. The "Guardian Angel" saga (which began with this issue) won several awards, including an Eagle Award for Best Story.

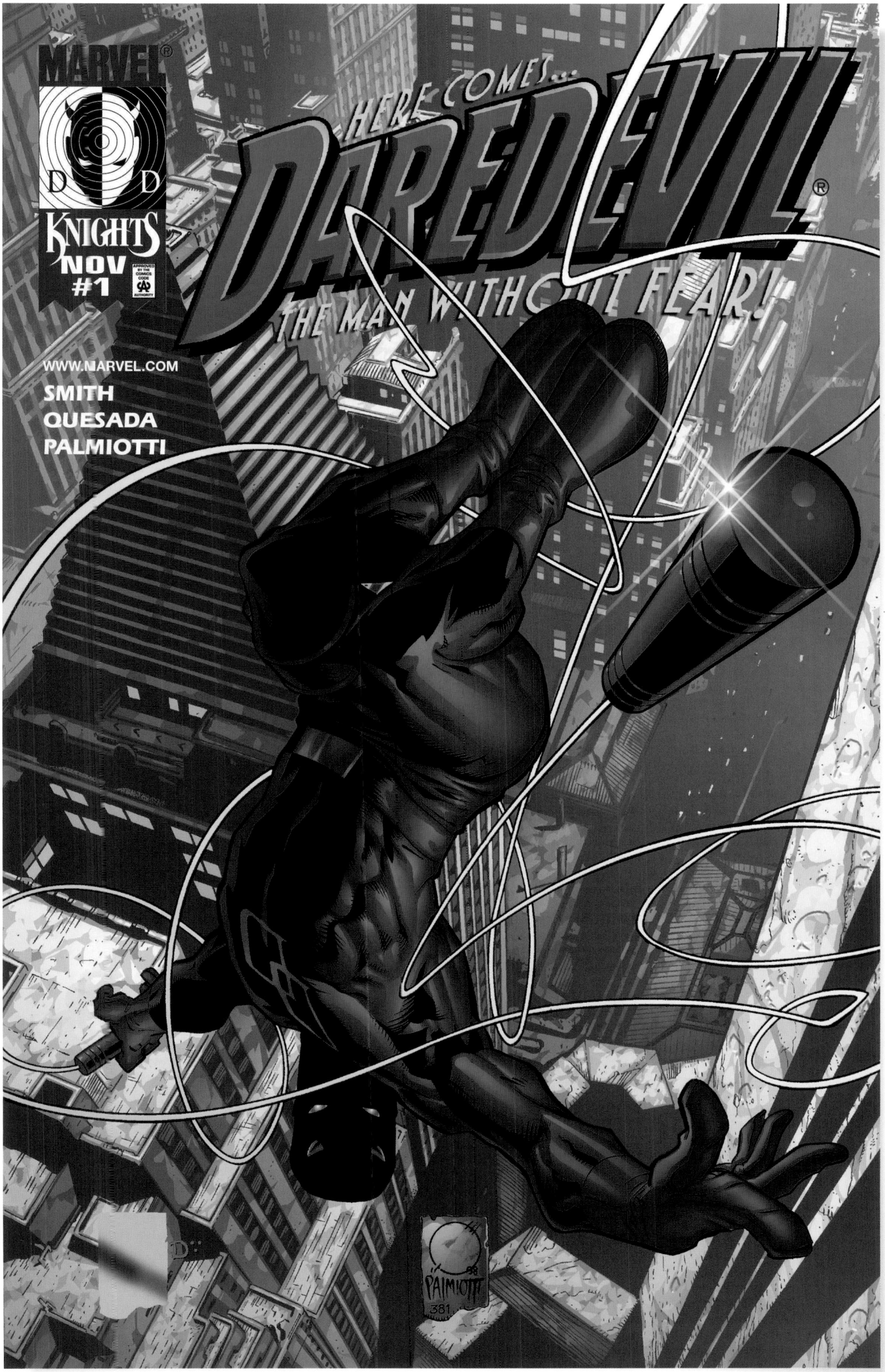
MARVEL
KNIGHTS
NOV
#1
HERE COMES...
DAREDEVIL
THE MAN WITHOUT FEAR!
WWW.MARVEL.COM
SMITH
QUESADA
PALMIOTTI

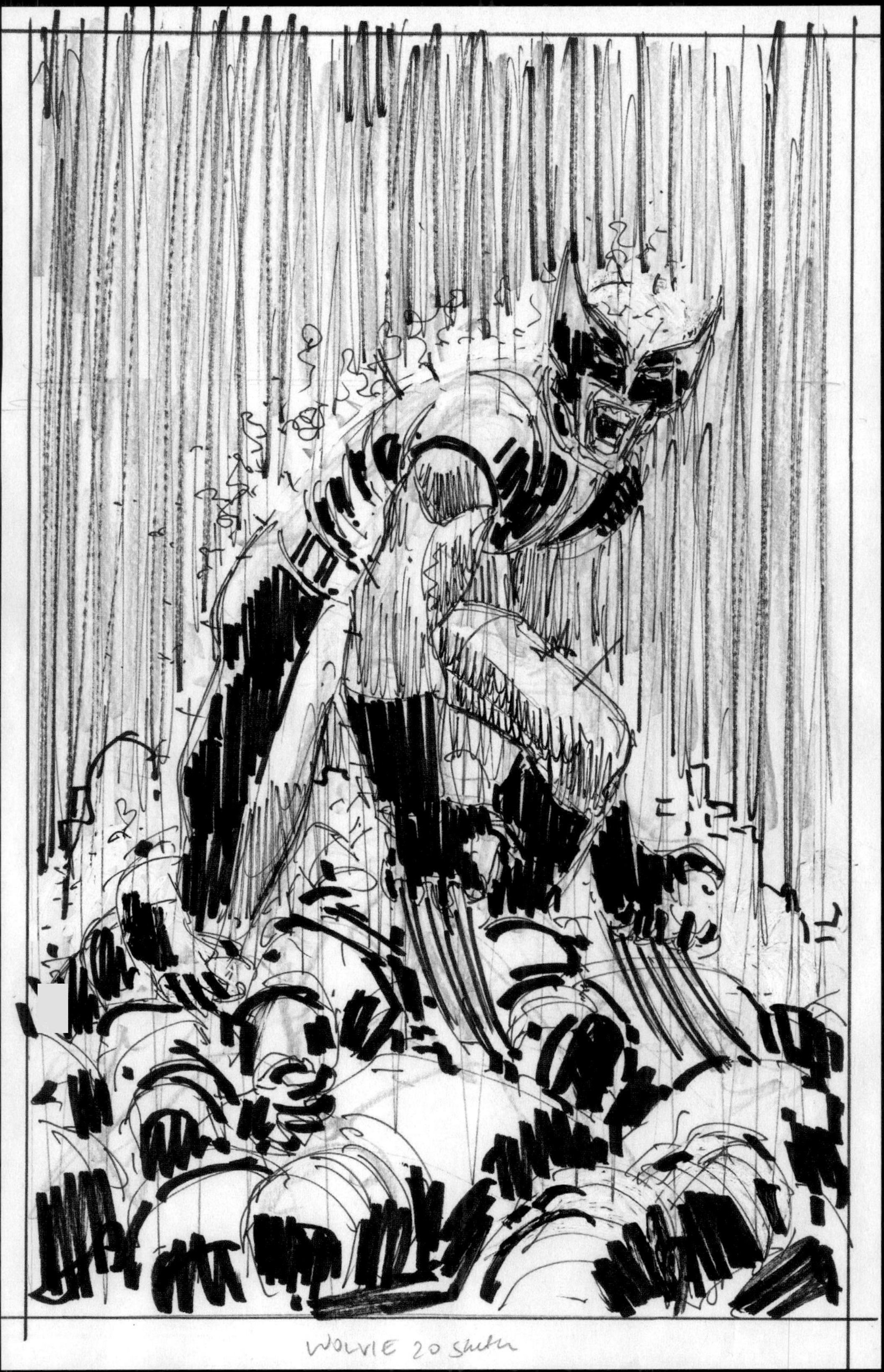
WOLVIE 20 sketch

1.

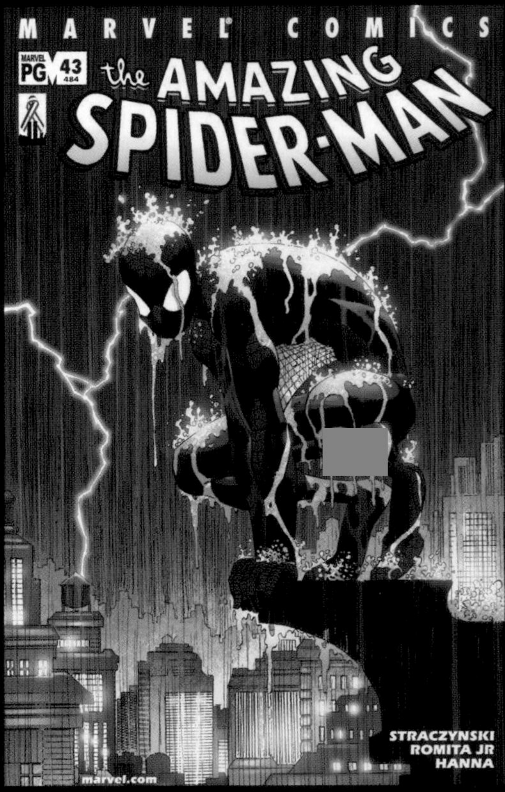
MARVEL COMICS
PG 43
the AMAZING SPIDER-MAN
STRACZYNSKI
ROMITA JR
HANNA
marvel.com

2.

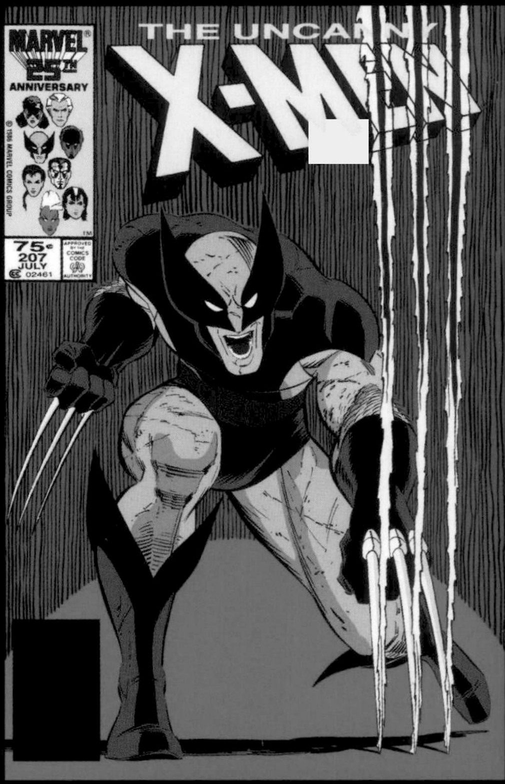
MARVEL 25TH ANNIVERSARY
75¢
207
JULY

3.

# JOHN ROMITA JR.

John Romita Jr. has been one of Marvel's top artists for over 40 years. From producing pages for Marvel UK as a young man, to his more recent work on Marvel's leading titles, John Romita Jr. has drawn just about every Marvel character going. While at first his art echoed the clean, commercial style of his father, Romita's art evolved during his run on *Daredevil* (1988–1990), becoming more confident, powerful, and increasingly filled with energy. It was a style that propelled him to the very top of his field. As art legend Joe Kubert said, "His style is one immediately recognizable, and the movement combined with impact and clarity of his storytelling is what cartooning is all about."

### 1. *WOLVERINE* #20

**December 2004**

This early sketch of Wolverine saw John Romita Jr. experiment with a different angle for the hero compared to the one finally used *(see p296)*. His loose pencil style still shows the raw power of his finished work.

### 2. *AMAZING SPIDER-MAN* #43

**September 2002**

Romita Jr. enjoyed two successful runs on *Amazing Spider-Man* and this cover exemplifies what made his second spell on the title so popular. It is a brooding, atmospheric work, perfectly bringing out the arachnid in Spider-Man, who was perched behind

### 3. *UNCANNY X-MEN* #207

**July 1986**

This cover showcases the dynamism of Romita's art during his first run on *Uncanny X-Men*. It also shows his use of inventive design and layout skills as Wolverine's claws tear dramatically through the cover.

### 4. *DAREDEVIL: THE MAN WITHOUT FEAR* #1

**October 1993**

Romita Jr. himself considers his work with Frank Miller on this title to be some of his best. This cover shows the highly detailed line-work Romita had developed during this period, as well as his ability to convey raw

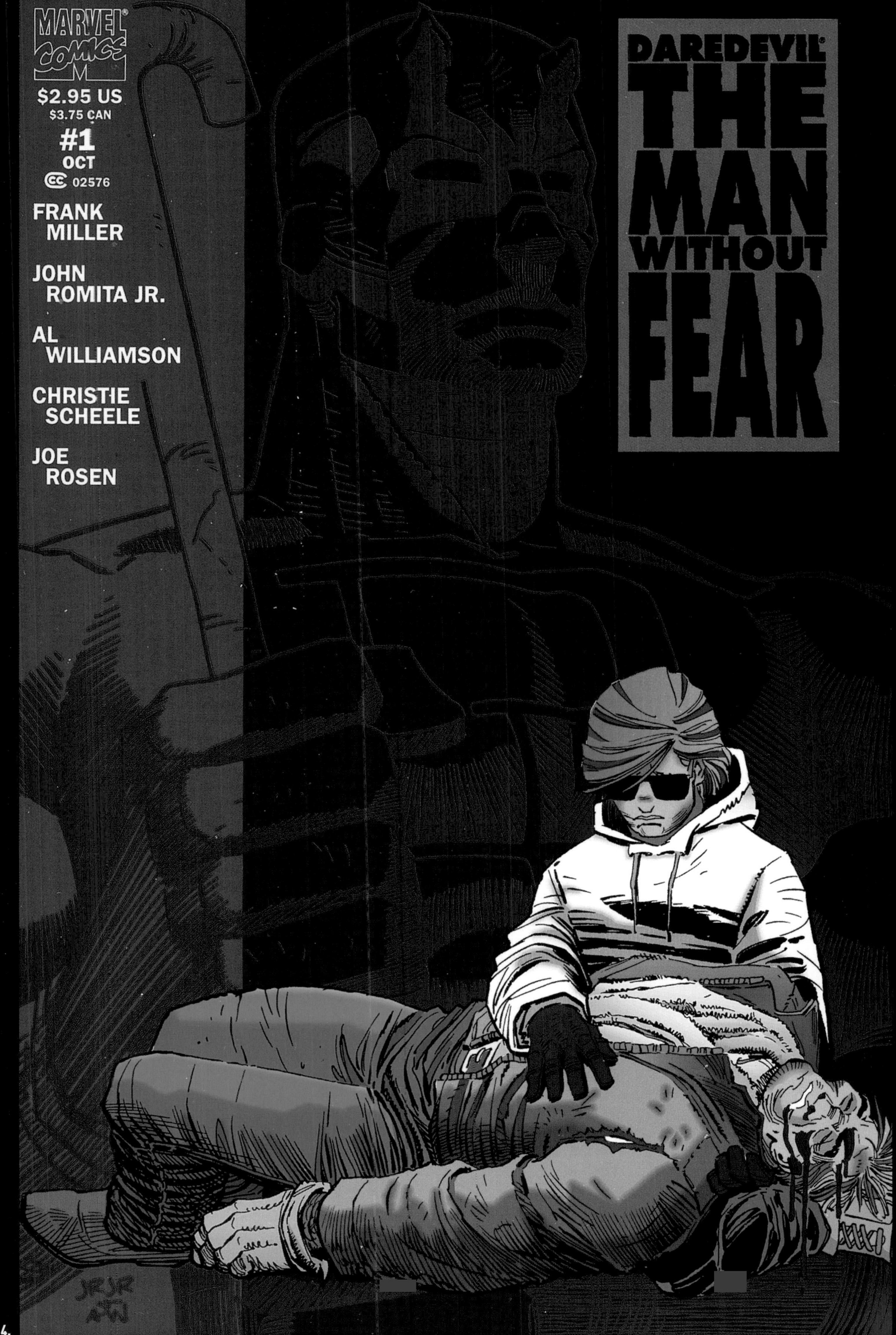
MARVEL COMICS
$2.95 US
$3.75 CAN
#1
OCT
CC 02576
FRANK MILLER
JOHN ROMITA JR.
AL WILLIAMSON
CHRISTIE SCHEELE
JOE ROSEN
DAREDEVIL®
THE MAN WITHOUT FEAR

***MARVEL KNIGHTS* #1** ▶

**July 2000**
**Artist**: Joe Quesada

The Marvel Knights imprint gained a team book with this issue, which brought together Shang Chi, Punisher, Dagger, Daredevil, and the Black Widow. The team had a more urban feel than other groups, and although they weren't officially a team, the heroes fought together against a number of foes. Joe Quesada illustrated the cover to the first issue and used the rope of Daredevil's Billy Club to add a sense of movement and energy to the atmospheric image.

MARVEL
HERE COMES...
DAREDEVIL
THE MAN WITHOUT FEAR!
KNIGHTS
DEC #3
WWW.MARVEL.COM
SMITH
QUESADA
PALMIOTTI

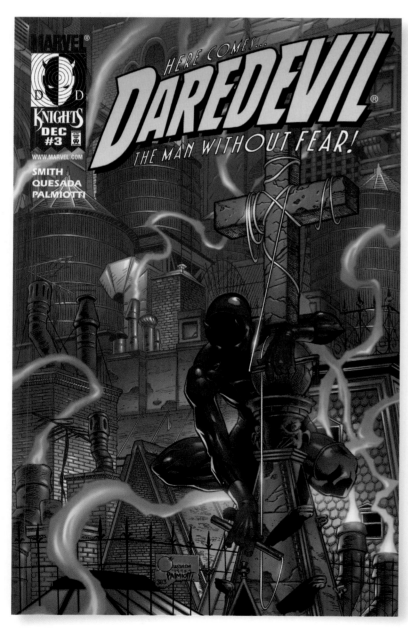

▲ ***DAREDEVIL* #3**

**January 1999**
**Artist**: Joe Quesada

This atmospheric Joe Quesada cover captures the story's religious elements. Matt Murdock's Catholicism had often played a major part in the comic's storylines. His beliefs were once again laid bare as the hero tried to protect a young baby he would soon come to believe could be the Messiah—or the Antichrist.

MARVEL
HERE COMES...
KNIGHTS
#8
SMITH
QUESADA
PALMIOTTI

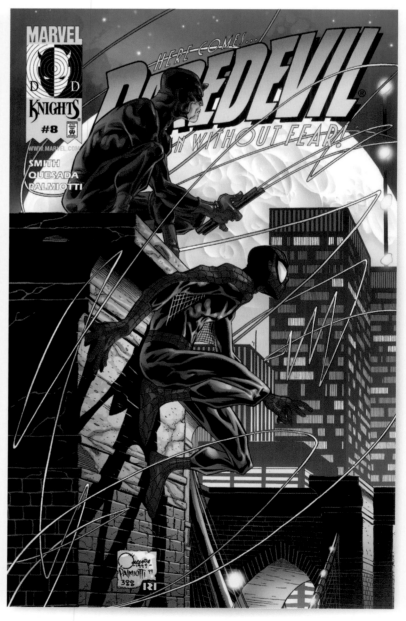

▲ ***DAREDEVIL* #8**

**June 1999**
**Artist:** Joe Quesada

Smith and Quesada's "Guardian Devil" epic came to a close this issue, which acted as an epilogue to the main saga. Quesada's cover, showing Spider-Man and Daredevil, was a calm change of pace after the tension and shocks of the previous issues. It reflects the melancholy nature of the climax, as Matt mourned Karen Page.

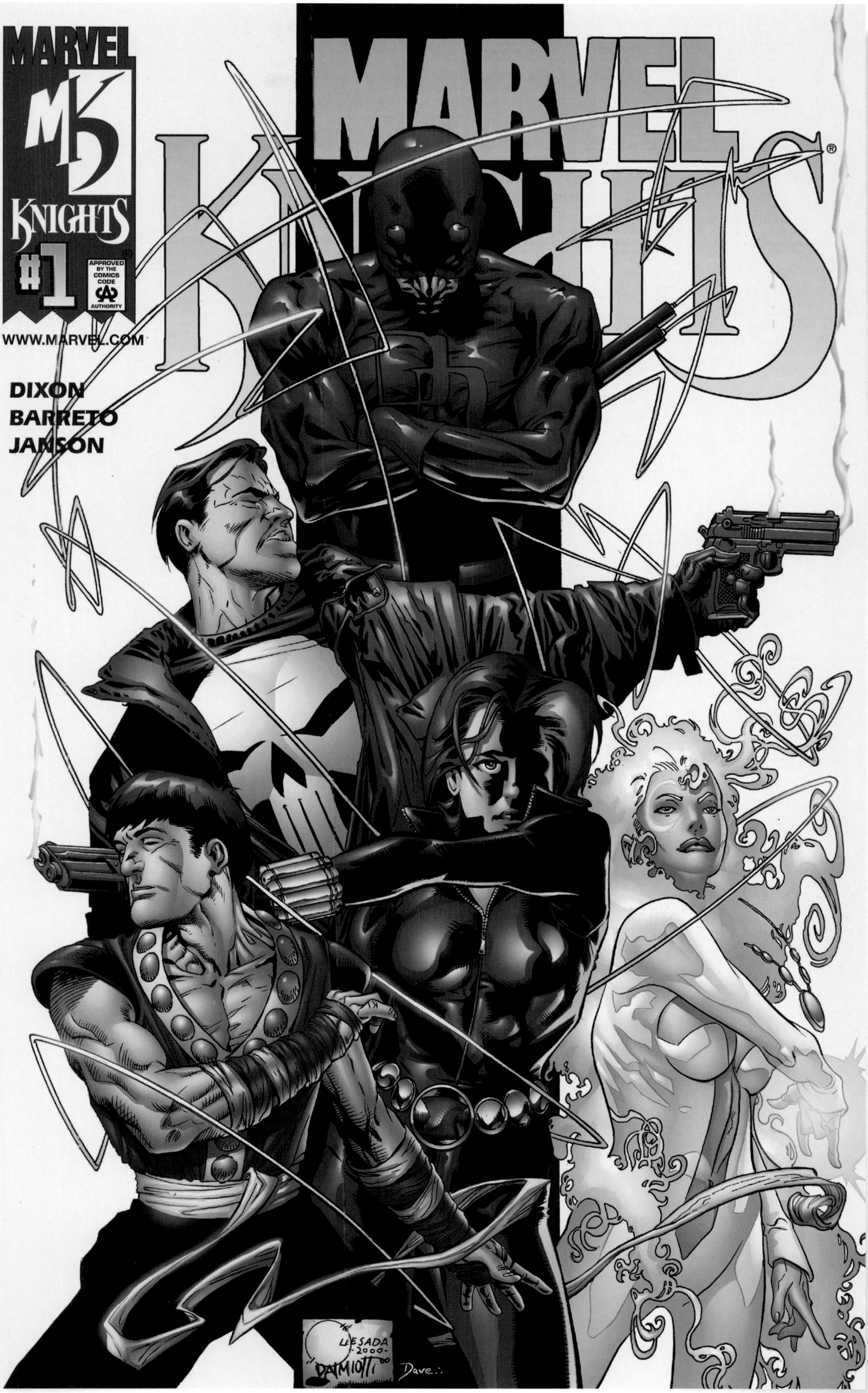
MARVEL
MK
KNIGHTS
#1
APPROVED BY THE COMICS CODE AUTHORITY
WWW.MARVEL.COM
DIXON
BARRETO
JANSON
MARVEL
KNIGHTS

MARVEL
KNIGHTS
#16
HERE COMES...
DAREDEVIL
THE MAN WITHOUT FEAR!
WWW.MARVEL.COM
BENDIS
MACK
MACK

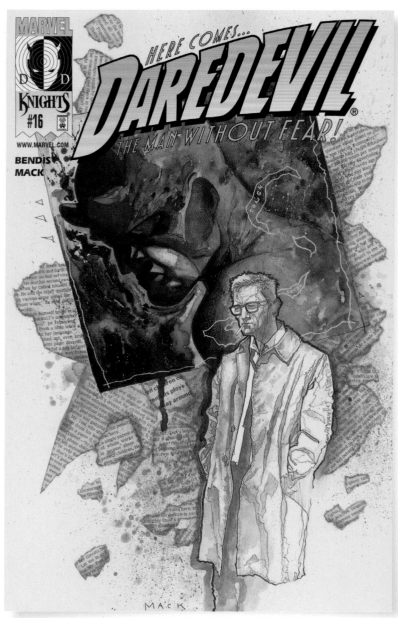

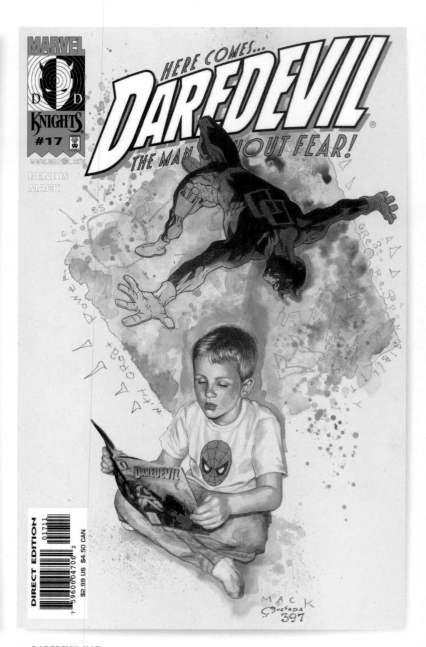

▲ ***DAREDEVIL* #16**

**May 2001**
**Artist:** David Mack

David Mack mixed collage and painting techniques to create high-impact covers for his short run on *Daredevil*. He also illustrated this four-part story, "Wake Up." Mack brought his unique vision to Brian Michael Bendis' tale of a young boy named Timmy and his turmoil after seeing his father, the villain Leap Frog, fight his hero Daredevil.

MARVEL
KNIGHTS
#17
HERE COMES...
DAREDEVIL
THE MAN WITHOUT FEAR!
BENDIS
MACK
DIRECT EDITION
$2.99 US $4.50 CAN
DAREDEVIL
MACK

▲ ***DAREDEVIL* #17**

**June 2001**
**Artist:** David Mack

Mack's second cover for the "Wake Up" story focused on the young protagonist, Timmy. The artist produced another dream-like montage for the cover, highlighting Timmy's admiration of heroes such as Daredevil and Spider-Man. Mack's painterly style brought storybook elements to the cover, which reflects Timmy's childish world view.

MARVEL KNIGHTS
18
BRIAN MICHAEL BENDIS • DAVID MACK
HERE COMES...
DAREDEVIL
THE MAN WITHOUT FEAR!
MACK
398
DIRECT EDITION
$2.99 US $4.50 CAN

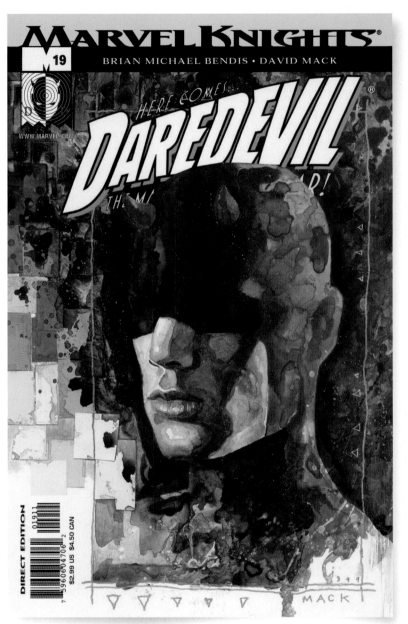

▲ *DAREDEVIL* #18

**July 2001**
**Artist:** David Mack

David Mack created another thoughtful cover as "Wake Up" reached its penultimate chapter. This time Mack produced a portrait of the Man Without Fear and his alter ego. The heroic depiction of the character reflects Timmy's obsession with the hero, which proved to be the main focus of the issue.

MARVEL KNIGHTS
19
BRIAN MICHAEL BENDIS • DAVID MACK
HERE COMES...
DAREDEVIL
WWW.MARVEL.COM
DIRECT EDITION
$2.99 US $4.50 CAN
399
MACK

▲ *DAREDEVIL* #19

**August 2001**
**Artist:** David Mack

"Wake Up" concluded with this issue and with one of David Mack's best covers. The elegant portrait of Daredevil has a grace and thoughtfulness not seen on many comic covers. In the story's thought-provoking climax, reporter Ben Urich learned of Timmy's troubled past and his shock at seeing Daredevil viciously defeat Leap Frog.

LATE CITY FINAL
MARVEL PG
BRIAN MICHAEL BENDIS • ALEX MALEEV
DAILY GLOBE
APRIL 18, 2002/ Cloudy, chance of rain,55/ Weather: Page 20
marvel.com
#32
DIRECT EDITION
$2.99 US $4.75 CAN

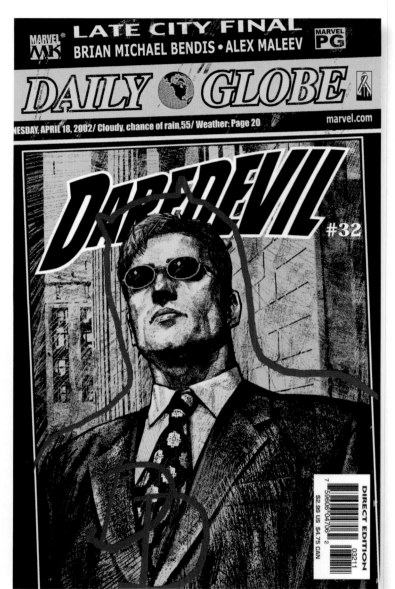

◀ ***DAREDEVIL* #32**

**June 2002**
**Artist:** Alex Maleev

Writer Brian Michael Bendis and artist Alex Maleev had a long and award-winning run on *Daredevil*, creating several twists along the way. This issue's cover reflects one of the biggest twists—the FBI started to suspect that Matt Murdock was Daredevil. Maleev had a fine arts background and his covers were often experimental, blending drawing with digital and photorealistic techniques.

PG 46
BRIAN MICHAEL BENDIS • ALEX MALEEV
HARDCORE
DIRECT EDITION
$2.99 US $4.75 CAN

◀ ***DAREDEVIL* #46**

**June 2003**
**Artist:** Alex Maleev

Typhoid Mary, one of Daredevil's deadliest and most complex foes, returned in this issue, with Alex Maleev providing a sensual new interpretation of the villain for the cover. Bendis and Maleev managed to create a series of stories that broke new ground for the Man Without Fear—without turning their backs on the character's rich history.

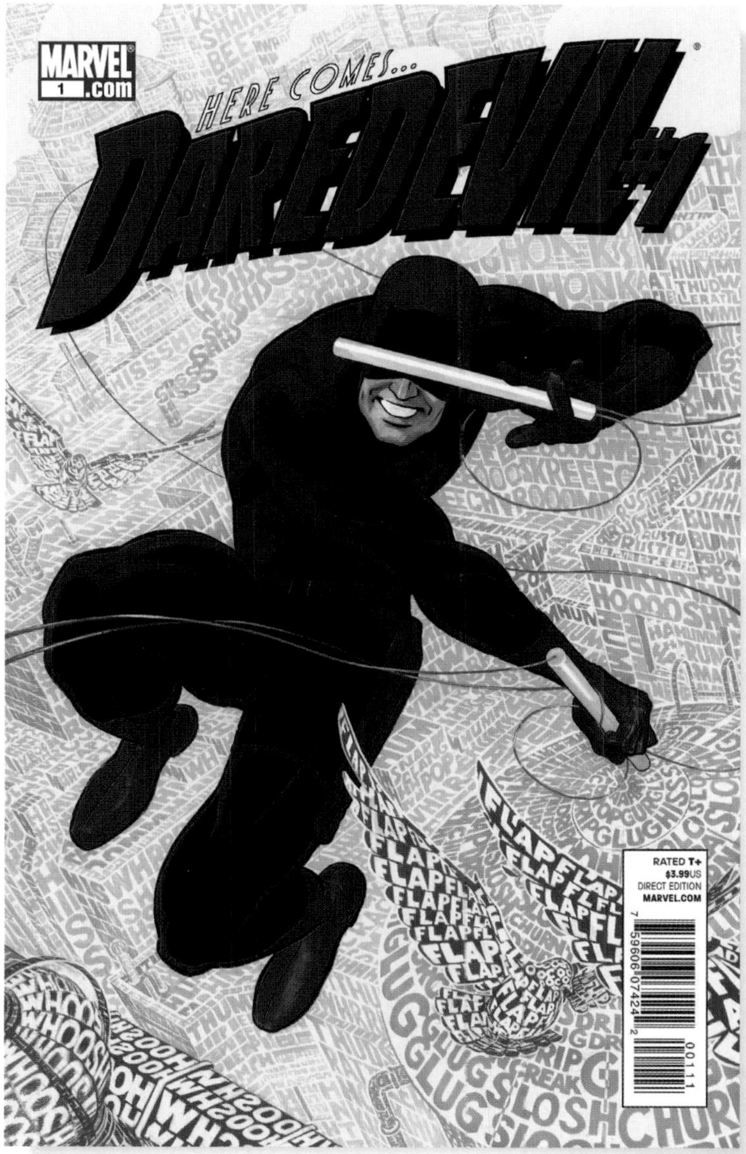
MARVEL
1 .com
HERE COMES...
DAREDEVIL #1
FLAP
GLUG
RATED T+
$3.99US
DIRECT EDITION
MARVEL.COM

◀ *DAREDEVIL* #1

**September 2011**
**Artist:** Paolo Rivera

After years of dark stories, Daredevil's adventures took a new direction with this relaunch. Artist Paolo Rivera and writer Mark Waid brought back a sense of daring adventure to the Man Without Fear. Rivera's simple yet effective cover shows a smiling Daredevil in motion. The artist also found a clever new way of illustrating Daredevil's radar sense by surrounding the hero with words instead of images.

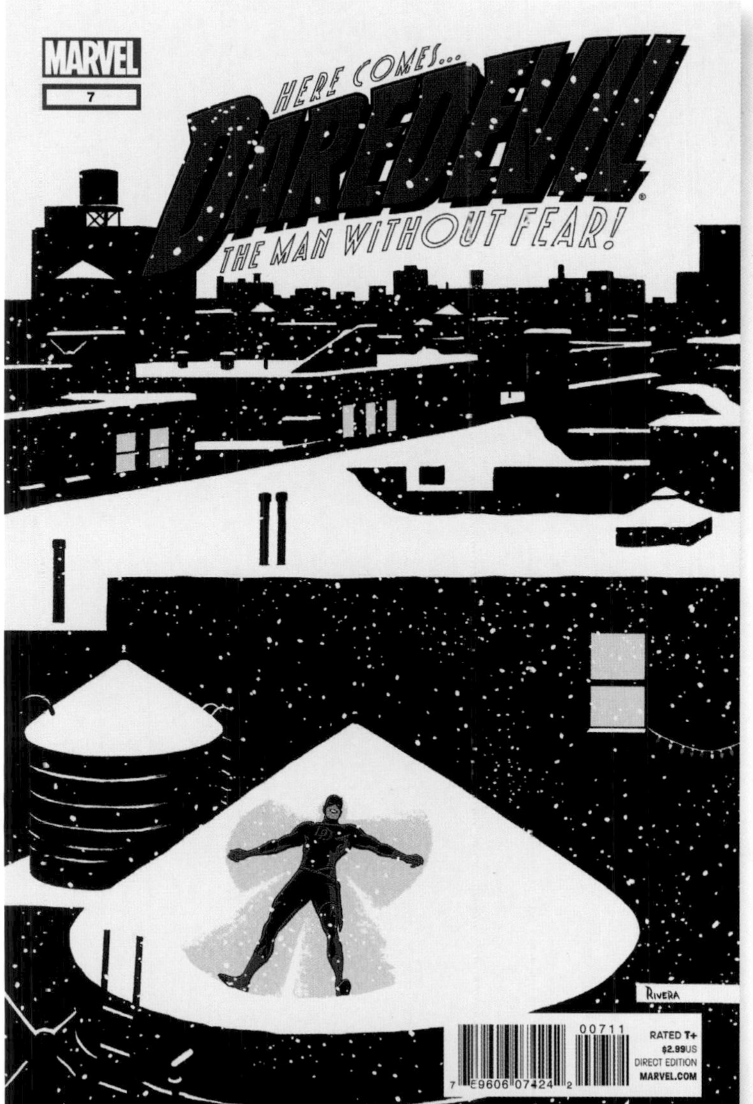
MARVEL
7
HERE COMES...
DAREDEVIL
THE MAN WITHOUT FEAR!
RIVERA
RATED T+
$2.99US
DIRECT EDITION
MARVEL.COM

◀ *DAREDEVIL* #7

**February 2012**
**Artist:** Paolo Rivera

The image of Daredevil making a snow angel hints at the hero's near-death during an attempt to save a group of children caught in a snowstorm. Rivera's bold use of color—especially black and white—resulted in another eye-catching cover for one of the title's most critically acclaimed runs. The comic received a prestigious Eisner Award in 2012 for Best Single Issue.

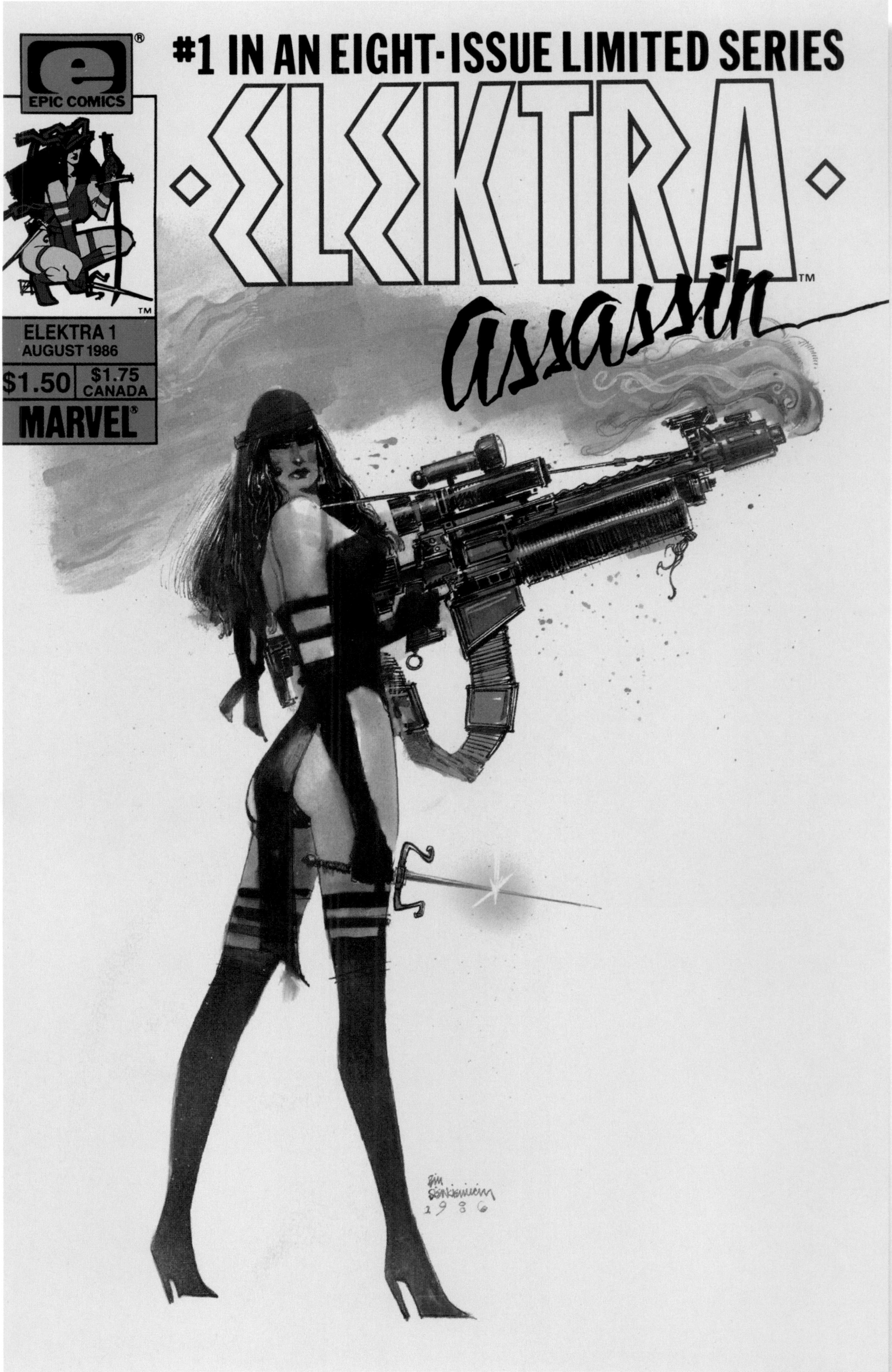

#1 IN AN EIGHT-ISSUE LIMITED SERIES
EPIC COMICS
ELEKTRA
Assassin
ELEKTRA 1
AUGUST 1986
$1.50
$1.75 CANADA
MARVEL

***ELEKTRA* #1 ▶**

**September 2001**
**Artist:** Greg Horn

Elektra regained her own book in 2001 with Greg Horn providing many beautifully painted covers for the series. His artwork often featured Elektra in a combative pose—this first cover shows her wielding her deadly sai. Horn's realistic approach to the work added a layer of cold beauty to the complex character.

MARVEL KNIGHTS
1
BRIAN MICHAEL BENDIS • CHUCK AUSTEN
VIOLENT CONTENT
WWW.MARVEL.COM
ELEKTRA
DIRECT EDITION
$3.50 US $5.25 CAN

***THUNDERBOLTS* #1 ▶**

**February 2013**
**Artist:** Julian Tedesco

Julian Tedesco was inspired by the look of the Thunderbolts' leader, the Red Hulk, on this eye-catching cover. The book saw the Red Hulk joining forces with some of Marvel's deadliest heroes—Elektra, Punisher, Venom, and Deadpool. The anti-heroes are tinted red on the covers to reflect the color of their leader, the Red Hulk.

MARVEL NOW!
THUNDERBOLTS
#1
WAY • DILLON • GURU eFX
PARENTAL ADVISORY
$2.99US
DIRECT EDITION
MARVEL.COM
JOIN THE REVOLUTION
001

**◀ *ELEKTRA: ASSASSIN* #1**

**August 1986**
**Artist:** Bill Sienkiewicz

The cover to the first issue of *Elektra: Assassin* saw artist Bill Sienkiewicz at the top of his game, creating a unique vision of the femme fatale and using a white background to give Elektra's red costume maximum impact. The series, written by Frank Miller, was published by Marvel's Epic imprint, which offered an outlet for more adult-oriented material, often featuring experimental visuals.

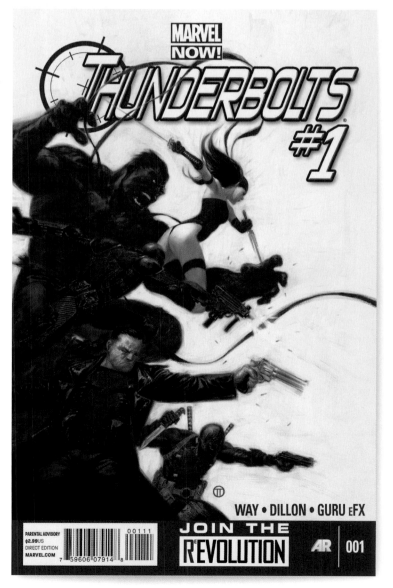

MARVEL COMICS
FANTASTIC 1ST ISSUE!
GHOST RIDER
$1.95 US
1
MAY
A SPIRIT REBORN!

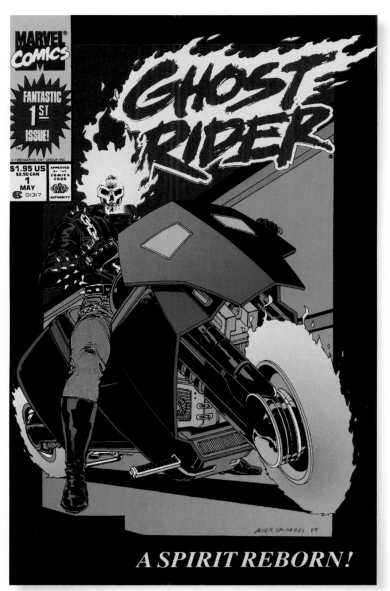

◀ *GHOST RIDER* #1

**May 1990**
**Artist:** Javier Saltares

A new Ghost Rider burst into action, as Javier Saltares revealed the new-look spirit of vengeance on the cover of the debut issue. The new title—featuring teenager Dan Ketch as the Ghost Rider—proved to be a smash hit, and it became one of the most popular Marvel comics of the time.

RISE OF THE MIDNIGHT SONS
MARVEL COMICS
GHOST RIDER & BLAZE
SPIRITS OF VENGEANCE
$2.75 US
1
AUG
Part 2 of 6

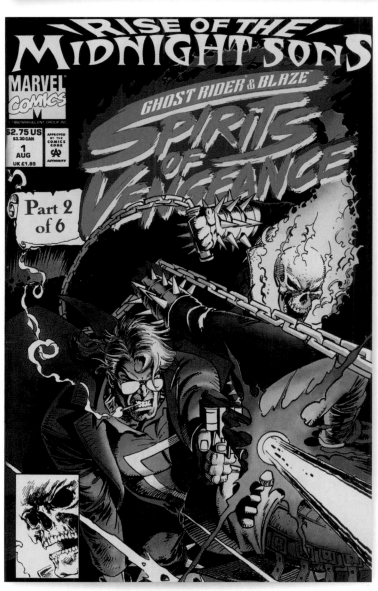

◀ *SPIRITS OF VENGEANCE* #1

**August 1992**
**Artist:** Adam Kubert

Adam Kubert's dramatic cover saw Johnny Blaze, the original Ghost Rider, team up with the latest incarnation. Kubert was a master of creating action scenes and dynamic movement, and he instills both characters with a sense of deadly energy in this cover portrayal.

MARVEL COMICS
GHOST RIDER
2099
$1.50 US
1
MAY

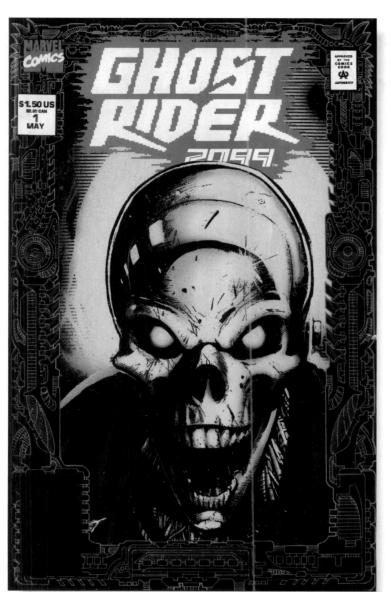

◀ *GHOST RIDER 2099* **#1**

**May 1994**
**Artist:** Chris Bachalo

*Ghost Rider 2099*'s first cover was an early work by Chris Bachalo, who created a new version of the Spirit of Vengeance, set in the far future. The frame around the main image is metallic ink, reflecting the cyberpunk nature of the new hero.

MARVEL COMICS
1
E A R T H
KRUEGER
LEON
REINHOLD

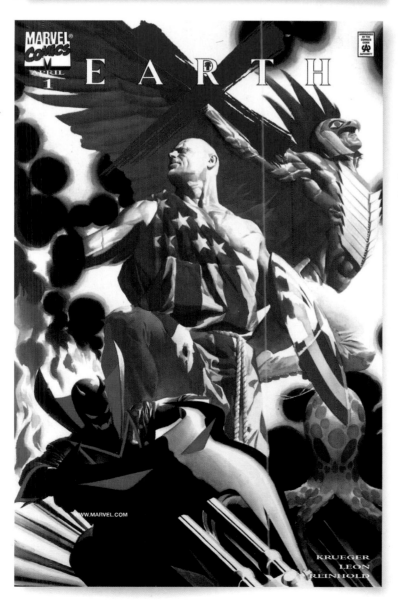

◀ *EARTH X* **#1**

**April 1999**
**Artist:** Alex Ross

Alex Ross' beautiful, painted art graced the cover of *Earth X*, a new series set in a dark future of the Marvel Universe. The cover for the debut issue showcases some of the strange alternate versions of the Marvel characters seen in the series, with the Earth X version of Captain America at the center.

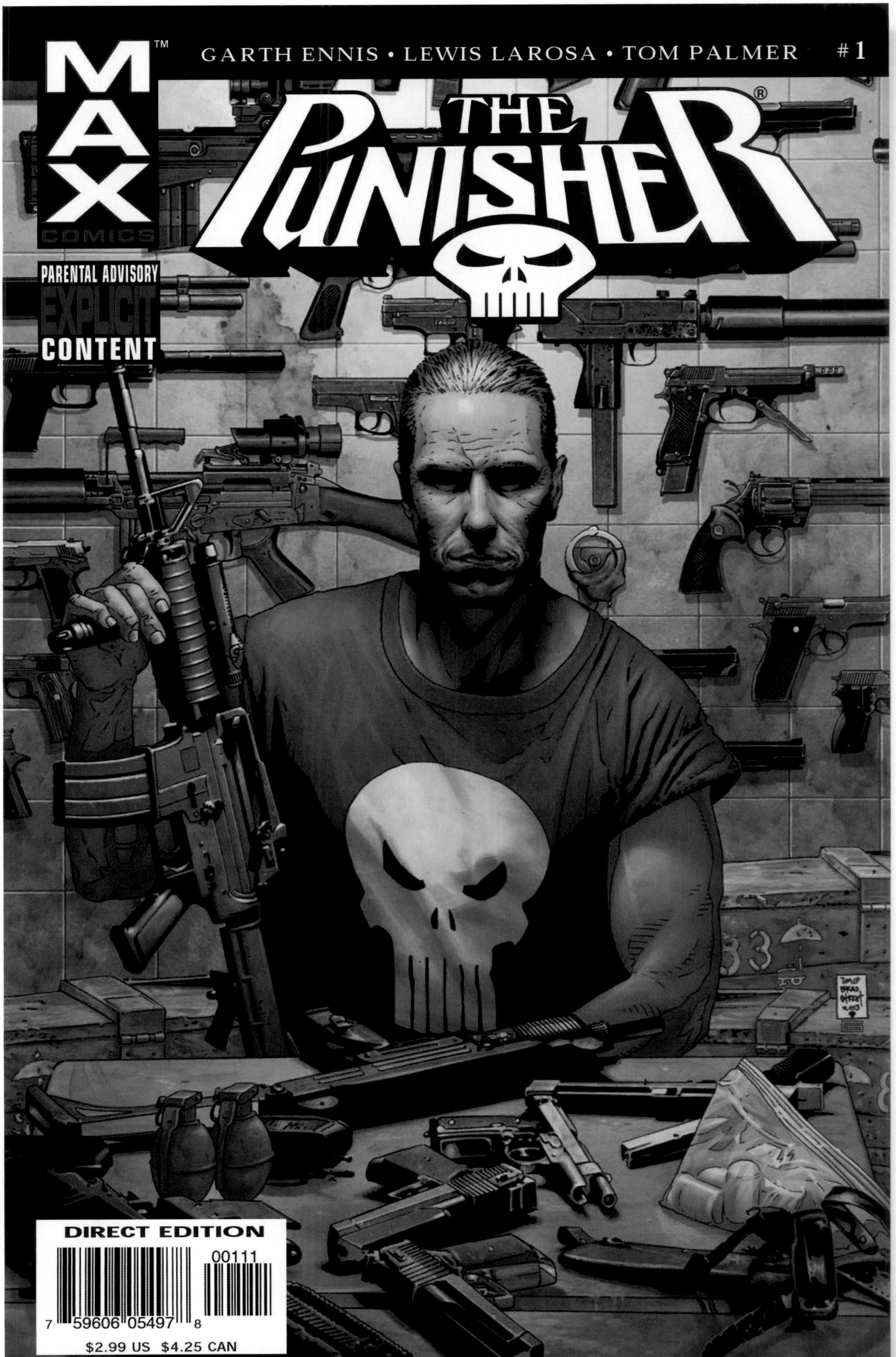
MAX
COMICS
GARTH ENNIS • LEWIS LAROSA • TOM PALMER
#1
THE PUNISHER
PARENTAL ADVISORY
EXPLICIT
CONTENT
DIRECT EDITION
00111
7 59606 05497 8
$2.99 US $4.25 CAN

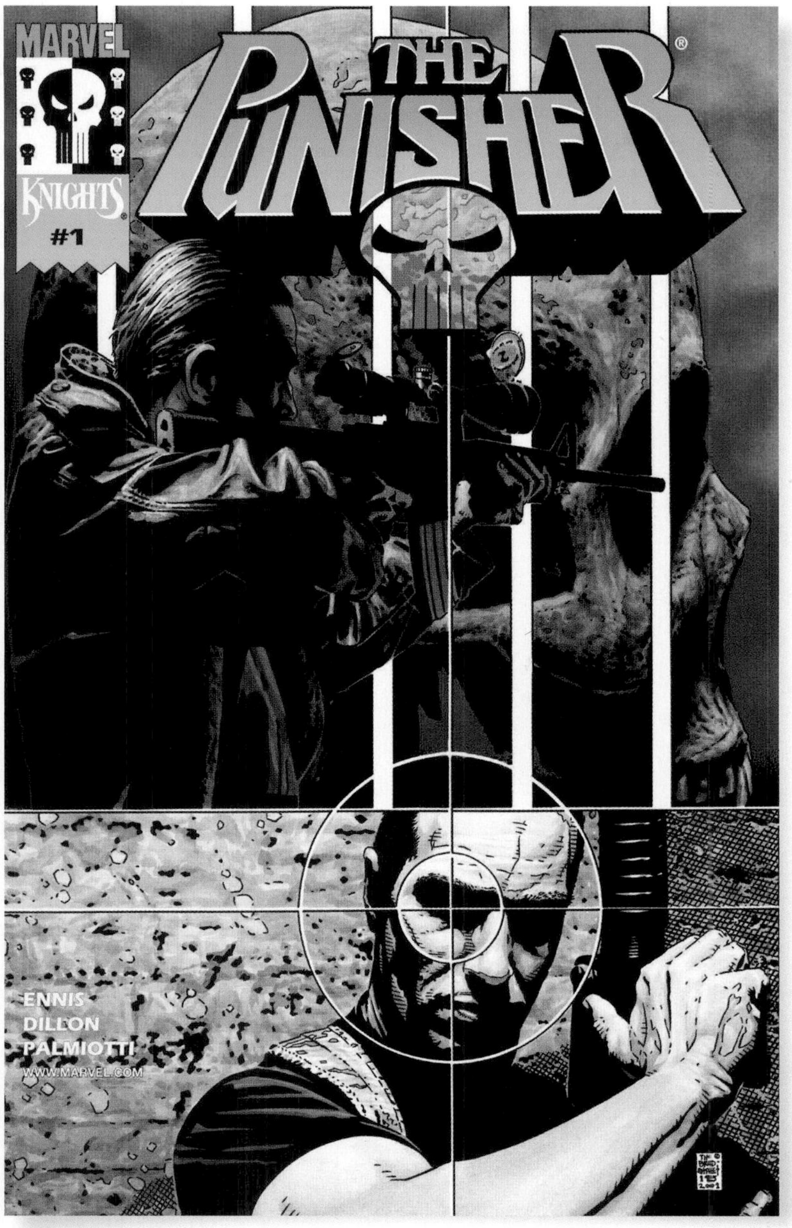
MARVEL
THE PUNISHER
KNIGHTS
#1
ENNIS
DILLON
PALMIOTTI
WWW.MARVEL.COM

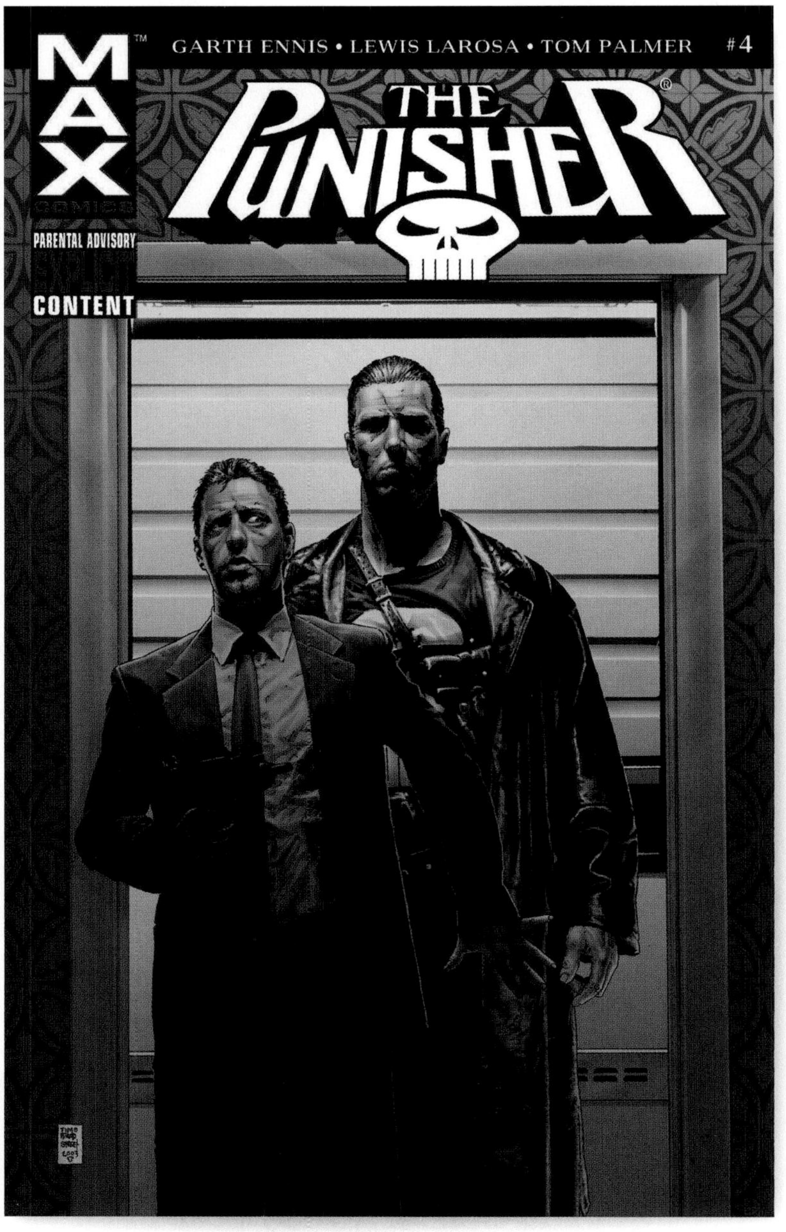
MAX COMICS
GARTH ENNIS • LEWIS LAROSA • TOM PALMER
#4
THE PUNISHER
PARENTAL ADVISORY
CONTENT

▲ ***PUNISHER* #1**

**August 2001**
**Artist:** Tim Bradstreet

This Tim Bradstreet cover was the perfect piece of art to help launch a new series of Frank Castle's adventures. Skulls and guns were big recurring themes for the vigilante hero and both were present here, as an assassin put the Punisher in his sights.

▲ ***PUNISHER* #4**

**May 2004**
**Artist:** Tim Bradstreet

While most of Tim Bradstreet's covers focused solely on the Punisher, this chilling visual selected the terrifying moment Frank caught up with a victim. Bradstreet's realistic art brought a sense of grim emptiness to the Punisher, making the hero look more ruthless than ever.

◀ ***PUNISHER* #1**

**March 2004**
**Artist:** Tim Bradstreet

Writer Garth Ennis had reinvigorated Punisher as part of the Marvel Knights imprint. However, a big part of the revamped title's success was due to Tim Bradstreet's realistic covers. This artwork helped to launch a new run of the Punisher's adventures—under the banner of Marvel's Max Comics imprint, reserved for graphic content. The image of Frank Castle's armory was a chilling reminder of the hero's deadly war on crime.

***AMAZING SPIDER-MAN* #294 ▶**

**November 1987**
**Artist:** Mike Zeck

Kraven the Hunter looks his insane best on this cover for "Kraven's Last Hunt," regarded as one of Spider-Man's key stories. Artist Mike Zeck depicts the crazed state Kraven was in. His desire to prove himself superior to Spider-Man reached its shocking conclusion in this penultimate chapter.

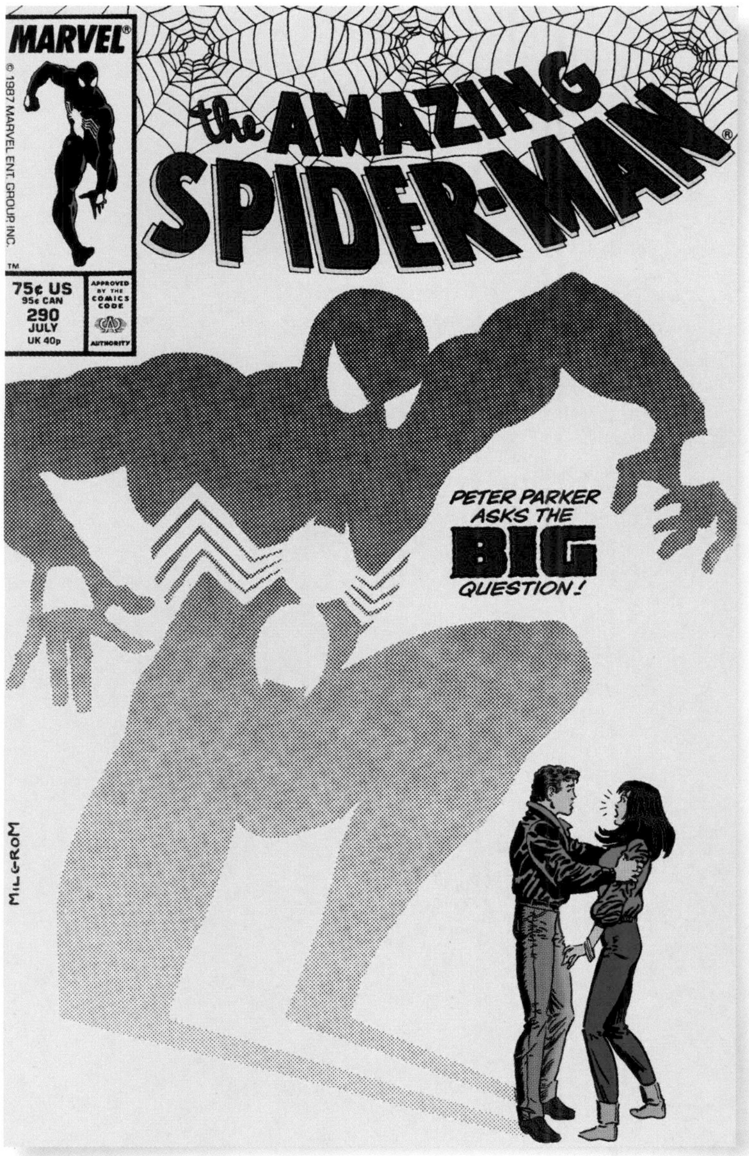
MARVEL
the AMAZING SPIDER-MAN
75¢ US
290
JULY
PETER PARKER ASKS THE BIG QUESTION!
MILGROM

**◀ *AMAZING SPIDER-MAN* #290**

**July 1987**
**Artist:** Al Milgrom

Al Milgrom's cover made pretty clear the big question Peter was going to ask inside. The use of white was perfect for focusing the attention on Peter and Mary Jane, reflecting the way a marriage proposal could make the rest of the world fade into insignificance. However, the shadow of Spidey looming over Peter and his bride-to-be adds a sinister edge to the piece.

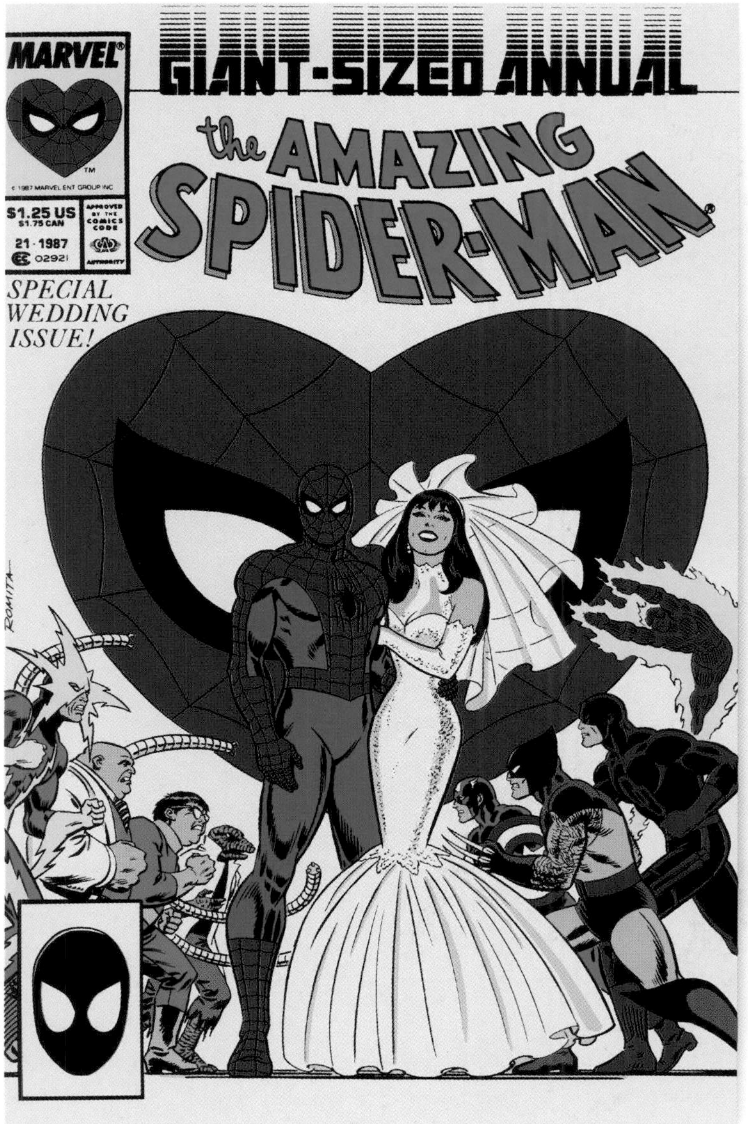
MARVEL
GIANT-SIZED ANNUAL
the AMAZING SPIDER-MAN
$1.25 US
21 · 1987
SPECIAL WEDDING ISSUE!

**◀ *AMAZING SPIDER-MAN ANNUAL* #21**

**1987**
**Artist:** John Romita Sr.

It was the wedding of the year—Peter Parker and Mary Jane—and Marvel put their top artist, John Romita Sr., on art duty for the cover. Central to the image is the happy couple, but with Spidey's foes facing off against his allies in the background, it looked like the wedding might not go according to plan.

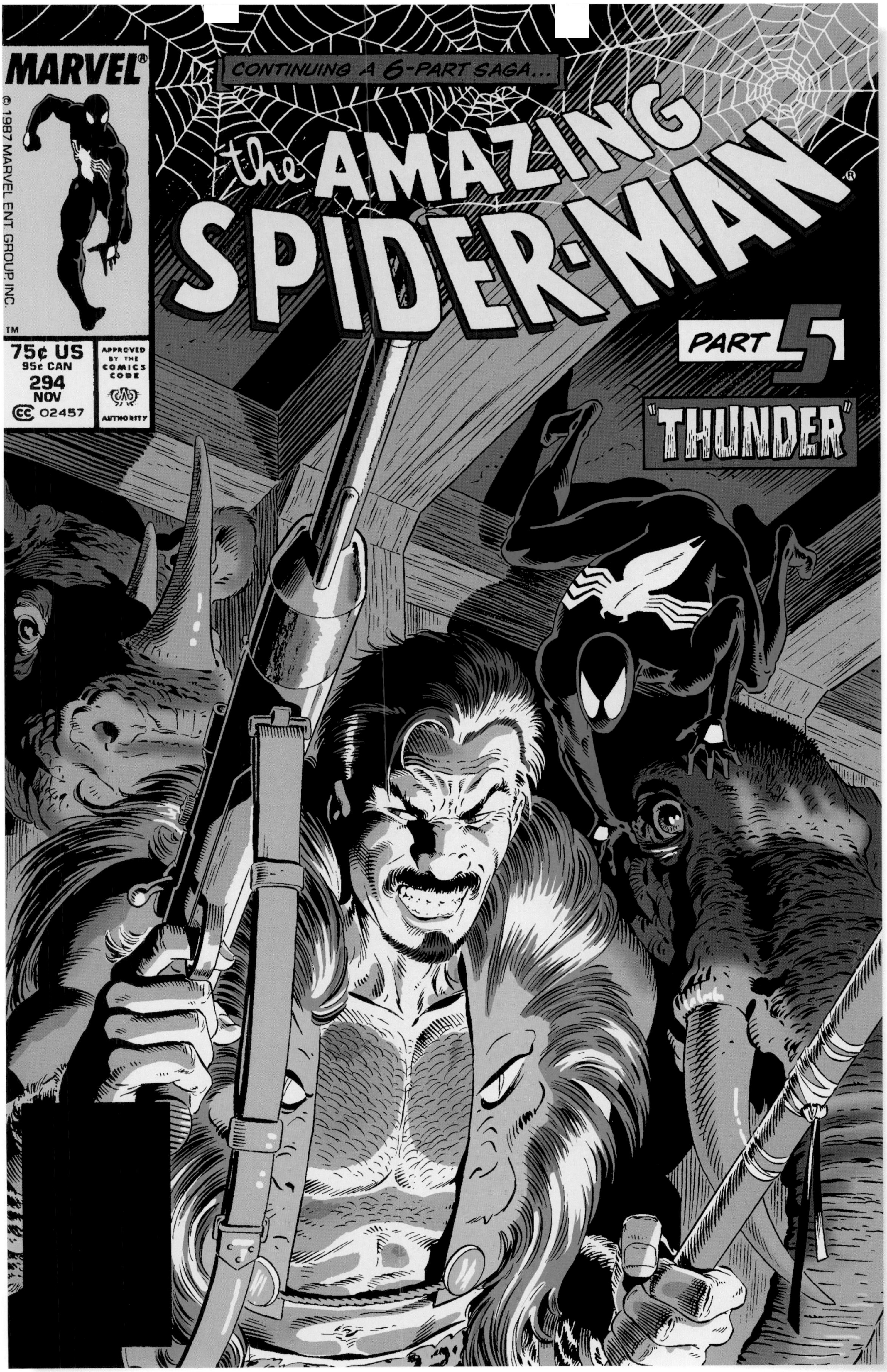
MARVEL®
© 1987 MARVEL ENT. GROUP, INC.
TM
75¢ US
95¢ CAN
294
NOV
CC 02457
APPROVED BY THE COMICS CODE AUTHORITY
CONTINUING A 6-PART SAGA...
the AMAZING SPIDER-MAN®
PART 5
"THUNDER"

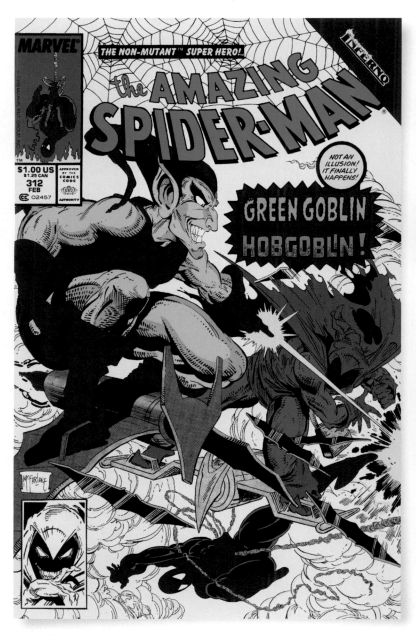

MARVEL
THE NON-MUTANT™ SUPER HERO!
INFERNO
the AMAZING SPIDER-MAN
NOT AN ILLUSION! IT FINALLY HAPPENS!
GREEN GOBLIN
HOBGOBLIN!
$1.00 US
$1.25 CAN
312
FEB
APPROVED BY THE COMICS CODE AUTHORITY

▲ ***AMAZING SPIDER-MAN* #312**

**February 1989**
**Artist:** Todd McFarlane

This Todd McFarlane cover features the Hobgoblin and the Green Goblin slugging it out with the webslinger caught in the middle. McFarlane's style makes the Green Goblin look crazier and more nightmarish than ever, while giving the fight scene a feeling of chaotic danger.

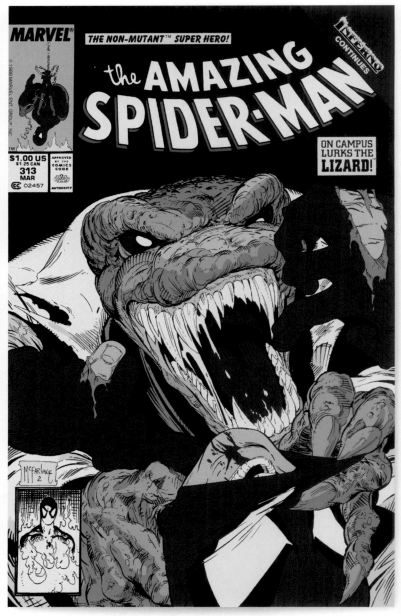

MARVEL
THE NON-MUTANT™ SUPER HERO!
INFERNO CONTINUES
the AMAZING SPIDER-MAN
ON CAMPUS LURKS THE LIZARD!
$1.00 US
$1.25 CAN
313
MAR
APPROVED BY THE COMICS CODE AUTHORITY

▲ ***AMAZING SPIDER-MAN* #313**

**March 1989**
**Artist:** Todd McFarlane

Todd McFarlane used his highly detailed technique to bring the Lizard to life on this cover. The close-up of the Lizard with its razor-sharp teeth, holding a seemingly beaten Spider-Man in his claws, creates a real sense of danger.

***SPIDER-MAN* #1** ▶

**August 1990**
**Artist:** Todd McFarlane

Following his huge success on *Amazing Spider-Man*, Marvel created a new Spidey title for Todd McFarlane to write and illustrate. McFarlane's debut cover illustration really adds the "spider" to Spider-Man, placing the hero in spider-like poses and adding intricate webbing detail. It became one of the most memorable modern-day images of Spider-Man and one of the biggest-selling Marvel comics of the decade.

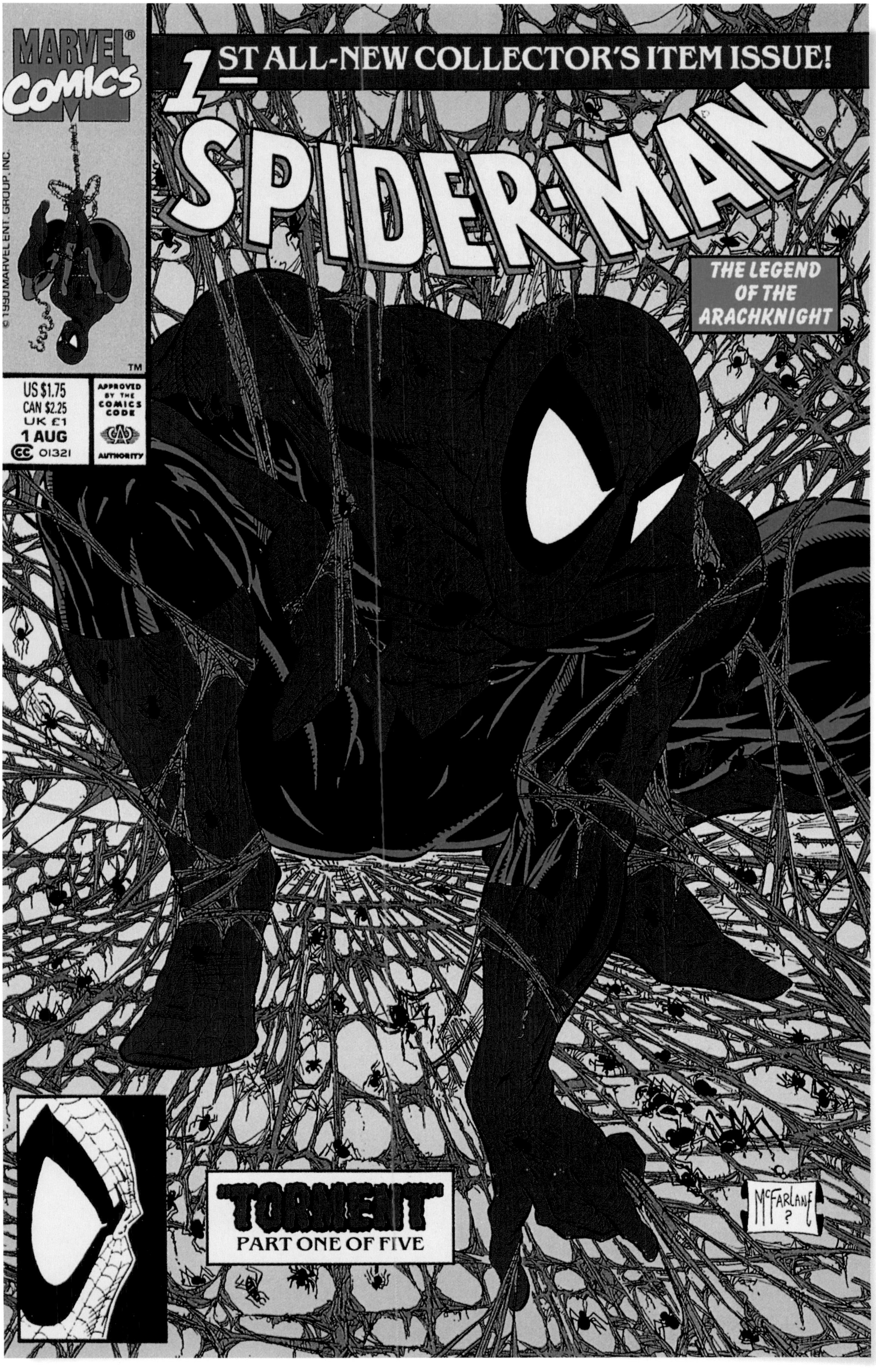
MARVEL COMICS
1ST ALL-NEW COLLECTOR'S ITEM ISSUE!
SPIDER-MAN
THE LEGEND OF THE ARACHKNIGHT
© 1990 MARVEL ENT. GROUP, INC.
US $1.75 CAN $2.25 UK £1
1 AUG
01321
APPROVED BY THE COMICS CODE AUTHORITY
"TORMENT"
PART ONE OF FIVE
McFARLANE

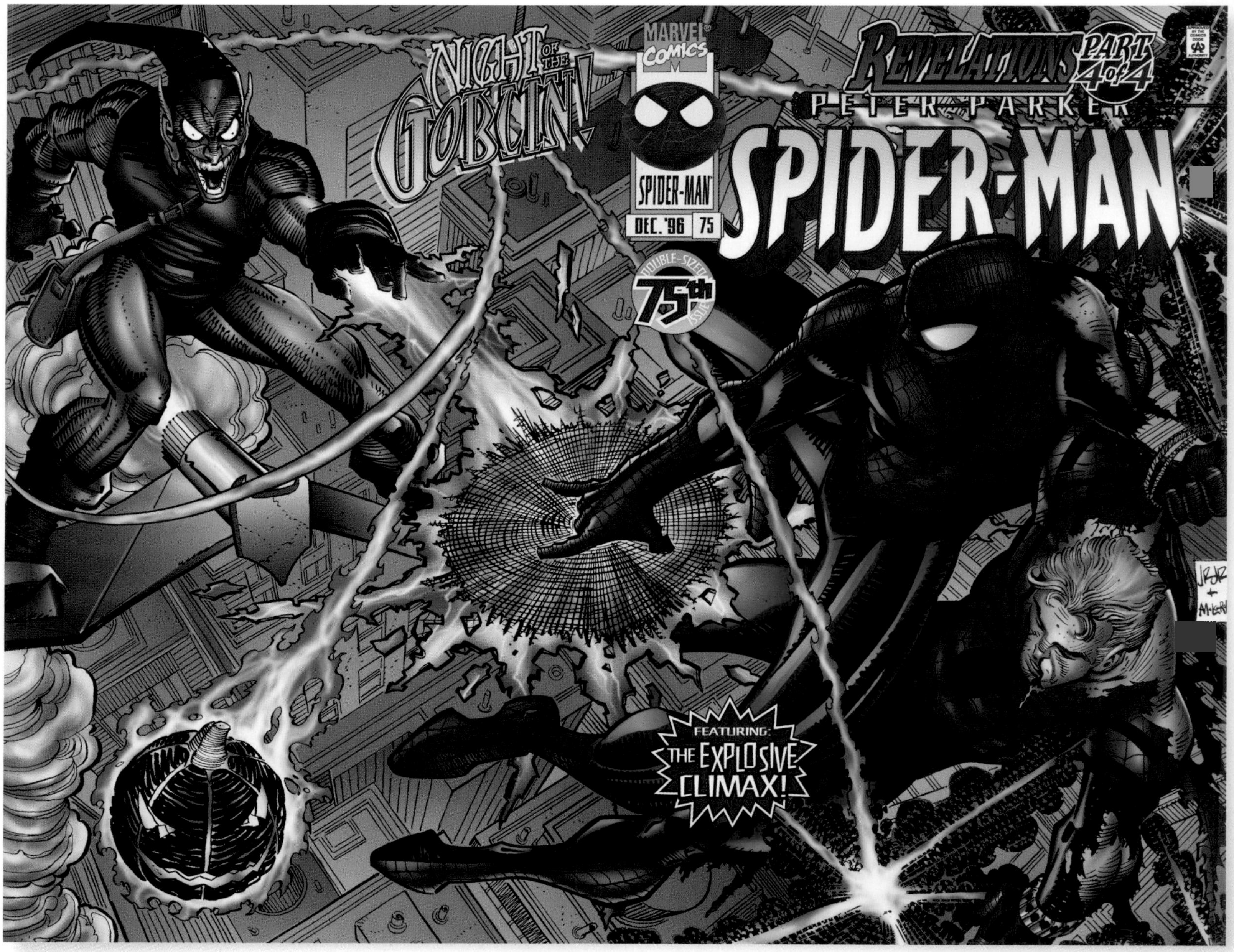
NIGHT OF THE GOBLIN!
MARVEL COMICS
SPIDER-MAN
DEC. '96 75
REVELATIONS PART 4 of 4
PETER PARKER
SPIDER-MAN
DOUBLE-SIZED 75th ISSUE
FEATURING:
THE EXPLOSIVE CLIMAX!

▲ *PETER PARKER: SPIDER-MAN* #75

**December 1996**
**Artist:** John Romita Jr.

The "Clone Saga," one of the most controversial Spider-Man epics of all time, came to a shocking conclusion in this issue, with John Romita Jr. producing an action-packed wraparound cover. Fans had been split when Ben Reilly (Peter Parker's clone) had become Spider-Man, but this issue saw the old order restored. The cover revealed some of the dramatic changes within, as Peter Parker returned as Spider-Man to face the original Green Goblin—a villain he had thought was long dead.

*AMAZING SPIDER-MAN* #30 ▶

**June 2001**
**Artist:** J. Scott Campbell

J. Scott Campbell's striking image heralded the start of a bold new era for *Amazing Spider-Man* as shocking secrets of Spidey's origin were revealed. Writer J. Michael Straczynski and artist John Romita Jr. took over the title, with Campbell creating a number of stylish covers. As the hero learned that his powers were linked to an ancient spider-god, Campbell's artwork put the "spider" back into Spider-Man.

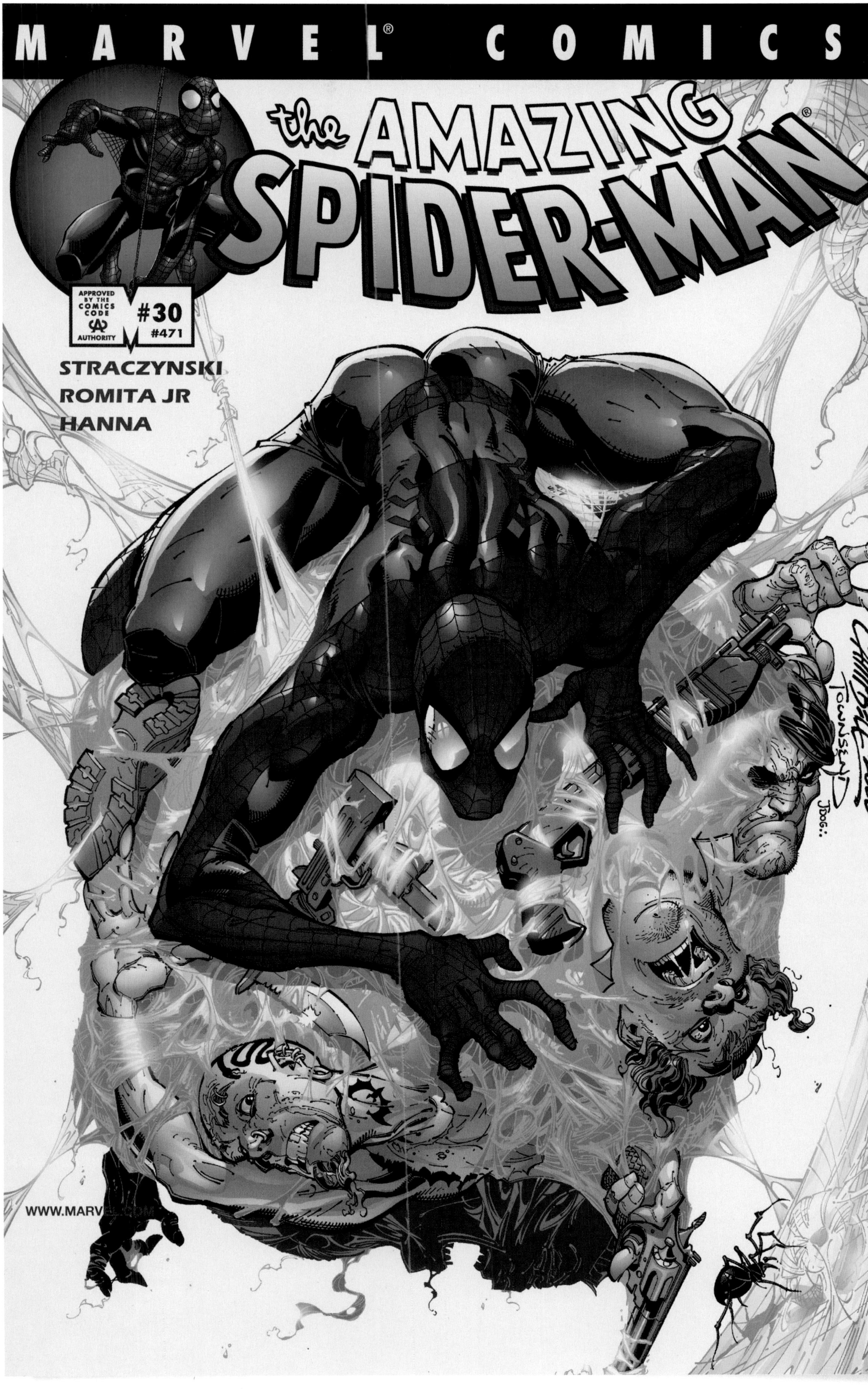
MARVEL® COMICS
the AMAZING SPIDER-MAN®
APPROVED BY THE COMICS CODE AUTHORITY
#30
#471
STRACZYNSKI
ROMITA JR
HANNA
WWW.MARVEL.COM

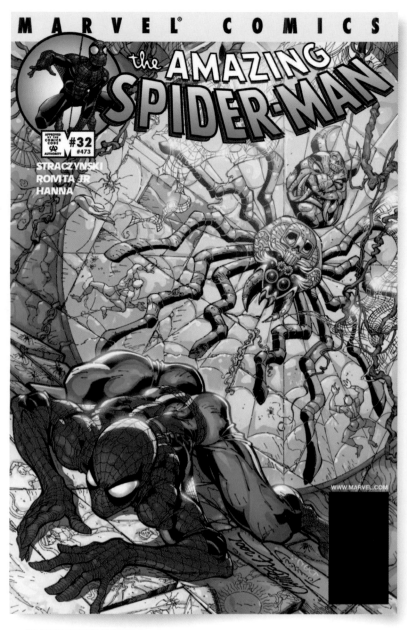

MARVEL COMICS
the AMAZING SPIDER-MAN
#32
#473
STRACZYNSKI
ROMITA JR
HANNA
WWW.MARVEL.COM

▲ *AMAZING SPIDER-MAN* #32

**August 2001**
**Artist:** J. Scott Campbell

J. Scott Campbell continued his run as cover artist on *Amazing Spider-Man* with another stunning piece. Campbell's cover hinted at the new, totemistic aspects of Spidey's origins that writer J. Michael Straczynski and artist John Romita Jr. were bringing to the title as they redefined Spidey's world.

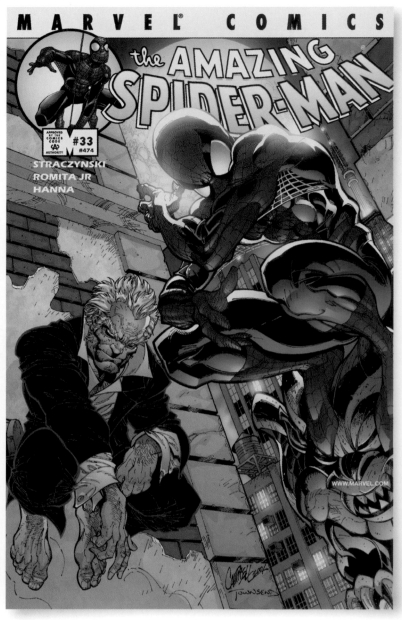

MARVEL COMICS
the AMAZING SPIDER-MAN
#33
#474
STRACZYNSKI
ROMITA JR
HANNA
WWW.MARVEL.COM

▲ *AMAZING SPIDER-MAN* #33

**September 2001**
**Artist:** J. Scott Campbell

Ezekiel, the man who had changed Spidey's life by telling him of his links to an ancient arachnid deity, appeared beside him on this cover. Campbell's depiction of Ezekiel looking like another, older "spider-man" was a sign that things were changing as one of the most original runs in the title's history continued.

*AMAZING SPIDER-MAN* #500 ▶

**December 2003**
**Artist:** J. Scott Campbell

*Amazing Spider-Man* went back to its original numbering for the 500th issue, with Campbell creating a truly dynamic cover featuring Spidey's most iconic enemies. The artist had burst onto the comic scene with his work for WildStorm, but his *Amazing Spider-Man* covers remain some of his best-known work. For this issue, he got to convey all the classic chaos and action that had made Spidey so popular.

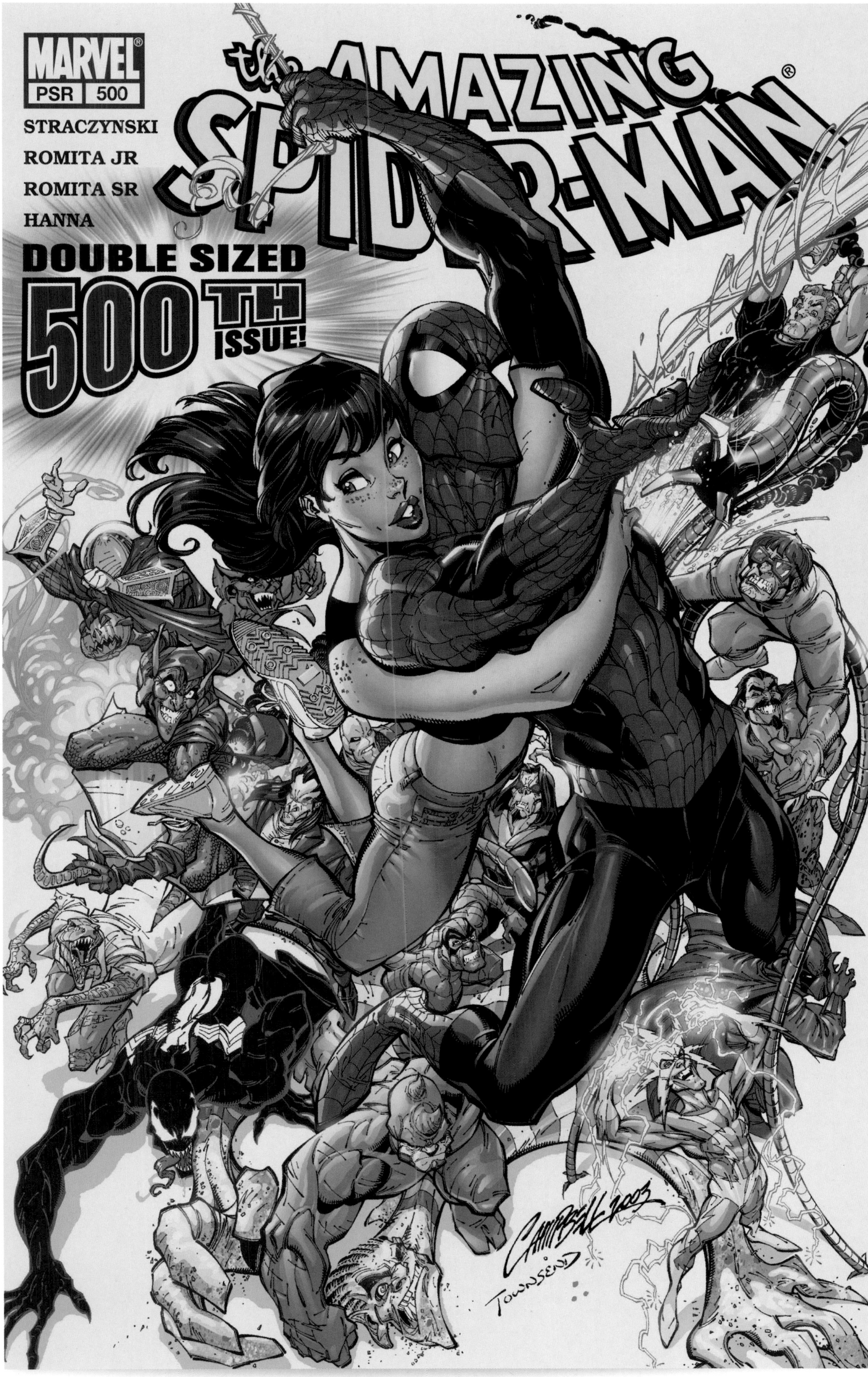
MARVEL
PSR 500
the AMAZING SPIDER-MAN
STRACZYNSKI
ROMITA JR
ROMITA SR
HANNA
DOUBLE SIZED
500 TH ISSUE!
CAMPBELL 2003
TOWNSEND

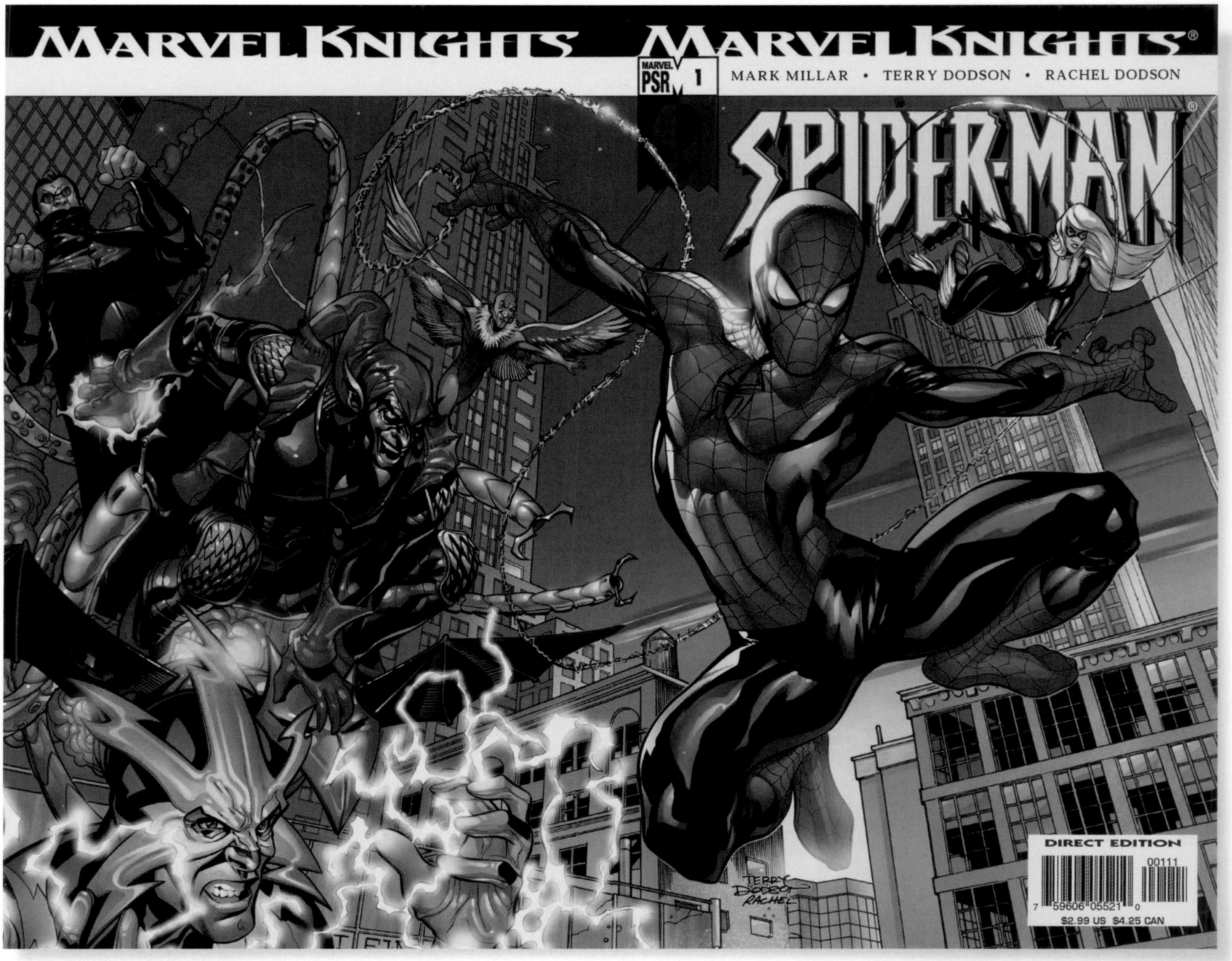
MARVEL KNIGHTS
MARVEL KNIGHTS
MARVEL PSR 1
MARK MILLAR • TERRY DODSON • RACHEL DODSON
SPIDER-MAN
DIRECT EDITION
$2.99 US $4.25 CAN

▲ ***MARVEL KNIGHTS SPIDER-MAN* #1**

**June 2004**
**Artist:** Terry Dodson

With the stellar creative team of writer Mark Millar and artist Terry Dodson at the helm, the launch of *Marvel Knights Spider-Man* was bound to be something special. Terry Dodson produced a wraparound cover for the first issue, featuring Spidey and the Black Cat on the front with four deadly foes pursuing them on the rear of the cover. Dodson gave Spidey's enemies a spectacular menacing edge.

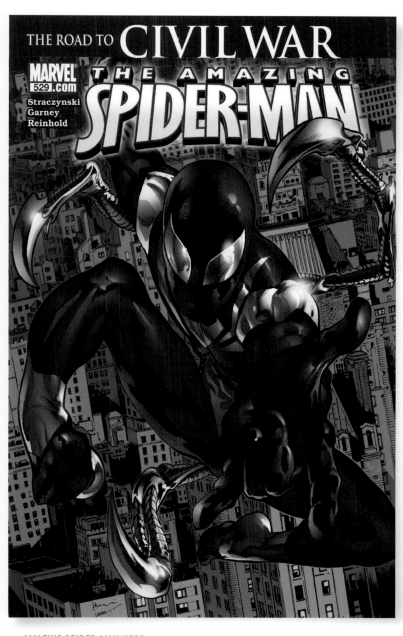

THE ROAD TO CIVIL WAR
MARVEL
529 .com
THE AMAZING
SPIDER-MAN
Straczynski
Garney
Reinhold

▲ ***AMAZING SPIDER-MAN* #529**

**April 2006**
**Artist:** Bryan Hitch

Spider-Man graced the cover of this issue in a shiny, new armored costume. Created fcr Spidey by Tony Stark, the suit would come to be known as the Iron Spider costume. Meanwhile, the strapline at the top also brings a sense of foreboding as the Civil War—when Super Hero would fight Super Hero—drew ever closer...

MARVEL
539 .com
STRACZYNSKI • GARNEY
THE AMAZING
SPIDER-MAN
BACK IN BLACK

▲ ***AMAZING SPIDER-MAN* #539**

**April 2007**
**Artist:** Ron Garney

Following the events of the Civil War, the world knew that Peter Parker was Spider-Man. Aunt May had also been shot, as Kingpin sought revenge on anyone who knew Spider-Man. Garney's cover image captures the webslinger's dark and vengeful mood perfectly.

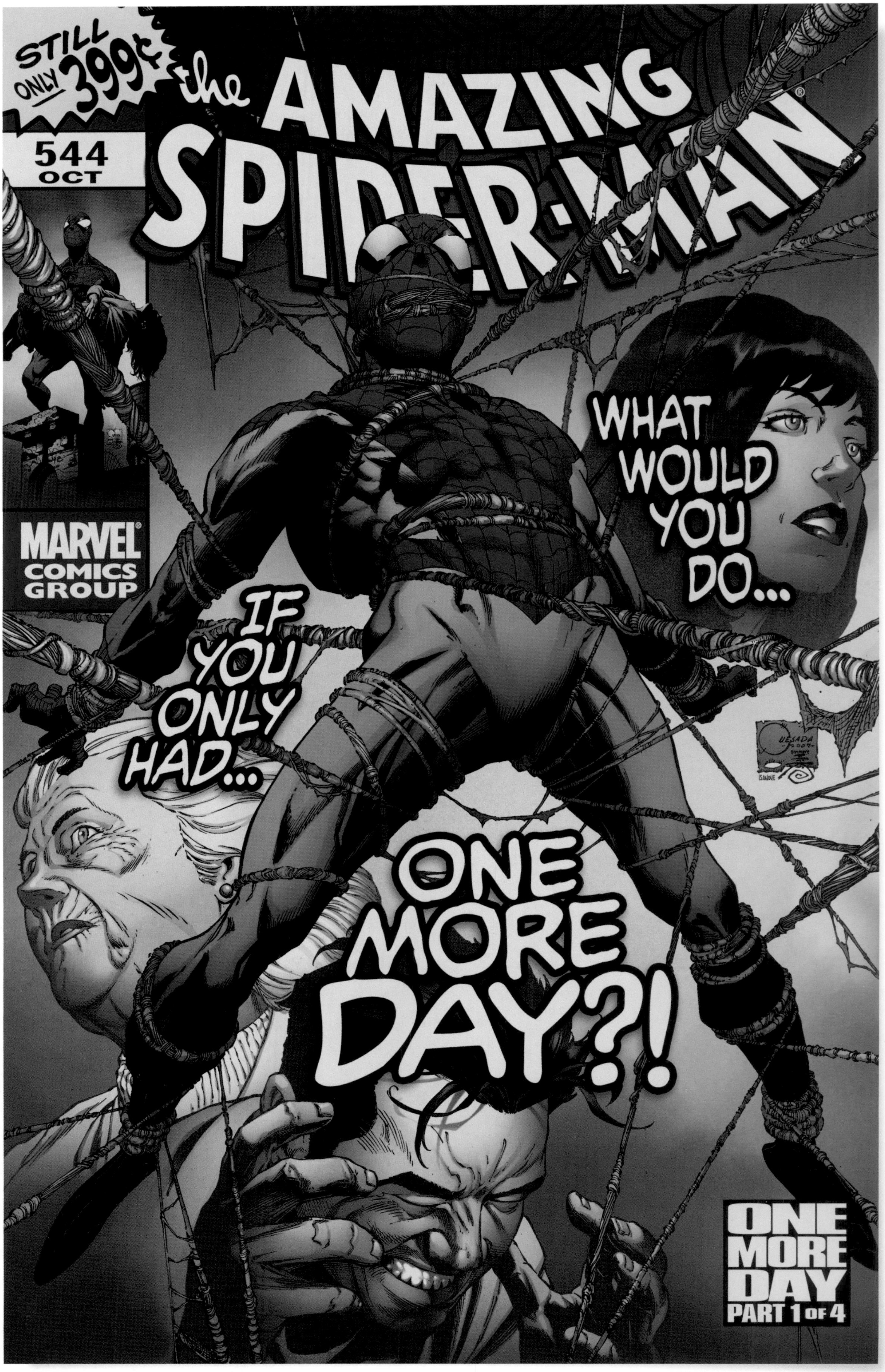
STILL ONLY 399¢
the AMAZING SPIDER-MAN
544 OCT
MARVEL COMICS GROUP
WHAT WOULD YOU DO...
IF YOU ONLY HAD...
ONE MORE DAY?!
ONE MORE DAY PART 1 OF 4

### *AMAZING SPIDER-MAN* #560 ▶

**July 2008**
**Artist:** Marcos Martin

The experimentation with cover design continued with a fun layout by Marcos Martin. The background image has strong echoes of pop artist Roy Lichtenstein's work, and revealed a new villain: Piper Dali, a.k.a. Paper Doll. This mutant villain possessed the novel ability to make her body as thin as paper.

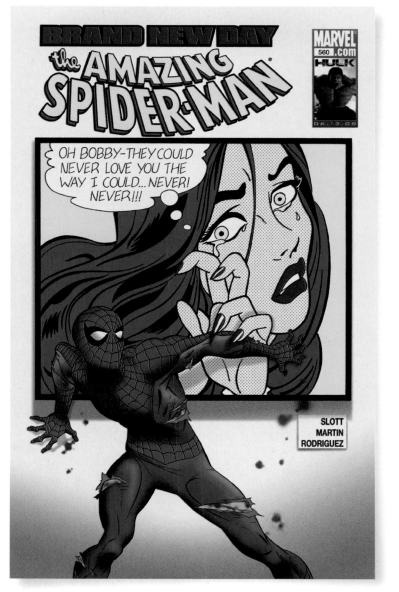

BRAND NEW DAY
the AMAZING SPIDER-MAN
MARVEL 560 .com
HULK
06.13.08
OH BOBBY-THEY COULD NEVER LOVE YOU THE WAY I COULD... NEVER! NEVER!!!
SLOTT
MARTIN
RODRIGUEZ

### *AMAZING SPIDER-MAN* #561 ▶

**August 2008**
**Artist:** Marcos Martin

Paper Doll's eyes stare out at the reader from Marcos Martin's high-concept, collage-style cover, reflecting the villain's obsession with movie star Bobby Carr. The cover also hints at the idea of Mary Jane Watson (Bobby Carr's girlfriend in this story) being the Super Hero Jackpot, although this would later be revealed as a case of mistaken identity.

MARVEL 561 .com
SPIDER-MAN
SLOTT
KILLER
MARTIN
ARR:
ut again?
ARITIES!
RODRIGUEZ

### ◀ *AMAZING SPIDER-MAN* #544

**November 2007**
**Artist:** Joe Quesada

"One More Day" was one of the most shocking storylines in Marvel's history as Spider-Man's marriage to Mary Jane was wiped out of existence. Quesada's powerful cover shows Spidey trapped by his own webbing—and torn between his love for Mary Jane and Aunt May. Spidey faced the hardest decision—to save Aunt May's life, he had to sacrifice his marriage to Mary Jane in a deal with Mephisto.

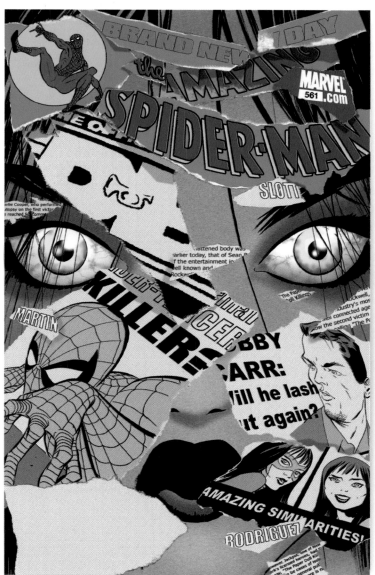

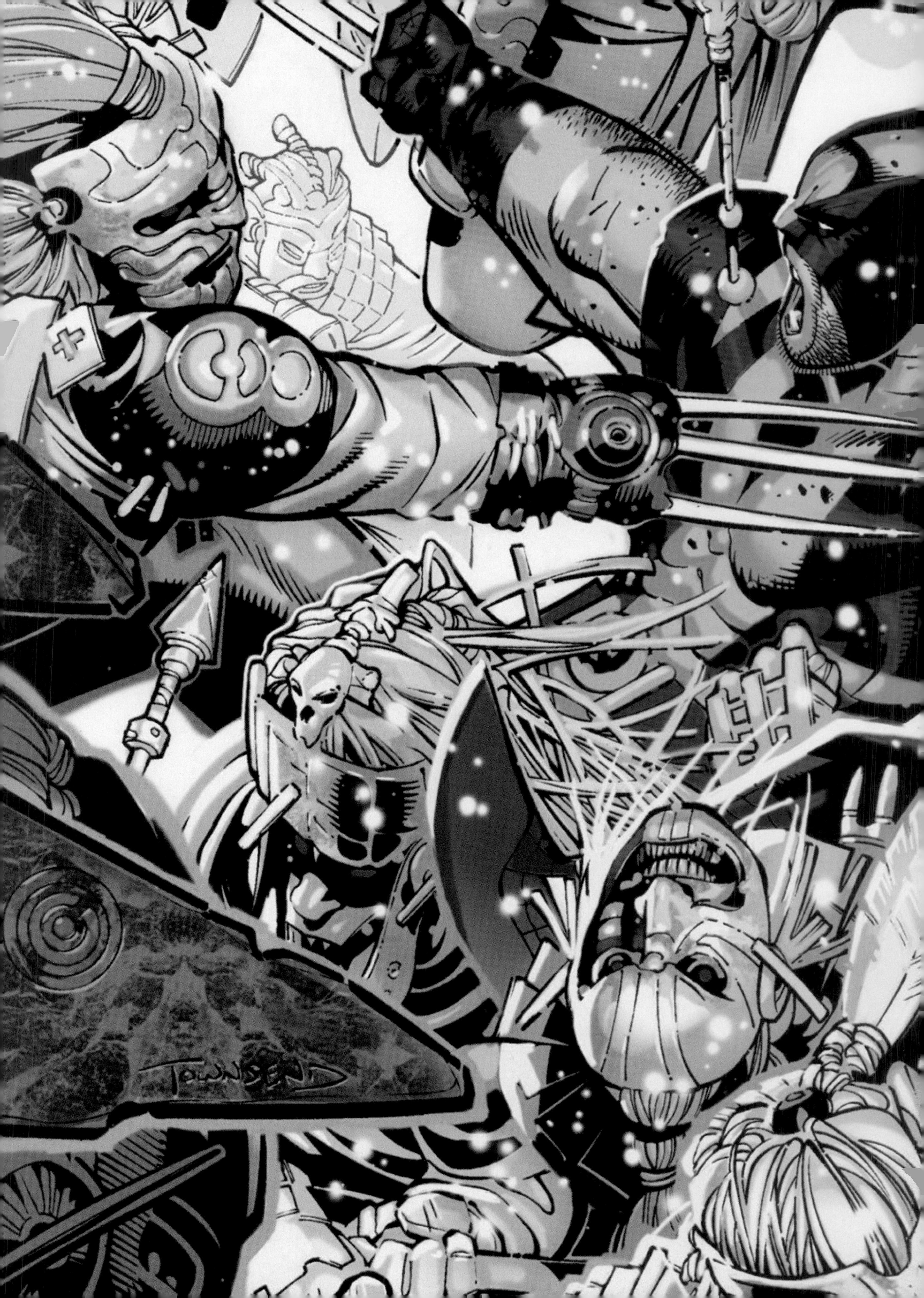
TOWNSEND

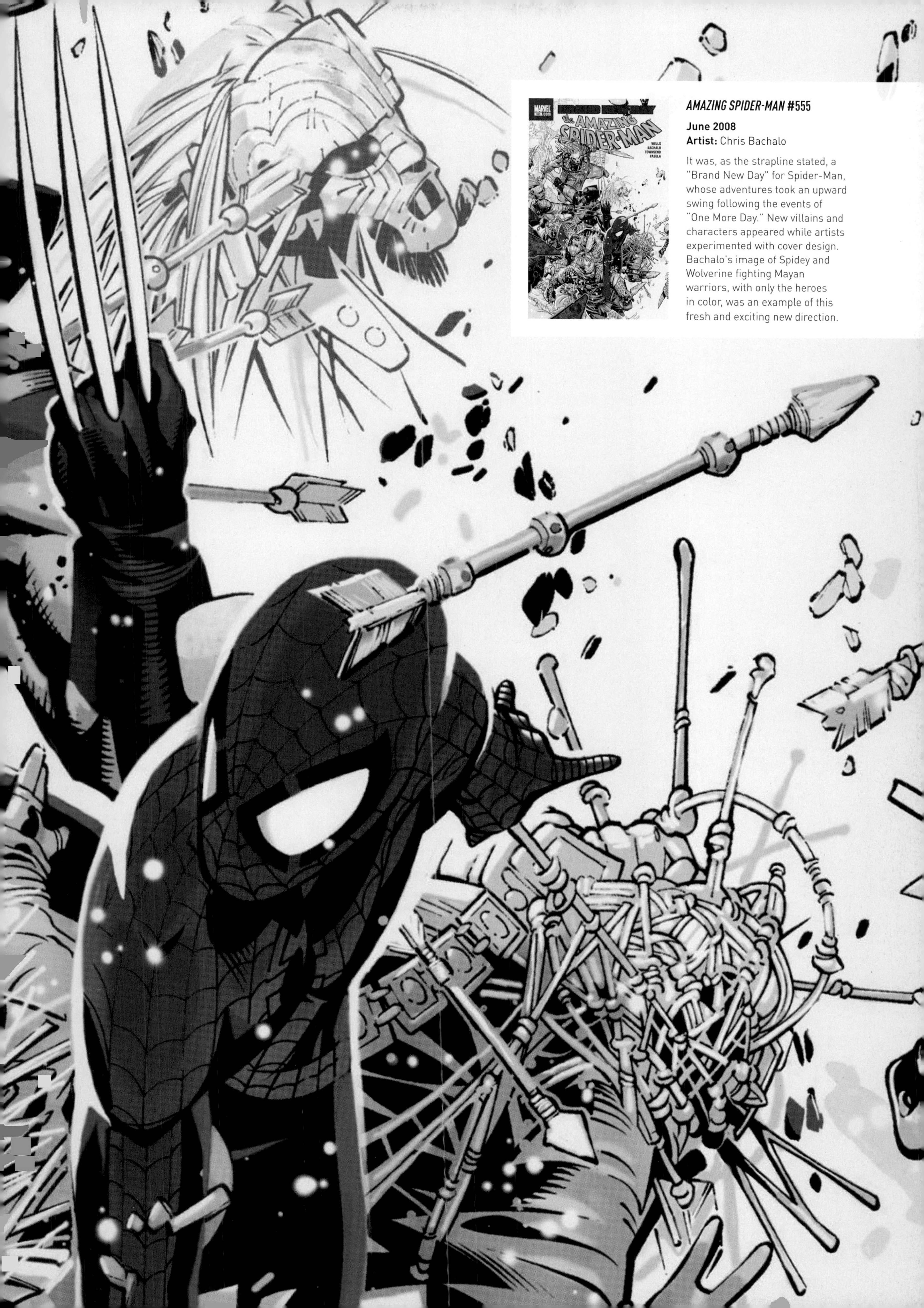

***AMAZING SPIDER-MAN* #555**

**June 2008**
**Artist:** Chris Bachalo

It was, as the strapline stated, a "Brand New Day" for Spider-Man, whose adventures took an upward swing following the events of "One More Day." New villains and characters appeared while artists experimented with cover design. Bachalo's image of Spidey and Wolverine fighting Mayan warriors, with only the heroes in color, was an example of this fresh and exciting new direction.

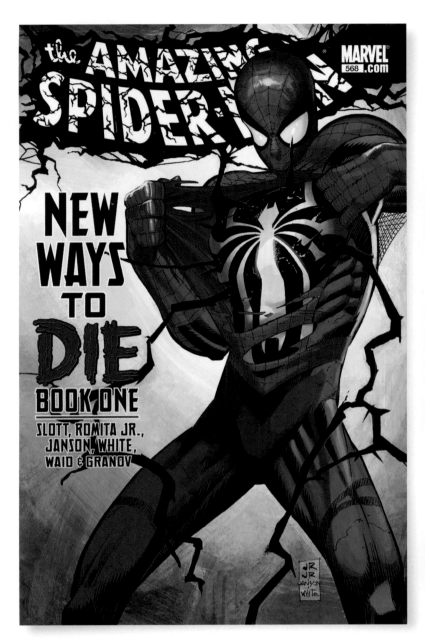

the AMAZING SPIDER-MAN
MARVEL
568 .com
NEW WAYS TO DIE
BOOK ONE
SLOTT, ROMITA JR., JANSON, WHITE, WAID & GRANOV

▲ ***AMAZING SPIDER-MAN* #568**

**October 2008**
**Artist:** John Romita Jr.

"The Brand New Day" era of Spider-Man saw Marvel experimenting with cover design, often employing interesting styles of typography, too. This cover, with "New Ways to Die" a prominent part of the artwork, reflected that trend. The dramatic image of Spidey revealing a Venom costume under his own clothes plays on a classic Super-Hero image, while the alien tendrils attacking the logo highlights the danger Venom represents.

MARVEL
575 .com
ULTIMATUM
11.2008
the AMAZING SPIDER-MAN
KELLY
BACHALO
TOWNSEND
MENDOZA

▲ ***AMAZING SPIDER-MAN* #575**

**December 2008**
**Artist:** Chris Bachalo

It was a great time for artistic experimentation on *Amazing Spider-Man,* as this striking cover demonstrated. Bachalo's close-up of Spidey being punched in the face by Hammerhead is a strong image, especially with Bachalo's own, stark coloring work. The image has an even greater impact when seen in conjunction with the cover of the following issue.

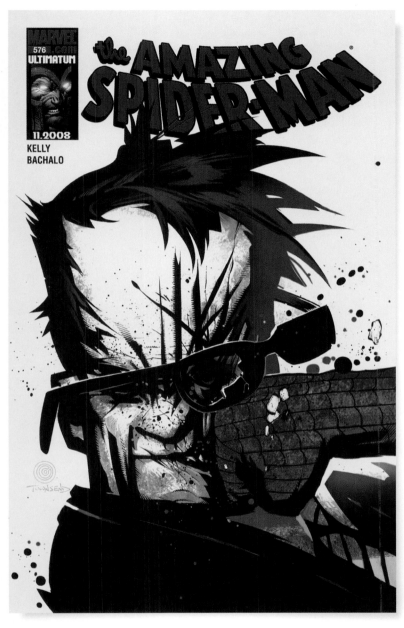

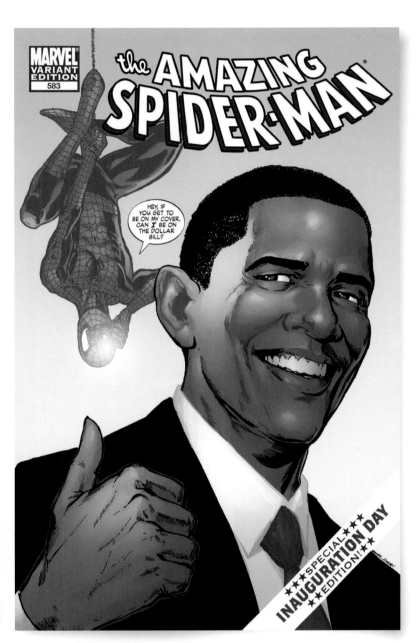

MARVEL .com
576
ULTIMATUM
the AMAZING SPIDER-MAN
11.2008
KELLY
BACHALO

▲ *AMAZING SPIDER-MAN* #576

**January 2009**
**Artist:** Chris Bachalo

The second part of the Hammerhead story had the webslinger's response to the previous issue's cover—Spidey punched Hammerhead right back! Over the coming months, other linking themes would appear on the covers, but this black, white, and red two-image punch-up was one of the most dramatic—and amusing.

MARVEL
VARIANT EDITION
583
the AMAZING SPIDER-MAN
HEY, IF YOU GET TO BE ON MY COVER, CAN I BE ON THE DOLLAR BILL?
★★★SPECIAL★★★
INAUGURATION DAY
★★EDITION!★★

▲ *AMAZING SPIDER-MAN* #583

**January 2009**
**Artist:** Phil Jimenez

Every now and again a cover comes along that sums up the mood of a particular moment in time. This "Inauguration Day" variant cover did just that. Phil Jimenez put US President Barack Obama (a self-confessed comic fan) on the front of *Amazing Spider-Man* to commemorate his inauguration. President Obama also guest-starred inside the issue as Marvel celebrated a key moment in US history.

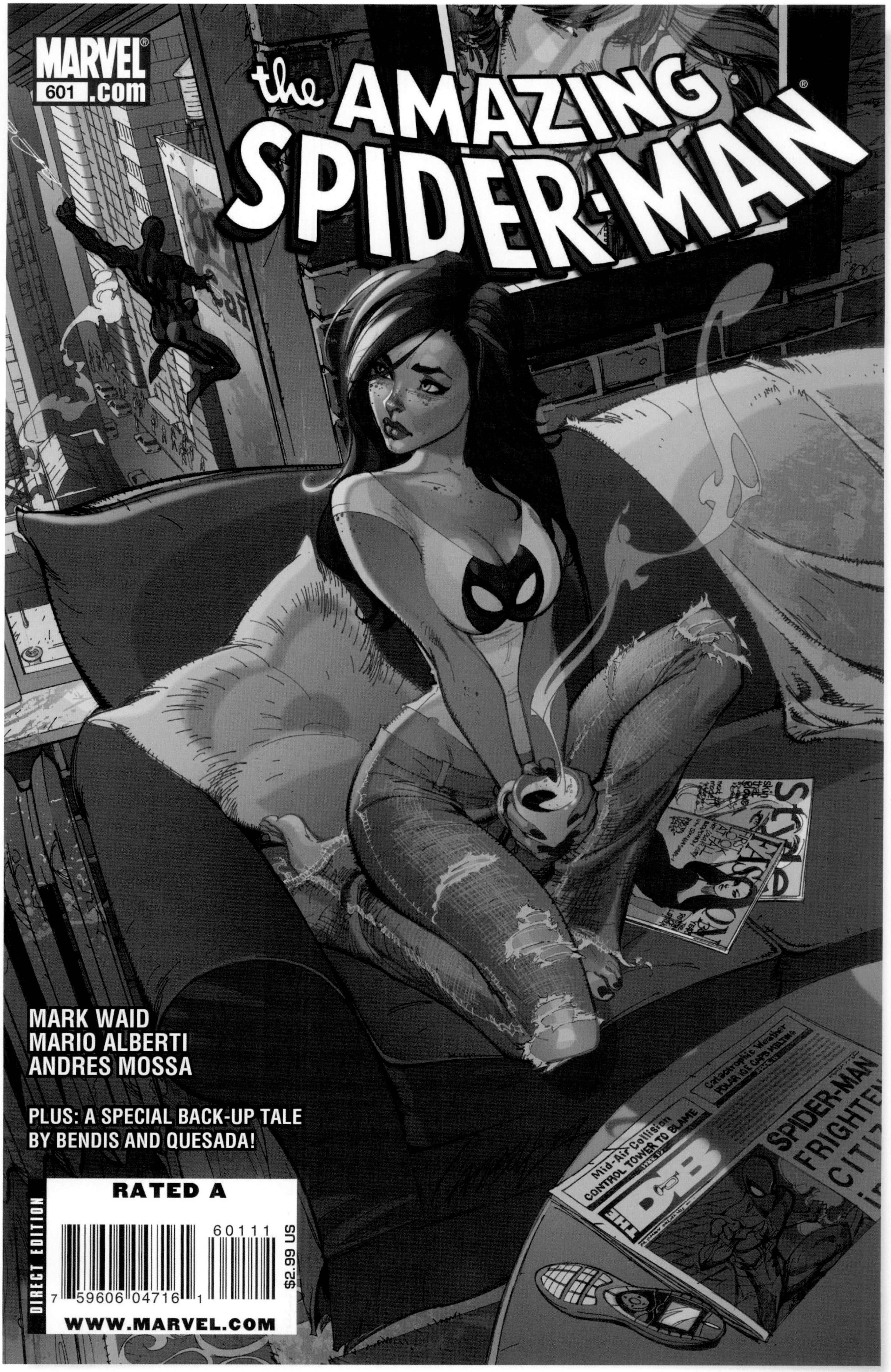
MARVEL
601 .com
the AMAZING SPIDER-MAN
MARK WAID
MARIO ALBERTI
ANDRES MOSSA
PLUS: A SPECIAL BACK-UP TALE
BY BENDIS AND QUESADA!
RATED A
DIRECT EDITION
$2.99 US
WWW.MARVEL.COM
Mid-Air Collision
CONTROL TOWER TO BLAME
SPIDER-MAN
FRIGHTEN

### ◀ *AMAZING SPIDER-MAN* #601

**October 2009**
**Artist:** J. Scott Campbell

J. Scott Campbell had always had a knack for drawing a great Mary Jane Watson, but this cover was something special. However, its appeal wasn't simply Campbell's winsomely pensive version of Spidey's ex. Readers were also thrilled by the inference that they were about to witness Peter and Mary Jane's first face-to-face meeting since "One More Day" had wiped their marriage from existence.

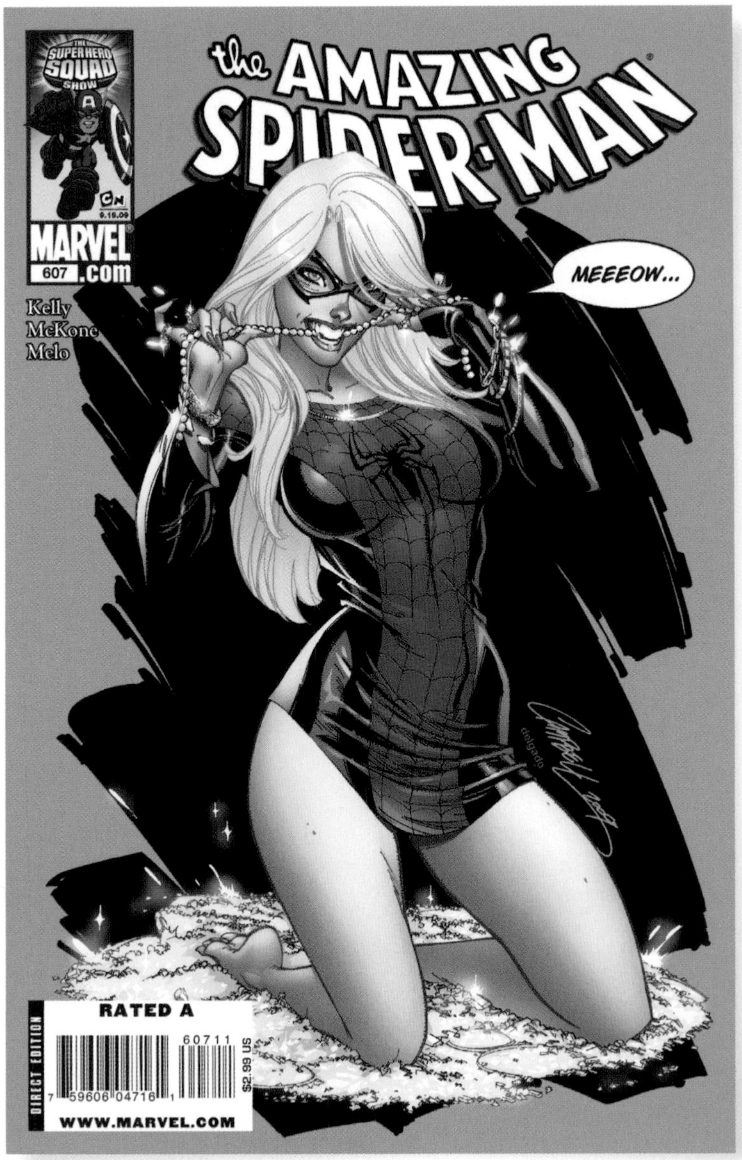
the AMAZING SPIDER-MAN
MARVEL
607 .com
Kelly
McKone
Melo
MEEEOW...
RATED A
DIRECT EDITION
WWW.MARVEL.COM

### *AMAZING SPIDER-MAN* #607 ▶

**November 2009**
**Artist:** J. Scott Campbell

Spidey and the Black Cat teamed up again this issue. Campbell's alluring cover hints that Felicia Hardy (the Black Cat) hadn't quite given up her criminal ways or her obsessional love of Spider-Man. It also suggests that the hero and Spidey might be a little more than friends in this issue...

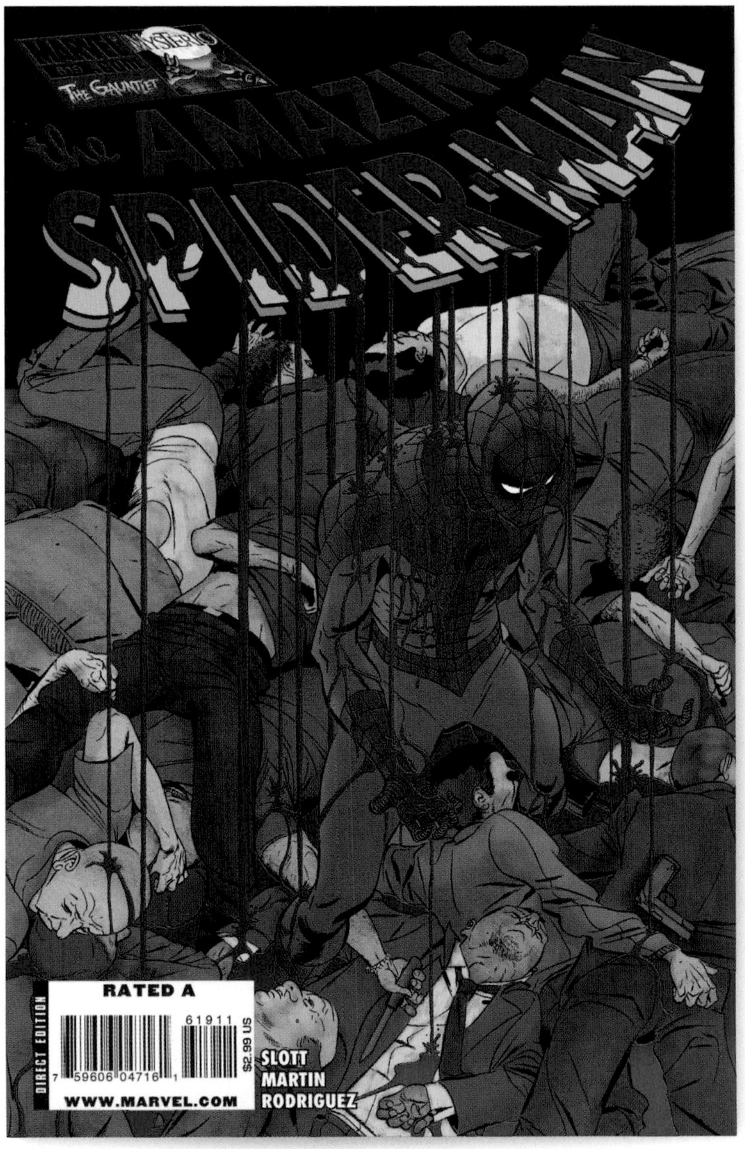
the AMAZING SPIDER-MAN
RATED A
DIRECT EDITION
WWW.MARVEL.COM
SLOTT
MARTIN
RODRIGUEZ

### *AMAZING SPIDER-MAN* #619 ▶

**March 2010**
**Artist:** Marcos Martin

Marcos Martin proved himself to be one of the most inventive artists in the business with this striking cover. As red ink dripped from the slanted logo, it seemed that Spidey's life was about to take a deadly turn. But the story inside involved master of illusion Mysterio, so, of course, nothing was as it seemed.

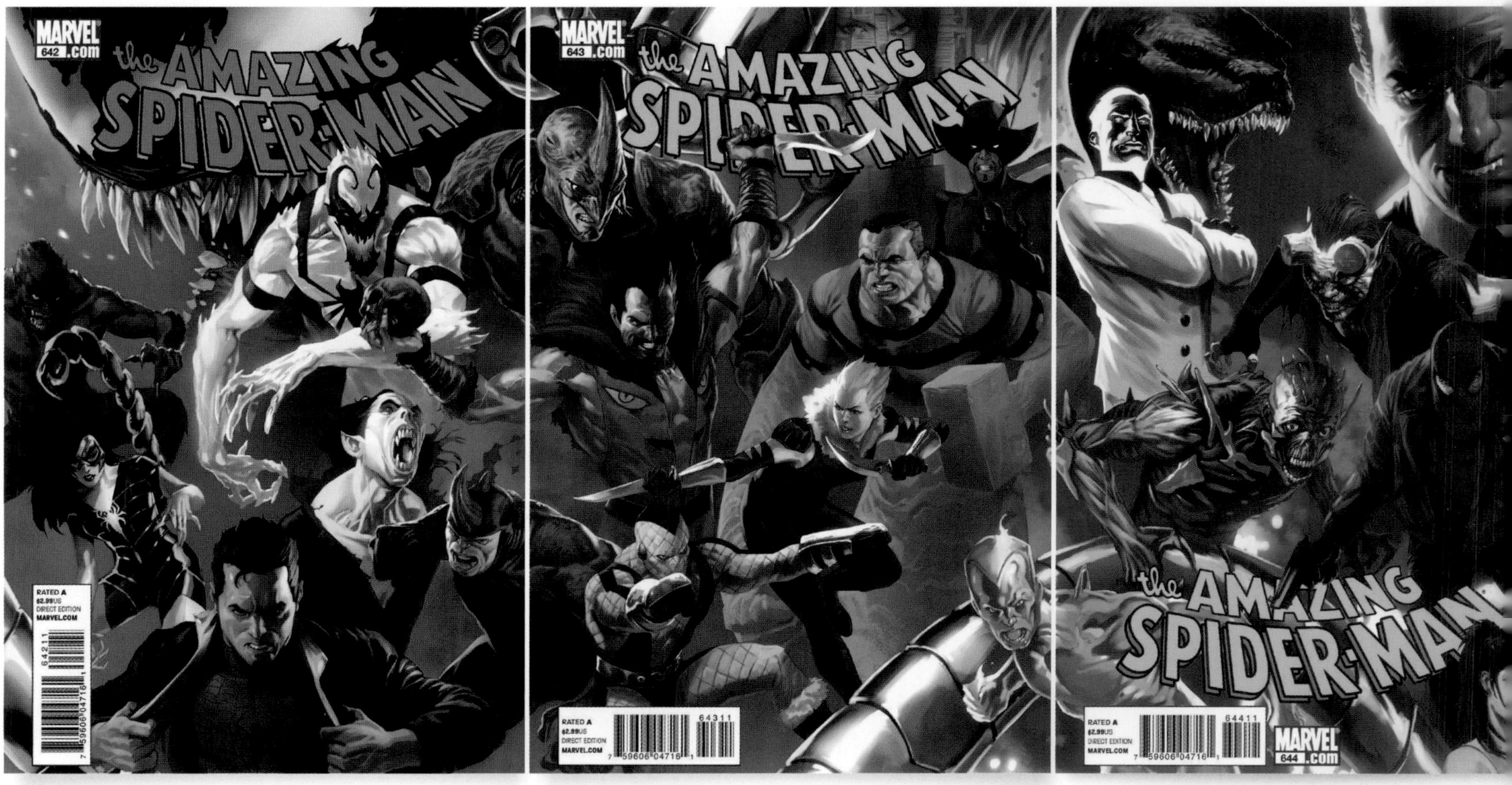
MARVEL
642 .com
the AMAZING SPIDER-MAN
MARVEL
643 .com
the AMAZING SPIDER-MAN
the AMAZING SPIDER-MAN
MARVEL
644 .com

▲ *AMAZING SPIDER-MAN #642–647*

**September–November 2010**
**Artist:** Marko Djurdjevic

The five-part "Origin of the Species" story saw Spider-Man and a host of villains trying to find a baby that Lily Hollister (aka Menace) had with Norman Osborn. There was a twist in the tale too, when Norman's son, Harry, was revealed as the baby's true father. This five-part series arc, and an epilogue to the end of Spidey's "Brand New Day" era, featured six interconnected covers by concept artist Marko Djurdjevic, showcasing the numerous villains appearing in the story. The covers were specially designed so they could be joined together to create one enormous, action-packed image.

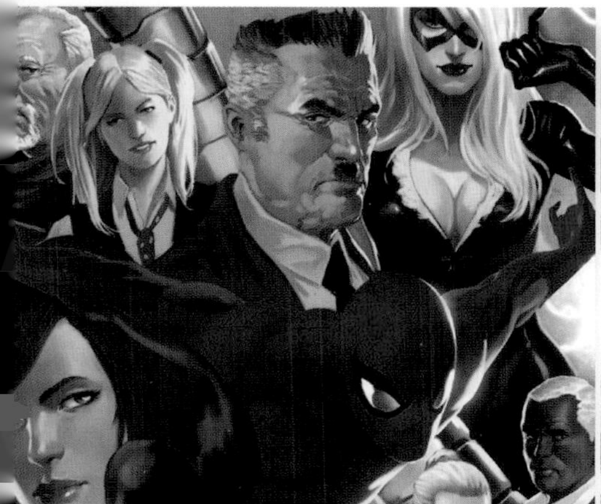
the AMAZING
SPIDER-MAN
MARVEL
645 .com
RATED A
$2.99US
DIRECT EDITION
MARVEL.COM

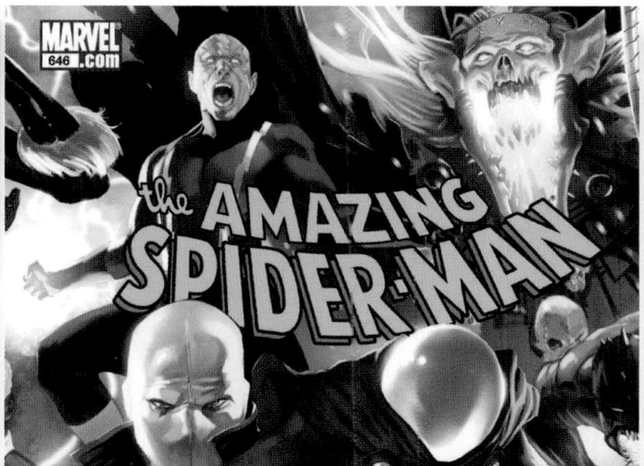
MARVEL
646 .com
the AMAZING
SPIDER-MAN
RATED A
$2.99US
DIRECT EDITION
MARVEL.COM

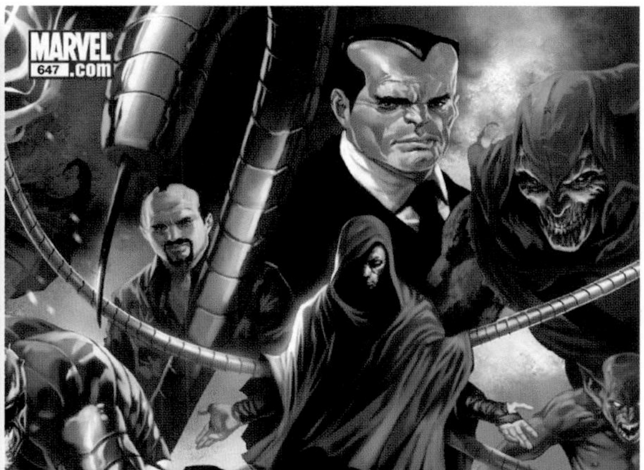
MARVEL
647 .com
the AMAZING
SPIDER-MAN
RATED A
$4.99US
DIRECT EDITION
MARVEL.COM

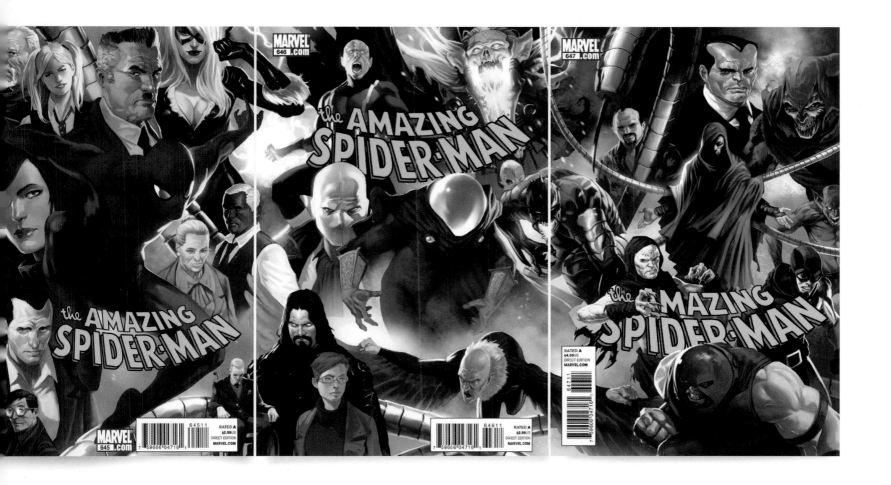

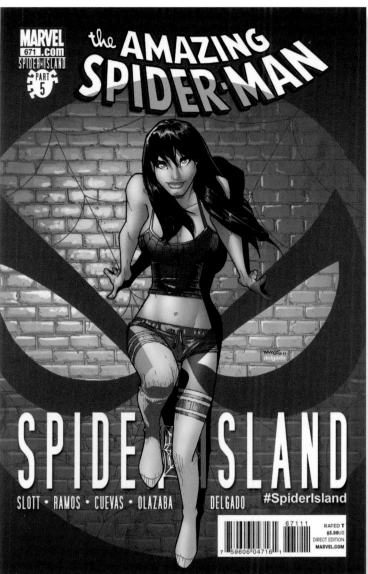

MARVEL
671 .com
SPIDER-ISLAND
PART 5
the AMAZING SPIDER-MAN
SPIDER-ISLAND
SLOTT • RAMOS • CUEVAS • OLAZABA • DELGADO
#SpiderIsland
RATED T
$3.99US
DIRECT EDITION
MARVEL.COM

**AMAZING SPIDER-MAN #700 ▶**

**February 2013**
**Artist:** Mr Garcin

Marvel used this fantastic collage from Mr Garcin (an artist who specializes in collages made from Marvel comics) for what, at the time, was going to be the last-ever issue of *Amazing Spider-Man*. Garcin's work was the perfect choice for the final issue, honoring the changing styles of the wall-crawling hero since his debut in 1963.

**◀ AMAZING SPIDER-MAN #671**

**December 2011**
**Artist:** Humberto Ramos

The "Spider-Island" epic crossover saw the entire population of Manhattan gain Spidey-like powers before transforming into giant spiders, thanks to the machinations of the Jackal and the Queen. This cover focuses on a new role for Mary Jane in the saga as she temporarily gained spider powers to rival those of Peter Parker.

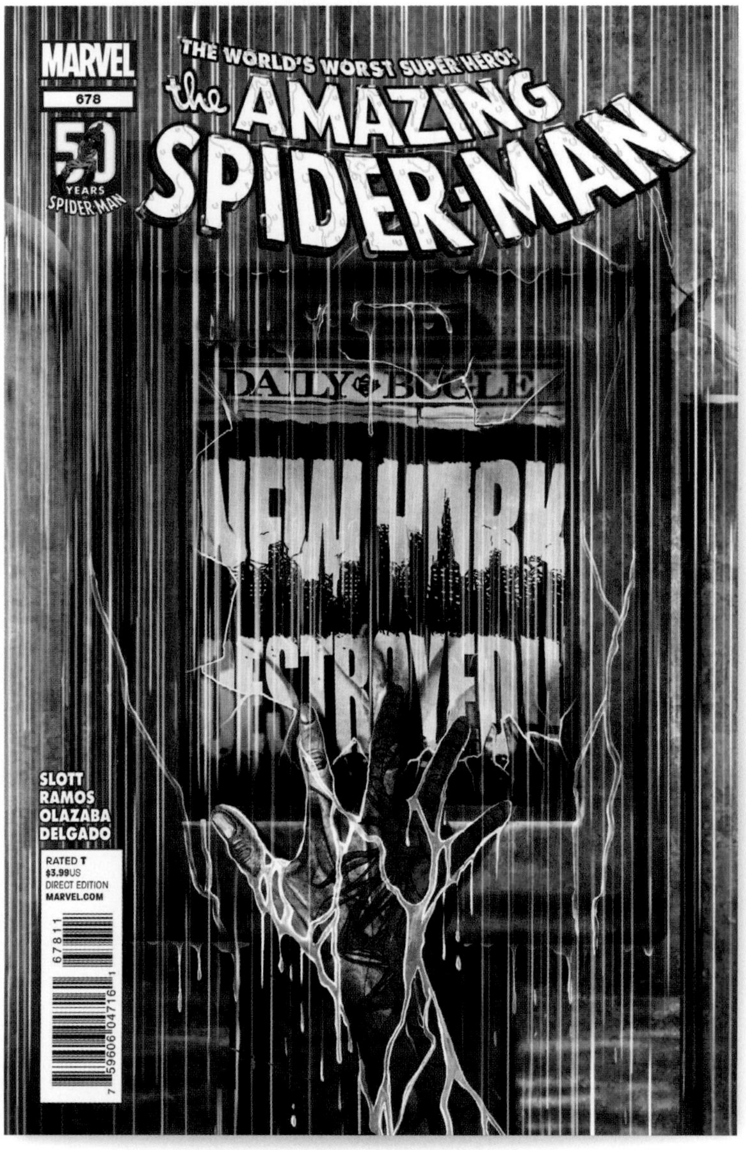

MARVEL
678
50 YEARS SPIDER-MAN
THE WORLD'S WORST SUPER HERO!
the AMAZING SPIDER-MAN
DAILY BUGLE
SLOTT
RAMOS
OLAZABA
DELGADO
RATED T
$3.99US
DIRECT EDITION
MARVEL.COM

**◀ AMAZING SPIDER-MAN #678**

**March 2012**
**Artist:** Mike Del Mundo

Mike Del Mundo's cover makes it clear that something bad happened, as Spidey's battered hand reaches toward a *Daily Bugle* bearing the headline "New York Destroyed" and a strapline altered to read "The World's Worst Super Hero." In the time-travel story inside, Spidey was convinced that something was going to destroy New York in the next 24 hours, unless he could stop it.

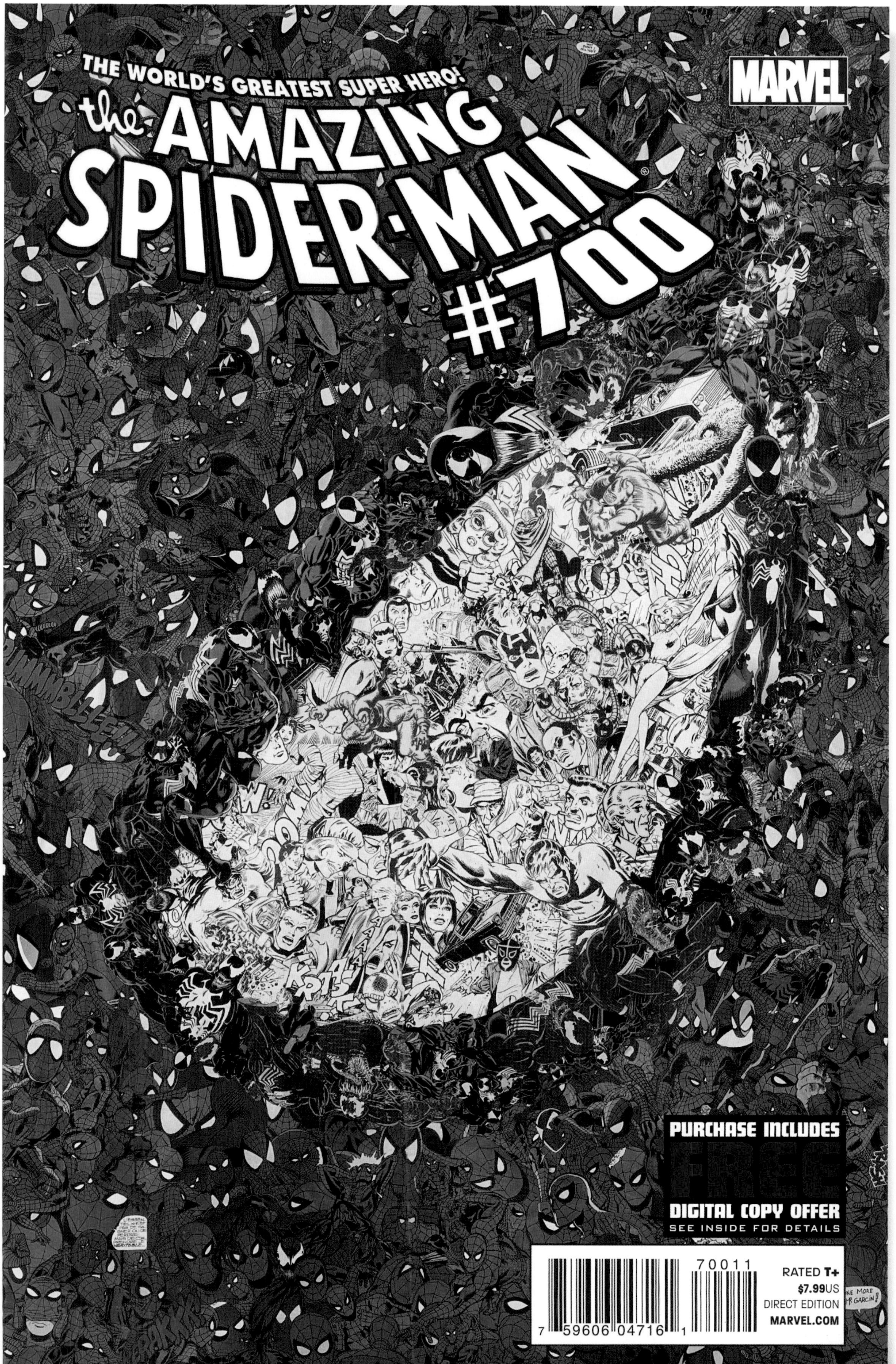
THE WORLD'S GREATEST SUPER HERO!
MARVEL
the AMAZING SPIDER-MAN
#700
PURCHASE INCLUDES
FREE
DIGITAL COPY OFFER
SEE INSIDE FOR DETAILS
RATED T+
$7.99US
DIRECT EDITION
MARVEL.COM

***AMAZING SPIDER-MAN* #1 ▶**

**June 2014**
**Artist:** Alex Ross

Marvel released a number of variant covers to celebrate Peter Parker's return as Spider-Man. Alex Ross painted this masterpiece as a variant for issue #1—it was one of several covers he created that also celebrated Marvel's 75th anniversary. Ross' image was a celebration of Peter Parker as Spider-Man and features all of the most important things in Peter's life.

THE SUPERIOR
SPIDER-MAN
No 1
MARVEL NOW!
DAN SLOTT • RYAN STEGMAN • EDGAR DELGADO
RATED T+
$3.99US
DIRECT EDITION
MARVEL.COM
JOIN THE REVOLUTION
PURCHASE INCLUDES FREE DIGITAL COPY OFFER
001

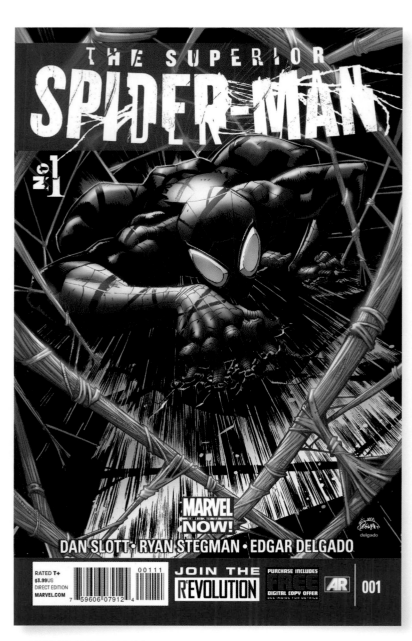

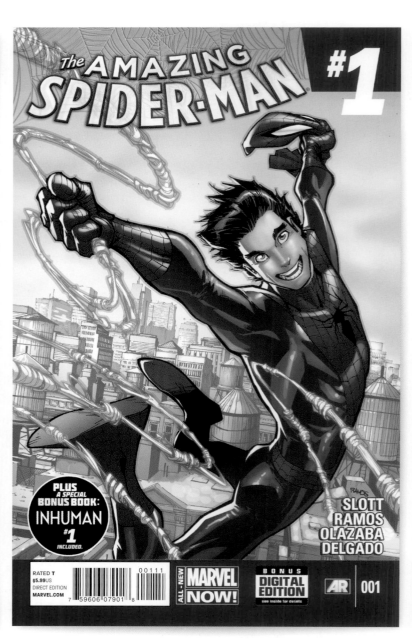

▲ ***SUPERIOR SPIDER-MAN* #1**

**March 2013**
**Artist:** Ryan Stegman

The old Peter Parker was dead—long live the new Peter Parker! With Doctor Octopus now masquerading as Peter, it was a time of great change for *Spider-Man* as *Superior* replaced *Amazing*. Ryan Stegman's cover showcases the new Doc Ock/Spidey as a different kind of webslinger, not just with a new costume but with a new superior—and deadly—attitude.

The AMAZING
SPIDER-MAN
#1
PLUS A SPECIAL BONUS BOOK:
INHUMAN
#1
INCLUDED.
SLOTT
RAMOS
OLAZABA
DELGADO
RATED T
$5.99US
DIRECT EDITION
MARVEL.COM
ALL-NEW MARVEL NOW!
BONUS DIGITAL EDITION
001

▲ ***AMAZING SPIDER-MAN* #1**

**June 2014**
**Artist:** Humberto Ramos

While it might appear as just a simple image of Spider-Man swinging through the city, the grin says it all—the real Peter Parker was back as Spider-Man. A whole new era of Spider-Man adventures was about to begin. It was one of the most upbeat Spidey covers in a long time.

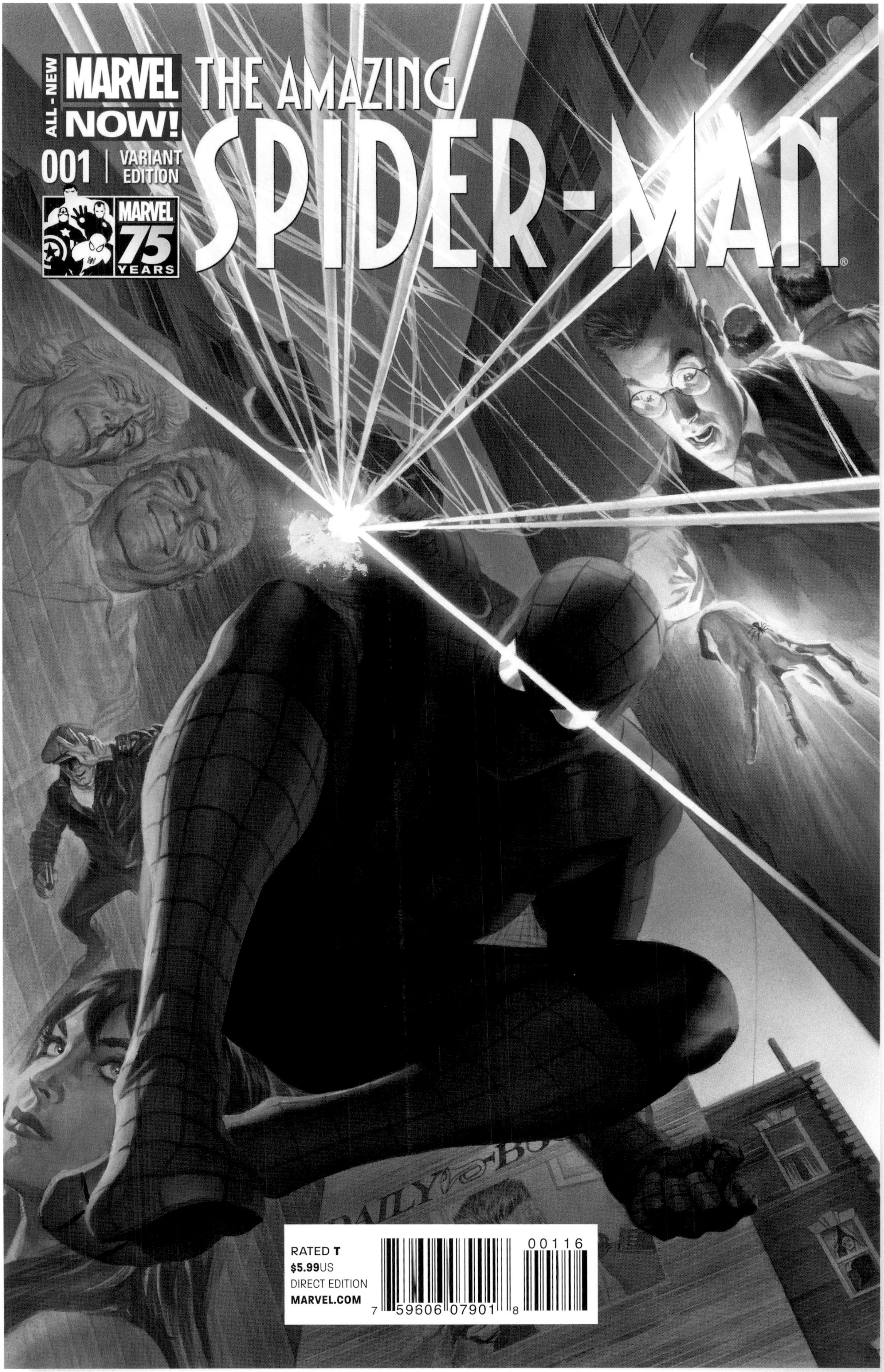
ALL-NEW MARVEL NOW!
001 | VARIANT EDITION
MARVEL 75 YEARS
THE AMAZING SPIDER-MAN
RATED T
$5.99US
DIRECT EDITION
MARVEL.COM

MARVEL COMICS
ALL NEW X-MEN LIMITED SERIES!
#1 AUG
DEAD-POOL

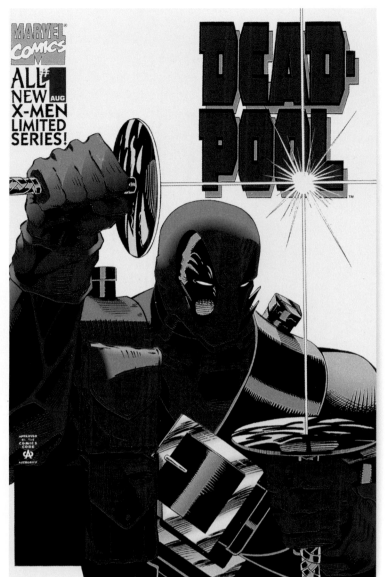

◀ *DEADPOOL* #1

**August 1994**
**Artist:** Ian Churchill

Ian Churchill illustrated the first cover to Deadpool's debut miniseries, focusing on a stylish body shot of the Merc with a Mouth. This early image is from a period when Deadpool was still more of an action star—albeit a slightly crazed one—in the style of Wolverine. In later years, Deadpool's style and stories would take a far more bizarre turn.

MARVEL COMICS
THE WORLD'S GREATEST COMICS!
DEADPOOL
DEC #11
THIS SUCKER IS 64 PAGES WITH ONLY 2 ADS...
...GUESS THAT'S WHY THEY CHEAPED OUT ON THE ROPE!
ALSO IN THIS ISSUE: AN UNIMPORTANT MESSAGE TO YOU, FROM THE EDITOR -- ABOUT ABSOLUTELY NOTHING!
KELLY WOODS

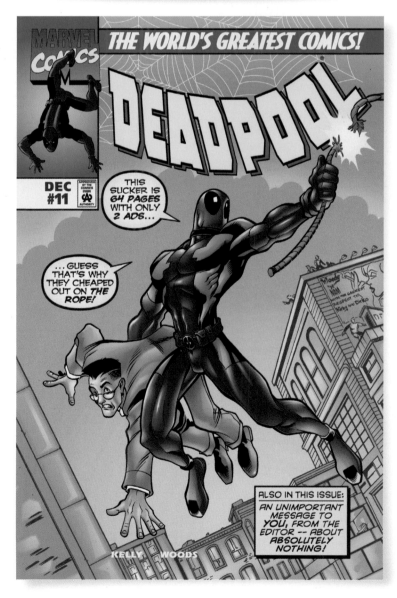

◀ *DEADPOOL* #11

**December 1997**
**Artist:** Pete Woods

By the time of his new ongoing series, Deadpool's adventures were starting to take a more humorous slant—as seen in this Pete Woods cover. The image is a homage to *Amazing Fantasy* issue #15 (August 1962; *see p50*), but it also reflects the story inside as Deadpool travels back in time to Spidey's early days. He even replaced the webslinger in an adventure that was a reworked version of *Amazing Spider-Man* issue #47 (April 1967).

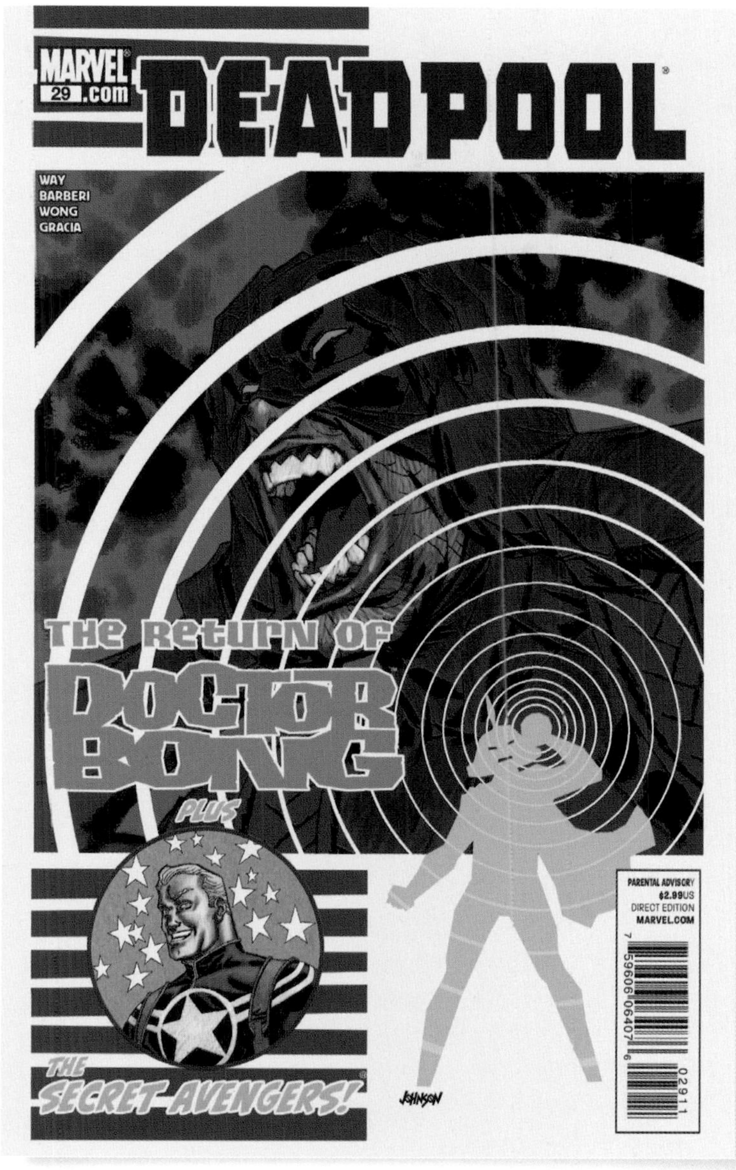
MARVEL
29 .com
DEADPOOL
WAY
BARBERI
WONG
GRACIA
THE RETURN OF
DOCTOR BONG
PLUS
THE SECRET AVENGERS!
JOHNSON
PARENTAL ADVISORY
$2.99US
DIRECT EDITION
MARVEL.COM

◀ *DEADPOOL* #29

**January 2011**
**Artist:** Dave Johnson

This issue harked back to *Howard the Duck* with the return of one of his old enemies, Doctor Bong. Dave Johnson's cover uses soundwaves emitting from Doctor Bong's helmet to maximum design effect. He also included a somewhat kitsch Steve Rogers' image, reflecting the way the title often satirized its stablemates.

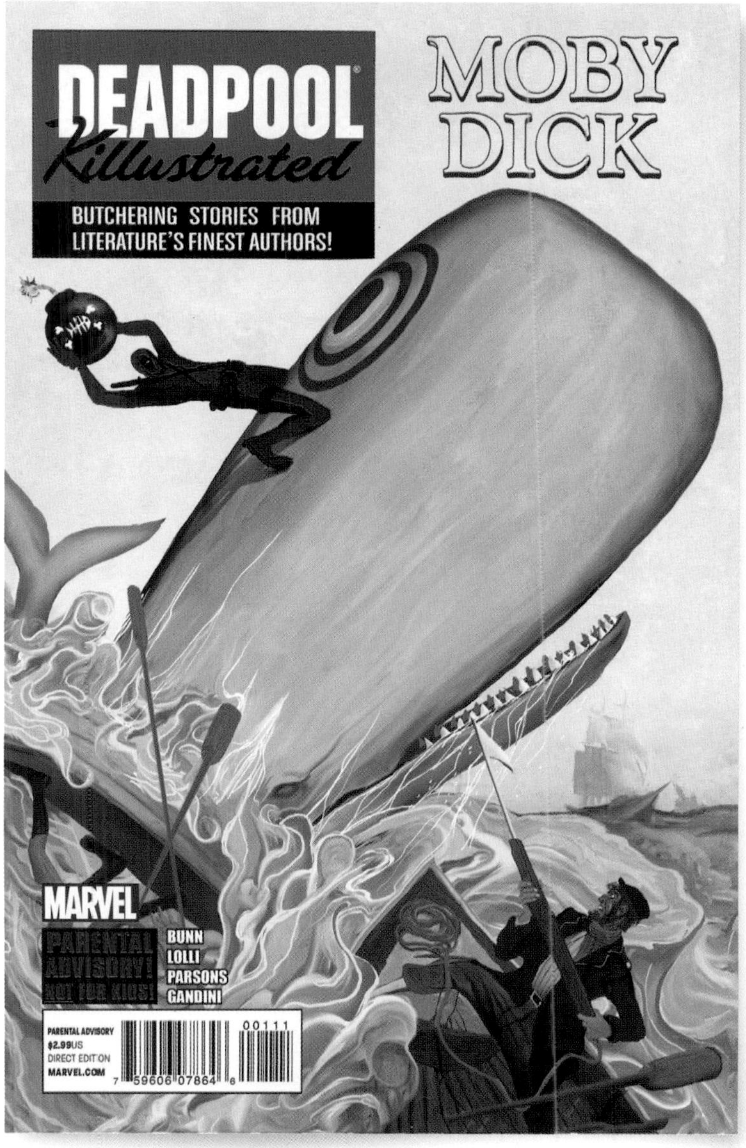
DEADPOOL
Killustrated
BUTCHERING STORIES FROM
LITERATURE'S FINEST AUTHORS!
MOBY DICK
MARVEL
PARENTAL ADVISORY! NOT FOR KIDS!
BUNN
LOLLI
PARSONS
GANDINI
PARENTAL ADVISORY
$2.99US
DIRECT EDITION
MARVEL.COM

◀ *DEADPOOL KILLUSTRATED* #1

**March 2013**
**Artist:** Mike Del Mundo

This cover followed Deadpool's shocking "realization" that he was just a fictional character and as such could never really die—unless he killed the literary archetypes of modern-day heroes and villains. Cue Deadpool literally hitting the classics. Each of the four issues took on the form of an old *Classics Illustrated* comics series cover (but humorously renaming them Deadpool "Killustrated"), starting with this *Moby Dick* homage.

**X-MEN: PHOENIX—ENDSONG #1 ▶**

**March 2005**
**Artist:** Greg Horn

Greg Horn cleverly portrayed Phoenix's deadly power in this image, as well as capturing the alien nature of the Phoenix Force. The red costume also indicates that this is the more deadly Dark Phoenix incarnation, while the flames behind reflect Phoenix's cycle of death and rebirth. A variant cover showed Phoenix in her original green costume.

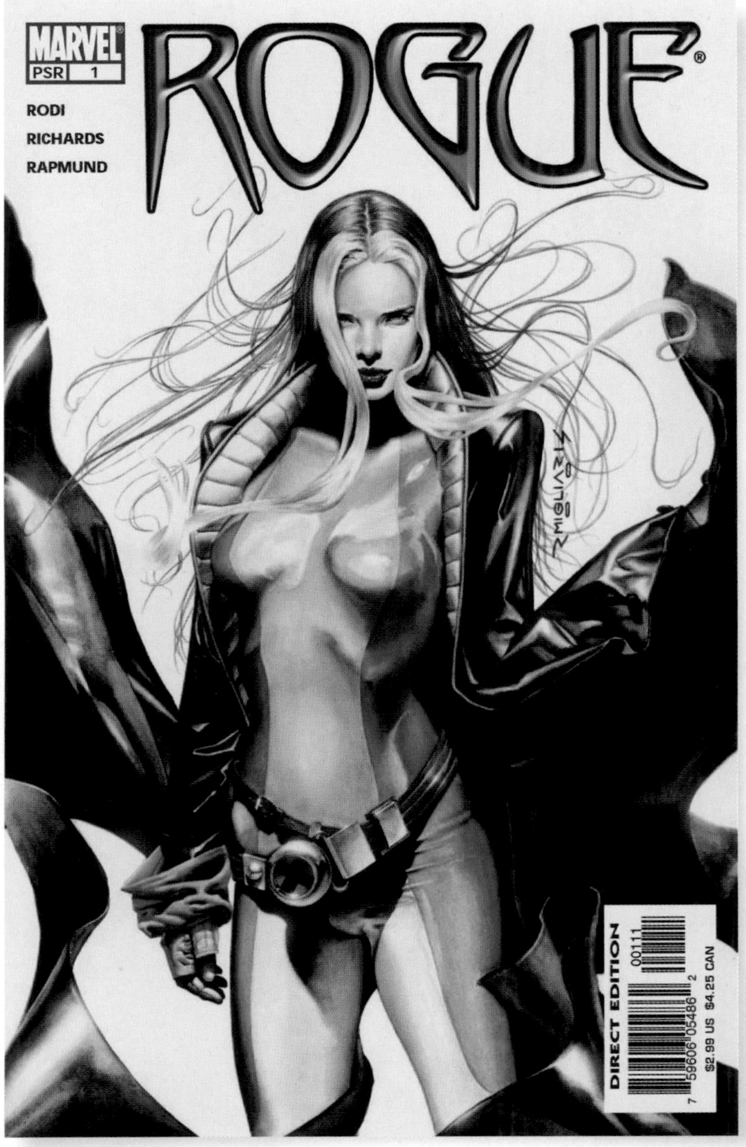
MARVEL
PSR 1
ROGUE
RODI
RICHARDS
RAPMUND
DIRECT EDITION
$2.99 US $4.25 CAN

**◀ *ROGUE* #1**

**September 2004**
**Artist:** Carlo Pagulayan

Carlo Pagulayan painted a number of beautiful covers for *Rogue's* third series, starting with this highly effective portrait. Pagulayan managed to capture not only Rogue's beauty, but also her aloofness and the alienation caused by her inability to touch anyone without harming them.

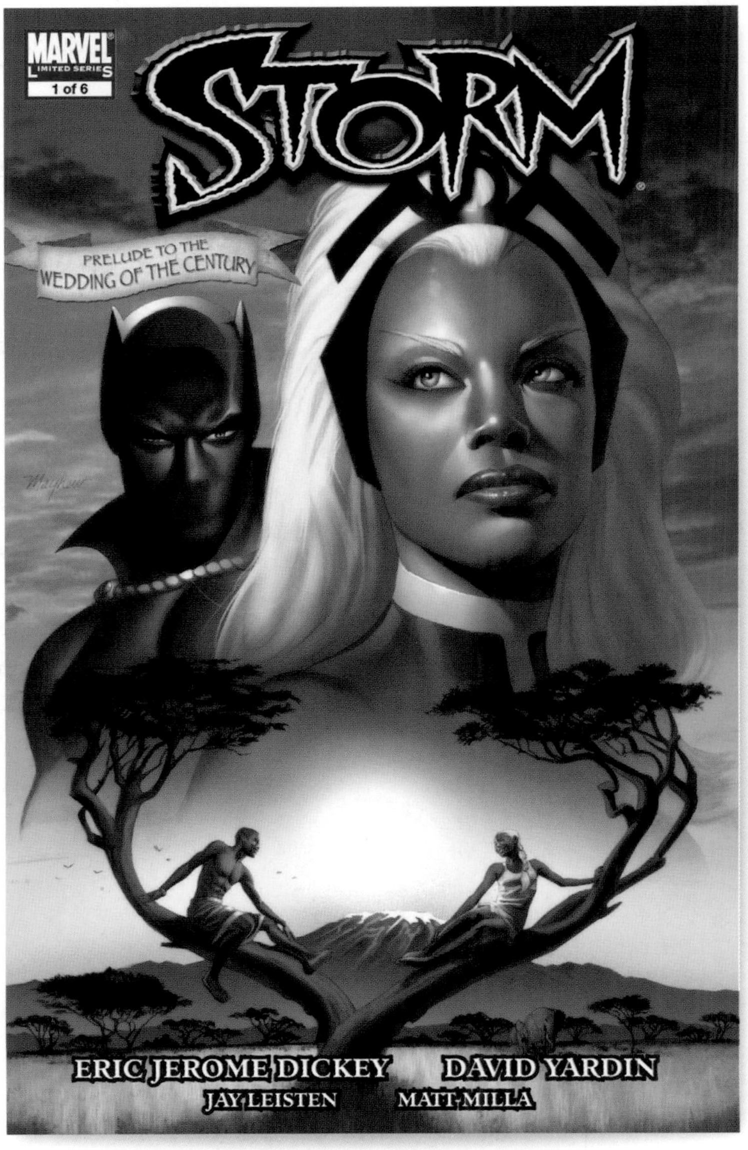
MARVEL
LIMITED SERIES
1 of 6
STORM
PRELUDE TO THE WEDDING OF THE CENTURY
ERIC JEROME DICKEY
DAVID YARDIN
JAY LEISTEN
MATT MILLA

**◀ *STORM* #1**

**April 2006**
**Artist:** Mike Mayhew

*Storm's* second series focused on Ororo Munroe's relationship with the Black Panther. The headshots of Storm and the Black Panther above a romanticized heart-shaped tree and their younger selves suggest that this series would reveal the previously untold story of their first meeting.

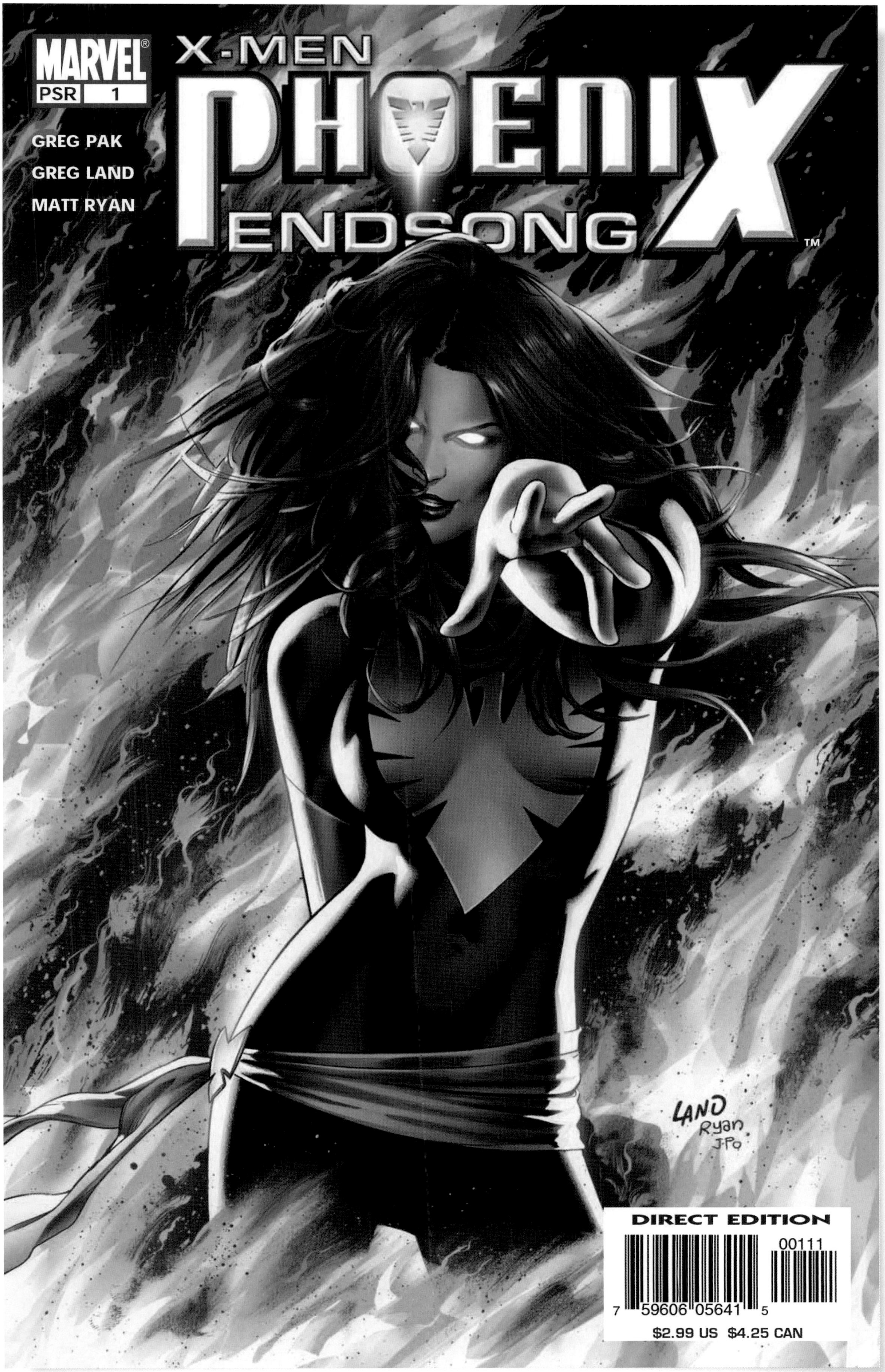
MARVEL
PSR 1
X-MEN
PHOENIX
ENDSONG
GREG PAK
GREG LAND
MATT RYAN
LAND
Ryan
J-Po
DIRECT EDITION
$2.99 US $4.25 CAN

MARVEL COMICS
WOLVERINE
$1.50 US
$2.00 CAN
24
MAY
APPROVED BY THE COMICS CODE AUTHORITY

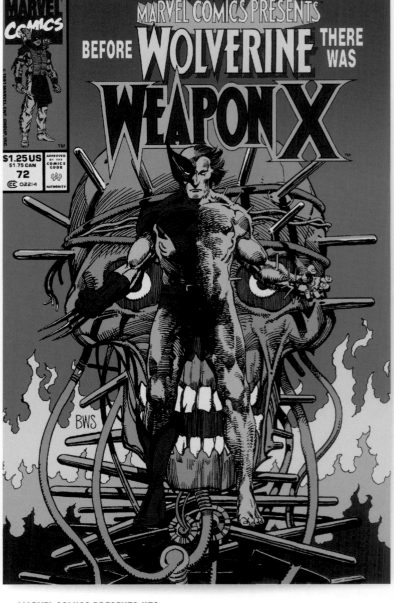

▲ ***WOLVERINE* #24**

**May 1990**
**Artist:** Jim Lee

Few artists can be said to have defined Wolverine as much as Jim Lee. While drawing the X-Men's own adventures, Lee also provided the occasional cover for Wolverine's solo title. This neon-lit masterpiece showing the hero in the far eastern island of Madripoor was one such cover. Lee's Wolverine looks truly deadly in this dark and dangerous image.

MARVEL COMICS
MARVEL COMICS PRESENTS
BEFORE WOLVERINE THERE WAS
WEAPON X
$1.25 US
$1.75 CAN
72
APPROVED BY THE COMICS CODE AUTHORITY
BWS

▲ ***MARVEL COMICS PRESENTS* #72**

**March 1991**
**Artist:** Barry Windsor-Smith

Barry Windsor-Smith provided covers for each of the 12 chapters of his epic "Weapon X" story, which was serialized in the *Marvel Comics Presents* anthology. This dramatic first cover hinted that the saga would reveal one of the biggest secrets from Wolverine's past—how he gained his Adamantium skeleton.

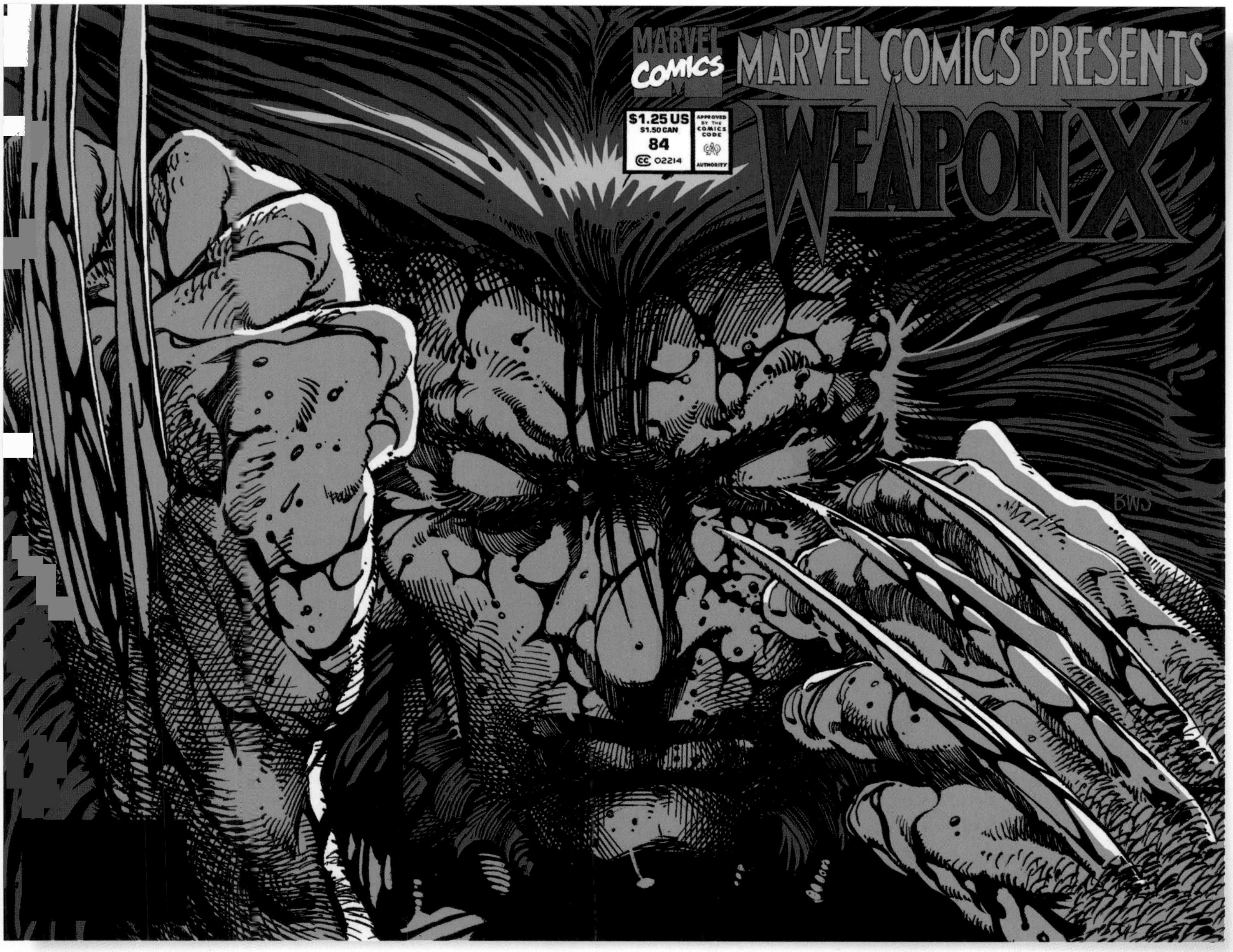
MARVEL COMICS
MARVEL COMICS PRESENTS
WEAPON X
$1.25 US
$1.50 CAN
84
02214
APPROVED BY THE COMICS CODE AUTHORITY
BWS

▲ ***MARVEL COMICS PRESENTS* #84**

**September 1991**
**Artist:** Barry Windsor-Smith

The wraparound cover to the final chapter of the "Weapon X" storyline features a close-up of Wolverine with blood seeping from his Adamantium claws as they pierce his own skin. Windsor-Smith's image combines the wildness of Wolverine with a sense of the character's humanity, while the story itself was a big influence on the *Wolverine* and *X-Men* movies.

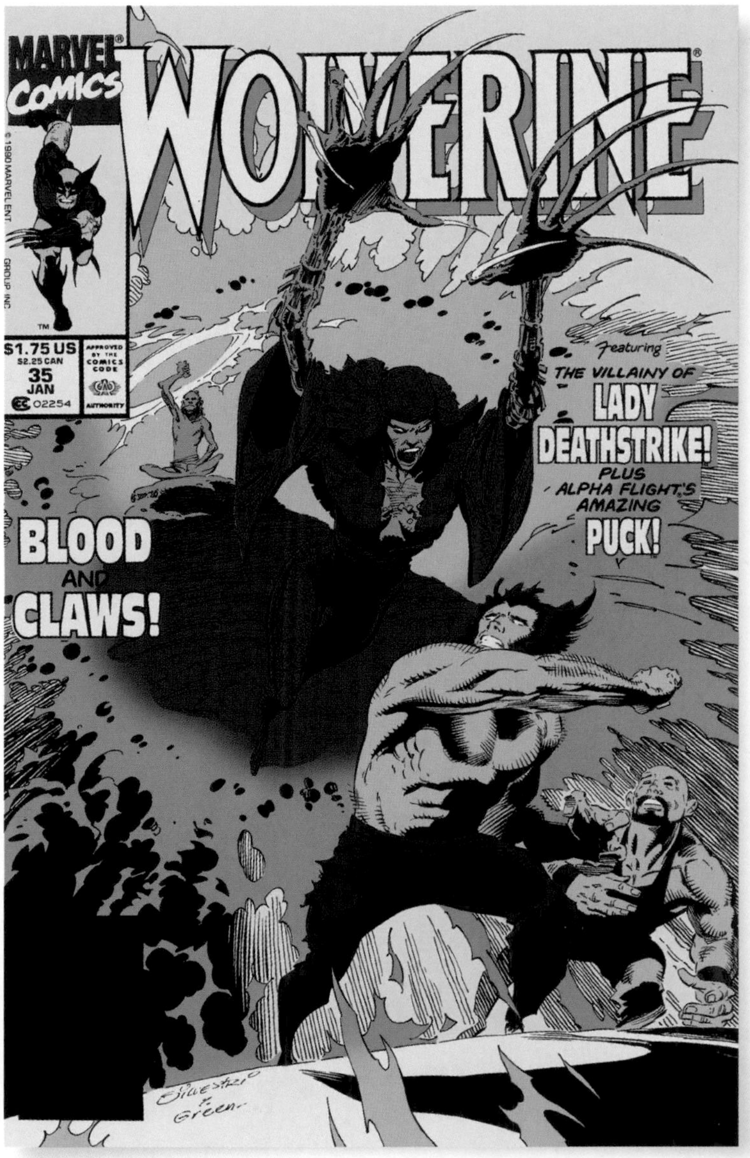
MARVEL COMICS
WOLVERINE
$1.75 US
$2.25 CAN
35
JAN
Featuring
THE VILLAINY OF
LADY DEATHSTRIKE!
PLUS ALPHA FLIGHT'S AMAZING
PUCK!
BLOOD AND CLAWS!

◀ *WOLVERINE* #35

**January 1991**
**Artist:** Marc Silvestri

Marc Silvestri illustrated one of the most critically acclaimed runs in *Wolverine*'s history and produced a number of action-packed covers during that time. This early Lady Deathstrike image is a prime example of Silvestri's dynamism and the gritty feel he brought to Wolverine's adventures.

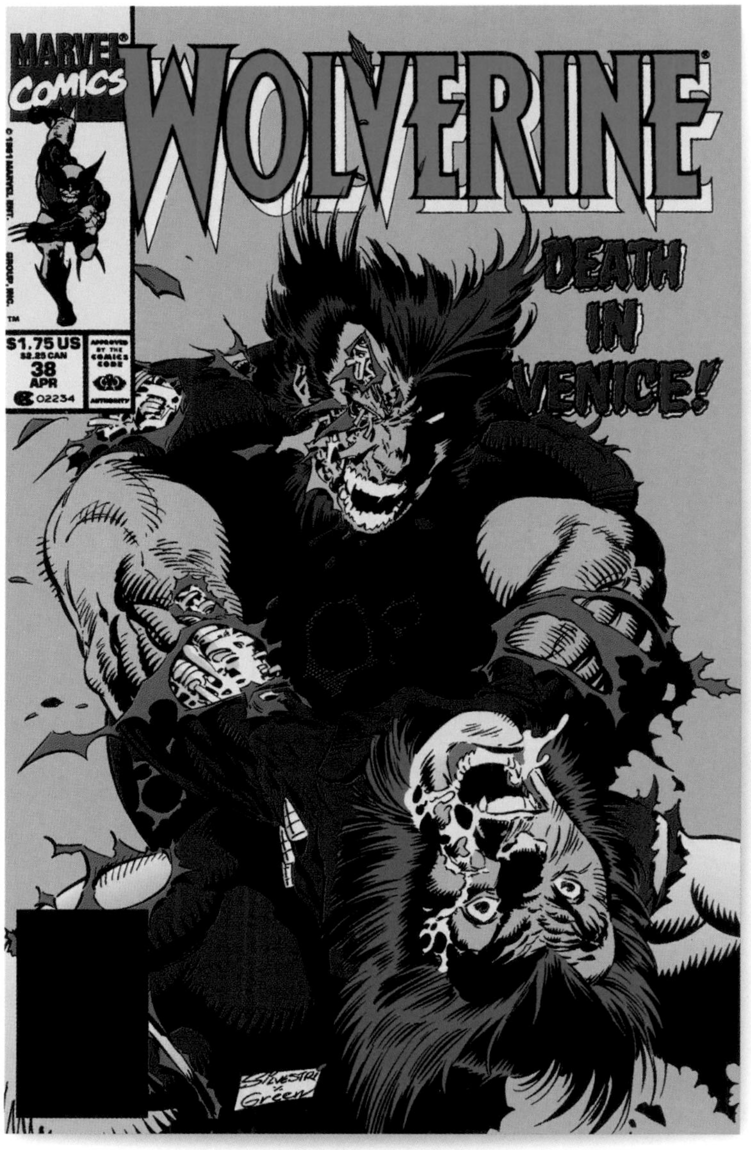
MARVEL COMICS
WOLVERINE
$1.75 US
38
APR
DEATH IN VENICE!

◀ *WOLVERINE* #38

**April 1991**
**Artist:** Marc Silvestri

"Albert" was one of the more interesting additions to the Wolverine mythos. He started life as a simple android duplicate of Wolverine, programmed to kill the mutant, but soon became an interesting character in his own right. This dramatic cover depicts an early showdown between Wolverine and his duplicate.

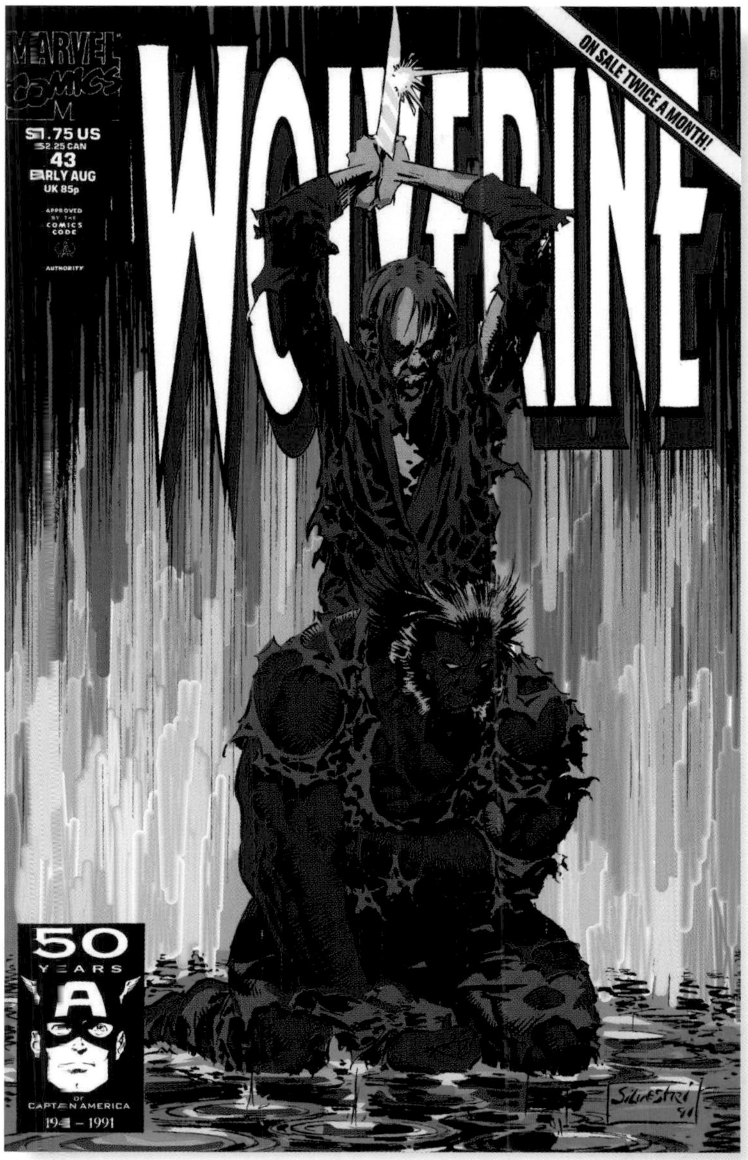
MARVEL COMICS
WOLVERINE
ON SALE TWICE A MONTH!
$1.75 US
$2.25 CAN
43
EARLY AUG
UK 85p
50 YEARS OF CAPTAIN AMERICA
1941 – 1991
SILVESTRI

◄ *WOLVERINE* #43

**August 1991**
**Artist:** Marc Silvestri

This atmospheric Marc Silvestri cover is all about color and texture. Here Silvestri used a rain effect and a strong red to create eye-catching artwork. The central pose reflects the story inside, with Wolverine seeking revenge on an insane killer who had tortured a wolverine in the Central Park Zoo.

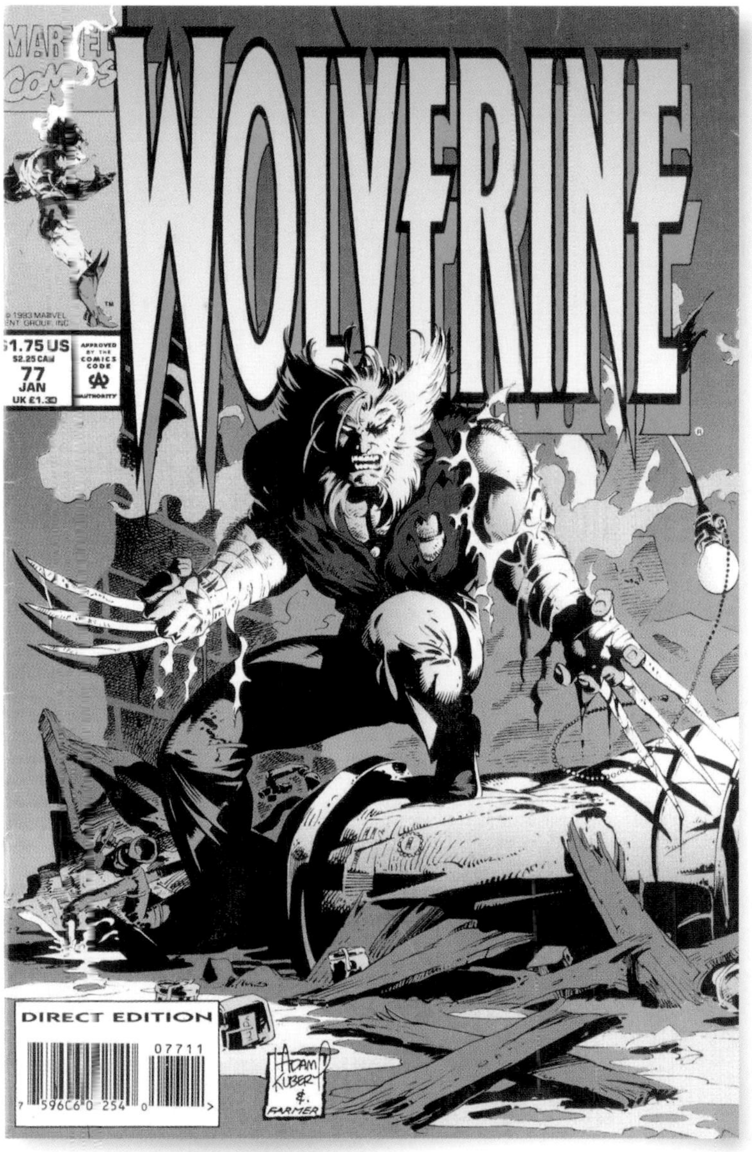
MARVEL COMICS
WOLVERINE
$1.75 US
77
JAN
DIRECT EDITION
ADAM KUBERT & FARMER

◄ *WOLVERINE* #77

**January 1994**
**Artist:** Adam Kubert

Adam Kubert produced many outstanding images of Wolverine. This classic cover features the mutant suffering after Magneto had ripped the Adamantium from his body. The bandages around Logan's wrists, the result of his bone claws slicing through his skin with every trademark "snikt," added a new, painful dimension to the always troubled hero.

***WOLVERINE* #87** ▶

**November 1994**
**Artist:** Adam Kubert

Adam Kubert's action scene of Wolverine and Gambit leaping from the rooftops is eye-catching enough, but the addition of overlaid sniper rifle sights gives the whole scene an extra sense of danger. Splitting the logo in two also cleverly helps to direct the reader's attention to the center of the action.

MARVEL COMICS
$1.75 US
$2.25 CAN
79
MAR
UK £1.30
WOLVERINE

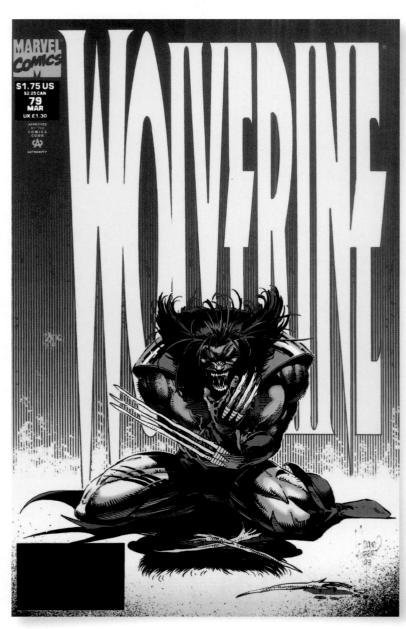

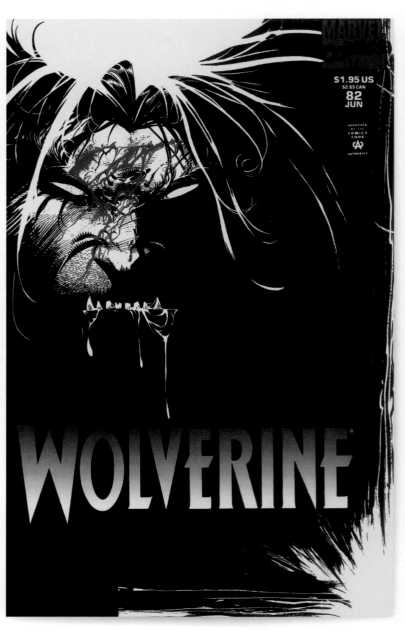

▲ ***WOLVERINE* #79**

**March 1994**
**Artist:** Adam Kubert

With its extended logo and shocking image of Wolverine in pain, clutching his broken claws, this classic cover shows a key moment in Wolverine's life. Kubert brought out the pain Wolverine was experiencing after his enemy Cyber snapped off three of his claws. Seeing the previously almost-indestructible Wolverine in agony was a big shock for long-term fans.

$1.95 US
$2.65 CAN
82
JUN
WOLVERINE

▲ ***WOLVERINE* #82**

**June 1994**
**Artist:** Adam Kubert

This relatively simple image was one of the most effective *Wolverine* covers that year. The stark black and white of the main image makes the blood on Wolverine's forehead and his yellow eyes even more striking. Moving the logo to the bottom of the cover was an innovative decision.

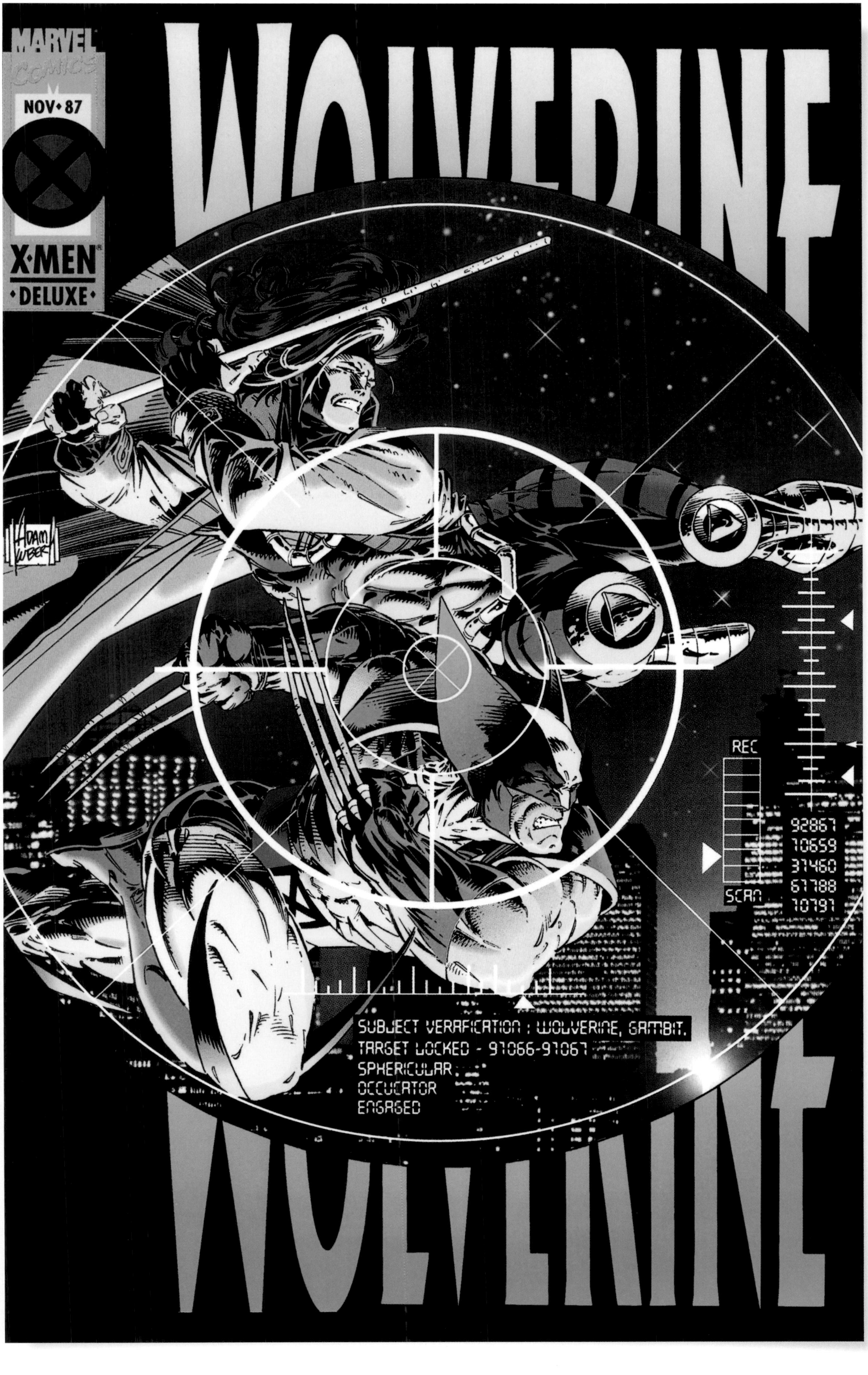
MARVEL COMICS
NOV • 87
X-MEN DELUXE
WOLVERINE
REC
SCAN
92867
10659
37460
61788
10791
SUBJECT VERAFICATION : WOLVERINE, GAMBIT.
TARGET LOCKED - 97066-97067
SPHERICULAR
OCCUCATOR
ENGAGED
WOLVERINE

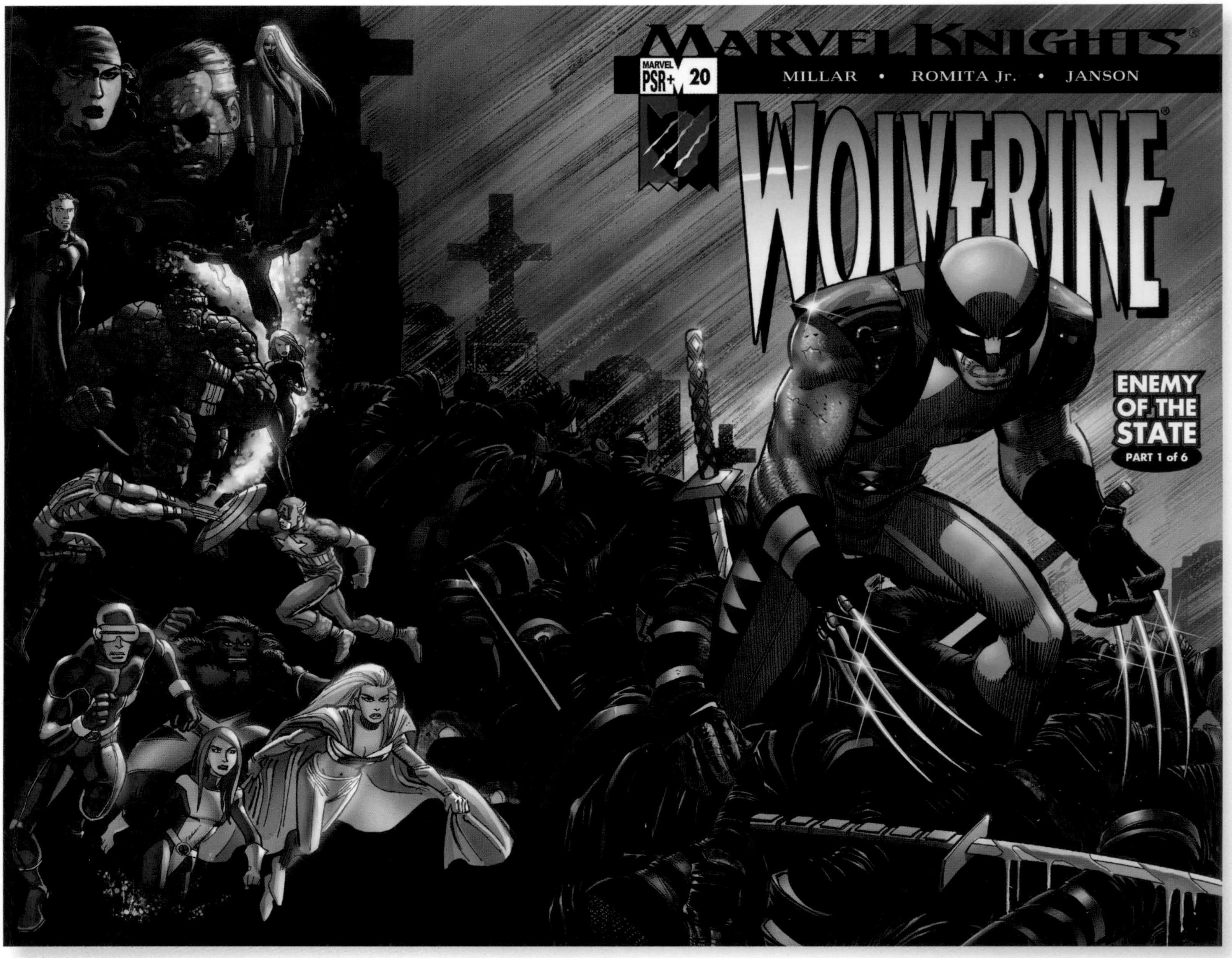
MARVEL KNIGHTS
MARVEL PSR+ 20
MILLAR • ROMITA Jr. • JANSON
WOLVERINE
ENEMY OF THE STATE
PART 1 of 6

▲ *WOLVERINE* #20

**December 2004**
**Artist:** John Romita Jr.

John Romita Jr. was Marvel's leading artist when he teamed up with one of their biggest writers, Mark Millar, to create "Enemy of the State," a shocking story in which Wolverine is brainwashed by ninja assassins from the order known as the Hand. Romita Jr.'s wraparound cover portrays a bloodthirsty Wolverine after his run-in with the ninjas, who would soon brainwash the hero into being their deadliest member.

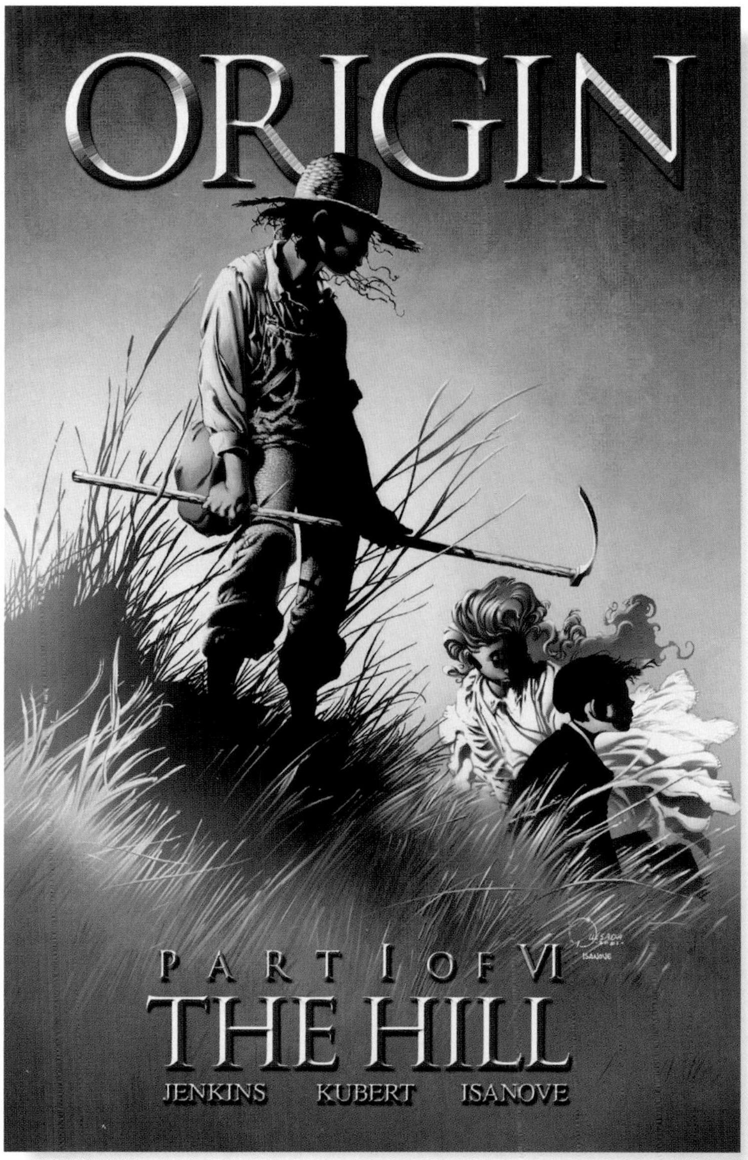
ORIGIN
PART I OF VI
THE HILL
JENKINS KUBERT ISANOVE

◀ *ORIGIN* #1

**November 2001**
**Artist:** Joe Quesada

It was the story that some thought would never be told—the origin of Wolverine. It was up to Marvel's then Editor-in-Chief and award-winning artist, Joe Quesada, to create something special for a story this big. His atmospheric cover, with the distinctive color work of artist Richard Isanove, is reflective of the story's 19th-century setting. Separate chapter headings on each of the four covers achieves a cinematic look.

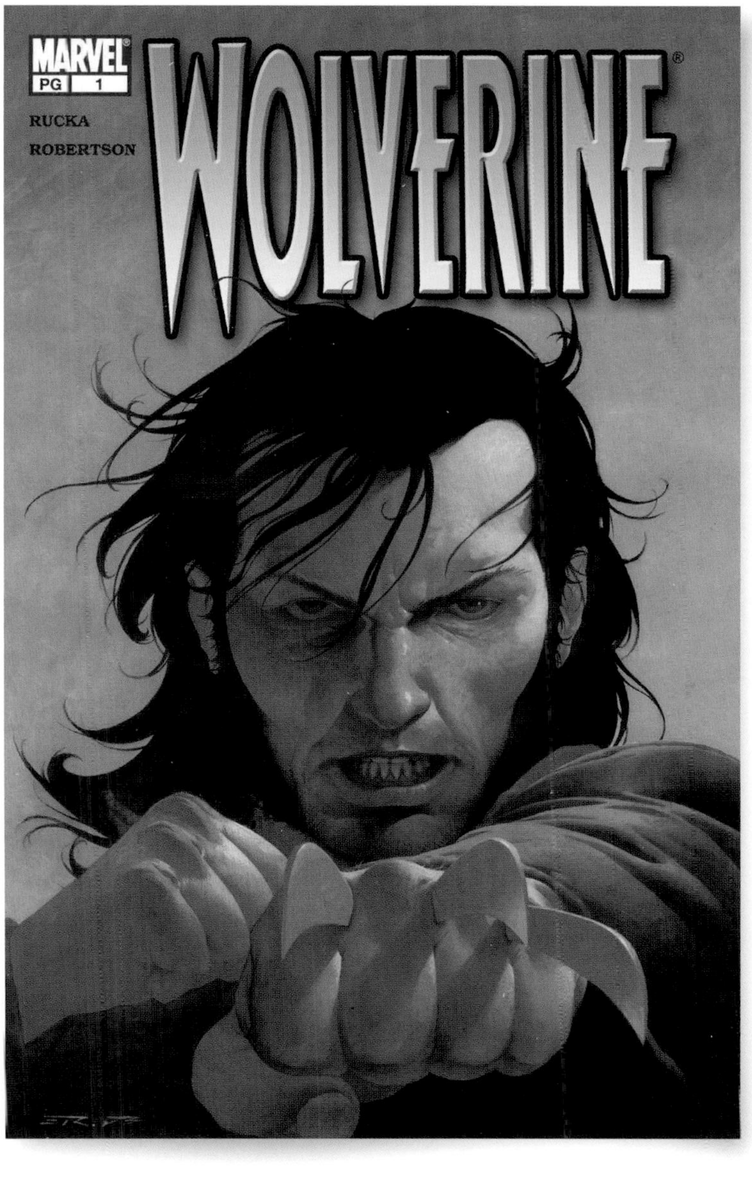
MARVEL
PG 1
RUCKA
ROBERTSON
WOLVERINE

◀ *WOLVERINE* #1

**July 2003**
**Artist:** Esad Ribic

Wolverine's third series went in a grittier and darker direction than the previous run. Esad Ribic's close-up of Logan might show Wolverine's claws, but it was a more everyday image of him than his usual costumed X-Men persona. The story inside was more "thriller" than "Super Hero," as Wolverine sought vengeance for a girl who was murdered after turning to him for help.

*UNCANNY X-MEN* #268 ▶

**September 1990**
**Artist:** Jim Lee

Even by Jim Lee's high standards, this was a special cover—and a very special issue. The central image promised a team-up that comic book fans would love. This time it was Wolverine, Black Widow, and Captain America fighting alongside each other—and looking exceptionally heroic. The issue had a surprise in store too, as it was revealed that the three heroes had first met during World War II.

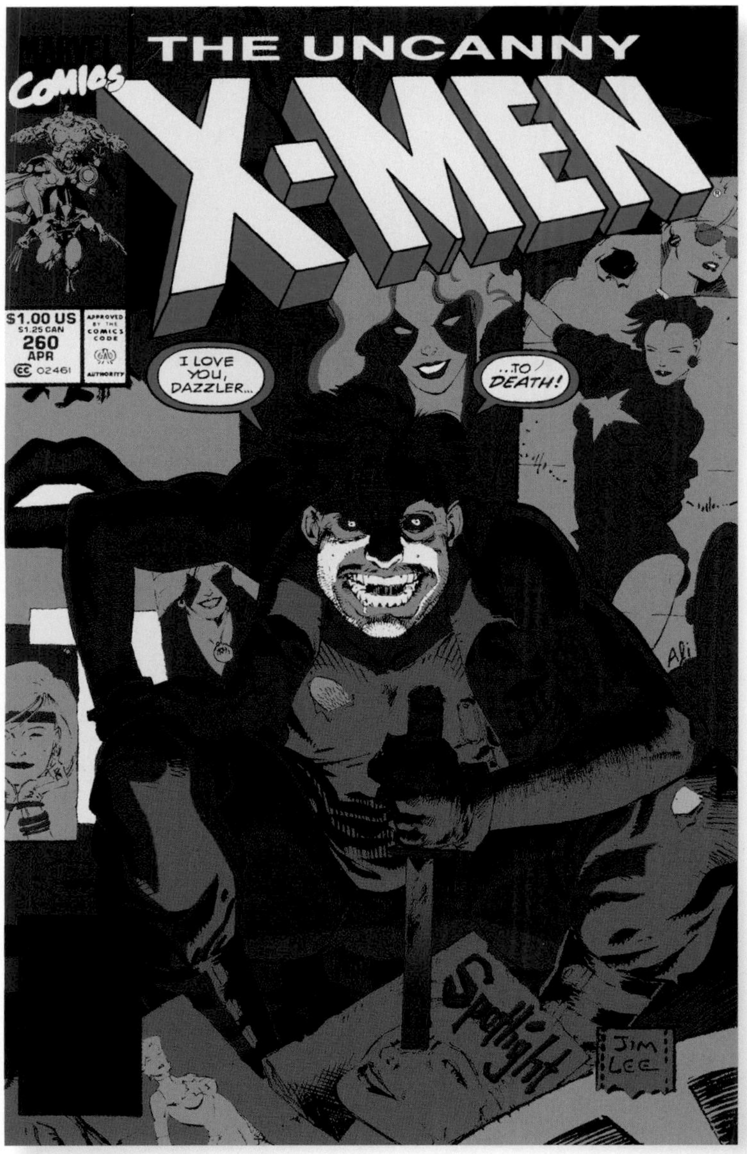
MARVEL COMICS
THE UNCANNY
X-MEN
$1.00 US
260
APR
I LOVE YOU, DAZZLER...
...TO DEATH!
Spotlight
JIM LEE

◀ *UNCANNY X-MEN* #260

**April 1990**
**Artist:** Jim Lee

Jim Lee reinvigorated the X-Men in the late 1980s. His sleek, action-packed style won him countless awards and he quickly became one of the most popular artists in the business. While Lee excelled at group shots of the X-Men, he could also produce atmospheric pieces such as this cover, showing a psychopath obsessed with Dazzler.

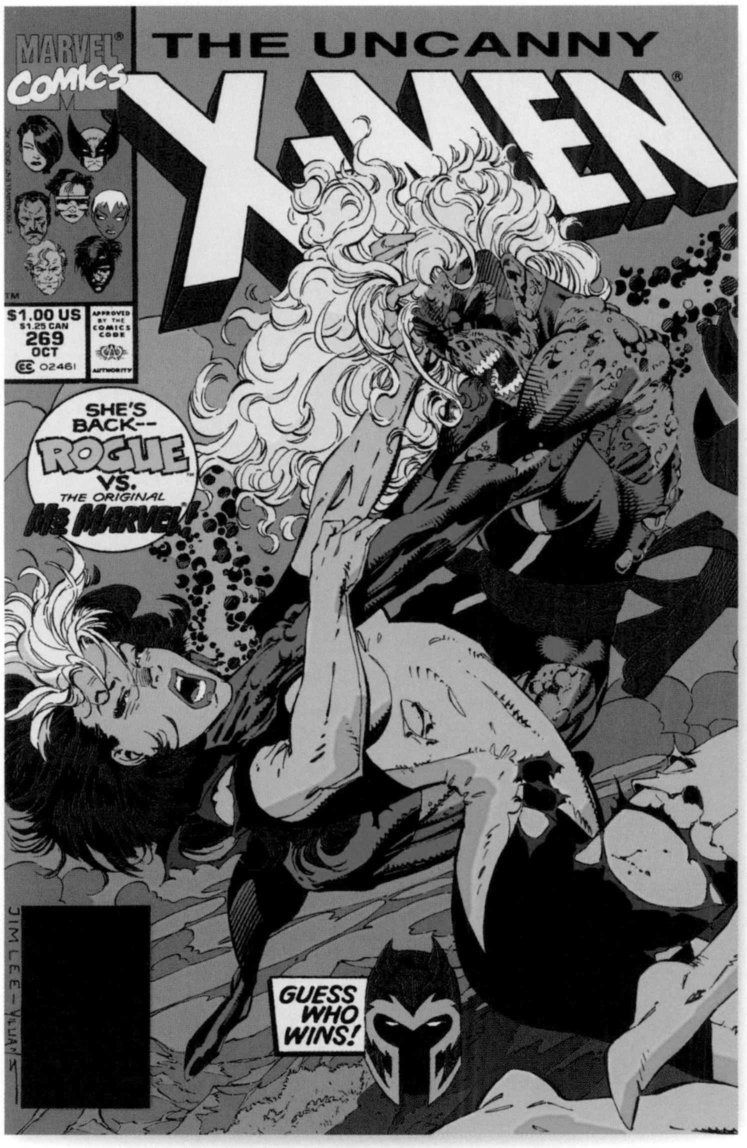
MARVEL COMICS
THE UNCANNY
X-MEN
$1.00 US
269
OCT
SHE'S BACK--
ROGUE
VS.
THE ORIGINAL
MS. MARVEL!
GUESS WHO WINS!

◀ *UNCANNY X-MEN* #269

**October 1990**
**Artist:** Jim Lee

Rogue and Ms. Marvel went way back. When Rogue was a villain, she accidentally stole Ms. Marvel's powers and memories. The two characters had met since, but this cover promised a much deadlier meeting. The image of Magneto's head at the bottom of the page, next to the words "Guess who wins!" suggested the meeting would have a surprise ending.

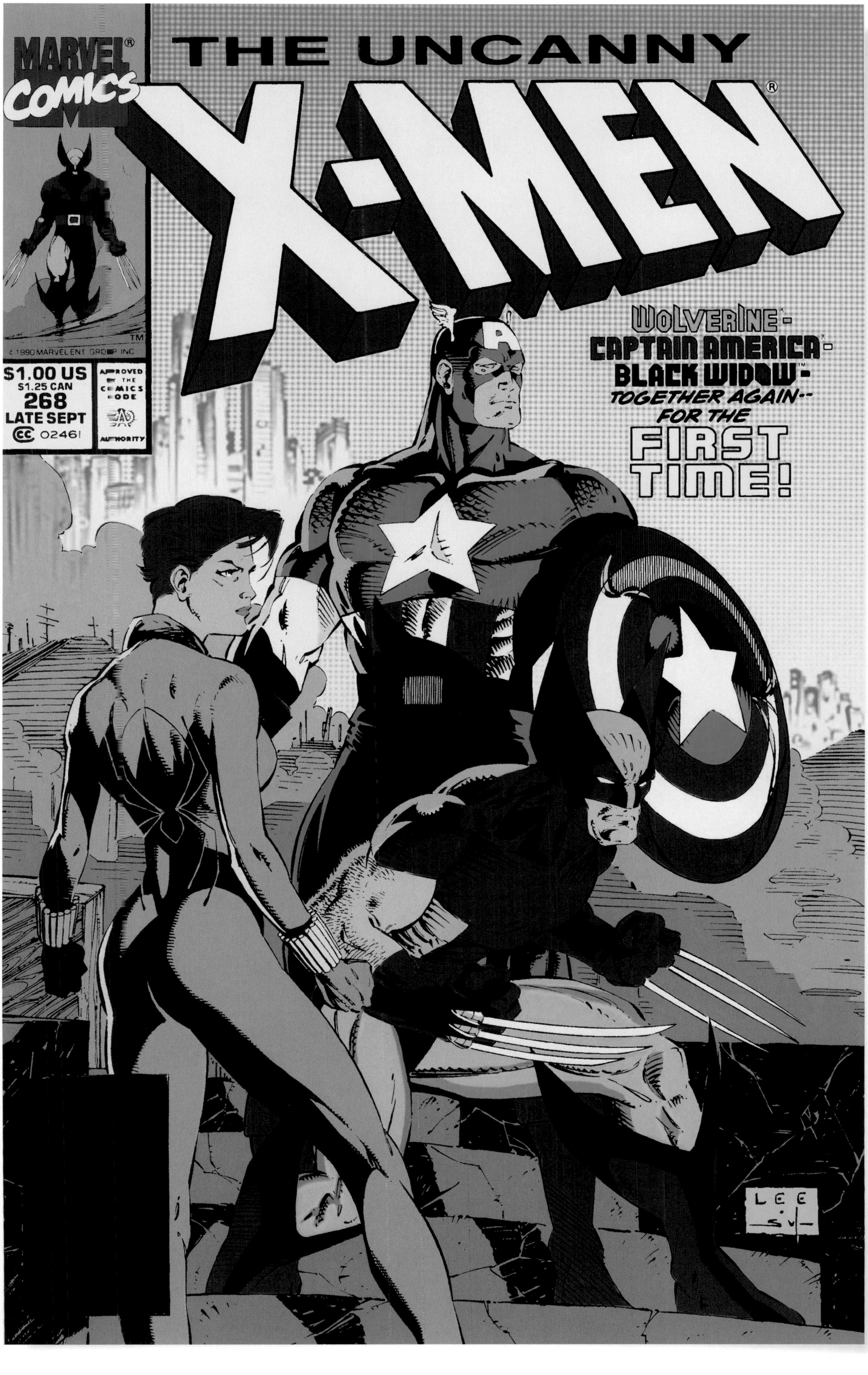
MARVEL COMICS
THE UNCANNY
X-MEN
© 1990 MARVEL ENT GROUP INC
$1.00 US
$1.25 CAN
268
LATE SEPT
APPROVED BY THE COMICS CODE AUTHORITY
WOLVERINE–
CAPTAIN AMERICA–
BLACK WIDOW–
TOGETHER AGAIN--
FOR THE
FIRST
TIME!
LEE

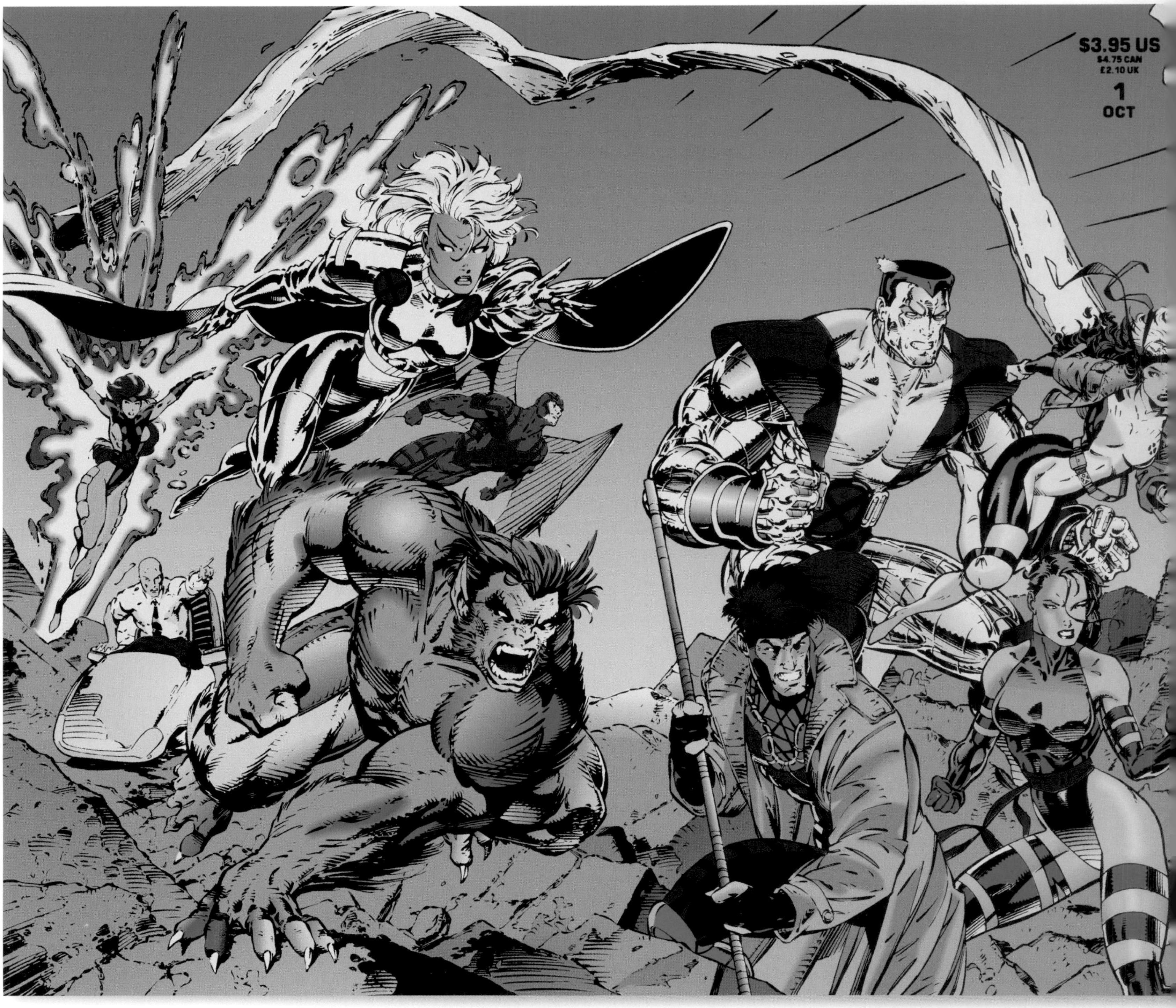
$3.95 US
$4.75 CAN
£2.10 UK
1
OCT

▲ ***X-MEN* #1**

**October 1991**
**Artist:** Jim Lee

Following the success of his work on *Uncanny X-Men*, Jim Lee was at the helm for the launch of the first new X-Men series since 1963. To celebrate this, Lee created a huge fold-out cover for the first issue. Each segment was released as a variant cover, but another edition was released with all the parts intact to fold out. The issue was a massive success and became the bestselling comic of the year.

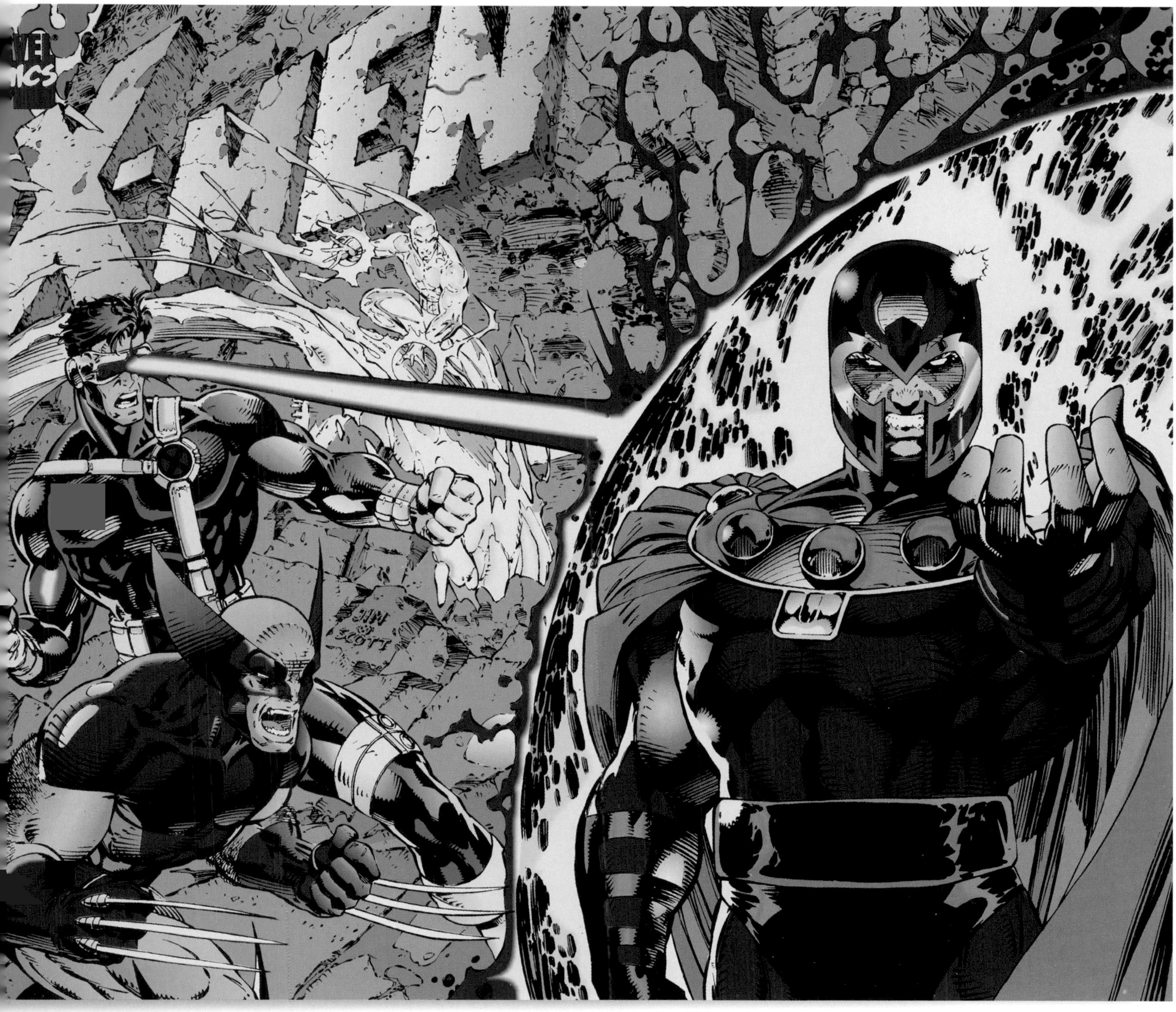

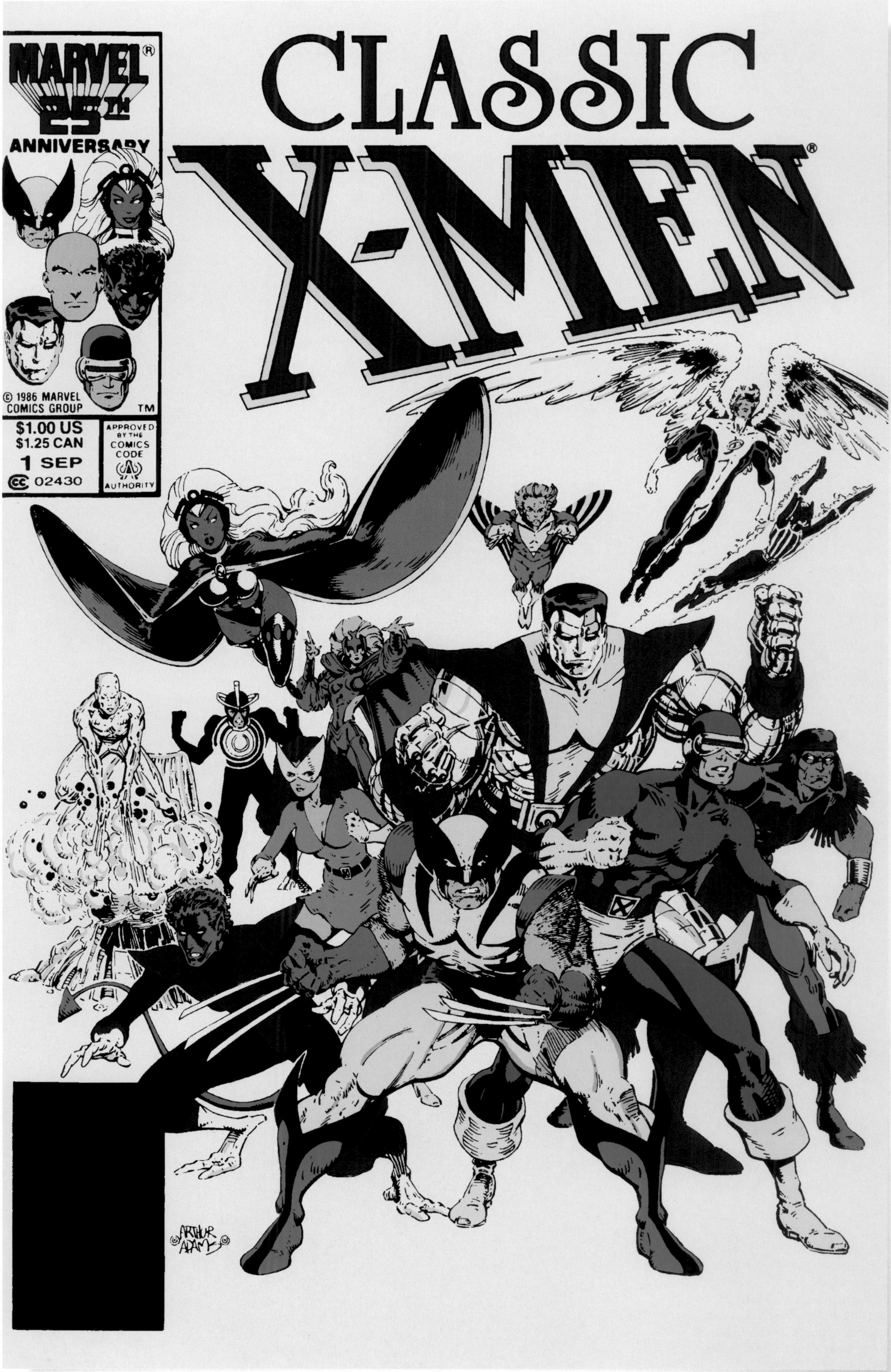
MARVEL 25TH ANNIVERSARY
© 1986 MARVEL COMICS GROUP
TM
$1.00 US
$1.25 CAN
1 SEP
02430
APPROVED BY THE COMICS CODE AUTHORITY
CLASSIC
X-MEN
ARTHUR ADAMS

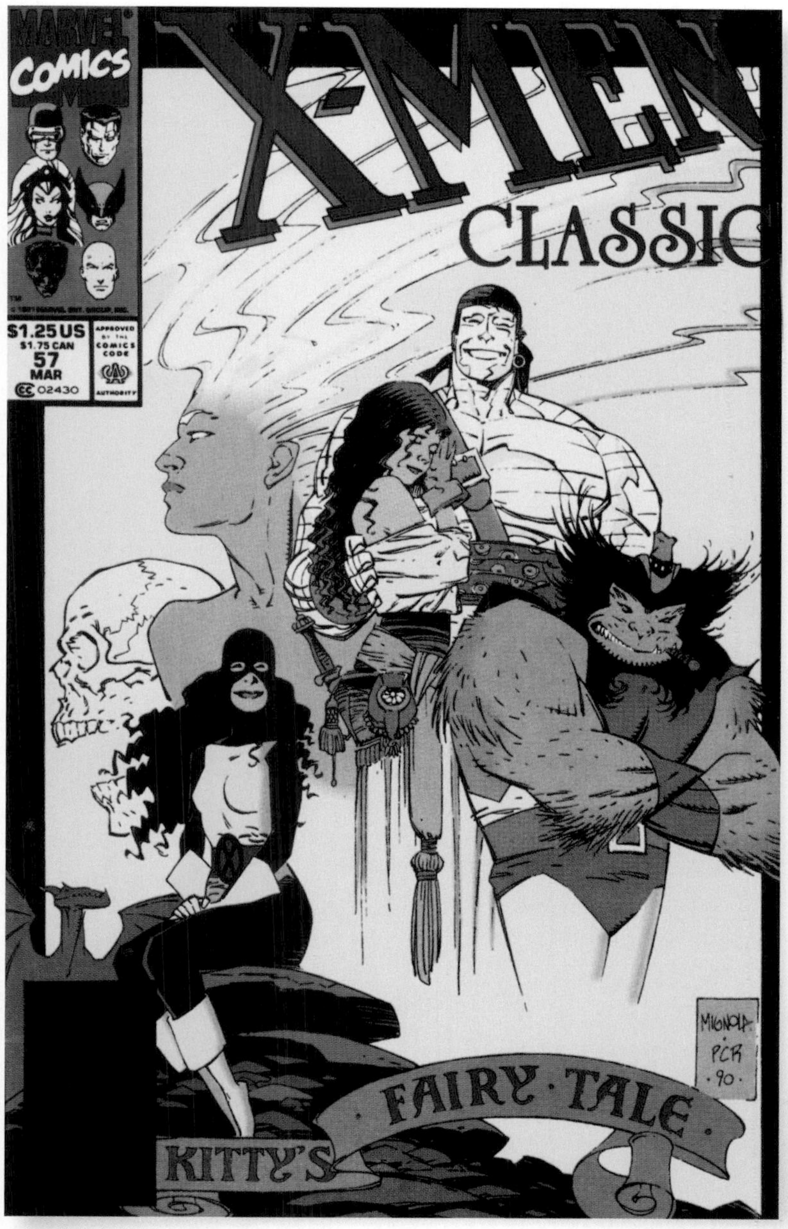
MARVEL COMICS
X-MEN
CLASSIC
$1.25 US
$1.75 CAN
57
MAR
KITTY'S FAIRY·TALE
MIGNOLA PCR ·90·

▲ *X-MEN CLASSIC* #57

**March 1991**
**Artists:** Mike Mignola and P. Craig Russell

This reprint of *Uncanny X-Men* issue #153 (January 1982) featured a beautiful new cover by Mike Mignola and P. Craig Russell. The two artists were masters of fantasy illustration and the perfect choice for this issue, which was based around a bedtime story Kitty Pryde told to the young Illyana Rasputin. While this reprint series had started as *Classic X-Men,* it changed its title to *X-Men Classic* from issue #46.

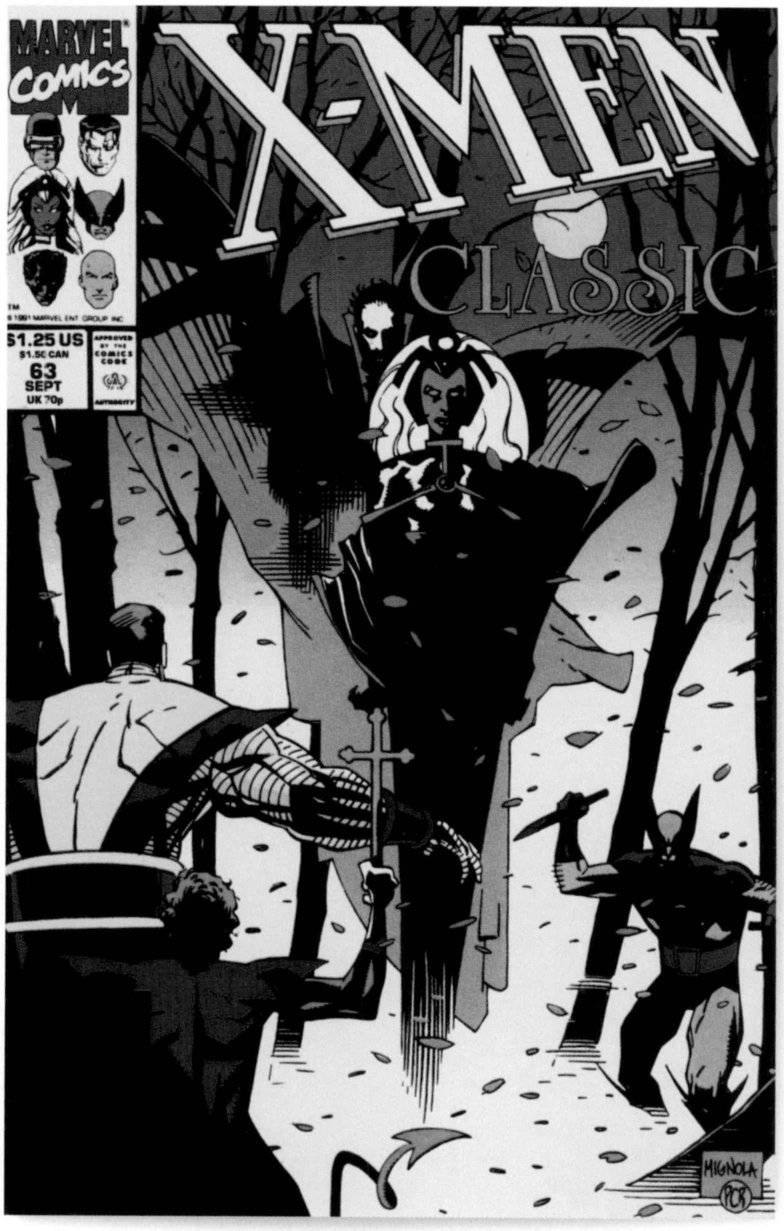
MARVEL COMICS
X-MEN
CLASSIC
$1.25 US
63
SEPT
MIGNOLA PCR

▲ *X-MEN CLASSIC* #63

**September 1991**
**Artists:** Mike Mignola and P. Craig Russell

Mike Mignola and P. Craig Russell created another masterpiece based on a classic X-Men story—*Uncanny X-Men* issue #159 (July 1982)—where the team met Dracula, who was attempting to make Storm his vampire bride. Mignola and Russell's work for these covers was so good, the series was collectible for the covers alone.

◀ *CLASSIC X-MEN* #1

**September 1986**
**Artist:** Art Adams

*Classic X-Men* had a series of stunning covers created by some of the best artists in the business. Each issue reprinted an old X-Men story, but also contained a second story by John Bolton. The first issue's cover, by Art Adams, was a celebration of the X-Men, with all the mutants who appeared in the classic *Giant Size X-Men* issue #1 (May 1975) brought together in one stunning image.

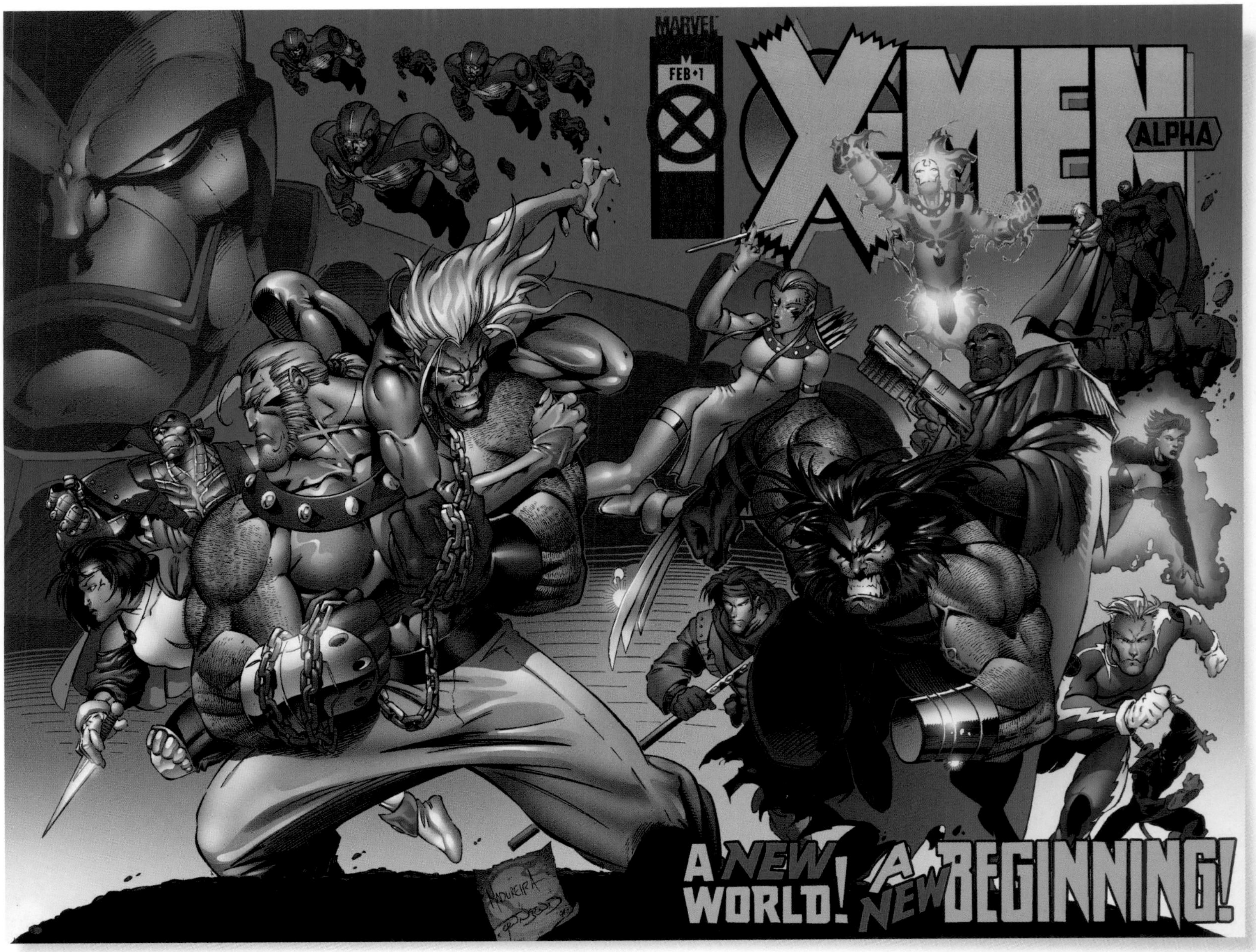
MARVEL
FEB • 1
X-MEN
ALPHA
A NEW WORLD! A NEW BEGINNING!

▲ ***X-MEN: ALPHA* #1**

**February 1995**
**Artist:** Joe Madureira

The "Age of Apocalypse" was one of the *X-Men* comics' biggest storylines. Set in a reality in which Professor X had been killed and had never formed the X-Men, it was a massive multi-part epic the like of which had never been seen before. Joe Madureira created an amazing image of the alternate versions of the X-Men for the first issue, *X-Men: Alpha*. The cover had shiny holofoil added to the art to make it even more eye-catching.

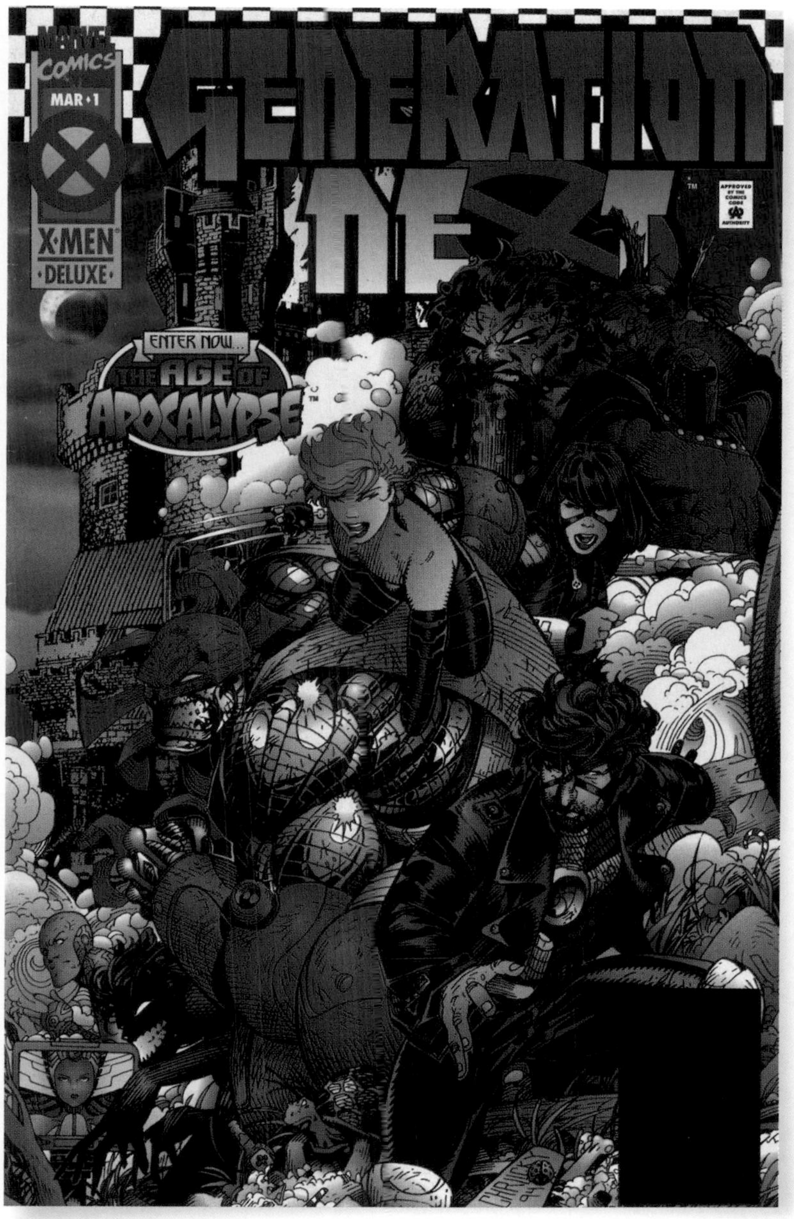
MARVEL COMICS
MAR 1
GENERATION
NEXT
X-MEN
DELUXE
ENTER NOW...
THE AGE OF APOCALYPSE

▲ *GENERATION NEXT* #1

**March 1995**
**Artist:** Chris Bachalo

All the X-line of comics were replaced by "Age of Apocalypse" versions during the event. Chris Bachalo was already producing wonderful art for *Generation X*, a new team of teen mutants, when he created this "Age of Apocalypse" cover for its replacement title *Generation Next*. The sight of the Generation X team in their Age of Apocalypse incarnations created an intriguing and memorable image.

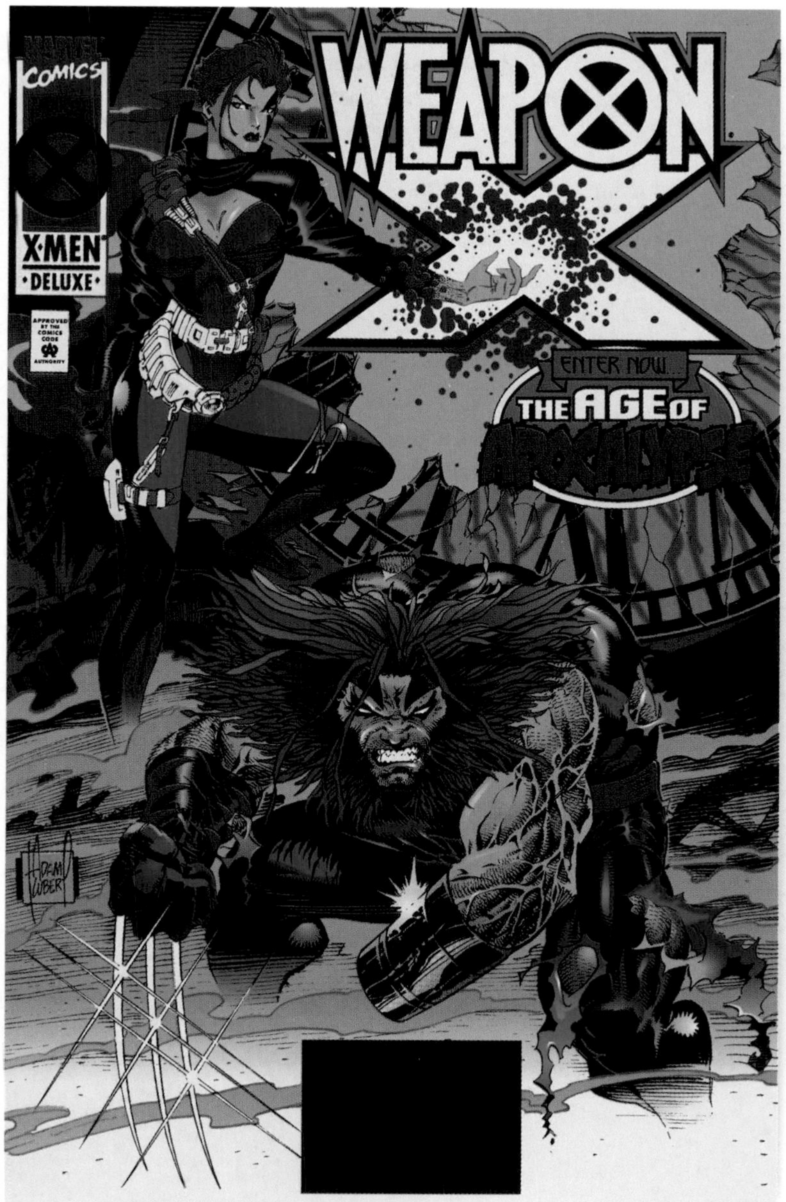
MARVEL COMICS
WEAPON
X
X-MEN
DELUXE
ENTER NOW...
THE AGE OF APOCALYPSE

▲ *WEAPON X* #1

**March 1995**
**Artist:** Adam Kubert

Perhaps the most shocking image from the early "Age of Apocalypse" covers was the sight of a one-handed Wolverine. The cover for the first issue of *Weapon X* had another shock for comic fans—the image of Jean Grey with Logan. In this dark reality the two were lovers, although events in the series soon forced them apart.

MARVEL
E IS FOR EXTINCTION
ONE OF THREE
NEW X MEN
JUL 2001 114 GRANT MORRISON ■ FRANK QUITELY ■ TIM TOWNSEND

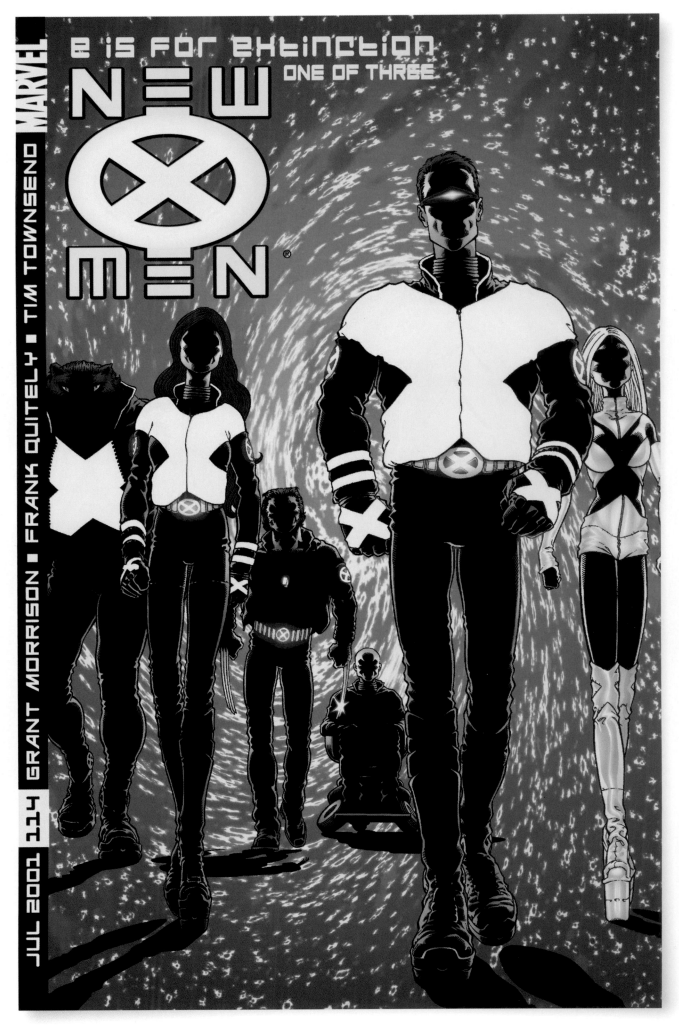

▲ *NEW X-MEN* #114

**July 2001**
**Artist:** Frank Quitely

It was all change for the X-Men in this issue as writer Grant Morrison started his epic run on the title, joined by artist Frank Quitely. The logo was redesigned for the new era and the title renamed *New X-Men*. Quitely's image of Cyclops and the X-Men moving purposefully forward, dressed in their new paramilitary uniforms, signified a real change in style for the heroes.

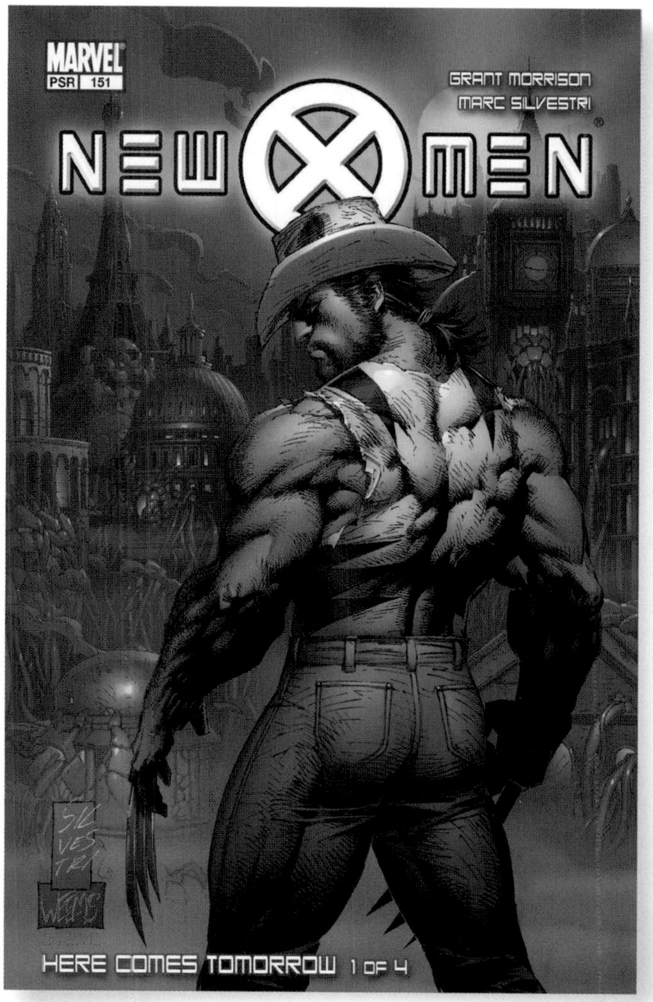
MARVEL
PSR 151
GRANT MORRISON
MARC SILVESTRI
NEW X MEN
HERE COMES TOMORROW 1 OF 4

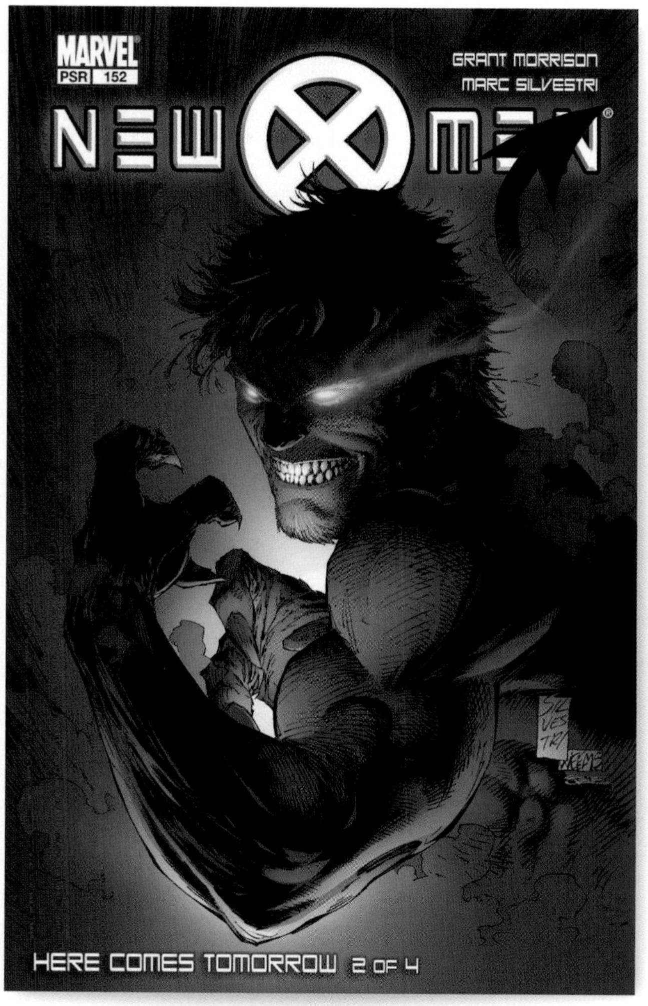
MARVEL
PSR 152
GRANT MORRISON
MARC SILVESTRI
NEW X MEN
HERE COMES TOMORROW 2 OF 4

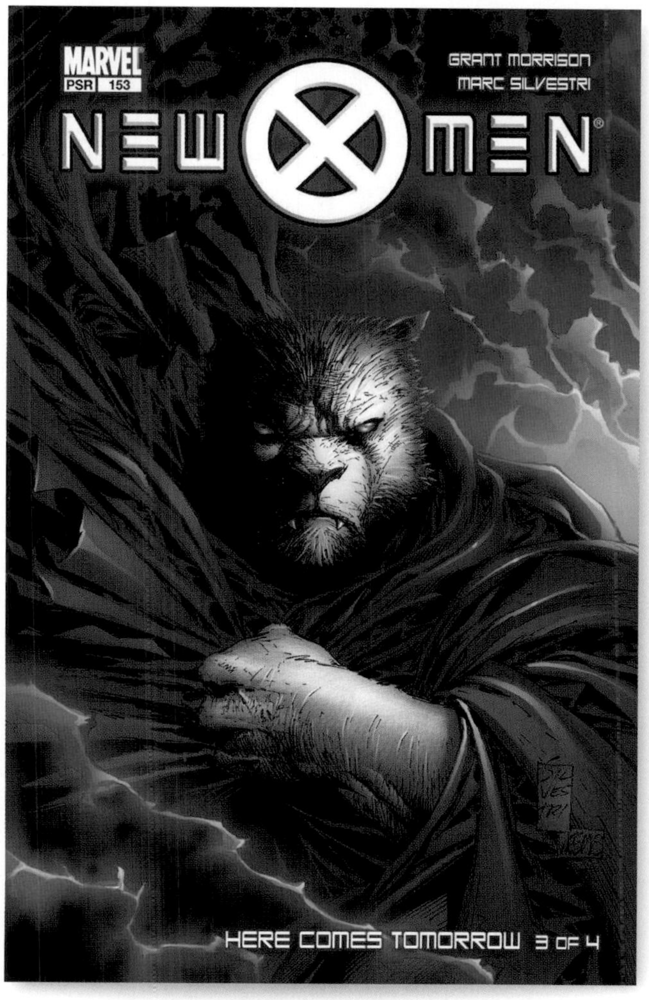
MARVEL
PSR 153
GRANT MORRISON
MARC SILVESTRI
NEW X MEN
HERE COMES TOMORROW 3 OF 4

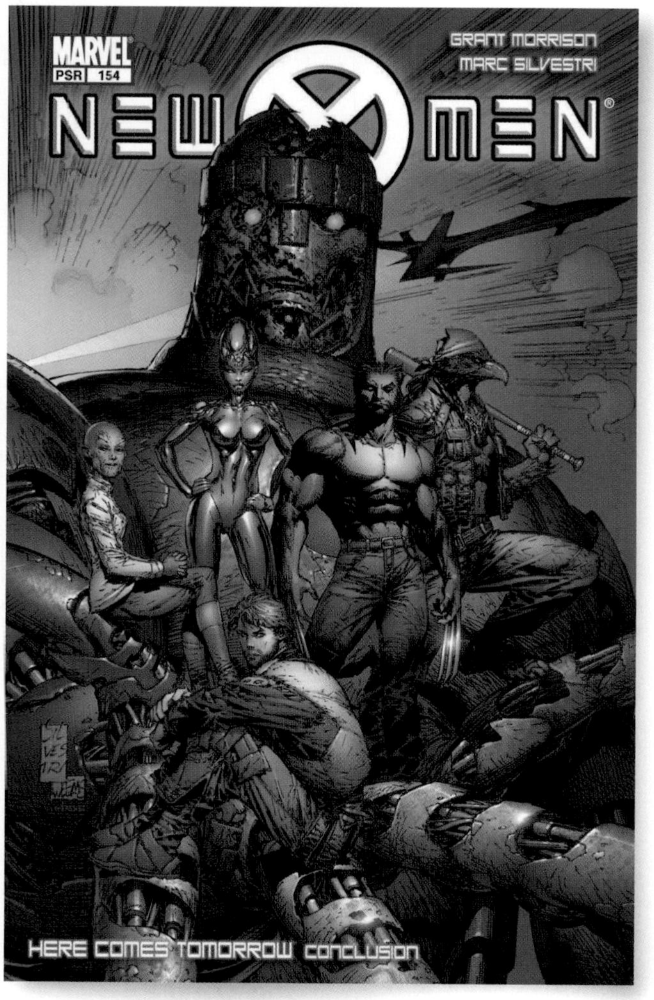
MARVEL
PSR 154
GRANT MORRISON
MARC SILVESTRI
NEW X MEN
HERE COMES TOMORROW CONCLUSION

▲ *NEW X-MEN* #151–154

**March 2004**
**Artist:** Marc Silvestri

These four issues were an epic conclusion to Grant Morrison's time as writer on *New X-Men*. Marc Silvestri, one of the leading artists in the business at the time, returned to Marvel for these issues and created a series of stunning covers. The first three are futuristic incarnations of Wolverine, Beast, and Nightcrawler, while the final shows a dark, future version of Wolverine and his new X-Men team.

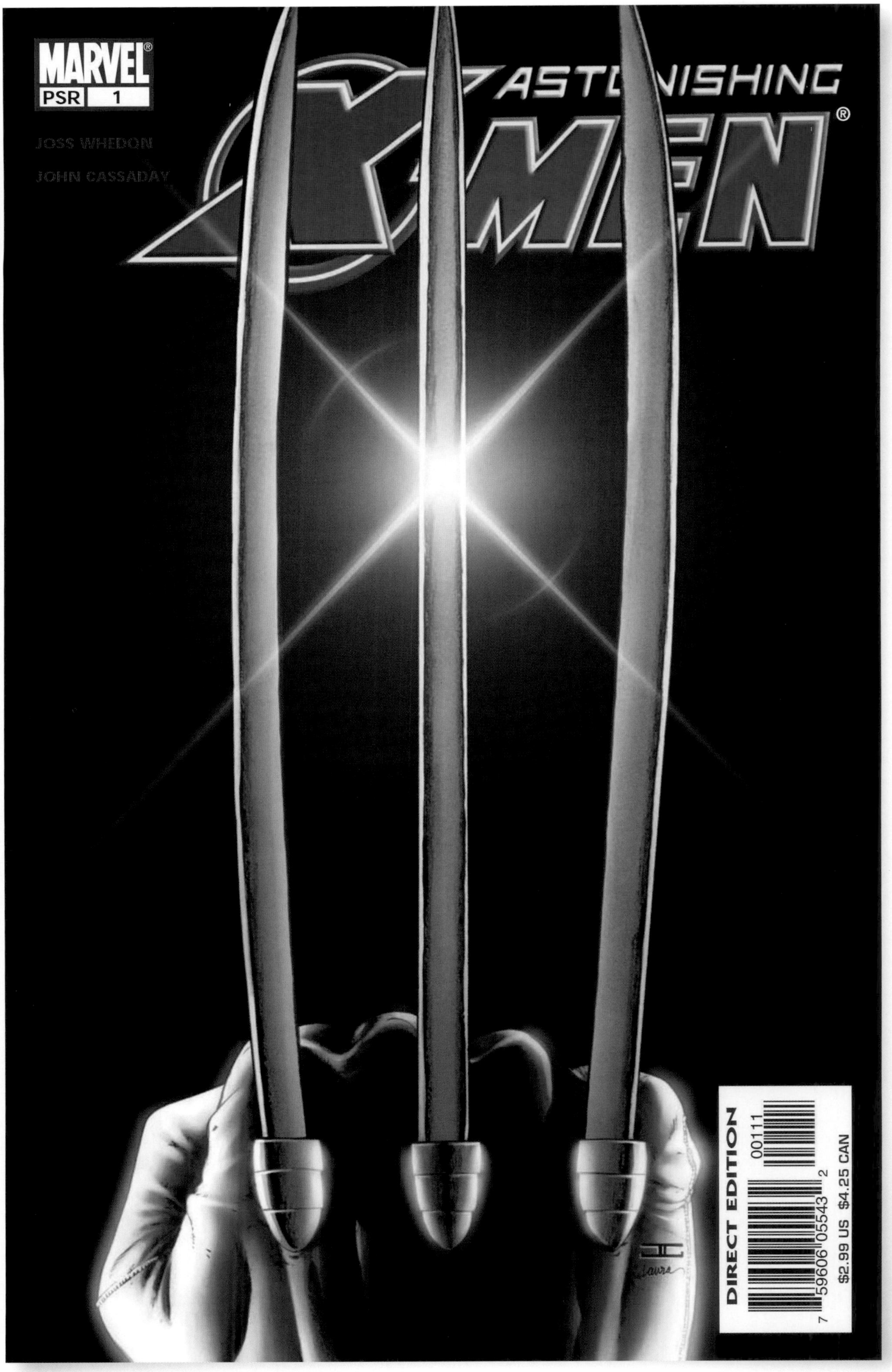
MARVEL
PSR 1
ASTONISHING
X-MEN
JOSS WHEDON
JOHN CASSADAY
DIRECT EDITION
$2.99 US $4.25 CAN

▲ ***ASTONISHING X-MEN* #1**

**July 2004**
**Artist:** John Cassaday

When artist John Cassaday joined forces with movie writer-director Joss Whedon, the result was one of the best X-Men comics of all time. Cassaday created a number of stylish covers for *Astonishing X-Men*, starting with this close-up of Wolverine's claws, the light shining off the middle claw providing an eye-catching flash.

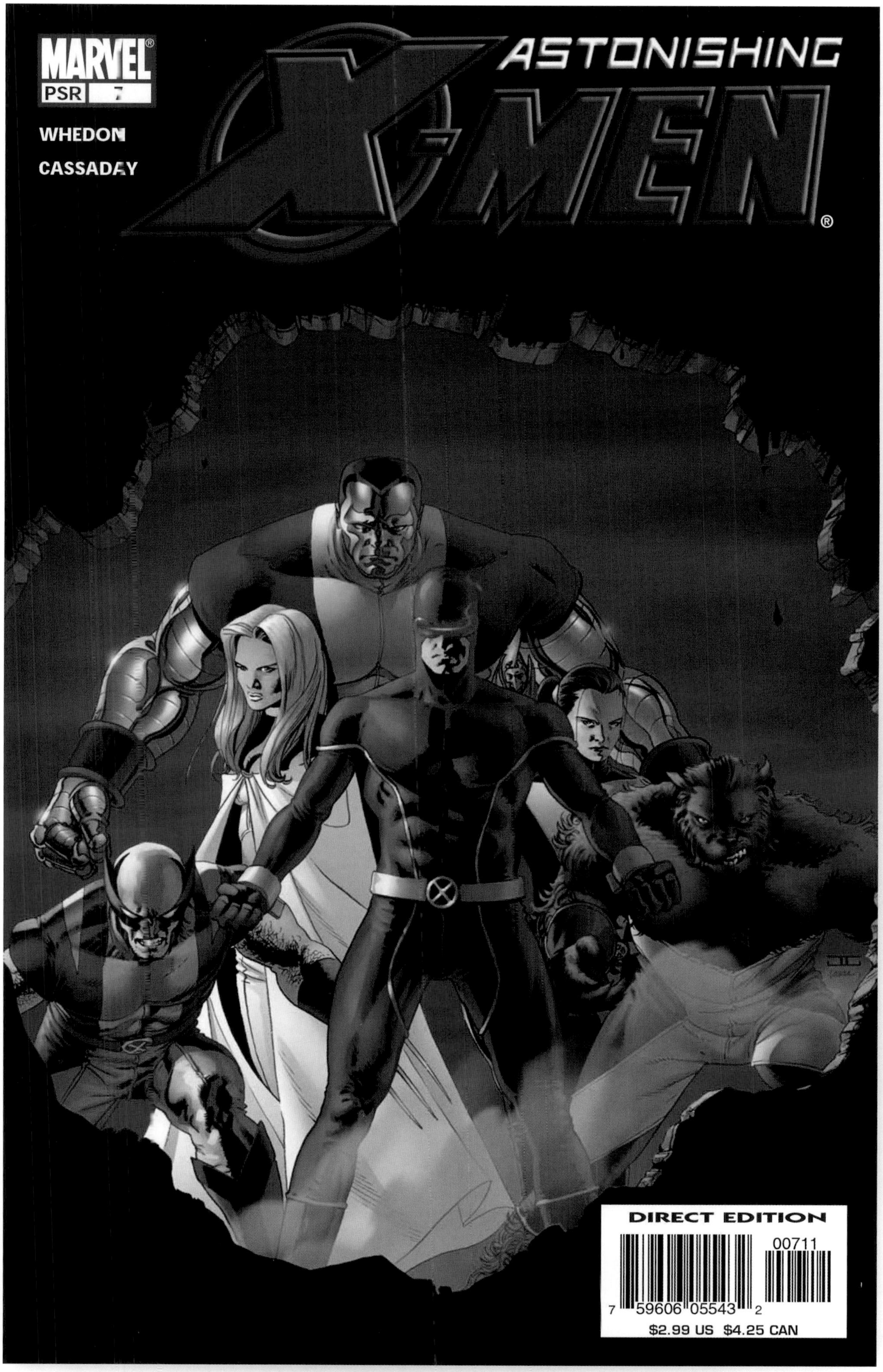
MARVEL
PSR 7
WHEDON
CASSADAY
ASTONISHING X-MEN
DIRECT EDITION
$2.99 US $4.25 CAN

▲ *ASTONISHING X-MEN* #7

**January 2005**
**Artist:** John Cassaday

Writer Joss Whedon made Cyclops one of his star characters during his run on *Astonishing X-Men*, with John Cassaday portraying Cyclops in a far more heroic light than he had in the time leading up to the series. This issue reflects Cyclops' resurgence under this team, with Cassaday's cover showing the team seconds after Cyclops' optic blasts had done their job.

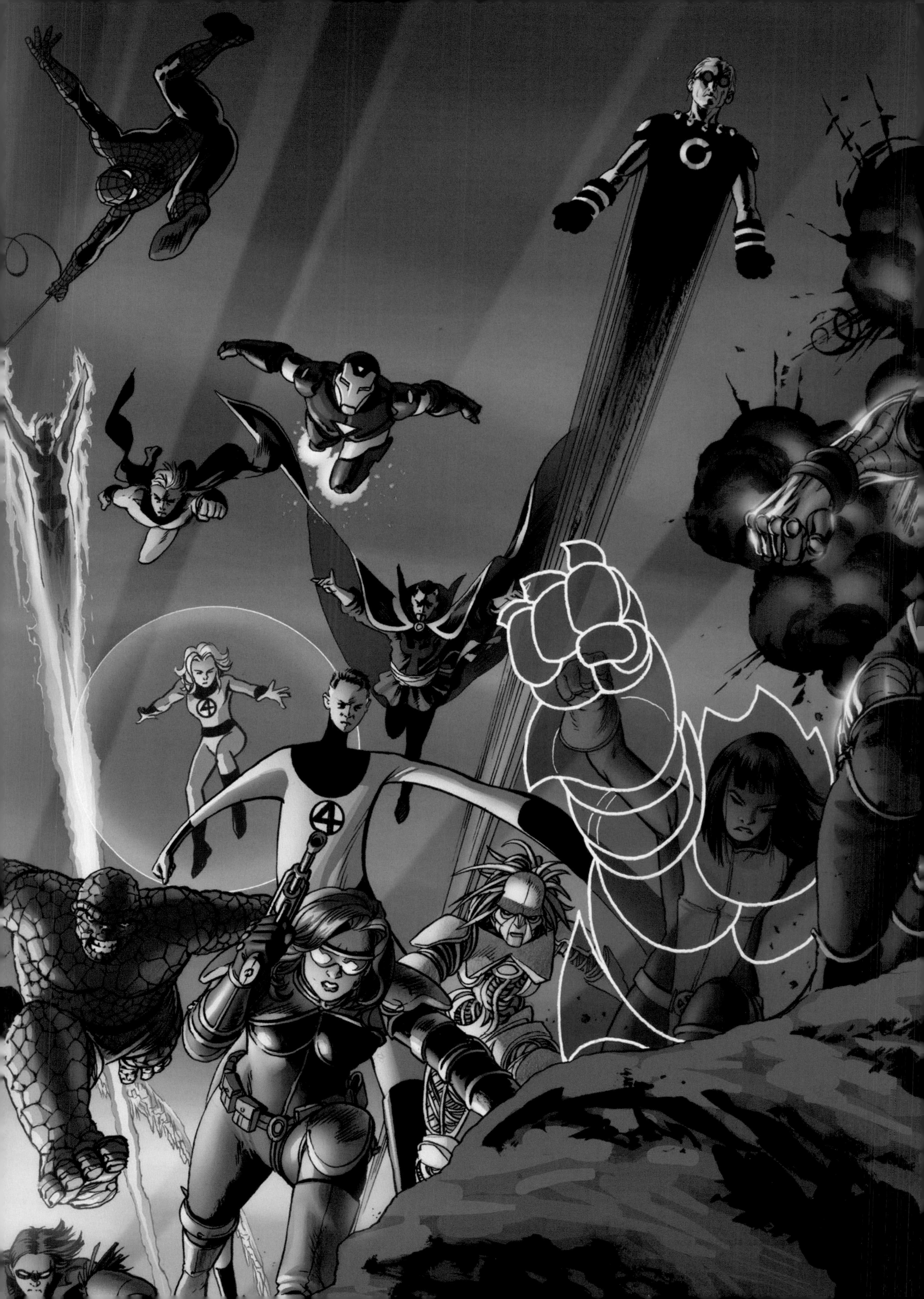

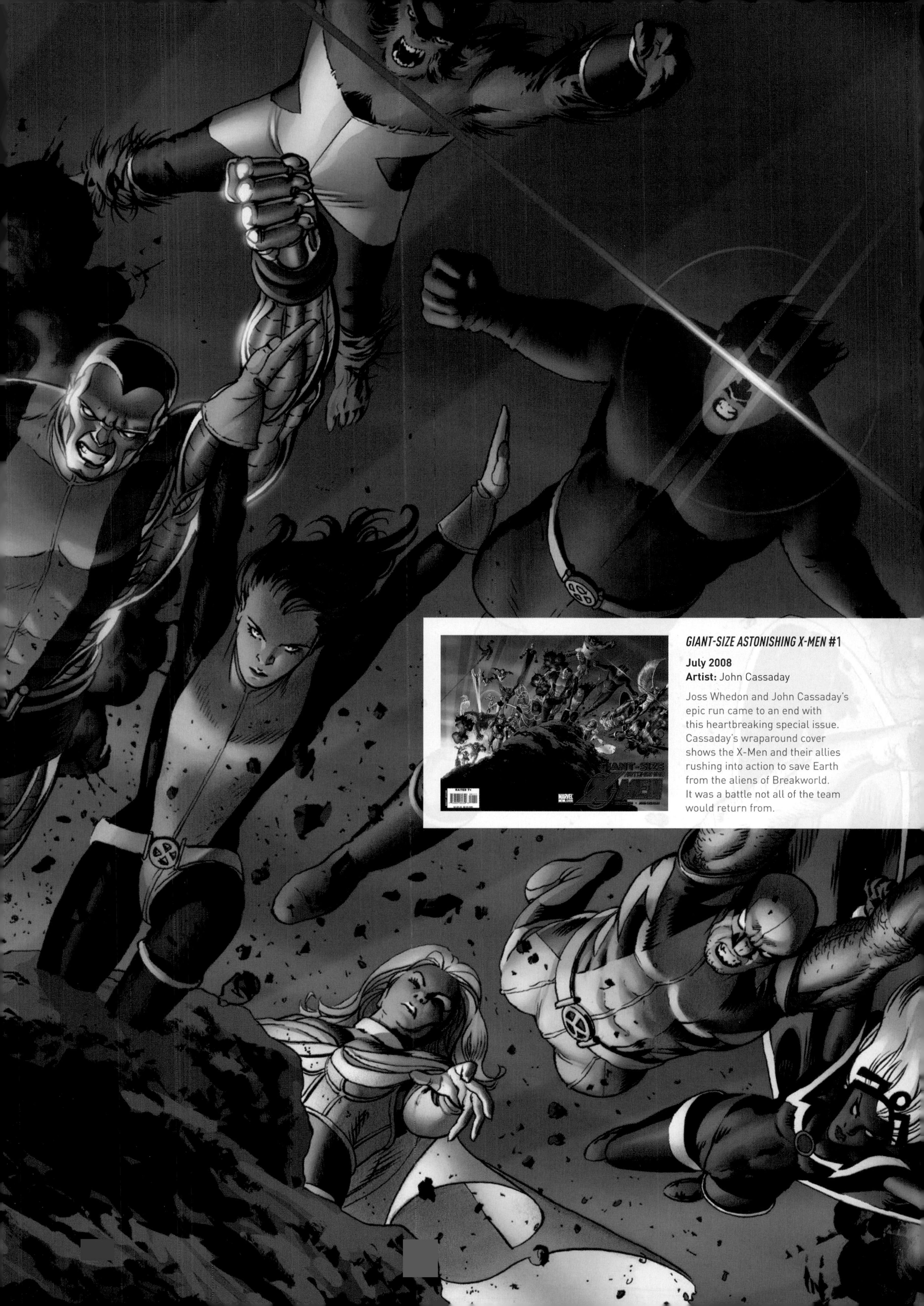

*GIANT-SIZE ASTONISHING X-MEN* #1

**July 2008**
**Artist:** John Cassaday

Joss Whedon and John Cassaday's epic run came to an end with this heartbreaking special issue. Cassaday's wraparound cover shows the X-Men and their allies rushing into action to save Earth from the aliens of Breakworld. It was a battle not all of the team would return from.

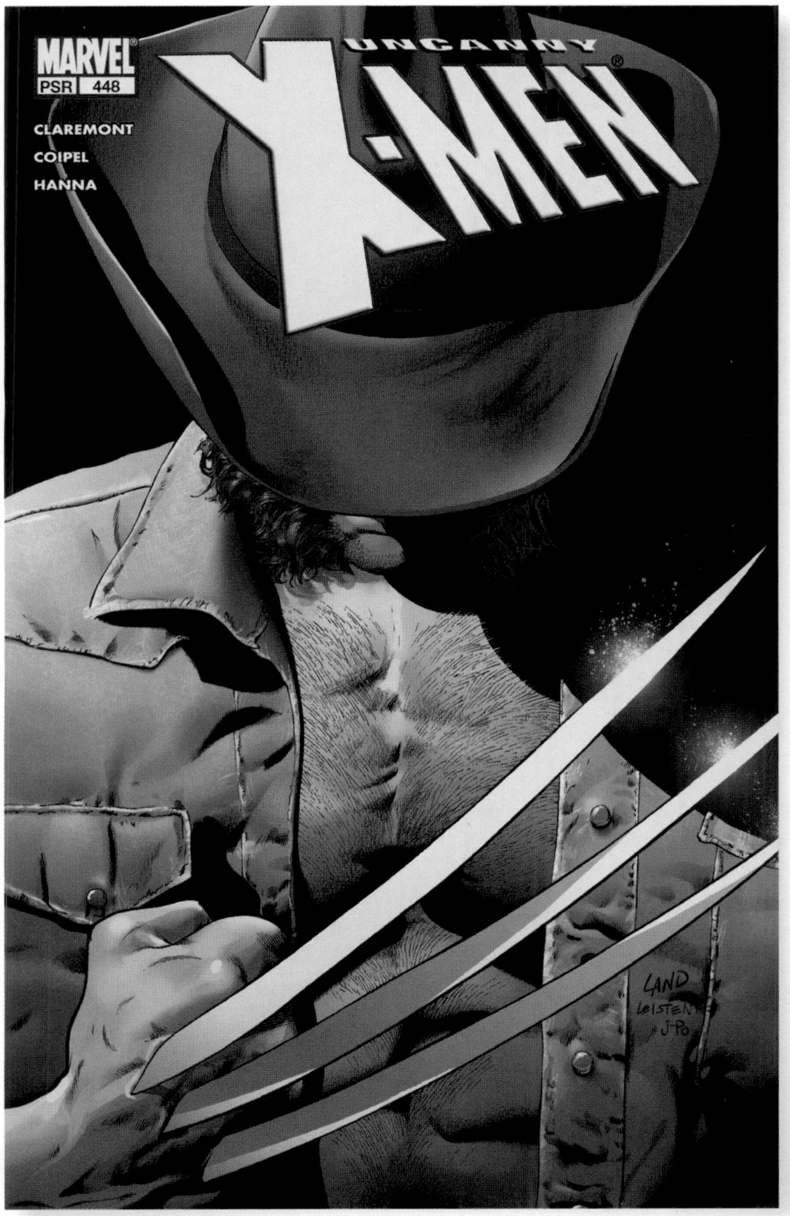
MARVEL
PSR 448
UNCANNY
X-MEN
CLAREMONT
COIPEL
HANNA

▲ *UNCANNY X-MEN* **#448**

**October 2004**
**Artist:** Greg Land

Greg Land brought his realistic style to *Uncanny X-Men* to create this moody close-up of Wolverine. It was one of the few Wolverine covers to keep the hero's face hidden. The concealed features, coupled with the sight of Wolverine's claws, add an element of mystery and danger.

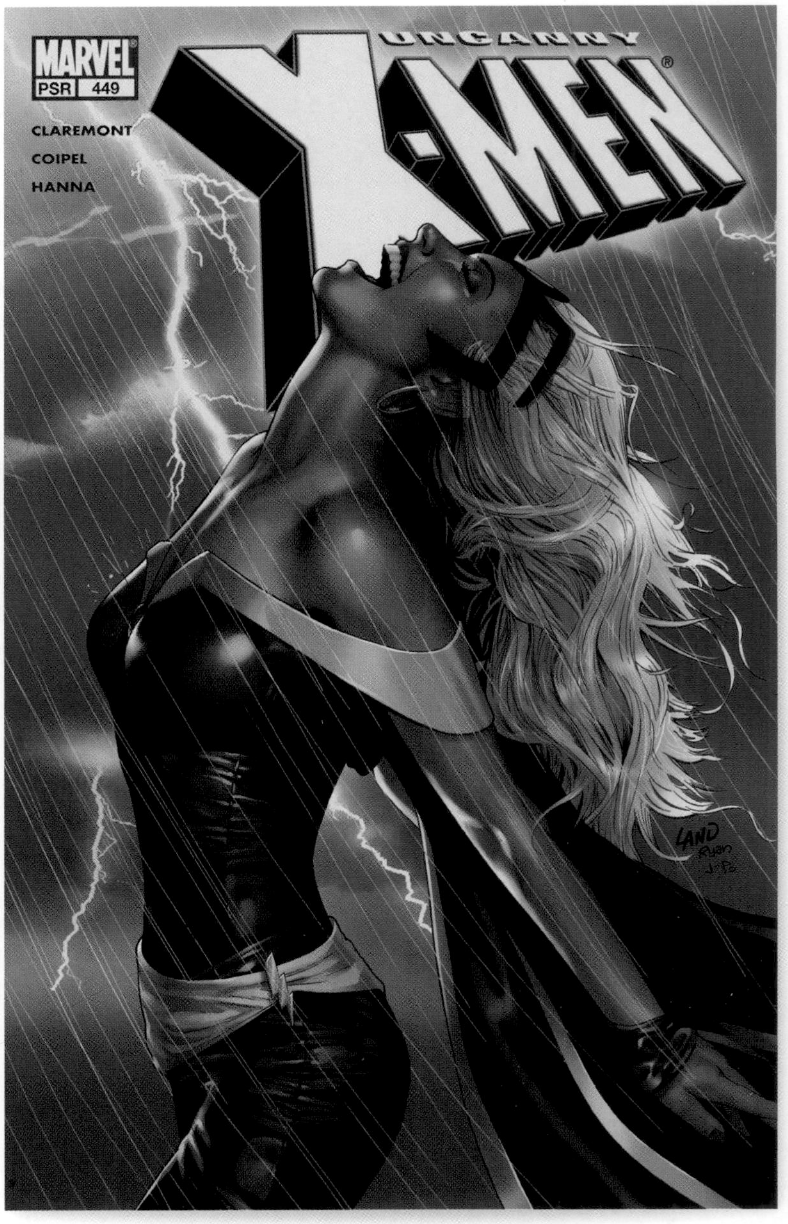
MARVEL
PSR 449
UNCANNY
X-MEN
CLAREMONT
COIPEL
HANNA

▲ *UNCANNY X-MEN* **#449**

**November 2004**
**Artist:** Greg Land

Land produced a wonderful portrait of Storm for this issue, showing Ororo Munroe embracing her connection to the elements. Ororo Munroe had always been a character who seemed happiest in wide open spaces, and this cover reflects her pleasure at being alone with the storm-ridden sky.

*UNCANNY X-MEN* **#466** ▶

**January 2006**
**Artist:** Chris Bachalo

Rachel Summers, the daughter of Jean Grey and Scott Summers from the horrifying parallel Earth of "Days of Future Past," was the focus of this cover. Bachalo's use of flames around both her and the logo is symbolic of one of the books' deadliest stories, as Shi'ar Death Commandos were sent to Earth to execute every member of the Grey family.

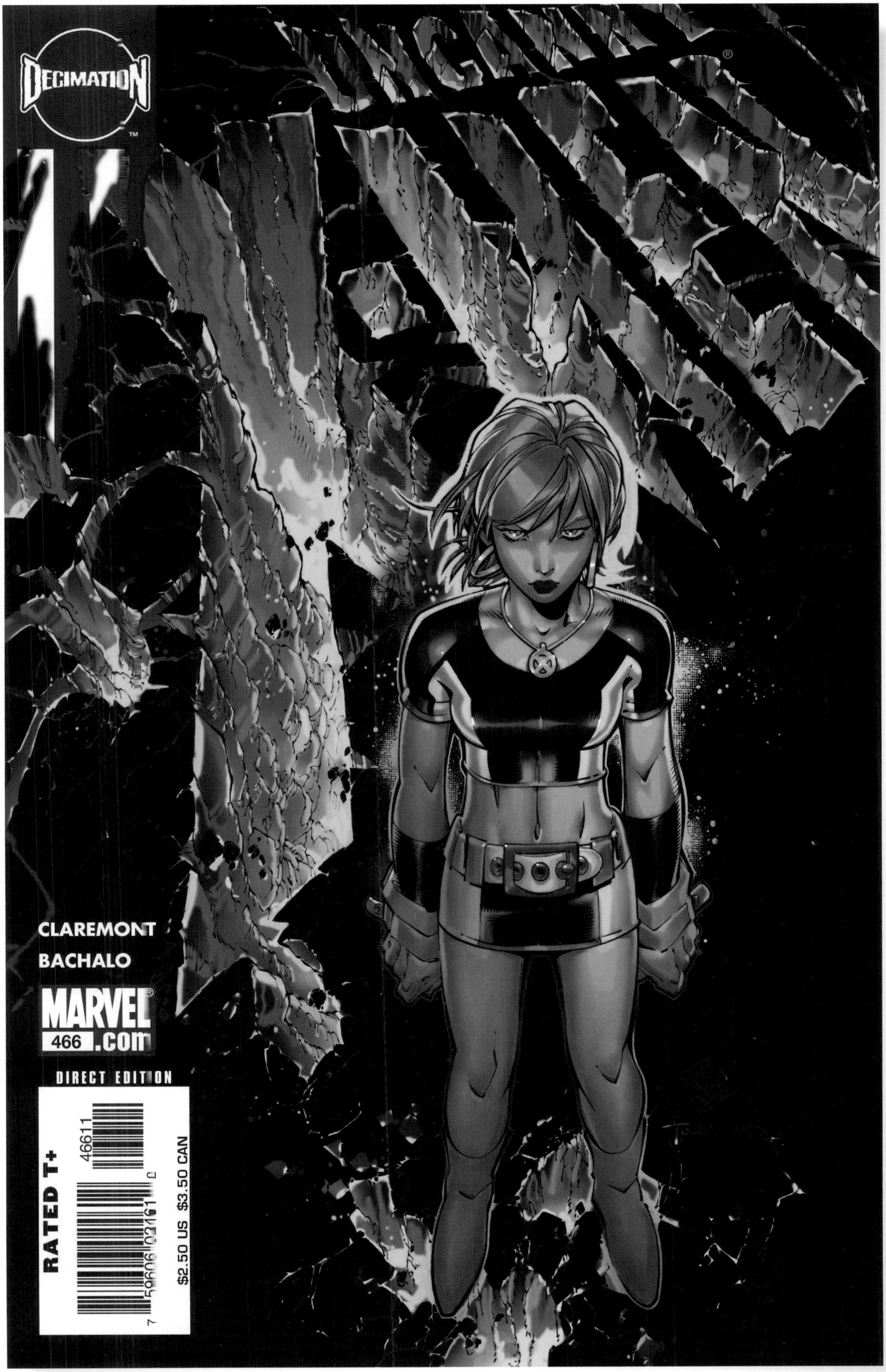
DECIMATION
CLAREMONT
BACHALO
MARVEL
466 .com
DIRECT EDITION
RATED T+
$2.50 US $3.50 CAN

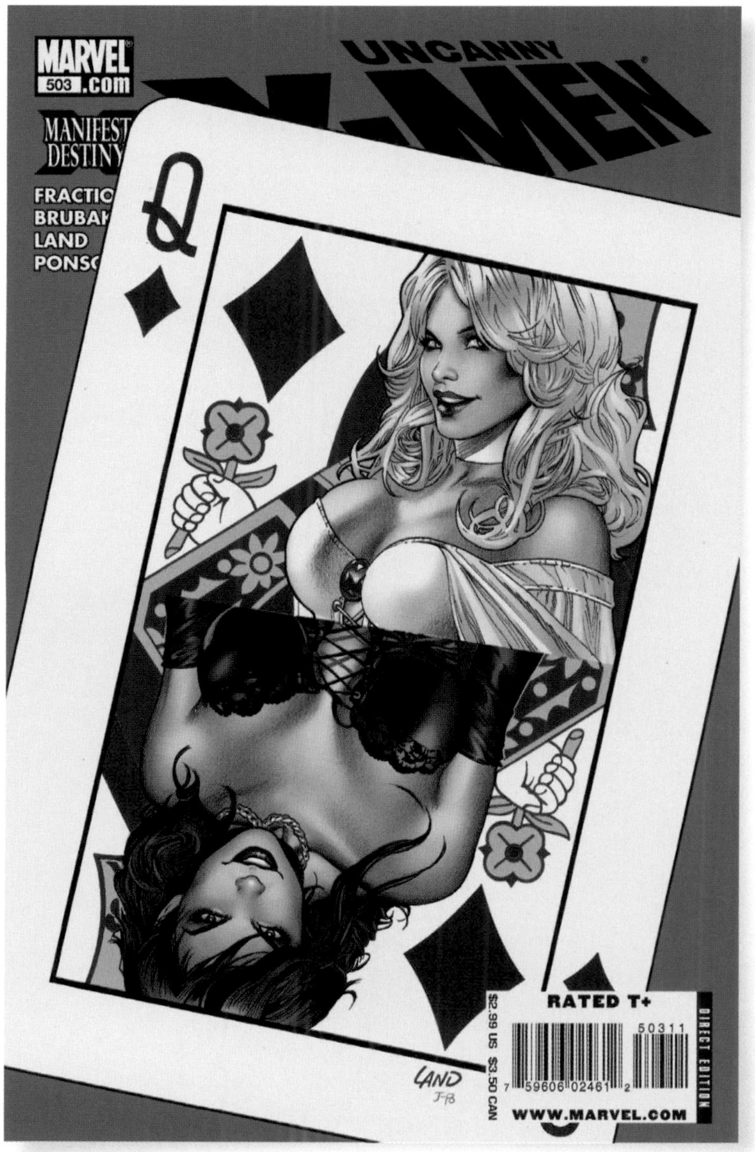
MARVEL
503 .com
UNCANNY
X-MEN
MANIFEST
DESTINY
Q
RATED T+
$2.99 US $3.50 CAN
DIRECT EDITION
WWW.MARVEL.COM
LAND

**◀ *UNCANNY X-MEN* #503**

**December 2008**
**Artist:** Greg Land

Cyclops' ex-wife Madelyne Pryor made a return in this issue. A clone of Jean Grey, Madelyne had turned into the Goblin Queen years before. The X-Men believed her to be dead, but Greg Land's cover hints at her return—and her role as the new Red Queen, the opposite of Emma Frost's old position as the Hellfire Club's White Queen.

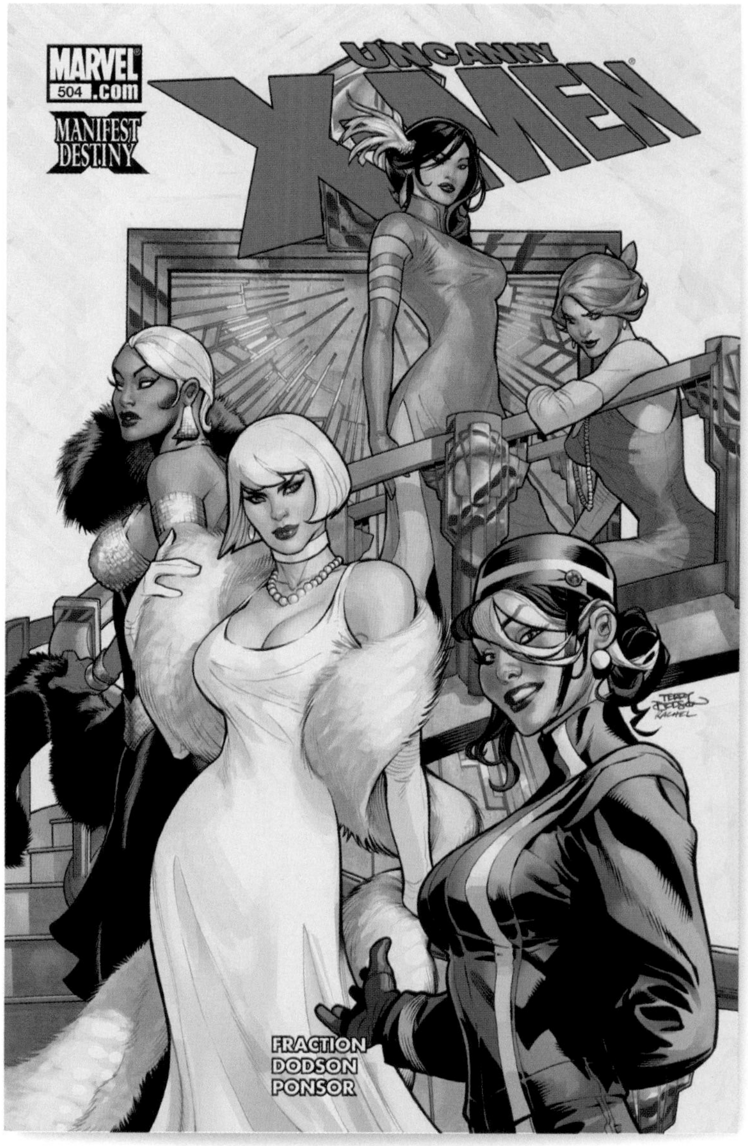
MARVEL
504 .com
UNCANNY
X-MEN
MANIFEST
DESTINY
FRACTION
DODSON
PONSOR

**◀ *UNCANNY X-MEN* #504**

**January 2008**
**Artist:** Terry Dodson

This 1920s-style cover showcases Terry Dodson's attention to detail and skill in drawing female characters. Dodson's depiction of the female X-Men wearing unusual attire turned out to be because it was an image from Cypclops' mind, as his telepathic lover, Emma Frost, entered it to find out why he had been acting so strangely.

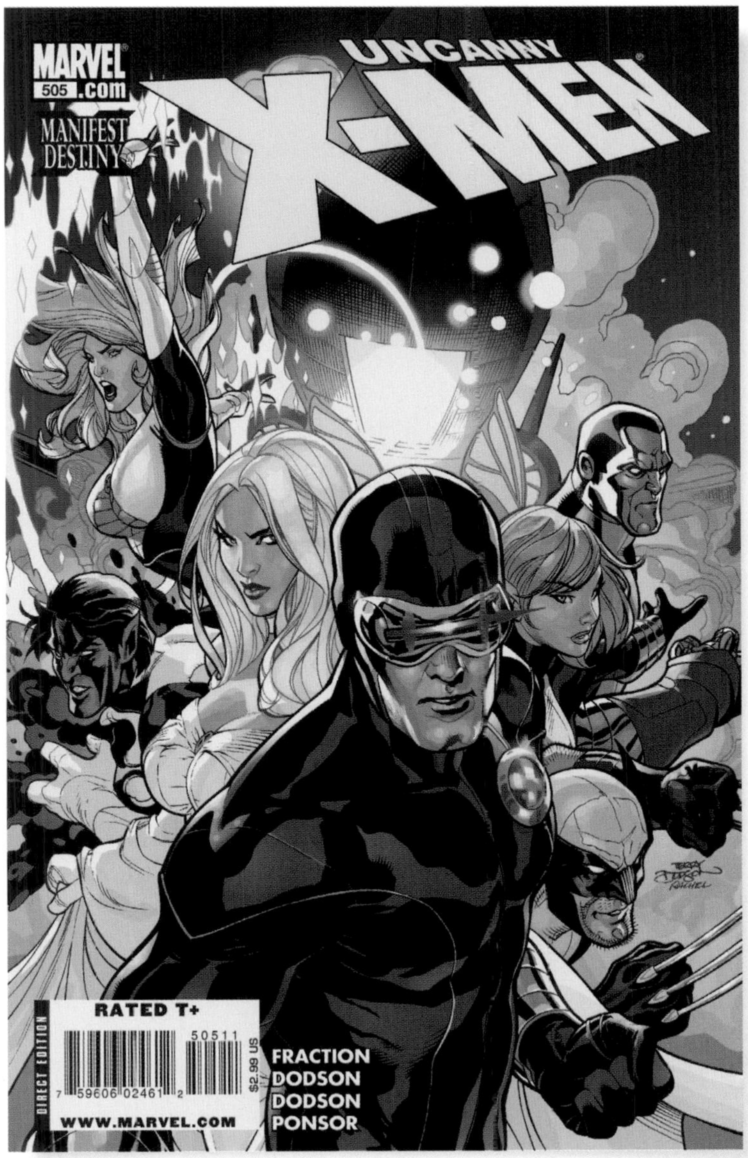
MARVEL
505 .com
UNCANNY
X-MEN
MANIFEST DESTINY
RATED T+
DIRECT EDITION
$2.99 US
WWW.MARVEL.COM
FRACTION
DODSON
DODSON
PONSOR

◀ *UNCANNY X-MEN* #505

**February 2008**
**Artist:** Terry Dodson

Despite the cover showing a group pose of the X-Men, this issue focused on the individual adventures of the team, rather than one big story. Dodson created a dramatic group shot, with the leader Cyclops in the forefront and the Blackbird aircraft taking off in the background.

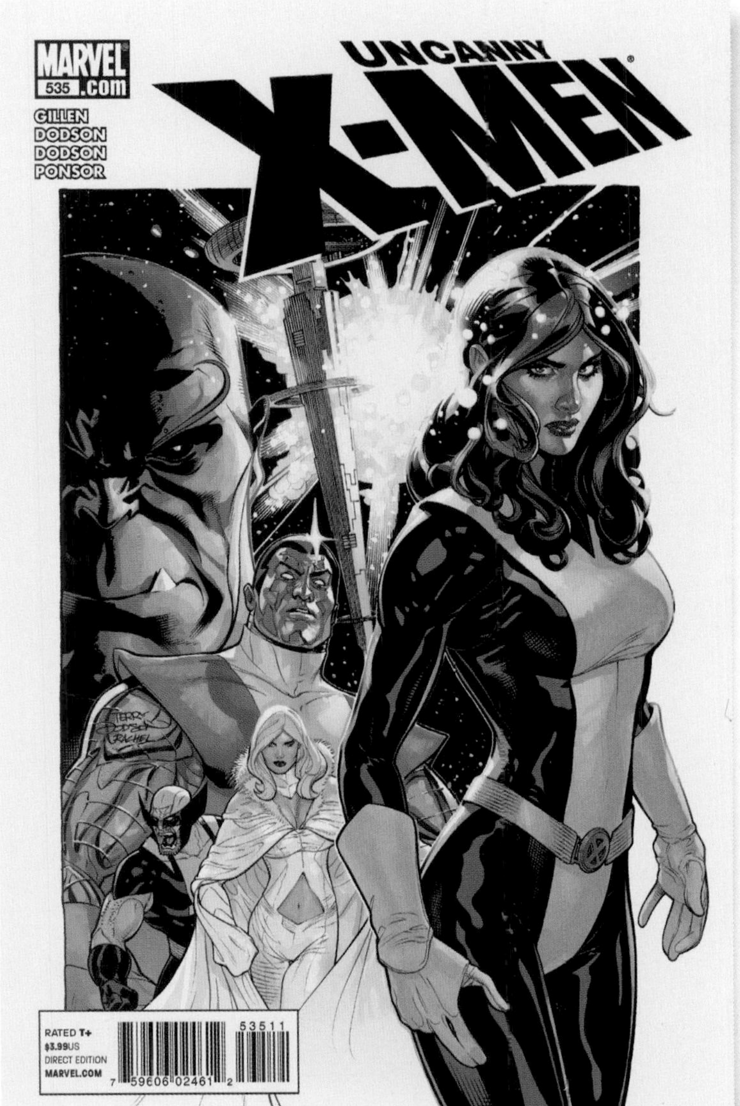
MARVEL
535 .com
UNCANNY
X-MEN
GILLEN
DODSON
DODSON
PONSOR
RATED T+
$3.99US
DIRECT EDITION
MARVEL.COM

◀ *UNCANNY X-MEN* #535

**June 2011**
**Artist:** Terry Dodson

A follow-up to Joss Whedon's *Astonishing X-Men* series sees Kitty Pryde as the focus on the cover. With the aliens from Breakworld returning, it was only natural that Kitty would be involved—in the previous series it seemed she had given her life to save Earth. The cover, which also shows the alien Ord and the S.W.O.R.D. space station, reflected the intergalactic scope of the new story.

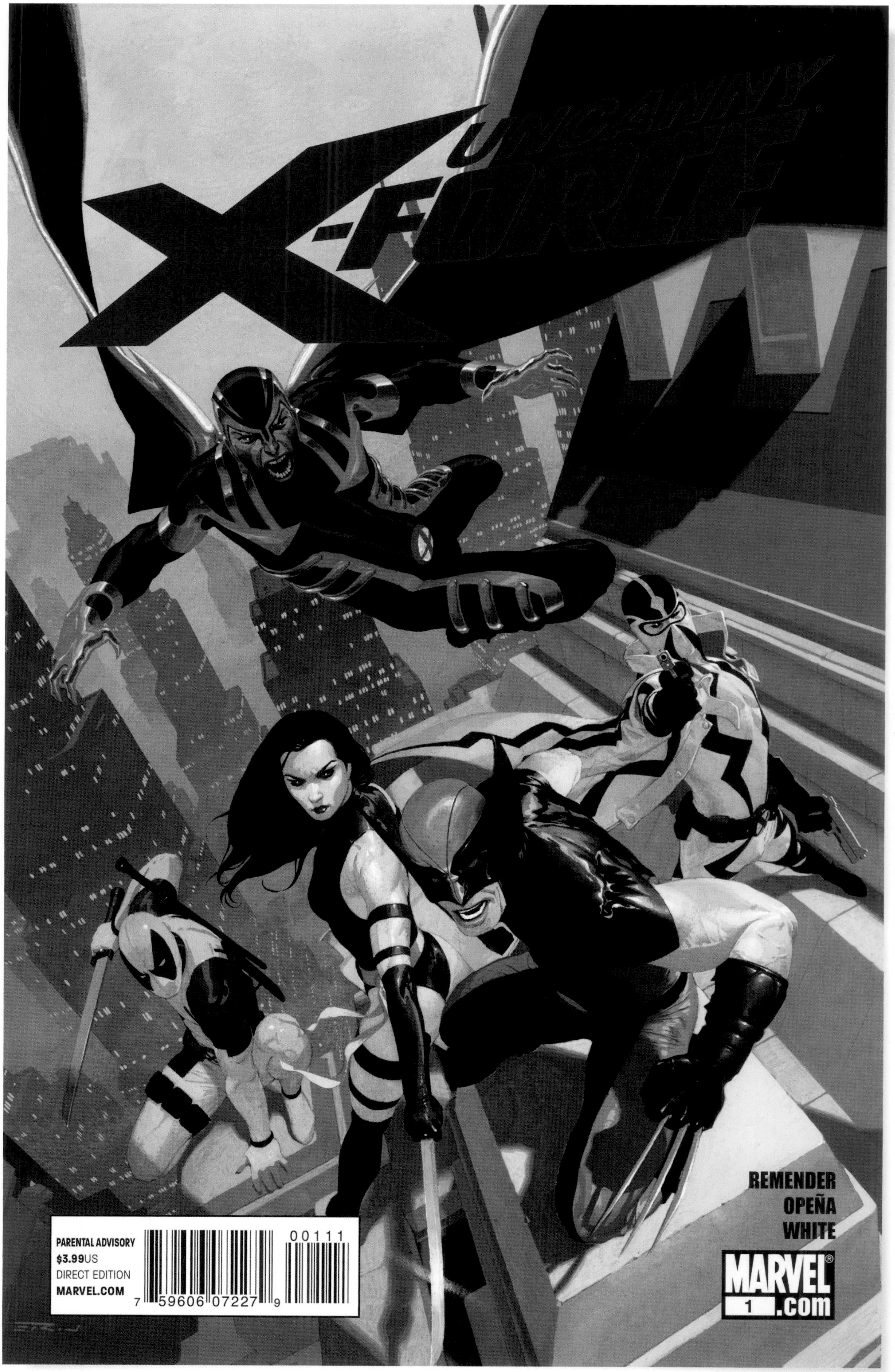
UNCANNY
X-FORCE
REMENDER
OPEÑA
WHITE
MARVEL
1 .com
PARENTAL ADVISORY
$3.99US
DIRECT EDITION
MARVEL.COM
00111
7 59606 07227 9

◀ ***UNCANNY X-FORCE* #1**

**December 2010**
**Artist:** Esad Ribic

The first issue of the new *Uncanny X-Force* series saw Wolverine again leading a team of killers—"a Black Ops" version of the X-Men. The new series had the team trying to stop one of the X-Men's deadliest enemies—Apocalypse—from returning. Ribic's dynamic and moody art was a perfect fit for this new grouping, bringing out the deadly nature of X-Force in one tough group shot.

THE FINAL EXECUTION SAGA
#31
MARVEL
UNCANNY
X-FORCE
REMENDER
NOTO
MARTIN
PURCHASE INCLUDES
FREE
DIGITAL COPY OFFER
SEE INSIDE FOR DETAILS
PARENTAL ADVISORY
$3.99US
DIRECT EDITION
MARVEL.COM

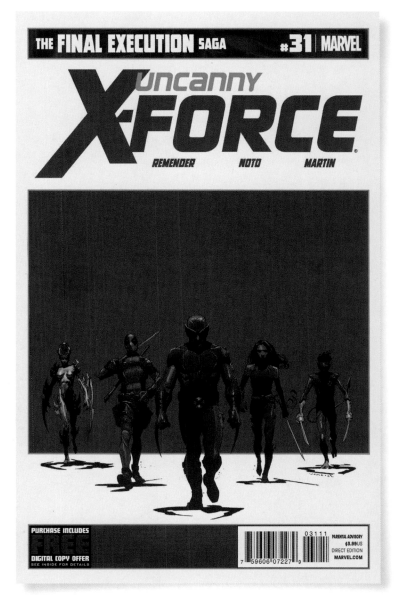

***UNCANNY X-FORCE* #31** ▶

**November 2012**
**Artist:** Jerome Opena

The "Final Execution" saga was the swan song for *Uncanny X-Force*. In this issue, Wolverine's son, Daken, formed a new Brotherhood of Evil Mutants to destroy the X-Force team. Jerome Opena's stylish two-tone cover reflects the dark nature and mood of the team as they prepared for their final battle with the Brotherhood.

SAM HUMPHRIES
MARVEL NOW!
RON GARNEY
UNCANNY
X-FORCE
#1
PARENTAL ADVISORY
$3.99US
DIRECT EDITION
MARVEL.COM
JOIN THE
REVOLUTION
PURCHASE INCLUDES
FREE
DIGITAL COPY OFFER
AR
001

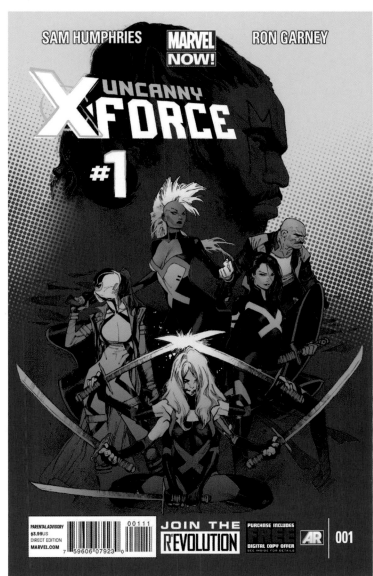

***UNCANNY X-FORCE* #1** ▶

**March 2013**
**Artist:** Olivier Coipel

A new X-Force team was introduced in this issue. Olivier Coipel's cover shows a group shot of the new team, which featured surprise members, such as the villain Spiral. It also promises the return of former X-Men member Bishop—shown looming in the background—without revealing whether he would return as a hero or a villain.

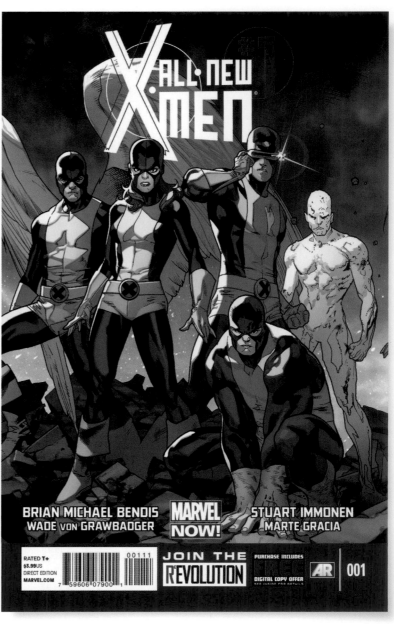

REGENESIS
#03
MARVEL
WOLVERINE and the X-MEN
AARON
BACHALO
TOWNSEND
REMEMBER WHEN WOLVERINE WAS COOL? ME NEITHER.
RATED T+
$3.99US
DIRECT EDITION
MARVEL.COM

▲ *WOLVERINE AND THE X-MEN* #3

**February 2012**
**Artist:** Chris Bachalo

*Wolverine and the X-Men* quickly became a favorite X-book for many fans. The stories were set in the Jean Grey School for Higher Learning, where Wolverine was headmaster. Chris Bachalo provided a suitably surly image of the popular Kid Omega (Quentin Quire) for the cover, which captured Kid Omega's rebellious attitude perfectly.

ALL-NEW X-MEN
BRIAN MICHAEL BENDIS
WADE VON GRAWBADGER
MARVEL NOW!
STUART IMMONEN
MARTE GRACIA
RATED T+
$3.99US
DIRECT EDITION
MARVEL.COM
JOIN THE R̈EVOLUTION
PURCHASE INCLUDES FREE DIGITAL COPY OFFER
AR
001

▲ *ALL-NEW X-MEN* #1

**January 2013**
**Artist:** Stuart Immonen

This new series reinvigorated the whole mutant world by bringing the original five X-Men through time into the present day. Stuart Immonen portrayed the youth and innocence of the young mutants on the cover of the first issue, instantly intriguing readers who wanted to see what would happen when the young mutants met their older selves.

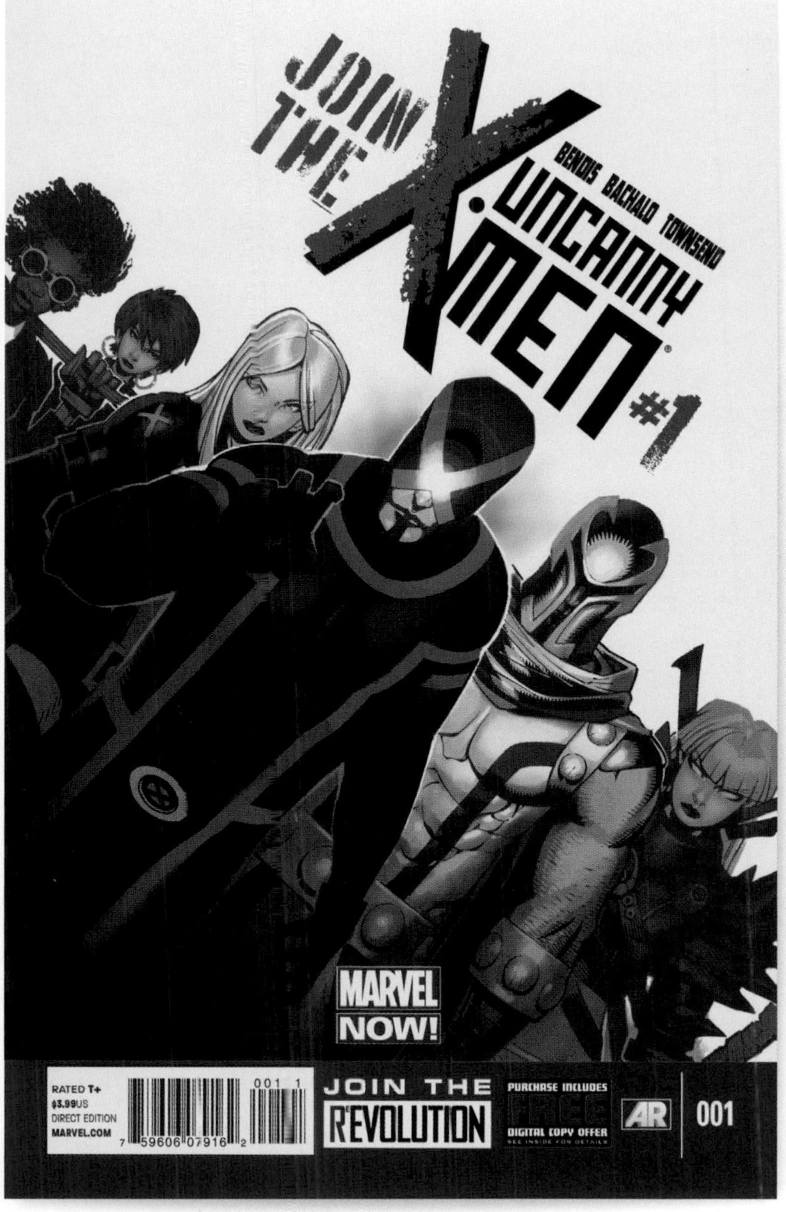
JOIN THE X
BENDIS BACHALO TOWNSEND
UNCANNY X-MEN #1
MARVEL NOW!
RATED T+
$3.99US
DIRECT EDITION
MARVEL.COM
JOIN THE REVOLUTION
PURCHASE INCLUDES
DIGITAL COPY OFFER
AR
001

▲ ***UNCANNY X-MEN* #1**

**April 2013**
**Artist:** Chris Bachalo

Bachalo's angled cover of the debut issue of a new *Uncanny X-Men* series reflects Cyclops' skewed view of the world—a world that now considered him a Super Villain. Cyclops' new visor was especially startling. The "X" represented the man Cyclops had killed while possessed by the Phoenix Force—his old mentor, Professor X.

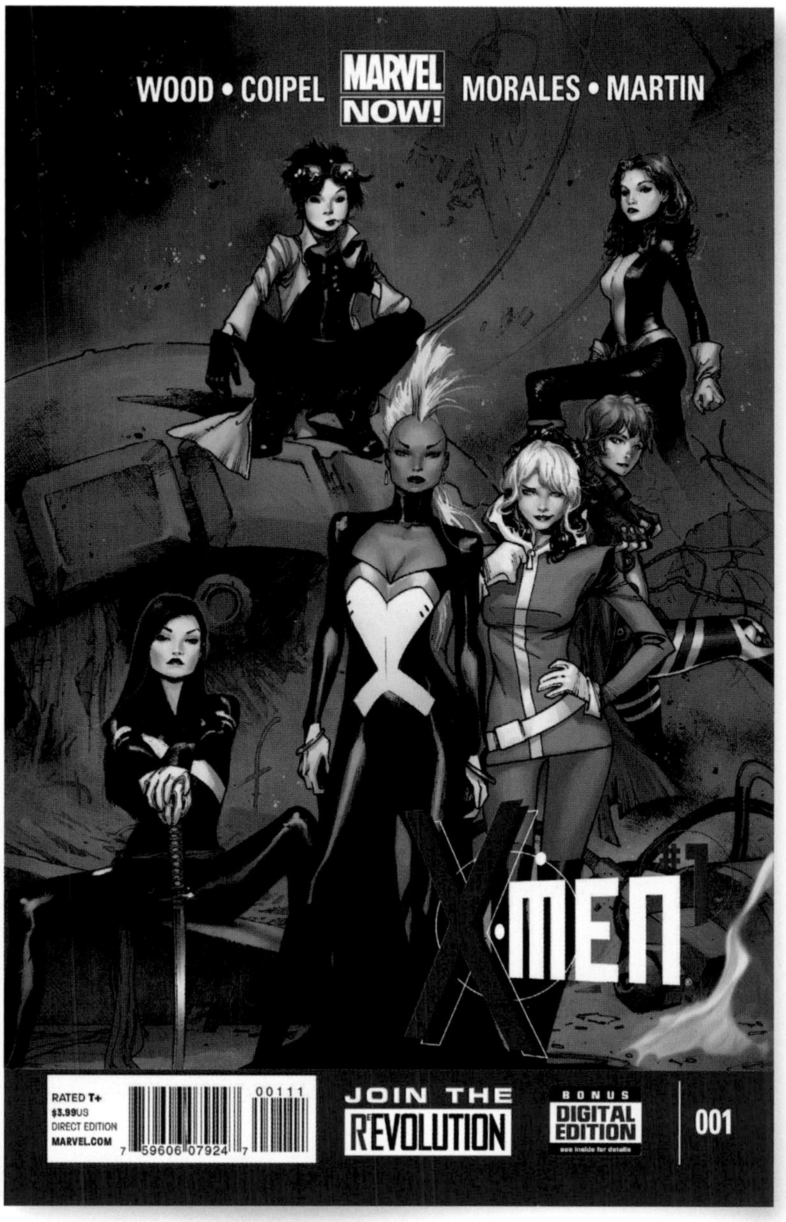
WOOD • COIPEL
MARVEL NOW!
MORALES • MARTIN
X-MEN
RATED T+
$3.99US
DIRECT EDITION
MARVEL.COM
JOIN THE REVOLUTION
BONUS
DIGITAL EDITION
001

▲ ***X-MEN* #1**

**August 2013**
**Artist:** Olivier Coipel

It was time for the women to take charge in the new *X-Men* series. While the *X-Men* comics had always included strong female characters, this was the first time they were featured in their own series. Coipel's eye-catching cover shows a dynamic group shot of the team, with Storm at the front, proving her leadership skills.

LONDON, NEW YORK, MUNICH,
MELBOURNE AND DELHI

**Senior Editor** Sadie Smith
**Project Art Editor** Owen Bennett
**Edited by** Jo Casey, Beth Davies, David Fentiman,
Gaurav Joshi, Tori Kosara, Catherine Saunders,
Chitra Subramanyam
**Designed by** Neha Ahuja, Karan Chaudhary
**Senior Pre-Production Producer** Jennifer Murray
**Senior Producer** Alex Bell
**Managing Editor** Laura Gilbert
**Managing Art Editor** Maxine Pedliham
**Publishing Manager** Julie Ferris
**Art Director** Lisa Lanzarini
**Publishing Director** Simon Beecroft

First published in Great Britain in 2014 by Dorling Kindersley Limited,
80 Strand, London WC2R 0RL
A Penguin Random House Company

10 9 8 7 6 5 4
007-195851-Oct/14

A CIP catalogue record for this book is available from the British Library

ISBN: 978-1-4093-4751-4

Printed and bound in China by Leo Paper Products

Discover more at
**www.dk.com**

**marvel.com**
© 2014 MARVEL

## ACKNOWLEDGEMENTS

**Dorling Kindersley would like to thank:** David Gabriel, Jeff Youngquist, Joseph Hochstein,
Mark Annunziato, Brian Overton, Sarah Brunstad and George Beliard at Marvel; Chelsea
Alon at Disney; Adi Granov for writing the foreword.

**Alan Cowsill would like to thank:** Nick Abadzis, James Britnell, Glenn Dakin, Aletia and
Gary Gilbert, James Hill, Adam Levine, Dan Rachael, Richard Starkings and Dean White
for answering the questions, and Matt McAllister, Maggie Calmels, Richard Jackson,
Ben Robinson, John Tomlinson, Colin Williams and the folk at Eaglemoss. Special thanks
to my Mum and Dad for buying me *Mighty World of Marvel* issue #1.

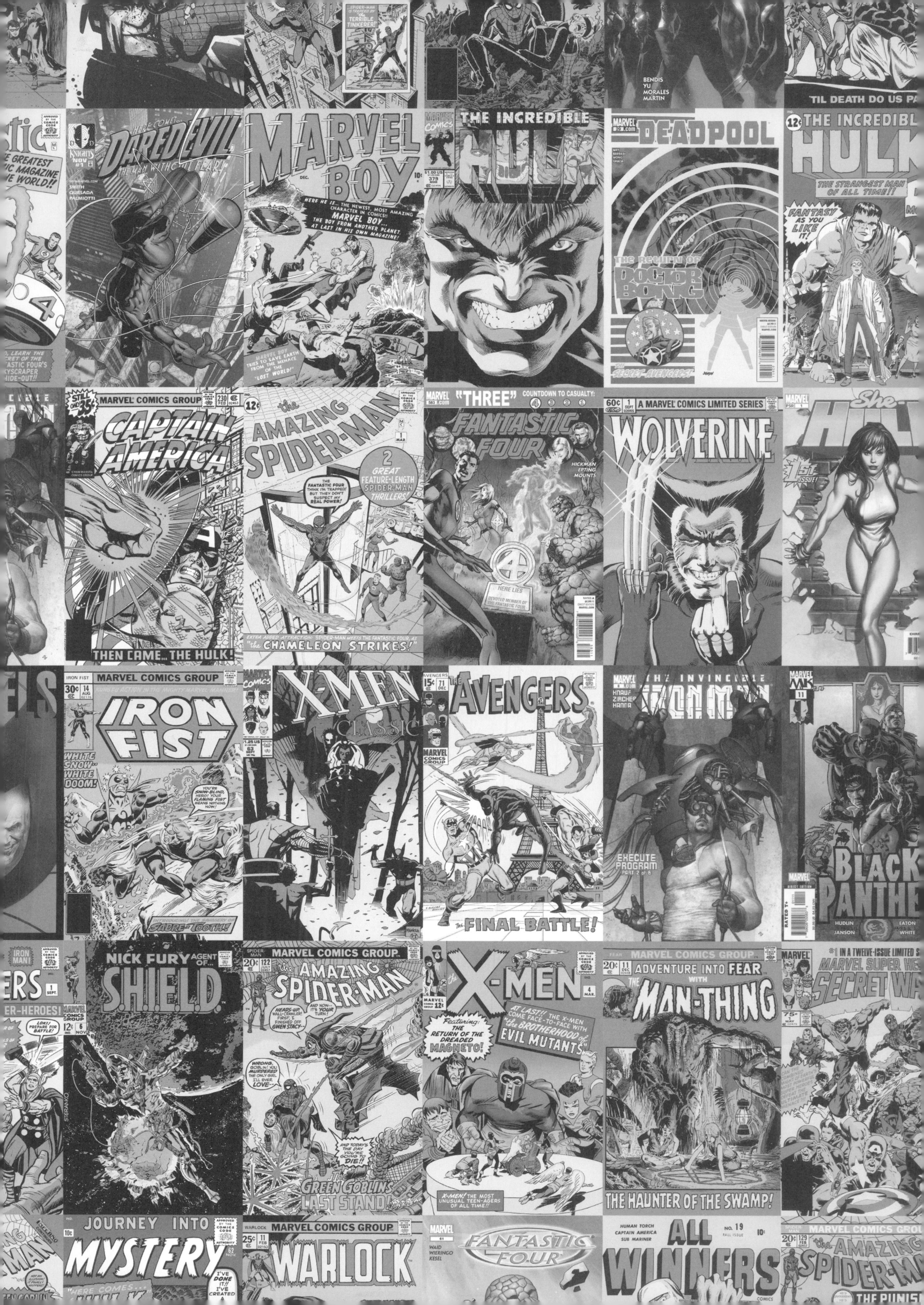

SPIDER-MAN IS TRICKED BY THE TERRIBLE TINKERER!
BENDIS
YU
MORALES
MARTIN
'TIL DEATH DO US PART
THE GREATEST COMIC MAGAZINE IN THE WORLD!!
LEARN THE SECRET OF THE FANTASTIC FOUR'S SKYSCRAPER HIDE-OUT!
DAREDEVIL
THE MAN WITHOUT FEAR!
SMITH
QUESADA
PALMIOTTI
MARVEL BOY
HERE HE IS... THE NEWEST, MOST AMAZING CHARACTER IN COMICS!! MARVEL BOY, THE BOY FROM ANOTHER PLANET, AT LAST IN HIS OWN MAGAZINE!
MARVEL BOY TRIES TO SAVE EARTH FROM THE MENACE OF THE "LOST WORLD!"
THE INCREDIBLE HULK
DEADPOOL
THE RETURN OF DOCTOR BONG
SECRET AVENGERS
THE INCREDIBLE HULK
THE STRANGEST MAN OF ALL TIME!!
FANTASY AS YOU LIKE IT!
MARVEL COMICS GROUP
CAPTAIN AMERICA
THEN CAME... THE HULK!
THE AMAZING SPIDER-MAN
2 GREAT FEATURE-LENGTH SPIDER-MAN THRILLERS!
THE FANTASTIC FOUR THINK I'M TRAPPED! BUT THEY DON'T SUSPECT MY REAL POWER!
EXTRA ADDED ATTRACTION: SPIDER-MAN MEETS THE FANTASTIC FOUR AS "the CHAMELEON STRIKES!"
"THREE"
COUNTDOWN TO CASUALTY:
FANTASTIC FOUR
HICKMAN
EPTING
MOUNTS
HERE LIES
DEVOTED MEMBER OF THE FANTASTIC FOUR
A MARVEL COMICS LIMITED SERIES
WOLVERINE
SHE-HULK
1ST ISSUE!
IRON FIST
MARVEL COMICS GROUP
IRON FIST
WHITE SNOW — WHITE DOOM!
YOU'RE SNOW-BLIND, HERO! YOUR FLAMING FIST MEANS NOTHING NOW!
INTRODUCING THE SAVAGERY OF SABRE-TOOTH!
X-MEN CLASSIC
AVENGERS
FINAL BATTLE!
THE INVINCIBLE IRON MAN
EXECUTE PROGRAM PART 2 of 6
BLACK PANTHER
HUDLIN
EATON
JANSON
WHITE
NICK FURY AGENT OF... S.H.I.E.L.D.
STERANKO
LOKI! PREPARE FOR BATTLE!
MARVEL COMICS GROUP
THE AMAZING SPIDER-MAN
HEADS-UP, WALL-CRAWLER! FIRST, I FINISHED OFF GWEN STACY--
AND NOW-- IT'S YOUR TURN!
WRONG, GOBLIN! YOU MURDERED THE ONLY GIRL I'LL EVER LOVE--
AND TODAY'S THE DAY YOU'RE GOING TO DIE!
THE GREEN GOBLIN'S LAST STAND!
X-MEN
AT LAST!! THE X-MEN COME FACE-TO-FACE WITH THE BROTHERHOOD OF EVIL MUTANTS!
Featuring: THE RETURN OF THE DREADED MAGNETO!
X-MEN! THE MOST UNUSUAL TEEN-AGERS OF ALL TIME!!
MARVEL COMICS GROUP
ADVENTURE INTO FEAR WITH THE MAN-THING
THE HAUNTER OF THE SWAMP!
#1 IN A TWELVE-ISSUE LIMITED SERIES
MARVEL SUPER HEROES SECRET WARS
JOURNEY INTO MYSTERY
I'VE DONE IT!! I'VE CREATED
HERE COMES...
MARVEL COMICS GROUP
WARLOCK
WAID
WIERINGO
KESEL
FANTASTIC FOUR
HUMAN TORCH
CAPTAIN AMERICA
SUB MARINER
ALL WINNERS
NO. 19
FALL ISSUE
MARVEL COMICS GROUP
THE AMAZING SPIDER-MAN
THE PUNISHER